Lowering
THE BAR

THIS BOOK WAS PUBLISHED WITH THE SUPPORT OF THE

Anonymous Fund for the Humanities

of the

UNIVERSITY OF WISCONSIN–MADISON.

Lowering
THE BAR

*Lawyer Jokes and
Legal Culture*

MARC GALANTER

THE UNIVERSITY OF WISCONSIN PRESS

The University of Wisconsin Press
1930 Monroe Street
Madison, Wisconsin 53711

www.wisc.edu/wisconsinpress/

3 Henrietta Street
London WC2E 8LU, England

Library of Congress Cataloging-in-Publication Data
Galanter, Marc, 1931–
Lowering the bar : lawyer jokes and legal culture / Marc Galanter.
p. cm.
Includes bibliographical references and index.
ISBN 0-299-21350-1 (cloth : alk. paper)
1. Lawyers—United States—Humor. 2. Lawyers—United States—Public opinion.
3. Lawyers–Complaints against–United States. I. Title.
K184.G35   2005
340′.02′07—dc22   2005005443

for

ALAN DUNDES (1934–2005)

friend and teacher

Ben Zoma said: Who is wise?
He who learns from all men.

—PIRKE AVOT IV: I

CONTENTS

ILLUSTRATIONS

ACKNOWLEDGMENTS

Jokes are an ambient medium filled with variation and surprise. Even to feign mastery over one province of the joke domain requires the support and guidance of a great network of informants. I am indebted to many people who shared jokes with me, led me to sources, helped me to decode them, and provided helpful feedback. Those I can identify are named below. Along with their anonymous counterparts, they merit total absolution from responsibility for any errors of fact or taste: Al Alshuler, Ann Althouse, Gordon Baldwin, Susan Bandes, Richard Bauman, Joel Berman, Bill Breslin, Bill Broder, Mia Cahill, Paul Campos, Jerome Carlin, Elizabeth Chambliss, Simon Chapman, Ross Cheit, James Clapp, Carol Clover, Christie Davies, Robert Diamond, Alan Dundes (and his band of students), Julia Eckert, Lauren Edelman, Cynthia Fuchs Epstein, Howard Erlanger, Edgar Feige, Marvin Frankel, Clark Freshman, Lawrence M. Friedman, Eve Galanter, Rachel Galanter, Sarah Galanter, Seth Galanter, Ken S. Gallant, Nancy Glasberg, Jona Goldschmidt, Richard Gordon, Robert Gordon, Marigay Graña, Gillian Hadfield, Lisa Harinanan, John P. Heinz, Jack Heller, Lynne Henderson, Jan Hoem, Beth Hoffman, J. Gordon Hylton, Herbert Jacob, Richard Jacobson, Richard M. Jaeger, John Kidwell, Julian Killingley, J. T. Knight, Giselinde Kuipers, Jack Ladinsky, Paul Lermack, Lisa Lerman, Alan Lerner, John Leubsdorf, Jethro Lieberman, Laura Macaulay, Stewart Macaulay, Jane Mansbridge, Stephen M. Masterson, Brian McConnell, Roy M. Mersky, David Nelkin, Mark Osiel, Steve Piotrowski, Nancy Reichman, Ed Reisner, Alison Dundes Renteln, Paul Rheingold, Deborah Rhode, Len Riskin, Marlyn Robinson, Tom Russell, Michael Saks, Ted Schneyer, Philip G. Schrag, Marge Schultz, Ronen Shamir, Fred Shapiro, Amy Singer, Joan Sklaroff, Morton Sklaroff, Neil Smelser, Dan Stewart, Mark Suchman, Carol Tan, Joseph Thome, Elizabeth Thornberg, Edward Tiryakian, Gretchen Viney, Maria Volpe, Clifford Westfall, David B. Wilkins, George Wright, Deborah Wu.

Transforming this abundant harvest into a book was made possible by many kinds of support. The library staff at the University of Wisconsin Law School—and especially Michael Morgalla—have been unfailingly helpful. The scope of my research was broadened by the opportunity to consult materials at the New York Public Library, the Schmulowitz Collection at the San Francisco Public Library, and the British Library. The Print Department of the British Museum was extraordinarily gracious in facilitating my search for visual counterparts to the textual material. In the captions to the illustrations in the text, the BM reference number identifies the location of that illustration in the *Catalog of Political and Personal Satires Preserved in the Department of Prints and Drawings in the British Museum.*

Much of the text was composed while I was a fellow at the Center for Advanced Study in the Behavioral Sciences, Stanford, California, a most congenial setting for research and reflection. I am grateful for the hospitality of the center and for the National Science Foundation's Grant #SBR-9601236 that supported my stay there. The University of Wisconsin–Madison has provided generous support through the Evjue-Bascom Professorship and, most recently, the John and Rylla Bosshard Professorship at the University of Wisconsin Law School.

Over the years, Lisa Harinanan, Allison Lynn, Aaron Stites, Angela Frozena, and Jennifer Grissom capably supplied indispensable research assistance. Brenda Balch, Collette Isachsen, and Theresa Dougherty grappled patiently and skillfully with numberless iterations of the manuscript.

Earlier versions of several parts of the manuscript were delivered as the Robert S. Marx Lecture at the University of Cincinnati ("The Faces of Mistrust: The Image of Lawyers in Public Opinion, Jokes, and Political Discourse," *University of Cincinnati Law Review* 66:805–45 [1998]), the 1999 Clifford Symposium on Tort Law and Social Policy at DePaul University College of Law ("The Conniving Claimant: Changing Images of Misuse of Legal Remedies," *DePaul Law Review* 50:647–65 [2000]), the Lansdowne Lecture at the University of Victoria (2001), and the Uri and Catherine Bauer Lecture at Cardozo Law School ("Changing Legal Consciousness in America: The View from the Joke Corpus," *Cardozo Law Review* 23: 2223–40 [2002]). Another bit appeared as "Lawyers in the Laboratory: or, Can They Run through Those Little Mazes? *Green Bag 2d* 4: 251–56 (2001).

At various stages of its development I enjoyed the opportunity to present parts of this material to student, faculty, and professional groups at Auburn Theological Seminary; Brown University; the Center for Advanced Study in the Behavioral Sciences; the Center for the Study of Law and Society, University of California, Berkeley; the University of Chicago; DePaul University; the University of Exeter; Georgetown University; the 2000 W. G. Hart Conference at the Institute of Advanced Legal Studies, London; Harvard University; the 1999 International Humor Conference in Oakland, California; the University of Iowa; the Law Librarians Association of Wisconsin; the 1999 meeting of the Law and Society Association; the London School of Economics and Political Science; the University of Southern California; Southern Methodist University; Stanford University;

the State Bar of Wisconsin; the University of Texas; the University of Toronto; and the University of Wisconsin–Madison.

Finally, I want to express my appreciation for the remarkable scholarly generosity of Alan Dundes, who patiently guided me though my clumsy first steps in working with folklore material, liberally shared his immense knowledge of jokes and related matters, and by his example emboldened me to develop a sense of independent judgment in these matters. I am grateful, too, for the unfailing support and encouragement of Bill Broder, who helped me over the many obstacles, external and internal, between writing and publication.

Lowering
THE BAR

Introduction

Few who are exposed to American media and popular culture of recent decades will have missed the eruption of a great frenzy of joking about lawyers. The profusion of lawyer jokes has even inspired "meta-jokes" that play with the question of their descriptiveness and provocativeness. In late 1997, Chief Justice William Rehnquist, speaking at the dedication of a new building at the University of Virginia Law School, began by noting the presence of both lawyers and nonlawyers:

K2   In the past, when I've talked to audiences like this, I've often started off with a lawyer joke, a complete caricature of a lawyer who's been nasty, greedy and unethical. But I've stopped that practice.

    I gradually realized that the lawyers in the audience didn't think the jokes were funny and the non-lawyers didn't know they were jokes.[2]

From ancient Greece and the New Testament to our own day, lawyers have long been objects of derision.[3] From time to time, attacks on lawyers have intensified and entered the political arena. In early modern England, lawyers were condemned for avarice and greed, for stimulating unneeded litigation and then prolonging it. Historian E. W. Ives reports lawyers were despised for their willingness to wrench the law to serve their causes, but "the most frequently heard of all the charges against the lawyers" was their partiality to the rich. He quotes an attack made in 1583: "The lawyers . . . handle poor men's matters coldly, they execute justice partially, & they receive bribes greedily, so that justice is perverted, the poor beggared, and many a good man in[j]ured thereby. They respect the persons and not the causes; money, not the poor; rewards and not conscience."[4] As lawyers outstripped the clergy in influence, they became the subject of "ferocious satirical abuse,"[5] eventually occupying the "role which in earlier literature had been filled by monks, friars, usurers and the diabolical Jesuits."[6]

From the late sixteenth century "the numbers, influence, and wealth of common lawyers and the volume of litigation were all growing very rapidly" and "both the vehemence and volume of recorded anti-lawyer comment" increased steadily.[7] By the mid-seventeenth century, litigation was widely viewed as a social evil, attributable to the presence of "multitudes of . . . irresponsible lawyers."[8]

Lawyers were viewed as parasites who consumed rather than promoted the nation's wealth.[9] The presence of lawyers in large numbers evidenced the severity of the nation's sickness. Schemes for regulation of the profession competed with cries for outright abolition.[10]

In postrevolutionary America, lawyers were again the targets of fierce contempt. "There existed a violent universal prejudice against the legal profession as a class" and its members "'were denounced as banditti, as blood-suckers, as pick-pockets, as wind-bags, as smooth-tongued rogues. . . . The mere sight of a lawyer . . . was enough to call forth an oath.'"[11] In March 1789, two months before the Constitutional Convention convened in Philadelphia, future president John Quincy

1. Blessings of Brittain—or A Flight of Lawyers (BM 12862. Williams, 1817). A swarm of legal dignitaries, judges, barristers and clerks descends on Westminster Hall, the seat of the higher courts, on the First Day of Term.

Adams, then a Harvard senior, addressed a college "conference": "The profession of the Law labours under the heavy weight of popular indignation; . . . it is upbraided as the original cause of all the evils with which the Commonwealth is distressed." Later that year he wrote to his mother, Abigail: "The popular odium which has been excited against the practitioners in this Commonwealth prevails to so great a degree that the most innocent and irreproachable life cannot guard a lawyer against the hatred of his fellow citizens."[12]

We live in another epoch of heightened antilawyerism. In terms of violence and vituperation, contemporary attacks on lawyers are mild in comparison to earlier sieges. But the recurrence of many of the same grievances and complaints suggests that the current eruption is neither random nor unique. Episodes of elevated anti-lawyerism are never entirely new; they draw on old themes and employ old images and tropes. But they are never just reruns, for such episodes are not just about lawyers: they are about people's responses to the distinct features of a particular legal system and the wider society that surrounds it.

A future historian looking back at our time may find one of the distinctive and peculiar features of late twentieth-century America to be the consternation about law that gripped much of American society in the 1980s and persisted through the turn of the century. America, it was endlessly repeated, has too much law, too many lawyers, too much litigation, and an obsessively contentious population that sues at the drop of a hat. "Everyone knows" that the United States is the most litigious nation on earth, indeed in human history, and many believe that excessive resort to law marks America's moral decline and entails enormous costs that portend economic disaster in an increasingly competitive world.

These images of law's maladies and afflictions coexist with a deep-seated belief that law is a wonderful thing. In the abstract, law is celebrated: the rule of law is regarded as a defining, essential, and valuable feature of our society. As an every-day presence, law generally meets a commonsensical acceptance, qualified by a sanguine recognition of its shortcomings. Our legal culture manages to contain multiple and conflicting visions of law. It is the cornerstone of our commonwealth; it is a costly, erratic, but indispensable resource for dealing with many workaday problems; it is a malign and dangerous presence.[13] By legal culture I refer to the shared, overlapping, and sometimes conflicting beliefs, expectations, and aspirations that Americans hold about law, lawyers, and litigation. The legal culture is not a fixed set of beliefs but, like literary or culinary culture, a shared repertoire from which we fashion responses to our lives and our society.

In this book I explore American legal culture by probing some of its less examined manifestations, especially the great stream of jokes about lawyers that has overflowed in recent years. The jokes are juxtaposed with other outcroppings of legal culture—public opinion as expressed in surveys; the discourse about law among political, media, and business elites; and the portrayal of law and lawyers in the media. These are different soundings of the same submerged complex of legal culture that undergirds American institutions.

To understand public images and perceptions of lawyers, we have to consider not only the flesh and blood lawyers that populate the world but the virtual lawyers that appear in television dramas, in news reports and punditry, in novels, in movies, in advertisements, and as the butt of jokes. Real and imaginary lawyers interact—like the people and the toons in *Who Framed Roger Rabbit?* (1988)—and sometimes it is hard to tell them apart.[14] The fusion of real and imaginary lawyers is not new, but we have had a great increase in exposure to both.

A convenient overall measure of feelings about lawyers is provided by changing public response to a Gallup poll inquiry asking people to rate the honesty and ethical standards of lawyers. In 1976, 27 percent rated lawyers low or very low. By 1994, this had risen to 47 percent.[15] In 1976 public opinion about lawyers' ethics was bell-shaped, with about as many rating them above average as below average. But by 1994, the 47 percent who rated them poorly were balanced by only 17 percent who thought their ethics better than average. Most of the change occurred after 1992.

In reading the polls' story of declining regard for lawyers, we should be wary of assuming that opinion about the legal profession has fallen from its normal plane of respect to a historic low. The "historic low" reading comports with the scenario favored by many lawyers, including eminent judges, in which the profession has fallen from an earlier state of grace into an abject and debased condition.[16] In this view, the proliferation of hostile lawyer jokes is a mark of the decline in lawyers' professionalism. I shall argue that this view is mistaken. For now, just recall that public estimation of lawyers was far less favorable at earlier points in American history. In the years following the Revolution, during the Jacksonian era, and in the years after the rise of industrialism, there were strong currents of hostility to lawyers that have not been outdone by contemporary lawyer bashing.

What is singular about the current sense of decline is the high elevation from which descent is measured. The period around 1960 may well have been the historic high point of public regard for law and lawyers. It was certainly an era of favorable portrayal by the media. In movies such as *Witness for the Prosecution* (1957), *Anatomy of a Murder* (1959), *Compulsion* (1959), *Inherit the Wind* (1960), *Judgment at Nuremberg* (1961), and *To Kill a Mockingbird* (1962), and on television with *The Defenders* (1961–65) and *Perry Mason* (1966–72), lawyers ranged from the benign to the heroic.[17] Steven Stark regards the lawyers portrayed in shows like *The Defenders* and *Owen Marshall* (1971–74) as "television's great benevolent authority figures."[18] To Anthony Chase, the portrayals in films like *To Kill a Mockingbird* represent "a complete integration of the virtuous-lawyer archetype in popular culture—an elaborated image unprecedented . . . [in] American mass cultural iconography."[19] In that film, and in the massively influential novel on which it was based, Atticus Finch, a lawyer in a small Alabama town during the 1930s, appointed to defend a poor black man accused of raping a white woman, courageously exposes himself to personal and professional risk to foil a lynching and to resist intimidation. Marshaling all his professional skill for this uphill battle, Finch demolishes the prosecution's case, but succeeds only in prolonging the jury's deliberation beyond the perfunctory. The jury convicts his client, who is killed trying to flee.

The tale of Atticus Finch's struggle has been a massive presence in American popular culture. For two generations, it has been one of the most frequently required books in American secondary schools. A 1991 survey of lifetime reading habits found that among the books mentioned as having "made a difference" in respondents' lives, Harper Lee's *To Kill a Mockingbird* ranked second only to the Bible.[20] The figure of its lawyer protagonist, Atticus Finch, resonates at many locations on the cultural spectrum. When, in 2003, the American Film Institute generated a list of the "top 100 movie heroes," Atticus was number one, outranking Indiana Jones, James Bond, Rick Blaine (the Humphrey Bogart character in *Casablanca*), and Rocky Balboa among others.

No figure in contemporary popular culture, with the possible exception of Abraham Lincoln, rivals Atticus Finch as an icon of the good lawyer. Within the profession, too, his story carries a powerful symbolic charge. For law and film scholar Michael Asimow, Atticus Finch is the "patron saint" of all lawyers who rise above exclusive concern with the bottom line. "He is a mythic character. He is everything we lawyers wish we were and hope we will become."[21] For decades, *To Kill a Mockingbird* has been the site of pitched battles among contending views of lawyerly virtue.[22]

In the real world of the 1960s, the civil rights struggle and its many progeny inspired many young lawyers to view the law as a shining sword with which to vanquish the long-festering problems of exclusion, poverty, and oppression. Benign and inventive courts could thread their way to a solution of society's most intractable problems with the help of energetic, public-spirited lawyers representing the silent and powerless. Legal services for the poor burgeoned, and the ideal of lawyers as valiant and dedicated warriors for justice ramified into environmental law, consumer law, and other "public interest" salients.

Lawyers were riding a wave of favorable regard of the whole panoply of social institutions.[23] As that wave broke up in the course of Vietnam War protests and the challenge to established authority in the early 1970s, scathing denunciations of the legitimacy and effectiveness of law gained prominence. In 1971 the editor of *The Rule of Law* discerned "a full scale assault on legal and political authority" and described as commonplace the view that "law in the United States is in bad shape both in theory and in practice."[24] The same year the editor of another collection reported with evident satisfaction wide agreement that "the legal system . . . is collapsing and can no longer be saved in its present form," and an establishment bar group sponsored an anguished examination of "Is Law Dead?"[25]

The "death of law" was short lived. The Watergate crisis (1972–74) accelerated the decline of public confidence in elites and, in particular, discredited lawyers who figured so prominently among the Watergate villains, but at the same time it revived allegiance to the rule of law.[26] The resolution of the crisis inspired appreciation that "the system worked." Criticism of legal institutions for failure to serve the public interest was taken up by a section of the legal establishment. The "public interest law" and "access to justice" movements that flourished during the 1970s sought to give voice to unrepresented groups, to enlarge the modalities for securing justice, and to inspire lawyers to embrace these neglected responsibilities.[27]

A decade of attacks on lawyers for abuse of ordinary clients, self-serving alliances with the powerful, and failure to implement equal justice culminated in a remarkable 1978 address by President Jimmy Carter, who took the occasion of the one hundredth anniversary dinner of the Los Angeles County Bar Association to deliver a critique of the legal system.[28] Beginning with an excerpt from *Bleak House,* President Carter excoriated "excessive litigation and legal featherbedding" and chastised lawyers for aggravating rather than resolving conflict. These familiar complaints were interwoven with another set of themes that have been notably absent from recent political rhetoric about the legal system. President Carter declared that legal services were, more than any resource in our society, "wastefully [and] unfairly distributed." Lawyers were particularly to blame for failing to make justice "blind to rank, power, and position." He deplored that "lawyers of great influence and prestige led the fight against civil rights and economic justice." Devoted to the service of dominant groups, lawyers had failed to discharge their "heavy obligation to serve the true ends of justice." In short, lawyers had fallen woefully short of their calling to be votaries of justice in an imperfect world. Carter called on them to embrace the theme of "Access to Justice," which was the official theme of the American Bar Association for 1978. Although the tones were critical, the song was one of optimism and hope: lawyers' rededication to their high calling combined with institutional redesign could vindicate the promise of connecting law to the pursuit of a just society.[29] Although the president's observations did not elicit a warm reception from the bar or the media, his criticism of the bar met with general public approval.[30]

A similar "public justice" critique infused the work of the Kutak Commission, set up by the American Bar Association in 1977, in the wake of Watergate, to revise the rules of ethical conduct for lawyers.[31] The major theme of the new Model Rules proposed by the commission was enlargement of the public duties of lawyers and limitation of their license for adversary combat.[32] The commission sought to accentuate the duties of lawyers that transcended their responsibilities to clients—for example, by limiting confidentiality to enable lawyers to blow the whistle on client wrongdoing, by imposing a duty of fairness in negotiations by requiring disclosure of material facts, and by mandating that lawyers devote a portion of their time to pro bono publico work.[33] The commission's proposals aroused fierce opposition from various sectors of the bar and were vitiated at a series of ABA meetings in 1982 and 1983.[34]

In the late 1970s, at the time that Carter and the Kutak Commission were calling the profession to account for its failure to pursue justice for the public, the first murmurs were heard of what was to become a great roar of denunciation of the legal system.[35] Eminent judges, lawyers, and academics opined that American society was suffering from an excess of law in the form of "legal pollution" or a "litigation explosion." The popular press echoed this concern, reporting that "Americans in all walks of life are being buried under an avalanche of lawsuits."[36] Led by the chief justice of the United States, important sections of the legal elite began to express their unhappiness with the enlargement of the legal system and the multiplication of rights. Chief Justice Warren Burger criticized lawyers for commercialism, for incompetence, and for excessive adversariness that produced court congestion and runaway litigation.[37] He mounted a broad attack aimed at curtailing litigation and replacing adversarial confrontation with a "better way."[38]

By the mid-1980s, the discourse about lawyers and civil justice in America was dominated by what I call the "jaundiced view." Our civil justice system was widely condemned as pathological and destructive, producing untold harm. A series of factoids or macro-anecdotes about litigation became the received wisdom: America is the most litigious society in the course of all human history; Americans sue at the drop of a hat; the courts are brimming over with frivolous lawsuits; resort to courts is a first rather than a last resort; runaway juries make capricious awards to undeserving claimants; immense punitive damage awards are routine; litigation is undermining our ability to compete economically.[39] Although a litigious populace and activist judges were also blamed, lawyers, as the promoters, beneficiaries, and protectors of this pathological system, held pride of place among the culprits responsible.

The Enlargement and Withdrawal of the Legal World

Both the proliferation and prominence of lawyer jokes and the emergence of the jaundiced view were responses to a massive transformation of the legal system. In the course of a generation, there was a dramatic change in scale of many aspects of the legal world: the amount and complexity of legal regulation; the frequency of litigation; the amount and tenor of authoritative legal material; the number, coordination, and productivity of lawyers; the number of legal actors and the resources they devoted to legal activity; the amount of information about law and the velocity with which it circulated.

These changes in the legal world in turn reflected changes in the surrounding economy and society. Compared to 1960, the American population in the 1980s was larger, older, more affluent, more educated, and more diverse.[40] It enjoyed a higher level of social services, higher life expectancy, and higher expectations of institutional performance.[41] At the same time, it had much less confidence in government, business, and other major institutions.[42] The economy expanded.[43] More Americans worked. There was a pronounced shift away from the making of goods to the providing of services.[44] In particular, there was an immense multiplication of financial transactions.[45] The economy was internationalized.[46]

The number of lawyers grew rapidly. Throughout the middle of the twentieth century, the number of lawyers per capita had remained roughly the same— and roughly the same as the number of physicians. But starting in the 1960s the proportion of lawyers in the population increased steeply, tripling from 1965 to the end of the century and greatly outstripping the number of physicians.[47] Society's spending on law increased markedly. The portion of the national income and product derived from legal services roughly doubled from 1960 to 1985.[48]

Not only were there more lawyers, there was more law. The amount of law increased exponentially. There were more federal regulatory statutes, more agencies, more staff, more enforcement expenditures, and more rules.[49] The body of authoritative legal material grew immensely as did the amount of commentary that glosses it.[50] After a long period of stability in the legal workplace, a rapid succession of new technologies—photoreproduction, computerization, on-line data services, overnight delivery services, electronic mail, and fax machines—multiplied the amount of information that could be assembled and manipulated by legal actors.[51]

Starting around 1960, after a thirty-year period in which the rate of civil litigation in the United States was low by historic standards, the amount of litigation began to rise.[52] Total civil filings in the federal courts grew from 59,284 in 1960 to 273,670 in 1985.[53] Comparable figures for the state courts are not available, but a sense of the growth of state judicial activity can be gathered from the number of lawyers employed by state courts, from 7,581 in 1960 to 18,674 in 1985.[54] Courts, federal and state, acquired more staff, clerks, and professional administrators.[55] These larger staffs were equipped with new information technologies, which increased the "production" of these institutions even faster.

Even more significant than the quantitative growth of the law was a gradual but pronounced change in its tenor. Before World War II, American law in practice provided little remedy for have-nots against dominant groups. Lawrence Friedman described the late nineteenth-century tort system as a "system of non-compensation" in which few claims were brought and plaintiffs faced an array of doctrinal, practical, and cultural barriers to recovery.[56] Studying personal injury cases in New York City over a forty-year period, Randolph Bergstrom concluded that "the injured had few reasons to think that lawsuits would offer a ready source of sustenance in 1870, less still in 1910."[57] My own review of pre-World War II disasters showed that compensation was uncertain and meager.[58] Successful claims by those in subordinate positions against bosses and authorities were few and far between.

But after World War II, courts and legislatures extended legal protections and remedies for more of life's troubles and problems to more and more people, including those who earlier were largely excluded from it—injured workers and consumers, blacks, women, the disabled, prisoners, and so on. Compensation for many of life's troubles became routine, through social insurance (ranging from social security disability payments to federal insurance of bank deposits) and through use of the litigation system.[59] Expectations of remedy and compensation rose.[60] Legal representation of claimants was more available and more proficient.[61] There was more "litigation up" by outsiders and clients and dependents against authorities and managers of established institutions and a corresponding shrinkage of the leeways and immunities from legal accountability of the powerful.

This enlargement of remedy was accompanied by (or some might say accomplished by) a cultural shift: the expansion and elaboration of the notion of rights. Broad sections of the public came to believe that the law would secure them remedy and vindication.[62] Although any particular bit is contested, the general direction remains clear—rights, and remedies for their violation, continue to grow. Law has become the master wall-to-wall orderer of our social life, and lawyers, as its custodians, have become "the dominant profession in American society."[63]

But the other side of rights is control and accountability. Whole areas of governmental activity that were not previously thought needful of close articulation with legal principles are now subjected to judicial oversight.[64] These include large sections of the criminal justice system, including police, prisons, and juvenile justice; and other institutions dealing with dependent clients such as schools,[65] mental hospitals, and welfare agencies.[66] Government entered into areas of life previously unregulated by the state (for example, in the great proliferation of environmental, health, and safety regulation) or in which regulation had not been closely linked to the application of legal principles. In the area of health care, for example, regulation of entitlement to treatment and provider compensation has proliferated. Similarly, the employment relationship has been legalized, through the welfare state's job and income security programs and through civil rights acts and wrongful discharge litigation.[67] Nor are our amusements exempt: much of the sports pages is devoted to reports of legal rulings and maneuvers. In each of these areas—health care, employment, sports—regulation by legal institutions inspires answering legalization by bodies within these social fields, who promulgate rules, hold hearings, and give decisions in a legal manner.[68] As public standards penetrate into every corner of social life, the amount of private regulatory activity is multiplied rather than reduced.[69]

The increased pervasiveness of law is reflected in popular perception of the ubiquity of law and its intrusion into areas previously immune from its impingement—for example, in stories about suits by children against their parents. A cartoon portrays an incredulous father who asks his son across the table, "You say if I make you drink your milk, you'll sue me?"[70] This theme presents itself seriously in the continuing controversy about the legal limitation of parental authority. Similarly, figure 2 epitomizes an uncomfortable sense that the world has been legalized—that our world of primal experience has been penetrated, permeated, colonized, and somehow diminished by a derivative and unprofitable layer of the legal. This unease—and recoil—manifests itself in many ways, from the wry reflection of these cartoons to widespread popular concern about the legal explosion,[71] excessive litigation, and too many lawyers to recondite anxieties about the "bureaucratization of the world,"[72] the "juridification of the social spheres,"[73] and the "colonization of the life-world."[74]

Life becomes more legalized. Legal norms and institutions are invoked to regulate dealings with intimates as well as to exert leverage on remote entities.[75] Modern society throws up more predicaments in which we find ourselves affected by actors that we have no leverage to control and hold accountable. Modern technology increases the power of faraway actions to impinge on us. Increasingly, our transactions and disputes are not with other persons, but with corporate organizations.[76] A greater portion of our dealings and our disputes are with remote actors. The growth of knowledge enables us to trace out these connections and establish responsibility for ramifying consequences. Education and wealth make more of us more competent in using institutions. We use law more, both in its overt forms of legislation, regulation, and litigation and in our internalized standards and our anticipation of others' expectations.

But law is not free. The law's enlarged responsiveness to the concerns of ordinary people is countered and rationed by the mounting cost of resort to an increasingly complex system. The system is more inclusive, but all parts of it have grown. During the era of expanding responsiveness to victims and outsiders, there was even greater growth in legal activity on behalf of dominant groups: litigation by businesses increased more rapidly than litigation by individuals; legal expenditures by businesses and government increased more rapidly than expenditures by

"Interesting. Have your lawyer call my lawyer."

2. Cartoon by Robert Mankoff (© The New Yorker Collection 1985, from cartoonbank.com. All rights reserved.)

individuals; the large firm sector of the legal profession that provides services for corporations and large organizations grew and prospered more than the small firm sector that services individuals.[77]

Increasingly, law is shaped by and for large organizational actors, for artificial persons rather than natural ones.[78] In the past century purposive corporate organizations (political/business/associational) displaced spontaneous "communal" or "primordial" institutions (such as families, religious fellowships, networks of transactors, neighbors, and friends) as the predominant forms of organizing human activity.[79] More of our lives consist of dealings with these corporate actors. They are, by virtue of their scale and rationality, effective players of the legal game and enjoy enduring and cumulative advantages over individuals.[80] More and more of the legal world is devoted to servicing them—whether we measure this by expenditures on legal services[81] or by the total effort expended by lawyers.[82] Increasingly the law has become an arena for routine and continuous play by organizations, an arena that individuals enter briefly in life emergencies. At the same time ordinary people as well as elites consume ever more and increasingly vivid images of the legal.

These trends entwine in curious ways. The legal system has grown prodigiously; law has become more elaborate and more visible; it occupies a larger part of the symbolic universe. The law proliferates new symbols of rights and entitlements—enlivening consciousness and heightening our expectations of vindication. At the same time it becomes more menacing and more forbiddingly difficult and costly to invoke.

The higher expectations that individuals bring to the law provoked a massive recoil. Unease among elites about the expansion of law joined with corporate interest in curtailing liability to fuel campaigns deriding law and lawyers. These intensified in the mid-1980s. Corporate spokesmen and their political allies mournfully recite the woes of a legal system in which Americans, egged on by avaricious lawyers, sue too readily, and irresponsible juries and activist judges waylay blameless businesses at enormous cost in social and economic well-being. The legal system, we are told, is "crazy" and "demented"; it has "spun out of control."

At the same time law and lawyers suddenly became much more visible. As late as the 1970s, information about the working of legal institutions was limited in content and restricted in circulation. The operations of law firms were shrouded in confidentiality. When Erwin Smigel studied Wall Street lawyers in the late 1950s he encountered massive institutionalized reticence. Older and conservative lawyers, he reported, "thought of their organizations in much the same manner as clergymen think of the church—as an institution that should not be studied."[83] The world of law practice was preferredly opaque. "Talking about clients and fees just isn't done, not even when lawyers gather among themselves."[84] The taboo on information about partnership agreements, finances, relations with clients, even their identity, was mirrored in bans on advertising, solicitation, and promotion.[85] The turnabout came quite abruptly in the late 1970s as a curious by-product of the Supreme Court's 1977 *Bates* decision, ruling that sweeping restrictions on lawyer advertising violated the First Amendment.[86] *Bates* liberated lawyers to talk to the press about their practices, for they no longer feared being accused of advertising. This new access to lawyers combined with enlarged curiosity about law and lawyers to revolutionize legal journalism.[87] Reporting about lawyers in general publications like the *New York Times,* the *Wall Street Journal,* and the news weeklies became more frequent, detailed, and intrusive.[88] A new kind of legal trade press provided a steady diet of detailed backstage information about law firm structure, hiring policies, marketing strategies, clients, fees, and compensation.[89] Contemporary observers noted that "law and lawyers are becoming demystified. The rites of secrecy have passed."[90] Not only were law firms more open, but the operations of the courts were less shrouded, and many core legal activities became more accessible. This openness is dramatized by the Freedom of Information Act, by open meeting laws, by courtroom television, and by interviewing of jurors.[91] Scholarship, journalism, and commerce all used the new accessibility of lawyers to penetrate into previously off-limits, backstage areas of legal life. Information that just a few years earlier would have been available only to a few insiders now circulated freely.

As the old system of professional reticence collapsed many eager hands moved to feed an enlarged public appetite for material about the legal arena. Movies and television were increasingly free of the censorship that had barred unfavorable portrayals of the legal system.[92] The wildly popular *L.A. Law* arrived on prime time television screens in 1986 and quickly became a barometer of public appetite for lawyer stories. A great surge of lawyer shows on TV[93] was accompanied by the emergence of best-selling legal thrillers, beginning with Scott Turow's *Presumed Innocent* in 1987 and continuing with the meteoric ascent of John Grisham after the publication of *The Firm* in 1991.[94]

Unlike earlier contingents of imaginary lawyers, many of those who have arrived since 1980 are both more deeply flawed and more three-dimensional. They are seen in not only the courtroom/counseling "frontstage" of lawyering, but the backstage areas as well; and their advocacy for clients is enmeshed in a setting of tactical maneuver, political constraints, and career strategy—not to mention a personal quest for fulfillment or redemption. These fictive lawyers encounter complex questions with few clear blacks and whites but many shades of gray, ethical dilemmas that often have no satisfying resolution. The lawyer is portrayed not as an unalloyed hero, but as the occupant of a crucial but morally ambiguous and precarious role.[95]

The imaginary lawyers on television are not a likely source of the public's negative picture of lawyers. The portrayal of lawyers on television series is more favorable than the public's perceptions of actual lawyers—or even than the perceptions of lawyers themselves.[96] Indeed, researchers suggested that the favorable TV image of attorneys, "especially their prowess in arguing cases in court," may result in inflated and unrealizable public expectations of attorneys.[97]

In the old regime of restricted information about the law in action, the legal order could be perceived in terms of its esteemed frontstage qualities—as formal, autonomous, rule-determined, certain, professional, learned, apolitical, and so forth. Everyone knew it was not exactly that way in his or her own corner, but private and fragmented knowledge of local deviations did not challenge the received picture of the system as a whole. Professionals and outsiders could maintain cherished images of the legal world even while aware of much that the dominant paradigm labeled atypical and deviant. But the profusion of information about the workings of law challenged these relatively stable and comfortable views and made it more difficult to dismiss discretion, bargaining, improvisation, and politics as extraneous to the law.[98]

LEARNING FROM LAWYER JOKES

Where many groups feel threatened by social and legal changes, and others are disappointed in the law's unfilled promises, the underlying and ineradicable themes of hostility toward lawyers are available to decipher and explain these troubling developments.

Jokes about lawyers have been around for a long time, and in the 1980s they acquired a prominence and currency they had not enjoyed earlier.[99] By the mid-1980s, observers noted an increase in the frequency and intensity of joking about lawyers. In 1986, a Los Angeles lawyer identified lawyer jokes as contributing significantly to the pervasive negative image of the profession and admonished lawyers to "recognize the inherent destructiveness of lawyer jokes and [to] resolve not to tolerate them."[100] A year later, Alan Dundes, the leading student of joke cycles, noted the onset of a wave of lawyer jokes.[101] The following year the annual meeting of the California bar included a workshop on the spread of lawyer jokes entitled "Why Are They Laughing?"[102] Observers noted the "spate of lawyer jokebooks," "radio talk shows across the country . . . feeding the frenzy, vying with each other in barrister-bashing," and "the emergence of a virtual mini-industry in legal humor."[103]

Lawyer jokes had their moment in the media sun in 1993, when a disgruntled client's shooting of eight people in a San Francisco law office led the president of the California Bar Association to call for a moratorium on lawyer bashing: "There's a point at which jokes and humor are acceptable and a point at which they become nothing more than hate speech."[104] His plea provoked an outpouring of media comment, almost all of it hostile. Animosity toward lawyers is perennial. Its expressions and intensity change, drawing upon a great cultural repertoire of antilawyer observations and sentiments.[105] At the turn of the twenty-first century, between five hundred and one thousand jokes about lawyers were circulating in the United States. Any such number is arbitrary, for just how many there are depends on how one distinguishes lawyer jokes from other jokes and similar items from one another. The point is that we are not dealing in dozens or in thousands. There are many ways to impose some order on this mass of material. One could organize it by form, sorting out narratives from riddles, or by source, or by time of their appearance. Because I want to relate the jokes to other expressions about lawyers and law, I have tried to organize them thematically rather than formally or historically.

As one listens to the jokes, it becomes apparent that a number of themes and figures recur repeatedly. I have organized some of the common themes into nine clusters. Five of these focus on substantive complaints about the things lawyers do, namely, that they are (1) corrupters of discourse, (2) economic predators, (3) fomenters of strife, (4) betrayers of trust, and (5) enemies of justice. The other four clusters focus not on the deeds of lawyers but on their character and standing and on our response to them. They characterize lawyers as (6) allies of the devil, (7) morally deficient, (8) objects of scorn, and (9) candidates for elimination.

"There's one thing about the law I always wanted to know but was afraid to ask: Where in the hell do all the lawyer jokes come from?"

3. Cartoon by Eldon Dedini in S. Gross, ed., *Lawyers! Lawyers! Lawyers!* (© Eldon Dedini 1994)

These categories in turn can be organized into two waves, an enduring core of topics and themes that have been well established for several centuries and a set of new thematic areas that have flourished since 1980. A few precursors of these new themes were present earlier, but their development as major parts of the lawyer joke corpus is quite recent. The two waves correlate in an inexact way with a division between what lawyers do and what they are. The clusters in the enduring core focus on substantive gripes about lawyer behavior. The exception is the allies of the devil cluster, which summarizes evaluations of lawyers by invocation of the symbols of hell, sin, and the devil. The clusters in the new territories focus not on lawyers' deeds but on their character, standing, and abundance. Again, there is an exception, in the betrayal cluster. Mainly, the old clusters are about things that lawyers do, while the new clusters are about what they are. In addition to the nine categories, my archive (described below) contains a cluster of jokes about particular demographic subsets of lawyers (such as women and Jews) and a small set of meta-jokes (i.e., jokes about lawyer jokes). I have designated each category with a letter which is used to identify the jokes in that category in text and in the Register of Jokes (appendix).

The Enduring Core

A. *Discourse:* Lawyers lie incorrigibly. They corrupt discourse by promoting needless complexity, mystifying matters by jargon and formalities, robbing life's dealings of their moral sense by recasting them in legal abstractions, and offending common sense by casuistry that makes black appear white and vice versa.

B. *Economic Predators:* Lawyers are economic predators; they are greedy, money-driven monopolists. They charge outrageously high fees, misread social exchanges as professional consultations, shamelessly pad their bills. They are parasitic rent-seekers who don't really produce anything, but merely batten on the productive members of society, often in alliance with the undeserving—opportunistic malingerers in one version, the privileged and powerful in another.

C. *Allies of the Devil:* Lawyers are associated with the devil, hell, sin, and irreligion.

D. *Conflict:* Lawyers are aggressive, competitive hired guns, incurably contentious, unprincipled mercenaries who foment strife and conflict by encouraging individual self-serving and self-assertion rather than cooperative problem solving.

J. *Enemies of Justice:* Lawyers are indifferent to justice and willingly lend their talents to frustrate it.

The New Territories

F. *Betrayers of Trust:* Lawyers are opportunistic, manipulative, self-serving deceivers who, under color of pursuing large public responsibilities, take advantage not only of hapless opponents but of clients who entrust their fortunes to them, and even partners, friends, and family.

G. *Moral Deficiency:* Lawyers are morally obtuse, callous, insensitive, deficient in ordinary human sentiments and lacking in common decencies.

H. *Objects of Scorn:* These stories address neither the deeds of lawyers nor their deficiencies of character, but their low reputation. Once identified as objects of universal scorn, lawyers can be despised precisely because of the shared contempt for them.

I. *Death Wish:* These jokes envision and celebrate the death, removal, or absence of lawyers. One set dramatizes lawyers in the aggregate as a pestilential affliction.

Other Clusters

E. *Demography:* These jokes focus on the personal identity of lawyers (women, Jews, etc.).

K. *Meta-jokes:* Jokes about lawyer jokes.

Some jokes fall neatly into one of these clusters, while others touch on several themes. For convenience, I have assigned each joke a home in one cluster. Each cluster is a composite, consisting of a number of specific and partially overlapping

"The judicial rulings are over here. That section is all lawyer jokes."

4. Cartoon by Sidney Harris (© The New Yorker Collection 2002, from cartoonbank.com. All rights reserved.)

complaints. In each cluster, there is a spectrum, from complaints about mistreatment of specific individuals (clients, opponents) to wrongdoing that has large public consequences. The jokes, as we shall see, tend to focus on the individual grievance side; the public effects of lawyers' shortcomings are dealt with indirectly.

Each of these clusters points to the dark side of things that may otherwise appear as virtues or at least useful qualities for lawyering. In the sins of discourse we can recognize the inventiveness of lawyers, their obsession with precision and relevance. In economic predation, we can appreciate the lawyer's prowess as an agent of redistribution. Fomenting conflict mirrors the lawyer's zealous advocacy and insistence on vindicating rights. The betrayal complaint proclaims regard for the lawyer as a potent ally, coupled with anxiety and resentment that he is an undependable ally. The jokes, as we shall see, reveal that the qualities and actions for which lawyers are despised are closely related to the things for which they are esteemed.[106] Beneath their surface of ridicule and condemnation, the jokes exhibit equivocal feelings about lawyers and the legal world.

Can we learn anything from the jokes about the enlarged legal world and our response to it? An op-ed piece in the legal press mocks the idea that lawyer jokes have any wider significance and attributes their popularity simply to their being funny.[107] But of course that begs the question of why this is funny now to a lot of people rather than bizarre or disgusting or pointless. Even if we grant a significant role in life to sheer accident and randomness, to regard an enduring social product like jokes as undeserving of inquiry seems a gratuitous denial of the sociological imagination. This book proceeds on the opposite premise, that the persistence of the social practice of telling, appreciating, and publishing jokes may reveal something about our society and ourselves that may otherwise elude us. As Alan Dundes puts it: "No piece of folklore continues to be transmitted unless it means something—even if neither the speaker nor the audience can articulate what that meaning might be. In fact, it usually is essential that the joke's meaning not be crystal clear. If people knew what they were communicating when they told jokes, the jokes would cease to be effective as socially sanctioned outlets for expressing taboo ideas and subjects. Where there is anxiety, there will be jokes to express that anxiety. . . . Remember, people joke about only what is most serious."[108]

In *An American Dilemma,* his classic study of American race relations, published in 1944, Gunnar Myrdal took patterns of jokes as revealing the hidden fault lines of social life. Noting the prominence of joking by whites and blacks about each other, he observed:

> It is no accident that . . . jokes play a particularly important role in the lives of the Southerners, white and black, and specifically in race relations. It should not surprise us that sex relations are another field of human life with a great proliferation of jokes. . . . When people are up against great inconsistencies in their creed and behavior, which they cannot, or do not want to, account for rationally, humor is a way out. It gives a symbolic excuse for imperfections. . . . The main "function" of the jokes is thus to

create a collective surreptitious approbation for something which cannot be approved explicitly because of moral inhibitions.[109]

Half a century after Myrdal found jokes expressive of the "deep seated ambivalence" of American race relations, law and lawyers joined race and sex as one of the great staples of joking in the United States.[110] Analysis of these jokes can, I believe, enable us to chart our legal imagination.

Because the enterprise of extracting intellectual treasure from such ignoble low grade ore may encounter more than a little skepticism, it may be helpful to review some of the methodological choices and problems that are involved in this undertaking.

Although I have always had a fondness for jokes, my interest in lawyer jokes started with an interest in lawyers rather than in jokes per se. For thirty years I have been studying patterns of litigation in the United States and have been interested in lawyers as players in the litigation game. I have been particularly concerned with the widespread perception that the United States is in the throes of a "litigation explosion" and the notion that lawyers are to blame for many of society's ills. Lawyer jokes attracted my attention as an increasingly prominent part of the rhetorical assault on lawyers and the legal system.

I started out by collecting lawyer jokes that struck me as telling or clever or outrageous. When the thought of writing about them came over me, I enlarged my collecting to include jokes that seemed to be ubiquitous even though I found some of them less engaging. As I began to see some patterns in the jokes, I added still others that seemed to fit those patterns. I soon realized that many of the jokes were quite old, while others were young, and that some had done long service as lawyer jokes while others were recent (and in some cases marginal) conscripts to the lawyer joke corpus. It finally dawned on me that lawyer jokes were not a distinct realm but an inseparable part of a much larger complex of jokes.

My literary searches began with the dozen or so collections of lawyer jokes published since 1982. Then I started looking at general joke collections and books of anecdotes for speakers, particularly older books. Although there are few bibliographic aids in this area, there are lots of books. I have now found and reviewed almost one thousand printed collections. In addition to books, my sources included several disk and CD-ROM collections, compilations on the Internet, and pickings from several e-mail joke lists. I searched for stories on "lawyer jokes" in the Nexis News Library, and in a few cases where I was particularly interested I did searches to find instances of particular jokes. As my obsession became known to friends, colleagues, and students, I was the grateful recipient of many texts and leads.

I have ended up with "jokographies" of about three hundred jokes, listing all the instances of the joke that I have been able to find, together with their (mostly printed) sources.[111] These three hundred include a significant chunk of the stories that circulate as lawyer jokes today.[112] The discussion here focuses on the United

States in the past thirty years, but the database is broadly representative of the lawyer joke corpus throughout the English-speaking world over the past two centuries. The joke population is not neatly separated into national compartments. Jokes move around the English-speaking world with surprising speed, sometimes undergoing local adaptation but often not.[113]

My archive is an unsystematic sample. It oversamples what might be called the core of very frequently encountered lawyer jokes in circulation in the last two decades. It also oversamples jokes that I found engaging because they concerned women lawyers or large firms, mentioned justice, or seemed to have dropped out of the joke corpus. Since I kept adding items to the list, some of the late additions are thinner in documentation than they deserve.

I have organized these jokes in clusters of stories around certain themes. Obviously there could have been fewer or more themes, but the ten (or eleven, counting meta-jokes) that I ended up with impose enough order to make the material manageable without squandering energy in futile deliberation about classification. Many stories straddle several themes. Of course, both the scheme and these assignments are mine and not those of the tellers/listeners.[114]

I take this corpus of lawyer jokes as reflective of popular consciousness or legal culture and treat these themes as components of it. But themes, corpus, consciousness, and culture are analytic constructs, not features experienced by the actors or resources available to them. Few if any tellers or hearers of jokes have a sense of the forebears, longevity, variants, and relations of the jokes they tell or hear. For example, if we note that a contemporary set of lawyer jokes derives from earlier jokes about Jews or mothers-in-law or politicians, this transformation may be revealing even though it is hidden from all but a few of those who tell or hear them. Individuals have partial and overlapping knowledge of a selection of the whole fund of shared material, which contains related, competing, and inconsistent themes. This kind of unknowing subliminal participation in a textual "tradition" is not peculiar to jokes. Like the carriers of literary and culinary traditions, some know more and some know less, but no participant has a mastery over the whole complex.[115] A certain level of overlap and sharing must exist to enable the enterprise to flourish, so it is possible to draw at least some conclusions about this collective body of sentiment and perception even though no participant's collection corresponds to that imaginary composite whole.

What is a joke?

The subject here is not all legal humor, but jokes.[116] Some riddles and a few definitions are included, but mostly I focus on narrative jokes (including anecdotes that have the structure of jokes).[117] Robert Hetzron provides a useful working definition: "A joke is a short humorous piece of oral literature in which the funniness culminates in the final sentence, called the punchline. In fact, the main condition is that the tension should reach its highest level at the very end. No continuation relieving the tension should be added."[118]

What is a lawyer joke?

Many of the jokes discussed in this book can, with slight modifications, be told about other groups as well as about lawyers. Indeed many originated as stories about golfers, Jews, mothers-in-law, or other protagonists and have been "enlisted" or "conscripted" into the corps of lawyer jokes. Some of these switched jokes have been adapted to lawyers by adding some specific distinguishing characteristics.[119] In contrast to these switched stories, many others, almost two-thirds of those discussed here, are indigenous to lawyers.[120] That is, they turn on specific features of the legal setting and have only limited applicability to other protagonists. Lawyer jokes then cover a range from indigenous jokes through adapted jokes to those which are switched without any significant modification.[121] Many widely circulated lawyer jokes are of the latter type. As we shall see, the long-established clusters that make up the enduring core of lawyer jokes are dominated by indigenous stories, while the latecomer categories that comprise the new territories of lawyer joking consist almost entirely of switched jokes.

For the purpose at hand, that is, using the jokes as a register of perceptions of lawyers, switched jokes are no less useful than indigenous or adapted ones. Tellers and listeners are probably unaware of and are certainly uninterested in their impure origins. The fact that a joke is told about lawyers indicates that tellers expect listeners to see it as revealing or confirming something about lawyers, and the fact that the joke endures in that form indicates that this expectation is fulfilled.

Lawyer jokes vs. jokes about lawyers

One significant troop of tellers and listeners are lawyers themselves.[122] I do not attempt here to distinguish "jokes about lawyers" from "lawyer jokes." It may be that there are some jokes told mainly by lawyers and others that are told entirely by nonlawyers. My guess is that most of the jokes here are told by various sorts of tellers to varied audiences. Unfortunately, the method of collecting material employed here does not enable me to address these matters directly. I do, however, discuss the discourse within the legal profession about lawyer jokes. That discourse may give us some clues about the relation of lawyers to lawyer jokes as an institution. It would not be surprising if lawyers have domesticated and transformed some lawyer jokes, just as Jews have reworked many jokes from anti-Semitic stories told by hostile outsiders into ironic self-observations.[123] It is possible that such a process of transformation is occurring, and that it is connected to changes in lawyers' sense of professional identity.

The lawyer joke corpus

This book focuses on the body of jokes about lawyers that is circulating in the United States and the way that it has changed in the last quarter century. An ever-changing array of jokes is being told and heard, read and thought about, remembered and misremembered, and forgotten. An omniscient observer might mark exactly what is being told, by whom, to whom, in what social settings, and what hearers and readers make of it, and so forth. But obviously we have to settle for a rough approximation of this imagined reality.

Recorded jokes and oral transmission

Some of the jokes presented here are taken directly from the oral tradition and most from published reports of that tradition. The joke corpus contains much that might be called folklore and much that might be called popular culture. I treat the joke corpus as an amalgam of folk, popular, commercial, and literary elements, and I make no effort to separate them or to privilege any over the others. The oral tradition is not an uncorrupted stream of "original" material that exists prior to and independent of the various published media. Oral, written, and broadcast sources feed upon and influence one another. In telling jokes, orality has retained a primacy that is absent in many other cultural forms. Although jokes are preserved in various written media as well as in oral transmission, contemporary cultural usage decrees that the "reality" of these jokes resides in their oral transmission and the authentic "text" is the oral one. Hetzron observes, "It is true that jokes may appear printed, but when further transferred, there is no obligation to reproduce the text verbatim, as in the case of poetry. Moreover, such secondary transmission will be viewed as equivalent to the original, unlike in other prose where a nonverbatim transmission is considered to be a 'report,' a 'synopsis,' a 'paraphrase,' but not an authentic original piece."[124]

The various recorded versions are presented here as indicators of what is abroad in the composite multimedia "tradition" I refer to as the lawyer joke corpus. Published jokes are like recipes, as opposed to the dishes themselves. Joke collections are like cookbooks; they are not collections of dishes, but of recipes. A collection of recipes provides a handy but inexact guide to what is being prepared and eaten. Although items may linger in the cookbook literature even after they fall out of favor with diners and cooks, on the whole changes over time in the contents of cookbooks reflect changes in culinary behavior.

"Switching"

In the course of oral transmission, jokes are modified by tellers, mostly inadvertently and/or incrementally, but sometimes deliberately to adapt a joke to new circumstances or even new topics. Joke books and other commercial media, in turn, do not just passively record what is circulating in the oral tradition. Typically they impose the coherence and formality of writing instead of speech. In addition, these publications are the site of entrepreneurial "switching" in which a joke about Texans or mothers-in-law or politicians is refurbished as a joke about lawyers. In the 1930s Milton Wright described the rise of professional gag-writing that accompanied the ascendence of radio: "The humor industry today is a manufacturing industry. The manufacturing process is switching, The raw material is old jokes. The finished product is new jokes."[125] Or, as Eddie Davis puts it, "The comedy writer does not steal. He switches. He pares a joke down to its core, then molds a new ripe artificial fruit around it."[126]

Switching may be less systematic and pervasive in the case of extended narrative jokes than in the gags and routines of performance comedy, but it is a prominent feature of the publication of jokes. It is particularly present in topical collections of jokes, where the compiler/editor/author may enlarge his stock by "switching" jokes about other topics or groups to insert the desired element.[127] This is evident in many of the collections of lawyer jokes published in the United States since the genre resurfaced in 1982.[128] Some appear to be simply compilations of material already circulating as jokes about lawyers, while others introduce many items that appear not to have circulated earlier as lawyer jokes.[129] Two books in particular, Larry Wilde's *Ultimate Lawyer's Joke Book* (1987) and the pseudonymous Blanche Knott's *Truly Tasteless Lawyer Jokes* (1990), seem to be responsible for grafting onto the corpus of lawyer jokes a large number of items that had circulated as jokes about politicians, mothers-in-law, Texans, Jews, and others. For any given item, it is always possible that the switch took place among tellers in the oral tradition and was merely recorded by these compilers. But the quantity of "new" material in these books and, in some cases, its close correspondence to nonlawyer material in the authors' earlier publications suggest that a good deal of the switching took place at the compiler's desk.[130]

It should be emphasized that switching is selective rather than indiscriminate. Some attempted switches just don't "take" and disappear from view; others flourish and may grow more prominent than the original version. But what "takes" is not controlled by the teller or writer; it has to strike a responsive chord in the listeners/readers. So just which items negotiate the transition from their original subjects to new ones tells us something about social perceptions. For example, jokes about Jews as devious and untrustworthy partners have been readily revamped as jokes about lawyers, but none of the many Jewish jokes about extended and precarious chains of deductive reasoning has made a successful transition, even though we might suppose they would fit with the many jokes about lawyers' peculiarities of discourse.[131] But once a joke has been successfully switched, those who encounter it in its new raiment may be unaware of its origin and perceive it as native to its new setting.[132]

Print media and the oral tradition

Print media preserve and disseminate (parts of) the oral tradition. They feed shamelessly on earlier collections; they enlarge the corpus by "switching"; and they elaborate the oral tradition by expanding and standardizing the repertoire of tellers. Very few jokes circulate in the oral tradition that do not show up in published form. I was prepared to report that among the three hundred lawyer jokes discussed here, there was only one that I have never encountered as a lawyer joke in any recorded form. But my delay in preparing the manuscript provided time for that story to cross the print barrier.[133] Lawyer jokes may be unrepresentative in this respect, for there are fewer inhibitions about recording animosity toward lawyers than toward currently sensitive targets like blacks, Jews, or women. Joking about lawyers can be less clandestine.[134]

Representativeness

Can we estimate the overall currency of a joke from evidence about its appearances in print? Oral and printed instances may occur in different proportions, but there is some correlation. Consider the lawyer jokes told to sociologist Jennifer Pierce by "secretaries, paralegals, attorneys, and other legal workers" during the fifteen months in 1988–89 that she was conducting research on law firms in the Bay Area.[135] Pierce reports twelve jokes that she was told in the course of her interviews and the number of times she was told each one. All of them appear in print and the most frequently told ones are abundantly represented.[136] Similarly, of the lawyer jokes collected by Alan Dundes's students in 1988–90 and those I collected from student and general audiences on numerous occasions in the mid-1990s, there are none that are not represented in the print media.

I conclude that when a joke is told a lot, it will turn up in print a lot. One cannot exclude the possibility that there are some hidden gems that circulate orally but do not surface in print or on-line media, but surely not many. We cannot, however, infer the converse, that when something turns up in print it is an active part of the oral tradition. The exigencies of publication—the need to fill pages, the attraction of out-of-copyright material, the sheer ease of mindless copying—may give dead jokes an afterlife in print. Plenty of items do disappear from the written corpus. I think it is safe to conclude that if an item turns up in print repeatedly it is probably circulating orally. (Of course some items, like extended "lists," are better adapted to written rather than oral transmission.)[137] It is more difficult to know what to make of a long absence after appearance in print. The written record contains a number of instances of jokes not surfacing in print for a lifetime, then reappearing.[138]

Tracing changes over time

For several reasons it is difficult to gauge changes in the quantity and character of jokes. They are primarily an oral medium and the retrievable record may reflect a changing and unrepresentative fraction of the whole. With the proliferation of recorded materials (published, photocopied, faxed, online), a larger portion of all joking behavior may now leave a documentary trace. This is especially so because earlier inhibitions about recording and disseminating obscene and scatological material have relaxed considerably in the past forty years. But taking into account these difficulties in assessing joking in the past, it seems clear that the profusion of biting, critical jokes about lawyers that have circulated in recent years was simply not present in earlier periods. Leaving aside the obscene and scatological, which would have had difficulty obtaining entry to respectable media, the recorded sources from the years before 1980 provide little evidence of the aggressively hostile humor that is commonplace today.[139]

The individual jokographies enable us to see when a joke appears; when lawyers join (or replace) others as the protagonists of a joke; which groups lawyers share jokes with; and, in some cases, when a joke disappears. Individual stories and even whole themes sometimes simply stop circulating. Dropouts, like the appearance of new jokes, are evidence of changing perceptions.

We cannot tell from this material how long any joke circulated orally before being recorded. This duration of this "gap" may well have changed with the proliferation of "print" media and the change in attitudes about "dirty" material. The existence of this unmeasurable gap requires constant qualification of statements about the times that jokes appear and change. The dates given are reliable indicators of the time *by which* a joke was in circulation, but the duration of its prepublication circulation remains unknown.[140]

Nor does this collection of texts tell us who is telling these jokes to whom in what settings, and what meanings tellers and hearers imbue them with. Jokes do not have a single fixed meaning. They can be told with very different intonations. The tone and setting of their telling may convey hostility, amused disdain, or self-mockery. Lawyers and nonlawyers, men and women, educated and uneducated, rich and poor encounter different bundles of jokes and may hear very different messages in a given joke.

> A jest's prosperity lies in the ear
> Of him that hears it, never in the tongue
> Of him that makes it.[141]

Does the joke corpus tell us about the legal culture?

Do these stories give us a reliable reading of what Americans think about lawyers? Obviously they are only one source among many, and it is a source that has its own biases. Jethro Lieberman and Tom Goldstein observe that the image of lawyers in books, dramas, and daily reports is systematically biased toward critique rather than appreciation. On the other hand, students of movies and TV testify to the favorable portrayal of lawyers in those media. The joke corpus falls at the critical end of the spectrum, since jokes by their nature focus on flaws, weaknesses, and pretensions. As a medium of fathoming life in its entirety, jokes have severe limitations. They are short, permitting no development of character; they are one-dimensional, unable to reflect the human situation in its complexity; and as comic productions that diminish rather than ennoble their subjects, they evade profound dimensions of human existence.[142]

But other features of jokes make them a good indicator of perceptions of society and its lawyers. First, since jokes may carry messages that are not fully apparent to teller and listener, they may evade the censorship that would screen out open expression of scandalous and reprehensible views. Second, the sentiments they express have to be shared rather than idiosyncratic; they register not transient and individual perceptions of lawyers but shared perceptions that have been ratified and confirmed by successive tellings. The persistence of jokes is a useful indicator of enduring patterns of sentiment because jokes are labile social productions, remade at each telling, and neither controlled nor supported by organizational sanctions or authoritative text. Thus they represent a shared and enduring collective representation even if that may be subject to different readings.

Third, jokes remain the possession and voice of individuals. While the production of music and even fairy tales is administered by formal organizations, there is no Time Warner or Disney of jokes. The small scale and cheapness that make them unattractive as a profit center leave jokes as one of the redoubts of individual expression. For this reason the perspective on lawyers in jokes is different from that in media more subject to corporate packaging and corporate control.

I conclude that jokes do tap a vein of genuine shared sentiment, even though some themes that are important in other manifestations of public opinion may be poorly represented in the joke corpus. In what follows, we shall be dealing with jokes not in isolation but in juxtaposition with other expressions about lawyers and the legal system.

In most instances I provide the full text of only a single version of each joke. Switches and minor variations are traced in the endnotes and summarized in the Register of Jokes (appendix). Occasionally, a second version is provided. I have no rigid policy for choosing which of the many versions to include in full text. I have a bias in favor of old ones; although they are sometimes stilted, they demonstrate that the basic story has been in place for a long time. For the sake of variety, I have mixed older and newer versions and have included some British, Australian, Canadian, Irish, and Indian versions along with American ones.

The jokes presented here are representative texts of jokes told over a long period. Each story is presented verbatim and in its entirety as it appeared in the original source. By contemporary standards, and in some cases by the standards of their own day, many are offensive in their reference to African Americans, Jews, women, and other groups. I proceed in confidence that the readers of this book deserve and prefer an unvarnished and uncensored view of our legal (and general) culture, past and present. The stories reprinted here tell us not only what struck (at least some) people as funny and worth retelling, but what passed as sufficiently respectable to be publishable. We can assume that until the later part of the twentieth century the oral tradition, incompletely mirrored by these published materials, contained other materials which could not pass this test of respectability.

In giving the jokes verbatim, I sacrifice any claim to originality in the hope of ascending to the fourth and fifth levels detailed a century ago in a much-quoted and possibly apocryphal exchange between the formidable President of Columbia University, Nicholas Murray Butler, and Professor Brander Matthews.

K3   "In the case of the first to use an anecdote," said Professor Mathews, "it is originality; in the case of the second, it is plagiarism; third, lack of originality; fourth, it is drawing from a common stock."

"Yes," replied Nicholas Murray Butler, "and in the case of the fifth, it is research."[143]

Jokes provide a rough gauge of common attributions of traits to various social groups and perceptions of the stature of various sorts of behavior. And they give us a useful baseline by which to assess change. The jokes reprinted here should not be taken as revealing what their tellers or listeners "really" thought or think. Jokes are neither transparent nor univocal; they contain multiple and ambiguous ideas and they can be told in manners and settings that make them subject to very different interpretations. They may express sentiments that their tellers or listeners propound but, like songs and poems, their content may not correspond to the convictions of teller or listener.

PART I

THE ENDURING CORE AND ITS RECENT ACCRETIONS

CHAPTER I

❧

Lies and Stratagems

The Corruption of Discourse

A1 How can you tell if a lawyer is lying?
His lips are moving.[1]

I was surprised to discover that this is a rather recent addition to the lawyer joke corpus, appearing in print first in 1986. It derives from a joke about husbands which has been around since at least the 1940s. Although sometimes told about men, women, salespeople, criminal suspects, economists, politicians, and others,[2] it has become predominantly a lawyer joke—at least in the United States.

It joins a large company of jokes that blame lawyers for misusing and corrupting language, perverting discourse by promoting needless complexity, mystifying matters by jargon and formalities, robbing life's dealings of their moral sense by recasting them in legal abstractions, and offending common sense by casuistry that makes black appear white and vice versa. Lawyer indulgence in the sins of discourse has been a grievance since ancient times, giving rise to an assembly of jokes that contains some of the most venerable specimens, but regularly attracts new additions.[3]

LYING AND DISHONESTY

One group of old stories plays on the similarity of the sounds of "liar" and "lawyer."[4]

A2 As a minister and a lawyer were riding together, the minister asked, "Do you ever make any mistakes in your pleading?" "Oh, yes," the lawyer replied. "And what do you do in those cases?" "Well," said the lawyer, "if they are important mistakes I correct them, and if they are small ones I pay no attention to them, but just go on. And do you every make any mistakes in your preaching?"

"Oh, yes," said the clergyman, "and I observe the same rule as you do. For instance, one Sunday not long ago I meant to say to my congregation that the devil is the father

31

of all liars and my tongue slipped and I said 'all lawyers' instead. But the mistake was so small that I let it go at that."[5]

This play on the closeness of the vowel sounds joins an even older story that plays on the overlap of forms of the verbs "to lie" and "to lay" and connects the lawyer's propensity to lie with his ability to represent either side:

A3   In Chancery, one time, when the Councel of the parties set forth the boundary of the land in question, by the plot and the Councel of one part said, we lie on this side, my Lord, and the Councel of the other part said, we lie on this side. The Lord Chancellor Hatton stood up and said, "If you lie on both sides, whom will you have me believe?"[6]

The "two sides" story turns up in a number of variants:

A3   In the 1920s, a plaintiff brought suit against the City of New York after he claimed to have been injured from falling into an open manhole.

During the trial, Dr. Willard Parker, appearing as an expert witness for the plaintiff, testified that the plaintiff "had been so badly hurt that he could lie on only one side."

Whereupon the city attorney joked, "I suppose, doctor, you mean he would make a very poor lawyer."[7]

If this originated in courtroom dialogue, it did so long before the date in this text, for the same exchange between counsel and Dr. Parker had been published in 1871. A more common variant involves the critical rejoinder of a rival professional:

A3   The lawyer was endeavoring to pump some free advice out of the doctor.
"Which side is it best to lie on, Doc?"
"The side that pays you the retainer."[8]

Another variant observes that lawyers enjoy good health even though, contrary to medical advice, they lie on both sides.[9] The "two sides" story makes a double dig: lawyers are not only liars, but they are also indifferent to the merits of the disputes and have no compunction about using their art against the meritorious side if it is to their advantage.

A6   A man was giving evidence in a lawsuit and the defendant's lawyer asked him, "Didn't you tell the defendant that you would testify for him if he would pay you better?" "That I did," admitted the man. "And let me ask you, wouldn't you be on the other side yourself if they'd offered you a bigger fee?"[10]

A6   A lawyer was walking down the street and saw two cars smash into one another. Rushing over, he said, "I saw everything and I'll take either side."[11]

There is a hint here that the lawyer is sufficiently resourceful to come up with something whatever the position in which he finds himself—a theme discussed below.[12]

Other stories make clear that fashioning lies is the essence of the lawyer's role:

within the plate: Pub. Jan.ᵗ 26ᵗʰ 1801 by R.ᵈ Ac.ᵐᵉ N.ᵒ Piccadilly.

Filler of Caricatures lent out for the Evening.

A COUNCILLER.

5. A Counciller (BM 11702. Rowlandson, 1801)

A7   "Have you a lawyer?" asked the judge of a young man brought before him.
          "No, sir," was the answer.
          "Well, don't you think you had better have one?" inquired His Honor.
          "No, sir," said the youth. "I don't need one. I am going to tell the truth."[13]

A8   The judge halted proceedings and leaned forward from the bench. "Look here, my
          man," he said to the defendant, "I granted you the right to plead your own case, but
          you're lying so clumsily that I really think you ought to get a lawyer."[14]

Another old joke, still current, hints that lying is what lawyers naturally and properly do:

A4   Farmer—"An' how's Lawyer Jones doing, doctor?"
          Doctor—"Poor fellow, he's lying at death's door."
          Farmer—"That's grit for ye; at death's door, an' still lying."[15]

A sixteenth-century joke anthology tells of a lawyer disabled by newly acquired honesty:

A9   A certain lawyer, after many cases which he always won, became a monk. And when,
          after he had been put in charge of the monastery's affairs and had been the loser in
          many cases, he was asked by the abbot why he was completely changed as an arguer, he
          replied: "I don't dare to lie as I did formerly, so that I now lose all my cases. You should
          get another man in my place, who cares more for worldly and temporary things than for
          eternal and heavenly ones."[16]

A nineteenth-century lawyer, advised that a beard was unprofessional, quipped:

A9   Right . . . a lawyer cannot be but barefaced.[17]

A century later the suggestion recurs that lawyers are *supposed* to be dishonest:

A10   Her lawyer is honest, but not enough to hurt her case.[18]

Through the centuries lying and dishonesty are identified as a qualification for
being a lawyer and an expertise that lawyers can be expected to display:[19]

A9   An old lady walked into a lawyer's office lately, when the following conversation took
          place:
              Lady—Squire, I called to see if you would like to take this boy and make a lawyer of
          him.
              Lawyer—The boy appears rather young, madam—how old is he?
              Lady—Seven year, sir.
              Lawyer—He is too young—decidedly too young. Have you no boys older?
              Lady—O yes, sir, I have several; but we have concluded to make farmers of the
          others. I told my old man I thought this little feller would make a first rate lawyer, and
          so I called to see if you would take him.
              Lawyer—No, madam; he is too young yet, to commence the study of the profession.
          But why do you think this boy any better calculated for a lawyer than your other sons?

Lady—Why, you see sir, he is just seven years old to-day. When he was only five, he'd lie like all natur; when he got to be six, he was as sassy and impudent as any critter could be; and now he'll steal everything he can lay his hands on![20]

For some parents it is the inability to lie that is a source of disappointment.

A9 A man, a lawyer, made a great ado over the breaking of his imported briar pipe. When he saw the fragments of the old friend on the floor, he exclaimed:

"Who could have does this wilful thing?"

His son, six years old, spoke up: "Father I cannot tell a lie! I did it to see what was inside."

"Alas," cried the now doubly-distressed man, "I did hope to make you a lawyer, my son; but I see it is never to be."[21]

A13 A countryman applied to a solicitor for legal advice. After detailing the circumstances of the case, he was asked if he had stated the facts exactly as they had occurred. "O, ay sir," rejoined he, "I thought it better to tell you the plain truth; you can put the lies to it yourself."[22]

According to a variant of this story, that is precisely the lawyer's job:

A13 A gentleman that had a suit in Chancery was called upon by his counsel to put in his answer, for fear of incurring a contempt. "Well," says the client, "and why is not my answer put in then?" "How should I draw your answer," saith the lawyer, "without knowing what you can swear?" "Hang your scruples," says the client again; "pray do your part of a lawyer, and draw me a sufficient answer: and let me alone to do the part of a gentleman, and swear it."[23]

A14 "Papa, do lawyers tell the truth?" "Certainly, my boy; they will do anything to win their case."[24]

Honest lawyers have for many centuries been believed to be rare creatures. Both Ben Jonson and Benjamin Franklin are credited with the couplet:

A15 God works wonders now and then;.
Behold! A lawyer and an honest man[25]

The scarcity of honest lawyers theme is elaborated in many stories. Some have dropped out as the social setting changed:

A16 At a railroad dinner, in compliment to the fraternity, the toast was given: "An honest lawyer, the noblest work of God!" But an old farmer, in the back part of the hall, rather spoiled the effect by adding, in a loud voice: "About the scarcest."[26]

Yet another victim of Richard Nixon is a story that dropped out with the demise of the Democratic "solid South":

A17 A young graduate in law, who had some experience in New York City, wrote to a prominent practitioner in Arkansas to inquire what chance there was in that section for such a one as he described himself to be. He said: "I am a Republican in politics, and an honest young lawyer." The reply that came seemed encouraging in its interest: "If you are a Republican the game laws here will protect you, and if you are an honest lawyer you will have no competition."[27]

But the most popular and enduring of these "no honest lawyer" stories is a prose rendition of the "God works wonders" couplet (A15), above:

A18   A stranger, passing through the churchyard, who noticed this inscription, is reputed to have exclaimed, "What! Two of them buried in the same grave?"[28]

Another turns on the epitaph of lawyer John Strange:

A19   There is an old story of a lawyer named Strange and his wife having a conference as to the things he wished done after he had departed this life.
"I want a headstone put over me, my dear," said the lawyer, "with the simple inscription—'Here lies an honest lawyer.'"
The wife expressed surprise that he did not wish his name put on the headstone.
"It will not be needful," he responded, "for those who pass by and read that inscription will invariably remark: 'That's Strange.'"[29]

This in turn has been extended into a ethnic joke about the English:

A19   An Englishman who has heard the story essayed to repeat it to his friend.
"I heard a good one the other night," he says, "a very good one, indeed. There was a barrister by the name of—his name was—well, I don't just think of the name now, ye know; but it's of no consequence whatever. You see, he was telling his widow—that is, his wife—what to do after he died, and he says: 'I want this inscription on my monument: "here lies an honest barrister." You'll get the point in a moment. It's very funny.' Well, his wife says: 'How in the world is that going to tell who you are?' Says he: 'Well everybody that reads the inscription will say: "That's devilish singular."'"[30]

WORKERS IN THE MILLS OF DECEIT

The jokes about lawyers' departure from truth reflect a firm public belief. A 1987 Gallup poll asked a national sample of adults about the truthfulness of various groups of people. Only 6 percent thought lawyers always tell the truth, while 87 percent thought they sometimes or often say things they know are not true.[31]

But departure from truthfulness need not be seen as a failing; indeed, it may be seen as essential to the lawyer's task:

A21   Lawyer: Well, if you want my honest opinion—
Client: No, no. I want your professional advice.[32]

The opposition of "honest opinion" and "professional advice" suggests that the lawyer is seen as operating in a realm disconnected from the sphere of personal morality.

A22   After serving a week on a jury, a man was asked:

"You must have listened to so much law in the past week that you are almost a lawyer yourself now."

"Yes," said the juryman, "I am so full of law that I am going to find it hard to keep from cheating people after I get back to business."[33]

It is expected that the lawyer's professional persona will not be controlled by the constraints of personal morality.

A9   A lawyer, in addressing a jury, made a statement that greatly exasperated his opponent, who sprang to his feet and exclaimed, "Sir do you say that as a lawyer, or as a man? If you say it as a lawyer, all is right; but if you say it as a man, you tell a falsehood."[34]

The task of the lawyer may be not to reveal the truth but to obscure it:

A23   "This law is a queer business."

"How so?"

"They swear a man to tell the truth?"

"What then?"

"And every time he shows signs of doing so some lawyer objects."[35]

Through inadvertence or oversight the lawyers may fail to expose the truth, which does not necessarily inspire universal regret.

"I urge this jury not to let the evidence prejudice you against my client."

6. Cartoon by Arnie Levin (© 2004, from cartoonbank.com. All rights reserved.)

A24   An old colored man, who had been crippled in the railroad service, served for many
years as a watchman at a grade crossing in the outskirts of an Alabama town. By day he
wielded a red flag and by night he swung a lantern.

One dark night a colored man from the country, driving home from town, steered his
mules across the track just as the Memphis flier came through and abolished him, along
with his team and his wagon. His widow sued the railroad for damages. At the trial the
chief witness for the defence was the old crossing watchman.

Uncle Gabe stumped to the stand and took the oath to tell the truth, the whole
truth, and nothing but the truth. Under promptings from the attorney for his side, he
proceeded to give testimony strongly in favor of the defendant corporation. He stated
that he had seen the approaching team in due time and that, standing in the street, he
had waved his lantern to and fro for a period of at least one minute. In spite of the
warning, he said, the deceased had driven upon the rails.

Naturally, the attorney for the plaintiff put him to a severe cross-examination. Uncle
Gabe answered every question readily and with evident honesty. He told just how he had
held the lantern, how he had swung and joggled it and so forth and so on.

After court had adjourned the lawyer for the railroad sought out the old man and
congratulated him upon his behavior as a witness.

"Gabe," he said, "you acquitted yourself splendidly. Weren't you at all nervous while
on the stand?"

"I suttinly wuz, boss," replied Uncle Gabe. "I kep' wonderin' whu wuz gwine happen
ef dat w'ite genelman should ax me if dat lantern wuz lighted."[36]

In the legal realm there is no premium on honesty. Quite the opposite, the
legal process is seen as a setting in which lying may win the day. Here is an old
version of the most common variant of a very widespread story:

A25   Judge (to witness)—"Do you know the nature of an oath?"
Witness—"Sah?"
Judge—"Do you understand what you are to swear to?"
Witness—"Yes, sah; I'm to swear to tell de truf."
Judge—"And what will happen if you do not tell it?"
Witness—"I 'spects our side'll win de case, sah."[37]

In another variant a young lad responds that he supposed "he would go where all
the lawyers went."[38] In yet another, the witness innocently provides a cynical
operational definition of the oath:

A25   The other day a colored man fresh from "Ole Virginy," was on the witness stand and
the judge asked him:
"Do you know what an oath is?"
"Yes, sah; when a man swears to a lie he's got to stick to it."[39]

The dismal "truth" about the fate of truth in the legal process is typically placed
in the mouth of an innocent, low status outsider: the uneducated Negro or

hillbilly in the U.S., the Irishman or a child in Britain, the aboriginal in Australia. Unschooled in the mythic picture of the legal system that is acquired by adults of stature and respectability, he is unable to see beyond the everyday imperfection of legal institutions.[40] It takes a certain ingenuousness to fail to see the emperor's clothes.

Lawyers differ in their sense of obligation to resist acknowledgment of the divergence of advocacy from truth-seeking. Half a century ago a distinguished Boston practitioner, Charles P. Curtis, outraged many lawyers by urging that lawyers follow Montaigne's advice to "recognize the knavery that is part of [their] vocation." Curtis proposed that on rare occasions it is "one of the functions of the lawyer to lie for his client."[41] But even when truthful "a lawyer is required to be disingenuous. He is required to make statements and arguments which he does not believe in. . . . When he is talking for his client, a lawyer is absolved from veracity down to a certain point of particularity. And he must never lose the reputation of lacking veracity, because his freedom from the strict bonds of veracity and of the law are the two chief assets of the profession." This posture commends itself because "the administration of justice is no more designed to elicit the truth than the scientific approach is designed to extract justice from the atom."[42] Henry S. Drinker (1880–1965), one of the high priests of legal ethics, wrote of the "amazement and indignation" with which he read "this insidious essay."[43] Unable to bring himself to believe that Curtis "really in his heart of hearts believes such extraordinary statements," Drinker supposed "he is moved to make them from an unconscious fear of appearing stuffy."[44] Drinker affirmed that law was indeed a noble profession, disfigured by an occasional malefactor, but peopled by good souls who "hate falsehood, dishonesty and all that is ignoble."[45]

Many thoughtful lawyers now incline more toward the view found in the jokes and in popular culture in general. In this view lawyers' obligations involve a complex blend of truth-telling and concealment ordained by a distinctive "role morality" in which their duties as advocates deflect and qualify the conventional imperatives of truthfulness.[46]

The Drinker view is still invoked more than occasionally. Thus Independent Counsel Kenneth Starr took time from his pursuit of President Clinton to deliver a bar lecture in which he expressed concern that the foundations of American society were threatened by a decline in lawyers' observance of their obligation to tell the truth.[47] In a notable conflation of real and imaginary lawyers, he argued that "times have changed." Quoting Daniel Webster on the honesty of lawyers, he skipped ahead to 1960 when Atticus Finch, the fictional hero of the novel *To Kill a Mockingbird*, "strove to find the truth while defending a black man wrongly accused of rape in a segregated town." To "this noble and trustworthy soul" Starr contrasts "the character Bruiser in John Grisham's book *The Rainmaker* and the Al Pacino character in the film *Devil's Advocate*. "Popular culture now sees lawyers as anything but seekers of truth and justice." Although "many of us question whether this modern-day portrayal of lawyers is fair . . . we must concede, our profession has changed." Having fallen, Starr exhorts the profession to rise again: "The path away from the seedy world of John Grisham's Bruiser, and a road map for reclaiming the moral high ground of Atticus Finch," is simply to embrace the principle that "lawyers have a duty not to use their skills to impede the search for truth." A leading legal ethicist, Geoffrey Hazard, quickly responded that "Mr. Starr's claim is not only ludicrous; it is pernicious," citing many occasions on which it is legitimate and even obligatory for lawyers to obstruct the search for truth.[48] Indeed, Atticus Finch himself seems to hold a more nuanced view, for at the story's climax he acquiesces in the sheriff's reporting a "justified" killing as an accidental suicide.[49]

Although Starr agrees with Drinker's ideal of truth-seeking lawyers, he seems to concur with Curtis and Hazard and the joke corpus that descriptively lawyers do manage and massage the truth. It is one thing to say lawyers are sophists and must follow the curious rules of that calling; it is another to deny it and claim they are called to be philosophers. Some may dismiss such claims of authenticity as just another piece of advocacy useful at the moment. But we should never underestimate the capacity of people to believe the best of themselves.

ELOQUENCE, PERSUASIVENESS, RESOURCEFULNESS

If courts are forums not of truth but of contending stories, much depends on the lawyer. Lawyers are not only unconstrained by the truth; they can marshal their eloquence and resourcefulness to make arguments that are obscure, improbable, and outrageous. They are unrestricted by requirements of consistency:

A26   The *Vermont Mercury* has the following excellent defence lately made to an action by a down east lawyer:—"There are three points in the case, may it please your honour," said the defendant's counsel. "In the first place, we contend that the kettle was cracked when we borrowed it; secondly, that it was whole when we returned it; and, thirdly, that we never had it."[50]

This familiar "inconsistent defenses" story is told of other protagonists, as well as lawyers.[51] But the setting is often a court or another arena of accusation, defense, and judgment. The joke seems to say that this is the legal model—you need not have a consistent and coherent story; rather, you have to have a point that will beat the other side.[52] Of course, having a number of points does not guarantee success:

A27   Not long ago, in the Court of Appeals, an Irish lawyer, while arguing with earnestness his cause, stated a point which the court ruled out.
   "Well," said the attorney, "if it plaze the coort, if I am wrong in this, I have another point that is aqually as conclusive."[53]

The joke corpus pays tribute to the lawyer's eloquence and persuasiveness.

A28   A man in North Carolina, who was saved from conviction for horse-stealing by the powerful plea of his lawyer, after his acquittal by the jury, was asked by the lawyer:
   "Honor bright, now, Bill, you did steal that horse, didn't you?"

"Now, look a-here, Judge," was the reply, "I allers did think I stole that hoss, but since I hearn yore speech to that 'ere jury, I'll be doggoned if I a'n't got my doubts about it."[54]

On the evidence of the published sources this has enjoyed a steady popularity for over a century, most recently as a joke about O. J. Simpson:

A28   "Man that Johnnie Cochran is a smooth talking lawyer. . . . Even O.J. thinks he's innocent."[55]

The jokes are laced with appreciation of the lawyer's resourcefulness, his ability to come up with something to say on behalf of the most apparently hopeless case:

A29   Prisoner: "Before I plead guilty or not guilty, I would like to ask the court to appoint a lawyer to defend me."
Judge: "You were caught in the actual commission of a crime, with the merchandise on you, a gun in your hand and your victim on the floor. What could a lawyer possibly say in your defense?"
Prisoner: "That's it—I'm curious also to hear what he could possibly say!"[56]

The lawyer is capable of abrupt reversals. There are stories of a lawyer writing successive treatises on opposite sides of a constitutional dispute; of the lawyer who assured his client that he could prove unconstitutional the same law he had recently proved constitutional.[57] And, not least, the drunken lawyer who mistakenly made a devastating argument for the wrong side:

A30   Counsel in a . . . condition of haziness hurriedly entered the Court and took up the case in which he was engaged; but forgetting for which side he had been fee'd, to the unutterable amazement of the agent, delivered a long and fervent speech in the teeth of the interests he had been expected to support. When at last the agent made him understand the mistake he had made, he with infinite composure resumed his ordination by saying: "Such, my lord, is the statement you will probably hear from my brother on the opposite side of the case. I shall now show your lordship how utterly untenable are the principles and how distorted are the facts upon which this very specious statement has proceeded." And so he went over the same ground and most angelically refuted himself from the beginning of his former pleading to the end.[58]

A30   An absent-minded attorney rose to defend a client, and, intent on winding up the proceedings promptly and reaching the country club, got off on the wrong foot.
"This man on trial, gentlemen of the jury," he bumbled, "bears the reputation of being the most unconscionable and depraved scoundrel in the state. . . ."
An assistant whispered frantically, "That's your client you're talking about."
Without one second's hesitation, the lawyer continued smoothly, " . . . but what outstanding citizen ever lived who has not been vilified and slandered by envious contemporaries?"[59]

7. The Old Bailey Advocate Bringing Off a Thief (BM 7593. ?1789).
Barrister places his foot in mouth of Truth as he tramples her prostrate body, beneath which lies the prostrate body of Justice with
broken sword and scales. The inscription reads: "Did not the Felon
firmly fix his hope / On flaw or jaw, and so escape the rope, / Justly
he'd meet that Fate without reprieve, / (Which come when
Advocate fails to deceive,) / Or, doom made sure for want of
quibbling aid, / He'd quit bad ways to seek an honest trade."

Jokes about resourcefulness, dogged tenacity, and improvisation are readily switched to lawyers. In this old joke, the lawyer replaces the Jew (or Irishman or Cajun) who enlarges the options while being intensely self-regarding.[60]

A31   Three college roommates got together regularly over the years, even though their professional lives differed widely. One had become an attorney, one a professor of Italian literature, and one a zoologist. When they next met up, each one looked pretty gloomy, and it turned out that each had been told by his physician that he had only six weeks to live. Understandably, the conversation turned to the way in which each intended to live out his last days.

"I'm going to Rwanda," said the zoologist. "I've always wanted to see the rare mountain gorilla in its native habitat."

"Italy for me. I want to see where Dante was born, to be buried near the great man. And you?" asked the professor, turning to the third friend. "What would you like to see?"

"Another doctor," decided the lawyer.[61]

A new mutation shifts the scene to the afterlife:

A31   Three good friends were driving along on the highway one Saturday: a doctor, a teacher, and a lawyer. All of a sudden, a brand-new SUV cut them off. In an attempt to miss the shiny big vehicle, the driver swerved to the left and hit the median. The car flipped several times and all three friends died instantly.

They all found themselves in the line waiting to get into Heaven. The doctor asked the others, "Hey, what do you all want people to say at your funeral? I want them to say, 'She was a great doctor, and she never let down any of her patients.'"

The teacher said, "I want people to remember me as a great educator, so I would want to hear people say, 'He was a wonderful teacher, a great role model for children, and he changed countless lives throughout his career.'"

Then the lawyer said, "I'd like people to say, 'Look! He's moving!'"[62]

The drive and innovativeness of lawyers, along with their resourcefulness and eloquence, are depicted in this story, originally about a speechwriter, switched to the setting of the large law firm.

A32   A senior partner at a major New York law firm . . . was asked by the Manhattan Chamber of Commerce to address its membership. Accepting months in advance, he forgets about the engagement until, cleaning off his desk late one Friday evening, he notices the date scheduled in his calendar for the following Monday. With a big weekend at the beach house on tap, there's no time to write a speech. Instead, he calls in a bright young associate.

Partner: Smith, I have to address the Chamber on Monday night and because of a client commitment all weekend, I can't do it myself. You'll have to write it for me. Have it on my desk by noon Monday.

Associate: But sir, my girlfriend and I have reservations at—

Partner: On my desk at noon. No ifs, ands, or buts.

Comes Monday at twelve, the speech is delivered, freshly typed and bound in a neat plastic folder. The partner, on his way to a client meeting that will last until the evening, stuffs the speech in his briefcase without reading it. Later that night, standing before the audience of five hundred business executives (many clients and potential clients), he delivers the speech, which turns out to be a literary pearl filled with humorous anecdotes, wonderful insights, and bright observations on the law, business, and modern society. Near the end, it reaches a crescendo that has the audience on the edge of its seats.

"Before I leave you tonight," the partner reads, "I want to share with you my ultimate vision for using the law not only to resolve disputes, but to create a new chapter in the history of mankind. A chapter of unparalleled peace and prosperity worldwide. To accomplish this, I will suggest that"—he turns the page, curious himself to read this remarkable plan, only to find, in capital letters, IMPROVISE, YOU SON OF A BITCH.[63]

Not only do we admire the nerve, resourcefulness, and eloquence of the associate, but we also wonder if the senior partner, so justly punished for his arrogance, will manage to come up with something to save the day.

Perhaps the most striking thing about the lawyer's discourse is his ability to use language to reshape things, not least the law itself. King Louis XII of France is reported to have said: "Lawyers use the law as shoemakers use leather; rubbing it, pressing it, stretching it with their teeth, all to the end of making it fit their purposes."[64] Some centuries later in *Gulliver's Travels,* Jonathan Swift had his hero, describing England, recount to the Houynyms: "There was a Society of Men among us, bred up from their youth in the Art of proving by words multiplied for the Purpose that White is Black and Black is White, according as they are paid. To this Society all the rest of the People are Slaves."[65]

A widely published lawyer joke focuses on this kind of linguistic manipulation:

A33   The Search Committee is interviewing the three finalists for the presidency of the University: a mathematician, a sociologist and a lawyer. The mathematician is ushered in first and the committee members pepper him with questions about his views on the state of higher education, the University's financial prospects, and his theories of educational leadership. Just as he is about to leave, a previously silent elderly member of the committee asks, "Excuse me, sir, but can you tell us how much is two and two?" "Well," says the mathematician, "that is really a complex question, but for present purposes we can say that if you take an abstract two and add another abstract two, you get an abstract four."

The next candidate is the sociologist and after he is quizzed on his views about administering the University, just as he is about to leave, the same committee member pipes up with the same question, "how much is two and two?" After pondering for a moment, the sociologist responds, "that is an empirical question that requires very careful collection and analysis of data, but roughly the range is from three to five with a mean of about four."

After he leaves, the lawyer enters and is questioned about his views at great length. Just as he turns to leave and opens the door of the committee room, the elderly member manages to say "Excuse me, just one more question: how much is two and two?" The lawyer stops in his tracks, closes the door, turns and slowly approaches the committee. In a soft voice he asks "How much do you want it to be?"[66]

This story is the most significant addition to the *Discourse* cluster in recent times. It is not a very old addition, first appearing as a lawyer joke in 1982.[67] For at least thirty years before that, it had flourished as an anti-Communist joke in the Soviet Union and Eastern Europe.[68] The point was the authorities' insistence on falsifying reality and the servility or opportunism of the applicant:

A33   What does two times two make?
             Whatever the Party says.[69]

Since its arrival in the lawyer joke corpus, it has occasionally turned up about politicians, accountants, and economists, but it has been predominantly a lawyer joke.[70]

Two plus two is an excellent example of what I call an adapted joke. It is not merely a switch in which a lawyer has been substituted for a politician or employer as the protagonist. The lawyer version typically reveals a distinctive twist that makes it specific to the lawyer theme. What is distinctive about the lawyer protagonist is his readiness to put his ability to reshape reality at the service of the "client." He is solicitous: How much do *you* want it to be? He closes the door and speaks softly or pulls down the shades and checks for hidden microphones to protect confidentiality. In contrast to the laborious mechanical responses of the other candidates, he seeks out the need that lies behind the question. He immediately takes the request as expressing some purpose of the questioner and indicates his eagerness to serve that undisclosed purpose. This responsiveness to clients is the thing that people value most in lawyers—the lawyer as entirely focused on your problem and entirely committed to be *your* champion.[71] As we shall see there is anxiety about whether he will be a distracted or faithless champion.

Among lawyers, this portrayal is specific to Americans. In the UK the "how much do you want it to be" trope is associated with accountants from at least 1990.[72] The *two plus two* joke arrives, apparently from Australia, in 2000.[73] A lawyer earlier in the series provides a legalistic answer, citing a case that "proves" the answer is four. In another Australian version, the penultimate respondent is a lawyer who "thought that in general it would be considered four, but that they should have counsel's opinion." The punch line is put in the mouth of an accountant whose response is not accompanied by any of the solicitude or body language of the American lawyer versions.[74]

The joke places the lawyer squarely among the proponents of "indeterminacy." In the Communist joke, the truth is malleable. For the lawyer, too, responding is not a search for a unique, objectively right answer. If there is objective truth, it does not control the answer. As one observer of the legal scene puts it: "Lawyers make claims not because they believe them to be true, but because they believe them to be legally efficacious. If they happen to be true, then all the better."[75] The stock in trade of the lawyer is that he is the master rather than the slave of the authoritative text. He uses his art to fashion an answer not to conform to the dictate of a dominant ruling group (as in the Communist joke), but to suit the purposes of a specific interlocutor.

Earlier critics derided lawyers as the votaries of an illusory certainty. Sixty years ago, in a famous polemic, Yale law professor Fred Rodell decried the law as a pretense, a fraud, a hoax, mumbo-jumbo, "a scheme of contradictory and nonsensical principles built of inherently meaningless abstractions" that exercises a superstitious hold over the populace. "The legal trade . . . is nothing but a high-class racket." Lawyers are soothsayers, modern medicine men, "purveyors of streamlined voodoo," priests of mystification.[76] On the culpability of lawyers for this state of affairs, Rodell vacillates. At times he portrays them as self-deceived: "The lawyers, taken as a whole, cannot by any means be accused of *deliberately* hoodwinking the public. . . . They, too, are blissfully unaware that the sounds they make are essentially empty of meaning."[77] Yet elsewhere he depicts them as knowing conspirators: "For the lawyers know it would be woe unto the lawyers if the non-lawyers ever got wise to the fact that their lives were run, not by The Law, not by any rigid and impersonal and automatically applied code of rules, but instead by a comparatively small group of men, smart, smooth, and smug—the lawyers."[78] As we shall see, other critics portray lawyers as errant priests of the true church of social justice. But Rodell portrays them as the idolatrous priests of a false religion, which he thinks can be dismantled by eliminating lawyers.

Rodell's portrayal of lawyers as the source of the mythic reification of legal rules and as captives of the law's empty mysteries makes important empirical claims about the beliefs and behavior of lawyers and lay people, claims that are at least incomplete and very likely seriously mistaken. Fifty years ago, David Riesman observed that lawyers "are feared and disliked—but needed—because of their matter-of-factness, their sense of relevance, their refusal to be impressed by magical 'solutions' to people's problems. Conceivably, if this hypothesis is right, the ceremonial and mystification of the legal profession are, to a considerable degree, veils or protections underneath which this rational, all too rational, work of the lawyer gets done."[79] Mystification and jargon do not necessarily imply that lawyers are enchanted by the law. Rather than believers that the law has a single true meaning, lawyers are as likely to be virtuosi of indeterminacy. Jethro Lieberman confides that:

> The only secret that the lawyer really possesses about the law is that no one can ever be certain of what the law is. . . . The lawyer is accustomed to the ways of bending and changing rules to suit his (or his client's) purposes, to dance in the shadows of the law's ambiguities. Rules hold no particular terror for the lawyer, just as the sight of

blood holds no terror for the surgeon. Because he operates a system of rules, the lawyer becomes indifferent to them in the way that a doctor becomes indifferent to the humanity of the body that is lying on the operating table.[80]

Hot Air: Lawyer Talk as Fakery and Bombast

Admiration for the lawyer's eloquence and inventiveness is balanced by a countertheme: although the lawyer is fluent and never at a loss for something to say and although his verbosity can dominate encounters, it is often empty, mindless, and fraudulent. Sometimes the fakery is innocuous bluff, as in this old story of the young lawyer's attempt to conceal his involuntary idleness. Here is a version published in 1915, still found in current collections with only minor changes:

A34   The young lawyer had opened his office that very day and sat expectant of clients. A step was heard outside, and the next moment a man's figure was silhouetted against the ground-glass of the door. Hastily the legal fledgling stepped to his brand-new telephone, and taking down the receiver, gave every appearance of being deep in a business conversation.

"Yes, Mr. S.," he was saying, as the man entered, "I'll attend to that corporation matter for you. Mr. J. had me on the `phone this morning and wanted me to settle a damage suit, but I had to put him off, as I'm so busy with cases just now. But I'll try to sandwich your matter in between my other cases somehow. Yes, yes. All right. Good-bye."

Hanging up the receiver, he turned to his visitor, having, as he thought, duly impressed him.

"Excuse me, sir," the man said, "but I'm from the telephone company. I've come to connect up your instrument."[81]

Where argument fails, there is always bombast:

A35   Samuel Seigal, the famous professor of law, was lecturing on courtroom procedure. "When you're fighting a case," he said, "if you have the facts on your side, hammer on the facts. If you have the law on your side, hammer on the law."

"But if you don't have the facts or the law," asked a student, "what do you do?"

"In that case," the professor said, "then hammer on the table.[82]

This is the modern dress of a much older story:

A35   An old lawyer was giving advice to his son, who was just entering upon the practice of his father's profession. "My son," said the counselor, "if you have a case where the law is clearly on your side, but justice seems to be against you, urge upon the jury the vast importance of sustaining the law. If, on the other hand, you are in doubt about the law, but your client's case is founded in justice, insist on the necessity of doing justice, though the heavens fall."—"But," asked the son, "how shall I manage a case where both law and justice are dead against me?"—"In that case, my son," replied the lawyer, "talk round it."[83]

Where the old version looks askance at lawyers for treating justice as just another resource, the modern version omits it entirely.

Although they are impressed, even dazzled, by lawyers' ability to talk, lay people harbor suspicions about the substance of that talk.

A36   The lawyer was cross-examining a witness to a robbery. "When did the robbery take place?" he asked.

"I think—" began the witness.

"We don't care what you think, sir. We want to know what you know."

"Then if you don't want to know what I think, I may as well leave the stand. I can't talk without thinking. I'm not a lawyer."[84]

Indeed, the lawyer's talk may come to the exclusion of thinking:

A37   Client to attorney: "How come the other side has two lawyers, and I only have one?"

Attorney: "It's not unusual. When one lawyer is talking, the other one is thinking."

Client: "Well, so who's doing your thinking?"[85]

The propensity of the lawyer to miss the central substance while exercising his cleverness is shown in a recent story, frequently presented as a series of questions "actually asked of witnesses by attorneys during trials."

A38   Q: "Doctor, before you performed the autopsy, did you check for a pulse?"

A: "No."

Q: "Did you check for blood pressure?"

A: "No."

Q: "So, then it is possible that the patient was alive when you began the autopsy?"

A: "No."

Q: "How can you be so sure, Doctor?"

A: "Because his brain was sitting on my desk in a jar."

Q: "But could the patient have still been alive nevertheless?"

A: "It is possible that he could have been alive and practising law somewhere."[86]

Although it is possible that some actual incident provided the germ of the story, it is impossible to say whether the joke has crystallized out of the "true story" or whether the joke (a nice extension of the theme of lawyers not thinking or using their brains) inspired a creative recounter to add the "true story" element.[87]

The lawyer's talk may make little contribution to the result:

A39   One of the justices of the Supreme Court tells of a young lawyer in the West who was trying his first case before Justice Harlan. The youthful attorney had evidently conned his argument until he knew it by heart. Before he had consumed ten minutes in his oratorical effort the justice had decided the case in his favor and told him so. Despite this, the young lawyer would not cease. It seemed that he had attained such a momentum that he could not stop.

Finally Justice Harlan leaned forward and, in the politest of tones, said:

"Mr. Smith, despite your arguments, the court has concluded to decide this case in your favor."[88]

The lawyer may have little of substance to contribute, but his negativity is matched by his immodesty.

A40   A lawyer dies and goes to Heaven, where he is brought before God. "A lawyer, eh?" Says God (who seems to be a Canadian). "We've never had a lawyer in Heaven before. Argue a point of the law for my edification."

The lawyer goes into a panic and says, "Oh, God, I cannot think of an argument worthy of your notice. But I'll tell you what . . . you argue a point of the law and I'll refute it."[89]

Lawyers' talk may be discounted as mere hot air:

A41   The secretary of the Bar Association was very busy and rather cross. The telephone rang.

"Well, what is it?" he snapped.

"Is this the city gas works?" said a woman's soft voice.

"No, madam," roared the secretary, "this is the San Francisco Bar Association."

"Ah," she answered in the sweetest of tones, "I didn't miss it so far, after all, did I?"[90]

Even where the lawyer's verbal performance is of high quality, it may contain little of value to the client. Among the few newer lawyer jokes that originated in Britain is a story about parliamentary answers that became a lawyer joke in the late 1980s and has spread throughout the English-speaking world. This elaborated version is from Australia:

A42   A couple of blokes set off in a balloon. They're determined they are going to stay up longer than anyone else in ballooning history. But two days later there's a huge storm that wrecks all their radio equipment. And while they're being buffeted around, their food falls overboard. Worse still, they don't know where they are. They might be anywhere. On the other side of the world. So they decide to lose altitude until they come in sight of land. Down they go, very slowly, descending through the clouds. And they sigh with relief because they're over land. Peering down from the basket they see cars and think, "Well, they're driving on the left side of the road. That means we're probably in the UK or Australia. And they're playing tennis. So it must be a civilised country."

They come within hailing distance of the tennis court and call out to one of the players, "Hello, down there!"

The two fellows stop playing tennis and look up. "Yeah, what do you want?"

"Where are we?"

"You got any money?"

"Yes, what do you want with money?"

"Throw it down," says the man on the ground. So they throw a wallet down and one of the blokes on the ground picks it up, takes the money out, splits it with the fellow on the other side of the net and puts the wallet in his pocket. Finally he says, "Now, what was your question?"

"Where are we?"

"You're in a balloon."

At that moment they rise above the clouds and the two partners look at one another helplessly. "That was useless," said one.

"No, at least we know where we are."

"What do you mean we know where we are?"

"Well, we're over a civilized country. They drive on the left hand side of the road. And those two fellows are lawyers."

"How can you tell they're lawyers?"

"Well, first of all, they wouldn't do a thing for us until we paid them. And what they said was absolutely true and totally useless."[91]

After a decade as a lawyer joke, this story acquired an elegant coda expressing lawyer exasperation with the elevated expectations of clients:

A42

A man is flying in a hot air balloon and realizes he is lost. He reduces height and spots a man down below. He lowers the balloon further and shouts: "Excuse me, can you help me? I promised my friend I would meet him half an hour ago, but I don't know where I am."

The man below says: "Yes. You are in a hot air balloon, hovering approximately thirty feet above this field. You are between 40 and 42 degrees N. latitude, and between 58 and 60 degrees W. longitude."

"You must be a lawyer," says the balloonist.

"I am" replies the man. "How did you know?"

"Well," says the balloonist, "everything you have told me is technically correct, but I have no idea what to make of your information, and the fact is I am still lost."

The man below responds, "You must be a client."

"I am," replies the balloonist, "but how did you know?"

"Well," says the man, "you don't know where you are, or where you are going. You have made a promise which you have no idea how to keep, and you expect me to solve your problem. The fact is you are in the exact same position you were in before we met, but now it is somehow my fault."[92]

It seems a safe bet that this client version of the *balloon* story originated among lawyers. The same is true of an even newer version, which uses the joke to expose the tensions between junior and senior lawyers and appears in chapter 5.

MASTERS OF STRATAGEM

Analyzing the "trickster" element in the public image of lawyers, Marvin Mindes found the public not much inclined to characterize lawyers as manipulative, tricky, and evasive, ranking these tenth, thirteenth, and fourteenth among eighteen qualities that he inquired about. Lawyers themselves found even less resonance in these descriptions, ranking them thirteenth, seventeenth, and fourteenth, respectively. But, strikingly, lawyers perceived that the public attributed these qualities to them, ranking them as eighth, sixth, and seventh, respectively, in their reading of the public's view of the profession.[93]

A number of jokes depict the lawyer as the author of clever stratagems to extricate clients from difficult or desperate situations:

A43 A businessman consulted his attorney about collecting a five-hundred dollar debt from a former associate.

"Have you a note or anything which proves that he owes you the money?" the lawyer wanted to know.

"No, I'm sorry to say."

"Then the only thing for you to do is write him a note asking for the thousand dollars he owes you."

"But all he owes me is five hundred dollars."

The attorney smiled. "Exactly. He will write and tell you so, and then we'll have the proof we need to use in court."[94]

The lawyer uses his rhetorical skills to help the client evade his just punishment:

A44 A lawyer was defending a man accused of housebreaking, and said to the court:

"Your Honor, I submit that my client did not break into the house at all. He found the parlor window open and merely inserted his right arm and removed a few trifling articles. Now, my client's arm is not himself, and I fail to see how you can punish the whole individual for an offense committed by only one of his limbs."

"That argument," said the judge, "is very well put. Following it logically, I sentence the defendant's arm to one year's imprisonment. He can accompany it or not, as he chooses."

The defendant smiled, and with his lawyer's assistance unscrewed his cork arm, and, leaving it in the dock, walked out.[95]

Both the lawyer and judge in this story illustrate the famous witticism of Thomas Reed Powell: "If you . . . can think about a thing that is inextricably attached to something else without thinking of the thing which it is attached to, then you have a legal mind."[96]

Of course, the lawyer is not a disinterested problem-solver; he makes sure that his own interests are advanced, even if it consumes all the benefit to the client.

A45 A man checked in at a prominent hotel in one of our large cities. At the desk, he said to the clerk, "Would you mind putting this hundred dollar bill in the safe? I'll pick it up in the morning. Hate to carry large bills around."

The clerk took the bill. Next morning when the guest asked for his hundred dollar bill, the clerk shrugged off the demand. "Hundred dollar bill? You never gave me a hundred dollar bill. Have you a receipt for it?"

"No," said the guest, "but I know I gave it to you."

"Sorry," said the clerk, "but your memory's at fault."

The guest walked down the street until he saw a lawyer's office. He went in and consulted the attorney, who said, "Tell you what, we'll use psychology. Pick up some friend who knows you; get another hundred dollar bill, and return to the same clerk. In the presence of your friend, ask the clerk if he'll put the hundred dollar bill away for you. Then you and your friend leave. You, alone, return in an hour. Say to the clerk, 'Let me have that hundred dollar bill now.' The clerk, knowing you have a witness, will hand over the money. Now find your friend, the witness, and go back to the hotel an hour later. Step up boldly and say, 'May I have the hundred dollars I gave you this morning while my friend was here with me?' You'll have the clerk trapped."

The psychology clicked. The guest got all his money back. He returned to the lawyer and told him how successful the advice was. "And now, what is your fee?"

"A hundred dollars," said the lawyer.[97]

Sharpening the flats.

8. Sharpening the flats. Illustration by Harry Furniss for A'Beckett's *The Comic Blackstone*, 1887.

The lawyer taking the whole of the stakes seems to be an American addition to a British story, told of John Philpott Curran (1750–1817), an Irish barrister, parliamentarian, and Master of the Rolls. The British story culminates with the countryman returning "exultingly to thank his counsel, with both hundreds in his pocket."[98]

A46   In a desperate act, Felix, a bank teller, quietly let himself into the vault and filled his briefcase with $100 bills, then fled home. He quickly came to his senses and realized the enormity of his action.

He phoned his attorney and said, "I've stolen $50,000 from the bank I work for! I don't know what came over me! What should I do?"

"Steal $50,000 more and bring it to me," the attorney directed calmly.

Felix was astounded, but he did it, and after he brought her the cash, she wrote the following letter, which served to get the man off:

"Gentlemen: Your teller, Felix Fingers, took $100,000 from your bank. The hard-pressed family, despite their most valiant efforts, was unable to raise more than $50,000, which they offer to return if you will not prosecute. . . ."[99]

In the earliest printed version of this joke, the lawyer explicitly takes half of the stolen amount as his fee.[100] More recent versions leave to our imagination what happens to the portion not returned.

A new story attributes to the lawyer a preternatural shrewdness or discernment that enables him to extricate a client from an apparently hopeless plight.

A47   It seems a man got turned in by his neighbour who saw him having sex with a goat. He was arrested and told to get a lawyer. He had a choice of two. It was a small town. One lawyer was very expensive. He usually won his case by having costly out of town experts testify. The other was cheap. His forte was jury selection, he could usually get a juror or two that would be sympathetic to his client. The defendant chose the less expensive lawyer.

The first day of the trial the witness was told to tell the jury exactly what he saw on the morning of March 15th. He stated that he happened to look out his kitchen window about 8 A.M. and he saw farmer Brown drop his pants and have sex with a tan-coloured goat. And when he finished the goat turned around and licked his penis. At this time a front-row juror was heard to say to another juror, "You know, a good goat will do that."[101]

The lawyer's stratagems may not be on behalf of clients, but solely for his own gain, including the pleasure of besting rival professionals:

A48   NASA was interviewing professionals to be sent to Mars. Only one could go—and couldn't return to Earth.

The first applicant, an engineer, was asked how much he wanted to be paid for going. "A million dollars," he answered, "because I want to donate it to M.I.T."

The next applicant, a doctor, was asked the same question. He asked for $2 million.

"I want to give a million to my family," he explained, "and leave the other million for the advancement of medical research."

The last applicant was a lawyer. When asked how much money he wanted, he whispered in the interviewer's ear, "Three million dollars."

"Why so much more than the others?" asked the interviewer.

The lawyer replied, "If you give me $3 million, I'll give you $1 million, I'll keep $1 million, and we'll send the engineer to Mars."[102]

Usually the three competitors in this truly international story are rival contractors and are contrasted by ethnicity or provenance rather than occupation.[103] The cunning scheme remains the same, but the lawyer version is distinctive in that his rivals are not business competitors but unselfish souls imbued with benevolence for others—in contrast to the self-serving chicanery of the lawyer.

But sometimes the rivalry among professions can involve outdoing the other in guile.

A49   Seems there were three lawyers and three MBAs traveling by train to a conference. At the station, the three MBAs each buy tickets and watch as the three lawyers buy only a single ticket. "How are three people going to travel on only one ticket?" asks an MBA. "Watch and you'll see" answers a lawyer.

They all board the train. The MBAs take their respective seats but all three lawyers cram into a restroom and close the door behind them. Shortly after the train has departed, the conductor comes around collecting tickets. He knocks on the restroom door and says, "Ticket, please." The door opens just a crack and a single arm emerges with a ticket in hand. The conductor takes it and moves on.

The MBAs see this and agree it was quite a clever idea. So after the conference, the MBAs decide to copy the lawyers on the return trip and save some money (being clever with money and all that). When they get to the station, they buy a single ticket for the return trip. To their astonishment, the lawyers don't buy a ticket at all. "How are you going to travel without a ticket?" asks one perplexed MBA. "This time we can't tell you," says one of the lawyers, "it's a professional secret."

When they all board the train the three MBAs cram into a restroom and the three lawyers cram into another one nearby. The train departs. Shortly afterward, one of the lawyers leaves his restroom and walks over to the restroom where the MBAs are hiding. He knocks on the door and says, "Ticket please."[104]

In later versions, it is the lawyers who are conned by engineers or by paralegals.[105] Although the jokes portray the lawyer as comfortably at home in the world of cunning and deceit, he is as often the vanquished as the victor in these games.

The lawyer is clever and resourceful; he has the wit to see opportunities and the audacity to grasp them. The lawyer draws on a fund of gamesmanship, but the jokes don't attribute great brilliance or sagacity to the lawyer. Lawyers are not credited with (Sherlock) Holmesian deduction or rabbinic wisdom. Although many jokes have been switched from Jews (and rabbis) to lawyers, it is noteworthy that the many stories of prodigious "talmudic" reasoning have not been associated with lawyers.

THE LAWYER OUTSMARTED

The lawyer's schemes and ruses are not always successful. Stories about clever stratagems are outnumbered by stories that show the lawyer undone by witnesses, shrewd jurors, guileful clients, assorted rustics, and even by blondes.

The badgering lawyer defeated by the rustic or blue-collar witness is a very old theme:

A50   A humorous fellow, a carpenter, being subpoena'd as a witness on a trial for an assault, one of the counsel, who was very much given to browbeat the evidence, asked him what distance he was from the parties when he saw the defendant strike the plaintiff.

The carpenter answered, "Just four feet five inches and a half."

"Prithee, fellow," said the counsel, "how is it possible you can be so very exact as to the distance?"

"Why, to tell you the truth," says the carpenter, "I thought perhaps that some fool or other might ask me, and so I measured it."[106]

In the following story, the witness in an Indian court is a Sikh, a group often assigned the "yokel" role in Indian humor.

A51   Joginder Singh was testifying in the witness box and the defence counsel was attacking him viciously to make him change his statement.

"You mean to say you timed it exactly at five minutes?"

"Yes."

"Are you sure it was five minutes only?"

"Yes."

"Well, we'll check out your wonderful sense of time. I'm going to test you. Don't look at your watch and tell me when five minutes are up, starting—now!"

After exactly five minutes Joginder Singh called out, "Five minutes!"

The defence lost the case and later the lawyer asked Joginder Singh, "How did you do it?"

"I am seeing the clock on the wall in backside of you!"[107]

Sometimes the witness's assault is more than verbal.

A52   After being badgered and tongue-lashed by the plaintiff's lawyer for a good fifty minutes, the man on the witness stand, who was defending himself against charges of assault and battery, still insisted that he did no more than push the plaintiff.

"I want to know just how hard you pushed him," demanded the lawyer. "Will you please step down and demonstrate on me the sort of push you gave my client?"

The defendant jumped down with alacrity. He headed straight for his tormentor, jarred him with a stiff left hook, lifted him a foot off the ground with a terrific uppercut, grabbed him before he could fall, and tossed him halfway across the room. He then turned to the judge and explained, "I pushed the plaintiff just about one-tenth as hard as that, Your Honor."[108]

Or the lawyer may be undone by his misreading of the jury:

A53   The defendant's lawyer, determined at all cost to save his client from the electric chair, surreptitiously approached one of the jurors.

"I'll make it worth your while," said the lawyer, "if you'll see to it that the jury brings in a verdict of manslaughter in the second degree."

The trial proceeded, and the jury retired. After seven hours they brought in the verdict, "manslaughter in the second degree," and the defendant was given a long prison term.

The lawyer, going to pay off the juror, thanked him warmly.

"It was pretty hard," admitted the juror. "At first they were all for acquittal, but I managed to talk them out of it."[109]

A54   A noted criminal defense lawyer was making the closing argument for his client accused of murder, although the body of the victim has never been found. The lawyer dramatically turned to the courtroom's clock and, pointing to it, announced, "Ladies and gentlemen of the jury, I have some astounding news. I have found the supposed victim of this murder to be alive! In just ten seconds, she will walk throught the door of this courtroom."

A heavy quiet suddenly fell over the courtroom as everyone waited for the dramatic entry.

But nothing happened.

The smirking lawyer continued, "The mere fact that you were watching the door, expecting the victim to walk into this courtroom, is clear proof that you have far more than even a reasonable doubt as to whether a murder was actually committed." Tickled with the impact of his cleverness, the cocky lawyer confidently sat down to await acquittal.

The jury was instructed, filed out, and filed back in just ten minutes with a guilty verdict.

When the judge brought the proceedings to the end, the dismayed lawyer chased after the jury foreman: "Guilty? How could you convict? You were all watching the door!"

"Well," the foreman explained. "Most of us were watching the door. But one of us was watching the defendant, and he wasn't watching the door."[110]

The lawyer who regards himself as a master of strategy may find himself outfoxed by deceptively simple types:

A55   A big-city lawyer was representing the railroad in a lawsuit filed by an old rancher. The rancher's prize bull was missing from the section of his ranch where the railroad passed through. The rancher wanted to be paid the fair value of the bull. Before the case began, the attorney for the railroad cornered the rancher and tried to get him to settle out of court. The lawyer did his best selling job, and finally the rancher agreed to take half of what he was asking. After the rancher had signed the release form and taken the check, the young lawyer couldn't help but gloat a little over his success.

"You know," he said to the rancher, "I hate to tell you this, but I really put one over on you. There's no way I could've won the case. The train's engineer was asleep at the switch and the fireman was back in the caboose when the train went through your ranch that day. I didn't have a single witness to put on the stand. I bluffed you!"

"Well," replied the old rancher, "to tell you the truth, young feller, I was a little worried about winning that case myself. That darned bull came home this morning."[111]

Sometimes even the lawyer's own clients may outdo him in guileful stratagem.

A56   A defendant in a lawsuit involving a large sum of money was talking to his lawyer.
"If I lose the case, I'll be ruined," he said.
"It's in the judge's hands now," said the lawyer.
"Would it help if I sent the judge a box of cigars?"
"Oh, no," said the lawyer "This judge is a stickler for ethical behavior. A stunt like that would prejudice him against you. He might even hold you in contempt of court. In fact, you shouldn't even smile at the judge."
Within the course of time, the judge rendered a decision in favor of the defendant.
As the defendant left the courthouse with his lawyer he said, "Thanks for the tip about the cigars. It worked."
"I'm sure we would have lost the case if you had sent them."
"But I did send them."
"You did?"
"Yes. That is how we won the case."
"I don't understand," said the lawyer.
"It's easy. I sent the cigars to the judge, but enclosed my opponent's business card."[112]

This story parallels an anecdote told about Sir Matthew Hale (1609–76), a practitioner and judge who rose to be chief justice of the King's Bench:

> A disposition to side with the poor against the rich and powerful was his fault and it once completely entrapped him. A courtier, having a cause to be tried, procured a person to go to the chief justice, as from the king, and speak in favor of his adversary. He gained his point, "for Sir Matthew could never think very well of any one that came so unduly recommended."[113]

The client may deal with the lawyer strategically from the outset as depicted in this widely published joke in which the canny client is often a Jew or Scot:

A57   A shrewd and thrifty farmer got into a boundary dispute with his neighbor. The battle waxed from warm to hot and the farmer sought legal aid.
After stipulating that there was to be no fee unless there were grounds for legal action, he gave the lawyer a detailed and elaborate account of the trouble.

"Fine!" the lawyer said. "The case is air-tight. The other fellow hasn't got a leg to stand on. My advice is ten dollars, and for a forty dollar retainer I'll start a suit at once."

"No," said the farmer. "No, I guess you better not. I gave you the other fellow's side."[114]

In devising a strategy to frustrate his client's antagonist, the lawyer runs the risk that the newly educated client will turn it on the lawyer to evade his fee. The lawyer hoist on his own petard theme is the longest-running lawyer joke. For over five hundred years it has taken various forms, many descended from an anonymous fifteenth-century French play, *The Farce of the Worthy Master, Pierre Pathelin, the Lawyer*.[115] In the spate of jokebooks that accompanied the Italian Renaissance:

A58   A doctor [of Law] said to a peasant, "If you are willing to pay me one ducat, I will teach you how to litigate so that you will always win." He promised he would pay him one ducat and the doctor said to him, "Always deny, and you will win." Then he asked him for the ducat, and the peasant immediately denied having promised it to him.[116]

In one line of descent from Pathelin, the lawyer coaches his client to recite a nonsensical response to all questions, defeating the claims of his adversary by what might be called an idiocy defense, as in this seventeenth-century English rendition:

A58   There was an unthrift in London, that had received of a Merchant certain Wares, which came to fifty pounds, to pay at three moneths; and at three moneths. But when he had it he consumed and spent it all: so that at the six moneths end there was not any left to pay the Merchant: Wherefore the Merchant arrested him. When he saw there was no other remedy, but either to pay the debt, or go to prison, he sent to a subtill Lawyer, and asked his Counsell how he might clear himself of that debt. What wilt thou give me, (quoth he) if I do? Five marks (quoth the other) and here it is: and as soon as you have done, you shall have it. Well, said the Lawyer, but thou must be ruled by my counsell, and do thus: When thou commest before the Judge, whatsoever he saith unto thee, answer thou nothing, but cry Bea still, and let me alone with the rest. So when he came before the Judge, he said to the Debter, Dost thou owe this Merchant so much money? Bea (quoth he). What, beast? (quoth he) The answer to that I aske thee. Bea (quoth he again.) Why how now? quoth the Judge, I think this fellow hath gotten a sheeps tongue in his head: for he answereth in the sheeps language. Why, Sir, quoth the Lawyer, do you think this Merchant that is so wise a man, would be so foolish, as to trust this Ideot with fifty pounds worth of ware, that can speak never a word? No, Sir, I warrant you—And he persuaded the Judge to cast the Merchant in his own suit. And so the Judge departed, and the Court brake up. Then the Lawyer came to his Client, and asked him his Money, since his promise was performed, and his debt discharged. Bea (quoth he.) Why, thou needs't not cry Bea any longer, but pay me my money. Bea, (quoth he again). Why thou wilt not serve me so, I hope, (quoth the Lawyer) now I have used thee so kindly? But nothing but Bea could Master Lawyer get for his paines, and so was faine to depart with a flea in his ear.[117]

In another line of stories, the lawyer's formula is not the client's incompetence but a procedural or evidentiary demand. One variant deals with the relationship between the established older lawyer and his entourage, including rivalry with ambitious young lawyers.

A58   About seventy years ago there was a lawyer, here in the United States, who had won great successes as a trial lawyer. His ability in court was the talk of his profession, and many a young lawyer would have given a good deal to know how the older man won such honors. There was one young attorney in particular who was envious of the older man.

It chanced that the two men found themselves together one day, in a stagecoach bound for a city in which a circuit judge was to sit. Both lawyers were bound to the sessions of court. The younger man lost no time in striking up an acquaintance with his older and more famous colleague, and in the course of their conversation said to him:

"Mr. Jones, you are a prominent and successful attorney, while I am but a beginner in the law. Will you not tell me the secret of your great success before judge and jury."

"Young man," said Jones, "my success has been won at the cost of long, hard work. However, I am willing to tell you my secret on one condition."

Without waiting to hear what that condition might be, the younger man agreed, and Jones said:

"I will tell you my secret, and you will pay all my expenses during the three days we shall be together during the sitting of the court. Agreed? Yes; well, my secret is this, I deny everything and demand proof."

They stayed three days attending court, and the older man occupied the best room in the inn, ate the best food and plenty of it, drank the finest liquors and smoked the most expensive cigars—all of which went on the bill.

The court sessions were over, and the two lawyers stood in the hotel office while the innkeeper made out their bills. There was a great big one for the older lawyer, and a little one for the younger man. The former took his bill and, without even looking at it, handed it to the other man.

"What's this?" said the young lawyer.

"My bill, which you agreed to pay."

"Why," the young man came back at him, "I deny everything and demand proof."

"Young man," said the older lawyer, "you don't need any lessons from me."[118]

Most modern renditions follow the original Renaissance script of the client turning the lawyer's trick against him. Most frequently the client demands the lawyer "get some witnesses" but some retain the original "sheep's tongue" response:

A58   A sheep-herder was accused of having robbed a store. He was caught with the goods so his lawyer said, "Our defense will have to be insanity. I will contend that the loneliness out there for weeks at a time with the sheep caused you to lose your mind. When I put you on the stand and ask you questions, you answer each one by saying 'Ba-a-a.'"

The defendant agreed. His lawyer asked, "What is your name?" and the prisoner replied, "Ba-a-a." "What is your age?" Again, "Ba-a-a." The jury was convinced and freed the accused.

Out in the courthouse corridor, the attorney said to his client, "And now how about paying me my fee/" The other said, "Ba-a-a."[119]

No matter how formidable on his home ground in the courtroom, the lawyer may find it difficult to translate his ascendency into everyday settings:

A59   A lawyer and a blonde are sitting next to each other on a long flight from L.A. to N.Y. The lawyer leans over to her and asks if she would like to play a fun game. The blonde just wants to take a nap, so she politely declines and rolls over to the window to catch a few winks. The lawyer persists and explains that the game is really easy and a lot of fun. He explains, "I ask you a question, and if you don't know the answer, you pay me $5, and vice-versa."

Again, she politely declines and tries to get some sleep. The lawyer, now somewhat agitated, says, "Okay, if you don't know the answer you pay me $5, and if I don't know the answer, I will pay you $500!"

Figuring that since she is a blonde that he will easily win the match [sic]. This catches the blonde's attention and, figuring that there will be no end to this torment unless she plays, [she] agrees to the game. The lawyer asks the first question. "What's the distance from the earth to the moon?" The blonde doesn't say a word, reaches in to her purse, pulls out a five dollar bill and hands it to the lawyer.

Now, it's the blonde's turn. She asks the lawyer: "What goes up a hill with three legs, and comes down with four?" The lawyer looks at her with a puzzled look. He takes out his laptop computer and searches all his references. He taps into the Airplane with his modem and searches the Net and the Library of Congress.

Frustrated, he sends Emails to all his coworkers and friends he knows. All to no avail. After over an hour, he wakes the blonde and hands her $500. The blonde politely takes the $500 and turns away to get back to sleep.

The lawyer, who is more than a little miffed, wakes the blonde and asks, "Well, so what IS the answer!?" Without a word, the blonde reaches into her purse, hands the lawyer $5, and goes back to sleep.[120]

A60   Johnny Cochran was duck hunting in Montana recently, when he attempted to cross a fence into a field to retrieve a duck he had shot. A farmer suddenly pulled up in his pick-up truck, jumped out, and asked Mr. Cochran what he was doing on his property. "Retrieving this duck I just shot," he replied. "That duck is on my side of the fence, so now it's mine," replied the farmer. Mr. Cochran asked the farmer if he recognized who he was talking to. "No," replied the farmer, "I don't know, and I don't care." "I am Johnny Cochran, famous lawyer from Los Angeles," came the reply. "I am the lawyer that got O. J. Simpson off. I'm the reason he is a free man today. And if you don't get me that duck, I can sue you for your farm, your truck, and everything else you own. I'll leave you penniless on the street." "Well," said the farmer, "in Montana the only law we go by is the three kicks law." "Never heard of it," said Johnny. The farmer said, "I get to kick you three times, and if you make it back to your feet and are able to kick me back three times, that duck is yours." Cochran thought this over. He grew up in a tough neighborhood and figured he could take the old farmer. "Fair enough," he said. So the farmer kicked Johnny violently in the groin. As he was doubling over, the farmer kicked him in the face, and when he hit the ground, he kicked him hard in the ribs. After several moments, Johnny slowly made it back to his feet. "Alright, now it's my turn," said Johnny. "Aw, forget it," said the farmer. "You can have the duck."[121]

Finally, the lawyer who attempts to push his skills of discursive manipulation beyond conceptual boundaries risks being the victim of his own overreaching.

A61   A Charlotte N.C. lawyer purchased a box of very rare and expensive cigars then insured them against fire among other things. Within a month, having smoked his entire stock-pile of these great cigars and without yet having made even his first premium payment on the policy, the lawyer filed a claim against the insurance company. In his claim, the lawyer stated the cigars were lost "in a series of small fires." The insurance company refused to pay, citing the obvious reason: that the man had consumed the cigars in the normal fashion.

The lawyer sued . . . and won! In delivering the ruling the judge agreed with the insurance company that the claim was frivolous[;] however[,] the judge stated that the lawyer held a policy from the company in which it had warranted that the cigars were insurable and also guaranteed that it would insure them against fire, without defining what is considered to be "unacceptable fire," and was obligated to pay the claim. Rather than endure a lengthy and costly appeal process, the insurance company accepted the ruling and paid $15,000.00 to the lawyer for his loss of the rare cigars lost in the "fires."

NOW FOR THE BEST PART . . .

After the lawyer cashed the check, the insurance company had him arrested on twenty-four counts of ARSON!!!! With his own insurance claim and testimony from the previous case being used against him, the lawyer was convicted of intentionally burning his insured property and sentenced him to twenty-four months in jail and a $24,000.00 fine.[122]

THE ASCENDENCY OF LAWYER TALK

Discourse jokes are solidly indigenous. They arise from and refer to the legal setting; only a handful have been switched to lawyers. They are also the oldest of our joke clusters. At least two-thirds of jokes discussed here were in circulation before 1940; a sizable contingent were current before 1900. With the coming of the great explosion of lawyer jokes after 1980, some new material has accrued to the *Discourse* cluster, but the themes were well established long ago. The bitterness and hostility that have entered into the lawyer joke corpus are largely located elsewhere, at least so far as we can find them in the texts. (Of course even these *Discourse* stories can be told with a hostile edge or may appear to have such an edge when juxtaposed with other types that arrived later.)

Looking back at this selection of jokes about the lawyer's discursive powers, we find a firm sense that lawyers are detached from ordinary canons of truth. Beyond that we find something of an "on the one hand / on the other hand" quality. Lawyers are fluent and resourceful, do amazing things with language, and are eager to put their art at the service of clients. While doing so they are looking out for themselves. They are so enclosed in a world of talk that they miss substance for form and often descend into senseless bombast; they overreach and clients and others turn the tables on them—outsmarting them and exposing their empty bluster. Although the tone overall is critical and mocking, there is an admixture of appreciation for their fluency, resourcefulness, cleverness, and attentiveness to clients.

The contemporary discussion of lawyers' sins and shortcomings adds a new dimension. The dominant role of lawyers in American public life has long been noted. Alexis de Tocqueville found they resembled "the hierophants of Egypt" as exclusive interpreters of an occult science.[123] One hundred thirty years later, historian Jerold Auerbach observed, "Law is our national religion: lawyers constitute our priesthood," a condition he blamed on America's "consuming individualism, unrelenting contentiousness, and discordant heterogeneity."[124] In *The High Priests of American Politics,* Mark Miller finds that American political institutions "have adopted lawyers' ways, lawyers' language, as well as lawyers' approaches to problem solving."[125] They emphasize procedure and process, rules and precedents; they take a rights-focused, case-by-case incremental approach to substantive social problems.

Opting for Chinese food for lunch, the law partners decide in principle to share their dishes and, accordingly, before ordering, negotiate a comprehensive pre-victual agreement.

9. Cartoon by Mort Gerberg (© The New Yorker Collection 1992, from cartoonbank.com. All rights reserved.)

So not only are lawyers guilty of various discursive sins, but the cumulative effect of their increasing presence undermines and drives out other forms of thought. Legal talk becomes the dominant discourse. Vice President Al Gore defended himself against charges of improper fundraising by insisting "counsel tells me there is no controlling legal authority that says that is any violation of any law."[126] The domination of legal discourse is noted resentfully by a movie critic: "What American has not uttered a curse in his heart against lawyers. We have created them in numbers beyond reason; and allowed them into every corner of our lives. Like priests in the Middle Ages, they hover over the essential rites of our civilization, talking, talking, talking. . . . They have altered intellectual life and public discourse. . . . At times, legal reasoning begins to supplant reason itself, and the triumphs and defeats of lawyers replace justice."[127] The sentiment is ratified by an editorial writer who observes, "The strange election of 2000 . . . certified the ascendency of lawyers in the moral and political life of the United States. . . . Everywhere people are learning to speak the language of lawyers for the purpose of understanding their own predicament."[128] These resentments of lawyers' wider effect on public life do not show up as *Discourse* jokes but as other kinds of attacks on lawyers. The complaints we shall examine are not just about discrete misdeeds of lawyers but about the role they play in contemporary society. The recurrence of the analogy between contemporary law and lawyers and medieval religion and priests suggests, however faintly, that the resentment of lawyers may reflect the ebbing of other sources of coherence and meaning in modern society.

CHAPTER 2

The Lawyer as Economic Predator

ONLY THE LAWYER WINS

Public imagination has long envisioned the basic figure of two litigants contending over a valuable object while the process of law consumes their resources and impoverishes both. In *Poor Richard's Almanac* for 1742, Benjamin Franklin counsels:

B1 Honest Men often go to Law for their Right; when Wise Men would sit down with the Wrong, supposing the first Loss least. In some Countries the Course of the Courts is so tedious, and the Expence so high, that the Remedy, Justice, is worse than, Injustice, the Disease. In my Travels I once saw a Sign call'd The Two Men at Law; One of them was painted on one Side, in a melancholy Posture, all in Rags, with this Scroll, I have lost my Cause. The other was drawn capering for Joy, on the other Side, with these Words, I have gain'd my Suit; but he was stark naked.[1]

The beggar in the following story bases his strategy on the same insight:

B1 A beggar posted himself at the door of the Chancery Court, and kept saying: "A penny please, sir! Only one penny, sir, before you go in!" "And why, my man?" inquired an old country gentleman. "Because, sir, the chances are, you will not have one when you come out," was the beggar's reply.[2]

Both Franklin and the beggar know the sad truth that the remedies and protections of the law are not free. Indeed, they are often so costly that they are worthless. They are costly because, among other things, the same law that promises a remedy to the aggrieved guarantees to the other party a full complement of protections in the form of procedural niceties. Like ships taking on pilots to navigate treacherous coastal waterways, claimants and defendants take aboard lawyers to guide them through the intricacies of the law. The suit becomes a contest between these competing champions, each equipped with the capacity to foil and frustrate the other. Summoning witnesses, investigating and proving contested facts, obtaining copies of records must all be paid for. But the greatest expense is the fees of the lawyers themselves. The Civil Litigation Research Project found that in ordinary civil litigation some 99 percent of individuals' out-of-pocket expenses were payments to lawyers to cover fees and expenses.[3]

Lawyers are thus the "gatekeepers" of the legal system. Inability to afford one effectively rules out resort to the law in many matters. But having a lawyer is no guarantee of success. The value of the matter in dispute may be outweighed by the lawyer's fees and other expenses. Often this is not apparent until there has been a heavy investment. Once these sunk costs are paid, there is an incentive for parties to invest even more in the hope of recouping something. There is also an incentive for lawyers paid fixed fees (by the hour or the engagement) to encourage further investment in chancy causes.[4] Encouraged by his lawyer, the claimant may find himself consumed by his cause:

B1

"I guess you heard about Ezry losin' his farm?" said the man who was showing him around.

"No I hadn't," said the visitor. "How did it happen?"

"Wal," said the local man, "Ezry got the idea that his neighbor's fence was encroachin' on his land, and he got to broodin' on it. Finally, he went to see a lawyer who thought so, too."[5]

The apparent winner may himself be a victim (of the lawyer):

B1

"I sent you an account of $25 for collection," said a man coming into the office of a Dakota lawyer.

"Yes, you did."

"What success have you had?"

"Sued him last week and got it."

"That's good. Give me the money and tell me the amount of your fees and I will pay you."

"My fees are $50. I have given you credit for the $25 collected—pay me another $25 and we'll be square."

"What!" gasped the man, "I don't see where I made anything by collecting the debt."

"Nothing, my dear sir, from a money point of view, but you have the satisfaction of knowing that a dishonest man has been brought to justice! You can use your own pleasure about paying that $25 now; I took the precaution to commence suit against you for the amount this morning."[6]

B3

Said a lady to her friend, "When we got our divorce, we divided everything we had equally between us. Two children stayed with me, two went to my ex-husband."

"What happened to the property?" asked a friend.

"That was shared equally between his lawyer and mine."[7]

Both stories, one from the U.S. frontier, and the other from present-day India, converge on the theme that the lawyers are the chief or sole beneficiaries of litigation.

B3   Two travellers . . . quarreling about the possession of an oyster, submit their difference to a lawyer. Having heard the matter in dispute, the lawyer whipp'd out his knife, opened the oyster, swallow'd the fish, gave the plaintiff and defendant each a shell and gravely went his way.[8]

The visual equivalent of this very old story is a famous nineteenth-century print entitled "The Lawsuit," which depicts plaintiff and defendant straining to pull a cow in opposite directions while a fat lawyer seated on a milking stool is milking the cow into his bucket.[9] Client response to the tendency of lawyers to end up with everything in their pockets ranges from resignation to resistance, as shown in the next two stories.

B5   The sick man had called his lawyer. "I wish to explain again to you," said he weakly, "about willing my property."
The lawyer held up his hand reassuringly.
"There, there," said he, "leave that all to me."
The sick man sighed resignedly. "I suppose I might as well," said he, turning upon his pillow. "You'll get it anyway."[10]

B6   "I'll have you understand," declared the wealthy young man, "that all the money I've got I got through hard work." "Aw, go on!" said his friend scornfully. "I happen to know that it was all left to you by your rich uncle." "Sure it was," agreed the other. "But don't you ever think it wasn't tough work getting it away from the lawyers."[11]

All these counsels of prudence—that law impoverishes, that it is better to lump it than to pursue a grievance, that it is better to settle a case than fight to the end, that law impoverishes litigants, that only lawyers come out ahead, and so forth— are very much alive today. Of course, they are invoked selectively and balanced by folk wisdom about the necessity of standing up for your rights and by tales of claimants who win outrageous undeserved sums.

TAKING IT ALL

Many suspect that material gain is the principal motivation of lawyers. Lawyers are proverbially unwilling to move without the stimulation of a fee:

B7   It is said, that in former days, an eminent counsellor was called on for his professional advice, by a countryman, who entered on the consultation thus: "Mr. A., my father died and made his will." The lawyer professed himself utterly unable to understand him; the countryman in vain endeavoured to make himself understood; and took his departure, surprised at the dullness of one reputed to be singularly acute. Meeting with a friend, he expressed to him his disappointment: his friend, more knowing, at once inquired whether he had given a retaining fee to the lawyer? "No," was the reply; "I left that for another opportunity." His friend advised him to return, and by no means to postpone that preliminary step. He did so; placed a shining guinea in the learned gentleman's hand, and began once more, "My father died, and made his will." The lawyer stopped him, saying, "Oh! I understand you now; you mean, your father made his will, and then died." From that time forward, the client found no cause to complain that his counsel was either dull of apprehension or negligent of his interests. Hints should not be thrown away.[12]

There are many stories about the unwillingness of lawyers to proceed without a fee.[13] And, once payment has ended, so do his attentions:

B7   A blustering attorney was trying to keep his client from the gallows and wept before the jury, and after a windy argument won his case. When the jury came in with a verdict of "not guilty" the client was surrounded by a weeping wife and relatives, who were all making quite a stir in the court room, when the Judge, as well as the defendant's attorney, walked into the side room to get away from the commotion. The Judge turned to the lawyer and said, "Why don't you continue weeping with the rest of your crowd?" The attorney, realizing the pointed remark, turned to the Judge and said, "No, my pay is stopped."[14]

Not the client's need, but his ability to pay determines the level of service the lawyer will render:

B8   A man accused of stealing two thousand dollars went to a lawyer to retain him for his defense. The lawyer said:

"Now that you are here, you had better make a clean breast of it to me. Did you take the two thousand dollars?"

"I did," said the client.

"How much of it is left?"

"I've got only ten dollars of it left."

The lawyer rose and buttoned his coat. "In that case," he said, "you had better plead guilty and throw yourself on the mercy of the court."

"I suppose I'll have to," said the man. "How much for that advice?"

"Ten dollars," said the lawyer.[15]

Other times, as in real life, ability to pay determines whether the lawyer will render any services at all:

B9   A prisoner charged with embezzlement appeared in court without counsel.

"How does it happen you have no lawyer?" asked the judge.

"Well, I did engage an attorney," explained the prisoner, "but as soon as he found out that I had not stolen the $10,000, he would have nothing to do with my case."[16]

A similar idea occurs in the form of a cynical portrayal of the

B10   lawyers creed: a man is innocent until proven broke.[17]

The lawyer's exactions may be seen as part of a system of pay-offs.

B11   Judge: "Have you anything to offer to the court before sentence is passed on you?"
Prisoner: "No, judge. I had ten dollars, but my lawyers took that."[18]

Lawyers are eager to extract everything the client has. Successful extraction is not automatic, but takes effort and strategy on the lawyer's part. A long line of jokes detail how lawyers manage to do this while maintaining their professional dignity and their pose of devotion to the client's interest and indifference to their own:

B12   An attorney, on being called to account for having acted unprofessionally in taking less than the usual fees from his client, pleaded that he had taken all the man had. He was thereupon honourably acquitted.[19]

Like several other jokes, this was often told as a story about the distinguished lawyer Rufus Choate (1799–1859). In a memoir by the junior lawyer who handled the case in question, Choate, "with a rich smile mantling over the lower part of his face," ends the exchange: "You took all he had, did you? Well, I've nothing to say to that—that's strictly professional."[20] The story flourished in both the U.S.

*"I'm certain I speak for the entire legal profession when
I say that the fee is reasonable and just."*

10. Cartoon by Leo Cullum (© The New Yorker Collection 1995, from cartoonbank.com. All rights reserved.)

and in Britain, where it was told of several barristers.[21] This story has expired, not having broken into print since 1949.[22] The lack of current appeal (in the U.S. at least) may reflect the demise of prescribed minimum fees after the United States Supreme Court declared in 1977 that bar associations' minimum fee schedules violated antitrust laws.[23]

A long and vigorous joke tradition holds that the charges of lawyers and doctors (and the services to be rendered) are calculated with an eye to the customer's purse rather than his problem.[24] Thus the lawyer, with the connivance of an understanding judge, contrives to extract the maximum in this story, published by Ambrose Bierce in 1898, about a probate proceeding:

B13   "Your Honor," said an Attorney, rising, "what is the present status of this case as far as it has gone?"

"I have given a judgment for the residuary legatee under the will," said the Court, "put the costs upon the contestants, decided all questions relating to fees and other charges; and, in short, the estate in litigation has been settled, with all controversies, disputes, misunderstandings and differences of opinion thereunto appertaining."

"Ah, yes, I see," said the Attorney, thoughtfully, "we are making progress we are getting on famously."

"Progress?" echoed the Judge "progress? Why, sir, the matter is concluded!"

"Exactly, exactly; it had to be concluded in order to give relevancy to the motion that I am about to make. Your Honor, I move that the judgment of the Court be set aside and the case reopened."

"Upon what ground, sir?" the Judge asked in surprise.

"Upon the ground," said the Attorney, "that after paying all fees and expenses of litigation and all charges against the estate there will still be something left."

"There may have been an error," said his Honor, thoughtfully. "The Court may have underestimated the value of the estate. The motion is taken under advisement."[25]

A shorter criminal law version circulates more widely.

B14   "Why do you want a new trial?"

"On the grounds of newly discovered evidence, your Honor."

"What's the nature of it?"

"My client dug up $400 that I didn't know he had."[26]

It is not clear whether this is a modification of Bierce or whether Bierce was inspired by this story or some ancestor.

B15   A businessman was involved in a costly lawsuit which carried the threat of imprisonment. "I know the evidence is strongly against my innocence," he told his attorney, "but I have $50,000 in cash to fight the case."

"As your lawyer I can assure you," said the attorney, "you'll never have to go to prison with that amount of money."

And he didn't. He went there broke.[27]

However dire the client's fate, these stories emphasize that the lawyer is always eager to maximize his return. For example,

B16   A Western lawyer entered a condemned client's cell. "Well," he said, cheerfully, "good news at last."

"A reprieve?" exclaimed the prisoner eagerly.

"No, but your uncle has died, leaving you $5,000, and you can now go to your fate with the satisfying feeling that the noble efforts of your attorney in your behalf will not go unrewarded."[28]

The lawyer's propensity to expand the services provided in order to empty the pocket of the client is codified in a light bulb joke, whose punch line also raises the question of the rationing of justice.

B17   Q. How many lawyers does it take to change a light bulb?
A. How many can you afford?[29]

Another response harks back to the theme of the lawyer consuming the stakes.

B18   It only takes one lawyer to change your lightbulb to his lightbulb.[30]

A PRODIGIOUS PREDATOR

One of the enduring sources of resentment of lawyers is that, like doctors, undertakers, and auto repair shops, they flourish on the troubles of others. And, they are experts to whom we defer to define those troubles and prescribe a remedy. The combination of diagnosis and prescription affords great opportunity for overreaching.

B19   An opulent farmer applied to an attorney about a lawsuit, but was told he could not undertake it, being already engaged on the other side; at the same time he gave him a letter of recommendation to a professional friend. The farmer, out of curiosity, opened it, and read as follows:

"Here are two fat wethers fallen out together,
If you'll fleece one, I'll fleece the other,
And make 'em agree like brother and brother."

The perusal of this epistle cured both parties, and terminated the dispute.[31]

Folklorists Herbert Halpert and Gerald Thomas assembled forty versions of this tale (including both rhyming and all-prose versions) dating from 1566. Half came from Ireland and Wales; the others from North America, Scotland, England, France, and Finland.[32]

Typically a single lawyer is capable of doing the shearing unassisted:

B20   An eminent Scottish divine met two of his own parishioners at a house of a lawyer, whom he considered too sharp a practitioner. The lawyer ungraciously put the question, "Doctor, these are members of your flock; may I ask, do you look upon them as white sheep or as black sheep?" "I don't know," answered the divine drily, "whether they are black or white sheep; but I know, if they are long here, they are pretty sure to be *fleeced*."[33]

B21 "How are you getting along in the law business, old man?"

"I have one client."

"Is he rich?"

"He was."[34]

The prospering on the troubles of others theme is pointedly present in one of the few jokes about the practice of divorce law:

B22 A young lawyer's wife was fretting over the bareness of their home.

"We need furniture, drapes, carpets everything," she wailed. "Cheer up, my dear," comforted her husband. "I have an excellent divorce case pending. I represent the wife, and the husband has plenty of money. As soon as I finish breaking up their home, we can fix ours up."[35]

The following lawyer as extractor joke has been in favor for well over a century. Two distinct versions have continued quite unchanged since the late nineteenth century and two new ones have been added more recently:[36]

B23 A lawyer had his portrait taken in his favorite attitude standing with his hands [sic] in his pocket. An old farmer remarked that the portrait would have been more like the lawyer if it had represented him with his hand in another man's pocket, instead of his own.[37]

Although this *portrait* version is the oldest, it seems to be fading away and has been published in the United States only once since the 1940s. It has been overtaken by the following *two speakers* version:

B23 George Ade had finished his speech at a recent dinner party, and on seating himself a well known lawyer rose, shoved his hands deep into his trousers' pockets, as was his habit, and laughingly inquired of those present:

"Doesn't it strike the company as a little unusual that a professional humorist should be funny?"

When the laugh had subsided, Ade drawled out:

"Doesn't it strike the company as a little unusual that a lawyer should have his hands in his own pockets?"[38]

The first "professional humorist" to deliver this punch line was Mark Twain, but it is most frequently attributed to the no-longer-celebrated George Ade (1866–1944).[39] Yiddish humorist Sholem Aleichem appears in a Jewish-American version. These notables are sometimes paired with famous lawyers: Twain with William M. Evarts and Joseph H. Choate, Sholem Aleichem with Louis Marshall.[40]

By 1956, yet another version was in print:

B23 The lawyer had ordered a special suit made to order and when he went for the final fitting he was delighted at the wonderful cut, the marvelous texture of the cloth, and the magnificent styling and lines of the design. But when he went to put his money into the pockets, he found there weren't any.

"But why no pockets?" he protested to the tailor.

"It shouldn't make any difference," the tailor answered. "Who ever heard of a lawyer with his hands in his own pockets?"[41]

In the mid-1990s, a very condensed form of *pockets* appears as quip about

B23   the weather being so cold that lawyers put their hands in their own pockets.[42]

That the lawyer is indeed a prodigious predator, outranking all manner of competitors, has been proclaimed in books, films, and on stage. In *The Beggar's Opera* (1728), John Gay has the Peachums sing the following reflection on a possible challenge to their daughter Polly's dowry:

> A Fox may steal your Hens, Sir,
> A Whore your Health and Pence, Sir,
> Your Daughter rob your Chest, Sir,
> Your wife may steal your Rest, Sir,
> A Thief your Goods and Plate.
> But this is all but picking,
> With Rest, Pence, Chest and Chicken;
> It ever was decreed, Sir,
> If Lawyer's Hand is fee'd sir,
> He steals your whole Estate.[43]

The same thought is put in the mouth of the distinguished jurist Lord Mansfield (1705–93):

B24   A man was brought before Lord Mansfield, charged with stealing a silver ladle, and the counsel for the crown was rather severe upon the prisoner for being an attorney. "Come, come," said his lordship, "don't exaggerate matters; if the fellow had been *an attorney*, he would have *stolen the bowl* as well as the ladle."[44]

And more recently, in the mouth of Theodore Roosevelt:

B24   When President Theodore Roosevelt was trying to persuade his son to become a lawyer, he used the following argument: "A man who never graduated from school might steal from a freight car. But a man who attends college and graduates as a lawyer might steal the whole railroad."[45]

Not to be outdone in cynical knowledge, Don Corleone in *The Godfather* (1969) observes: "A lawyer with his briefcase can steal more than one hundred men with guns."[46] Hence the lawyer has long been ranked with predators of fabled scale and ferocity:

B25   Lawyer: "When I was a boy my highest ambition was to be a pirate."

Client: "You're in luck. It isn't every man who can realize the dreams of his youth."[47]

The pirate trope reappeared in a recent proceeding challenging the fees of the lawyers who represented the State of Wisconsin in its claim to recover health care costs from the manufacturers of cigarettes. Objectors to the size of the fees cited a 1917 case in which the Supreme Court of Wisconsin condemned a contract by which a lawyer solicited clients among flood victims for another lawyer. Justice E. Roy Stevens wrote: "Attorneys are entitled to good pay, for their work is hard, but they are not entitled to fly the black flag of piracy. Such contracts as are here in question tend to make the lawyer forget his high duty as a minister of justice and to convert him into a mere grubber for money in the muck-heaps of the world. They also tend to make the name of lawyer a proverb and a byword among lay-men."[48] Some contemporary lawyers are less punctilious about the pirate image, perhaps in hope of becoming "a proverb and a byword" in their own right. Flamboyant plaintiff's lawyer Melvin Belli (1907–96) installed a flagpole on the roof of his office, so that he could run up the Jolly Roger whenever he won a case, much to the embarrassment of his more respectable colleagues.[49]

The lawyer is such a formidable predator that he can turn the tables on even the most feared beasts in the urban jungle:

B26   Two muggers met in an alley, one of them breathless.

    "I just tried to mug a lawyer," the man panted.

    "Cripes," said the other. "He get anything?"[50]

Again, the earliest turnabout story seems to be an Ambrose Bierce fable:

B26   Two Footpads sat at their grog in a roadside resort, comparing the evening's adventures.

    "I stood up the Chief of Police," said the First Footpad, "and got away with what he had."

    "And I," said the Second Footpad, "stood up the United States District Attorney, and got away with—"

    "Good Lord!" interrupted the other in astonishment and admiration, "you got away with what that fellow had?"

    "No," the unfortunate narrator explained, "with a small part of what I had."[51]

As a debate on "Is it wrong to cheat a lawyer?" concluded, it is "not wrong, but too difficult to pay for the trouble."[52] For a century, muggers, burglars, and pickpockets have been bested by lawyers, who have not only talked them out of their swag, but also poached on their prey and occasionally made them into clients.[53]

B26   Burglar: "Talk about hard luck, I broke into a lawyer's house last night an' he got the drop on me an' advised me to get out."

    Pal: "Huh! Yer got off dead easy."

    Burglar: "Easy nothing! He charged me $10 for advice."[54]

Usually, the lawyer prevails without explicitly charging fees, but other enterprising professionals manage to sell insurance or real estate to their would-be victimizers.[55] The endurance and spread of the theme of the fellow-predator's regard for the lawyer's extractive abilities are displayed in this pair, the first from England in 1887 (and the U.S. in the 1920s), the second from India in 1990:

B27   A couple of pickpockets followed a gentleman for some distance with a view of availing themselves of the first opportunity to relieve him of his purse. He suddenly turned into a lawyer's office. "What shall we do now?" asked one. "Wait for the lawyer," said the other.[56]

B27   Two pick-pockets [are] outside a theka [tavern]. After they had ordered their drinks, they saw a car pull up on front of a house on the other side and fat sethji [moneylender] step out of it. Said one pick-pocket to the other, "Looks like a nice shikar [quarry]. Let's polish him off before we enjoy our drink."

"Don't be silly," replied the other, "He has gone into the house of a lawyer. When he comes out, his pocket will have already been picked by his host."[57]

The extractive propensities of lawyers are summarized in riddles comparing them with bloodsuckers:

B28   What is the difference between a lawyer and a vampire?
A vampire only sucks blood at night.[58]

But the most widespread and distinctive of the *Predator* jokes is based on an equation with that emblematic predator the shark. The term "shark," suggesting a combination of skill and deception (as in "pool shark" or "card shark"), was used to refer to a pickpocket or rapacious swindler by the early eighteenth century and was seafarers' slang for lawyers by the early nineteenth century.[59] The first connection with "professional courtesy" is in 1900:

B29   Two lawyers, while bathing at Santa Cruz the other day, were chased out of the water by a shark. This is the most flagrant case of want of professional courtesy on record.[60]

By 1945 the professional courtesy theme was the basis of an elaborate narrative:

B29   A minister, a scientist, and a lawyer were adrift on a life raft in the tropics. At last they sighted land. But the wind died down while they were still a short way off the beach. The lawyer, the only one who could swim, volunteered to go ashore with a line and pull the raft to land. The minister knelt and prayed for his safety.

Then the lawyer dived in. His companions saw the black fin of a shark making straight for him. The shark disappeared, then came up on the other side, having passed under the swimmer. Shortly they saw an even bigger shark darting toward him, but this one also swerved just in time.

After the lawyer had reached shallow water, the minister said to the scientist, "There, you Doubting Thomas, there is proof of the power of prayer."

"Power of prayer, hell!" retorted the scientist. "That was just professional courtesy."[61]

This shark joke is occasionally switched to other formidable types such as Mafia capos, Jewish mothers, and Robert Maxwell, but overwhelmingly it is told of lawyers.[62] Starting in the 1970s, the sharks salute the lawyer by formally escorting him.[63] The shark image is ambiguous, however. It testifies to the ferocity and power of the lawyer, but who is the prey? Is it the opposing party? Or is it the client as well? At least some lawyers have embraced the shark image as a totem, flaunting it on T-shirts, signboards, and even in advertisements.[64] In a newspaper advertisement (figure 11a) adorned with a drawing of a smiling shark with sunglasses, striped tie, and briefcase, a lawyer counseled potential clients: "Sometimes, all it takes is the sight of a dorsal fin to get people moving. Sometimes, all it takes is a letter from us."[65]

Trust Me

This attention-getting T-shirt was our best-seller at every lawyer's convention. Orange on black. 100% heavy preshrunk cotton. Sizes M, L, XL, XXL. State size.

SHARK T-SHIRT ITEM #0675 $18.50

11. The shark image is domesticated by lawyers and turned into an ironic icon of the trade. (Just Litigation ad reproduced with permission of Walter Moore. Trust Me T-shirt reproduced from the For Counsel holiday catalog with permission.)

A recent spin-off from the *professional courtesy* story gives the same fin image a less benign reading. Taking the point of view of the devoured opposing party, it invokes the "even worse than" trope to demote the lawyer from moral equality with the shark.

B30   A doctor took his family on vacation to the ocean. When they were walking on the beach, the doctor became hysterically frightened when he saw a fin sticking up in the water. Trying to calm him down, his wife said, "Honey, that's just a shark. You've got to stop imagining there are lawyers everywhere."[66]

These well-established themes have flourished and been elaborated in the great surge of lawyer joking that began in the 1980s.

Fee Simple

People do not think they get good value from lawyers. In a 1974 survey, 68 percent of a national sample of Americans thought "most lawyers charge more for their services than they are worth."[67] A 1984 survey found that 61 percent of a national sample disagreed with the statement that lawyers' fees were "quite reasonable in light of the services they provide clients."[68] Only 29 percent agreed. In a 1990 survey, a national sample of adults was asked to rate "the value you get for your money" for lawyers' fees. Only 5 percent thought they got good value; 41 percent average value; and 55 percent poor value.[69] Resentment of lawyers' fees seems to be rising. In *National Law Journal* surveys in 1986 and 1993, respondents who had hired a lawyer were asked whether they were charged a fair fee or overcharged. From 1986 to 1993, those who thought the fee fair decreased from 66 percent to 47 percent, while those who said the lawyer charged too much rose from 28 percent to 43 percent.[70]

"Impressed? Well, wait until I tell you about this next case."

12. Cartoon by Charles Barsotti (© The New Yorker Collection 2002, from cartoonbank.com. All rights reserved.)

Traditionally lawyers charged by assessing an inclusive unitemized fee for the matter at hand, such as arguing a case or writing a will. Many of the older jokes above refer to this kind of fee-setting. As different fee arrangements developed, they too were commented on in the joke corpus.

The contingency fee, in which the lawyer charges a specified portion of the amount recovered by the client, was condemned in England and elsewhere as incompatible with professional dignity and a dangerous incentive to overzealous representation. Although prohibited in most legal systems, it has flourished in the United States, where it was an established feature of the legal scene by the mid-nineteenth century.[71] In his study of personal injury litigation in New York City, historian Randolph Bergstrom found that the contingency fee was little used in 1870, but much in use by 1890 and pervasive by 1910.[72] From its inception, it has been accompanied by accusations of illegitimacy. Attacks on the contingency fee have recurred with regularity, often in conjunction with campaigns against plaintiffs' lawyers for degrading professional standards by fomenting meritless litigation, ambulance chasing, and accident faking.[73]

A small set of jokes focus directly on the contingency fee relationship. Like the contingency fee itself, these jokes are confined largely to the United States. Here is an 1883 version:

B31   A New Yorker asked Wm. M. Evarts what he would charge for managing a certain law case.

"Well," said Mr. Evarts, "I will take your case on a contingent fee."

"And what is a contingent fee?"

"My dear sir," said Mr. Evarts, mellifluously, "I will tell you what a contingent fee to a lawyer means. If I don't win your suit I get nothing. If I do win it you get nothing. See?"[74]

A century later the same story is still current:

B31   "I'll take this case on contingency."

"What's contingency?

"If I lose, I get nothing."

"And if you win?"

"You get nothing."[75]

Other stories express the resentment of the size of the lawyer's share of the recovery:

B32   An Englishman while passing along the main street in a small town in Maine stepped in a hole in the sidewalk and, falling, broke his leg. He brought suit against the city for one thousand dollars, and engaged Hannibal Hamlin for counsel. Hamlin won his case, but the city appealed to the supreme court. Here also the decision was for Hamlin's client. After settling up the claim, Hamlin sent for his client and handed him one dollar.

"What's this?" asked the Englishman.

"That's your damages, after taking out my fee, the cost of appeal, and several other expenses," said Hamlin.

The Englishman looked at the dollar and then at Hamlin. "What's the matter with this?" he asked; "is it bad?"[76]

Although Hamlin (1809–91), once a practicing lawyer, governor of Maine, and one of Abraham Lincoln's vice presidents, has long departed public consciousness, the joke is still around:

B32   A man walking along a city street fell through an open sewer hole and broke his leg. He engaged a famous attorney, brought suit against the city for twenty thousand dollars and won the case. The city appealed the case to the Supreme Court, but again the lawyer won the decision. After the claim was settled the lawyer sent for his client and handed him a dollar bill. "What's this?" asked the man, looking at the dollar. "That's your damages, after deducting my fee, the cost of the appeal and other expenses," replied the attorney. The man looked at the dollar again, turned it over and carefully scanned the other side. He then looked up at the lawyer and said, "What's the matter with this dollar? Is it counterfeit?"[77]

Implicit in the condemnation of the lawyer's charges is the contrast between what is for the lawyer a routine occasion for the exercise of his craft but for the claimant a life emergency. Again, a century has brought little change from this 1895 version:

B33   Litigant—"You take nine-tenths of the judgement? Outrageous!"
        Lawyer—"I furnish all the skill and eloquence and legal learning for your cause."
        Litigant—"But I furnish the cause."
        Lawyer—"Oh, anybody could do that."[78]

B33   The man looked at the check he received after winning his suit against the city.
        "Wait a minute!" he said to his attorney. "This is only a third of the full amount!"
        "That's right," said the attorney. "I took the rest."
        "You!" screamed the man. "I was the one who was hurt!"
        "You forget. I provided the intelligence required to build the case, the expertise to find precedents, and the oratory to convince the jury. Any asshole could fall down a manhole."[79]

The role of underappreciated contributor can be shifted from lawyer to client:

B34   Patrick Murphy, while passing down Tremont Street, was hit on the head by a brick which fell from a building in process of construction. One of the first things he did after being taken home and put to bed was to send for a lawyer. A few days later he received word to call, as his lawyer had settled the case. He called and received five crisp, new, one-hundred dollar bills.
        "How much did you get?" he asked.
        "Two thousand dollars," answered the lawyer.
        "Two thousand, and you give me $500? Say, who got hit by that brick, you or me?"[80]

These stories take the contingency fee as the occasion to complain of the size of the lawyer's fee, but register no complaint about the contingency device itself.

The public generally regards it as an essential safeguard. In a 1985 survey, some 77 percent agreed that this method of paying the lawyer "gives everyone, even poor people, access to the courts because they don't have to pay the lawyer anything in advance, or anything at all if they lose the lawsuit." Only 9 percent disagreed with this viewpoint.[81] In another survey, conducted in late 1986 at the height of the furor about the liability crisis, some 73 percent of the public agreed that it was important to retain the contingency fee system.[82] Attachment to the contingency fee is inversely related to income and education: the most prosperous and educated people and those in top jobs were less attached.[83]

The pattern of lawyer jokes provides indirect but telling confirmation of the survey data showing public acceptance of the contingency fee as an institution. Although there is resentment of the lawyer's cut, there is an acceptance of its necessity and appreciation of the benefits of the arrangement.[84] Its enemies are not those who avail of it or who fear they might have to use it. Peter Karsten observes that its late nineteenth-century critics included "railroad attorneys, physicians facing malpractice suits, treatise writers, law journal editors and jurists."[85] A century later the contingency fee is assailed by a comparable alliance of adverse economic interests and professional notables.

Compared to the proliferation of jokes about lawyers' overcharging, relentless billing, and predatory practices, the contingency fee jokes are relatively mild and infrequent. The resentment of lawyers' fees is not particularly focused on the contingency fee: individual clients are far more exercised about hourly, retainer, and percentage fees in divorce, property transactions, and probate, while corporate clients complain about superfluous billing at excessive hourly rates. The first print appearance of the best known story about billing is in the dissenting opinion of a judge on the U.S. Court of Appeals in a 1980 case:

B35 An immediately deceased lawyer arrived at the Pearly Gates to seek admittance from St. Peter. The Keeper of the Keys was surprisingly warm in his welcome: "We are so glad to see you, Mr. [X]. We are particularly happy to have you here, not only because we get so few lawyers up here, but because you lived to the wonderful age of 165." Mr. [X] was a bit doubtful and hesitant. "Now, St. Peter, if there's one place I don't want to get into under false pretenses, it's Heaven. I really died at age seventy-eight." St. Peter looked perplexed, frowned, and consulted the scroll in his hand. "Ah, I see where we made our mistake as to your age. We just added up your time sheets!"[86]

The timing of this addition to the corpus of lawyer jokes is not surprising, for the hourly fee did not become widespread until the 1960s and 1970s.[87] Since its appearance (by 1980), this single story about abuse of hourly fees has appeared in the print and electronic media far more often than all the various contingency fee jokes combined.[88]

As the purchase of durables on the installment plan became widespread, the installment payment idea was used to twit professionals for the material concerns that lay just beneath the surface of their professional attentions. For example,

B36   "Here's my bill," said the lawyer. "Please pay down $100, and $25 a week thereafter for ten weeks."

"Sounds like buying an automobile," said the client.

"I am," returned the attorney.[89]

Although the lawyer bills clients assiduously, there may be pleasure in thinking (even if it is not so) that he earns less than those who contribute visibly to the well-being of society. This item switches to lawyers just as lawyer earnings are taking off.

B37   A . . . plumber . . . had been working at the lawyer's house for only a short time when he corrected the problem and presented him with a bill. After some quick calculating in his head the lawyer exclaimed, "Why, that's over two hundred dollars an hour. Even I don't make that." "I know," said the plumber. "I didn't make that either when I was a lawyer."[90]

THROWING THE METER

In addition to public bemusement and outrage at the amount of lawyers' charges, lawyers have another persistent problem: what is it that they can charge for? Where

S. GROSS

"If we were lawyers this would be billable time."

13. Cartoon by Sam Gross (© 2004, from cartoonbank.com. All rights reserved.)

does the social leave off and the professional begin? A series of jokes portray lawyers using the blurriness of this boundary to exploit clients and evade social obligations. These stories suggest that the lawyer's social life is inauthentic, feigning genuine commitment to others as a strategy for obtaining clients. In short, being a lawyer impoverishes or even obliterates him as a social being.[91]

The lawyer turns the occasion of an indisputable social claim invoked by a neighbor or tradesman into a technical consultation, so that he can offset his fee against the claim:

B38 Between a Protestant clergyman and a Roman Catholic lawyer, who had very good feeling towards each other, the following occurrence took place not far from Bath: "If," asked the clergyman, "a neighbour' dog destroy my ducks, can I recover damages by law?" "Certainly," replied the lawyer, "you can recover; pray, what are the circumstances?" "Why, Sir, your dog, last night, destroyed two of my ducks." "Indeed,

14. Cartoon by Aaron Bacall in S. Gross, ed., *Lawyers! Lawyers! Lawyers!* (© A. Bacall 1994)

then you certainly could recover the damages; what is the amount? I'll instantly discharge it." The demand of four shillings and six pence was made and paid, when the lawyer immediately made a demand of his fee, six shillings and eightpence, which, unless instantly paid, he should adopt legal means to recover.[92]

The classic joke on this subject involves a claim by the butcher:

B38   A vigorous looking man once came into the office of Max D. Steuer and said that he wanted to consult him about a certain case.

Steuer asked him to be seated.

"I am a butcher," commenced the visitor. "About a week ago a dog ran into my store and snatched from the counter a five pound steak. It was worth three dollars, and I want to know if the owner of the dog is responsible."

"He certainly is," Steuer replied.

"If so," said the butcher slyly, "please pay the three dollars. It was your dog."

Steuer opened his wallet and handed him three dollars.

"Thank you," said the butcher, triumphantly, and rose to leave the office.

"Wait a moment," said the eminent jurist. "My minimum fee for legal advice is five hundred dollars."[93]

More generally, the lawyer is suspected of turning social exchanges with clients into services to be charged to clients, as in this 1739 tale:

B39   A worthy old gentleman in the country having employed an attorney, of whom he had a pretty good opinion, to do some law business for him in London, he was greatly surprised, on his coming to town, and demanding his bill of law charges, to find that it amounted to at least three times the sum he expected; the honest attorney assured him, that there was no article in his bill, but what was fair and reasonable. "Nay," said the country gentleman, "there's one of them I am sure cannot be so, for you have set down three shillings and four-pence for going to Southwark, what is the meaning of that, Sir?" "Oh, Sir," said he, "that was for fetching the chine and turkey from the carrier's that you sent me for a present out of the country."[94]

B40   The renowned attorney Samuel Untermeyer was accustomed to taking an early morning walk around Central Park in New York. For a period of several weeks on each of those excursions, a neighbor greeted him with these words: "Isn't it a good morning, Mr. Untermeyer?"

Untermeyer would invariably reply: "Yes, it certainly is."

After several weeks of this abbreviated dialogue, Untermeyer sent the greeter a bill for fifty dollars for "advice services rendered."

The next time the greeter came upon Mr. Untermeyer in the park at the usual time and place, he said, "It's a good morning, Mr. Untermeyer, and this time I'm telling you, not asking you."[95]

A young Welsh girl was more cautious in dealing with future Prime Minister Lloyd George.

B40   When Lloyd George was a young country solicitor in Wales he was riding home in his dogcart one day, and came upon a little Welsh girl trudging along so wearily that he offered her a ride. She accepted silently, and all the way along, although the future statesman tried to engage her in conversation, he could not get her to say anything more than "Yes" or "No."

        Some days afterward the little girl's mother happened to meet Mr. Lloyd George, and said to him smilingly, "Do you remember my little girl riding with you the other day? Well, when she got home she said, 'Mamma, I rode from school with Mr. Lloyd George, the lawyer, and he kept talking to me, and I didn't know whatever to do, for you know Mr. Lloyd George, the lawyer, charges you whenever you talk with him, and I hadn't any money.'"[96]

Lawyers are accused of charging for social greetings, chat about the weather, and pointers during golf matches.[97] But even the eighteenth-century charge for fetching the client's gift is outdone by the recent report of the large Los Angeles firm that charged clients for the flowers it sent to their funerals.[98]

Sometimes the exchange is not with an avowed client, but arises in a social encounter. The classic is the following:

B41   A doctor was fuming when he finally reached his table at a banquet after breaking away from a woman who sought his advice on a health problem. "Do you think I should send her a bill?" he asked a lawyer who was sitting next to him.

        "Why not?" the lawyer replied, "You rendered professional services by giving advice."

        "Thanks," physician said. "I think I'll do that."

        When the doctor went to his office the next day to send a bill to the annoying woman he found a statement from the lawyer. It read: "For legal services $25."[99]

That the lawyer's response is not idiosyncratic, but an expression of his professional mindset, is made clear in a recent offshoot:

B42   I consulted a lawyer to find out if I needed a lawyer. He said no and sent me a bill for $300. Two days later, I was at a party and met another lawyer. I told him how all I did was ask the first guy if I needed a lawyer and he socked it to me for $300. "Can he do that?" I asked. "Yes," the second lawyer said. The next morning he sent me a bill for $300 for legal advice.[100]

Of course, others can play the game of blurring the line between sociability and professional consulting. The lawyer's defense is as good as his offense. An older British story shows the lawyer adept at using the law to thwart attempts to secure free legal advice:

B43   A story is told of a close fisted business man who, wanting advice on a knotty point of commercial law, invited a solicitor to dinner, and in the course of the meal elicited the opinion he required. On his return home, however, the lawyer, feeling that he had been done, sent in a bill for advice given. To this the merchant retaliated with a bill for dinner and wine. Not to be outdone, the solicitor reported the merchant to the Excise for selling intoxicants without a licence, and obtained the reward due from that Department to an informer.[101]

Once a relationship with the client is established, what activities can the lawyer charge for? The lawyer's labor is partly thought—and thought may occur away from court or office in the midst of the lawyer's private life. This is a problem that has bedeviled lawyers since they first started to market advice rather than paperwork or courtroom advocacy:

B44   "I'm beginning to think my lawyer is too interested in seeing how much money he can get out of me."
"Why?"
"Just listen to this bill: 'For waking up at night and thinking about your case—$5.'"[102]

Although this joke predates hourly billing by several generations, it has become more troubling in the era of hourly fees. The pressure to bill hours is revealed in the sad report of a high-powered woman litigation partner at a large Miami firm who lost primary custody of her children to a stay-at-home ex-husband. At the hearing:

> One mother testified that she saw Ms. Hector read lawbooks while attending a school performance.
> Ms. Hector said she did not read while her child was on stage. "I probably took a lawbook," she said, "so that I could bill hours and still be there."[103]

Although one court is reported to have rejected a request for fees for thinking about a case during travel to the courthouse, billing for thinking about the client while showering or engaging in other grooming activities is encouraged by many firms.[104] A secretary in a large firm reports seeing a memo from a partner that advised "if you even *think* about a file, whether in your car, in the shower, or on the golf course, its gets a minimum fifteen-minute charge."[105] An associate in a large Washington office recalls being prompted, "When you're taking a dump, you're always thinking about a client."[106]

But suppose the purported service is totally valueless?

B45   A corporate executive received a monthly bill from the law firm that was handling a big case for his company. It included hourly billings for conferences, research, phone calls, and everything but lunch hours. Unhappy as he was, the executive knew that the company would have to pay for each of these services. Then he noticed one item buried in the middle of the list: For crossing the street to talk to you, then discovering it wasn't you at all—$125.[107]

This joke, which was told about lawyers by 1945, mirrors an older story about medical students being instructed about fees, in which one asks the expert, "What do you charge for passing a patient on the street?"[108]

Since legal services are discursive, the provision of the services and the discussions that frame that provision may bear sufficient resemblance to tempt the service provider to throw the meter earlier in the interaction than the would-be client anticipates.

B46   Client. You have an item in your bill, "Advice, Jan. 8, $5." That was the day before I retained you.

Lawyer. I know it. But don't you remember, on the 8th I told you you'd better let me take the case for you?

Client. Yes.

Lawyer. Well, that's the advice.[109]

This nineteenth-century story anticipates an increasingly popular contemporary joke:

B46   A man went to see a lawyer and asked what his least expensive fee was. The lawyer replied, "$50 for three questions."

15. The Lawyer Winding Up His Accounts (BM9814. 1801). Lawyer makes up itemized account of charges to expedite collection from client who is bound to lose his cause. A devil assists and complains of overwork.

Stunned, the man asked, "Isn't that a lot of money for three questions?"

"Yes," the lawyer said. "What is your final question?"[110]

Lawyers frequently share jokes with doctors, politicians, Jews, and mothers-in-law. The *three questions* story is told about only one other group, a group that intersects with the lawyer joke corpus only in this single instance: fortune tellers, clairvoyants, and Gypsies.[111] It is difficult to tell which version appeared first, but the recent wave of jokes about lawyers has given the lawyer version more prominence. The joint tenancy of this joke suggests that clients turn to lawyers, as to clairvoyants, to learn things about their situation that lie beyond the boundaries of their own knowledge and vision. But, the joke tells us, it is difficult to negotiate entrance into such a relationship. Instead of meeting the would-be client in a safe zone, the clairvoyant/lawyer insists on squeezing immediate advantage from the intimidated and inexperienced client.

SEXPLOITATION: PREDATION AS SEX / SEX AS PREDATION

For the most part, the jokes in the *Economic Predators* category are old, long predating the contemporary explosion of jokes about lawyers. Of the fifty or so jokes discussed earlier in this chapter, only eight appeared after 1980. The themes that animate these jokes have been in place for a long time. At least a third of these jokes were in circulation before 1900 and two-thirds before 1950. But one new theme has emerged as a feature of jokes about the economic exactions of lawyers—the fusion of sexual and economic predation, which I refer to as sexploitation. It is possible that jokes of this sort were present earlier but remained unrecorded because of the censorship that prevailed in the written media. If so, one would expect bowdlerized versions to mark their place. Since they are not present, I conclude that this theme had not developed earlier.

A whole cycle of stories in which the roles of sexual and economic predator are combined, often with overtones of betrayal, have emerged since the 1980s. The message is that what lawyers do is "screw" people, merging that term's connotations of fraudulent extraction and of copulation.

The single old and indigenous lawyer joke, dating back to 1910 or earlier, that explores this territory was joined in the 1980s by switches of many sexploitation jokes told earlier about other kinds of protagonists but now newly enlisted as jokes about lawyers.

B47   The elderly spinster hired a young lawyer to prepare her will. "I have ten thousand dollars set aside," she explained, "and I want to spend it on myself. Nobody in this town has ever paid any attention to me, but they'll sit up a take notice when I die." Warming to the subject, she cackled, "I want to spend all of eight thousand dollars on the biggest, fanciest funeral this town has ever seen!"

"Well," said the lawyer, "that's a lot to pay for burying in these parts, but it's your money, madam, and you're entitled to spend it any way you like. Now what about the other two thousand?"

"I'll take care of that!" the old woman replied with a broad smile. "I've never been to bed with a man, and I aim to try that at least once before I'm through. As you can see, I'm not much to look at, but I figure for two thousand dollars I can get me a man that's young enough and handsome enough to please me."

That night, the lawyer reported the conversation to his wife. As they discussed the situation, the wife casually mentioned how nice it would be to have the two thousand dollars.

Minutes later, they were on their way to the spinster's house, the wife driving. As the lawyer stepped from the car, he instructed his wife: "Pick me up in two hours."

Returning at the prescribed hour, the wife tooted the horn. No response from the house. She then blew a prolonged blast. An upstairs window was raised and the lawyer thrust out his head. "Come back in four days," he shouted. "She's decided to let the county bury her."[112]

Here the lawyer is not portrayed as a sexual predator. The lust is the spinster's; his motive, so far as we can tell, is purely economic. The lawyer is literally equated with a prostitute—providing sexual favors for gain rather than desire. What the joke displays is not his thrusting libido but his greed and opportunism. Exploiting the opportunity offered by the client's vulnerability, he cultivates her neediness to run up the bill far beyond what the client anticipated.

Direct sex for gain exchanges are infrequent, but not entirely absent:

B48   At the Dulles Airport departure gate, Kirinsky was bidding farewell to the man for whom he was handling a big case. Harrison, who was also boarding the plane to New York, overheard the lawyer saying, "You've been a wonderful host, Andy. Thanks for the use of your guest room."

"And thank your wife. She's great in bed. I really enjoyed making love to her."

"It's nothing. Have a good trip."

Once on the plane, Harrison approached the lawyer. "Excuse me," he said, "but I couldn't help overhearing. Did you really enjoy making love to his wife?"

"No," said the lawyer, "but I really need this case."[113]

This is yet another 1980s switch to lawyers, this one from a joke about the man who doesn't want to insult a good friend.[114] In the lawyer version, the motivation shifts from commendably accommodating a friend to crass self-serving. This equation of lawyering with prostitution surfaces elsewhere in the joke corpus.[115]

The lawyer's characteristic vice is not sex for gain but gain as sex. Gain—especially gain from exploitation, i.e., from "screwing" someone—is eroticized. Thus, we are not surprised when the lawyer spurns intimates to boost productivity:

B49   An architect, an artist, and a lawyer were discussing whether it was better to have a spouse or a lover.

The architect said he enjoyed time with his spouse, building a solid foundation for an enduring relationship.

The artist said he enjoyed time with his lover, because of the passion and mystery he found there.

The lawyer said, "I prefer to have both."

"Both?"

Lawyer: "Yeah, If you have both a spouse and a lover, they will each assume you are spending time with the other, and you can go to the office and get some work done."[116]

A line of jokes develops the notion that screwing (in its economic exploitation sense) is the characteristic and defining activity of the lawyer. The simplest of these, and also the oldest, is a play on words, much in evidence since the early 1980s:

B50   What is the difference between a lawyer and a rooster?

When a rooster wakes up in the morning, its primal urge is to cluck defiance.[117]

To play his role as sexual-economic predator, the lawyer should be worldly, sexually adventurous, uninhibited, and opportunistic:

B51   A Baptist minister had the misfortune of being seated next to an attorney on his flight home. After the plane was airborne, the flight attendant came around for drink orders. The attorney asked for a whiskey and soda, which was brought and placed before him. The attendant then asked the minister if he would also like a drink. The minister replied in disgust, "I'd rather savagely ravish a brazen whore than let liquor touch these lips." The attorney then handed his drink back to the attendant and told her with delight, "I didn't know there was a choice!"[118]

Here, the worldly sophisticate puts down the Puritanical bluenose and displays his own sexual avarice. The lawyer clearly identifies with the pursuit of this-worldly gratification and displays his alacrity in pursuing it.[119]

B52   A handsome young man turned off a number of young ladies he met in a bar. "Listen," the bartender said, "don't tell them you're a plumber. These chicks want to meet professional men. Next time say you're a lawyer."

Moments later a women sat next to the man and asked his occupation.

"Lawyer," he said.

"You must have many interesting cases to talk about," she replied. "Why don't we go up to my apartment and you can fill me in?"

Soon they were in bed and he was laughing. "Why are you laughing?" she asked.

"This is great. I've only been a lawyer for an hour and I'm already screwing somebody."[120]

This descends from a line of jokes about the instantaneous effects of conversion. For instance, a Jewish convert to Roman Catholicism explains, "I've only been a Gentile for twenty minutes and already I hate those Jews."[121] The lawyer version arrives in 1987, apparently derived through a political variant.[122]

B53   Two lawyers are sitting in a bar drinking when a stunning blonde in a skin-tight, low-cut dress slinks by. One of them stares for a moment, then turns to his buddy and says, "Boy, would I like to screw her!"

        The other lawyer asks, "Out of what?"[123]

In circulation by 1992, this joke is told almost exclusively of lawyers.[124] A story about the woman whose successive husbands are disabled from consummating the marriage by various professional tics has been adapted to affirm that screwing is the lawyer's characteristic activity.[125]

B54   A mature woman was in the pastoral study counseling for her upcoming fourth wedding.

        "Father, how am I going to tell my husband that I am still a virgin?"

        "My child, you have been a married woman for many years. Surely that cannot be."

        "Well, Father, my first husband was a psychologist, and all he wanted to do was talk, and the next one was in construction and he always said he'd get to it tomorrow. The last one was a gynecologist and all he did was look. But this time, Father, I'm marrying a lawyer and I'm sure I'm going to get screwed."[126]

The same theme animates another new switch to the lawyer joke corpus.

B55   In a long line of people waiting for a bank teller, one guy suddenly started massaging the back of the person in front of him. Surprised, the man in front turned and snarled, "Just what the hell are you doing?"

        "Well," said the guy, "you see, I'm a chiropractor, and I could see that you were tense, so I had to massage your back. Sometimes I just can't help practicing my art."

        "That's the stupidest thing I've ever heard," the guy replied. "Look, I'm a lawyer. Am I fucking the guy in front of me?"[127]

Jokes about predation, emphasizing the economic exactions of the lawyer, often contain betrayal themes as well. The lawyer misuses a position of trust to gain an unfair advantage—to screw the other both metaphorically and often literally. In what might be called "double discharge" jokes, the lawyer opportunistically parlays financial dealings into sexual exploitation.

B56   Milt and Ernie established a law practice together, and not long after that, Ernie was the best man at Milt's wedding to Gabby, a gorgeous blonde. Ernie thought she was the most desirable woman he'd ever seen, and he went from flirting with her over the phone to sending her flowers, to begging her for a date; but each time, his partner's wife demurely resisted his advances. Finally he offered her a thousand dollars for a few sweet hours together, and that did the trick. Gabby arranged for a time for him to come by the house, and Ernie had barely closed the front door before she was pulling his clothes off. He just had time to put the thousand dollars on the hall table before she took him by the hand and led him upstairs.

        Ernie had only been gone for a few minutes when Milt's Audi pulled into the driveway. "Aha!" he exclaimed as he stepped in the door. "I see my partner was here today."

Gabby paled and was about to confess all when Milt went on cheerfully. "For once that son-of-a-bitch kept his word. He borrowed a thousand bucks from me last week and said he'd drop it off today—and damned if it isn't right here on the hall table."[128]

This is an old and widespread tale, found in Boccaccio and Chaucer, about the friend who corrupts a wife with money borrowed from her husband.[129] The most popular contemporary version, of which the previous story is an instance, involves a friend or fellow-worker of the husband, repaying a loan or delivering his pay.[130] A similar story of a faithless emissary features comparable gamesmanship and compromises the lawyer's professional obligation:

B57 The lawyer went to the whorehouse and, flashing one thousand dollars, asked for Becky Smart. He was shown to the attractive young hooker, and had a great time with her.

The next night, the lawyer returned and, once again putting one thousand dollars on the table, asked the madam for Becky Smart. Once again, he had a great time.

This went on every night for a week. On the seventh night, the lawyer was dressing and Becky said, "Listen, big guy—where you from?"

16. Symptoms of Crim Con!! (BM 8925. Cruikshank, 1796). Barrister importunes young female client while her husband dozes.

"White Plains," he said. "Woodlands Avenue."

"Really!" said the whore. "That's amazing! I just won a paternity suit with a guy who lives on Woodlands!"

"I know," said the lawyer. "He's my client—and here's the last of the seven grand he owes you."[131]

The presentation of the lawyer as an exploitative sexual predator is combined with the theme of professional rivalry in a story that is revealing about elite attitudes toward lawyers:

B58   A doctor, an engineer, and a lawyer go out hunting in the woods one day. Each of them brings along his hunting dog, and they spend most of the morning arguing about which of the dogs is the smartest. Early in the afternoon, they discover a clearing in the forest. In the middle of the clearing is a large pile of animal bones.

Seeing the bones, the doctor turns to the others and says, "I'm going to prove to you two that my dog is the smartest. Watch this!" He then calls his dog over and says, "Bones! See the bones? Go get 'em!" The dog rushes over to the pile, rummages around for a bit, and then proceeds to build a replica of the human skeleton, perfect down to the last detail. The doctor grins smugly; after all, his dog has just built a human skeleton from animal bones.

The engineer, however, is totally unimpressed. "That's nothing," he says. "Watch this." He calls his dog over, and points out the pile. "Bones! Get the bones!" The dog rushes over, tears down the skeleton, and in its place builds a perfect replica of the Eiffel Tower. It even has a little French flag waving at the top. The doctor is forced to agree that the engineer's dog is, in fact, smarter than his own.

The lawyer, however, is still not impressed. "My dog is smarter," he says. "Watch." He then calls his dog over, points to the pile, and says simply "Bones." The dog rushes over to the pile, tears down the tower, eats half the bones, buries the other half, screws the other two dogs, and takes the rest of the afternoon off.[132]

Mirroring their masters, the other dogs are constructive, even creative; the lawyer's dog is destructive and predatory. He not only contributes nothing, but appropriates the others' deserved rewards, and violates them "personally." (This late twentieth-century dog may be a descendant of the larcenous lawyer's dog who for centuries has preyed on the butcher.)[133] In some versions the other dogs are completely devoured by the lawyer's dog or their efforts are demolished by the lawyer's dog. The lawyer's relation to the rival professionals here is strikingly different from the *two plus two* joke (A33), where the lawyer's accommodating response contrasts with the mechanical and unhelpful answers of the other professionals.

Like the *three questions* joke (B46), *dogs* is distinctive in the groups that share it with lawyers—in this case not fortune tellers and clairvoyants but government workers and trade unionists, who match the lawyer in destructiveness and self-indulgent despoliation. The joke's targets are, in short, a rogue's gallery of the slackers and knockers blamed for hobbling free-enterprising America.

B58   Four men were bragging about how smart their dogs were. The first man was an Engineer, the second an Accountant, the third man a Chemist, and the fourth a Government worker.

To show off, the Engineer called to his dog, "T-Square, do your stuff!" T-Square trotted over to the desk, took out some paper and a pen and promptly drew a circle, a square, and a triangle. Everyone agreed that T-Square was pretty smart!

But the Accountant said his dog could do better. He called his dog and said, "Spreadsheet, show 'em how smart you are!" Spreadsheet went out into the kitchen, and returned with a dozen cookies. He divided them into four equal piles of three cookies each. Everyone agreed, that was good!

But the Chemist said his dog could do even better. He called his dog and said, "Measure, do your thing!" Measure got up, walked over to the fridge, took out a quart of milk, got a ten-ounce glass from the cupboard and poured exactly eight ounces without spilling a drop. Everyone oohed and ahhed and were quite impressed! Then the three men turned to the Government Worker, and said, "What can your dog do?"

The Government Worker called to his dog and said, "Coffee Break, do your stuff!!" Coffee Break jumped to his feet, ate all the cookies, drank the milk, crapped on the paper, sexually assaulted the other three dogs, claimed he injured his back while doing so, filed a grievance report for unsafe working conditions, put in for Worker's Compensation, and went home for the rest of the day on sick leave!!!![134]

The linkage is mirrored in *Wall Street Journal* columnist Paul Gigot's observation, in 1992, just as *dogs* was becoming an emblematic joke about lawyers, that

17. Cartoon by Steve Kelley (© 2003 Steve Kelley, The Times-Picayune)

"lawyers have replaced trade unionists as the chief scourge of American business."[135] The joke captures the intense indignation of professionals and business people who feel attacked, hemmed in, and overcharged by lawyers. It reflects resentment of the emergence of medical malpractice, product liability, civil rights, wrongful discharge, and other sorts of litigation that expose America's managers and authorities to unwonted and unwarranted accountability.

If lawyers were once seen as pillars of the establishment, by the late 1980s they were scorned by major sections of elites as enemies of prosperity and order. They are not alone in these sentiments. Americans generally believe that there are too many lawyers, that they have too much influence and power in society, and that they are principally responsible for a litigation explosion in the United States.[136] And those with more wealth and education believe these things in much larger numbers.[137]

The *dogs* story paints the lawyer's predation on a wider canvas. It is not just that lawyers victimize individual clients or opponents, but that they destroy social assets and unravel the social fabric. This is a complaint that has been around a long time: In 1782, H. St. John Crèvecoeur, in his widely read *Letters of an American Farmer*, spelled out the parasitic and destructive character of the lawyer:

> Lawyers are plants that will grow in any soil that is cultivated by the hands of others, and when once that have taken root they will extinguish every vegetable that grows around them. The fortunes they daily acquire in every province from the misfortunes of their fellow citizens are surprising. The most ignorant, the most bungling member of that profession will, if placed in the most obscure part of the country, promote litigiousness and amass more wealth than the most opulent farmer with all his toil. . . . What a pity that our forefathers who happily extinguished so many fatal customs and expunged from their new government so many errors and abuses both religious and civil, did not also prevent the introduction of a set of men so dangerous. . . . The value of our laws and the spirit of freedom which often tends to make us litigious must necessarily throw the greatest part of the property of the Colonies into the hands of these gentlemen. In another century, the law will possess in the North what now the church possesses in Peru and Mexico.[138]

In the late 1970s, as significant sections of America's elites recoiled from the expansion of legal remedies, these themes resurfaced. In an article entitled "Will Lawyering Strangle Democratic Capitalism?" Laurence H. Silberman, later to become a federal judge, detailed how "the legal process, because of its unbridled growth, has become a cancer which threatens the vitality of our forms of capitalism and democracy" and "the harmful impact of an ever expanding legal process on our society." The profligate creation of new individual rights was weakening the "intermediate institutions [families, churches, schools, corporations, labor unions, and political parties] . . . that are indispensable pillars of a pluralistic democracy." In addition, "litigation of all kinds [was] becoming a major structural impediment to our economy."[139] Overuse of lawyers, Silberman declared, contributed to the competitive advantage enjoyed by our economic rivals in Japan and Europe.[140] According to the executive vice president of the Insurance Counselors Association of Texas, "Each year at the beginning of June, 100,000 law school graduates with visions of faultily-designed football helmets dancing in their heads, descend upon American commerce and industry like a plague of locusts."[141] A decade later, the lawyers as parasites idea reached for academic respectability when a University of Texas finance professor proclaimed that countries with the highest lawyer populations suffered from impaired economic growth and that each American lawyer decreased the output of goods and services by one million dollars annually.[142] Weak data, peculiar research design, and absence of controls for other influences on economic growth led to the rapid demolition of this theory, but not before it had been adopted as part of the campaign to diminish the civil justice system.[143]

The economic cluster is the largest of all the categories of lawyer jokes. Some new items have been switched to lawyers, but overall this cluster remains overwhelmingly composed of jokes that are indigenous to the legal setting. The major exception is the new theme of sexual exploitation that has been grafted on since 1980. Of the twelve sexploitation jokes given above, only three seem indigenous to the legal setting and nine have been switched to lawyers. Not all of the switches will prove enduring additions to the lawyer joke corpus. As the repertoire of lawyer jokes is enlarged and the demand for joke material shifts from lawyers to others, many jokes attached to lawyers in the boom years of antilawyerism may face an early retirement.

THE JUSTICE TARIFF

The persisting sense of grievance about legal fees is multilayered. First, there is the widespread and recurrent perception that lawyers charge unfairly: they overcharge for what they have done, charge for services they have not rendered, and charge for things they shouldn't charge for. These grievances form one of the oldest, largest, and most enduring limbs of the body of lawyer jokes. These grievances are so persistent and enduring because they trace fault lines that are intrinsic to the nature of legal services and the structure of lawyer-client relations. And they resonate with more profound misgivings about the way that legal work is institutionalized.

One of these is the notion that legal fees are themselves a nasty, harmful, and unjustified institution. In 1843, John W. Pitts published a little book that both anticipates and illuminates current discontents.[144] Pitts thought lawyers were driven by self-interest both to make laws prolix and complicated and to "excite strife, confusion and debate."[145] As the dominant group of legislators, lawyers made law complex and generated a need for lawyers to vindicate the rights that they established.[146] These rights are then diminished by the very need for professional lawyers, who extract fees for securing these rights for their clients. What the justice parties obtain is thus flawed and incomplete, for a portion of their entitlement is diverted to the lawyers, who add no value. Thus, for Pitts, every legal entitlement is diminished by the presence of an occupational group that is paid for vindicating it. This "justice tariff" (my phrase, not his) is an affront to liberty, which is "the power of enjoying rights without paying for them." For Pitts, "Fees at the bar, from their first institution up to this hour, have been the source of more numerous and more malignant evils in the countries where they have been tolerated than all the wars, pestilence, famines, tornadoes & earthquakes that ever harassed these lands."[147] Beneath Pitts's bluster lie some of the deep roots of resentment of lawyers, growing from the necessity of using and paying lawyers to secure what people regard as already rightfully theirs.

Legal philosopher Max Radin discerned an ancient theme that "justice is a man's right. That is what society is for. It should be free as air."[148] As Jake Warner, one of the founders of Nolo Press, a leading publisher of do-it-yourself legal material, puts it, "There's a reason people hate lawyers. . . . It's because they have a monopoly on what rightfully belongs to everyone."[149] A long tradition holds that the need for lawyer intermediaries is not natural but is itself an outgrowth of lawyers' corruption of legal discourse. It is because lawyers have made law complex and mysterious that they can levy the justice tariff.

Lawyers' fees are offensive not only because they levy a tariff on justice, thereby diminishing and distorting it. The true offense of lawyers is to take something of ineffable value like justice—one of the things in life that should not be in the market—and debase it by commercializing it. Although the jokes (and other manifestations of public opinion) propose no alternative model, they echo a persistent sense that lawyers' expertise should not be a commercial service.[150] In mocking lawyers because they are successful merchants and not priests of justice, we resonate with some of the passion of the medieval satirist who execrated lawyers for abandoning religion for gain:

> Many study the law these days, not for justice,
> But because avarice wishes to acquire more goods.
> I beg Christ to confound the jurists;
> They are no psalmists, but the harpists of Satan.
> The lawyer, the doctor, and the whore are always alert;
> If anyone offers them a higher fee, they slip away and follow him.[151]

When lawyers flourish in the marketplace, the profession appears to have fallen from a purer nobler calling. Another medieval critic set the standard for anti-lawyer invective:

> That once venerable name and glorious profession of advocate is now debased by notorious venality, and sells its miserable and abandoned tongue, buys litigation, dissolves legitimate marriages, breaks friendships, revives the ashes of sleeping disputes, violates contracts, calls settlements into question, shatters legal traditions, and in setting its nets and snares for the capture of money destroys all justice. . . . The lawyer should give freely of what he has freely received, should plead for the orphan and widow, for the good of the commonwealth, for the liberty of the Church, demanding

nothing, undertaking obligations voluntarily, "delivering the poor from the hand of them that are stronger than he; the needy and the poor from them that strip him."[152]

As we shall see, this account of the lawyer's failings has many echoes in contemporary popular views of lawyers. From the 1960s into the early 1980s, critics ranging from Ralph Nader to Jimmy Carter excoriated lawyers for their cooptation by the powerful and their deflection from the promotion of justice.[153] In our time, this "public justice" critique has abated, and has been displaced by prominent attacks on lawyers as parasites subverting the economy.

Public dissatisfaction with the profession has its counterpart among lawyers who bemoan the decline of their calling from true professionalism into commercialism. Distress about the decline from a noble profession infused with civic virtue to crass commercialism has been a staple of concern in legal circles in the United States for over one hundred years.[154] At the end of the nineteenth century there was already a sense that the profession had fallen from its former high estate and, by too close an embrace of business, had become merely a branch of commerce. In 1895 a law journal said the bar "has allowed itself to lose, in large measure, the lofty independence, the genuine learning, the fine sense of professional dignity and honor. . . . For the past thirty years it has become increasingly contaminated with the spirit of commerce which looks primarily to the financial value and recompense of every undertaking."[155] Such admonitions multiplied in the 1990s, which saw a remarkable flowering of lament about the demise of professional virtue.[156] Both the lay public's charge of economic predation and the profession's discomfort about commercialism reflect that sense of paradox or contradiction that something as ineffable and "priceless" as justice is bought and sold.

CHAPTER 3

🙠

Playmates of the Devil

Most of the jokes in the *Discourse* and *Economic* categories focus on some disagreeable or outrageous behavior of lawyers, displaying some specific nasty trait, like dishonesty, arrogance, greed, or disloyalty. But some sorts of lawyer jokes do not detail specific items of nastiness; instead they summarize the lawyer's shortcomings in a judgment of general moral deficiency. The oldest and most widespread of these are jokes about lawyers' association with the devil, sin, hell, and irreligion.

THE DEVIL'S OWN

The connection with the devil is proclaimed by the legend of St. Ives (Yves, Ivo, Yvo, Evona; 1253–1303, canonized in 1347), who was sent to paradise as ambassador of the Breton legal fraternity to petition God to grant the lawyers a patron saint. After the heavenly archivist found no lawyers in the roll of saints[1]

C1   God said to him: "Maître Yves, as you observe, we cannot give you for patron a saint who pleaded in his lifetime, but in order to show Our good will in the matter, you shall go blindfolded along the passage where my saints have their statues, and you may there select one of my Elect by placing your hand upon his image; that one, whether good or indifferent . . . shall be your patron saint."

    Carrying out this command, the honest Breton tied a heavy bandage over his eyes, and step by step, with arms extended, went down the passage, racking his brain for some inspiration to guide him in making a suitable choice.

    At last, with some hesitation, he came to a halt, and passing his hand over a head, "Brow, bald and receding," said he, "mouth cynical, this must surely be an attorney, if indeed it is not a president or even a judge. Well, here goes! For better or for worse. I will select him as the lawyer's patron."

    Immediately an immense burst of laughter broke from the ranks of the Elect, who through curiosity had come to assist at the ceremony. Yves de Kermartin, anxious to discover his choice, tore the bandage from his eyes, and with one glance at the statue uttered a cry of dismay. It was worse than a president, it was much worse than a judge, it was even much worse than an attorney; it was no less than . . . Satan. . . .

You ask, no doubt, how his Satanic Majesty came to be there. The reason is, that Saint Michael is represented there, as on earth, overcoming the devil, and paring his diabolical lordship's claws. The Breton had mistaken the devil for an angel.

"Ah ! My poor man," said God, "your luck has played you a bad turn this time. But as I would not have such a patron to represent the Bar, especially the Bar of Brittany, henceforth I enroll you among my Elect, and the lawyers will no longer be without a patron."

At that moment, it is said, the gentleman from Breton died at his home in Trequier, the 19th day of May, 1303, and this is how . . . Saint Yves the glorious friend of God became the lawyer's patron saint.[2]

Tracing the origins of "the lawyer-devil type in English literature," E. F. J. Tucker finds "the major influence seems to stem from the morality drama of the fifteenth century in which the legal profession is virtually always on the side of vice."[3] The lawyer-devil equation became conventional by Shakespeare's time. Dean Swift, chiding lawyers for pleading wrongful causes, called them the devil's children.[4]

The devil connection was emphatically present in the early days of the American republic. Indeed the editor of an 1832 book of jests complains of the indecency and the "hackneyed character" of its predecessors, including the "standing jest . . . [that] the doctor is in league with the undertaker, the attorney with the devil," and promises his readers a collection that "combine[s] wit and humour, without indelicacy . . . [and] excite[s] pleasure in the mind, without leaving an injurious impression on the heart."[5] The "standing jest" of which this editor complained proved robust:

C2   A country attorney happened to be at a tavern with an honest peasant, and was very facetious at the countryman's expense. They nevertheless agreed to try for a bottle of wine who could make the best rhyme. The lawyer enquired the peasant's occupation, who cheerfully informed him he was a weaver, upon which the lawyer wrote the lines:
The world, tho' large, is but a span;
It takes nine weavers to make one man.
The weaver in his turn, enquired the lawyer's occupation, and being informed:
"I thought," said he, "you were of the law by the glibness of your tongue, but since you have rhymed about the world, so will I too," and then he wrote,
The world is wide, and full of evil
And half a lawyer makes a devil.[6]

A companion jest has remained unchanged since this 1871 version.

C3   "Did you present your account to the defendant?" inquired a lawyer of his client.
"I did, sir."

Printed for & Sold by BOWLES & CARVER.   No.69 St.Paul's Church Yard. LONDON.

A LAWYER AND HIS AGENT.

18. A Lawyer and His Agent (BM3765 c.1760). Smiling devil pays friendly visit to lawyer, possibly admonishing him for overreaching in his wickedness.

"And what did he say?"

"He told me to go to the devil."

"And what did you do then?"

"Why, then, I came to you."[7]

Not only were lawyers associated with the devil, but the latter was himself often described as a lawyer, the grand master of the profession's deceptive arts.

C2   A grave old country blade coming before a judge and taking his oath on a cause was bade to have a care what he swore to, lest he went to the devil. "I fear not that," replied he, by way of retort, "for I have given him my oldest son, and he ought to be content with one out of a family." "How's that?" says the judge; "Pray explain yourself." *"Why, truly, I have made him a lawyer and you know the devil was a lawyer from the beginning."*[8]

The exchange continues with the judge suggesting that the countryman means a liar, but the witness responds that *"we in the country know no difference between a lawyer and a liar."*

The identification of the lawyer with the devil is far less ferocious than the medieval identification of Jews with the devil. Medieval society shared a "general conviction . . . of the Jew as an alien, evil, antisocial and antihuman creature, essentially subhuman . . . and . . . answerable for the supreme crime of seeking to destroy by every subversive technique the fruits of . . . Christian civilization."[9] In this cause he was "the devil's associate, accepting his counsel and leadership, actively cooperating with him as his terrestrial agent."[10] In an age when the devil's agency was credited as highly efficacious, the association was more than metaphorical; the Jew was "sorcerer, murderer, cannibal, poisoner, blasphemer, the devil's disciple in all truth."[11]

The identification of the lawyer with the devil, though it has its roots in the same nexus of ideas, is more metaphoric than literal. The legend of St. Ives involves an inadvertent embrace of a representation of Satan, not a deliberate alliance with him. The medieval satirist who reproved money-hungry lawyers as "no psalmists, but the harpists of Satan," goes on to compare them with doctors and whores who also follow the money.[12] Although occasionally lawyers were blamed for a host of social ills, the jokes suggest that they are accepted as a kind of piquant side dish at the social feast, a relish that contributes a distinct flavor if it lacks nutritive value and is likely to cause stomach distress. The lawyer is rarely viewed as an active principle of evil to be eradicated. His wickedness, at least in small doses, was tolerable and his antics a source of amusement. Law practice was a stage in the downward journey, not its consummation.

C4   A small boy in an Austin, Texas Sunday school was asked: "Where do the wicked finally go?" "They practice law a while and then they go to the Legislature," was the reply of that observant youth.[13]

Headed for Hell

The sign of the lawyer's moral standing is his postmortem destination. The traffic between earthly and infernal stations is described in a story, popular in nineteenth-century America, and still found in the U.K.:

C5   A gentleman in the country who had just buried a rich relation, who was an attorney, was complaining to Foote, who happened to be on a visit to him, of the very great expenses of a country funeral, in respect to carriages, hatbands, scarfs, etc. "Why, do you bury attorneys here?" asked Foote gravely. "Yes, to be sure we do, how else?" "Oh, we never do that in London." "No!" said the other, much surprised; "how do you manage?" "Why, when a patient happens to die, we lay him out in a room over night by himself, lock the door, throw open the sash, and in the morning he is entirely off." "Indeed!" said the other in amazement. "What becomes of him?" "Why, that we can't exactly tell, not being acquainted with supernatural causes; all that we know of the matter is, there is a strong smell of brimstone in the room the next morning."[14]

A long series of jokes establish that many lawyers are to be found in hell and few, if any, in heaven. Hell is on the lawyer's itinerary. The lawyer's work leads there; it is a place where lawyers can penetrate and conduct operations:

C6   Two old codgers had become involved in a land dispute, and it was brought into the county court to be decided. After a decision had been rendered by the county judge, the losing farmer assailed the winner with:
      "You may think you're purty smart now, but this ain't the end. I'm a-goin' to law ye to the district court about this."
      "When you do, I'll be thar," said the other complacently.
      "And if I lose that, I'll law ye to the supreme court of this state," howled the loser.
      "I'll be thar when ye do," said the other easily.
      "And if I don't get the decision there, I'll law ye to the United States Supreme Court."
      "I'll be thar, too," repeated the winner.
      "And after that I'll law ye to hell," shrieked the other.
      "That's all right. My attorney will be there when ye do."[15]

Will this lawyer make a special trip to hell, or is the client just relying on the fact that he is fated to arrive there eventually?

C7   "What are you waiting for?" said a lawyer to an Indian, who had paid him money.
      "Receipt," said the Indian.
      "A receipt," said the lawyer, "a receipt! What do you know about a receipt? Can you understand the nature of a receipt? Tell me the nature of one, and I will give it to you."
      "S'pose mabe me die; me go to heben; me find the gate locked; me see 'postle Peter; he say, 'Indian, what you want?' Me say, 'Want to get in.' He say, 'You pay A that money.' What me do? I hab no receipt. Hab to hunt all over hell to find you." He got his receipt.[16]

19. The Lawyer's last Circuit (BM 3452. Baker ?1819). Demons hail lawyer being carried off by Death. The inscription reads: "In his Office with Writs and Parchments hung round / Midst Letter and Lawsuits Old Justice was found / His eyeballs were sunk, whilst his hands grasp'd his fees, / For Old Nick would no more be put off with sham Pleas, / On shelves Bills in Chanc'ry were rang'd pile o'er pile, / With Demurrers, Decrees, and Injunctions to file / But his Petition's answer'd—his Orders are past / And Death's struck a Docket against him at last! / No more he'll declare, or for Clients e'er plead, / Though Issue was join'd, his Cause did not succeed, / His Counsel, 'twas plain, could not lend him relief, / Though doubly he fee'd him—he threw up his Brief, / His false Witness heard—to gain time then he try'd, / But Chief Justice Death a fresh Trial denied; / His Costs are all tax'd—final judgment is past, / And Old Nick with a CA SA [writ to take into custody till the plaintiff's claim is satisfied] has got him at last, / The news through the regions of Pluto soon fled, / And on Earth it was whisper'd "Old Justice was dead," / Whilst thousands flock'd round, none believing the tale, / 'Till they saw his poor Clients their sad loss bewail, / His Creditors met—but soon clamorous grew, / For his Assents [sic] wouldn't yield e'en the Devil his due, / To find him they swore—yet the road none could tell / Though 'tis said that the Lawyer's last Circuit's to Hell."

C8   A certain sharp attorney was said to be in bad circumstances. A friend of the unfortunate lawyer met Douglas Jerrold, the English wit, and said, "Have you heard about poor R? His business is going to the devil."

"That's all right—then he is sure to get it back again," said Jerrold.[17]

If hell is not foreordained, the lawyer is certainly in danger of ending up there, a result that inspires recent additions to this cycle:

C9   In Pittsburgh an M.D. was summoned to a courtroom where an attorney had had a seizure. After examining his still form the doctor rose to go. "Is Lawyer Cobb out of danger?" asked the judge.

"He's dead," said the physician. "But I'm afraid he is far from being *out of danger.*"[18]

C10   As the lawyer slowly came out of the anesthesia after surgery, he said, "Why are all the blinds drawn, doctor?"

"There's a big fire across the street," the doctor replied. "We didn't want you to think the operation had been a failure."[19]

The lawyer population of hell is considerable according to a story often told as an anecdote about various nineteenth-century notables, including Abraham Lincoln, Ulysses S. Grant, and Lorenzo Dow. The story is still going strong after a century and a half:

C11   Lorenzo Dow, an evangelist of the last century, was on a preaching tour when he came to a small town one cold winter's night. He entered the local general store to get some warmth and saw the town's lawyers gathered around the pot-bellied stove, discussing the town's business. Not one offered to allow Dow into the circle.

Dow told the men who he was and that he had recently had a vision where he had been given a tour of Hell, much like the traveler in Dante's Inferno. When one of the lawyers asked him what he had seen, he replied, "Very much what I see here: all of the lawyers, gathered in the hottest place."[20]

The lawyers' unfavorable position in the next world is a mirror image of the privileged position they arrogate to themselves in this one.

The abundance of lawyers in hell means that it is uniquely free of one of the torments of life on earth, "the law's delay."

C12   Why does it take only two weeks to get a trial date in Hell? There are plenty of lawyers to handle the load.[21]

But hell's advantage is qualitative as well as quantitative. Hell is home to a great concentration of legal talent:

C12   An attorney observed a boy about nine years of age, diverting himself at play, whose eccentric appearance attracted his attention. "Come here my lad," said he. The boy accordingly came, and after chatting a bit, asked the attorney what case was to be tried next. "A case between the Pope and the Devil," (answered the attorney) "and which do you suppose will gain the action?" "I don't know," said the boy, "I guess 'twill be a pretty tight squeeze; the Pope has the most money, but the devil has the most lawyers."[22]

This story faded away early in the last century, but was soon replaced by another story of the devil as litigant:

C12   A scoffing young attorney came to a Rabbi and said: "Heaven and hell, you will agree, are no doubt separated by a wall. Should this wall accidentally fall down, who, in your opinion, would rebuild it? The righteous would insist that the wicked do it; the latter would likely refuse the job. If this case should come up before a judge, which do you think would emerge the winner?"

"It seems to me," said the Rabbi, "that any fair-minded judge would render a verdict against the wicked, since the likelihood is that the wall would crumple from the fires of hell rather than from what is taking place in paradise. On the other hand I realize that hell will surely contain a predominance of glib-tongued attorneys and I should therefore not be surprised if they would win the case."[23]

To the lawsuit between heaven and hell, this story adds an earthly contest between religious authority and cynical lawyer that mirrors the celestial struggle. Another

"Can I see that 'National Law Journal' when you're through with it?"

20. Cartoon by Mort Gerberg (© The New Yorker Collection 1996, from cartoonbank.com. All rights reserved.)

branch of the broken fence story dropped this frame and shifts the focus to the absence of lawyers in heaven, a venerable theme.

ABSENT IN HEAVEN

In another telling of his legend, when St. Ives arrived at the entrance to paradise, St. Peter tried to expel him: "A lawyer indeed! and what is that? such a calling is quite unknown in the Divine Kingdom."[24]

Lawyers have remained scarce in heaven to this day.

C13   A man who had a case in court said that if he lost it in the Common Pleas he would appeal to the Supreme Court, and from there to the United States Court, and from there to heaven. "Certainly, then," replied a gentleman, "you will be defeated; for you will not be present to answer for yourself, and no attorney is ever admitted there!"[25]

C13   In a lawsuit, between two members of the same church, counsel for one of the parties suggested that the brethren ought to defer their differences for adjustment to the higher court above; to which the client responded that the same idea had occurred to him, but there seemed to be an insuperable obstacle in the way—he couldn't contrive any way to get his lawyer there.[26]

But lawyers are resourceful and difficult to control:

C13   There is a pleasant story of a lawyer who, being refused entrance into heaven by St. Peter, contrived to throw his hat inside the door; and then, being permitted by the kind saint to go in and fetch it, took advantage of the latter's fixture as doorkeeper to refuse to come back again.[27]

Subsequently St. Peter adjusted his standards to deal with lawyers:

C13   Recently a teacher, a garbage collector, and a lawyer wound up together at the Pearly Gates. St. Peter informed them that in order to get into Heaven, they would each have to answer one question. St. Peter addressed the teacher and asked, "What was the name of the ship that crashed into the iceberg? They just made a movie about it." The teacher answered quickly, "That would be the Titanic." St. Peter let him through the gate. St. Peter turned to the garbage man and, figuring Heaven didn't REALLY need all the odors that this guy would bring with him, decided to make the question a little harder: "How many people died on the ship?" Fortunately for him, the trash man had just seen the movie and answered, "about 1,500." "That's right? You may enter." St. Peter then turned to the lawyer. "Name them."[28]

C14   While a number of lawyers and gentlemen were dining in Wiscasset, a few days since, a jolly son of the Emerald Isle appeared and called for dinner. The landlord told him he should dine when the gentlemen were done.

"Let him in among us," whispered a limb of the law," and we will have some fun with him."

The Irishman took a seat at the table.

"You was not born in this country?" said one.

"No, sir, I was born in Ireland."

"Is your father living?"

"No sir, he's dead."

"What is your occupation?"

"A horse jockey, sir."

"What was your father's occupation?"

"Trading horses."

"Did your father ever cheat anyone while here?"

"I suppose he did cheat many, sir."

"Where do you suppose he went?"

"To heaven, sir."

"Has he cheated anyone there?"

"He has cheated one, I believe, sir."

"Why did they not prosecute him?"

"Because they searched the whole kingdom of Heaven, and couldn't find a lawyer."[29]

All of these seem to have fallen out of the joke corpus, the last one after a successful hundred-year run. But the thought lives on in more contemporary vehicles. The following story (obviously a cousin of the rabbinic story related in the last section) has been extremely popular over the past sixty or so years.

C15   Once upon a time, so the story goes, the fence broke down between HEAVEN and HELL. St. Peter appeared at the broken section of the fence and called out to the devil . . . "Hey, Satan, it's your turn to fix it this time."

"Sorry," replied the boss of the lower regions. "My men are too busy to go about fixing a mere fence."

"Well, then," scowled St. Peter, "I'll have to sue you for breaking our agreement."

"Oh yeah," echoed the devil, "WHERE ARE YOU GOING TO GET A LAWYER?"[30]

After being firmly crystallized for half a century, a new version suddenly appeared in 1997:

C15   An engineer died and went to heaven. St. Peter looked at his computer printout and said, "I'm sorry, your name isn't here. The down elevator is to the right," and so, the engineer went to hell.

He found hell to be everything it was supposed to be. It was hot and dirty; it didn't have plumbing. It was terrible. So he got himself a corner office and started working.

Before long they had air conditioning, running water, electricity, cars, dishwashers, the whole works. It got so good there, God heard about it. God said to his secretary, "Get me Lucifer on the phone." In a minute she said, "The Devil on line two." God picked up the phone and said, "God here. What's this I hear about your fixing the place up and starting to compete directly with me. You're disregarding our original agreement."

The Devil says, "I know; it didn't start out that way. I got this engineer down here, and things just got out of hand."

God says, "Yeah, I heard about him; he's one of Pete's screw-ups. He's supposed to be up here. I'll tell you what I'll do. You send him up to me and put the place back the way it was by the end of the month, and we'll forget all about it. If not, I'm going to sue."

The Devil laughs and says, "Where in heaven are you going to find a lawyer?"[31]

The shortage of lawyers in heaven not only impairs the enforcement of divine rights, but restricts the provision of services to the inhabitants:

C16   A devout couple were about to get married when a tragic car accident ended their lives. When they got to Heaven they asked St. Peter if he could arrange for them to be married, since it was what they'd hoped for in life. He thought about it and agreed but said they'd have to wait.

About 100 years later, they discovered that, perhaps, it would be better not to spend all eternity together. They returned to St. Peter and said, "We thought we'd be happy forever but now believe we have irreconcilable differences. Is there any way we can get divorced?"

"Are you kidding?" said St. Peter. "It took me 100 years to get a priest up here to marry you. I'll never get a lawyer."[32]

The lawyer element here is a recent addition that supplements or in some cases supplants the much older story about the inability to find a clergyman in heaven.[33]

The absence of lawyers in heaven, we saw, formed part of the legend of St. Yves. Like the lawyer who entered by the hat trick, he proved hard to dislodge:

C17   Dying, [Yves] presented himself at the gate of paradise in a train of many nuns. Of these St. Peter demanded: "Who are you?" "Nun." "Enter then; heaven is full of your sisters." Then addressing himself to St. Yves: "and you?" "Lawyer." "Come in; we have never had till now a man of the law." St. Yves found his way in all right, but a day arose when there was a pettifogging inquiry into his title deeds, and the effort was made to expel him from paradise. "I will not resist," said the saint, "but it is necessary that service of the writ of my expulsion shall be made upon me by a bailiff." Needless to say, the legend concludes, they were never able to find a bailiff in heaven.[34]

The arrival of the first lawyer in heaven disrupts the association of rewards with deserts:

C17   A priest, a doctor and a lawyer are killed in a bus crash and all arrive at heaven together. The priest is just awed. Heaven is really heavenly. The streets are lined with mansions and paved with gold.

St. Peter puts his arm around the priest and says, "Michael, it's wonderful to have another priest here. Come, I'll show you your new home."

Nestled on a grassy knoll is a charming cottage. Roses grow over the doorway and birds sing in the surrounding trees. "It's everything I ever wanted," says the priest. "May I continue on with you to see where my friends are going to live?"

"Certainly," says St. Peter. The sun is shining, flowers are blooming and the air is fresh and clean. As they progress, the lawns and gardens get more magnificent and the houses more palatial.

Stopping before a forty-room mansion, St. Peter says, "Dr. Bob, you have spent your life caring for your fellow man and this home, with twelve bathrooms, fifteen fireplaces and a staff of twenty is yours for eternity. You need never work again."

"Thank you," says Dr. Bob. "I am a little tired after my life's work. I think I'll take a short nap."

St. Peter, the lawyer, and the priest walk on, and the neighborhood continues to improve. Rounding a bend, they see a magnificent mansion on a knoll, surrounded by a garden of blooming flowers. The priest wonders if the mansion might be the home of one of the saints, or even of the Lord Himself.

As they mount the marble stairs to the front door, St. Peter says to the lawyer, "Son, this is your eternal home."

The attorney nods, and without saying a word, opens the door. The priest catches a glimpse of a hallway paved with lapis lazuli and gold, and as the lawyer disappears inside, St. Peter shouts after him, "If you want anything, just pick up the red phone. It's connected to my office. And if, for any reason, I'm unable to satisfy your needs, use the white phone. It's a direct line to God."

As they walk away, the priest is lost in thought.

"Do you mind if I ask a question," he says.

"Go right ahead," replies St. Peter.

"Well, I don't mean to complain," says the priest, "but I'd like to know why that lawyer deserves more of a reward than Dr. Bob or myself."

"That's easy," says St. Peter, "We get a lot of priests, and a few doctors, but that man was our first lawyer."[35]

This is the lawyer version of an old tale about the arrival of a rich man in heaven which provokes song and dance because of the rarity of such an event.[36] It has also been applied to such suspect categories as admiral, senator, congressman, doctor, sales manager, and jazz musician.[37] But since 1982, when it first appeared as a lawyer joke, it has been predominantly told about lawyers. The rarity of lawyers confers on them a kind of prodigal son celebrity. Their mere presence elicits a special solicitude that provokes resentment among those whose rectitude and deservingness are habitual and predictable.

A KINGDOM OF THIS WORLD

Since their postmortem prospects are so unpromising, it is not surprising that lawyers seek to make the best of it here.

C18   William Nibbs was a South Carolina lawyer of ordinary standing, but is remembered as having said one good thing. He had managed a case successfully for the Rev. Mr. Lilly, and called for his fee. Mr. Lilly jestingly replied, "Why, Mr. Nibbs, I thought you gentlemen of the bar were not in the habit of charging us ministers for your services."

"Ah! With regard to that," said Mr. Nibbs, "you look for your reward in the next world; we lawyers expect ours in this."[38]

More than a century later, the changes are minor:

C18   The priest settled into a chair in the lawyer's office.
"Is it true," said the priest, "that your firm does not charge members of the clergy?"
"I'm afraid you're misinformed," said the attorney. "People in your profession can look forward to a reward in the next world, but we lawyers have to take our reward in this one."[39]

Is the implication that the lawyer will experience punishment rather than reward in the next world? Or just that he is skeptical whether reward is to be expected beyond the world at hand? Although many features of the law have religious roots and some lawyers regard the practice of law as an expression of religious mission or calling, the joke corpus portrays the lawyer as, at best, very much of this world.[40] This tension has been long noted by Christian thinkers whose view of the practice of law was summed up in the proverb, "Bonus jurista, malus Christista" (a good lawyer is a bad Christian).[41]

The contrast between the lawyer and the follower of Christ is dramatized in an old and still popular story:

C19   An old farmer was on his deathbed. He requested that two lawyers from a neighboring town be sent for. When they came he motioned them to take seats, one on each side of the bed. He looked from one to the other for a few moments, and then with his last breath exclaimed: "I die content, like my Savior, between two thieves."[42]

The sense of opposition between the law and religion is displayed in these old stories:

C20   "Don't you want to be a Christian?" a Sunday-school teacher asked one of the members of her class.
"No, ma'am," was the ready response. "My papa wants me to be a lawyer."[43]

C20   A prominent figure in the legal world has recalled a conversation of his student days with a North Country farmer who was interested enough to ask if he was studying for the ministry.
"Oh, no," replied the student, "I'm not going to be a minister I'm going to be a lawyer."
"Man, man," said the farmer, with a slow shake of the head, "Jist the opposite!"[44]

Especially in jokes that circulate among lawyers, the law is efficacious, while religion is ineffectual or too remote to address the realm of earthly well-being and justice entrusted to the lawyer.

C21   In a case of an assault by a husband on his wife, the injured woman was reluctant to prosecute and give her evidence. "I'll have him to God, me lord," she cried. "Oh, dear, no," said the judge; "it's far too serious a matter for that."[45]

In these jokes, skepticism about the efficacy of religious actors, ceremonies, and God himself is typically articulated not by lawyers but by judges, the godly authorities of the earthly legal order. In yet another version of the *oath* story (A25), when a child witness responds that if she doesn't tell the truth she will go to hell, the judge says "Let her be sworn . . . she knows more than I do."[46]

C22   A colored man at Marshalltown, Iowa, was brought into the Justice Court. Despite the efforts of his attorney the offender was bound over to await the action of the Grand Jury. When court convened the negro's counsel was not present. The case was called and the judge asked the defendant if he had an attorney.

"Well, suh, I had one," he said, looking, "but I ain't seen him since I was done up before the Justice, an' I guess he's done absconded, suh."

"Well, do you wish to employ another attorney?" asked the Court.

"No, suh," was the answer. "I ain't got no money. I'se willin' to let God Almighty look after my case."

"The Court will appoint a lawyer to assist your counsel," was the reply from the bench.[47]

C23   A defendant who had been convicted of murder was before the court for sentencing. As usual, the judge asked if he had anything to say before the sentence was pronounced. The defendant said:

"As God is my judge, I didn't do it. I'm not guilty." To which the judge replied:

"He isn't, I am. You did. You are."[48]

In the same vein,

C22   A judge . . . in sentencing a prisoner to death, observed: "Prisoner at the bar, you will soon have to appear before another, and *perhaps* a better judge."[49]

Similarly, it was reported that an Irish judge admonished a witness "you may think to deceive God, sir, but you can't deceive me."[50]

A newly emerged story suggests that where religious counsel is efficacious it is because it leads to action in the realm of secular legality.

C24   Wilfred Benton was an active layperson at the Grace Presbyterian Church. He went to see his minister, Carl Wattling, for advice. Wilfred complained that he was severely depressed—business was bad, his wife had left him, the bill collectors were after him, and he was on the verge of a nervous breakdown.

The minister gave him what solace he could, then said "Go home, pick up the Bible and open it at random. Ask the Lord for guidance. Then read the first two words you see. They will provide the advice you need for your situation."

"Just the first two words I happen to see?" repeated Wilfred.

"That's right," said the pastor.

Pastor Wattling did not hear from Wilfred for several months. Then one day while in town, the minister saw Wilfred drive up in a Rolls Royce. He got out of the car with a beautiful young woman on his arm. The minister walked up to him and said "Well, I see your situation has changed. You look very prosperous."

"Yes," replied the man. "I took your advice, went home, opened the Bible at random and read the first two words."

"Well, what were the two words that served you so well?" asked the minister.

"Chapter Eleven," replied Wilfred.[51]

The relative authority of law and religion is explicitly addressed in the following story.

C25   Two ladies once had a dispute as to which was the most influential, the clergy or the bench.

"I think the bench is the most influential," said one, "because the Judge can say: 'You shall be hanged.'"

"But," said the other, "the clergyman can say: 'You shall be damned.'"

"Ah, yes," said the first, "but when the Judge says, 'You shall be hanged' you are hanged."[52]

The primacy of earthly law has an echo in the Jewish tradition in the famous talmudic story of Akhnai's oven, in which the rabbis, debating the fitness of a particular style of oven, uphold rule by a majority of jurists over God's direct intervention.

2 Supp.   We have been taught: Say a man made an oven out of separate coils [of clay, placing one upon another], then put sand between each of the coils—such an oven, R. Eliezer declared, is not susceptible to defilement, while the sages declared it susceptible. The oven discussed was the oven of Akhnai—"snake" [so called because it precipitated arguments as numerous as the coils of a snake].

It is taught: On that day R. Eliezer brought forward every imaginable argument, but the sages did not accept any of them. Finally he said to them, "If the Halakhah [binding law] agrees with me, let this carob tree prove it!" Sure enough, the carob tree was uprooted [and replanted] a hundred cubits away from its place. "No proof can be brought from a carob tree," they retorted.

Again he said to them, "If the Halakhah agrees with me, let the channel of water prove it!" Sure enough, the channel of water flowed backward. "No proof can be brought from a channel of water," they rejoined.

Again he urged, "If the Halakhah agrees with me, let the walls of the house of study prove it!" Sure enough, the walls tilted as if to fall. But R. Joshua rebuked the walls, saying, "When disciples of the wise are engaged in halakhic dispute, what right have you to interfere?" Hence, in deference to R. Joshua they did not fall, and in deference to R. Eliezer they did not resume their upright position; they are still standing aslant.

Again R. Eliezer said to the sages, "If the Halakhah agrees with me, let it be proved from heaven!" Sure enough, a divine voice cried out, "Why do you dispute R. Eliezer, with whom the Halakhah always agrees?" But R. Joshua stood up and protested, "'It [the Torah] is not in heaven' (Deut. 30: 12). We pay no attention to a divine voice, because long ago, at Mount Sinai, You wrote in the Torah, 'After the majority must one incline' (Exod. 23: 2)".

[Subsequently] R. Nathan met [the prophet] Elijah and asked him, "What did the Holy One do in that moment?" Elijah: "He laughed [with joy], saying, 'My sons have defeated Me, My sons have defeated Me.'"[53]

The coda presents God as amused at the usurpers. There is no report that the Christian god is similarly entertained by his displacement from the legal world. There are lawyers who are religious,[54] but they are entirely absent from the joke corpus. In the jokes the lawyer stands apart from religion. He is worldly and un-impressed with religion rather than actively opposed to it. But his responsibilities

"Just a minute! I happen to be a lawyer. . ."

21. Cartoon by Frank Cotham (© 2004, from cartoonbank.com. All rights reserved.)

and ambitions put him at cross-purposes with those who see life as preparation for the hereafter.

For many centuries the man of religion was the single most frequent target of jokes. When religion was the most prominent source of order and meaning in people's lives, joking about priests or preachers was a way of expressing doubts and anxieties about that order and meaning. Now that law has moved to a more central position and rivals where it does not displace religion as a source of order and meaning, the jokes more frequently target lawyers as surrogates for our ambivalence about the increasingly secularized and legalized world.

Overall, the ascent of lawyers has been part of the desacralization of the world. Tracing the role of lawyers in early modern European culture, William Bouwsma concludes:

> Lawyers represented the growing assumption that life in the world is only tolerable when it is conceived as a secular affair and that the world's activities must be conducted according to manageable principles of their own rather than in subordination to some larger definition of the ultimate purpose of existence. By applying this assumption to solve the constantly changing problems of their societies lawyers were, in a manner far more effective than that of any abstract philosopher, the supreme secularizers of their world.
>
> . . . The lawyer['s] . . . role was to foresee and provide against as many as possible of the dangers that might lie ahead, and thus it reflected both distrust of the future and, at the same time, some confidence in the ability of men to plan ahead and to control the unfolding of their earthly lives. . . . [R]esort to lawyers implied the reverse of fatalism.[55]

Not only was the law drained of its supernatural connections, but it became an agency for secularizing other sectors of social life:

> By imposing their own secularism on the machinery of social life, they helped to accustom their contemporaries to think in secular terms, thus contributing in a fundamental way to the secularization of every other dimension of human concern.[56]

CHAPTER 4

Conflict

Lawyers as Fomenters of Strife

Lawyers have long been associated with discord and strife. They are frequently portrayed as aggressive, competitive hired guns, unprincipled mercenaries who foment strife, prolong conflict, and promote disorder by encouraging individual self-serving and self-assertion rather than cooperative problem solving.

Lawyers are also thought to be naturally argumentative. Just as children with an inclination to lie are steered toward legal careers, so are those who are contentious and intrusive:

D1   "What profession is your boy going to select?"

"I'm going to educate him to be a lawyer. He's naturally argumentative and bent on mixing into other people's troubles, and he might just as well get paid for his time."[1]

Because it is ingrained, the lawyer's combativeness is reflexive and often pointless:

D2   "It is my understanding that you called on the plaintiff," stated Counselor Lutkin.

"I did," replied the witness.

"What did he say?"

The prosecutor leapt to his feet and slammed down his book, vehemently objecting to the question. He denounced the question as irrelevant, misleading, and tending to incriminate an entirely innocent party. He accused Lutkin of using illegal tactics, and of being a wholly immoral person, guilty of malicious practices by daring to try to introduce such testimony. He continued, questioning the legitimacy of Lutkin's birth, the decency of his mother, and the marital conduct of his wife.

Lutkin, boiling with rage, jumped for the prosecutor's throat, and court attendants were forced to subdue the two antagonists, but not before they'd bloodied each other's noses and blackened each other's eyes.

A Cheap Beating.

22. A Cheap Beating (BM 13154 Cruikshank 1818). Barrister punches tailor.

·The judge, after restoring order, ruled that Lutkin would repeat the question and directed the witness to answer.

The court fell into a deep silence, waiting to hear the crucial testimony.

Wiping blood from his upper lip, Lutkin said, "I repeat, then: What did he say?"

The witness answered, "He didn't say anything. He wasn't home."[2]

Lawyers may be criticized for insufficient as well as excessive combativeness, recalling the observation that the qualities for which lawyers are despised are close to the ones for which they are esteemed. Here the lawyer is reproached for failure to be as aggressive and demanding as the client would like:

D3   Her lawyer phoned Mrs. Gitkin and said excitedly, "I told you when I took your divorce case that I would rather avoid lengthy litigation and try to make an out-of-court settlement. Well, I've just concluded a meeting with your husband's attorney and we have worked out a settlement that, I believe, is eminently fair to both of you!"

"Fair to both!" exploded Mrs. Gitkin. "For that, I had to hire a lawyer! That I could have done myself!"[3]

Full often we're Told and true it may be
That two of a Trade can never agree

The Learned A———S or a legal Construction of Rogues and Vagrants

23. The Learned A____s or a legal Construction of Rogues and Vagrants (BM 12916 ?B. Heath 1817). Two barristers fight with umbrellas, based on an 1817 incident involving opposing counsel in a case involving the construction of the Police Act regarding vagrants, rogues and vagabonds.

The lawyer's failure to live up to the role of being zealous champion and hard-ball negotiator on behalf of the client is an instance of what Richard Raskin in his analysis of Jewish jokes calls "role fiasco."[4] Perhaps beneath the surface there is a hint of exemplary deviance—the lawyer's departure from the client's stereotype may be in the client's best interest—at least if that interest lies in achieving a resolution rather than punishing the opponent.[5] But the client's discontent in this story catches something important in the behavior of lawyers and client perceptions of it. Contrary to the popular myth of lawyers as unrelentingly contentious and combative, there is evidence that lawyers often "cool out" clients, advise them against aggressive moves, counsel compromise and conciliation, and downplay adversary combat. Studying the application of a new statute favorable to consumers, Stewart Macaulay found that for the most part lawyers acted as mediators rather than aggressive champions.[6] In a much cited 1967 article entitled "The Practice of Law as a Confidence Game," Abraham Blumberg indicted criminal defense lawyers for allowing themselves to become coopted by the court organization, so that they became "double agent[s]" cynically manipulating their clients.[7] Austin Sarat and William Felstiner observed divorce lawyers undermining their clients' drive to adversary trial. The method of disposition was raised early and often and "in those conversations the lawyers' message is overwhelmingly pro-settlement. They consistently emphasize the advantages of informal as opposed to formal resolution. Adjudication is presented in an unfavorable light, as an alternative to be avoided."[8] In each of these instances we see lawyers for individual one-shot litigants disappointing their clients' expectations of untrammeled advocacy by a zealous champion. *Fair to both* reflects both the client's disappointment with the lawyer who seems insufficiently adversarial and the lawyer's exasperation with the client who craves a shooting war.

If lawyers are valued for pursuing conflict on behalf of individual clients, their prowess in contention makes us uneasy, for once let loose the conflict they engender is a destructive force, threatening social order.

D4   Three professional men . . . were debating the advantages and disadvantages of their respective professions in terms of what they do for society. They consisted of a physician, an architect and a lawyer. Since each of them could propound many reasons why they were valuable to society, the discussion, although animated, gradually stalemated. Eventually the physician broke the stalemate by suggesting divine origin for his profession. After all, the first successful surgery is talked about very early in the Book of Genesis when the Lord takes Adam's rib and creates Eve. The architect was not to be outdone. He also claimed divine origin for his profession and said that his divine origin was even pre-eminent because even before this initial surgery, there was first chaos and confusion. Then the Lord created heaven and earth and formed the sun, the moon and the stars, and in this act of creation there was architecture. So his was the most pre-eminent profession. The lawyer was bewildered; what could he say? Never at a loss for words, however, he piped up very quickly, and said: "Who do you think was responsible for the chaos and confusion?"[9]

This story is now firmly established as a lawyer joke, but that is a new development in its career. It starts out in the 1930s as a joke about communists and is soon told about politicians generally.[10] In a number of early renditions, the first professional in the series is an American lawyer, who argues, "Man would never have survived the first days of creation if he hadn't had a few laws to govern him."[11] Politicians have remained the target in Britain, Australia, and India, but in the United States lawyers joined politicians in the public imagination as figures capable of unleashing powerful forces of disorder.[12] The course of this turnabout is revealed by the timing and the provenance of the version recounted above, one of the very first in print in which the lawyer has moved to the final position as author of chaos. It was told at a conference in London on product liability, by a lawyer from New York who reported that the story was "making the rounds in the United States," and he segues into his topic by noting that "chaos and confusion" can be found "right here in product liability law."[13] This is 1977, just at the culmination of the first product liability insurance crisis, at the very crux of the turn against law, or at least against the expansion of legal remedy, by America's legal and business elites. During the preceding year Chief Justice Warren Burger's Pound Conference had pronounced American law dangerously overextended, and the terms "tort reform" and "alternative dispute resolution" entered our vocabulary.[14]

PROMOTERS OF CONFLICT

The joke corpus unreservedly subscribes to the observation that "lawyers have an economic interest in generating and prolonging conflict."[15] Not only do lawyers reap advantage from others' conflicts and troubles, but they require them to prosper:

D5   At a revival meeting, a young lawyer was called upon to deliver a prayer. Totally unprepared, he got to his feet, and these words tumbled out: "Oh, Lord, stir up much strife amongst thy people lest Thy humble servant perish."[16]

The lawyer joke corpus is rich in depictions of lawyers as impresarios of contention, who manage to benefit from the conflict they instigate.

D6   "Father," asked the little son, "what is a lawyer?"
       "A lawyer? Well, my son, a lawyer is a man who gets two men to strip for a fight and then runs off with their clothes."[17]

The very presence of lawyers, and particularly their confrontation with one another promotes strife:

D7   There was a small town with just one lawyer and he was starving for lack of business. Then another lawyer moved to town and they both prospered.

D7   A small town that can't support one lawyer can always support two.[18]

The eagerness of lawyers to promote conflict is codified and stigmatized in jokes about their connection with ambulances. The term "ambulance chaser" was current by 1897.[19] But although *Conflict* jokes frequently depict the personal injury lawyer, jokes about ambulances do not appear in print until somewhat later.

D8   Two attorneys, one decidedly glum of countenance, met on the street.
      "Well, how's business?" the first asked of the dismal one.
      "Rotten!" the pessimist replied. "I just chased an ambulance twelve miles and found a lawyer in it."[20]

D8   Did you hear about the lawyer who was so successful he had his own ambulance?[21]

D8   My lawyer had a bad accident.
      An ambulance backed over him.[22]

Conversely, an insurance man in a state that enacted no-fault auto insurance was reported to have quipped:

D8   Things have gotten so bad for an attorney friend of mine with the new setup, he has had to sell his ambulance.[23]

Once there is conflict, the lawyer cynically protracts and enlarges it in pursuit of gain.

D9   Two friends, who hadn't seen each other for some time, met. One was on crutches.
      "Hello," said the other man. "What's the matter with you?"
      "Streetcar accident," said the man on crutches.
      "When did it happen?"
      "Oh, about six weeks ago."
      "And you still have to use crutches?"
      "Well, my doctor says I could get along without them, but my lawyer says I can't."[24]

More generally, some stories point directly to the role of the lawyer in "constructing" the clients' injury.

D10   "Are you badly injured?"
      "Can't tell till I see my lawyer!"[25]

Recently, the injured party has acquired medical credentials.

D10   A car ran through a stop sign at an intersection and rammed into the side of another car. The errant driver quickly rushed over to the disabled vehicle and saw that the driver's door was open and the driver was sprawled on the pavement.
      "Are you all right?" the first driver asked, observing that the man was slowly getting to his feet and brushing off his clothes.
      "How should I know?" retorted the angry driver. "I'm a doctor, not a lawyer."[26]

Of course, the lawyer is expected to favor litigation rather than amiable resolution, but his motives may be more complex. The proclivity to litigate is both depicted and mocked in an old story, attributed to Joseph Choate, who was reportedly fond of telling this story as a lesson for those with a leaning toward litigation.

D11   "It's this way," explained the client. "The fence runs between Brown's place and mine. He claims that I encroach on his land, and I insist that he is trespassing on mine. Now, what would you do if you were in my place?"

      Lawyer: "If I were in your place, I'd go over and give Brown a cigar, have a drink with him, and settle the controversy in ten minutes. But, as things are, I advise you to sue him by all means. Let no arrogant, domineering, insolent pirate like Brown trample on your sacred rights! Assert your manhood and courage. I need the money!"[27]

THE CONNIVING CLAIMANT

Stories like those in the previous section that locate the impetus to exaggerate the injury in the lawyer were at one time greatly outnumbered by stories of conniving claimants who seize the opportunity to "construct" or magnify an actionable injury.

D12   A New York lawyer tells of an old and well-to-do farmer in Dutchess county who had something of a reputation as a litigant.

**"Our case is up next. By the way,
you look great!"**

24. Cartoon by Jerry Marcus (© 2004, from cartoonbank.com. All rights reserved.)

On one occasion this old chap made a trip to see his lawyers with reference to a lawsuit he intended to bring. He sat down with one of them and laid out his plan at great length. The lawyer said: "On that statement you have no case at all." The old fellow hitched his trousers nervously, twitched his face, and hastily added:

"Well, I can tell it another way."[28]

D12   The late Thomas B. Reed used to tell this story of an enterprising client by whom he was retained to prosecute an action. On talking with the plaintiff's witnesses, Mr. Reed found that their stories were far from consistent, so he reported the fact to his client, and advised that the suit be dropped. The client was somewhat perturbed, but told the attorney he would have a talk with the witnesses and let him know next morning what he had decided to do. True to his word he dropped in bright and early wearing the cheerful look of one who has fought the good fight. "I've seen those witnesses," he exclaimed, "and they say they must have been mistaken."[29]

These stories of fabrication of evidence in the litigation context are matched by stories of fabrication and exaggeration of injury.

D13   "Did ye get damages fer being in that railway accident, Bill?"
        "Sure; fifty dollars for me and fifty fer the missus."
        "The missus? I didn't hear she was hurt."
        "She wasn't; but I had the presence o' mind to fetch her one on the head with me foot."[30]

D13   Levi's son Abe was in a train going from Boston to New York; the train got wrecked, and about five hundred killed and wounded, but Abe escaped without a scratch. So he telegraphed home to his father and told him of his good luck in escaping from injury. When his father got the telegram he was wild, and exclaimed: "Abe in a railroad accident and not hurt! He must be crazy!" So he sent back this message: "Dear Abe, go and hire some Irish bummer to break your face—we must get some damages."[31]

D14   Ikey came upon a crowd at the crossing, the wreckage of an automobile and two men gasping on the ground.
        "Vat was it; an engine?" he asked one of the victims.
        "Yes," he answered feebly.
        "Did they blow der whistle?"
        "No."
        "Did dey ring the bell?"
        "No."
        "Has der claim-agent been here yet?"
        "No."
        "Do you mind if I lie down here mit you?"[32]

Fake victim jokes reflect public awareness of accident faking for purposes of gain, an undertaking that descended from earlier schemes that accompanied the rise of fire and life insurance. Faking of accidents to collect compensation is a

25. Litigation (BM 15639 Landseer c.1828). "A sudden thought strikes me!" Fashionable ape client conveys his sudden inspiration to ape barrister. (The conniving claimant of another day!) The inscription, from Pope, reads: "In such a cause, the Plaintiff will be hiss'd, / 'My Lord,'—The Judges laugh—& 'you're dismiss'd.'"

distinctively American contribution which arose in the last quarter of the nineteenth century. When faking flourished in the early years of the twentieth century, it was often associated in the public mind with Jews. Joke D13 depicts what Ken Dornstein in his book *Accidentally, on Purpose* describes as a prevalent type of fraud involving professional accident fakers or just random passersby who would insert themselves into genuine trolley accidents and then pretend to be injured. He recounts an early instance of "this basic, unorganized fraud" in the aftermath of an 1893 trolley accident in the Italian Market section of South Philadelphia. Under the headline "Foreigners Feign Trolley Injuries" the *Philadelphia Press* reported that when two trolley cars collided: "The glass in both cars was broken and the passengers were thrown from their seats to the floor. . . . Within two or three minutes, the wrecked cars were filled with a crowd of men, all of whom appeared to have received some injury. But as there were several times as many of the injured as there had been passengers in both cars, the trolley men did not give them any encouragement and tried to put them off the cars. The foreigners resisted, and a lively fight was breeding when a couple of policemen appeared and drove the foreigners off."[33] Accident faking appeared on the scene at the same time as, and was often confused with, ambulance chasing by lawyers.

Even if the injury is genuine, it may be the basis for malingering:

D15 "When will your father's leg be well so he can come to work?"
     "Not for a long time, I think."
     "Why?"
     "'Cause compensation's set in."[34]

The malingering theme has recently reappeared in a new joke:

D16 [Jesus walked into a bar.] He approached three sad-faced gentlemen at a table, and greeted the first one: "What's troubling you, brother?" he said. "My eyes. I keep getting stronger and stronger glasses, and I still can't see." Jesus touched the man, who ran outside to tell the world about his now 20–20 vision. The next gentleman couldn't hear Jesus' question, so The Lord just touched his ears, restoring his hearing to perfection. This man, too, ran out the door, probably on the way to the audiologist to get a hearing-aid refund. The third man leapt from his chair and backed up against the wall, even before Jesus could greet him. "Don't you come near me, man! Don't touch me!" he screamed. "I'm on disability."[35]

Not all victims are connivers, however. Some victims, especially ethnic and racial outsiders, may be so naive or intimidated that they perceive themselves as targets of claims rather than as claimants.

D17 Up in Minnesota Mr. Olsen had a cow killed by a railroad train. In due season the claim agent for the railroad called.
     "We understand, of course, that the deceased was a very docile and valuable animal," said the claim agent in his most persuasive claim-a[gent] gentlemanly manner,

"and we sympathize with you and your family in your loss. But, Mr. Olsen, you must remember this: Your cow had no business being upon our tracks. Those tracks are our private property and when she invaded them, she became a trespasser. Technically speaking, you, as her owner, became a trespasser also. But we have no desire to carry the issue into court and possibly give you trouble. Now then, what would you regard as a fair settlement between you and the railroad company?"

"Vall," said Mr. Olsen slowly, "Ay bane poor Swede farmer, but Ay shall give you two dollars."[36]

And not all connivers are claimants. Potential defendants may engage in denial, ruses, or intimidation to avoid liability:

D17   After standing in front of the store for several minutes, seemingly undecided what to do, he entered and asked for the proprietor, and then began:

"My ole woman was gwine 'long yere las' night an' fell down on your sidewalk and busted her elbow."

"Ah! Well, being you are a poor man I'll make the charges as light as possible!"

"But dat hain't de case, sah. A lawyer tells me that you is 'sponsible fur dat slippery sidewalk, an' dat I kin git damages."

"Exactly; but you don't understand the matter. In the first place you must fee your lawyer and put up for court expenses. Then you prove that I own the sidewalk. Then you prove that your wife was not guilty of contributory negligence. Then you prove that your wife didn't bust her elbow by falling down stairs. Then I appeal the case and the higher court grants a new trial. By that time your wife and her busted elbow are dead and buried, and you are married again, and you offer to settle for five pounds of brown sugar."

"Fo' de Lawd! but has I got to wade frew all dat?"

"All that and more. The grocery business is cut so close that I shall probably be bankrupt by April, and then what good will a judgment do you?"

"Dat's so, dat's so."

"Or the case may hang in the Supreme Court until both of us are dead."

"I see. And you would gin two pounds of brown sugar to settle de case now?"

"Well, yes."

"Den you may do it up, an arter dis de ole woman takes de oder side of de street or we dissolve partnership! I 'spected ebery minit you war gwine to tist it around to levy on my household goods, an' if I'm two pounds of sugar ahead I want to close de case to once afore you bring in a bill for contributory piracy."[37]

D18   A reporter on a Kansas City paper was among those on a relief train that was being rushed to the scene of a railway wreck in Missouri. About the first victim the Kansas City reporter saw was a man sitting in the road with his back to a fence. He had a black eye, his face was somewhat scratched, and his clothes were badly torn—but he was entirely calm.

The reporter jumped to the side of the man against the fence. "How many hurt?" he asked of the prostrate one.

Printed for & Sold by BOWLES & CARVER.   No. 69 St. Paul's Church Yard, LONDON.

A FLAT BETWEEN TWO SHARPS.

"*Law is like a* new fashion, *folks are bewitched to get into it* — *It is also like* bad weather, *most people are very glad when they get out of it.*"

26. A Flat between Two Sharps (BM 3763. c.1760). Solicitor and barrister mock bewildered country client before Westminster Hall.

"Haven't heard of anybody being hurt," said the battered person.

"What was the cause of the wreck?"

"Wreck? Haven't heard of any wreck."

"You haven't heard of any wreck? Who are you, anyhow?"

"Well, young man, I don't know if that's any of your business, but I am the claim-agent of this road."[38]

As these stories suggest, defendants may connive to deny injury and blame the victim.

D18   Son: Papa! Papa! The lid to our coal-shoot was left open and a man fell down inside. What should I do?

Father: Quick! Put the cover on it. I'll call a cop and have him arrested before he can sue us.[39]

The heavy Jewish presence in these conniving claimant jokes reflect a once widespread (and perhaps persisting) belief that Jews are overeager to pursue legal remedies and to invoke the legal system to obstruct remedy for others:

D19   Two Jewish gentlemen were playing golf. They had wagered a dollar a hole on the contest and the battle was waxing fast and furious. One saw the other pick his ball up out of a bad lie and throw it out on the fairway.

"Moe," he yelled, "you can't do that."

"Vy can't I?"

"It gives in the rulebook that you can't pick your ball up."

"Vell, I did it, didn't I?"

"But vat if you should win this match and my money by such actions. Vat would I do then?"

"Sue me."[40]

In the first half of the twentieth century Jews were widely regarded as only partly within the moral community, unconstrained by a common morality and with an inappropriate affinity for opportunistic use of formal legal controls. Whether there was a basis for the perception of Jewish readiness to sue,[41] its shadow lives on in such items as:

D19   What's a Jewish car accident?

No damage to the automobile, but everyone inside has whiplash.[42]

D19   Q: Did you hear about the new Japanese-Jewish restaurant?

A. It's called So-sumi.[43]

The provenance of these stories suggests that their currency is now largely intra-ethnic, among Jews themselves. And today the notion that some people have inappropriate recourse to legal remedies has been de-ethnicized into a generalized worry about frivolous cases and the "litigation explosion."

The most pervasive and enduring of these Jewish claimant jokes alleged a propensity to set fires to commercial premises in order to collect insurance. The accusation is one with a long history. Joshua Trachtenberg recounts the lethal association of Jews with fires in medieval Europe:

> Fire swept rapidly through the tinderbox towns of those days, and the populace was justifiedly in dread of a conflagration. But the responsibility was so consistently laid upon the Jews—entire communities were time after time ravaged and expelled, even when the fire did not first break out in the Jewish quarter—that we cannot ascribe this circumstance solely to the cupidity or passion of the mob. If, as was often the case, it was asserted that the guilty arsonists were witches in league with the devil, then the Jews could not escape the taint of complicity, supported as this suspicion was by their purported intention to destroy Christendom by whatever means.[44]

In the early twentieth century jokes about insurance fires started by Jewish businessmen were common in both England and the United States, reflecting what many regarded as a "notorious fact."[45]

D20   Ikey saw his friend Jakey in the smoking-car when he entered, and sat down in the same seat.

"How was that fire in your place last week, Jakey?" he inquired.

Jakey started nervously.

"Sh!" he whispered. "It vas next week."[46]

D21   A citizen who maintained a pawnshop took out a fire insurance policy. The same day a blaze broke out that destroyed the building and its contents.

The insurance company tried in vain to find sufficient grounds to refuse payment, and was obliged to content itself with the following letter appended to the check:

"Dear Sir: We note that your policy was issued at ten o'clock on Thursday morning and that the fire did not occur until three-thirty. Why this unseemly delay?"[47]

The theme that ties together these stories of conniving claimants is that misfortune is good fortune, for the victim or for those near and dear to him.

D23   Loeb and Weinstein were discussing the affairs of a fellow textile merchant. "Did you hear about Schwartz?" asked Loeb.

"Hear what? How's business for him?"

"Finished. Over the weekend his warehouse burned to the ground."

"Such a nice guy, Schwartz," responded Weinstein, "and finally he gets the good luck he deserves."[48]

D23   "Can he recover, doctor?" asked a woman whose husband had been hurt in a railway accident.

"I fear not, madame," replied the doctor; "but you can. You should get at least twenty thousand dollars from the company"[49]

D23   The agent for one insurance company was a wide-awake guy and as he gave Mrs. Stanton a check for the insurance payment on her late husband, he put in a strong pitch for her to take out some insurance on her own life.

"Why, I do believe I will," she said. "My husband had such good luck with his."[50]

A recent update of the last story brings the gender politics into the foreground:

D23   A new-made widow called at the office of an insurance company for the money due on her husband's policy. The manager said:

"I am truly sorry, madam, to hear of your loss."

"That's always the way with you men," said she. "You are always sorry when a poor woman gets a chance to make a little money."[51]

Another prototypical conniving claimant was the "gold digger," who sought "heart balm" from wealthy men for breach of promise to marry, seduction, or other misdeeds.

D24   "Well, may I hope then, dearest, that at some time I may have the happiness of making you my wife?"

"Yes, I hope so, I am sure," she replied. "I am getting tired of suing fellows for breach of promise."[52]

D24   "I have met a lovely girl, who tells me she will be perfectly satisfied with $50 a week."

"With or without?"

"With, or without what?"

"Attorney's fees."[53]

Jokes about the gold digger flourished from early in the century. In the 1930s, a great wave of antipathy to these "heart balm" suits led to their legislative abolition in a number of states.[54]

Since the Second World War, the entire cluster of conniving claimant stories, including the Jewish fire stories and golddigger stories, have largely disappeared. There are only a few notable exceptions. One is the single fire-for-profit story that has survived:

D25   Two Jews meet in Miami Beach. "Hello, Einhorn," says one. "How are you feeling? Everything okay? Or are you down here for your health?"

"Not exactly. You see, Finkelstein, by me in the shop there was a big fire. So when I collected the insurance, I thought I would come down here for a little rest, before I open again. But, Finkelstein, what are you doing here right in the middle of your busy season?"

"Well, it happened like by you. Except by us we had a big flood. While the insurance company is arranging to pay off, I thought I would come down here for a while."

At this point, Einhorn looks at him quizzically and asks, "Listen, how to make a fire we all know, but how do you make a flood?"[55]

This joke is no longer exclusively told about Jews and has recently been switched into a lawyer joke:

D25 A lawyer and an engineer were fishing in the Caribbean. The lawyer said, "I am here because my house burned down and everything I owned was destroyed. The insurance company paid for everything."

"That is quite a coincidence," said the engineer, "I'm here because my house and all my belongings were destroyed by a flood, and my insurance company also paid for everything."

The lawyer looked somewhat confused and asked, "How do you start a flood?"[56]

In a switch that occurs with some frequency in contemporary joking, the lawyer takes the place of the conniving Jewish businessman.[57]

Another survivor is the story of the claimant who is testifying about his impairment:

D26 A . . . story is told of the late Lord Birkenhead in his early days at the Bar. He was acting for a tramway company, one of whose vehicles had run down a boy. According to the statement of counsel the boy's arm was hurt, and when he entered the witness-box his counsel made him show that it was so much injured that he could no longer lift it above his head. In due course "F.E." rose to cross-examine, which he did very quietly. "Now, my boy," he said, "your arm was hurt in the accident?" "Yes, sir," said the boy. "And you cannot lift your arm high now?" "No, sir." "Would you mind," said "F.E." very gently, "just showing the jury once more how high you can raise your arm since the accident?" The boy lifted it with apparent effort just to the shoulder level. "And how high could you lift it before the accident?" asked "F.E." in the most innocent manner, and up went the arm straight over the boy's head.[58]

I recall hearing this in law school in the 1950s (the point was not the chutzpah of the claimant, but the cleverness of the cross-examining lawyer), and it is current today in the law school setting.

A final "survivor" is a robust example of the conniving claimant that emerged a generation or more later than its companions, and is frequently told of Jewish or Irish protagonists:

D27 Abraham Goldberg, a Chicago Jew, has a collision with the heavy limo of his Irish neighbor, the multimillionaire Jim McCormick. Goldberg claims that he's paralyzed from the waist down and is awarded damages of one million dollars. As McCormick makes the payment, he says: "Now look, Abe. Here is my check. But I warn you: Great pleasure you won't get from this money. I'm going to watch you like a hawk. The moment I see you taking a single step, you will not only have to return the money, but you'll go straight to jail." And so it was. Goldberg travels to the casino in Atlantic City. Who is staying in the room next to him? Jim McCormick. Goldberg travels to Tahiti. Who has the bungalow next to his on the beach? Jim McCormick. Goldberg travels to Switzerland and finds McCormick waving to him from the adjacent chalet. Until McCormick's private investigators inform him that Goldberg has purchased a ticket on Air France. No sooner has Goldberg been lifted out of his wheelchair and been installed in his first class seat, than he hears from behind the ironic voice of McCormick: "Hello, Abe, where to this time? To Paris? Les Folies Bergeres?" "No, Jim," answers Goldberg, "this time we're going to Lourdes. And there you will witness the greatest miracle of our time."[59]

Life almost managed to match this scenario. In 1989, a Texas woman brought suit against the Steak & Ale restaurant, where a waiter had dropped "a large tray of double-plated dinners on her," and she claimed that as a result she was confined to a wheelchair. In the midst of the trial in May 1991, the parties agreed on a two-million-dollar settlement, which was orally approved by the judge. A month later she was observed walking in high heels "without apparent difficulty" in another San Antonio restaurant. Steak & Ale hired private detectives who videotaped her for five days, during which she neglected to use a cane, walker, or wheelchair. The trial court refused to allow Steak & Ale to withdraw its consent to the settlement agreement on the ground that it was final. However, the Supreme Court of Texas found that although the trial judge had approved the settlement at the time of the trial, he did not "render judgment" by preparing and signing the agreement until after Steak & Ale's June 18 request to withdraw—even if "the trial court believed that he had rendered judgment during the May 14 hearing."[60] The settlement was nullified and the plaintiff sent away empty-handed. There is surely a lesson here for claimants: in no case should Lourdes be omitted from the post-settlement itinerary!

LITIGATION FEVER

The disappearance of this whole cycle of stories about conniving claimants (and, less frequently, defendants) scheming for undeserved legal advantage does not mean that such activity has become less salient. On the contrary, popular lore overflows with accounts of unfounded claims and malingering claimants. Twenty years ago, at the onset of concern about the "litigation explosion," *U.S. News & World Report* reported that

> Americans in all walks of life are being buried under an avalanche of lawsuits.
> Doctors are being sued by patients. Lawyers are being sued by clients. Teachers are being sued by students. Merchants, manufacturers and all levels of government—from Washington, D.C., to local sewer boards—are being sued by people of all sorts.
> This "epidemic of hair-trigger suing," as one jurist calls it, even has infected the family. Children haul their parents into court, while husbands and wives sue each other, brothers sue brothers, and friends sue friends.[61]

A few years later columnist Jack Anderson reported:

> Across the country, people are suing one another with abandon; courts are clogged with litigation; lawyers are burdening the population with legal bills. . . .
> This massive, mushrooming litigation has caused horrendous ruptures and dislocations at a flabbergasting cost to the nation.[62]

In a similar vein eminent judges, lawyers, and academics registered dismay at American litigiousness and warned about its consequences.[63] Pundits and politicians retailed "horror stories" of outlandish claims and grotesque verdicts: tales of absurd and outrageous awards to burglars and psychic fakers, and stories of havoc visited on beleaguered Little Leagues and abandoned day care centers. These stories reported that the system had "spun out of control" and America's substantial and productive citizens were the victims of unchecked litigiousness. Upon examination by journalists and scholars, these resilient stories turned out to be embellishments where they are not complete fictions.[64] Although the events they recount are far from typical of what goes on in the civil justice system, they captured widespread attention and credence.

The conniving claimant, once portrayed in stories that depicted bizarre deviations from the normal, is now presented as emblematic of a new and alarming normality. The notion that deviants or outsiders are misusing the legal system is generalized into the notion that frivolous cases are the normal and typical stuff of the legal system.[65] Sociologist of law John Lande, who interviewed senior executives in publically held companies on their views about litigation, found "they were virtually unanimous that there has been a litigation explosion and the vast majority believed that most suits by individuals against businesses are frivolous."[66] With this, the conniving claimant figure has departed the joke arena, for in this new and debased normality, unfounded or exaggerated claims are unexceptional;

"When will I be old enough to start suing people?"

27. Cartoon by Bruce Eric Kaplan (© The New Yorker Collection 1993, from cartoonbank.com. All rights reserved.)

since they do not deviate from the expected, they lack the element of surprise to function as jokes. So stories of outlandish claiming flourish, no longer as jokes but as fables of decline. For example, former Vice President Dan Quayle, conveys our fallen condition in the following account:

> We have become a crazily litigious country. Today a baseball comes crashing through a window, and instead of picking it up and returning it to the neighbor whose kid knocked it through—and who pays the glazier's bill in a reasonable, neighborly way— the "victim" hangs on to the baseball as evidence and sues the neighbor. (Or the baseball's manufacturer. Or the glassmaker. Or usually all three.) Several lawyers are soon billing hours, and the civil docket has been further crowded by one more pointless case that's probably going to be part of the 92 percent of cases that get settled before they come to trial—but not before a huge amount of time and money has been wasted on everything from "discovery" to picking a jury that will be discharged before it ever deliberates this case that shouldn't have gotten started in the first place. In America we now sue first and ask questions later.[67]

Such fables feed on and give expression to popular concerns about litigation. Their currency does not depend entirely on spontaneous welling up from the folk; instead they are broadcast and disseminated by multimillion-dollar campaigns spawned by a minor industry of lobbyists, consultants, think tanks, and "tort reform" groups whose pronouncements are parroted by politicians and pundits.[68]

Paradoxically the industrious projection of the image of unrestrained litigiousness and rampant overclaiming turns out to be a self-fulfilling prophecy. Persuading many that substantial compensation is readily obtainable encourages resort to lawyers.[69] And it reinforces the sense that the system is so routinely abused by exaggerated and deceptive claiming that one would be a sucker not to play the game.[70]

This feverish enthusiasm for litigation is blamed squarely on lawyers. As concern about excessive litigation mounted, then Chief Justice Warren Burger knew who to blame: "The entire legal profession . . . [has] become so mesmerized with the stimulation of the courtroom contest that we tend to forget that we ought to be healers—healers of conflicts. . . . Healers, not warriors. . . . Healers, not hired guns."[71]

The chief justice was anticipated in the joke corpus. Ignoring other values and disdaining the possibilities for amicable resolution, the lawyer is quick to see every situation as an occasion for staking claims threatening suit:

D30   "I educated one of my boys to be a doctor and the other a lawyer," said Father Corntassel.

"You should be very proud of them," announced his visitors. "That seems like an excellent arrangement."

"I don't know about that," replied the aged agriculturist. "It looks as though it was going to break up the family. I got run into by a locomotive, and one of 'em wants to cure me, and the other wants me to go lame so he can sue for damages."[72]

D31   A lawyer and a doctor go golfing. On one of the holes, the doctor gets hit in the head with a wild ball. An apologetic golfer rushes over and asks the doctor how he is. The doctor begins to say that he's fine when the lawyer interrupts, "He has a huge lump on his head. We want five thousand dollars or we'll sue." The golfer responds, "But I yelled fore!" At which point, the lawyer says, "We'll take it."[73]

Lawyers not only exaggerate plausible claims, they use unjustified claims to fend off the rightful claims of others:

D32   Billy, Bobby and Joe had a spree in the fruit orchard. They tore all the fruit from the trees, gorged themselves, then threw fruit and generally vandalized the place. When the farmer caught them, he called the sheriff and had them taken into custody. When the boys appeared before the judge after spending a night in jail, he asked them if they had learned their lesson. The first boy replied, "Yes, sir. All that fruit made me sick. My dad's a doctor, and he told me never to do that again!" The second boy was from a military family, "My dad told me that if I ever get in trouble with the law again, I can kiss West Point goodbye!" The third boy told the judge, "You bet I won't do it. My dad's a lawyer, and I'm gonna sue that farmer for damages to my pants that got tore jumping his fence!"[74]

To the public, the lawyer is someone who promotes conflict for personal gain. Most respondents to public opinion surveys blame lawyers for the presence of too much litigation and specifically pinpoint the cause as lawyers' self-interest. Seventy percent of respondents to a 1992 CBS/*New York Times* poll agreed that "lawyers encourage too many lawsuits in order to make money for themselves." Only 19 percent preferred the response "by encouraging lawsuits, lawyers help injured people get the compensation they deserve."[75]

As in the *crutches* story (D9), lawyers collude with their clients for mutual (and undeserved) gain. But when their interests are not in harmony, the lawyer has no hesitation in managing the client's case to suit his own purposes. As a classic story, which has flourished for a century and a half, has it:

D33   A Chancery barrister, into whose hands had fallen the lucrative practice of his father-in-law, one morning gleefully announced to the latter that he had brought to a successful termination a cause which had been pending in the Court of Chancery for many years, "You blockhead," said the legal veteran, "it was by this suit that my father was enabled to provide for me, and I to portion your wife; and if you had exercised common prudence, it would have furnished you with the means of providing handsomely for your children and grandchildren."[76]

A related story dispenses with the Dickensian props:

D34   A businessman was involved in a lawsuit that dragged on for years. One afternoon he told his attorney, "Frankly, I'm getting tired of all this litigation." The lawyer replied, "Nonsense. I propose to fight this case down to your last nickel."[77]

Although bringing lawsuits is only a small part of what most lawyers do, litigation and the threat and maneuver that accompany it are seen as defining the lawyer's identity. In a discerning study of the metaphors used in lawyers' talk, Elizabeth Thornberg detects a metaphorical fixation on adversary combat. Metaphors that emphasize the combative, noncooperative aspects of war, sports, and sex are "used in dead earnest" and form "a major part . . . of public lawyer discourse about litigation."[78] For example, litigators may be "battle-tested" "hired guns" who undertake "frontal assaults" or "preemptive strikes," "play hardball," "go to the mat" with their opponents, and "screw them to the wall."[79]

Where the lawyer as litigator challenges other persons of status and accomplishment, it provokes more than transient resentment. Doctors are among the leading carriers of lawyer jokes and their animus is reflected in the joke corpus. The lawyer's need for medical attention provides a convenient setting for professional revenge:

D36   The doctor took one glance at his new patient. "You'll have to call in another physician," said he.

"Am I as sick as all that?" gasped the patient.

"No, but you're the lawyer who cross-examined me last March when I was called to give expert testimony in a certain case. Now, my conscience won't permit me to kill you, but I'm hanged if I want to cure you, so good day."[80]

After the great increase in malpractice litigation, starting in the 1960s, the doctor changes roles from expert witness to defendant, and his response becomes more ominous.

D36   A patient on the operating table was just about to be put under. He was screaming hysterically, "Tell me Dr. Green isn't my surgeon! He can't be! No, no, no!"

The operating room team had him almost under control when Dr. Green entered, took one look at his patient and said: "Well, well, if it isn't that nice lawyer who tried to get me on that trumped-up malpractice suit last year!"[81]

A sketch by Art Buchwald elaborating this theme circulates on the Internet as a lawyer joke:

D36   It had to happen sooner or later. Lawyer Dobbins was wheeled into the emergency room on a stretcher, rolling his head in agony. Doctor Green came over to see him.

"Dobbins," he said, "What an honor. The last time I saw you was in court when you accused me of malpractice."

"Doc. Doc. My side is on fire. The pain is right here. What could it be?"

"How would I know? You told the jury I wasn't fit to be a doctor."

"I was only kidding, Doc. When you represent a client you don't know what you're saying. Could I be passing a kidney stone?"

"Your diagnosis is as good as mine."

"What are you talking about?"

"When you questioned me on the stand you indicated you knew everything there was to know about the practice of medicine."

"Doc, I'm climbing the wall. Give me something."

"Let's say I give you something for a kidney stone and it turns out to be a gallstone. Who is going to pay for my court costs?"

"I'll sign a paper that I won't sue."

"Can I read to you from the transcript of the trial? Lawyer Dobbins: 'Why were you so sure that my client had tennis elbow?' Dr. Green: 'I've treated hundreds of people with tennis elbow and I know it when I see it.' Dobbins: 'It never occurred to you my client could have an Excedrin headache?' Green: 'No, there were no signs of an Excedrin headache.' Dobbins: 'You and your ilk make me sick.'"

"Why are you reading that to me?"

"Because, Dobbins, since the trial I've lost confidence in making a diagnosis. A lady came in the other day limping . . ."

"Please, Doc, I don't want to hear it now. Give me some Demerol."

"Nervous, Doctor? Never treated a personal injury lawyer before?"

28. Cartoon by Dave Carpenter (© 2004, from cartoonbank.com. All rights reserved.)

"You said during the suit that I dispensed drugs like a drunken sailor. I've changed my ways, Dobbins. I don't prescribe drugs anymore."

"Then get me another doctor."

"There are no other doctors on duty. The reason I'm here is that after the malpractice suit the sheriff seized everything in my office. This is the only place that I can practice."

"If you give me something to relieve the pain I will personally appeal your case to a higher court."

"You know, Dobbins, I was sure that you were a prime candidate for a kidney stone."

"You can't tell a man is a candidate for a kidney stone just by looking at him."

"That's what you think, Dobbins. You had so much acid in you when you addressed the jury I knew some of it eventually had to crystallize into stones. Remember on the third day when you called me the 'Butcher of Operating Room 6?' That afternoon I said to my wife, 'That man is going to be in a lot of pain.'"

"Okay, Doc, you've had your ounce of flesh. Can I now have my ounce of Demerol?"

"I better check you out first."

"Don't check me out, just give the dope."

"But in court the first question you asked me was if I had examined the patient completely. It would be negligent of me if I didn't do it now. Do you mind getting up on the scale?"

"What for?"

"To find out your height. I have to be prepared in case I get sued and the lawyer asks me if I knew how tall you were."

"I'm not going to sue you."

"You say that now. But how can I be sure you won't file a writ after you pass the kidney stone?"[82]

The rivalry and animosity between doctors and lawyers attract further additions to the joke corpus, some of which flourish while some fail. The following "joke in progress," which seems a deliberate composition that has not been smoothed out by retelling, made a brief on-line appearance:

D37   Two doctors were discussing a case in the psych ward. The first doc asked what had triggered such a profound depressive psychosis in the patient. The second one answered, "He's a lawyer. One day at home, he started to think about how much money he'd screwed his partners and clients out of over the last few years. He laughed so hard he defecated in his pants. When he smelled the foul odor he had created, he checked for the source. Finding his trousers full of the stuff, he thought he was leaking. This caused him to go into shock and faint. When he woke up, he found he had fallen on his arm, breaking it." The first doc asked, "He went mad because he broke an arm?" The second medico answered, "No, he went mad because he couldn't figure out how to sue himself!"[83]

Here the lawyer's incorrigible contentiousness is his undoing at the culmination of a story combining themes of predation, betrayal, moral insensibility, and scatology.

After its brief on-line appearance, this story sank into obscurity, possibly because it tried to touch so many bases that it is diffuse and anticlimactic. In contrast, the following story with its strong narrative movement and deft punch line is a successful switch to the lawyer-doctor conflict. Obviously it can be told either way.

D38   Two attorneys boarded a flight out of Seattle. One sat in the window seat, the other sat in the middle seat. Just before takeoff, a physician got on and took the aisle seat next to the two attorneys. The physician kicked off his shoes, wiggled his toes, and was settling in when the attorney in the window seat said, "I think I'll get up and get a Coke."

"No problem," said the physician, "I'll get it for you."

While he was gone, one of the attorneys picked up the physician's shoe and spat in it. When he returned with the Coke, the other attorney said, "That looks good, I think I'll have one too."

Again, the physician obligingly went to fetch it and while he was gone, the other attorney picked up the other shoe and spat in it. The physician returned and they all sat back and enjoyed the flight. As the plane was landing, the physician slipped his feet into his shoes and knew immediately what had happened.

"I don't feel quite as fulfilled when I've saved a lawyer."

29. Cartoon by Frank Cotham (© The New Yorker Collection 2003, from cartoonbank.com. All rights reserved.)

"How long must this go on?" he asked. "This fighting between our professions? This hatred? This animosity? This spitting in shoes and pissing in Cokes?"[84]

THE LAWYER AS HEROIC CHAMPION

Many lawyers like to imagine themselves as champions who ride out to battle on behalf of the oppressed and misused. Popular culture ratifies this image.[85] From Mr. Tutt to Perry Mason to John Grisham, imaginary lawyers extend themselves to rescue the innocent.[86] The emphasis on this theme in story and film has no counterpart in the joke corpus. The few stories that reflect this theme of the lawyer as heroic benefactor of the weak have long passed out of circulation in the United States. Here are two extended tales that once enjoyed some currency:

D39   John Gough tells a story of a Southern planter who had got into financial difficulty. Those were the days of the Fugitive Slave Law, when planters could hunt their fugitive slaves over the North, and take them back. This planter, considering how he might extricate himself from his embarrassments, got trace of one of his fugitive slaves—a favourite girl, almost white, who had been brought up in his house, and got a good deal of education there along with his daughters. She had made her escape to the North, and settled in Philadelphia, where she had married a white man, a storekeeper, by whom she had several children.

The planter went to Philadelphia, taking all necessary evidence with him, sent for the storekeeper, and told him he had come to recover a slave of his, whom the storekeeper had married.

The man was thunderstruck. Perhaps his wife had revealed to him her past history, and he knew of the dreadful law; but would suppose that the planter had long since lost all trace of the runaway girl.

The unhappy man demanded evidence, but there was no difficulty about that; the planter laid before him incontrovertible proof that the girl was his runaway slave, and therefore, in the eye of the law, his property.

"You are, of course, aware also," said the planter, "that as the children follow the condition of the mother, your children are also legally my property."

The unfortunate storekeeper staggered as if he had been shot. He knew, the moment the planter said it, that this was the law; but he had not at first realised its application.

The shock was so terrible that he seemed to lose the power of both thought and utterance.

The planter said: "I do not wish to be hard upon you. I am willing to sell you both your wife and her children; but it will cost you three thousand dollars. I am sorry to come upon you in this way; but I have to look after my own interests, and I must either have that money, or take your wife and children with me."

The man entreated a night to think about it, and see if anything could be done.

The planter agreed.

The unhappy man went to a legal friend and told him the case. The lawyer said: "There is no recourse. You must pay that three thousand dollars tomorrow."

"It is impossible," said the man. "I haven't three thousand dollars in the world."

The lawyer considered. Philadelphia lawyers have a reputation for smartness; and this one, after cross-questioning the storekeeper and going home with him and seeing his wife, ultimately said he would undertake the case and do his best. "But," he added, "that three thousand dollars will have to be paid."

Next day he went to the planter's hotel, taking three thousand dollars with him. He saw the planter, and said he had come to pay him the money, and get the deed of sale.

The planter was delighted—the money suited him best. The papers were duly made out, signed, and handed over to the lawyer, who handed over the three thousand dollars in return.

"A very handsome girl she has been," said the lawyer referring to the storekeeper's wife, who had been the principal subject of the negotiation. "Intelligent; highly educated too."

"That's so," said the planter, as he put the roll of dollar bills into his pocket. "That fact is, that girl was brought up in my house, and educated like one of my own daughters."

"That's just the point I was going to refer to," said the lawyer. "I am going to bring an action against you for that." The planter stared.

"Yes," continued the lawyer, "it is a penal offence in your State, as you know, to educate a slave, and I think this is a case where the law ought certainly to be put in force." The planter moved uneasily in his chair. He saw that the lawyer had him.

"And yet," said the lawyer, "I would not like to be hard upon you. If you like to hand back those three thousand dollars I shall let you off."

The planter bit his lip; he knew that an action against him would involve worse consequences than the loss of three thousand dollars; and, at last, with the best grace he could, handed back the money.

He returned to the south a wiser and sadder man; while the lawyer carried the news to the storekeeper and his wife, and also handed over to the grateful family the deed of sale, which secured them against future risk.[87]

D39   One of the most prominent lawyers of America was walking one day through a small village near his country home, and was attracted by the sale of the effects of a poor widow, whose home was being sold at auction. The article that was being put up was a sugar bowl. When it had been sold, the widow said to the purchaser:

"Wait a moment; don't take it yet. I want to take out the sugar and put it into something else."

But the purchaser, who was the village skinflint, objected. He said that when he bought the sugar bowl the contents went with it. An argument ensued. The purchaser looked about the room, and spied the lawyer. He said:

"There's Mr. Atterbury, our neighbor, who is a lawyer; I'll leave it to him. Haven't I a right to the sugar as well as the bowl, Mr. Atterbury?"

The lawyer got up in his best court room manner and delivered a long address, citing legal precedents and authorities, to the effect that undoubtedly the sugar must go with the bowl. Thereupon the old skinflint, rubbing his hands in glee, said to the widow, "There, didn't I tell you so?" And he grabbed the bowl.

But Mr. Atterbury had more to say. He turned to the purchaser and said:

"Wait a moment; you asked my legal advice, in the presence of all these witnesses, and you got it. My fee, sir, is one hundred dollars. And unless you pay me on the spot, sir, I shall bring suit against you for the full amount and costs."

The old skinflint saw that he was caught, and paid the cash—which, of course, the lawyer turned over immediately to the poor woman.[88]

A single Lincoln anecdote seems to be the major contemporary representative of this theme:

D39   It was Abraham Lincoln's habit to discourage unnecessary lawsuits, though it cost him a pretty penny. One day a man stormed into his office and demanded that he bring suit for $2.50 against a debtor. Lincoln gravely demanded ten dollars as a retainer. Half of this he gave to the poor defendant, who immediately confessed judgment and paid the $2.50. Thus the suit was terminated to the entire satisfaction of everyone concerned.[89]

Even where lawyers do not rise to these heights of beneficence, their capacity for contention and confrontation may be seen as an asset, especially by clients

"My lawyer finally got me on the endangered-species list!"

30. Cartoon by Mick Stevens (© The New Yorker Collection 1996, from cartoonbank.com. All rights reserved.)

who are inexperienced in asserting themselves or feel themselves overpowered by a more formidable adversary. Thus lawyers may pursue remedies where parties hesitate to envision them:

D40   Friend: "Your voice surprises me."
        Vocalist: "I studied and spent one million dollars to learn to sing."
        Friend: "I would love to have you meet my brother."
        Vocalist: "Is he a singer, too?"
        Friend: "No, he's a lawyer. He'll get your money back."[90]

And lawyers may help subordinates to confront dominant parties.

D41   The real-estate mogul was delighted by the comely new receptionist, and proceeded to turn all of his charms upon her. Within a few weeks, however, he grew extremely displeased at her growing tardiness. "Listen, baby," he roared one morning, "we may have gone to bed together a few times, but who said you could start coming in late?"
        The secretary replied sweetly, "My lawyer."[91]

Tales of lawyers empowering clients are still current, but plot and characters have changed. Those empowered are less dramatically victimized than the widows and tenants of the earlier stories; their opponents are less monstrously villainous. The lawyer is not a beneficent patron, but a resource available to ordinary people to deal with the troubles and disappointments of everyday life.

CHAPTER 5

The Demography of the World of Lawyer Jokes

THE HEMISPHERIC PRISM

As we complete the first part of our tour of the classic core of joking about lawyers, let us pause to survey the terrain over which we have traveled. The contours of that terrain, we shall see, have changed very little even as new waves of jokes have enlarged and reshaped the lawyer joke corpus.

Jokes about lawyers tend to be generic. Geographical markers are infrequent and never essential to the story. Nor are the jokes located at specific points of time; they exist in a timeless present. That lawyers' practices are specialized (by field of law and especially by type of client) goes largely unremarked in the lawyer joke corpus. The jokes credit lawyers with the moral elasticity to represent either side of a dispute and the agility to switch from one side to the other.[1] But they ignore that lawyers in fact frequently specialize in representing particular types of clients and tend to develop strong attachments to rhetorical stances and policy positions that favor that class of clients (injury victims, corporate polluters, insurers, white collar criminals.)[2] Robert Rosen observes that "doctors specialize by disease, lawyers by side."[3] Jokes about doctors reflect the lines of specialization, frequently revolving around comparison of surgeons, internists, psychiatrists, and so forth. But there are no jokes at all contrasting different kinds of lawyers, and few that are specifically aimed at particular kinds of legal specialists.

Although they are in these respects undifferentiated, the lawyers depicted in the jokes do display definite features. In the world of lawyer jokes, lawyers are almost without exception white males of no discernible ethnicity. There is no reflection of the changing composition of the increasingly diverse profession. In the real world almost three-quarters of lawyers are in private practice. In the joke world, virtually all lawyers have been and remain private practitioners. There are no government lawyers (apart from judges and an occasional prosecutor), no in-house corporate lawyers, no legal services or public interest lawyers.[4]

Apart from some railroad lawyers in the older jokes, the lawyers in the jokes represent individual clients, not large impersonal corporations. In contrast, most of what real world lawyers do is supply services to these organizational clients rather than to individuals. In their classic study of the Chicago bar, John Heinz and Edward Laumann estimated that in 1975 "more than half (53 percent) of the total effort of Chicago's bar was devoted to the corporate client sector, and a smaller but still substantial proportion (40 percent) is expended on the personal client sector."[5] When the study was replicated twenty years later, the researchers found that there were roughly twice as many lawyers working in Chicago, and about 61 percent of the total effort of all Chicago lawyers was devoted to the corporate client sector and only 29 percent to the personal/small business sector.[6] The pronounced shift to servicing of organizations is not confined to Chicago, but is quite general. Census data reveal that from 1967 to 1992 expenditures on legal services by individuals increased 261 percent, while law firms' income from businesses increased by 555 percent.[7] Business expenditures on legal services grew at well over twice the rate of increase of individual expenditures.[8]

The provision of legal services to individuals and to corporate bodies is done by different lawyers, differently organized. Lawyers in the United States nominally form a single profession. But it is a profession that is intensely stratified. With due allowance for exceptions, the upper strata of the bar consist mostly of large firms whose members are recruited mainly from prestigious law schools and who serve corporate clients; the lower strata practice as individuals or small firms, are drawn from less prestigious schools, and service individual clients. Law practice is a bifurcated structure, organized around different kinds of clients. Heinz and Laumann characterized these strata as the "two hemispheres of the profession. Most lawyers reside exclusively in one hemisphere or the other and seldom, if ever, cross the equator."[9] In the corporate hemisphere, a wider range of services is supplied over a longer duration, there is more specialization and coordination, research and investigation are more elaborate, and tactics can be more innovative and less routine.[10] "Fields serving big business clients," Heinz and Laumann found, enjoyed the most prestige "and those serving individual clients (especially clients from lower socioeconomic groups)" the least.[11] Again differentials in prosperity and prestige are invisible in the world of lawyer jokes. In the jokes, there is little discernible hierarchy among lawyers who (with few exceptions) relate to one another as peers.

During the last twenty-five years, while lawyer jokes have multiplied and flourished, the legal profession has undergone dramatic change. There are many more lawyers. Many remain sole practitioners or work in small practices, but an ever-greater portion practice in ever-larger large firms.[12] As they have grown, these firms have become more rationalized and businesslike, more diverse and less socially exclusive, and more visible. The law firms that service corporations and other organizations have multiplied, grown, and flourished, while the sectors of the profession that serve individuals have been relatively stagnant in earnings and growth.[13]

With very few exceptions the practices depicted in the jokes are small practices. Although labels like "Wall Street lawyer" occasionally surface, the large corporate law firm that has increasingly dominated both legal practice and the news about law appears only rarely. Among the three hundred or so jokes recounted in this book, I could identify only eight in which the setting was arguably a large firm and about as many in which the client is a large organization.[14] (About half of the latter group are dropouts that are no longer in circulation.) In effect the imagery is that of the personal service hemisphere. The corporate hemisphere of the legal profession is not absent, but it is seen dimly through the prism of the world of personal service. Only in the small (but growing) number of jokes that address the tension between partners and junior lawyers do we sense the presence of the rationalized, hierarchic, market-oriented world of large firm practice.

The jokes' portrayal of what lawyers do reflects this individual client vantage point. There is little preventative or planning work (apart from preparing wills). Lawyers' work is reactive; they are engaged to respond to various emergencies and predicaments that fracture the rhythm of everyday life. The jokes favor litigation, especially criminal cases. In real life, only a small portion of lawyers' effort is devoted to litigation, but it looms larger in the jokes. Of the jokes in which we can identify the work the lawyer is engaged in, something like a quarter involve litigation, far larger than the portion of their efforts that actual lawyers spend on such work. In the real world, all criminal work absorbs something like a tenth of the efforts of the entire bar.[15] About one-third of jokes involving litigation refer to criminal proceedings, but this is considerably more balanced than the depiction of lawyers in television and movies where they are overwhelmingly concerned with criminal law.[16]

WOMEN IN COMBAT

Few lawyer jokes target or even mention women lawyers. The great stock of lawyer jokes was formed at a time when women lawyers were rare.[17] As recently as 1971 women made up only 3 percent of the legal profession. Twenty years later they were 20 percent of a much-expanded profession and a much larger portion of younger lawyers.[18] These changes are only dimly reflected in the general body of lawyer jokes. In some recent published collections, a few *hes* have been changed to *shes*, but it is not clear that very many of them are told that way. Sources that are more indicative of how these jokes are told register little integration of women. For example, in a set of over 180 items found on the Internet at the beginning of September 1994, only one identified the lawyer as a woman (a joke about female prosecutors, which was also the only prosecutor joke).

There are a few jokes specifically about women lawyers in which the gender of the lawyer is connected to the point of the joke. Of those few, most focus on the issue of combativeness:

E1   How can you tell the difference between a woman lawyer and a pit bull?
      Lip gloss.[19]

E2   Question: What's the difference between female prosecutors and terrorists?
Answer: You can negotiate with terrorists.[20]

The threatening character of the woman lawyer was registered almost as soon as the first women lawyers appeared.

E3   "Would you marry a woman lawyer?"
"No, indeed. The ordinary woman can cross-examine quite well enough."[21]

The underlying message is that lawyering involves an intensification of aggressive, combative, intrusive traits that are out of place in a woman and that these traits are manifested in even more exaggerated form when the lawyer is a woman.[22]

"So you went to law school, and now you want to practice law. I think that's cute."

31. Cartoon by Michael Goodman (© Michael Goodman)

These jokes reflect precisely a widely reported inclination among male lawyers to attribute excess aggression to their female colleagues. One woman lawyer complained, "You hardly ever met a man practicing law who didn't regale you with stories of the horrible experiences he had with ballsy, nasty, aggressive women lawyers and how different you were."[23] Male lawyers told Cynthia Epstein that women lawyers were "too harsh and unbending," "more intransigent than men," and "less human, less compassionate, and less accommodating."[24]

But this "indictment of women lawyers as 'too tough'"[25] is only one side of the coin; at the same time, they are suspected of being insufficiently tough. Jennifer Pierce describes this as a double bind: "Women lawyers face contradictory messages . . . When they adopt gamesmanship strategies they are criticized for 'unladylike' and 'shrill' behavior, but when they are 'nice' or 'pleasant' they are judged 'not tough enough' to be good lawyers."[26]

The paradox that binds women lawyers reflects the tensions in the relation of lawyers to conflict. Concern about lawyers' aggression and combativeness is accompanied by an offsetting appreciation of their ability and willingness to fight and some anxiety about insufficient zeal. This tension creates a tangle for women lawyers that is summed up in this ambiguous riddle:

E4   What do you get when you cross a feminist with an attorney? A lawyer who won't screw you.[27]

On the surface this repeats the charges that feminists are antisexual and woman lawyers deficient in female sexuality. But there is another twist here. "Screwing" has become a shorthand expression for the aggressive and predatory activity that is a defining characteristic of lawyers. A lawyer who won't screw you may be appreciated as a lawyer who would not abuse clients, opponents, or peers. But at the same time a lawyer incapable of the damaging aggression for which lawyers are feared (and valued) is not equipped with the full powers of the lawyer; she is, literally, impotent.

A second and related theme surfaces in the current joke canon: the woman lawyer is an obsessive workaholic who suppresses both romance and family for her career.

E5   The lawyer and her husband were having a late dinner one night.
      "I just don't understand," she said. "The law specifically states one thing, yet Judge Asherman made a point of disallowing—"
      "Honey," said her husband, "for once—just once—why can't we talk about something other than the law or a case you're working on?"
      "I'm sorry," she said. "What would you like to talk about?"
      "How about sex?"
      "Okay," she said. After a moment, she asked, "How often do you think Judge Asherman has sex?"[28]

The obsessive workaholism of male lawyers never attracted this joke, which has been applied to varied monomaniacs from stockbrokers to sports fans since (at least) the 1960s.

E6   Finally yielding to her husband's pleas, the workaholic attorney agreed to have a baby. During her maternity leave she decided to take the newborn to the zoo, and made the mistake of passing too close to the gorilla cage. A hairy arm reached out and plucked the baby out of the stroller, and the huge ape proceeded to eat the child before her very eyes.

A policeman arrived and spent over an hour trying to calm the hysterical woman, but nothing seemed to work. Finally he put an arm around her shoulders and reasoned, "Lady, don't take it so hard. You and your husband can always have another baby."

"Like hell!" the lawyer snapped. "You think I've got nothing better to do than fuck and feed gorillas?"[29]

These anti-sex-and-family stories again reflect a sore point in the professional and personal identity of women lawyers. Much of the resistance to women's attainment of central roles in modern law practice is on the grounds that they are less committed to their role and practice and more susceptible to having these commitments compromised by competing responsibilities as mothers. But if she demonstrates that she is dedicated to her work, then she admits to abandoning her feminine nurturing qualities.[30]

How do hard-driving ambitious women lawyers fare in a traditionally male professional realm?

E7   Three young women have all been working eighty-hour weeks for six straight years in the struggle to make partner in the law firm, and the cutoff date is fast approaching. Each one is brainy, talented, and ambitious but there's only room for one new partner. At a loss as to which one to pick, the senior officer finally devises a little test. One day, while all three are out to lunch, he places an envelope containing $500 on each of their desks.

The first woman returns the envelope to him immediately.

The second woman invests the money in the market and returns $1500 to him the next morning.

The third woman pockets the cash.

So which one gets the promotion to partner? The one with the biggest tits![31]

This is another widespread story that is a recent recruit to the lawyer joke canon.[32] The theme of a hiring contest in which qualification is subverted by nepotism or sexual attraction has been around since women entered the white-collar workplace. Earlier versions typically depicted the boss selecting a secretary.[33] The law firm version is distinctive in that the women are competing for a position that potentially involves a relationship of professional equality with their male bosses. But the joke asserts or concedes or celebrates (depending on how it is told) that male lawyers, despite their pretensions to meritocratic objectivity, still see female lawyers as sexual objects and ignore their professional accomplishments. This adds another dimension to the bind of the woman lawyer. To flaunt her physical attractions would be unprofessional, but to exhibit her professional acumen to the exclusion of feminine charms is defined as precisely the kind of aggressiveness and single-mindedness that is the target of the jokes above.

JEWS AND OTHER OUTSIDERS

If gender surfaces in lawyer jokes occasionally the jokes pay little heed to ethnic identity. There are no jokes (known to me) about black or Hispanic lawyers

"For God's sake, Mildred. You're a lawyer, not a lawyerette!"

32. Cartoon by George Jartos in S. Gross, ed., *Lawyers! Lawyers! Lawyers!* (© George Jartos 1994)

(although the older jokes are full of black clients, usually criminal defendants and witnesses). In older versions of some jokes, lawyers were occasionally identified by obviously Jewish or Irish surnames, but jokes in which the point turns on ethnic identity are extremely rare.[34]

This is not because the presence of such ethnic outsiders in the real world of law went unremarked or uncontested. Black lawyers, shouldering "a crippling burden of handicaps," were simply excluded from the higher echelons of law practice.[35] Although there was lingering prejudice against Irish (and other Catholic) lawyers, Jews were the first "minority" to join the legal profession in numbers that elicited unease in the legal establishment.[36] Warnings against "the great flood of foreign blood . . . sweeping into the bar" and immigrants with "little inherited sense of fairness, justice and honor as we understand them" were followed by sustained campaigns to stem the entry of these undesirables.[37] The foremost

"Do you know Kimberly, my attorney?"

33. Cartoon by Edward Frascino (© The New Yorker Collection 1989, from cartoonbank.com. All rights reserved.)

authority on legal ethics of the interwar years affirmed the necessity of protecting the bar against the menace of "Russian Jew boys" who had "come up out of the gutter . . . and were merely following the methods their fathers had been using in selling shoe-strings and other merchandise."[38]

The image of Jewish lawyers was two-sided. Jews figured both as heroic civil liberties lawyers in Progressive fiction and as the archetypal shyster in Samuel B. Ornitz's *Haunch, Paunch and Jowl* (1923).[39] Although excluded from the higher echelons of the profession, Jews became a major section of lawyers in many larger cities. In New York Jews comprised half of the bar by the 1930s, although *Fortune* reassured its readers that

> 50 per cent of New York lawyers does not mean 50 per cent of New York's lawyer *power*. The most important office law business in America such as the law business incidental to banking, insurance, trust-company operation, investment work, railroading, patents, admiralty, and large corporation matters in general is in the hands of non-Jewish firms. Jewish legal activity will be found most commonly in litigation. In other words, Jews are largely to be found in those branches of law which do not interest non-Jewish lawyers. . . . [who] tend to prefer the fat fees and regular hours and routine, solicitor-like labors of their office to the active, combative professional service of the law courts.[40]

Barriers to Jewish entry into elite law firms began to give way in the 1950s. By the early 1960s, exclusion had softened into concern about having "too many" Jews.[41] A sociologist who conducted a detailed examination of Wall Street lawyers reported in 1968 the "tremendous lessening of discrimination—especially toward Jews" since he had gathered data a decade earlier.[42]

In Chicago, Jews made up a third of the bar in 1975, but were disproportionately present in small practices and low status specialities.[43] There are no data from which to gauge the population of Jewish lawyers nationwide, but more than one in six law students was Jewish around 1960.[44] But as law school enrollments expanded dramatically (and Jewish population remained static), the proportion of Jews in the profession has fallen.[45] At the same time, the collapse of discrimination has increased the presence of Jews in the higher echelons of the profession. A 1995 survey of partners in the highest-billing law firms found that 22 percent were Jewish.[46]

The jokes about conniving claimants proclaim that Jews are more combative, more ready to resort to the legal system (and to invoke its protection), and even inclined to manufacture claims (by setting fires and faking whiplash). Curiously, although such images haunted the bar worthies who decried their entry to the profession, these images did not spawn jokes about Jewish lawyers. Despite the movement to exclude them, little note is taken of Jewish lawyers in the joke corpus. The animus against Jews in the profession was projected by their rivals at the establishment bar rather than by the wider populace who might admire or even seek out "a smart Jewish lawyer."

The conflicts about Jewish presence at the bar left little residue in the joke corpus. I have found only three jokes that turn on the lawyer's Jewish identity, none of them in circulation today.

E9 A story is told at the expense of Joseph Choate, the great lawyer, now ambassador to the Court of St. James. On a very important case, Edward Lauterbach, an eminent Jewish attorney, was associated with him. They won their case and when it came to deciding upon the fee, Mr. Choate, the Christian, asked Mr. Lauterbach, the Jew, what he thought they ought to charge. Mr. Lauterbach said he thought $5,000 would be a fair charge. Mr. Choate replied that it shouldn't be less than $15,000. Said Mr. Lauterbach: "Almost thou persuadest me to be a Christian."[47]

The mocking reference to the Jew tempted to abandon his religion to enjoy the greater fees of a Christian lawyer is obvious, but the Jewish lawyer's response is ironic—as if to say you guys say we are out for a buck and drive a hard bargain, but behind your cloak of respectability you outdo us. And note that the editor read the joke contemporaneously as "at the expense of . . . Choate."[48]

From the Jewish side comes the suggestion that Jewish lawyers may be more proficient and that their efforts may be "carrying" their Gentile colleagues:

E11 Jackson, Waybrook, Buchanan, and Isaacs was one of the finest law firms in the city. One day a friend of Eli Isaacs asked, "Why does your name appear last, Eli? Everyone knows that Jackson is ga-ga. Waybrook spends most of his time in the country, and Buchanan never won a case in court. Your name should be first!"
"You forget something," Isaacs smiled.
"What's that?"
"My clients read from right to left."[49]

Apart from these ironic comments on the relations of Jewish lawyers and the legal establishment, the joke corpus contains almost nothing on Jewish lawyers— and for that matter about lawyers of any ethnic flavor. A single story that appears only once, as part of a famous 1928 "underground" collection, is worth noting:

E10 Cohen and Murphy had been partners for twenty years when suddenly Cohen got it into his head that he wanted to be in business by himself.
"I don't know, Murph," he said. "I ain't got nottin' against you, but I'd like to try for myself. So I made up my mind we should split."
Murphy accepted his decision gracefully.
"Of course," he said, "we'll part friends."
"Positively the best," said Cohen. "And now let's call in Feldman, our lawyer, and have him draw up the dissolution papers."
Feldman, when he heard the news, was grief-stricken. "After twenty years," he moaned. "Of course, I'm getting paid for doing this, but nothing hurts me so much as to have to draw up these papers breaking up this fine partnership. But, Cohen, since you made up your mind, as the Latin phrase has it, yens de goy [screw the gentile]."[50]

Although it admits of various readings, one that is close to the surface is the classical canard about Jews as clannish outsiders who will betray others and favor their own. Realizing the worst nightmares of those elite lawyers who scorned Jews as incapable of disinterested professionalism, the lawyer here subverts professional norms in favor of narrow ethnic loyalty. We don't know who told this joke or with what intent. All we know is that it did not survive and was not replaced by other jokes about "clannish" Jewish lawyers.

Of course it is possible that the animus against Jewish lawyers is codified in stories about "shysters"[51] and "ambulance chasers." Dornstein shows how much the campaigns against the evils of ambulance chasing were dominated by "concern about names" and often focused on exposing Jewish attorneys as the chief perpetrators of unethical practices.[52] There is hardly a trace of this in contemporary "ambulance" jokes,[53] but some "Jewish" jokes use the ambulance-chasing script:

E11   What's a Jewish Nativity scene?
       Seven lawyers surrounding a car crash.[54]

The current campaigns to delegitimize "trial lawyers" and "contingency fee lawyers" never invoke the ethnic motif, but it is possible that many in the audience find sufficient cues to awaken the older stereotypes.

Other minorities do not appear at all. There are no visible jokes about Irish, Polish, black, Hispanic, or Asian lawyers. Although ethnic characters appear in jokes about clients, defendants, and witnesses, the stories about lawyers are ethnically undifferentiated. It is the traits of the lawyer, not the differences among lawyers, that engage the tellers and listeners. The only primordial characteristic that shows up in the joke corpus is gender—and such jokes are few and appear infrequently. At the same time the world of lawyer jokes has expanded by absorbing jokes that were earlier told about ethnics. Certain categories of lawyer jokes involve heavy borrowing from jokes about Jews. There are also numerous switches from jokes about groups that are stereotyped as dumb (Irish, Poles) or undesirable (Mexicans, blacks), as well as from politicians, spouses, and mothers-in-law. That ethnicity is not displayed in lawyer jokes may be due in part to contemporary political correctness which makes ethnic jokes unacceptable in certain settings.

SENIORS AND JUNIORS

One demographic characteristic that seems to be emerging into greater prominence in lawyer jokes is age. Stories about seniors instructing and exploiting young lawyers and about juniors turning the tables on their senior colleagues have been around for a long while.[55] But recent developments in the profession have given them a new prominence. Since 1970 the profession has grown rapidly; as larger new cohorts of lawyers arrived, the profession became younger (and, as noted earlier, more female).[56] At the same time, law firms were growing larger, more hierarchic, more diverse, and more competitive and businesslike. Partners no longer enjoyed the secure tenure that had once marked the world of large firms.

The tensions between striving associates and established (and increasingly insecure) partners are reflected in stories that circulate largely within the world of law practice.

An "underground" publication aimed at associates includes the following story:

E13   Thomas Dewey was the former New York governor who, according to press accounts, defeated Harry S. Truman for president in 1948. He was also a founder of the law firm Dewey, Ballantine, Bushby, Palmer & Wood.

One Saturday, Attorney Dewey called the office in an effort to find an associate to do some work for him. After getting a young associate on the phone, Mr. Dewey explained what he needed and then emphasized that it had to be done immediately. The associate responded that he couldn't possibly take on more work because he already expected to be at the office all weekend completing a project that was due on Monday.

Attorney Dewey, not believing what he was hearing from the associate, asked, "Do you know who this is?" When the associate replied that he did not, he was told, "This is Thomas Dewey." After a short pause, the associate asked, "Do you know who *this* is?" When Mr. Dewey said that he didn't, the associate hung up the phone.[57]

E14   A young associate was invited to a party at the home of an august senior partner at his firm. The associate wandered awestruck through the house, especially amazed at the original artworks by Picasso, Matisse, and others adorning the walls. As the associate stood gazing at one Picasso, the senior partner approached, and put his arm around the associate's shoulder. "Yes," he said, "if you work long and hard, day in and day out, six, seven days a week, ten, twelve hours a day . . . I could buy another one!"[58]

Perhaps the best of these is the newest variant of the balloon joke (A42), which displays not only the junior-senior gap but also the gender tension that often overlies it. Earlier, we saw how the original story shifted from the uselessness of parliamentary discourse to the unhelpfulness of legal advice and then to the fecklessness of clients. Now it is further transformed into a weapon in the war within the firm.

A42   A man in a hot air balloon realized he was lost so he reduced altitude and spotted a woman below. He descended a bit more and shouted, "Excuse me, can you help me? I promised a friend I would meet him an hour ago, but I don't know where I am."

The woman below replied, "You are in a hot air balloon hovering approximately thirty feet above the ground. You are between forty and forty-one degrees north latitude and between fifty-nine and sixty degrees west longitude."

"You must be a second-year associate," said the balloonist.

"I am," replied the woman, "How did you know?"

"Well," answered the balloonist, "everything you told me is technically correct, but I have no idea what to make of your information, and the fact is, I am still lost. Frankly, you've not been much help so far."

The woman below responded, "You must be a partner!"

"I am," replied the balloonist, "but how did you know?"

"Well," said the woman, "you don't know where you are or where you are going.

You have risen to where you are due to a large quantity of hot air. You made promises which you have no idea how to keep, and you expect me to solve your problems. The fact is you are in exactly the same position you were in before we met, but now, somehow, it's my fault."[59]

The current body of jokes about lawyers is not a picture of the profession but a screen on which people project their feelings about lawyers. The images on that screen depart quite sharply from a factual portrait of contemporary lawyering: lawyers are undifferentiated by specialty, large firms and corporate clients are rarities, minorities are absent, and women are only marginally present. It is a distinctly old-fashioned image of generalist sole practitioners and small partnerships representing individual clients, an image that differs sharply from the depiction of the law in other media. It is not the glamorous world of *L.A. Law*'s litigators or the gritty world of *Law and Order*'s prosecutors and defense attorneys, nor the tense hierarchy and testing of John Grisham's *The Firm*. It is perhaps most reminiscent of *The Defenders* or Mr. Tutt.[60] Images from the world of *Saturday Evening Post* covers are used to talk about discontents with the abundance of law and lawyers in a very different age.

PART 2

THE NEW TERRITORIES

CHAPTER 6

Betrayers of Trust

Our examination of the various clusters of jokes that make up the classic core of joking about lawyers has revealed many features of lawyers that might induce wariness in those who deal with them—their ability to double-talk, their recourse to clever stratagems, their greed, pursuit of self-interest, combativeness. If lawyers are equipped with these attributes, those who rely upon lawyers—clients, professional associates, kin—may wonder whether these powers will be employed on their behalf or will be turned against them. Can lawyers be trusted or need we fear that they will betray us? This is the subject of a new set of lawyer jokes that have flourished in the new era.

LAWYERS IN A WORLD OF DECLINING TRUST

Trust is widely acclaimed as a public good that enhances civic life, generates social capital, and lubricates the economy.[1] There is widespread agreement that trust (at least some forms) has declined dramatically in the United States over the past thirty or forty years. Positive responses to the question "Most people can be trusted" fell from 58 percent in 1960 to 37 percent in 1994.[2] Confidence in almost all political and social institutions has experienced a corresponding decline.[3] The portion of Americans who responded that "the government in Washington" can be trusted "to do what is right" *most of the time* or *just about always* fell from 76.4 percent in 1964 to 28.9 percent in 1992.[4]

The trust that is measured by the "most people can be trusted" question does not exhaust the range of trust relationships that play a role in our lives. A number of observers have introduced a useful distinction between the personal, particularized, or thick trust characteristic of communal societies with their intense and constant interaction among the same people, and the impersonal, generalized, abstract, or thin trust that grows up alongside it in modern societies with their proliferation of loose, distant, and secondary relations. In the world we inhabit, our thick trust in the loyalty of kin and friends is complemented by our reliance on such people as airline pilots, restaurant staff, hospital personnel, and other drivers on the road. Notwithstanding the decline in personal trust, our faith that we can count on things to work and on people to do their jobs is constantly replenished. Kenneth Newton characterizes this as a shift in social trust "from the thick towards the thin. . . . [P]ersonal trust between known individuals has been supplemented by impersonal or abstract trust, taught by education, enforced and monitored by public rules and agencies, and (perhaps) by the mass media."[5]

Lawyers are implicated in the decline/change in trust in various ways. In an expansive flourish, a Democratic ex-cabinet secretary blames lawyers for "perpetrat[ing] loss of trust between doctor and patient," "slipp[ing] the cruel poison of distrust into society's most basic unit: the family," and "render[ing] . . . obsolete" the "sacred obligation" that "institutions once felt . . . to stand by their contracts."[6] Critics of the legal profession untiringly point out that lawyers induce mistrust and suspicion in their clients, deflecting candid and humane responses into socially destructive gaming. Lawyers "encourage their clients to think with selfish defensiveness, to imagine and prepare for the worst from everyone else"[7] and they "add suspicion and unnatural caution to all our relationships, whether personal or professional."[8] It is indeed the lawyer's stock in trade to point out to clients the many things that can go wrong, the hidden contingencies, the frailty of unsupported promises, and the need for external guarantees. The lawyer also proffers a cure for the fragility of "natural" trust: the legal system's array of devices for stimulating what we might call "artificial" trust—the contract, the lease, the license, whose provisions will be enforced (so we like to believe) by the lawsuit or the policeman. Like the provider of artificial hormones that supplement the diminished supply coursing through the body, the lawyer contrives enforceability to supplement the failing supply of reciprocity, moral obligation, and fellow-feeling.

As our economy and society generate ever more dealings among those bound by thinning webs of reciprocities or reputational controls, we become more reliant on the law's channeling and on its enforcement (and especially the threat of it) to induce compliance, discourage defection, and inspire confidence. Criminal penalties and civil remedies (and the expense and obloquy that attend them) increase the cost of opportunistic violation of agreements or public standards of care. By raising the cost of defection from justified expectations, law lowers the risk of reliance on others.

Lawyers contrive to provide "artificial trust" in a number of ways, including inventing security devices, devising lower transaction cost regimes, channeling transactions, and bonding their clients.[9] Although much of the world's business involves reliance on a strong admixture of nonlegal controls, these are increasingly interwoven with legal controls.[10] Because lawyers are producers and vendors of impersonal "thin" trust, they are beneficiaries of the decline of its low-cost rival, thick personal trust. As the demand for their product increases, lawyers prosper at the same time that they themselves are increasingly distrusted.

The wariness of lawyers revealed in the falling public estimations of lawyers' ethics is evident when the inquiry is specifically about trustworthiness. When (in 1991) a national sample was asked to volunteer "what profession or type of worker do you trust the least," lawyers were far and away the most frequent response. Almost as many (23 percent) spontaneously volunteered lawyers as the next two categories (car salesman, 13 percent; politicians, 11 percent) combined.[11]

But other survey evidence suggests that these expressions of lack of trust in lawyers should not be taken at face value. In a 1984 survey in which majorities of a national sample of adults expressed their views that lawyers charge unreasonable fees (61 percent) and recommend more legal work than is actually required (56 percent), some 71 percent agreed that "lawyers generally work very hard to protect the interests of their clients" (20 percent disagreed) and 64 percent agreed that "lawyers generally follow very high ethical standards in their work for their clients" (28 percent disagreed).[12] What we see is not unqualified condemnation of lawyers, but deep distrust combined with approval of lawyers' care for their clients.

In a 1993 survey, people thought lawyers were smart, knowledgeable, and good at problem-solving, but greedy, overpaid, and lacking in ethics and compassion. But when asked whether lawyers put their clients' interest first, the same respondents were sharply divided: 31 percent said this described lawyers; 35 percent said it did not; and 34 percent were undecided.[13]

LAWYER AND CLIENT

Old Croc.—" Now I will give you a joy ride and take you into the dark waters of English law and . . . "

N.B.—No figure in this cartoon represents any living person directly or indirectly.

34. Lawyer and Client. 1935 etching by English anti-lawyer crusader Percy E. Hurst.

THE BETRAYAL JOKE CLUSTER

In the world of jokes much is made of lawyers' lying, trickiness, cleverness (though often not so clever as they think), contentiousness, and unremitting economic exactions, but until recently the joke corpus had little to say directly about the trustworthiness of lawyers. Opponents might be tricked and clients fleeced, but no jokes specifically branded lawyers as betrayers of trust. But in the last twenty years a whole set of jokes have appeared that focus on the lawyer's proclivity to betray those who trust and rely upon him—clients, partners, friends, and family.

The lawyer's duplicity may be manifested in connection with the expectations of trust and reciprocity generated in casual encounters between strangers:

F1 A doctor and a lawyer in two cars collided on a country road. The lawyer, seeing that the doctor was a little shaken up, helped him from the car and offered him a drink from his hip flask. The doctor accepted and handed the flask back to the lawyer, who closed it and put it away. "Aren't you going to have a drink yourself?" asked the doctor. "Sure, after the police leave," replied the attorney.[14]

Here the lawyer, in the guise of making a compassionate gesture, is bettering his position by acting strategically. What appears to be a magnanimous gesture of fellowship is really part of a strategy to fasten responsibility on the other motorist (whose identity as a doctor introduces the familiar theme of professional rivalry). The lawyer remains cool and calculating in adverse circumstances and bests his rival professional by superior guile.

This story started out (between the arrival of the automobile and 1917) as a simple celebration of the gamesmanship of the clever driver.[15] It later became a joke about the sturdy rustic or prole outwitting the arrogant "smart" tourist, preppy, or ethnic outsider or about the Irish layman outwitting the priest.[16] For the past twenty years the principal protagonists have been lawyers and rabbis (outwitting priests) as the joke has reverted to its earlier "crafty guy wins" theme.[17]

F2 A lawyer named Sam and his accountant are backpacking in the woods. Suddenly, they spot a cougar twenty yards away. They stand there for a moment, then Sam starts removing his pack. His accountant whispers, "What are you doing?" "I'm going to run for it." "But you can't outrun a cougar!" "I don't have to," Sam says. "I just have to outrun you."[18]

This story, first spotted in print in 1983, has been a favorite of speech-making executives seeking to dramatize the exigencies of competition.[19] It surfaced as a lawyer joke in 1991. There is a "two lawyers" version as well as the professional rivalry version given here.[20] In both, fellowship quickly dissolves into single-minded self-preservation and indifference to the other. The lawyer displays not only selfishness but also superior resourcefulness. Penetrating beyond the apparent hopelessness of the situation, he comes up with a strategy for escaping from a tight spot by reconceiving the situation to discern a way out—as it happens at the expense of his companion. Although the lawyer may violate the canons of fraternity, he is a winner who reassures us that we may justifiably pursue our claims, even if the rightness of our cause is only relative, for, if someone has to lose, it might as well be the other guy.

The lawyer may also be involved in less momentous guilt-free loss shifting:

F3   Two lawyers are in a bank, when, suddenly, armed robbers burst in. While several of the robbers take the money from the tellers, others line the customers, including the lawyers, up against a wall, and proceed to take their wallets, watches, etc. While this is going on lawyer number one jams something in lawyer number two's hand. Without looking down, lawyer number two whispers, "What is this?" to which lawyer number one replies, "it's that $50 I owe you."[21]

From its earliest appearance in 1913, this was a joke about friends, usually Jewish.[22] The appearance of the two lawyers version above in 1995 was preceded by a client pays the lawyer version in 1993.[23]

F4   An ancient, nearly blind old woman retained the local lawyer to draft her last will and testament, for which he charged her two hundred dollars. As she rose to leave, she took the money out of her purse and handed it over, enclosing a third hundred-dollar bill by mistake. Immediately the attorney realized he was faced with a crushing ethical question: Should he tell his partner?[24]

This widely circulated story depicts the lawyer's unhesitating victimization of the trusting client, here one specified as particularly vulnerable, an old, nearly blind woman. The neat twist is that he completely misses the ethical violation against the client while sensing an ethical problem in concealing this rip-off from his partner—implying that the latter, as a fellow vulture, would happily share these ill-gotten gains.

This became a lawyer joke only in 1990 after a long career as a joke about the merchant (usually Jewish) instructing his son in business ethics.[25] But where the merchant's advice was hypothetical (i.e., suppose a customer overpaid) the lawyer joke from the start has been a narrative of past events; what is depicted is not just a larcenous inclination but a history of betrayal of the vulnerable.

As the *extra $100 bill* joke suggests, it is touch and go whether the bonds of partnership can restrain the lawyer's proclivity to take advantage of the vulnerable. Once this trait is acknowledged, fellowship is tinged with suspicion:

F5   The two partners in a law firm were having lunch when suddenly one of them jumped up and said, "I have to go back to the office—I forgot to lock the safe!" The other partner replied, "What are you worried about? We're both here."[26]

Again, this is an old joke, recorded as early as 1922, about business partners (usually Jewish) that first appears as a lawyer joke in 1989.[27]

Even where there is generosity and sharing, it cannot withstand the imperative of self-interest:

35. Councellor Double-Fee (BM 4238. 1768). Lawyer takes fees from opposing parties in a lawsuit. His speech balloon says "Open to all parties" and his hands are inscribed "open to all." On his desk are briefs for plaintiff and defendant in the same case. The accompanying text identified him as "Sir Bullface Double-fee."

F6   John and Joe had been law partners for many years, sharing everything, most especially the affections of their libidinous secretary, Rose. One morning, an agitated John came to Joe with the bad news, "Rose is pregnant! We're going to be a father!" Joe, the more reserved of the two, calmed his partner and reminded him that things could be much worse. They were both well-off, and could easily afford the costs of raising the child. Rose would have the best care available, her child would attend only the finest schools, and neither would want for anything. The child would have the benefit of having two fathers, both of which were caring and well-educated. Gradually, John got used to the idea of fatherhood. When the big day came, both were at the hospital awaiting the news of their offspring's birth. Finally, John could take no more and went outside to take a walk. When he returned an hour later, Joe had the news. "We had twins," said Joe, "and mine died."[28]

This first appears as a lawyer joke in 1988 after at least sixty years as a story about business partners (once again often Jewish).[29] This version is distinctive in its buildup of the generosity and sharing of the lawyers which is rudely punctured by the individualistic shift from "we" to "mine." The bonds of partnership and intimacy fail to constrain the lawyer's selfishness and opportunism.

F7   One morning at the law office, one attorney looked at the other and said, "Wow, you look really terrible this morning." The other lawyer replied, "Yeah, I woke up with a headache this morning and, no matter what I try, I can't seem to get rid of it." The first lawyer told him, "Whenever I get a headache like that, I take a few hours off during the day, go home, and make love to my wife. Works every time for me." Later that afternoon, the two lawyers met again. The first told the second, "You know, you look 100 percent better." The second replied, "Yeah, that was great advice you gave me. You've got a beautiful house, too."[30]

From early in the century through its first appearance as a lawyer joke in 1993 to the present, this was a "dumb" joke about the fellow worker who misunderstood the helpful advice and asked, "Is your wife home now?" or "What's your address?"[31] The lawyer in the 1994 version given here is the first protagonist to actually betray his benefactor rather than just contemplate it. Others quickly followed.[32]

    Another story of benevolence repaid has made a few print appearances as a lawyer joke:

F8   A young lawyer in a swank Beverly Hills restaurant spotted J. Paul Getty, the billionaire oil man. The lawyer went over to his table and said, "Mr. Getty, please forgive me for interrupting your lunch, but please. Mr. Getty, I'm expecting two of my clients to come in and I would consider it an enormous favor if sometime during our lunch, you could stop by my table and say, 'Hello, Bernie.' You don't know what it would mean to me. . . ."

    The lawyer returned to his table, where his clients joined him.

    Getty and his guest were finished and were on their way out of the restaurant when Getty remembered the young lawyer's request. He went back to the lawyer's table and, tapping him on the shoulder, said, "Hello, Bernie."

    The lawyer said, "Not now, Getty, I'm eating."[33]

Since at least 1971, a host of protagonists including Newfoundlanders, Ole the Norwegian, Paddy the Irishman, and ambitious young salesmen, executives, and advertising men have enlisted the help of super-celebrity politicians, tycoons, and entertainers and then rebuffed them.[34] That only two lawyers have joined this band suggests that this flourishing joke did not resonate enough with perceptions of lawyers to be firmly lodged in the lawyer joke corpus. It is impossible to know why this joke didn't "take" as a lawyer joke, but a couple of possible explanations come to mind. First, the joke is about a *young* man—and for the most part the lawyer is seen as seasoned and mature, not a novice. Second, the young man is bold and resourceful, but his stratagem of sacrificing the (illusory) friendship of a powerful patron for the merest increment of momentary advantage may just seem too heedless and crude to be convincingly lawyerlike.

F9   There once was a mobster who established a corps of loyal and dedicated employees, chief among whom were a deaf-and-dumb accountant and his brother, a lawyer. Both of them served the mobster for a number of years, and everything was fine until the chief decided to double check the books. Finding himself some two million dollars short, the boss flew into a rage and sent out a couple of thugs to round up the accountant and his brother, who could speak sign language and serve as interpreter. "You tell this son-of-a-bitch I want to know where my two million is!" he yelled. After a quick exchange with his brother, the lawyer reported that his brother had no idea what his employer was talking about. The mobster jumped to his feet, held a gun to the accountant's temple, and screamed, "You tell this bastard that if he doesn't sing, pronto, I'm going to blow his brains out—after I have a couple of my boys work him over!" This was duly translated to the quaking accountant, who explained to his brother in frantic sign language that the bills were hidden in three shoeboxes in his closet. "So whaddid he say?" interrupted the gangster. The lawyer turned back to him with a shrug. "He says you haven't got the balls."[35]

In this *Betrayal* tale the lawyer is not only engaged in dirty business to start with, but he proceeds to take advantage of the dependence of his client and his brother to betray both. The story is resonant with clients' anxieties over whether lawyers are really doing what they say they are doing. Here the lawyer rips off both antagonists by exploiting his monopoly on the channels of communication to falsify messages and aggravate conflict for his own economic advantage.[36] *Betrayal* here is coupled with *Economic Predation*. It is also a tale about the lawyer's moral obtuseness and lack of ordinary human attachments. This shows up as a lawyer joke in 1990, over a dozen years after its appearance as a story about the faithless translator.[37]

F10   Pete and Jerry had been law partners for many years. One day, Pete fell ill, and grew progressively worse. Medical specialists were called in from the world over, but no one could diagnose Pete's illness. The only thing that seemed certain was that Pete's death was imminent. As Pete lay in his last hours, he felt obligated to reveal a few secrets to

Jerry. "You know that million dollar settlement we got from Morgan last year? I never told you this, but it was really three million. I kept the other two million, and eventually gambled it away. Can you forgive me?" Jerry said that he would, without question. Pete then told him, "Well, you remember when your wife divorced you and got the big alimony judgement? It was me that gave her the inside information on your finances. I had been screwing her for years. How can you forgive me?" Jerry told his friend, once again, that it was forgotten. After Pete had told of several other transgressions, all of which Jerry forgave, Pete began to look at Jerry as saintly. "How can you be so forgiving, after the way I have cheated and lied to you for so many years?" Jerry answered, "For two reasons, Pete. First, because you will soon be dead, and there's no reason to hate you in the grave. And, secondly, because I poisoned you."[38]

This popular story has been told about spouses since before 1928[39] and about partners (often Jewish) since 1945.[40] The first lawyer poisoner appeared in 1991 (preceded by a client poisoning his lawyer in 1987). Since 1991, vengeance has been wreaked in the print record by six lawyers, five business partners, ten husbands, and two wives. No other new protagonists have appeared. Like his predecessors, the lawyer appears long-suffering and forgiving; he "turns the other cheek," but it is only appearance. Behind the scenes he responds forcefully and lethally to punish those who injure him. He feigns forgiveness while silently doing in his partner just as the partner feigned loyalty and exploited him. Tit for tat, what they share is treacherous infliction of ruinous damage.

In many of these stories the lawyer's betrayal has a phallic component: the lawyer has literally screwed someone he shouldn't have (the secretary or the partner's wife) or metaphorically screwed his partner or his client. The conflation of economic and sexual predation, which we saw earlier in the new "sexual" *Economic Predation* jokes, is condensed in the following riddle:

F11   Q: How does a lawyer say, "Screw you?"
           A: "Trust me."[41]

In more mundane ways, the lawyer has no compunction about using his power over others to forward his own interests:

F12   A paralegal, an associate and a partner of a prestigious N.Y. law firm are walking
           though Central Park on their way to lunch when they find an antique oil lamp. They rub
           it and a Genie comes out in a puff of smoke.
               The Genie says, "I usually only grant three wishes, so I'll give each of you just one."
               "Me first! Me first!" says the paralegal. "I want to be in the Bahamas, driving a
           speedboat, without a care in the world."
               Poof. He's gone.
               In astonishment, "Me next! Me next!" says the associate. "I want to be in Hawaii,
           relaxing on the beach with my personal masseuse, an endless supply of piña coladas and
           the love of my life."
               Poof. She's gone.

"You're next," the Genie says to the partner.

The partner says, "I want those two back in the library after lunch."[42]

This is one of the few jokes that is set in the world of modern large firm practice. Like *beautiful house* (F7), this was (and remains) a dumb joke, here about the stupid guy who undoes his mates' escape from a desert island.[43] A lawyer instance appears in print in 1996.[44] In 1997 the more instrumentalist workaholic version in the text above was circulating, apparently modeled on an earlier variant involving a movie producer who wants his director and writer on the set.[45]

BETRAYAL AS VIRTUE

Is the lawyer's treachery and proclivity to defect entirely negative? The earliest *Betrayal* joke to be switched to lawyers, and one of the most popular, portrays the lawyer's trickiness as not entirely without redeeming qualities:

F13   A very wealthy man, old and desperately ill, summons to his bedside his three closest advisors: his doctor, his priest, and his lawyer. "I know," he says, "they say 'you can't take it with you.' But who knows? Suppose they're mistaken. I'd like to have something, just in case. So I am giving each of you an envelope containing one hundred thousand dollars and I would be grateful if at my funeral you would put the envelope in my coffin, so that if it turns out that it's useful, I'll have something." They each agree to carry out his wish.

Sure enough, after just a few weeks, the old man passes away. At his funeral, each of the three advisors can be seen slipping something into the coffin. After the burial, as the three are walking away together, the doctor turns to the other two and says, "Friends, I have a confession to make. As you know, at the hospital we are desperate because of the cutbacks in funding. Our CAT scan machine broke down and we haven't been able to get a new one. So, I took $20,000 of our friend's money for a new CAT scan and put the rest of it in the coffin as he asked."

At this the priest says, "I, too, have a confession to make. As you know, our church is simply overwhelmed by the problem of the homeless. The needs keep increasing and we have nowhere to turn. So I took $50,000 from the envelope for our homeless fund and put the rest in the coffin as our friend requested."

Fixing the other two in his gaze, the lawyer says, "I am astonished and deeply disappointed that you would treat so casually our solemn undertaking to our friend. I want you to know that I placed in his coffin my personal check for the full one hundred thousand dollars."[46]

The *check in the coffin* in something like this form has been circulating for more than a hundred years, often but not exclusively as a joke about Jews.[47] The first lawyer, who appeared in 1964, is the lawyer son of a testator who requires that his coffin contain $100,000; the son removed the cash and substituted his check.[48] For the first time the joke figure is a lawyer and for the first time the money for deposit is supplied by the deceased. With the next lawyer protagonist in 1967, the joke is reconfigured into its now canonical form: the deceased is attended by a triad of friends or advisors, of different professions or ethnicities. There is an escalating diversion of funds for altruistic reasons, but the earlier deposits are not removed; and the joke figure reproaches the others.[49] In its several versions this has become one of the most widespread of the longer narrative jokes about lawyers. In this *take it with you* version the lawyer combines greed, formalism, manipulation and betrayal. He is a too-clever deceiver who betrays his client and outdoes his friends by a kind of crazy literalness. The betrayal is done in good form, but form is employed to undermine substance. On the surface the lawyer complies fully with the request. But his compliance is achieved by a daring extension of the conventional equation of check with cash that sabotages the intent of the promise—at the same time that it extends the zany logic of the deceased, for why should an afterlife where U.S. dollars are honored lack facilities for negotiating a check?

The lawyer's abysmal performance as a trustee is combined with adroit gamesmanship and moral pretension. The doctor and the priest divert part of the money for unimpeachably good causes, but they are guilt-stricken and apologetic. The lawyer appropriates it *all*, and for himself rather than for charitable purposes, and he makes no apologies—in fact he reproaches them for betrayal and presents himself as the one who faithfully honored the old man's trust. Ironically, the arch deviant uses his formal compliance to claim the most complete fulfillment of duty.

Still, I think this joke is permeated by admiration for the lawyer. The doctor and the priest are hesitant, inhibited do-gooders who end up wasting a lot of human treasure. If they believe the deceased's crazy premise, they are perpetrating an awful betrayal. If they don't believe it, they are foolish, wasteful, crippled by their conscientiousness. In contrast with their hesitant virtue, we have the lawyer's clear, decisive assertion of self-interest. He doesn't believe it and he is free of the inhibiting sentimentality of the others. They really don't believe it either, but they can't face up to the virtue of betrayal. It is the lawyer's unblinking rationality, beneath the guise of compliance, that stuns us. Recall David Riesman's observation that lawyers "are feared and disliked—but needed—because of their matter-of-factness, their sense of relevance, their refusal to be impressed by magical 'solutions' to people's problems."[50]

So, the lawyer deviates where the others should have. He is at once a disastrous failure as a trustee, an adroit con artist—and a model of how to deal with irrational demands, in contrast to the megalomania of the deceased and the sentimental paralysis of the other advisors.[51] The deceased by denying death would destroy resources that should be left to the living. Where the doctor and the priest "balance" the claims of the deceased and of the living, the lawyer embraces the claims of the living. But ironically his unabashed assertion of the claims of the living benefits only himself, while the hesitant assertions of the doctor and the priest do benefit deserving others.

The verdict on the lawyer here is complex: it is the lawyer that has the wit to see through sham, the courage to ignore it, and the resourcefulness to figure a way

The TRIPLE PLEA.

Law, Physick, and Divinity, ——
Contend which shall Superior be.
The Lawyer pleads He is your Friend,
And will your Rights & Cause defend.
The Doctor swears (deny't who will)
That Life and Health are in his Pills.
The grave Divine, with Look demure,
To Penitents will Heaven assure.

But mark these Friends of ours & see,
Where ends their great Civility.
Without a Fee, the Lawyer's Dumb;
Without a Fee, the Doctor — Mum;
His Rev'rence says, without his Dues,
You must the Joys of Heaven lose,
Then be advis'd: In none confide;
But take Sound Reason for your Guide.

Sold by J. Jarvis, Bedford-Court, Covent-Garden.

36. The Triple Plea (BM 1775. c.1725). The classical triad of professions so familiar today in jokes—doctor, lawyer, and priest—was then depicted as representing three threats of dependence and exploitation. The verse reads: "Law, Physick, and Divinity, / Contend which shall Superior be. / The Lawyer pleads He is your Friend, / And will your Rights & Cause defend. / The Doctor swears (deny't who will) / That Life and Health are in his Pills. / The grave Divine, with Look demure, / To Penitents will Heaven assure. / But mark these friends of ours & see / Where ends their great Civility. / Without a Fee, the Lawyer's Dumb; / Without a Fee, the Doctor Mum; / The Rev'rence says, without his Dues, / You must the Joys of Heaven lose. / Then be advis'd: in none, confide; / But take Sound Reason for your Guide."

LAW, PHYSICK, and DIVINITY,
Being in dispute, could not agree
To settle which among them three,
Should have the Superiority.
LAW pleads he does preserve men's lands,
And all their goods from ruinous hands.
Therefore of right challenges He,
To have the Superiority.

PHYSICK prescribes receipts for health,
Which men prefer before their wealth:
Therefore of right challenges He,
To have the Superiority.
Then strait speaks up the PRIEST demure,
Who of mens Souls takes care and cure.
Therefore of right challenges He,
To have the Superiority.

If JUDGES end this TRIPLE PLEA,
The LAWYERS shall bear all the sway,
If EMPERICS their verdict give,
PHYSICIANS best of all will thrive.
If BISHOPS arbitrate the case,
The PRIESTS must have the highest place.
If HONEST, SOBER WISE MEN judge,
Then ALL THE THREE a man may trudge.

For let men live in peace and love,
The LAWYERS tricks they need not prove.
Let them forbear excess and riot,
They need not feed on DOCTOR'S diet.
Let them attend what GOD does teach,
They need not care what PARSONS preach.
But if men FOOLS and KNAVES will be,
They'll be Astridden by ALL THREE.

FROM THE ORIGINAL PICTURE BY JOHN COLLETT, IN THE POSSESSION OF THE PROPRIETORS.

37. The Triple Plea (BM 3761. John Collett c.1760). Another rendition of the professional triad, summed up in the oval picture of "Harpies" and the open book on the table at left which reads: "Behold these Three, too oft by Fate design'd: / To poison, plunder and delude Mankind."

to do it adroitly. At the same time, he lacks a saving common sentimentality, ignores obligations to others, and acts solely to his own advantage. The lawyer is someone with qualities we would want on our side. He is a very desirable ally, but the betrayal jokes remind us that he is one with a dangerous propensity to abandon those who rely upon him.

I regard the *take it with you* version of *check in the coffin* as the most complex and sophisticated of current jokes about lawyers. Driven by the dying man's heroic denial of death, it has a basic premise that is engaging and immediately recognizable, has a long historic pedigree, and, at some level, tempts us into wishing there was something to it. The other friends' diversion of some of the funds to altruistic uses introduces the possibility that there may be some virtue in betrayal. The lawyer then outdoes them in diversion but makes no attempt to match their rationale of an offsetting obligation. The theme of escalating altruistic diversion provides the perfect foil for the depiction of the lawyer as supplied with an excess of penetrating rationality and a deficiency of fellow feeling. We are presented with two competing but incomplete forms of exemplary deviance: the friends act on a vision of higher uses for the treasure, but stumble because they are sentimental; the lawyer fully surmounts the irrationality of the deceased and the sentimentality of the friends, but disappoints because his clear-sighted rationality is entirely devoid of the benevolence that makes the friends endearing. We are shown a world in which the components of an exemplary response to the megalomania of the deceased—rationality and benevolence—are separately embodied in flawed carriers. All the needed pieces are present, but an optimum solution eludes us because of the deformation attendant to each specialized virtue. The lawyer embodies part of what we want, but he brings it to us fused with a self-centeredness we disdain and embrace.

This *take it with you* story is the most widespread of the several distinct lines of *check in the coffin* jokes.[52] Two of the other variants are also told about lawyers.[53] In one, the deposit of the money is explained not as part of the deceased's plan for financing in the next world, but as a respectful gesture by the mourners, inspired by family tradition or cross-cultural experience.

F13   An anthropologist had been studying an obscure Thai hill tribe when he contracted a particularly virulent case of jungle rot and was dead in a week. His heartbroken widow accompanied the casket back to Milwaukee, where she invited his three best friends to attend an intimate funeral. When the brief service was over, she asked each of the friends to place an offering in the casket, as had been the custom of the tribe he had been living with."It would mean a great deal to Harry," she whispered, then broke down into racking sobs. Moved to tears himself, the first friend, a doctor, gently deposited a hundred dollars in the coffin. Dabbing his cheeks, the second friend, a stockbroker, laid a hundred and fifty dollars on the deceased Harry's pillow. The third friend, a lawyer, scribbled a check for four hundred and fifty dollars, put it in the casket, and pocketed the cash.[54]

The basic figure is the same as *take it with you:* a dead man and three friends of different professions who are obliged to place money in his coffin. But beyond that, everything changes: the money to be deposited is the mourners' rather than the dead man's; the amount is a token rather than an immense sum; the first two friends comply fully rather than partially, and they are just tearfully sentimental, not purposefully altruistic. The lawyer perfects the gamesmanship aspect by not only using a check for his own contribution but gratuitously increasing the amount to cover the friends' contributions, which he then pockets as change. Instead of sabotaging the megalomaniacal and self-serving plans of the deceased, the lawyer's extractive behavior violates the dead man's heartfelt wish, exploits the generous impulses of his friends, and adds insult to injury by a pretense of magnanimity. By subverting the sentimental gesture that warms and unites the widow and mourning friends, he announces his inability to subordinate his self-serving to even a momentary salute to fellowship.

Take it with you appears as a lawyer story in 1964, before the emergence of the jaundiced view of the legal system and before the great boom in lawyer jokes sent jokesters looking for plausible switches. The *respectful gesture* version, after a long history as a joke about groups that are cheap and canny, appears as a lawyer joke in 1990 when the great wave of lawyer jokes is flowing swiftly.[55] Another *check in the coffin* lawyer story arrived on that wave, but seems to have vanished:

F13   A lawyer confided to his partner that years ago he had cheated one of his clients out of $10,000. That client had just died. "I made amends," said the lawyer. "I went to his funeral and wrote a check for $10,000 and put it in his coffin."[56]

Here, the trio of professionals is eliminated. The comparison with specific others is replaced by comparison with an implicit generalized other and the moral condemnation is intensified. As in the *take it with you* version, it is a client that the lawyer betrays. Here, the betrayal took place long ago. Now the lawyer, recognizing that breach, purports to repair his moral stature by making amends. But his attempt to do so involves yet another deceit, further compounded by the gap between the seriousness of his intention and the emptiness of his gesture. We are left to wonder whether his account is insincere (and so he is incapable of honesty even with his partner) or whether his deceitfulness is so ingrained that he is incapable of appreciating the absurdity and hollowness of his gesture. Either way, he is incapable of repentance. We move from crafty self-seeking to moral incorrigibility. While the *take it with you* story is very widespread and the *respectful gesture* is also popular, this *make amends* story surfaced in print only twice and does not seem to be in circulation.[57]

What Do the Jokes Tell Us?

This set of jokes is one of several newcomer categories that have recently swollen the already ample corpus of lawyer jokes. None of these betrayal jokes is originally or exclusively a lawyer joke. This category does not contain a single joke that is "indigenous" to law in the sense that it arises from or depends upon distinctive features of the legal setting and is told originally, only, or mainly about lawyers. Every one has been switched from a story about some other kind of protagonist. One or two generations ago almost all of these jokes were in circulation, but they were not connected to lawyers. They were jokes about friends, companions, spouses, or business partners.

These betrayal jokes have been refashioned as lawyer jokes and repeated because they contain characterizations that tellers and listeners wanted to attach to lawyers. The jokes are not a direct reflection of people's experience with lawyers, but a screen on which they project their feelings and judgments and anxieties about lawyers and law in a world in which lawyers are increasingly prominent and increasingly inescapable. Like iron filings that reveal the presence of an unseen magnetic force, these jokes enable us to locate a powerful current of unease about lawyers in which appreciation of their cleverness, potency, and resourcefulness accentuates anxiety about their trustworthiness and loyalty.

A large portion of the jokes in the *Betrayal* cluster are adapted from jokes that were predominantly told about Jews.[58] Lawyers have joined (or displaced) Jews as objects of these stories about clever, tricky, greedy, and untrustworthy operators who do not hesitate to betray intimates, dependents, and benefactors.[59] The lawyer, like the Jew, is a liminal figure, who is defined as proficient at self-serving and deficient in loyalty, especially to outsiders. In the lawyer setting, the question arises of what is included in the self-interest that is being served? Are lawyers going to exercise their cleverness on behalf of their partners and clients? Are these intimates exempt from the lawyer's proclivity for betrayal? Or are they likely to be targets of the lawyer's treachery?

These switches are recent: lawyer versions of the *check in the coffin* and *collision and flask* surfaced in print only rarely until they were joined by the others noted here in the late 1980s and the 1990s. Assuming that there is some lag between the time a joke circulates in the oral tradition and its appearance in print, we might estimate the arrival of this cluster as at most a few years earlier. But we are talking about the late 1980s.

Why did this cluster of jokes emerge at this time? Before we embark on explaining the lawyer-betrayal joke connection, we may want additional assurance that such a connection in fact exists. We have to deal with an alternative hypothesis: could it be that with the general decline of trust, *Betrayal* jokes are spreading to many kinds of protagonists and lawyers are just one of many targets? If so, the jokes would reflect only the general lack of trust rather than something specific to law and lawyers. To test whether the spread of these jokes has been general and therefore cannot be taken as specifically registering perceptions of lawyers, I have examined the publication history of each of the *Betrayal* jokes noted in this chapter. Lawyers have become the principal protagonists of these stories in some cases and important protagonists in others; jokes about the original protagonists usually continue, but the appearance of other new protagonists like doctors, businessmen, or politicians is infrequent and sporadic. Of course it is possible that there is *another* set of *Betrayal* jokes that have attached themselves to members of other groups. All I can say is that as an observer of the joke scene I have never encountered them.

The 1980s, when these *Betrayal* jokes arrived as a small part of a great tide of lawyer jokes, was a time of falling trust and of declining confidence in institutions, including the legal system. Less trusting of others and increasingly involved in transactions with strangers, people had more need to rely on lawyers for the assurance that the legal system can provide. It was a time of great expansion of the legal profession. There was increasing resort to lawyers and they were increasingly visible in public life, an exposure that was magnified by a proliferation of imaginary lawyers in the media. Public estimation of the honesty and ethical standards of lawyers fell. The jokes were accompanied and overshadowed by a mounting tide of "serious" criticism of lawyers and the legal system for unraveling public morality and depressing the national economy.

The combination of evidence that lawyers are highly distrusted with the appearance of a new set of jokes about lawyers as betrayers of trust led me initially to assume that this reflected a heightening of anxiety among clients and potential clients about whether lawyers could be relied upon to be loyal to them. However, reexamination of the jokes themselves suggests that there is both more and less involved than fear of unfaithfulness to clients. Who is the lawyer betraying in these jokes? Of the thirteen jokes discussed in this chapter, we can discern the relation of the figures in twelve. In two (*collision and flask* [F1] and *celebrity greeting spurned* [F8]) they are strangers (often rival professionals); in eight they are partners (*safe unlocked* [F5], *payment during robbery* [F3], *beautiful house* [F7], *mine died* [F6], *poisoned you* [F10]) or other professionals involved in the same enterprise (*partner undoes wishes* [F12], *sign language* [F9], *outrun bear* [F2]).[60] The only jokes in which the primary victim is the lawyer's client are *extra $100 bill* (F4) and two of the versions of *check in the coffin* (F13).

In *extra $100 bill,* the client is an inadvertent victim, but it is the lawyer's partner who he contemplates intentionally cheating. Also, the treachery has no connection with the lawyer's service to the client; it is in connection with the fee, joining the older and larger pool of stories about the lawyer overcharging, taking everything the client has, and so forth, reviewed in chapter 2. *Check in the coffin* is more complex: in the *respectful gesture* variant, the transaction is remote from representation of a client, as the lawyer is typically described as one of the deceased's closest friends.[61] In the *making amends* variant, there is a clear but unspecified betrayal of the client. But this variant, we noted, has never achieved any popularity. That leaves the most popular variant, *take it with you.* Here the lawyer is usually identified as "his [the deceased's] lawyer."[62] So we can think of the deceased as a trusting and vulnerable client, although the service requested is personal rather than specifically professional and strains the bounds of loyalty even for devoted and unselfish friends. Indeed, the lawyer's disloyalty there, although discredited by his unabashed self-serving, wavers toward the laudable. Nevertheless this story is the *only* joke in the entire lawyer joke corpus that depicts the lawyer thwarting the client's goals (as distinguished from fleecing the client or refusing to serve the impecunious client).[63]

Even in the few jokes that depict faithlessness to clients, there is also "betrayal" of professional peers, including the lawyer's partner not receiving a share of the ill-gotten extra $100 bill and the conscientious and altruistic doctor and priest outdone by the lawyer in the *take it with you* version of *check in the coffin*. This is even more clear in the *respectful gesture* version where the lawyer rips off the offerings of the generous fellow professionals.[64] Overall, the prime target of the lawyer's treachery is his partner or professional peer. And the damage wreaked on these tends to be far more serious as professional intimacy increases. Where the client can ill afford to lose the $100 bill, the lawyers (or other professionals) in *outrun bear, poisoned you,* and *sign language* are exposed to mortal danger. To the great fund of stories about lawyers' economic exploitation of their clients, *Betrayal* jokes make a quite minor addition, but they add to the joke corpus a theme almost entirely new in joking about lawyers: the propensity to betray partners and other professionals who are not opponents, but on the "same side." I conclude then that these jokes point less to the anxieties of clients dealing with professionals than to the anxieties of professionals dealing with one another in an increasingly competitive environment.

It is not surprising that such concern should appear at a moment when the legal profession, and in particular its upper reaches, was undergoing a massive transformation. During the 1980s, the number of lawyers increased dramatically. The world of staid clubby law firms—a world of assured tenure and little lateral movement, shrouded in confidentiality, cocooned by retainers from loyal long-term clients—dissolved. It was replaced by a world of rapid growth, increased competition for clients, mergers and breakups, movement from firm to firm, fear of defection, and pervasive insecurity.[65] Collegiality was replaced by wariness. Increasingly, lawyers were competitive not only with lawyers in other firms but "with their own partners and even associates coming up the ladder."[66] Established partners might be "pushed off the iceberg" by their colleagues. No longer shrouded in confidentiality, a new intrusive legal journalism exposed the stratagems of lawyers and the operations of law firms. Lawyers lamented the loss of collegiality within firms and the decline of civility at the bar. An outpouring of books and articles bemoaned the descent of the profession from civic virtue to commercialism.[67] These *Betrayal* jokes reflect tensions within the profession at least as much as the anxieties of its customers.

To confirm this it would be helpful to know who tells these jokes. We know that a very significant part of the telling of lawyer jokes is done by lawyers themselves. Professor A. W. B. Simpson even asserts that "although other people get into the act too, it is principally lawyers who tell jokes against lawyers."[68] Although Simpson offers no support for this observation, a scatter of evidence suggests that there is more than a little truth to it. Some lawyers profess outrage at lawyer jokes, but the press coverage of the lawyer joke phenomenon contains numerous references to the interest of lawyers in lawyer jokes. The proprietor of Nolo Press, which operates one of the longest-running and best-known Web sites for lawyer jokes, reports "most of the jokes come from lawyers."[69] The embrace of lawyer jokes includes law firms using them in brochures, newsletters, and Web sites and law schools using them in alumni promotions.[70]

Lawyers are not unique in consuming and producing jokes about themselves. There is abundant evidence that "minorities" (including Jews, African Americans, Polish Americans, the Irish in England) are important producers and consumers of jokes about their own groups.[71] One explanation of this phenomenon involves intragroup differentiation. In this view "the 'better' members of the ridiculed group" enjoy jokes that display the inferiority of their less educated, less emancipated, less assimilated, less respectable cousins.[72] Thus, the point of dialect stories told by second-generation American Jews "is precisely that the subject does not stand for all Jews. Rather than being anti-Semitic it is anti-greenhorn, anti-immigrant, anti-Old-World, and possibly anti-poor." That is, such jokes reflect the situation of the uneasy "second generation American Jew . . . who wished to separate himself sharply from the unassimilated immigrant, whose ways he viewed not only as old fashioned and irrelevant, but, most important, as an obstacle to his own efforts toward acceptance by the majority culture."[73] Another student of Jewish jokes takes this as exploding the notion that Jewish humor is self-mocking or masochistic, arguing that "invariably the object of ridicule is a group with which the raconteur disassociates himself. Joke-telling is a verbal expression which manifests social differentiation."[74]

This has a ready applicability to lawyers. The more diverse and internally conflictful the lawyer category, the more occasion for lawyers to employ jokes to disassociate themselves from others. My small stock of direct information here points in this direction. I interviewed a lawyer whose four-person California firm distributed handouts of lawyer jokes with its newsletters and at meetings of potential clients. Convinced that "a big percentage of the profession are a bunch of schmucks . . . trying to take advantage of clients," he reported that he personally uses lawyer jokes in presentations and conversations with clients to disarm the endemic suspicion of lawyers: "by telling jokes about lawyers you show that you are not one of those crooks, but one of the good guys."[75] Differentiation is similarly stressed at the outset in a beautifully illustrated brochure entitled, "We Are *Not* the Enemy," distributed by a large multicity firm based in New York that depicts a series of lawyer jokes:

> Lawyer jokes. Why are they so popular? We have a theory. Too many clients today do not get the representation they want and deserve. It doesn't have to be that way.
> Anderson Kill Olick & Oshinsky is different. Since our founding in 1969, we have never wavered from our principal objective—being responsive to clients' needs.

> Every lawyer at Anderson Kill Olick & Oshinsky is committed to ensuring client satisfaction. We take that responsibility seriously—and that's no joke.[76]

Jokes are used by lawyers to tell clients they are the good guys. I suspect that they are told among lawyers themselves to similar effect, identifying those present as above the antics and shenanigans of the lawyers in the jokes.[77]

But differentiation does not exhaust the function of lawyer jokes for lawyers. Gershon Legman observed that telling jokes acts to "absorb and control, even to slough off, by means of jocular presentation and laughter, the great anxiety that both teller and listener feel in connection with certain culturally determined themes."[78] Stanley Brandes, applying this to the case of Jewish dialect jokes, finds them an expression of "the collective Jewish-American uncertainty about its ethnic identity, and its fear of committing cultural suicide."[79] Similarly, lawyers' engagement with lawyer jokes can be imagined as an expression of anxiety about the fragility of their professional identity, threatened both by massive structural changes and by unrelenting attacks from other high-status groups. Hoist by the increasing legalization of society into an uneasy ascendency, lawyers wonder whether they can retain the privileges of professionalism along with the rewards of affluence. Jokes lend themselves to this exercise because, in Davies's words, they "are *ambiguous* comic utterances without a single clear meaning, and their relation to aggression or fear is variable and problematic. . . . Tendentiousness is not a quality of a joke as such but a quality of the teller. It is the teller who decides by choice of tone and context whether he or she is playing at or with aggression and whether the play is rough or friendly." Jokes enable us "to construct safe mock versions of real fears both to amuse [ourselves] and others. . . . Depending on context, one and the same joke can either inflame fears or else domesticate and master them."[80]

Although they attack lawyers, many lawyer jokes are infused with the sense that lawyers are clever, powerful, and important. Lawyer jokes offer a particularly appealing way of displaying these things because of a curious glitch in the culture that directs joking up the status scale rather than down. It has frequently been observed that lawyers are one of the groups that can be attacked without worry about offending norms of political correctness. *The Economist* observed that "the level of hostile humour" directed at lawyers "has increased noticeably since racist jokes went out of fashion. The sorts of jokes which, in less enlightened time, were directed at ethnic groups are now more commonly aimed at lawyers, particularly in America."[81] But this realignment has a curious effect."Those who are *fair* game for . . . ridicule" are those at high end of the status ladder: "men, WASPs, vocationally successful, physically slim, beautiful women and handsome men."[82] Since it is "incorrect" to ridicule down, being singled out as an acceptable target of jokes is a sign of high status and has the ultimate effect of boosting rather than lowering status. So lawyers' affable self-disparagement in turn translates into an assertion of status: we have so much status we can endure a firestorm of jokes.

A. W. B. Simpson observes that "all these jokes and criticisms make indirect reference to the supposed ideals of the legal profession. They presuppose these ideals; indeed they are indirect statements of them, coupled with the claim that lawyers in reality do not live up to them."[83] This observation fits many sorts of lawyer jokes, including those discussed in this chapter. I am less certain that it can be extended to other kinds of lawyer jokes, such as the *Objects of Scorn* and *Death Wish* jokes discussed in the following chapters. The "ideals" in question in our *Betrayal* jokes are the collegiality and faithfulness of lawyers in their dealings among themselves, a matter of low visibility and salience to others. This doesn't mean that these jokes are told by or appreciated only or mostly by lawyers. For others, these stories augment their sense of the quirks and transgressions of lawyers. One message that could be extracted is that these are guys you have to watch out for, for they have no compunction about doing in their own. If lawyers are such tricky and unprincipled guys, with a proclivity to turn on those close to them, a certain wariness may be justified. But it strikes me as significant that when imagination ranges freely, it envisions lawyers betraying other professionals rather than clients. Hearers may be amused and appalled at this portrait of ruthless instrumentalism, but it is less clear that they are threatened by it.

An Excess of Loyalty?

The *check in the coffin* should remind us that faithfulness to clients is a respectable virtue, but not necessarily the ultimate good. Students of legal ethics engage in intense debate about the extent and boundaries of the lawyer's obligation of loyalty to the client.[84] In a discussion of the contemporary wave of lawyer jokes, Roger Cramton suggests that in the eyes of the public the profession's problem is not disloyalty to clients, but excessive loyalty. Although he views public antipathy as unavoidable because it is the lawyer's role to be bearer of the bad news of "society's internal dissonance and division,"[85] he assigns part of the blame for the current upsurge of hostility to the ethos of the profession: "The dominant professional view has a normative structure that gives highest priority to loyalty to client and abhors betrayal of clients."[86] Cramton thinks that the bar's "self-centered and immoral position" against disclosure of client fraud is "at variance with general morality" and leads to "problems of overrepresentation and excessive zeal that properly concern the public."[87] Is the public actually exercised about this problem? The jokes that Cramton discusses do not raise the issue, and the joke corpus as a whole supplies only faint evidence of concern. There is a long line of jokes ridiculing the lawyer's eager and easy embrace of the client and his cause, the tendency of the lawyer to go "over the top" for the client and to be carried away by the momentum of his own argument.[88] But such jokes have been a placid backwater hardly disturbed by the great flood of contemporary joking about lawyers.

The notion that public animus against lawyers stems from their unqualified devotion to clients might seem to gain support from the 1997 film *The Devil's Advocate*, which updates the image of the lawyer as a confederate of the devil by promoting that worthy to managing partner of a Wall Street firm. What is it about lawyers that makes them so devilish? The film's answer is clear: greed is subsidiary; the distinctive sin of the lawyer is the love of winning which leads him to defeat justice by placing his preternatural cleverness in the service of the guilty. Lawyers' indiscriminate embrace of clients' unjust causes to feed their passion for winning is the sin of vanity. Pursuing victory for the loathsome client leads the brilliant young lawyer into the embrace of the devil, who is also, it turns out, his father.[89] (The way out of his grasp is unclear, for the ambiguous ending of the film suggests that the young lawyer's dramatic abandonment of the detestable client may be a more subtle pursuit of vanity, equally pleasing to the devil.)

On another screen at the local multiplex in 1997 was John Grisham's *The Rainmaker* (1997) in which a novice lawyer working out of a sleazy office develops an intense familial intimacy with his poor, vulnerable, and misused clients and becomes their guardian angel.[90] The lawyer's heroic role is built not on his untried and uneven skills, but on the intensity and purity of his identification with his clients. Utterly loyal to them, he is willing to lie, cheat, and steal where necessary to vindicate their rights, overcoming the fierce opposition of (equally unscrupulous) lawyers knowingly abetting a cruel and avaricious insurance swindle.[91]

It is no easier to extract an unambiguous message from a film than from a joke, and it is at least equally questionable how adequately it represents public opinion. Nevertheless, let me venture that the two films, taken together, seem to say that it is commendable for lawyers to go "over the top" for clients who are genuinely deserving victims, but abominable to do so for bad guys. Survey evidence shows that people are aware that villains are entitled to lawyers and that "somebody phas to do it," but many have reservations about the zeal of such representation.[92] People are distressed about lawyers' willingness to defend the guilty, but they are reluctant to condemn lawyers for going all out for their clients, even sleazy ones.[93] These movies concur with the survey evidence that the characteristic of lawyers that most engages Americans is lawyers' loyalty, zeal, and commitment to the client. But public estimation of the level of commitment that is present and that is desirable depends at least in part on the characteristics of the client.[94] As we shall see, the problem of the lawyer's level of engagement shades into the problems of disparities in the distribution of legal services.

CHAPTER 7

The Lawyer as Morally Deficient

The lawyer's problematic moral standing was long ago codified in terms of an association with the devil. Since the 1980s, this line of jokes has been renewed and expanded, as detailed in chapter 3. This period has seen an even greater growth in jokes about the moral deficiencies of lawyers that are phrased in a more secular idiom.

A Suspect Profession

Although lawyers enjoy high professional status, the nagging suspicions surrounding their moral standing that were manifested in the association with the devil and sin did not pass with the waning of belief in postmortem reckoning. Instead, doubts about the moral condition of lawyers have been restated in secular terms:

G1   Judge W—, who had been for many years a worthy occupant of the Federal bench in Michigan, fell into conversation a few days since in a barber's shop, with a plain, substantial looking, and rather aged stranger, from the neighborhood of Tecumseh. The judge being formerly well acquainted in that vicinity, took occasion to ask after certain of its citizens. "You know Mr. B. do you?" said the judge. "Very well!" was the reply. "He is well, is he?" "Quite well!" was the answer. Judge W. then remarked: "Mr. B. is a very fine man!" "Y-e-s!" said the old man," rather cautiously; "a fine man for a lawyer—you know we don't expect a great deal from them!"[1]

That beneath their exalted professional status lawyers are really indistinguishable from their most despised clients is implied by the popular play on the term "criminal lawyer." The classic is the exchange:

G3   Have you a criminal lawyer in this burg?
      We think so but we haven't been able to prove it on him.[2]

Other versions simplify the response to an epithet:

G3   "My uncle is a criminal lawyer."
        "Aren't they all?"[3]

Or simply

G3   "criminal lawyer" is redundant.[4]

Others add a New Age twist:

G3   What do you call an attorney who describes himself as a criminal lawyer?
        Self-aware.[5]

The convergence may be appreciated even by those who are empathic rather than hostile:

G3   "I understand your son, John, is an attorney?"
        "Yes, he is out west, and he's got lots of business," she answered with a mother's pride.
        "Is he a criminal lawyer?"
        "No, not yet," she said, as a shadow fell upon her wrinkled face. "Leastwise he ain't told me. But I'm afraid he will be. The law is so dreadfully tempting."[6]

Another common deflation of the lawyer's claim to status and respect is comparison with the "oldest profession." Such an equation is suggested in the following story, more frequently told of doctors:

G5   A young lawyer, walking along the street with his wife on his arm, was greeted by a beautiful young lady. The jealous young wife asked him who his girl friend was. "Can't remember her name," he said. "Just a girl I met professionally."
        "Whose profession, dear, yours or hers?"[7]

Although this story predates the current surge of antilawyer sentiment, the comparison with prostitution seems to have initially arrived in the United States soon after World War Two. It is tenacious because it resonates with three separate themes. First, the lawyer, eager for fortune and fame and bolstered by the maxim that even the most dastardly wrongdoer deserves zealous representation, is not fastidious about the clients he embraces. Chicago lawyer Don Reuben used to delight in telling law students: "A good lawyer is like a good prostitute. If the price is right you warm up to your client."[8] Others are less enthused by the parallel. An idealistic lawyer reported her frustration: "I was taught that a good lawyer can advocate any position; only a poor lawyer chooses her side. . . . But if that is so, then a good lawyer must be like a prostitute, who works well for anyone who pays her."[9] Second, the lawyer is seen as pliable and complaisant—a hired gun directed not by an inner compass but the dictates of the client. Finally, both prostitute and lawyer are seen as victimizing their clients.

The lawyer-prostitute equation is occasionally elaborated in extended lists. The polemic of an early twentieth-century Indian reformer compares the operations of "dancing girls" to those of *vakils* (attorneys) (table 1). Many of the items in his "serious" list are echoed in the "humorous" list circulating among contemporary American law firm associates (table 2).

Comparison of lawyers and prostitutes, to the disadvantage of the former, occurs in narrative jokes as well as a whole set of riddles:

G6   A lawyer had scheduled a business trip to New York, and a colleague has suggested he call on Miss Agatha Jane Foote while in town. "It'll be an unforgettable experience," the colleague promised. "She's no ordinary trollop, I assure you."

The first night of his New York stay, the lawyer took a cab and got out in front of one of the finest brownstones on Fifth Avenue. He rang the bell, and a maid ushered him in. After presenting his card, he was led into an elegantly furnished drawing room and invited to make himself comfortable. Miss Foote would be down shortly.

While waiting, the lawyer stepped over to a huge floor-to-ceiling bookcase and examined the gilt-bound works. Among the many tomes was a twenty-volume set of Corpus Jurus [sic].

A few moments later, Miss Foote stepped down the curved staircase in a most elegant evening gown. The lawyer stood stunned. She was indeed gorgeous!

But he was further stunned to find Miss Foote's conversation urbane, charming, and witty. He turned to the bookcase and remarked, "Miss Foote, I notice a set of Corpus Jurus [sic] on your shelves. Did you ever study law?"

"Yes," she replied, "I'm a graduate of the Columbia Law School."

"Is that so?" the lawyer continued. "Then how did you ever get into this business?"

"Oh!" Miss Foote shrugged, "I must have been very lucky."[10]

G7   What's the difference between a prostitute and a lawyer?
Nothing. You pay them both to screw you.[11]

Or

G8   A prostitute stops screwing you after you die.[12]

Or

G9   A prostitute doesn't pretend to care.[13]

The lawyer's pliability was an asset if not a virtue in *two plus two* (A33) where the lawyer responded, "How much do you want it to be?" But it can also signify the lawyer's utter lack of principle:

G10   What is the difference between a successful lawyer and a down-and-out-hooker?
There are some things a hooker just WILL NOT do for money.[14]

The prostitute, even though "down and out," preserves some remnant of natural virtue while the lawyer, despite being insulated by success, is unresisting in his abandonment of principle.[15] The comparison faintly echoes the trope of the prostitute with a heart of gold, the roots of which go back at least as far as the New

TABLE 1. A Comparison between the Vakils and the Dancing-girls [India, 1926].

1. Both insist on prepayment of less invariably and will never do business on Credit.

2. The Vakils sell their conscience for money.	2. The Dancing-girls sell their chastity for money.
3. The Vakils really care little for the interests of their clients.	3. The dancing-girls have no true love for their customers.
4. The Vakils engage touts and brokers in their service.	4. The dancing-girls engage go-betweens to run their trade in flesh.
5. Though retained wholesale by one for all his cases, yet would they take up cases from another.	5. Though engaged by one man, they would secretly welcome others.
6. Being always selfish, they will not care for the hardships and inconveniences of their clients.	6. Caring only for their own gains, they have little regard for the difficulties and anxieties of their customers.
7. The litigant world places implicit trust in Vakils.	7. The merry lovers place implicit faith in the dancing-girls.

8. Both never realize other's difficulties and wants. The greater the acquaintance with them, the greater the danger from them. They will boldly seize opportunities to grab the riches of others and convert them into beggars. Of course, there are rare exceptions among both classes. Just as there are honest men among Vakils, so there are honest women among the dancing-girls.

9. Both pile up their riches by causing ruin to families and hence their wealth does not last long.

10. Neither has any scruples whatever regarding the blood-relationship of those with whom they deal. Father and son may resort to one and the same Vakil or dancing-girl.

11. Vakils make a pompous display of their Law-books and Law Reports in courts.	11. Dancing-girls parade their jewels and skills in festivals and entertainments.
12. Vakils plead in proportion to their fees.	12. Dancing-girls love in proportion to the money paid them.
13. The pomp of Vakils consists in their big Law-Books and Reports beautifully arranged in glass almirahs.	13. The pomp of Dancing-girls lies in their drawing rooms furnished with velvet spring-Cots, Sofas, Pictures and the like.
14. Vakils are cordial and beam with smiles to their clients till they knock out their fees, but afterwards grow cold and contemptuous.	14. Dancing-girls deceive customers with an overflow of love during the first moments of their engagement, but afterwards turn them out without mercy.
15. Clients are taken in by the false hopes of success given by Vakils and stake their all in the protection of a case to spite their enemies.	15. Dancing-girls hide their defects and rotten diseases under Silk petti coats and Saries and fleece their customers of their last pie by flatteries and false love.
16. Vakils breed crime and litigation by rousing hatred and passion by their professional advice. Murders, riots, forgeries and family quarrels are mainly due to Vakils.	16. Dancing-girls kindle jealousies and passions by their curtain lectures and create dissensions in families and between friends resulting in murder, suicide, etc.

SOURCE: Mani 1926: chap. 14.

Testament. It also resonates with a broader reproach, whose literary apotheosis is found in George Bernard Shaw's *Mrs. Warren's Profession* (1894). The argument, as Shaw tells us in the preface, is that "we have great prostitute classes of men: for instance, dramatists and journalists, to whom I myself belong, not to mention the legions of lawyers, doctors, clergymen and platform politicians who are daily using their highest faculties to belie their real sentiments: a sin compared to which that of a woman who sells the use of her person for a few hours is too venial to be worth mentioning; for rich men without convictions are more dangerous in modern society than poor women without chastity."[16] A century later, law professor Paul Campos suggests that "lawyers are often compelled by their professional obligations to become something akin to emotional prostitutes; that is, to be persons whose public personae require the simulation of inauthentic affective states as a condition of their compensation. In . . . litigation the most common of these simulated emotions is outrage."[17] The lawyer's readiness to take up causes that "belie

TABLE 2. E-mail Circulating among Law Firm Associates (U.S., 1999).

Are you a prostitute or are you an associate at a law firm?

1. You work very odd hours.
2. You are paid a lot of money to keep your client happy.
3. You are paid well but your pimp gets most of the money.
4. You spend a majority of your time in a hotel room.
5. You charge by the hour but your time can be extended.
6. You are not proud of what you do.
7. Creating fantasies for your clients is rewarded.
8. It's difficult to have a family.
9. You have no job satisfaction.
10. If a client beats you up, the pimp just sends you to another client.
11. You are embarrassed to tell people what you do for a living.
12. People ask you, "What do you do?" and you can't explain it.
13. Your client pays for your hotel room plus your hourly rate.
14. Your client always wants to know how much you charge and what they get for the money.
15. Your pimp drives nice cars like Mercedes or Jaguars.
16. Your pimp encourages drinking and you become addicted to drugs to ease the pain of it all.
17. You know the pimp is charging more than you are worth but if the client is foolish enough to pay it's not your problem.
18. When you leave to go to see a client, you look great, but return looking like hell (compare your appearance on Monday A.M. to Friday P.M.).
19. You are rated on your "performance" in an excruciating ordeal.
20. Even though you get paid the big bucks, it's the client who walks away smiling.
21. The client always thinks your "cut" of your billing rate is higher than it actually is, and in turn, expects miracles from you.
22. When you deduct your "take" from your billing rate, you constantly wonder if you could get a better deal with another pump.

SOURCE: Laura Macaulay, e-mail message to author, June 9, 1999.

[his] real sentiments" depreciates the currency of speech just as the prostitute depreciates the external signs of love. Devotion that flows from contrivance rather than conviction arouses contempt, as expressed in a comparison that assesses the lawyer's expertise:

J15   A lawyer is an expert on justice like a prostitute is an expert on love.[18]

At the bottom of the prostitute analogy is the accusation of betrayal of justice. As one outspoken critic put it at the high point of New Left attacks on the legal system: "The system of justice, and most especially the legal profession, is a whorehouse serving those best able to afford the luxuries of justice offered to preferred customers. The lawyer, in these terms, is analogous to the prostitute. The difference between the two is simple. The prostitute is honest—the buck is her aim. The lawyer is dishonest—he claims that justice, service to mankind, is his primary purpose."[19]

The response to this is to cut back the claims of lawyering from serving justice by direct pursuit to serving it through acting as advocate, "special friend," and confidant of the client in an adversary system in which justice emerges from the clash of loyal partisans.[20] But critics point out that lawyers "do what they do not, like friends, for ineffable reasons but coolly for cold cash. . . . Most people do find some critical moral distinction lurking in the difference between the motives of the lover and those of the whore."[21] The response to this in turn, less often essayed, is to redefine prostitution as a high calling, worthy of at least metaphoric embrace. Charles Curtis, in his essay that scandalized ethical pillars of the profession by conceding that lawyers sometimes lie for their clients, extols law as a career that offers the greatest opportunity "for both the enjoyment of virtue and the exercise of vice, or, if you please, the exercise of virtue and the enjoyment of vice, except possibly the ancient rituals which were performed in some temples by vestal virgins, in others by sacred prostitutes."[22]

Looking Out for Number One

In their everyday profane activities, lawyers are portrayed as being acquisitive and grasping:

G12   Smithfield said to his wife, "It is about time we found out what Matthew wants to be when he grows up. Watch this."
He put a $10 bill on the table and explained, "That represents a banker."
Next to it he put a brand new Bible. "This represents a minister."
Beside that he placed a bottle of whiskey. "That represents a bum!"
The two of them then hid where they could watch the table without being seen. Pretty soon Matthew walked into the room, whistling, and noticed the three things on the table. He looked around to check that he was alone. Not seeing anyone, he picked up the money, held it to the light, then put it back down. He then thumbed through the Bible, and put that down. Then he quickly uncorked the bottle and smelled its contents.

In one quick motion, he stuffed the money into his pocket, put the Bible under his arm, chugged down the contents of the bottle, and walked out of the room, still whistling.

The father turned to his wife and whispered, "How about that? He's going to be a lawyer!"[23]

This was exclusively a joke about politicians from at least 1907, but since 1989 it has been a lawyer joke, perhaps marking the advent of an image of lawyers as people of unrestrained and voracious appetite.[24] It is one of a set of jokes that have been switched from politicians to lawyers.[25]

If the lawyer is grasping, his reach is for the superficial and materialistic, traits commonly associated with yuppies.

G13   The ambulance rushed to the scene of the accident where a lawyer lay amid the wreckage.

"Stay calm," said the paramedic, working frantically. "You've had a serious crackup."

"Oh, my Jag . . ." he moaned. "My poor, poor car."

"Look," said the paramedic. "I wouldn't worry about your car. Your left arm's been ripped off!"

The lawyer groaned, "Oh, my Rolex! My poor, poor Rollie!"[26]

This story was told about lawyers and other yuppies by 1990.[27]

Lawyers are depicted as single-mindedly self-serving, indifferent to their obligations to others, and willing to sacrifice others to achieve their ends.

G14   Two law partners were fanatically competitive golfers, letting absolutely nothing get in the way of their Saturday game. One Saturday Mrs. Jones grew increasingly anxious as dusk fell with no sign of her husband. As dinnertime came and went, she paced before the window, frantic with worry. Finally she heard the car pull into the driveway and rushed out. "Where've you been?" she cried. "I've been worried sick!"

"Harry had a heart attack on the third hole," her husband explained.

"Oh my God! That's terrible!" she gasped.

"You're telling me," agreed Jones. "All afternoon it was hit the ball, drag Harry, hit the ball, drag Harry. . . ."[28]

This is a well-known joke about fanatical golfers that is found all over the English speaking world.[29] When told of golfers, it depicts an obsession that eclipses the normal reaction of aiding a fallen friend. When the golfers are identified as lawyers, the lapse expresses a broader moral insensibility (nicely contrasted here with the concern and sympathy of the wife).

Not surprisingly, the lawyer is capable of lethal indifference to strangers, even famously virtuous ones.

G15   A corporate lawyer and Mother Theresa get stranded in a desert. Two weeks later, a rescue plane lands. The pilot finds Mother Theresa dead, while the lawyer is calmly resting with his hands under his head.

"This is awful," the pilot says. "Mother Theresa dead!"

"Yeah."

"Tell me, how come you survived and she didn't?"

The lawyer shrugs. "She never found the water hole."[30]

In contrast with Mother Theresa, who exemplifies selflessness, the lawyer is greedy, competitive, and lacking any sense of fellowship or generosity of spirit. This story of the lawyer's unwillingness to share information vital to survival mirrors (or mocks?) the lawyer's professional obligation to maintain the confidences of the client heedless of the social costs. The joke echoes the moral disapproval of the lawyer who claims he can't inform the police about the location of bodies because of his obligation to his client.[31]

His old friend the devil is enlisted to dramatize the lawyer's willingness to sacrifice others for his own aggrandizement:

G16   A lawyer is working late at night on a difficult case when in a puff of smoke the devil appears to him. The devil offers to make him the most powerful, wealthiest lawyer in the history of the world.

"I'll bet," says the lawyer, "and all I have to do is give you my soul."

"No," says the devil, "I only ask the right to damn to eternal suffering the souls of your wife and two young children!"

The man is dumbstruck, thinks for a moment, then looks at the devil. "All right," he says, "but what's the catch?"[32]

This joke is told mostly about lawyers, but occasionally about agents and others.[33] As a lawyer joke, this story has passed through two phases. When it first appeared in 1990, the devil proposed a straightforward Faustian bargain in which the lawyer would enjoy worldly success in exchange for his soul.[34] In this Faustian version, the lawyer's "what's the catch?" confirms his affinity for the devil. But starting in 1993, renditions like the one above emerged, in which horrors are visited on wives, children, and other innocents while the lawyer emerges unscathed. The new version shifts the focus from being the devil's playmate to the lawyer's horrifying indifference to those closest to him.[35]

No Redeeming Social Value

The unwillingness of the lawyer to extend himself for others betrays a deficient grasp of shared moral understandings about desert and obligation:

G19   The lawyer is standing at the gate to Heaven and St. Peter is listing his sins:

(1) Defending a large corporation in a pollution suit where he knew they were guilty.

(2) Defending an obviously guilty murderer because the fee was high.

(3) Overcharging fees to many clients.

(4) Prosecuting an innocent woman because a scapegoat was needed in a controversial case.

And the list goes on for quite a while.

The lawyer objects and begins to argue his case. He admits all these things, but argues, "Wait, I've done some charity in my life also."

St. Peter looks in his book and says, "Yes, I see. Once you gave a dime to a panhandler and once you gave an extra nickel to the shoeshine boy, correct?" The lawyer gets a smug look on his face and replies, "Yes."

St. Peter turns to the angel next to him and says, "Give this guy fifteen cents and tell him to go to hell."[36]

This is an old and widespread story about a miserly rich man whose refusal to take up his obligations to others is matched by St. Peter's refusal to accept the sufficiency of his token acts of charity.[37] It appeared as a lawyer joke in 1987, when a major part of the legal profession was enjoying unprecedented prosperity. Lawyers in the upper echelons of the profession, who had always been comfortable, could aspire to be rich. Although in the UK, Australia, and India this joke remains a story about a rich man, in the United States it has become predominantly a joke about lawyers.

G20   Mr. Wilson was the chairman of the United Way, which had never received a donation from the most successful lawyer in town. He called on the attorney in an attempt to make him mend his ways. "Our research shows that you made a profit of over $600,000 last year, and yet you have not given a dime to the community charities! What do you have to say for yourself?" The lawyer replied, "Do you know that my mother is dying of a long illness, and has medical bills that are several times her annual income? Do you know about my brother, the disabled veteran, who is blind and in a wheelchair? Do you know about my sister, whose husband died in a traffic accident, leaving her with three children?" The charity solicitor admitted that he had no knowledge of any of this. "Well, since I don't give any money to them, why should I give any to you?"[38]

This is an even more recent switch, appearing as a lawyer joke in 1991, after a career as a Jewish joke in which it migrated from its old country setting, underwent Americanization, and finally had the Jewish element effaced entirely.[39] The switch to lawyers occurred in the 1990s, when lawyers (or at least the upper echelons of the profession) were increasingly affluent—a condition displeasing to the public.[40]

In the following version the joke is re-Judaized: [41]

G20   A local Jewish Federation office realized that it had never received a donation from the town's most successful lawyer. The campaign director called the lawyer to persuade him to contribute: "Our research shows that out of a yearly income of at least $500,000, you give not a penny to tzedaka [charity]. Wouldn't you like to give back to the community in some way?"

The lawyer mulled this over for a moment and replied: "First, did your research also show that my mother is dying after a long illness, and has medical bills that are several times her annual income?"

Embarrassed, the Federation person mumbled, "Um . . . No."

The lawyer continued: "Or that my brother, a disabled veteran, is blind and confined to a wheelchair?"

The stricken Federation worker began to stammer out an apology.

The lawyer interrupted her apology, saying: "or that my sister's husband died in a traffic accident," the lawyer's voice rising in indignation, "Leaving her penniless with three children?!"

The humiliated Campaign director, completely beaten, said simply, "I had no idea. . . ."

On a roll, the lawyer cut her off once again: "So, if I don't give any money to them, why should I give any money to you?"[42]

The lawyer reveals his appalling indifference to family, but this is less an accusation that lawyers neglect their families than a convenient conventional measure of moral callousness.[43] The story also affords a showcase for the lawyer to display his rhetorical skill and turn the tables on the intrusive fundraiser.

38. St Dunstan Triumphant or The Big Wigs Defeated (BM 14636. Williams 1824). Lawyers' lack of charity is depicted in this struggle between a monk (St. Dunstan) and parishioners seeking to collect the parish poor rates from the Serjeants Inn. The lawyers, aided by the Devil, seek to uphold their claim that their establishment was exempt from parish poor-rates. The engraving was inspired by a newspaper report of the upholding of the lawyers' claims.

Even when he attempts to be charitable, the lawyer can't rise above self-interest.

G21   One afternoon, a wealthy lawyer was riding in the back of his limousine when he saw
       two men eating grass by the road side. He ordered his driver to stop and he got out to
       investigate. "Why are you eating grass?" he asked one man.
          "We don't have any money for food," the poor man replied.
          "Oh come along with me then."
          "But sir, I have a wife with two children!"
          "Bring them along! And you, come with us too," he said to the other man.
          "But sir, I have a wife with six children!"
          "Bring them as well!"
          They all climbed into the car, which was no easy task, even for a car as large as the
       limo. Once underway, one of the poor fellows says, "Sir, you are too kind. Thank you for
       taking all of us with you."
          The lawyer replied, "No problem, the grass at my home is about two feet tall."[44]

Most of these moral obtuseness stories portray the lawyer as deficient in common moral understandings rather than as the proponent of an alternative vision. But consider the following:

G22   One lovely spring morning a doctor, a priest and a lawyer are on the third hole at the
       Country Club and are fuming with impatience at the slow foursome just ahead of them.
       When they complain to a club official who happens by, he explains that the players
       ahead are the first blind golfers to play the course. The doctor, expressing his admiration
       for their determination, sheepishly says he's sorry for his impatience. The priest asks
       forgiveness for his failure to appreciate their special needs. The lawyer, however, is
       unappeased: "It's wonderful that they can play," he tells the official, "but why don't
       you make them play at night?"[45]

On the surface this is a moral obtuseness joke. The lawyer lacks the empathy and magnanimity that induces the others to tolerate a minor inconvenience to allow the disabled to share in the pleasures of golf. Unlike them, he refuses to write off an increment of well-being or advantage and proposes a more "efficient" solution that uses otherwise idle resources. But his solution is efficient at the expense of demeaning the recipients. It is rational, but not infused with empathy, fellow feeling, or generosity. So although the lawyer here is not exclusively self-regarding (like the lawyer in the *check in the coffin* [F13] story), he displays some of the same excessive rationality.

Play at night, like *check in the coffin*, portrays the lawyer as pursuing "rational" solutions impervious to the sentimental appeal of the obvious (but costly) solution. These stories are the contrary of those discourse stories that portray lawyers as obfuscating and bombastic. Here it is lawyers' cold rationality and lack of sentiment that puts us off.[46]

"HE JUST DOESN'T GET IT"

It has been argued that lawyers are morally challenged, that they do not share the general appreciation of moral obligation that others take for granted. (Indeed it is this that enables them to "come up with something to say" in behalf of the most hopeless causes and most odious clients.)

G23   Templeton was a loathsome young man, but one with such an orderly mind and clear grasp of the tax code that his year's billings were approaching the ten-million dollar mark, far exceeding those of any other junior partner. Yet his conduct was such that one day the president of the firm called him in for a reprimand.

"Your behavior and moral standards are reprehensible," the executive pointed out sternly. "You cheat on your expense account, you miss no chance to backstab the other junior partners, you've embezzled a substantial amount from the company, you get kickbacks from half your clients, and I just found out you've been sleeping with my wife. Now I'm warning you, Templeton—a few more missteps, and you're out!"[47]

This item, from one of the most influential topical collections of lawyer jokes, inadvertently provides a snapshot of switching in progress. The joke, current since at least the 1920s, typically about a bookkeeper, accountant, or business partner,[48] was switched to lawyers in the late 1980s. The version here musters such lawyerly terms as billings and clients, but negligently retains "president," "executive," and "company"—terms completely inappropriate in the law firm setting in which the story is supposedly placed. Subsequent versions discarded these anomalies.

The story has a message beyond the contrast between the senior's stern warning and the atrociously low standards demonstrated by his past toleration. One of the constants in the various versions of this story is the element of sexual aggression: the employee has ravished the senior's wife or daughter. By reacting so mildly to these provocations, the senior shows a readiness to subordinate his male honor to the bottom line. The switch of this story to lawyers has simply not "taken." Lawyers are regarded as devious and unfeeling, but lack of "balls" or insufficiency of aggression is not a point that supports jokes about lawyers.

G24   "Tell me," said the personnel director of a large corporation, "are you an honest attorney?"

"Honest?" the lawyer replied. "Let me tell you something. My father lent me ten thousand dollars for my education, and I paid him back in full after my very first case."

"I'm impressed," he said. "And what case was that?"

The attorney squirmed slightly. "He sued me for the money."[49]

This story, an indigenous joke that is told only about lawyers, arrived on the scene by 1982 at the outset of the great boom in lawyer jokes and has flourished since. It neatly combines the theme that the lawyer is no respecter of family obligations with his adeptness in putting a positive spin on a discrediting story.

The following story shows a lawyer who doesn't "get it" in another realm:

G25 The comely redhead was thrilled to have obtained a divorce and dazzled by the skill and virtuosity of her lawyer, not to mention his healthy income and good looks. In fact, she realized, she had fallen head over heels in love with him, even though he was a married man.

"Oh, Sam," she sobbed at the conclusion of the trial, "isn't there some way we can be together, the way we were meant to be?"

Shaking her by the shoulders, Sam proceeded to scold her roundly for her lack of discretion and good judgment. "Snatched drinks in grimy bars on the edge of town, lying on the phone, hurried meetings in sordid motel rooms—is that really what you want for us?"

"No . . . no . . ." she sobbed, heartsick.

"Oh," said the lawyer. "Well, it was just a suggestion."[50]

*"Stop making such a case of it!
A lot of young lawyers kick their fathers out of their law firms!"*

39. Cartoon by Boris Drucker in S. Gross, ed., *Lawyers! Lawyers! Lawyers!* (© Boris Drucker 1994)

IN THE LABORATORY

The single most prevalent of all current lawyer jokes is a story that sprawls across our categories:

G26 Why have research laboratories started using lawyers instead of rats in their experiments? There are three reasons: first, there are more of them; second, the lab assistants don't get attached to them; and third, there are some things a rat just won't do.[51]

The rats joke is a genuine innovation. The first printed version that I have found appeared in Tom Blair's column in the *San Diego Union-Tribune*, October 18, 1984:

G26 M. J. Crowley contends lawyers are replacing laboratory rats in popularity among scientific researchers. "There are more of them," says Crowley, "and you don't get so attached to them."

The preexisting item "some things a rat (or pig or prostitute) just won't do"[52] was soon added, and the joke in its canonical form—setup (a question in riddle versions) and three-part response—first appears in print in 1986.[53] This addition raises the critical ante. Stuart Taylor, a well-known commentator on the profession, asks: "So what is it that a white rat won't do, but many lawyers will do? . . . The joke rings true to a lot of people because of what many lawyers in this country—including many at the top of the profession—do for their clients: bend, distort, conceal, cover up, obfuscate, or misrepresent the facts, in ways that are simultaneously (1) regarded by ordinary people as just plain dishonest, and (2) defended by many lawyers and legal experts as embodying the finest traditions of the bar, and of legal ethics in our adversary system."[54]

The joke has been considerably elaborated, adding many invidious comparisons: rats are smarter, better looking, have feelings, and more dignity; lawyers are cheaper, more expendable, less missed, more harmful to society, arouse less compassion, and so forth. Starting in the early 1990s, some versions added a wonderful coda:

G26 One problem, though, is that no one has been able to extrapolate the test results to human beings.[55]

So many new elements were added that the 1998 Lawyer Joke-a-Day Calendar featured the rats joke in ten separate items.[56] In other media, the joke has metastasized into a comic list. Two examples provide an anthology of antilawyer sentiments:

G26   Why do behavioral scientists prefer lawyers to rats for their experiments?
   (1) There are more of the lawyers to work with; (2) lawyers are more expendable; (3) lawyers do more harm to society than rats; (4) lab assistants are less likely to develop a bond or feel sympathy for them; (5) rats arouse more feelings of compassion and humanity; (6) they multiply faster; (7) rats have an innate right to life and liberty; (8) animal rights groups will not object to their torture; (9) rats have more dignity; and (10) there are some things even a rat won't do.

40. An illustration of the Laboratory Rats joke in a law firm brochure depicts the caged lawyer with briefcase and Yuppie amenities including brie, Perrier, and a Rolex watch. (Illustration by Mark A. Frederickson for Anderson Kill Olick & Oshinsky brochure)

What is the only disadvantage to using lawyers instead of rats in laboratory experiments?

It's harder to extrapolate the test results to human beings.[57]

G26   TOP TEN REASONS WHY LAWYERS SHOULD REPLACE LAB RATS

10. There is an endless supply.
 9. Lab assistants don't get attached to them.
 8. It's more fun to shave and stick needles in lawyers.
 7. There are some things rats just won't do.
 6. It's fun to dispose of them when you're through.
 5. It's not "inhumane" treatment, when it comes to lawyers.
 4. No one cares when a lawyer squeals.
 3. We've seen what happens when they are allowed to breed freely.
 2. Lawyers belong in cages.

And the #1 reason lawyers should replace lab rats:

 1. Animal rights activists don't care if you torture them.[58]

Laboratory rats is frequently told by public speakers, often by lawyers themselves. It was one of the jokes most frequently recorded by researcher Jennifer Pierce in her 1988–89 interviews of secretaries, paralegals, and lawyers in the San Francisco Bay Area.[59] It has gained currency all over the English-speaking world.[60] In many of these foreign tellings, especially in Britain, it is presented as a report of developments in the United States, sparing (and perhaps warning) local lawyers.

The equation with rats is hardly confined to this story. Under the nom de plume of "The Rodent," a West Coast lawyer has satirized the profession in books and columns in legal newspapers.[61] An article in the *New York Times* reported that "the Internet is swarming with lawyer-rat animations."[62] When the new premises of a prominent Washington law firm were overrun with rats, a client, playing off another emblematic lawyer joke (B29), quipped: "You'd think . . . that the rats would only show up after business hours—as a professional courtesy."[63]

Although it has occasionally been directed at Mexicans, Poles, politicians, guitarists, and hockey players, this joke is overwhelmingly told about lawyers. Of the seventy versions I have collected, only eight are about nonlawyers.[64] *Rats* offers a convenient vehicle for voicing a number of interrelated points about lawyers in a wonderfully condensed fashion. The association with rats suggests both moral deficiency and betrayal; the response of the lab assistants depicts the low public regard for lawyers; their abundance suggests the need for something to be done about "too many lawyers"; "some things rats won't do" points to their moral deficiency. The setting reminds us that this is the revenge of the laboratory classes: scientists and doctors who preside in laboratories get to cut up the lawyers (who sue them and cut them up on cross-examination). Lawyers who obstruct finally make a positive contribution when reduced to experimental animals. The joke relishes the fantasy of the diminishment of lawyers and their wholesale removal from social life.

The laboratory rats joke provides a map of the themes of the new territories: lawyers are unreliable and traitorous, deficient in morality, universally scorned, and in such abundant supply that their removal is desirable. Rats are, after all, the prototypical pest that needs to be exterminated. We are left to imagine how this is to be accomplished, but we can assume that laboratory animals are not put out to pasture.

CHAPTER 8

Lawyers as Objects of Scorn

The fifteenth-century *Facetiae of the Mensa Philosophica,* literally jokes of the philosophers' table, tells of the

H1   two rustics [who] rescue a lawyer from the mud, but throw him back in when they learn he is a lawyer.[1]

Half a millennium later an American novelist imagines a young lawyer's response to the "gunn[ing] down of fourteen lawyers and clients":

> When people heard about the massacre, they at first were appalled, but then very quickly, seeking as one does cosmic explanations for tragedy on this scale, explained it to themselves by saying, with the radiance of sudden comprehension, "Ah, but they were lawyers."
>
> "In the same tone as they would say, 'after all, they were only dogs,'" Roger said. He had never thought of himself as a member of an undesirable social category.[2]

Unlike jokes about *Betrayal* and *Moral deficiency,* many jokes about lawyers do not refer to specific traits of lawyers or to specific grievances about lawyers, but instead assume and celebrate a more general and widely shared contempt for lawyers. Thus, in *laboratory rats* (G26), one of the standard reasons for the substitution of lawyers is that "lab assistants don't become attached to them." The humor plays off the already codified animus against lawyers and takes satisfaction in envisioning the antilawyer consensus. The identification of lawyers as objects of universal scorn itself becomes further reason to despise them.

CLOSING THE CIRCLE OF SCORN

H2   Q: What's the difference between a dead snake lying in the road and a dead lawyer lying in the road?

       A: There are skid marks in front of the snake.[3]

One of the best known jokes about lawyers, this seems to have originated or at least been popularized as a lawyer joke and has been switched to other victims only infrequently.[4] It combines the satisfaction of contemplating the death of a lawyer with the additional satisfaction of confirming that contempt for lawyers and the impulse to eliminate them is widely shared. This consensus is verified by the fact that the sense of fellow feeling for a snake, itself a symbol of deviousness and treachery, is at a higher level than that for lawyers.

That lawyers are a negative whose absence is to be celebrated is expressed in the following switch on an old story that appeared at the time of the run-up to the Gulf War:

H3   Did you hear that Sadam [*sic*] Hussain took a hundred lawyers hostage and said that if his demands aren't met he'll start releasing them one by one?[5]

The direct ancestor of this joke concerned a threat to kidnap or kill the recipient's wife, husband, or mother-in-law unless a certain sum was delivered, as in the following:

Percy E. Hurst

SOLICITOR WAITING FOR A CLIENT

N.B.—No figure in this cartoon represents any living person directly or indirectly.

41. Solicitor Waiting for a Client. 1935 etching by English anti-lawyer crusader Percy E. Hurst.

H3   My mother-in-law was kidnapped last week. The kidnappers said if we didn't send
      twenty-four thousand dollars quick we would have to take my mother-in law back.[6]

The lawyer version quickly entered the published jokebooks and was soon ab-
stracted from the specific Gulf War setting.[7]

H3   A cruise ship with 1,500 passengers, including 650 lawyers on board for a tax-free bar
      association meeting, is suddenly hijacked soon after leaving port. The hijackers read a
      detailed list of demands to the Coast Guard, threatening, "If our demands are not met
      by 5 P.M., we will release one lawyer every fifteen minutes, until they are."[8]

The consensus that lawyers are despised and avoided extends beyond tyrants
and criminals.

H4   A lawyer, a Jew, and a Hindu are traveling together and they are caught in a terrible
      snowstorm. They make their way to a farmhouse. The farmer says, "I'll let you stay here,
      but one of you will have to sleep in the barn."
          First the Hindu goes out to the barn, and in a few minutes, there is a knock on the
      farmhouse door. The Hindu says, "In my country, cows are a sacred animal. It would be a
      terrible sin for me to sleep in the same place as a cow."
          Then the Jew heads for the barn. In no time, there is a knock at the farmhouse door.
      The Jew says, "I'd stay in the barn, but my religion forbids me from sleeping with a pig."
          The lawyer has no choice and he heads for the barn. A few minutes later, there is a
      knock on the farmhouse door and there stand the pig and the cow.[9]

This goes beyond skid marks because not only are unattractive animals regarded
more highly than lawyers, but the animals themselves hold lawyers in such low
regard that they refuse to share a barn with one. After more than a decade of service as a Polish joke,[10] this was switched to lawyers by 1990. It has occasionally been
applied to national groups or other problematic professionals, such as politicians,
but it flourishes mainly as a joke about lawyers.[11]

A joke borrowed from a very different source takes up the theme of widespread
(or universal?) contempt:

H5   Did you hear about the post office having to cancel its commemorative issue honoring
      lawyers? It seems that it was too confusing—people didn't know which side of the stamp
      to spit on.[12]

For more than a generation this circled the world as a story about various ruthless
tyrants, including Hitler, Mussolini, and Stalin.[13] Since becoming a lawyer joke
(by 1992), it has been retired from active political service and reduced to registering that lawyers are widely despised. In its earlier incarnation, the joke always
pointed at a specific abominable and menacing individual against whom it was
imprudent to express hostility openly. The joke seems somewhat enfeebled by the
switch to lawyers who tyrannize over us only collectively and metaphorically and
who lack the power to retaliate for abusive attacks. Thus deflated it is now applied
to such figures as Bill Clinton and Tony Blair.

The theme of commemoration displaced by contempt reappears in this item, which surfaced briefly as a lawyer joke:

H6   Young Tad was walking along the deserted lake when he heard a cry for help. Spotting a capsized boat in the water with a man flailing his arms nearby, he ran to the pier, threw another rowboat in the water, and rushed toward the helpless figure. After pulling him in, Tad began rowing back to shore. When the panting man could finally speak, he said, "Young fellow, I'm attorney Jerry Goldsmith, and I'm one of the richest men in town. For saving my life, I want to get you something . . . anything you want."

    The boy thought for a moment, then said, "I'd like a nice funeral, if you please."

    "A funeral?" gasped the lawyer. "You can't be more than twelve years old! Why are you thinking about dying?"

    "Because when my dad finds out I saved a lawyer from drowning, he's gonna kill me."[14]

This joke, which seems to be older than the preceding item, originated as a story about a soldier or sailor saving an officer, but after World War II, it traveled the world and was attached to a much wider variety of political leaders, including not only dictators but also a number of highly polarizing democratic leaders (Bobby Kennedy, Nixon, Margaret Thatcher, Paul Keating, Clinton) and less frequently to lawyers.[15] Apart from those early military officers, both of these jokes were aimed at dominating public figures; only lawyers have joined this charmed circle as a group rather than as individuals.

SOUNDING THE DEPTHS

Unlike these recent "switches," the following story is old and "indigenous"—that is, set in a distinctively legal setting. It is part of the wider set of stories of the witness turning the tables on the aggressive cross-examiner.[16]

H7   Mr. Plowden, the well-known London magistrate, on his retirement from the bench was fond of relating the following as one of the choicest bits of his legal experience. In the course of a certain case he had to cross-examine the wife of a notorious burglar.

    "You are the wife of this man?" he asked.

    "I am," she replied.

    "And you knew he was a burglar when you married him?"

    "I did," she admitted.

    "But, how could you possibly marry such a man?" he demanded.

    "Well, it was like this," the witness explained confidentially. "I was getting old, and two chaps wanted to marry me, and it wasn't easy to choose between 'em, but in the end I married Bill there. The other chap was a lawyer, same as you, sir."[17]

In another version, the witness proudly compares his humble occupation (minstrel, laborer) with that of his father.[18] The point is that, despite its pretensions, lawyering is actually lower in the scale of worthy work than various menial, deviant, or even criminal occupations.

H8   Miss Gibson said to her third grade class, "I'm going to ask each of you what your father does for a living. Bobby, you're first. "

Bobby stood up and said, "My father runs the bank."

"Madeline?"

"My dad is a chef."

"Matthew?"

"My father plays piano in a whorehouse. "

Miss Gibson changed the subject to arithmetic.

After school, the teacher went to Matthew's house and rang the bell. Mathew's father opened the door.

"Your son, Matthew, is in my class," said the teacher. "He says you play piano in a whorehouse for a living?"

"No," said the father. "Actually, I'm an attorney, but you can't tell that to an eight-year-old kid."[19]

Before this appeared as a lawyer joke in 1986, it was directed at a secret police major in Hungary and a philosophy professor in Australia.[20] It has been principally a joke about lawyers but occasionally applied to politicians, bond salesman, and record company executives.[21]

H9   A fanatic fly fisherman, Bosman the big-city lawyer spent each vacation in search of the perfect trout stream. He finally came across an idyllic spot in the Wyoming foothills, one of its attractions being the sweet young thing who worked at the rundown motel down the highway. Each year Bosman returned in pursuit of both the fish and the girl, and he finally had his way with her.

When his Alfa Romeo pulled up in front of the motel the next year, Bosman was flabbergasted. There behind the desk sat the sweet young thing—with a baby on her lap. "Why, honey, Why didn't you tell me?" he stammered, "Why, I would have done right by you, fetched you and married you. . . ."

"My folks may not have much money or much schooling, but they've got their pride," replied the young mother. "When they found out about my condition we talked it over, and everyone allowed as how it was better to have a bastard in the family than a lawyer."[22]

This has been predominantly or exclusively a lawyer joke since the mid-1980s, but half a century ago the protagonist was the "light-skinned colored boy" who impregnated his white college sweetheart.[23]

A more extreme example of the "even lower than x" trope is this adaptation of the "no lawyers in heaven" theme:

H10   A very good man dies, and as a reward for a life well-spent, goes to heaven. When he arrives, St. Peter meets him at the gate. "Welcome," says St. Peter, "since you were such a good person in life, you may enter heaven." "Thank you," said the man. "But before I come in, could you tell me what kind of other people are here?"

"Well, all kinds," replied St. Peter.

"Are there any convicted criminals in heaven?" asked the man.

"Yes, some," said St. Peter.

"Are there any communists in heaven?" asked the man. "Yes, there are," replied St. Peter.

"Are there any Nazis in heaven?" asked the man.

"Just a few," said St. Peter.

"Well, are there any lawyers in heaven?" asked the man.

St. Peter replied, "What, and ruin it for everyone else?"[24]

This "even lower than x" trope is codified in a riddle that also introduces the notion that lawyers are scorned not only as individuals but in the aggregate, as a class.

H11   Why does California have the most lawyers and New Jersey the most toxic waste dumps?

New Jersey had first choice.[25]

Told earlier about various ethnic and occupational groups,[26] this riddle first surfaced in print as a lawyer joke in 1987, when Senator James Exon got in trouble

42. Villagers Shooting out their Rubbish (BM 13286. G. Cruikshank, 1819). The professional triad—parson, apothecary, and lawyer—are summarily expelled by villagers.

by telling a version in which lawyers were less desirable than queers. (It was not the lawyers who protested.) What is striking is how uniform is the pairing with toxic waste dumps.[27] These facilities are a perfect example of something that is a deadweight loss with no redeeming social value (and of course they are not sensitive to having jokes told about them).

H12   A man died and was taken to his place of eternal torment by the devil. As he passed sulfurous pits and shrieking sinners, he saw a man he recognized as a lawyer snuggling up to a beautiful woman.

"That's unfair!" he cried. "I have to roast for all eternity, and that lawyer gets to spend it with a beautiful woman."

"Shut up," barked the devil, jabbing him with his pitchfork. "Who are you to question that woman's punishment?"[28]

Before (and since) the switch to lawyers in 1990, this story has been directed at sages, political figures, and clergy.[29]

INTO THE SLIME

Another batch of *Scorn* jokes turns not on low social status but on association with low and disgusting creatures, substances, or body parts. The similarity that inspires these subhuman comparisons is sometimes spelled out, but in other cases the jokes refer to specific accusations against lawyers that are coded in the reference to these creatures: sharks (devouring predation), rats (betrayal, pestilence), snakes (cunning, deceit), vultures (scavenging), ticks (parasitic exploitation).

This type of joke has a long lineage. Seventeenth-century English polemicists compared lawyers to vipers, vermin, and caterpillars.[30] Perhaps the earliest narrative development of the comparison is in a long-forgotten anecdote about Sir William Jones (1746–94), linguistic genius and jurist:

H13   One day, upon removing some books at the chambers of . . . [Sir William Jones], a large spider dropped upon the floor, upon which Sir William, with some warmth said, "Kill that spider, Day; kill that spider!" "No, (said Mr. [Thomas] Day, with coolness,) I will not kill that spider, Jones; I do not know that I have a right to kill that spider. Suppose, when you are going in your coach to Westminster Hall, a superior Being, who perhaps may have as much power over you, as you have over this insect, should say to his companion, 'Kill that lawyer; kill that lawyer!' how should you like that, Jones? and I am sure, to most people, a lawyer is a more noxious animal than a spider."[31]

In the jokes about *Economic Predation* in chapter 2, contemporary comparisons of lawyers were made with ticks, leeches, and vampires. These turn on the superior powers of extraction attributed to lawyers, not just on the relative public estimation of lawyers, as in the spider story.

A scatter of recent items liken lawyers to snakes.[32] None has attained the popularity of this fully elaborated narrative joke:

H15   A blind rabbit and a blind snake met one another in the woods, hit it off pretty well and began to meet everyday after that. One day the snake said, "We've known each other for a long time now and I don't even know what you look like. Would you mind if I felt you?" The rabbit said fine. "Goodness," said the snake, "You are soft and warm and furry and you have big ears. Are you, by any chance, a rabbit?" "Yes, I am," said the rabbit. "And you—you are cold, slimy, have fangs and are squeezing the life out of me. Could it be that you are a lawyer?"[33]

Although it contains no reference to any legal actor, content, or setting, this story seems to have arisen in the late 1980s in reference to lawyers and is told almost exclusively about them.[34] The lawyer element is locked in not by reference to any legal features, but by the resonance of the physical features of the snake and their conventionally coded moral counterparts. In the version above, the snake is cold, slimy, and fanged, and squeezing the life out of the bunny. In other versions it is "scaly and slimy, and . . . [has] a forked tongue and no balls" or "slimy . . . [with] beady eyes . . . slither[ing], and . . . no balls." Lawyers are correspondingly portrayed as unsympathetic, cold-hearted, sneaky, dangerous, predatory, lying, cowardly, traitorous, and so forth.

The several punch lines of a popular riddle emphasize that lawyers' numbers far exceed their usefulness.

H16   What do lawyers and sperm have in common?
       Only one in three million does any real work.[35]

Or

       There's always more than you'd ever need.[36]

Or

       Each has a one-in-a-million chance of becoming a human being.[37]

These arrived on the scene in the early 1990s, as the concern about too many lawyers was reaching a crescendo.[38]

Another "lower than *x*" arrival from this period seems to be exclusively a lawyer joke.

H17   What is the difference between a catfish and a lawyer? One is a scum-sucking, bottom-feeding scavenger. The other is a fish![39]

Unsurprisingly, the lawyer is identified with the male organ:

H18   Q: What happens when a lawyer takes Viagra?
       A: He gets really, really tall.[40]

H19   A fellow walks into a bar with a ten-inch, scowling man on his shoulder. He orders a drink. The little man jumps off the shoulder, drinks a third of the drink and climbs back up. The fellow then orders a sandwich. The little man likewise devours a third of the sandwich. After this goes on for two more drinks, the bartender says, "Hey buddy, I don't usually pry into customers' private affairs, but what the heck is it with that little guy?" The customer replies, "Well, I found a bottle on the beach. When I uncorked it, out popped a genie. He gave me one wish. I asked for a ten-inch prick, and the genie shrunk my lawyer!"[41]

This is an extension of an older story based on wordplay in which the genie, asked for a "ten-inch penis," instead provides a ten-inch pianist.[42] Here the genie not only labels the lawyer as a prick, but deftly portrays the miniature lawyer as an economic predator (the contingency fee lawyer taking his one-third cut). At the same time that he is equated with a potent powerful phallus the joke gives play to a glorious fantasy of reducing the lawyer to a position in which he is dependent and controllable. It suggests that cutting lawyers down to size and controlling their power is a theme that runs through many of these *Scorn* jokes.

THE ANAL CONNECTION

The equation of lawyers with some inferior substance or subhuman creature culminates in a line of jokes that equates lawyers with the ultimate polluting and despised substance, shit. Both riddles and narratives on this theme arrived in the late 1980s:

H20   Why don't lawyers go to the beach?
        The cats keep trying to bury them.[43]

A narrative, featuring a caring, reassuring, and knowledgeable doctor, incorporates a vein of professional rivalry:

H21   A woman went to her doctor for advice. She told the physician that her husband had developed a penchant for anal sex, and she was not sure that it was such a good idea. The doctor asked, "Do you enjoy it?" She said that she did. He asked, "Does it hurt you?" She said that it didn't. The doctor then told her, "Well, then, there's no reason that you shouldn't practice anal sex, if that's what you like, so long as you take care not to get pregnant." The woman was mystified. She asked, "You can get pregnant from anal sex?" The doctor replied, "Of course. Where do you think attorneys come from?"[44]

Earlier the joke was told about bartenders and others, but since the late 1980s it has been principally a lawyer joke.[45]

H22   Did you hear about the lawyer from Texas who was so big when he died that they couldn't find a coffin big enough to hold the body?
        They gave him an enema and buried him in a shoebox.[46]

Like the ten-inch penis, this joke features a diminishment theme. The expansiveness of the lawyer is a function of bombast and waste; his substance is actually small. This item also reveals something about the mechanics of the switching and transmission of jokes. This story, dating from no later than the early twentieth century, is about the Irishman or Texan who (in a less explicit era) was described as having the devil or hot air squeezed out of him.[47] Gershon Legman, a great collector of dirty jokes, reports the enema version about a Texan in 1954. Blanche Knott, a stalwart joke editor and master switcher, printed the enema story in 1983 about "the Texan who was so big . . ." and in 1988 printed it in an Irishman version. In 1990, she conferred a law degree on the Texan and published that version in a topical collection of lawyer jokes, but reverted to the lay Texan in a general collection the following year.[48] In 1992, another topical book of lawyer jokes gives a different version, omitting the Texas connection.[49] The Knott-Texan version shows up on the Internet, in a lawyer-joke calendar, and (minus the Texas connection) in an Australian collection.[50]

Two less venerable items on the same theme were switched to lawyers in the early 1990s:

H23 Q: What is the difference between a lawyer and a bucket of shit?
      A: The bucket![51]

Women lawyers are not exempted from the fecal equation.

H24 A lawyer went on vacation to a western dude ranch. Awed by the scenery, she went for a twilight stroll among the cattle. Suddenly, the stepped in something soft.
      "Honey!" she shouted to her husband. "I'm melting."[52]

The next item combines the shit theme with the "even lower than x" trope:

H25 The scene is a dark jungle in Africa. Two tigers are stalking through the brush when the one to the rear reaches out with his tongue and licks the ass of the tiger in front. The startled tiger turns around and says, "Hey! Cut it out, all right!"
      The rear tiger says, "sorry," and they continue. After about another five minutes, the rear tiger again reaches out with his tongue and licks the ass of the tiger in front. The front tiger turns around and cuffs the rear tiger and says, "I said stop it."
      The rear tiger says, "sorry," and they continue. After about another five minutes, the rear tiger once more licks the ass of the tiger in front. The front tiger turns around and asks the rear tiger, "What is it with you, anyway?"
      The rear tiger replies, "Well, I just ate a lawyer and I'm trying to get the taste out of my mouth!"[53]

Lawyers are the only occupational group that has broken into the select circle of ethnic and national groups that have offended the tiger's palate in renditions of this joke.[54] The joke seems to be an adaptation of a story about a dog with a grudge against a college dean. After biting the dean, the dog bites a member of his staff "jest to git the taste out'n his mouth."[55]

Not all the "anal" stories are so gross and obvious. A recent switch on a well-known story provides an example of an elaborate "adapted" joke:

H26   It seems that there were two brothers; one went to business school and became a banker, the other went to law school and became a lawyer. As will happen in some families, they drifted apart. So much so, that they completely lost touch with each other; neither knew the address or phone number of the other.

The banker did very well. He became vice president of a large eastern bank, which had many, many branches. One day, the banker realized that they were soon approaching the lawyer's fiftieth birthday and he really ought to try to locate his brother. He set about this methodically, got a letter off to various bar associations, until finally his efforts were rewarded. He received a letter that his brother was vice president and general counsel for a small circus in an out-of-the-way place in Kansas. No phone number given. Directory assistance was of no help; the circus did not have a telephone.

So the banker flew to Kansas City and then took a bus to Topeka. At the bus station in Topeka, he asked a cab driver for help, and the latter allowed that for just $20, he could take the banker to the circus. And he did. He drove the banker to the outskirts of town and then to a smaller town, and then to a little village and at the far end of the

Boss's Lawyers

43. Boss's Lawyers is part of a 1988 book of savage drawings by Bill Berger and Ricardo Martinez entitled *What to Do with a Dead Lawyer*. This one clearly links the Scorn and Death Wish themes. (© Bill Berger and Ricardo Martinez, Ten Speed Press, 1998. Reprinted with permission.)

village was the circus. A sad sight. Covered with Kansas dust. All the trucks and trailers needed a paint job. Sad. Not second rate, not even third rate . . . And there he found his brother's trailer, with the brother's name on the door, followed by "Vice President and General Counsel."

The banker knocked on the door. The lawyer opened the door. They tearfully embraced, and each told the other what he had been doing the last twenty-five years. After about thirty minutes of this, the lawyer looked at his watch, and said, "Time to give the elephant an enema."

"WHAT?" asked the banker, as the lawyer dressed himself in a yellow rain slicker.

"Time to give the elephant his enema," repeated the lawyer.

"What ARE you talking about?" asked the banker.

"Come with me," said the lawyer. "You see, the circus has fallen on hard times. We didn't have the money for liability insurance. Last year, after the circus had its parade through a small town, an old man slipped on a 'deposit' the elephant left on the street. The old man broke his leg. We were sued; no insurance, and the large judgment which resulted all but wiped us out. We just couldn't afford another claim like that. It would put us out of business. And there is a parade this afternoon."

With that the lawyer walked outside, dressed in his rain slicker, grabbed a fire hose, inserted the nozzle into the elephant's rectum and turned on the hydrant. Almost immediately, the elephant had a most normal reaction; he sprayed the hapless lawyer from head to toe with fecal matter.

The banker stood there, out of range, and watched these proceedings in utter disbelief. First, he couldn't speak at all; then he said to his brother, "Please! You don't have to do that! Come back east with me. I have a good position with the bank. I can get you a CLEAN job as teller, maybe even as loan officer."

And the lawyer, wiping his face, answers, shouting, "WHAT?!! AND GIVE UP THE PRACTICE OF LAW???"[56]

This is the first lawyer version of a much-recorded joke in which the protagonist exclaims "What, give up show business?"[57] It is also one of the few jokes in the whole joke corpus in which the lawyer is identified as an in-house corporate counsel—possibly the only one in current circulation. But this attribution reflects the exigencies of plot rather than an interest in portraying anything specific regarding this kind of law practice.[58] This equation of law practice with being drenched in shit accentuates the contrast between the mundane traffic of practice and the aspiration or pretension to engage in noble work.

The Uses of Scorn

Like the jokes about lawyers as betrayers of trust and as morally deficient, the *Scorn* cycle contains few older jokes and relatively few items that are indigenous to the legal setting. The few older jokes have been overwhelmed by a vast growth from the mid-1980s, consisting mostly of switches, but with a minority of new indigenous jokes (*skid marks, blind rabbit, catfish*). Although these are in turn readily switchable, they serve almost exclusively as lawyer jokes. The sources of these stories are mostly from different groups—Texans, tyrants, mothers-in-law, Poles, and blacks, rather than from Jews or politicians or other professionals. Unlike the older core categories of lawyer jokes discussed in chapters 1–4, *Scorn* jokes refer in a summary way to the generic identity of lawyers, not to any particular behavior or to any specific set of lawyers. The indictment is general and unqualified. As a newsweekly put it: "Lawyers have become symbols of everything crass and dishonorable in American public life."[59]

This category is distinctly American, with some spillover to Australia and very recently to Britain. Where the jokes in the enduring core are found throughout the English-speaking world, *Scorn* jokes seem to be much less of a presence in the United Kingdom, Canada, and India. *Scorn* jokes arrived on the American scene as public opinion about lawyers was falling and public comment about their shortcomings and excesses was becoming respectable and modish. As the animus against lawyers became a visible feature of the social landscape, this was recorded and celebrated by the *Scorn* jokes.

"I am a member of the legal profession, but I'm not a lawyer in the pejorative sense."

44. Cartoon by Lee Lorenz (© The New Yorker Collection 1992, from cartoonbank.com. All rights reserved.)

Moral entrepreneurs grasped the opportunity to exploit the recoil against lawyers to advance various agendas. Thus, Frank Luntz, a prominent Republican political consultant, advised his charges to use scorn for lawyers as a political asset:

> Unlike most complex issues, the problems in our civil justice system come with a ready made villain: the lawyer. Few classes of Americans are more reviled by the general public than attorneys, and you should tap into people's anger and frustration with practitioners of the law.
>
> Attacking lawyers is admittedly a cheap applause line (right up there with announcing your birthday, anniversary, wedding, etc.), but it works. *It's almost impossible to go too far when it comes to demonizing lawyers.* . . .
>
> *Make the lawyer your villain by contrasting him with the "little guy," the innocent, hard-working American who he takes to the cleaners.* Describe the plight of the poor accident victim exploited by the ambulance-chasers and the charlatans—individuals who live off the misfortunes of others. . . .
>
> Don't forget that trial lawyers and their ilk tend to take themselves very seriously. Make fun of them mercilessly, and they will not know how to respond. They truly are one group in American society that you can attack with near impunity.
>
> If you are an attorney yourself, make a joke out of it. Be self-deprecating, even make a mock apology to your audience and you will surely endear yourself to them.[60]

In the same spirit, in 1997 Thomas J. Donohue, the new president of the U.S. Chamber of Commerce, launched a campaign against "class action suits and ambulance chasing trial lawyers, who suck billions of dollars out of consumers and companies."[61] The choice of a target, he explained, was that "the single, universal thing I get a positive response on—from small companies and big companies, from individual proprietors and multinationals—is that something has gone seriously wrong with our legal system, that we've become a society where there always must be someone who's wrong and there always must be someone to sue."[62]

It is unsurprising that *Scorn* jokes are directly related to currents of public opinion, for they are about public opinion rather than about lawyers. What messages do the currents of public opinion carry about lawyers? To explore this, we turn to the most prominent and most distinctive set of new jokes about lawyers.

CHAPTER 9

"A Good Start!"
Death Wish Jokes

Death Wish jokes are relatively new. Only a few are to be found in the published joke collections that predate the "modern" literature that begins in 1982. The major exception is a much-published British story, expressing judicial rather than public exasperation with lawyers.

11   A lawyer died in penniless circumstances and his friends decided to get up a subscription in order to give him a decent burial. One of them approached the Lord Chief Justice, explained the situation and asked for a shilling.

    "A shilling to bury a lawyer!" exclaimed the Lord Chief Justice.

    "Here's a guinea—bury twenty-one of them."[1]

This story, often attributed to an early nineteenth-century Dublin judge[2] has flourished as a lawyer joke since the mid-nineteenth century.[3] Through the years, it has been switched to a variety of undesirables, especially politicians and unwelcome immigrants, who are encouraged to take many of their fellows on their return journey.[4] The theme is removal: the departure of unwanted outsiders is equivalent to the burial of the annoying professional.

    There were a few other stories about the death of lawyers, but none proved as robust. An extended tale told by nineteenth-century humorist Eli Perkins about the virtue of eliminating lawyers seems to have disappeared without a trace.

12   In Akron, Ohio, where they have the personal damage temperance law . . . [a] rumseller, whom I will call Hi Church, because he was "high" most of the time, . . . had been sued several times for damage done by his rum on citizens of the town. One man came out drunk and smashed in a big glass window. He was too poor to pay for it, and the owner came against Church. A boy about sixteen got drunk and let a horse run away, breaking his arm. His father made Church pay the damage. A mechanic got drunk

and was killed on the railroad track, and his wife sued Church for $2,000 and got it. A farmer got drunk and was burned in his barn on the hay. His son sued Church and recovered $1,800. Church got sick of paying out so much money for personal and property damages. It ate up all the rumseller's profits.

Still he acknowledged the law to be a statute, and that it held him responsible for all the damage done by his rum. He used to argue, also, that sometimes his rum did people good, and then he said he ought to receive something back.

One day lawyer Thompson got to drinking. Thompson was mean, like most all lawyers, and when he died of the delirium tremens there wasn't much mourning in Akron. There wasn't anybody who cared enough for Thompson to sue for damage done. So, one day, Church, went before the Court himself.

"What does Mr. Church want?" asked the Justice.

"I tell yer what, Jedge," commenced the rumseller, "when my rum kill that thar mechanic Johnson and farmer Mason, I cum down like a man. I paid the damage and squared up like a Christian—now, didn't I, Jedge?"

"Yes, you paid the damage, Mr. Church; but what then?"

"Well, Jedge, my rum did a good deal to'ards killin' lawyer Thompson, now, and it 'pears ter me when I kill a lawyer, I kinder oughter get a rebate!"[5]

An ancient and widespread *Death Wish* story was occasionally extended to lawyers in the United States.

13   A blacksmith of a village in Spain murdered a man, and was condemned to be hanged. The chief peasants of the place joined together then begged the Alcade [*sic*] that the blacksmith might not suffer, because he was necessary to the place, which could not do without a blacksmith to shoe horses, mend wheels and such offices. But the Alcade said, "How then can I carry out the law?" A laborer answered, "Sir, there are two lawyers in the village, and for so small a place one is enough, you may hang the other."[6]

The old tale about the indispensable smith had appeared in an American collection in 1877 in virtually identical language, except that the surplus was of weavers rather than lawyers.[7] The version above, neatly switched to lawyers, appeared in an 1895 topical book of lawyer jokes and recurred, fully domesticated, a century later in the following form:

13   One of the most famous cases in Texas history involved a blacksmith charged with murder. When the jury returned a guilty verdict and ordered the man hung, the town had a problem—they only had one blacksmith and a lot of horses that needed shoeing. The city leaders finally resolved the issue by hanging the man's lawyer since they had plenty of lawyers.[8]

The last story from the prehistory of contemporary *Death Wish* jokes concerns an office-seeking lawyer.

14   A lawyer called the governor's mansion at 3:30 A.M., insisting that he must speak to the chief executive on a matter of extreme urgency. Eventually an aide decided to awake the governor.

"Well, what is it?" demanded the governor.

"Well, Governor," said the caller, "Judge Parker just died, and I want to take his place."

The response came immediately: "It's all right with me, if it's all right with the undertaker."[9]

This story, usually told about a generic office-seeker, first surfaced in 1922.[10] Beginning in 1958, it is sometimes specified to lawyers seeking to replace deceased judges, as in the version above.[11] Another version, which omits the contemplated demise of the applicant, sometimes involves lawyers:

14   A persistent party member once appeared before President Lincoln and demanded appointment to a judgeship as reward for some campaigning he'd done in Illinois. The President, aware of the man's lack of judicial attributes, told him it was impossible, "There simply are no vacancies at the present time," Mr. Lincoln said.

"There was 'reasonable doubt,' Ma'am, so we're hanging a few lawyers."

45. Cartoon by George Booth (© The New Yorker Collection 1996, from cartoonbank.com. All rights reserved.)

The man left. Early the next morning he was walking along the Potomac when he saw a drowned man pulled from the river and immediately recognized him as a federal judge. Without a moment of hesitation he presented himself to Mr. Lincoln while the President was eating breakfast, told him what he has seen, and demanded an immediate appointment to the vacancy.

Lincoln shook his head. "I'm sorry, sir, but you came too late," said the President. "I have already appointed the lawyer who saw him fall in."[12]

Although each of these stories involves the demise of a single lawyer, the idea of a superfluity of lawyers is present in *bury twenty-one* and in *hang the lawyer instead.* The disparagement is delivered by insiders—the judge, the governor being importuned, the townspeople threatened with loss. In none, does the story express a generalized public attack on lawyers.

In 1980, the connection between lawyers and *Death Wish* jokes was almost nonexistent. Of the four we identified, the *rebate* story seems not to have survived; *hang the lawyer instead* had last been published in 1895; and *bury twenty-one,* by far the most widely circulated of the three, had not appeared in print since 1942. Lawyers had begun to appear in the *check with undertaker* joke, but lawyer identity there added a plausible detail rather than providing a platform for expressing feelings about lawyers in general.

The Contemporary Onslaught

In the course of a decade, *Death Wish* jokes became the most frequently cited and most emblematic components of the current round of lawyer bashing. Among the best known examples are a set of riddles, which became lawyer jokes over the course of the 1980s.

15   What do you need when you have three lawyers up to their necks in cement? More cement.[13]

Although occasionally switched to other targets (IRS auditors, accountants, conductors, banjo players, Robert Maxwell, and Howard Cosell)[14] it was first and mostly told about lawyers.

16   What do you call six thousand lawyers at the bottom of the sea?
        A good start.[15]

This joke appeared in the early 1980s aimed at feminists, blacks, Iranians, and Jewish American Princesses as well as lawyers.[16] By 1990, the lawyer version achieved wide popularity.[17] Although occasionally told about others, it is predominantly a lawyer joke and the emphasis is on the large numbers of lawyers.[18]

17   Did you hear the good news and the bad news? The good news is that a bus load of lawyers just ran off the cliff. The bad news is that there were three empty seats on the bus.[19]

This joke, which has a longer prelawyer history, has flourished as a lawyer joke since its appearance in 1989.[20]

Other *Death Wish* jokes are elaborated in narrative form:

18   A client phones his lawyer. "I'm terribly sorry," the secretary says, "but Mr. Forsythe died this morning."

The next day, the client calls again. Patiently, the secretary reminds him the lawyer is dead. Day after day, the client keeps calling, and each time, the secretary tells him the same thing. Finally, she can't stand it anymore. "Why do you keep calling? I've told you a thousand times, Mr. Forsythe is dead!"

"I know," the client says. "I just love hearing it!"[21]

The client's pleasure here echoes a long tradition of enjoyment of the death or departure of leaders, found in the constituent who requests copies of the *Congressional Record* because "there is nothing I enjoy reading more" than the eulogies of dead members of Congress.[22] Absence is celebrated in the story of the emigré who never tires of hearing that communist periodicals are unavailable in Paris, the Israeli who calls repeatedly for news of Begin's resignation (and Begin who calls for repetition of the news that Ben-Gurion is no longer prime minister), and the ex-husband who enjoys hearing his ex-wife tell him they are no longer married.[23] Death enters as the cause of the agreeable absence with the demise of Stalin and later of East German dictator Walter Ulbricht.[24] In 1988, it was switched to lawyers, who remain the most frequent subject, but it has been extended to bank managers, stockbrokers, conductors and band leaders, agents, and ex-wives.[25]

In another variant, clients may seek more than verbal assurance of the lawyer's death:

19   Smith practiced law for sixty years. Finally, he drops dead. At the funeral, hundreds of people show up. A bystander turns to one and says, "What a turn-out."

The mourner says, "We were all clients of his."

"No kidding! All clients! And you all showed up to pay your respects!"

"Hell, no. We came to make sure he was dead!"[26]

The satisfaction may come from telling rather than hearing of the lawyer's death:

I10   A lawyer goes to the doctor because he is not feeling well. After examining him, the physician says to the lawyer, "Before I tell you anything, I would like for you to be examined by my colleague in the next office, just to get a second opinion." The lawyer is introduced to the other doctor, then goes through another complete physical examination. When it is over, the physician tells him to sit in the waiting room until the first doctor calls him back into his office.

A few minutes later he is brought in, and as the lawyer takes a seat across from the doctor's desk, he begins to feel a bit nervous. Both doctors are sitting there behind the desk, with very serious looks on their faces. The first doctor says to the lawyer, "My colleague and I have examined you and we have come to the same conclusion: You have a very rare and incurable disease. You will die in two weeks, and it will be a very slow and painful death."

The other doctor suddenly turns toward the first doctor, looking very surprised. "Why did you tell him that?"

"Well," replies the first doctor, "I felt that he had the right to know."

"Yeah," whines the other doctor, "but I wanted to be the one to tell him."[27]

Satisfaction with the demise of lawyers appears in this riddle which appeared in 1990 and has been predominantly about lawyers, although it has recently been switched to various other subjects as well: [28]

111   Q: Why are lawyers buried twenty-five feet under ground?
       A: Cause down deep they're really nice guys.[29]

Another instance of satisfaction in the death of lawyers is a switch from a well-known story about a death-bed conversion intended to diminish an enemy group instead of one's own.[30] A lawyer version has circulated on the Internet since 1995:

112   The old man was critically ill. Feeling that death was near, he called his lawyer.

"I want to become a lawyer. How much is it for that express degree you told me about?"

"It's $50,000," the lawyer said, "But why? You'll be dead soon, why do you want to become a lawyer?"

"That's my business! Get me the course!"

Four days later, the old man got his law degree. His lawyer was at his bedside making sure his bill would be paid.

Suddenly the old man was racked with fits of coughing, and it was clear that this would be the end. Still curious, the lawyer leaned over and said, "Please, before it's too late, tell me why you wanted to get a law degree so badly before you died?"

In a faint whisper, as he breathed his last, the old man said: "One less lawyer."[31]

LET'S KILL ALL THE LAWYERS

The oft-cited "The first thing we do, let's kill all the lawyers" is uttered by the thuggish Dick the Butcher and endorsed by Jack Cade, demagogue and leader of the rebellious mob, in Shakespeare's *Henry VI, Part II* (1590–91).[32] Despite its ignominious source, this passage has become an emblematic expression of hostility to lawyers, not only embodied as a familiar saying but inscribed on T-shirts and coffee mugs, and now the ur-text of a flourishing genre of *Death Wish* jokes about lawyers.

The stories in the previous section involve appreciation and commendation of bad things happening to lawyers. But the lawyer's demise may be actively promoted as well as passively enjoyed. The *skid marks* joke (H2), suggests that such aggression is normal and acceptable, and it is celebrated directly in a number of jokes newly switched to lawyers:

113   A stranger arrived in a town just as a funeral procession was passing by.

Behind the hearse marched a man who held on a leash a large, snarling dog with dagger-like fangs. And behind the man and dog followed seventy people, in single file.

"What's the story?" asked the stranger.

"That's my lawyer, in the hearse," said the man. "This is the dog that bit him to death."

Pause.

"Uh," whispered the stranger. "Could I borrow that dog?"

"Sure," said the dog owner. "Get in line. . . ."[33]

This is a switch from an older and still popular joke about the dog or mule (or other beast) that bit, kicked, or ate the subject's mother-in-law or wife or both.[34] Spouses and mothers-in-law were traditionally the major subjects of *Death Wish* jokes. The dog/mule story itself has roots in Renaissance Italy:

113   A Sicilian, hearing a friend mourning because his wife had hanged herself on a fig-tree, said to him: Give me, I beg you, a little cutting from that tree, so that I may plant it.[35]

The next two items, each switched from other sorts of undesirables in the early 1990s, move away from revenge on one's own lawyer to aggression against lawyers in general.[36]

114   Q: What's black and brown and looks terrific on a lawyer?
A: A Doberman.[37]

115   A man walked into a bar with his alligator and asked the bartender, "Do you serve lawyers here?"

"Sure do," replied the bartender.

"Good," said the man, "give me a beer and my 'gator will have a lawyer."[38]

This theme of generalized attack is pursued in a number of recent switches of elaborate narrative jokes:

116   A man walking along the beach found a bottle. When he rubbed it, lo and behold, a genie appeared.

"I will grant you three wishes," announced the genie. "But there is one condition. I am a lawyer's genie. That means that for every wish you make, every lawyer in the world gets the wish as well—only double."

The man thought about this for a while. "For my first wish, I would like ten million dollars," he announced.

Instantly the genie gave him a Swiss bank account number and assured the man that $10,000,000 had been deposited, "But every lawyer in the world has just received $20,000,000," the genie said.

"I've always wanted a Ferrari," the man said. "That's my second wish."

Instantly a Ferrari appeared. "But every lawyer in the world has just received two Ferraris," the genie said. "And now what is your last wish?"

"Well," said the man, "I've always wanted to donate a kidney for transplant."[39]

This is an ancient and widespread tale of the envious man who is granted any wish on condition that his rival shall receive double.[40]

117   A truck driver used to amuse himself by running over lawyers he would see walking down the side of the road. Every time he would see a lawyer walking along the road, he would swerve to hit him, and there would be a loud "THUMP," and then he would swerve back onto the road. This pastime was immensely enjoyable to the truck driver.

One day, as the truck driver was driving along, he saw a priest hitchhiking, so he thought he would do a good turn by offering the priest a lift. He pulled the truck over and asked the priest, "Where are you going, Father?"

"I'm going to the church five miles down the road!" replied the priest.

"No problem, Father! I'll give you a lift. Climb in the truck."

With that, the happy priest climbed into the passenger seat, and the truck driver continued down the road.

Suddenly, the truck driver saw a lawyer walking down the road, and instinctively he swerved to hit him. But then he remembered there was a priest in the truck with him, so at the last minute he swerved back to the road, narrowly missing the lawyer. However, even though he was certain he missed the lawyer, he still heard a loud "THUD."

Not understanding where the noise came from he glanced in his mirrors, and when he didn't see anything, he turned to the priest and said, "I'm sorry, Father. I almost hit that lawyer."

"That's okay," replied the priest. "I got him with the door!"[41]

In an earlier incarnation the truck driver was a Klansman and the target blacks.[42] The enthusiastic participation of the priest tells us that notwithstanding conventional disapproval of bigoted aggression, when directed against lawyers it is really meritorious.

118   A truck driver is passing through New York City and stops at a bar for a couple of beers. Shortly thereafter another man enters the bar, wearing a suit, bowler hat and bowtie, and carrying a briefcase. The bartender asks, "Are you a lawyer by any chance? You sure look like one." "Why yes, as a matter of fact I am," the man replies. Without another word the bartender pulls out a shotgun from under the bar and blows the lawyer away. The truck driver is stunned and asks the bartender for an explanation. "You must be from out of town, pal. It's lawyer season in New York City this time of year. You don't even need a license." "Sounds like a great idea to me," agrees the truck driver, who has recently lost his shirt in a nasty divorce and is nursing a serious grudge against the legal profession.

Upon leaving the bar, the truck driver doesn't get more than a mile down the street when he hits a pothole, blows a tire, and crashes his truck into a light pole. While trying to extricate himself from the cab of his truck, he sees a growing crowd of men and women in expensive suits surrounding his wrecked truck, thrusting their arms in through the broken windshield and waving their business cards in his face, all the while screaming at him not to move until an ambulance arrives. The truck driver reaches into his glove compartment, pulls out his handgun, leaps from the cab of his truck and opens fire on the now-scattering flock of attorneys, winging several of them in the process. As he pauses to reload, a policeman arrives on the scene and orders him to drop his weapon. He complies, whereupon the officer promptly handcuffs him and informs him that he is under arrest. "But they're in season, aren't they?" the truck driver protests. "Well, sure, but you can't bait them."[43]

This narrative may have been inspired by the humorous lists of "regulations for attorney season" that have been circulating since the late 1980s.[44] These lists, based on the conceit of lawyers as game to be hunted, contain such items as:

118

    4. It shall be unlawful to shout "whiplash," "ambulance", or "free Perrier" for the purpose of trapping attorneys.

    7. It shall be unlawful to use cocaine, young boys, $100 bills, prostitutes or vehicle accidents to attract attorneys.[45]

    The documentation on many of these new *Death Wish* items is thin with only a few versions, but the fact that so many jokes on this theme have been switched to lawyers in a short period suggests that there is some general resonance to the "kill the lawyers" theme.

"The men are excited about getting to shoot a lawyer."

46. Cartoon by Frank Cotham (© The New Yorker Collection 1998, from cartoonbank.com. All rights reserved.)

A Pestilential Affliction

Many *Death Wish* jokes underscore the abundance of lawyers and the desirability of getting rid of them by the busloads or the thousands. In the background is concern about the rise of the lawyer population, marked in the quip that:

119   By the year 2000, this country will have more lawyers than people.[46]

A number of very popular items outside the *Death Wish* category echo the themes that lawyers are numerous (like *sperm*, H16), their presence is a misfortune (like *toxic waste dumps*, H11), and their departure would be unmourned (as registered in the absence of *skid marks*, H2). And the *laboratory rats* (G26) joke, the single most prevalent of all current lawyer jokes, not only has an "elimination" theme, but is premised on the notion that lawyers are more plentiful than rats.

    That so many *Death Wish* jokes refer to the prevalence of lawyers directly or indirectly by referring to lawyers in large aggregates (busloads, thousands at the bottom of the sea) suggests that their abundance is one of the major sources of concern about lawyers. That the United States is uniquely cursed is explicit in the following joke that depicts the excess of lawyers as a distinctive and emblematic national trait.

120   A Russian, a Cuban, an American and a Lawyer are in a train. The Russian takes a bottle of the Best Vodka out of his pack, pours some into a glass, drinks it, and says: "In Russia, we have the best vodka of the world, nowhere in the world you can find Vodka as good as the one we produce in Russia. And we have so much of it, that we can just throw it away." Saying that, he opened the window and threw the rest of the bottle thru it. All the others are quite impressed. The Cuban takes out a pack of Havanas, takes one of them, lights it and begins to smoke it saying: "In Cuba, we have the best cigars of the world: Havana, nowhere in the world there is so many and so good cigars and we have so much of them, that we can just throw them away." Saying that, he throws the pack of Havanas thru the window. One more time, everybody is quite impressed. At this time, the American just stands up, opens the window, and throws the lawyer through it.[47]

    Although it became a joke about lawyers only recently, the story has a long history. During the Renaissance it appeared as a joke about the passenger on a ship in distress who, asked to throw overboard the heaviest thing that he can best spare, throws his wife.[48] During the twentieth century the ship was replaced by an airplane that would crash unless some passengers volunteer to jump out: a Frenchman leaps out, shouting "Vive la France," followed by an Englishman, who yells, "God save the queen." Then a Texan comes forward, shouts "remember the Alamo" and throws a Mexican out the door.[49] In other renditions, Indianans throw Kentuckians, Englishmen throw Irishmen, Greeks throw Americans, Israelis throw Arabs, Norwegians throw Swedes, Mrs. Thatcher personally throws the Irish prime minister, and so forth.[50]

In the Renaissance version, the joke is that the wife was more dispensable since she was less valuable than the baggage. In the modern version, it has become a joke about sacrificing a member of a less-valued neighboring group rather than oneself, while still claiming to be acting for a larger noble purpose. Often there is a suggestion that the devalued group is too numerous—that we could do just as well with fewer.

The lawyer version, which is first recorded in 1988, shifts the point once more. The theme is neither sacrifice nor ethnic cleansing, but superfluity. There is a potlatch element; each nation has something that is abundant to the point that it can be treated as disposable. There is a hint of silver lining here, for disposal in this ceremonial form carries an implication of value—the lawyers are the best of their kind, like the Cuban cigars, Russian vodka, and Swiss watches. The potlatch gesture acquires its grandeur from the value of the goods destroyed as well as the heedlessness of the destroyer.

That the lawyer is thrown out because he is superfluous rather than because he is a scoundrel is reinforced by the publication profile of a similar joke. When politicians in an airplane boast how many people their actions will make happy the pilot or a bystander proposes that throwing the politicians out would make even more people happy.[51] Although this joke has circulated since 1950, it has never to my knowledge been switched to lawyers. Thus, of the two similar stories about the dispatch of the unpopular figure, only one is switched to lawyers—the one adapted to include the theme of surplus.

The following story suggests that surplus may call for a more systemic solution:

121   A tourist wanders into a back-alley antique shop in San Francisco's Chinatown. Picking through the objects on display he discovers a detailed, life-sized bronze sculpture of a rat. The sculpture is so interesting and unique that he picks it up and asks the shop owner what it costs. "Twelve dollars for the rat, sir," says the shop owner, "and a thousand dollars more for the story behind it." "You can keep the story, old man," he replies, "but I'll take the rat."

The transaction complete, the tourist leaves the store with the bronze rat under his arm. As he crosses the street in front of the store, two live rats emerge from a sewer drain and fall into step behind him. Nervously looking over his shoulder, he begins to walk faster, but every time he passes another sewer drain, more rats come out and follow him. By the time he's walked two blocks, at least a hundred rats are at his heels, and people begin to point and shout. He walks even faster, and soon breaks into a trot as multitudes of rats swarm from sewers, basements, vacant lots, and abandoned cars. Rats by the thousands are at his heels, and as he sees the waterfront at the bottom of the hill, he panics and starts to run full tilt.

No matter how fast he runs, the rats keep up, squealing hideously, now not just thousands but millions, so that by the time he comes rushing up to the water's edge a trail of rats twelve city blocks long is behind him. Making a mighty leap, he jumps up onto a light post, grasping it with one arm while he hurls the bronze rat into San

Francisco Bay with the other, as far as he can heave it. Pulling his legs up and clinging to the light post, he watches in amazement as the seething tide of rats surges over the breakwater into the sea, where they drown.

Shaken and mumbling, he makes his way back to the antique shop. "Ah, so you've come back for the rest of the story," says the owner. "No," says the tourist, "I was wondering if you have a bronze lawyer."[52]

In this story, with its overtones of the Pied Piper, the equation of lawyers with rats focuses on lawyers as swarming pests from whom society may experience a miraculous deliverance. The story came more directly from Communist Eastern Europe:

121   Hordes of big brown rats have suddenly overrun the Soviet capital and the Politburo is holding an around-the-clock session trying to figure out what to do. Finally someone suggests a call to [President Lyndon] Johnson; those Americans can cope with any situation. Johnson listens to Brezhnev carefully and says: "Yes, we have a sure-fire remedy. But it will cost you one million dollars." Brezhnev reports to his associates, and the Politburo is outraged. "The price is too high. It is just like Americans to take advantage of hard-pressed customers!"

But the need became greater. Finally the decision is made to accept Johnson's terms. On the appointed day a big package is delivered by the American envoy to the assembled Politburo. Out of it jumps a big white rat. He runs from the room to the Moscow streets, and at once all the big brown rats follow him. The white rat makes a dash for the Moskva River, jumps in and drowns himself. The millions of brown rats jump after him; all are drowned. Moscow is relieved at last. In great joy Brezhnev gets on the hot line again, and shouts: "Mister President, it worked! Now, for ten million dollars, send us a white Chinaman!"[53]

This image of lawyers as a pestilential swarm is long encoded in our culture. In seventeenth-century England, John Lilburne urged Parliament to arrange "the ridding of this kingdom of those vermin and caterpillars, the lawyers, the chief bane of this poor nation."[54] A contemporary described the Inns of Court as "the devil's school of sophisticating and lying frauds and hypocrisies which bring forth a generation of vipers which destroy and eat up the commonwealth, their mother."[55] More than three centuries later a contemporary British critic warns against "a pestilence so pervasive, rampant, and destructive of the quality of life that it threatens to engulf us all. . . . the outbreak of lawyers."

In the U.S., the fountainhead of modern malaise, there are already 800,000 lawyers 70 percent of the world's total and they are expanding at the rate of 40,000 a year. Inevitably, the infestation has reached these shores, borne upon the same wind that blows American junk culture into our lives. The obvious solution [to the excess of lawyers in Britain] is a cull. What fun it would be to join the hunt, rounding up rural notaries, small town solicitors, and fat cat barristers, whipping them into the tumbrels, and trundling them screaming to their fate at the hands of the bloodthirsty mob. But we are a civilized people content to express ourselves through the market.

Lawyers, however, are a wily breed whose stock in trade is low cunning. Just as rats develop an immunity to poisons, members of the legal profession are prone to circumvent the rules. So it is that the lawyers who seek to prolong their existence and maintain their numbers by side-stepping natural selection and creating fresh carrion upon which to feed.[56]

Although the imagery wavers among lawyers as game to be hunted, rats to be poisoned, or counterrevolutionaries to be guillotined, the author is constant in his determination to eliminate or at least diminish their presence.

Parallel imagery flourishes in the United States. Unexpectedly, its contemporary revival was projected from within the legal establishment, most prominently by the chief justice of the United States, Warren Burger, when he warned in 1977 that "unless we devise substitutes for courtroom processes—and do so quickly—we may well be on our way to a society overrun by hordes of lawyers, hungry as locusts, and brigades of judges in numbers never before contemplated."[57] For the chief justice the hordes were a danger threatened by the excessive adversariness of our legal system and to be prevented by reforming that system. To other imaginations, the horde had already arrived and needed to be exterminated. Respectable

47. Where the Carcase is, there will the Birds of Prey be gatherd together. Or Symptoms of Term time (BM 15432. H. Heath, 1827). A great swarm of predatory lawyers swoop down to seize briefs from a pile before Westminster Hall.

mainstream voices echo the allusion to pests and measures to control them. Surveying "America's Legal Mess," pundit David Gergen concluded, "Clearly, we need to de-lawyer our society."[58] The chairman of the board of the National Association of Manufacturers recounts that "like a plague of locusts, U.S. lawyers with their clients have descended upon America and are suing the country out of business."[59] A former chair of the President's Council of Economic Advisers, lamenting slow growth, observed that "law schools have been flooding the nation with graduates who are suffocating the economy with a litigation epidemic of bubonic plague proportions."[60] Ex-politico commentator Ken Adelman observes that "America's lawyer population is breeding like maggots."[61] Another journalist reports, "The lawyers now swarming in Washington are picking the place clean. (One cannot but think of maggots.)"[62]

For full and uninhibited development of the pestilence imagery, we must turn to a 1994 cartoon book entitled *Final Exit for Lawyers,* devoted to the theme of lawyers as multitudinous and innately dangerous vipers:

> Rumor has it that they breed under rocks in the hot deserts of California, Nevada and Utah. From there they leave their nests and crawl their way through the underbrush to the rest of the world. Once arriving at their final destinations, they shed their skins, don suits and hang out shingles. They call themselves attorneys, lawyers or advocates, but they really cannot leave their ancestry too far behind, because when you least expect, they bare their poisonous fangs, and bite down hard.
>
> Their ability to procreate is phenomenal. The world is crawling with an excess of these dangerous creatures, and every year their population multiplies at a horrific rate. . . . to stop the propagation of this species . . . we have demonstrated our solutions to their overwhelming blight. Their final exit.[63]

The 70 Percent Legend

The great pestilential horde of lawyers that swarms and scuttles and slithers through the jokes mirrors a remarkable and persistent modern legend that reveals the sentiments that animate the jokes. It is widely believed that the United States is cursed with a population of lawyers that is vastly disproportionate to any possible usefulness. This notion is given concrete "story" form in the belief that almost all the lawyers in the world are in the United States. In theory, such an observation might be taken as evidencing superior realization of the rule of law in the U.S., but it is always presented as an alarming figure, suggesting a monstrous deviation from the rest of the world and insinuating that lawyers are a kind of cancerous excrescence on American society.

This "most of the lawyers" story achieved extraordinary prominence in August 1991, not long after the flowering of *Death Wish* jokes, when Vice President Dan Quayle ended a speech to the American Bar Association on the wrongs of our legal system with the rhetorical question, "Does America really need 70 percent of the world's lawyers?"[64]

Counting lawyers cross-nationally is a daunting undertaking. Not only is the data poor and spotty, but the comparison is plagued by apples and oranges problems, since the legal professions in various countries are not exact counterparts of one another, but cousins more or less distant and bearing greater or lesser resemblance. However the problems are resolved, it is clear that the 70 percent figure is very far from the mark. An informed guess would be something less than half of that. Counting conservatively, American lawyers make up less than a third and probably somewhere in the range of one quarter of the world's lawyers, using that term to refer to all those in the jobs that are done by lawyers in the United States, including judges, prosecutors, government lawyers, and in-house corporate lawyers.[65]

Nevertheless, Quayle's 70 percent figure was an immediate media triumph, resonating with the widespread animosity to lawyers. Parroted by George H. W. Bush and cabinet members, members of Congress, and media experts, this nugget became a familiar factoid in the rhetoric of the 1992 presidential campaign.[66] Although it was presented without any indication of how it was arrived at, it was not entirely without precedent.[67] It was a retread of an item that had surfaced almost a decade earlier, having no apparent terrestrial origin, that the United States had two-thirds of the world's lawyers.[68] The two-thirds item was retailed by Chief Justice Burger as part of his indictment of litigious America.[69] It was subsequently used by Justice Sandra Day O'Connor and others[70] and became part of the speeches of Governor Richard Lamm of Colorado about America's descent to doom.[71] Ross Perot, blaming his lawyers for the terms of his ill-fated contract with General Motors, complained: "As long as two-thirds of the world's lawyers are in this country you can expect every clause that these people will dream up. I wish more of these lawyers would become engineers and make something."[72] The two-thirds item had never been challenged, but it never made a big splash. Quayle's reformulation projected it into national consciousness. Just where Quayle's handlers picked it up is unknown, but they certainly had reason to know that it was a tall tale.[73] If Quayle himself did not realize at the time that it was a phony figure he surely knew by time he repeated it in his acceptance speech at the 1992 Republican convention, just a few weeks after an *ad hominem* dismissal of those who sought to assess the accuracy of "litigation explosion" lore: "Only those who benefit from the squandering of litigation resources are attempting to calculate to the decimal the total costs of all lawsuits or to determine whether Japan's scriveners should be counted in a census of the world's lawyers."[74]

Quayle's unwillingness to relinquish the 70 percent item is readily understandable: by his own account, it was the rhetorical high point of his public life. Reflecting on it in his 1994 book, he recounts: "I knew the speech—especially its line about America's having 70 percent of the world's lawyers—would be controversial." Unexpectedly, he reports, it led to "something completely new to my vice-presidency: an avalanche of good press, the best I would have in my four years in office. My line about the United States having 70 percent of the world's lawyers was the sound bite of the day, and over the next week or so, editorial pages took up the question of legal reform. . . . This was as good as anything that had come along in two and a half years. In fact, for a politician it doesn't get any better than this: good press for doing something that he strongly believes in."[75]

This item has shown a remarkable capacity to outlive its original rhetorical moment. Although most serious observers quickly concluded that it was meaningless or false,[76] editorialists, grievance-mongers, letters-to-the editor writers, and media pundits have kept it alive. In the media and political worlds, it is served up without shame or challenge.[77]

Not only has this item survived, but it has become a piece of genuine global folklore. In Britain, it is invoked as a marker to distinguish a Britain free of (but threatened by) litigation madness.[78] *The Banker* refers to "the U.S., the country with three quarters of the world's lawyers."[79] Correspondents in Washington conveyed the 70 percent story to readers of the *Independent* twice within days in March 1995.[80] It is equally welcome in up-market and down-market publications.[81] It is accepted without question by the BBC's chief American correspondent, who views the United States as degraded and paralyzed by its overpopulation of lawyers.[82] In Japan an American computer executive includes "three quarters of the world's total" lawyers in the U.S. as one of the reasons "Why Japanese Live Better Than Americans."[83] The *Straits Times* tells Singapore readers that "about three-quarters of the world's lawyers live in the [U.S.]."[84] A house magazine in a Spanish hotel room reports that "the United States has two-thirds of the two million lawyers in the world."[85]

If Dan Quayle's 70 percent story is the "political" counterpart of the "swarm" jokes, they also had their "scientific" champion in University of Texas economist Steven Magee, who claimed to ascertain the optimum number of lawyers and to prove that each of America's many excess lawyers cost the economy one million dollars of lost GNP annually. Again, serious research soon exploded these claims.[86]

The promulgation and, in many cases, ready acceptance of these legends about lawyers coincided with the profusion of jokes about the overabundance and superfluity of lawyers. Both stories and jokes point to genuine public unease about the number of lawyers and their increase. In 1986, 55 percent of the respondents to a *National Law Journal* survey believed that there were too many lawyers.[87] When the survey was repeated in 1993, this number had increased to 73 percent.[88] Generally, lawyers are thought to have too much influence and power in society, to be principally responsible for a litigation explosion in the United States, and to bring too many lawsuits, damaging the U.S. economy.[89] This sense of too many laws and too much litigation increased during the period when *Death Wish* jokes were becoming widespread.

These sentiments are not randomly distributed. If lawyers were once derided by ordinary people as pillars of the establishment, we have undergone something of a historic reversal. It is now "top" people—those with more education, higher incomes, and more exalted jobs—who are most critical of lawyers. In 1993, one pollster summed up his findings:

> By and large, those who see lawyers in a more favorable light than average tend to be downscale, women, minorities, and young. . . .
>
> Americans who are more critical than average tend to be more establishment, upscale, and male. The higher the family income and socioeconomic status, the more critical the adults are. Pluralities of college graduates feel unfavorably toward lawyers, while pluralities of non-college graduates feel favorably.[90]

While 55 percent of all respondents to the 1986 *National Law Journal* survey agreed that the country had too many lawyers, this sentiment was shared by 69 percent of college graduates, 68 percent of those earning over $50,000 annually, and 64 percent of the occupational category made up of professionals, executives, and managers.[91] Curiously, however, the members of these categories were at least as highly satisfied with the performance of their own lawyers as were respondents overall. The correspondence in time and theme of legends and jokes about the number and superfluity of lawyers suggests these are not happenstance items of trivia, but together proclaim the anxieties and concerns of large numbers of Americans, particularly members of elites, about the role of lawyers in American life.

WHY DEATH WISH JOKES FLOURISH

How can we account for the appearance of these jokes about pestilential swarms and killing lawyers, along with the folklore about the number of lawyers? What do they tell us about public perceptions of lawyers and the legal system? As noted earlier, the multiplication of these jokes and legends parallels increases in the population of lawyers, the amount and pervasiveness of legal regulation, and the visibility of both law and lawyers. It seems plausible that there is a connection, but what is it?

Let us first put aside some theories that I think we can safely dismiss. Many observers think lawyer jokes are a response to the public's unhappiness in their dealings with lawyers. In its simplest form "lawyer jokes arise from aggressive impulses caused by concrete complaints about the legal profession. Until these grievances are addressed in one fashion or another, lawyer jokes are *not* going to go away."[92] At the conclusion of a serious study of changing conditions of large firm practice, published in 1997, an Atlanta practitioner observed: "The increasing frequency with which truly tasteless and insulting jokes are told about lawyers by respected speakers at business and public meetings, not to mention on television and radio, is further evidence that the legal profession has lost status during the last thirty-five years. The public has noticed how many lawyers behave and the negative public reaction is affecting the entire profession."[93]

This implies that Americans are so exasperated by lawyers' bad behavior that their grievances have escalated into homicidal fantasies.[94] This seems implausible for several reasons. First, the reports by members of the public on their own experience using lawyers do not register any significant decline in satisfaction. Well over half of American adults have used lawyers and most of these report themselves satisfied. In a 1986 *National Law Journal* poll, almost half of American adults reported professional contact with a lawyer within the preceding five years.[95] Well over half of these users reported themselves "very satisfied" with the lawyer's performance and another quarter were "somewhat satisfied."[96] By 1993, the percentage of respondents who reported using a lawyer had risen to 68 percent.[97] Even with all these novice customers, the level of dissatisfaction was only slightly higher.[98] In comparison, 67 percent of the respondents in the 1993 ABA survey reported using a lawyer in the last ten years, and about two-thirds of them were satisfied.[99]

Second, the various "concrete complaints" (about fees, attentiveness, honesty, double-talk, contentiousness, and so forth) have been around for a long time. If concrete complaints were driving the great surge of lawyer jokes, we would expect the new additions to the lawyer joke corpus to reflect those grievances. But the new additions, which include jokes about the death of lawyers and the scorn for lawyers, are for the most part remote from "concrete complaints" about specific kinds of lawyer behavior.[100]

A further reason for doubt about the concrete complaints scenario is that those who are presumably best served and who have the least basis for concrete complaints about lawyers are the most intensely negative about lawyers and those most likely to have bad experiences with lawyers are the least negative. These better-off clients may come to lawyers with higher expectations, but they seem to report even higher levels of satisfaction.

A theory that focuses not on lawyer behavior but on changing public attitudes is advanced by Stephen Trachtenberg, the president of George Washington University. To him the stream of lawyer jokes reflects the loss of respect for and deference to the professions that resulted from the postwar spread of education and the increase in divorce and experience with divorce lawyers.[101] It is true that there has been a general decline in regard for almost all authorities and social institutions.[102] But these shifts in opinion have not been evenly distributed. This explanation fails to account for the relative increase in the number and the hostility of jokes about lawyers compared to other professionals.[103] The group whose plunge in public regard parallels that of lawyers is neither doctors nor accountants. It is politicians, which suggests that the source of animosity to lawyers is less their professional status than their connection to the governmental-regulatory complex.

Other theories focus on developments specific to the world of jokes. One theorist views the spread of increasingly cruel and violent humor throughout the popular culture of the United States, accelerating in the 1980s, as a reflection of "growing anxiety about the vulnerability of the human race in the context of global risks and dangers."[104] We might think the emergence of *Death Wish* jokes about lawyers is an instance of this more cruel and violent humor. There are several problems with this conjecture. First, the observation that jokes generally have become more cruel and violent in the most recent period requires considerable qualification, if it can be sustained at all.[105] Second, the premise of a historic increase in cruelty and violence in the world at large seems dubious. It is possible of course that improved communications have made large numbers of people more aware of the amount of cruelty and violence, so that the perceived level has increased even if the absolute level has decreased or stayed the same. And with higher expectations, much that was once the accepted order of things (e.g., slavery, physical abuse of wives and children, mockery of the handicapped) is now defined as cruelty deserving to be condemned and remedied. Third, the notion that most Americans are subjected to a net increase of risks and dangers strikes me as far-fetched.[106] If precariousness of life is the cause of such joking, it is difficult to see why the United States—and particularly its most privileged and comfortable—would be in the vanguard. Again, rising expectations of protection may lead to a perception of increased risk independently of any objective increase. Finally, the increased cruelty theory does not address the distribution of cruel and violent jokes: why lawyers and not doctors, bankers, or teachers?

It is frequently suggested that lawyer jokes have proliferated as a response to the inhibition of joking about minorities, women, and the disabled. As these longtime staples of the joking world have become taboo in many public and private settings, especially in the United States, lawyers as the quintessential nonvictims are the perfect surrogate for these protected categories. There may be something in this displacement notion, but it cannot account for the focus and energy of the across-the-board assault on lawyers. The great takeoff of hostile joking about lawyers came at a time when ethnic joking was flourishing.[107] Only a minority of the new lawyer jokes are switched from these taboo groups.[108] Also, the emergence of the nonjoke folklore tracking the same points about lawyers (their numbers, their cost, their destructive effects) suggests that any explanation specifically in terms of the economy of jokes will be insufficient.

The common element in the jokes we have examined is a fantasy about lawyers who are dead, heading in that direction, or otherwise removed from society. There is much attention to numbers—the more the better. What is the appeal? Perhaps it is revenge—seeing lawyers punished for their sins. But many are not specific about lawyers' misdeeds. And only a minority are about *killing* lawyers. Most don't portray aggression directly. Instead they contemplate with satisfaction the removal of lawyers from society. A book of cartoons is entitled *Dead Lawyers and Other Pleasant Thoughts;*[109] another cartoon sequence details "Eighty Uses for Dead Lawyers."[110] The posture is one of enjoyment and gratification, but it is largely passive. Recall the punch line of 'What do you call six thousand lawyers at the bottom of the sea?"—one of the most popular of all contemporary lawyer jokes: "A good start."

It is the removal of lawyers that is the central point, not killing them. What is so good about their absence? We are freed from their exactions. But their absence might mean more: it might release us from the constraints of law and permit unbridled anarchy. That might be what Dick the Butcher and Jack Cade wanted, but I think it is a misreading of the American temper. Americans don't want to be rid of law, but of "lawyers' law"—of formal, complex, "artificial" law that only lawyers can understand. The notion is that if we were only rid of these lawyers we could return to a better law—simple, natural, direct, and understandable. Lawyers are seen as obstacles interposed between us and a harmonious natural state of social order. A distinguished English lawyer noted that the legal profession "offended against the instinct that justice ought not to stand in need of the services of a middleman. The lawyer is an intruder into Eden; his presence an affront to the vision which men carry within them of a paradise lost, and hopefully to be regained, in which lambs and lions will congregate without specialist assistance."[111] In his survey of "Antilawyer Sentiment in the Early Republic," historian Maxwell Bloomfield reports widespread suspicion of the lawyer as an intruder who inserts himself into a self-regulating harmonious community, displacing substantive justice with artificial formality, self-interest, and high fees.[112]

As an influential antilawyer tract of the early nineteenth century put it: "God never intended his creature, man, should be under the necessity to carry a written book in his pocket, or a lawyer by his side, to tell him what is just and lawful; he wrote it on his mind."[113] The dream of a world without lawyers is an enduring dream of making language transparent, eliminating ambiguity and the need for interpretation. As one seventeenth-century proponent of abolishing lawyers asserted, "Neither [shall there be] any need to expound laws; for the bare letter of the law shall be both judge and lawyer trying every man's actions."[114]

But the increasing volume and complexity of law has swept us far from this idyll. The painful sense of personal violation induced by our dependence on lawyers is captured by a contemporary philosopher.

> Ours is a culture dominated by experts, experts who profess to assist the rest of us, but who often instead make us their victims. Among those experts by whom we are often victimized the most notable are perhaps the lawyers. If you as a plain person take yourself to be wronged and you wish to achieve redress, or if you are falsely accused and you wish to avoid unjust punishment, or if you need to negotiate some agreement with others in order to launch some enterprise, you will characteristically find yourself compelled to put yourself into the hands of lawyers—lawyers who will proceed to represent you by words that are often not in fact yours, who will utter in your name documents that it would never have occurred to you to utter, and you will behave ostensibly on your behalf in ways that may well be repugnant to you, so guiding you through processes whose complexity seems to have as a central function to make it impossible for plain persons to do without lawyers.[115]

What makes the dream of a lawyer-free world so salient now? We are enchanted by the image of a neighborly world of communal accord based on common sense and in harmony with a divinely inspired natural order. But at the same time our lives are woven into the highly technical, "global" world with its boundless web of unstable manmade complexity, specialization, indirect relations, and dependence on remote and unknown actors, a world whose central players are not natural human persons but artificial persons, a world whose dazzling promises of prosperity, excitement, and autonomy hold us in thrall. We have no intention of forsaking that big world, but we resent and fear many things that accompany it: the threat of economic convulsion rippling from a distant source; the need to navigate a labyrinth of rules; the dependence on intermediaries; the need for indirection, artifice, and formality. Lawyers seem the authors of those rules, the beneficiaries of our reliance on intermediaries, and partisans of artifice and formality. Even if we do not draw the easy conclusion that these vexations are an imposition by lawyers, they seem to have such an affinity that we think that eliminating lawyers would free us from the net of artifice in which we are ensnared and restore us to a world of spontaneous human order.

The profusion of *Death Wish* jokes about lawyers can best be explained, I submit, as a response to the increasing legalization of society, manifested both in the ubiquity of lawyers and the pervasiveness of law.[116] This explanation seems to fit with the timing of the arrival of these jokes, the distribution of targets among lawyers and other professionals, the presence of parallel legends, and various features internal to the jokes, namely, the relative indirection and lack of violence, and their emphasis on elimination of large numbers. The "eliminate lawyers and return to a world of natural harmony" interpretation of the *Death Wish* jokes is bolstered by the simultaneous flowering of the *Objects of Scorn* joke cluster. The chronology of the two sets of jokes is very similar: in each case less than a handful of jokes that predate 1980 were joined by a flow of new jokes from the mid-1980s.[117] These *Objects of Scorn* jokes not only heap scorn on lawyers by equating them with noxious substances or detested creatures, they announce and applaud the broad agreement on this low estimate of lawyers. By declaring and celebrating the consensus that lawyers are despised and scorned, they hint that a comradely, neighborly, unlawyered, "natural" social life is already present beneath the incrustations of legal formality.

Finally, a last item of evidence for the "legalization" theory is that *Death Wish* and *Scorn* jokes are distinctly and overwhelmingly American in origin and prevalence. These jokes hardly exist outside the English-speaking common law world. Within the common law world, the tenor of joking about lawyers in other countries is less aggressive and hostile than in the United States. In Britain, for example, jokes about lawyers' lying, greed, and trickiness are very much present, but *Scorn* and *Death Wish* jokes are encountered rarely and, when they are told, are frequently identified as American lawyer jokes.

But *Death Wish* and the other new categories of jokes do not stand alone. Their proliferation has been accompanied by the flourishing and growth of older categories of jokes about lawyers. All have prospered together—with a single exception. We turn now to the one component of the enduring core that has not flourished in the booming market for lawyer jokes—jokes about justice.

PART 3

THE JUSTICE IMPLOSION

❧

Enemies of Justice

In his review of ethnic humor, Christie Davies notes that "it is the phenomenon of the jokes that could be told but are not that calls for an explanation."[1] What is missing from the world of lawyer jokes? Consider how rare are jokes that even mention the subject of justice. Such jokes became scarcer during the second half of the twentieth century, leaving less than a handful of survivors.

DOING JUSTICE

The most prominent *Justice* joke that has survived is a story encountered throughout the English-speaking common law world for more than half a century.

J1 A businessman has to leave town before a lawsuit brought against him by a competitor was ended. So he told his lawyer to wire him the outcome as soon as it was over. Several days later he received a telegram: "Justice has triumphed." He hastened to wire back immediately: "Appeal at once!"[2]

The joke is permeated by a feeling that law ought to be the institutionalized pursuit of justice. Its divergence from this proper state is the dirty little secret that the joke reveals. This version, in which the "realistic" client delivers the deflationary line, is the oldest and most prevalent variant.[3] It was in circulation in this form by the 1920s. (By the 1940s it was joined by a version that located the exchange among lawyers, which will be taken up shortly.)

Whatever the client wants from the legal system, it is not justice. Recall the large troop of conniving claimants who manufactured or exaggerated claims, figures who have largely departed the joke corpus leaving behind only a few stragglers. In the conniving claimant era, there were also jokes in which overreaching clients pursued goals that violated the law and/or the lawyers' sense of fitness.

Many of these "more than justice" jokes have dropped out of the joke corpus. The oldest of these and the one with the longest run may have been a victim of

the postwar attrition of capital punishment and has not returned in the new capital punishment world of death-qualified juries and decades of appeals.

J2   "Do you think I'll get justice done me?" said a culprit to his counsel. "I don't think you
will," replied the other, "for I see two men on the jury who are opposed to hanging."[4]

J3   Lawyer—"Are you aware, sir, that what you contemplate is illegal?"
Client—"Certainly. What do you suppose I came to consult you for?"[5]

J4   "Your legal department must be very expensive."
"Yes," sighed the eminent trust magnate, "it is."
"Still, I suppose you have to maintain it?"
"Well, I don't know. Sometimes I think it would be cheaper to obey the law."[6]

None of these are currently in circulation. Nor is the following story, in spite of
being reprinted in a widely circulated 1987 book of lawyer jokes:

J5   "All right, sir," said the lawyer to his new client; "I'll take the case, I feel assured that I
can get you justice."
"Hang it all!" replied the litigant. "If that's the best you can do I'd better get another
lawyer."[7]

This joke resembles the client version of *appeal at once* in the client's rejection
of justice as (he thinks) the lawyer sees it. The lawyer is celebrating or predicting
the client's victory and calling it justice, but the client reads the lawyer's message
as a repudiation of his claim. If the client is seeking something more or other than
justice, what about the lawyer? Is he just being pompous and grandiose? Or is the
lawyer fully invested in the justice of the client's cause, even while the client
remains detached and cynical?

In *appeal at once* the joke is not only about overreaching *by* the client, it is
about the lawyer overreaching *for* the client, making such extravagant claims on
the client's behalf that even the client disowns them or sees through them. The
lawyer confirms that he is the devoted and uncritical ally of the client. He is not
only a hired gun, but a hired gun who deludes himself that he is a devoted champion of principle. This portrait of hypocrisy/self-delusion is often located in a
specific practice setting. It is one of the very few jokes in which the lawyer is
depicted in the service of large business clients. In many tellings the client is identified as a rich or important figure involved in a large or momentous case. In modern renditions, the client is variously described as a "businessman," a "financier," a
"billionaire" or the firm's "richest client." Sometimes the client is involved in shady
dealing which has resulted in charges of fraud, tax evasion, or insider trading.

The very earliest extant version of the joke (from 1910) displays the original
nexus with the outsize machinations of the robber baron era:

J1   An American corporation, not so very long ago, was engaged in litigation with a
South American republic over certain concessions. One day the head office in New York
received from its agent in the country a cablegram reading:—

"Courts have rendered just decision."

An hour later there went over the wires to the South the following:—

"Appeal at once to American Minister for diplomatic intervention."[8]

In retrospect, we can appreciate why this joke appears when it does, just as elite American lawyers (or many of them) abandon the stance of independent advocates and embrace the role of "client-caretakers," subservient to their corporate clients.[9] Theron G. Strong, a New York lawyer who kept a wonderful journal through that transition, observed in 1914 that relations with clients had "undergone a complete and marvelous change. The advent of the captains of industry, the multi-millionaires, the mighty corporations and the tremendous business enterprises, with all the pride of wealth and luxury which have followed in their train, have reversed their relative positions. . . . The lawyer no longer receives the obsequious client hat in hand, but is subject to the beck and nod of the great

MERKWÜRDIG, WIE MAN DAS INSTRUMENT MISS-
BRAUCHEN KANN, OHNE ES ZU ZERBRECHEN.
                                    JUDGE, NEW YORK

48. Law (as accordion) from the popular U.S. magazine *Judge*, probably from the 1910s or early 1920s, reprinted in Cornelis Veth, *Der Advokat in Der Karikatur* (Berlin 1927). My re-translation of the caption is: "It is remarkable how one can abuse this instrument without breaking it."

financial magnate, who, whenever he desires to see his lawyer, 'sends for him.'"[10] Lawyers on annual retainers to corporations, Strong thought, "become little more than . . . paid employee[s] bound hand and foot to the service of [the corporation] . . . [The lawyer] is almost completely deprived of free moral agency and is open to at least the inference that he is virtually owned and controlled by the client he serves."[11] Though somewhat diluted, the lawyer's subservience to the powerful client resonates throughout the history of this joke. The law firm's work displays many features of the representation of the rich and powerful: the law firm acts in the client's stead, sparing him the inconvenience of attending while he goes about his business elsewhere, and the firm puts forth Herculean efforts. It is exactly the scenario that public opinion visualizes as the lawyer going all out to bend the law to protect the wealthy and powerful.

In simple terms the story is: unscrupulous big shot cuts corners and gets in trouble; lawyer goes over the top for him, diminishing justice to the client's (and therefore his own) advantage, and wins the case. His message misfires because the businessman retains his judgment, whereas the lawyer's is permanently corrupted. Not only is the lawyer a hired gun who uses his abilities without scruple, but his lack of independence makes him lose any appreciation of justice.

The *client* version of *appeal at once* contains echoes of the overreaching client theme, in which the lawyer, portrayed as the representative or guardian of justice, fairness, and moderation, rebuffs or appraises the client animated by greed or vengeance.[12] But the lawyer in *appeal at once* is no longer the representative of justice, and the joke does not invite us to identify with him. The viewpoint is that of the detached observer who sees the lawyer's cynical hypocrisy or self-delusion, serving the client who is knowingly using the legal system to advance a discreditable cause. The lawyer is no longer in possession of independent judgment, but slavishly overidentifies with the client. Conniving claimant jokes faded away when it was no longer bizarre or surprising for the claimant to try to push the envelope. Similarly overreaching client jokes have withered with the expectation that the lawyer will resist or at least reprove those who seek "more than justice." In their stead *appeal at once* shows us the lawyer outdoing the client in thwarting justice without even the redeeming cynical self-awareness.

THE LAWYER AS ENEMY OF JUSTICE

In other stories the lawyer is a more active and self-aware producer of injustice. Nineteenth-century stories depict lawyers intimidating jurors with threats of physical violence by their clients and intimidating opponents with threats of their own.

J6   The following powerful, elegant, and classical appeal was made in a court of justice somewhere in Kentucky by one of the "learned heads" of the bar:—"Gentlemen of the jury,—Do you think my client, who lives in the pleasant valley of Kentucky, where the lands is rich and the soil are fertile would be guilty of stealing eleven little skains of cotting? I think not, I reckon not, I calculate not. And I guess, Gentlemen of the Jury, that you had better bring my client in not guilty, for if you convict him, he and his son John will lick the whole of you!"[13]

An occasional lawyer may happily trump up a case against an innocent party:

J7   "I want to engage your services," said an Arkansaw man to a lawyer.
"All right, sir, be seated. What is the case."
"There's a man in my neighborhood called Alex Hippen. I want you to prove that he stole a saddle."
"Did the saddle belong to you?"
"No."
"But then you are the prosecuting witness?"
"No, I don't propose to have anything to do with the case."
"Then why do you want me to prove that Hippin stole the saddle?"
"You see, I stole the saddle myself, and if I can prove that Hippin stole it, I'm all right."
"Ah, I see. We'll fix that. Of course we can prove that he stole it."[14]

Physical violence and outright fakery were surely overshadowed, in frequency at least, by the lawyer's willingness to help the client evade the law.

J8   "You are to give the prisoner the best advice you possibly can," Judge Epperberger told the court-appointed lawyer as the court recessed.
Several hours later, the court reconvened but the prisoner was nowhere to be found. A search of the building and the grounds was made, and he still could not be located.
"Where in God's name is he?" Epperberger demanded of the attorney.
"Well, Your Honor," answered the lawyer calmly, "I found out he was guilty as hell, so I told him to scram."[15]

More frequently, this helpfulness is the product not of incompetence, but of competence.

J9   "Why can't you take my case?'
"I'm a corporation lawyer and wouldn't know how to get you out of jail. If you'd come to me in the first place you'd never have got in there."[16]

This long-extinct story, one of the few that takes note of specialization within the profession, echoes a wonderful 1905 piece by Finley Peter Dunne, creator of Mr. Dooley, in which the new style of corporate lawyer is contrasted with the court-room orator who had previously dominated the profession:

> "Th' law to-day is not only a profissyon. It's a business. I made a bigger honoraryum last year consolidatin' th' glue inthrests that aftherwards wint into th' hands iv a receiver, which is me, thin Dan'l Webster iver thought was in th' goold mines iv th' wurrld. I can't promise to take a case f'r ye an' hoot me reasons f'r thinkin' ye'er right into th' ears iv a larned judge. I'm a poor speaker. But if iver ye want to do somethin that ye think ye oughtn't to do, come around to me an' I'll show ye how to do it," says he.[17]

Advice on evading the law can translate into high fees.

J10   The lawyer explained to the client his scale of prices:
"I charge five dollars for advising you as to just what the law permits you to do. For giving you advice as to the way you can safely do what the law forbids, my minimum fee is one hundred dollars."[18]

Or, as a lawyer in a *New Yorker* cartoon matter-of-factly explains it to his client:

J10   "If you want justice, it's two hundred dollars an hour. Obstruction of justice runs a bit more."[19]

Even more pervasively, the lawyer promotes injustice by his indifference to principle and readiness to switch sides: [20]

J11   Lawyer: "You have an excellent case, sir."
Client: "But a friend of mine said he had an exactly similar case, and you were the lawyer on the other side and you beat him."
Lawyer: "Yes, I remember that; but I will see that no such game is played this time."[21]

J12   The big business magnate entered the famous lawyers's office wearing a worried frown. "That law I spoke to you about is stopping a big deal of mine," he said, "and I'd like to know if you can prove it unconstitutional?" "Very easily," declared the lawyer. "All right; then get busy and familiarize yourself with the law," he was instructed. "No need to," replied the lawyer. "It's that same law you had me prove constitutional a couple of years ago."[22]

The joke evokes the pre-1937 era of "substantive due process" when courts regularly struck down regulatory legislation at the behest of business.[23] In contrast to the contemporary era of hourly billing, the lawyer here is uninterested in the prospect of logging lots of hours. The picture here combines the lawyer's total indifference to merits or principle, his ability to manipulate the law to come to any result, and his abject willingness to place his talent at the service of the rich client.

Life, as it often does, takes over where art falters. Kenneth Starr, former Solicitor General, judge, partner in a major law firm, Independent Counsel, and sometime prophet of the lawyer's transcendent duty to the truth, provides a contemporary real life version of the last story:

When Starr was Solicitor General in the Bush Justice Department, he . . . refused to okay a White House attempt to declare . . . [the federal whistleblower] law unconstitutional. He later boasted that saying no to the White House in this instance had been an act of principle for him.

In June of 1996, Starr appeared before the Supreme Court on behalf of Hughes [Aircraft], which had been accused by a whistleblower of defrauding the Air Force. He argued that the federal whistleblower law involved in this case should be held unconstitutional. (The Court ended up ruling for Hughes on a technicality.)[24]

Other stories emphasize the lawyer's eagerness to serve the powerful and the dependence of the powerful on their lawyers:

J13   Archbishop Ryan once attended a dinner given him by the citizens of Philadelphia and a brilliant company of men was present. Among others were the president of the Pennsylvania Railroad; ex-Attorney-General MacVeagh, counsel for the road; and other prominent railroad men.

Mr. MacVeagh, in talking to the guest of the evening, said: "Your Grace, among others you see here a great many railroad men. There is a peculiarity of railroad men that even on social occasions you will find that they always take their lawyer with them. That is why I am here. They never go anywhere without their counsel. Now they have nearly everything that men want, but I have a suggestion to you for an exchange with us. We can give free passes on all the railroads of the country. Now if you would only give us— say a free pass to Paradise by way of exchange."

"Ah, no," said His Grace, with a merry twinkle in his eye, "that would never do. I would not like to separate them from their counsel."[25]

That the lawyers are destined for hell is here pronounced by no less than an archbishop.[26] His Grace also contemplates with apparent equanimity that, either because of their deeds or because of their slavish dependence on their lawyers, the "railroad men" are headed for the same destination.[27] The constant attendance of lawyers on the powerful is a sign that neither is up to good.

None of these jokes has survived into the present, and the themes that animate them are rarely encountered directly in the contemporary canon. There is not a single joke in the current corpus that damns the lawyer for subservience to the rich and powerful, even though the public fully appreciates that the legal system operates to the advantage of those with more resources.[28] The lawyer's indifference to the merits and his accommodating elasticity are now so taken for granted that their depiction does not in itself violate our expectations of lawyers sufficiently to provide the surprise needed for a successful punch line.[29]

As with the overreaching client stories, these nefarious lawyer stories have died out with the singular exception of another version of *appeal at once*, which comes in two main variants:

J1   A lawyer went out West to try an important case and promised to let his partner in Charleston know the outcome as soon as possible. The call came and a happy voice said, "Justice has triumphed!" The partner replied, "File an appeal immediately."[30]

Here the lawyers are peers. But in other renditions the lawyers may be senior and junior, with the punch line uttered by a senior instructing an idealistic junior. Here is a version that I heard in India in the late 1950s:

J1   A fresh junior lawyer was despatched by his senior to argue his first case in a remote mofussil [hinterland] town. At the hearing the young lawyer prevailed. He was elated and immediately proceeded to the telegraph office and wired his senior "Justice is done."

Exhausted, he retired to his hotel and fell into a deep sleep. He was rudely awakened by a pounding on the door. It was a messenger with a return telegram, which he tore open hastily, to find the message "Appeal at once."[31]

All the *appeal at once* stories depict the widely felt disjunction of law and justice, but they differ in their judgment about the forces that maintain this disjunction. In the lawyer-lawyer stories, the response of the lawyer reveals him as a cynical scoundrel and active perverter of the system. The *lawyer peers* variant portrays the lawyers as part of a fraternity of cynical betrayers of justice. Their devotion to justice is revealed as a pretense. In the *senior-junior* variant the cynicism of the senior partner is contrasted with the innocence of the young aspirant, doomed to be coarsened by experience. Indeed, we see the novices' naive pursuit of justice manipulated by initiates to serve the schemes of the unjust.

Another *Justice* joke combines the messages of the two branches of *appeal at once:*

J14   The senior partner of a prestigious Pittsburgh law firm was speaking to the young wife of the company's newest partner.

"You know, Mrs. Baylock, your husband is an absolutely honest man. He seems passionately concerned with the attainment of justice."

"That's a wonderful quality," said his wife.

"Yes," said the boss, "if only he wasn't a lawyer."[32]

Here the hierarchy is emphasized—it is the "senior partner" and the "newest partner" of a "prestigious," presumably large and hierarchic, firm. The younger lawyer (represented by his wife) sees his legal work as a quest for justice; the senior lawyer reproves her as naive and reveals his vision that the attainment of justice and the practice of law are not only separate but antithetical. The pursuit of justice is innocuous, even admirable, in others, he implies, but for a lawyer it is a disability. Lawyers are presented here as priests of darkness; it is incumbent on them to deviate from justice and to lack the capacity to do so is an infirmity. This leaves open whether they depart from justice for their selfish advantage or to serve their clients. So two quite different readings of this joke are possible: in one, justice-seeking is a disability in the fraternity of the wicked; in the other, it is a disability to one whose job is to suppress his moral impulses to serve the selfish interests of others.

Though this crop of jokes seems to have withered, the theme of the lawyer's opportunistic relation to justice is currently expressed in the spate of lawyer-prostitute comparisons, especially

J15   A lawyer is an expert on justice as a prostitute is an expert on love.[33]

WHAT DOES LAW DELIVER?

Another line of stories focuses less on unscrupulous parties or whorish lawyers than on the failure of legal institutions themselves to secure justice. They pick up the theme of the disjunction between law and justice that animates *appeal at once.*

J16   Defendant (in a loud voice): "Justice! Justice! I demand justice!"
       Judge: "Silence! The defendant will please remember that he is in a courtroom."[34]

That awareness of the disjunction is more trenchant among the public than among legal professionals is suggested in an English anecdote:

J16   The great Lord Chief Justice Coleridge was in a hurry and called a cab.
       "Take me as quickly as possible to the Courts of Justice."
       "Where are they?" asked the man.
       "What! You, a London cabby and don't know where the Law Courts are!"
       "Oh! The Law Courts! I thought you said the Courts of Justice."[35]

But it may be the judge himself who insists on the distinction, as in a story usually told about Supreme Court Justice Oliver Wendell Holmes [1841–1935] (frequently with the renowned judge Learned Hand [1872–1961] as his straight man). Here are two current versions:

J16   When late in his career a friend parted with Holmes on the steps of the Supreme Court, saying, "Well, Sir, Good Bye— Do justice!" Holmes replied, "that's not my job! My job is to play the game according to the rules."[36]

"What are you—some kind of justice freak?"

49. Cartoon by Danny Shanahan (© The New Yorker Collection 1996, from cartoonbank.com. All rights reserved.)

J16   There is a story that two of the greatest figures in our law, Justice Holmes and Judge Learned Hand, had lunch together and afterward, as Holmes began to drive off in his carriage, Hand, in a sudden outburst of enthusiasm, ran after him, crying, "Do justice, sire, do justice." Holmes stopped the carriage and reproved Hand: "That is not my job. It is my job to apply the law."[37]

Dozens of versions, going back to 1926, have been collected by a law professor who proceeds on the assumption that later stories are distortions, many tendentious, of Holmes's "actual words."[38] It is quite possible that Holmes said something like this, and not less likely that he did so on more than one occasion. The anecdote is distinctive for two reasons. First, it puts the perception of the dissociation of law and justice in the mouth of a much admired judge rather than a party or observer. Second and more importantly, its contrarian embrace of the disassociation as inevitable or commendable, rather than as a regrettable departure from what ought to be, plays off the well known witticisms that pointed out the lack of correspondence between justice and the administration of law by inverting the judgment that animated them.

Contrarian commendation remains rare, at least in public avowal. Instead the dissociation is a conventional prod to courts to align the law to the requirements of justice.[39] Jokes addressed the various features that defeated such alignment, including the play of personal influence, the wiles of hotshot lawyers, and loopholes in the law.

J17   Two lawyers were conversing about a case, when one said: "We have justice on our side." "What we want," said the other, "is the Chief Justice."[40]

J9   A bank president was giving some fatherly advice to his son who was about to go to another part of the country to engage in some business for himself.

    "Son," said the father, "what I want to impress upon you at the beginning of your business career is this—Honesty is always and forever the best policy."

    "Yes, father," agreed the youth.

    "And, by the way," added the old man, "I would advise you to read up a little on corporation law. It will amaze you to discover how many things you can do in a business way and still be honest."[41]

J18   "Got a case in court, eh?"

    "Yes; and I'll win, too."

    "Both law and justice on your side, I suppose?"

    "Um! I don't know as to that, but I've got the highest priced lawyers."[42]

The assumption that the most renowned and expensive lawyers carry the day in spite of a case's merits may lead to inferences that undermine their persuasiveness, as in the following story about fabled New York lawyer Max Steuer.

J18   Max Steuer related that once he inquired of a prospective juror at a trial whether he had any opinion regarding the defendant's guilt or innocence.

"I have no doubt that he is guilty" replied the juror.

"What makes you say that?" asked Steuer.

"Because," replied the juror, "if he were innocent he would not have engaged a big lawyer like you."[43]

All of these stories dropped out of circulation well before the onset of the great lawyer joke explosion of the 1980s. But this does not mean that the thoughts that animated them have been abandoned or forgotten. Many of these are summed up in the notion that justice is rationed according to ability to pay and this has survived the decline of *Justice* jokes.

J19   John Horne Tooke's opinion upon the subject of law was admirable. "Law," he said, "ought to be, not a luxury for the rich, but a remedy to be easily, cheaply, and speedily obtained by the poor." A person observed to him, "How excellent are the English laws, because they are impartial and our courts of justice are open to all persons without distinction!" "And so," said Tooke, "is the London Tavern to such as can afford to pay for their entertainment."[44]

W. Carew Hazlitt, a late nineteenth-century student of jokes, in 1890 referred to Tooke's reply as a "capital observation" that "every one has heard."[45] The witticism outlived memory of its source. In 1961, an English judge reported:

50. From "Pigmy Revels" (BM 9636. G. Cruikshank, 1819). The "London Tavern" joke [J19] in "comic strip" form before any known appearance in print.

J19   Only a few weeks ago I was asked by a correspondent where I had said that *'The courts are open to all—like the Ritz Hotel'* and I was compelled to answer that it had been attributed to Mr. Justice Mathew but that thirty years ago it was attributed to Lord Bowen and also to Lord Justice Chitty.[46]

Earlier we encountered a number of stories that claimed to be reports of an actual courtroom incident. Usually these attributions are apocryphal, but in the following text we have an approximation of an actual address to a prisoner by an English judge, Sir William H. Maule (1789–1858) at Warwick Assizes in the mid-1850s.

J20   A prisoner having been found guilty of bigamy, the following conversation took place.
    Clerk of Assize: "What have you to say that judgment should not be passed upon you according to the law?"
    Prisoner: "Well, my Lord, my wife took up with a hawker and ran away five years ago: and I have never seen her since, so I married this other woman last winter."
    Justice Maule: "Prisoner at the Bar, I will tell you what you ought to have done, and if you say you did not know, I must tell you that the Law conclusively presumes that you did. You ought to have instructed your attorney to bring an action against the hawker for criminal conversation with your wife. That would have cost you about £100. When you had recovered substantial damages against the hawker, you would have instructed your proctor to sue in the ecclesiastical courts for a divorce a mensa atque thoro, you would have had to appear by counsel before the House of Lords for a divorce a vinculo matrimonii. The Bill might have been opposed in all its stages in both the Houses of Parliament, and altogether you would have had to spend about £1,000 or £1,200. You will probably tell me that you never had 1,000 farthings of your own in the world, but prisoner, that makes no difference. Sitting here as a British judge, it is my duty to tell you that this is not a country in which there is one law for the rich and another for the poor."[47]

Although there is some variation among the several texts claiming to be verbatim reports, there is no doubt about the historicity of the incident, which is credited as the "final impetus" that "precipitated" the enactment of the 1857 act that first made divorce available in England's civil courts.[48]

Justice Maule's ironic demonstration of legal equality producing vastly unequal results raises a persisting question. If lawyers, judges, and courts allot effort and access according to the resources commanded by the parties, what difference does it make that some parties are better fixed to command the services of lawyers and seize the opportunities afforded by the law? At one time there was a scatter of jokes on the theme of the rationing of justice, but all of them have faded away, with the exception of the following.

A well-known cartoon by J. B. Handelsman, published in the *New Yorker* on December 24, 1973, and reproduced in fig. 51, depicted a lawyer in his office addressing his client: "You have a pretty good case, Mr. Pitkin. How much justice can you afford?" The line juxtaposing "justice" and "afford" has entered the language as an "aphorism." The cartoon attained some renown; it was passed around law school libraries, displayed on the walls of lawyers' offices, remembered and misremembered in various ways (for instance, with the client behind bars).[49]

The plaintiff in an age discrimination suit entitled his 1983 memoir of the case *All the Justice I Could Afford.*[50] A *light bulb* joke (B17) with "how many [lawyers] can you afford" as the response line circulated by 1981. By the mid-1990s two former presidents of the American Bar Association recollected "an old joke [that] ends with a lawyer saying to his client, 'Well, how much justice can you afford?'"[51] A Texas lawyer described his fight against software piracy in China as recalling an American legal joke:

J21 The litigant . . . rushes indignantly into his lawyer's office, shouting that he wants "justice!" The lawyer calms him down, and then says: "Tell me, exactly how much justice can you afford?"[52]

His telling was repeated verbatim in an Irish newspaper a few months later in connection with a dispute about Ireland's blood transfusion tribunal.[53] A week

51. Cartoon by J. B. Handelsman (© The New Yorker Collection 1973, from cartoonbank.com. All rights reserved.)

later an essayist in an English paper refers to the joke, and the following year legal aid lawyers in Scotland held a conference entitled "How Much Justice Can We Afford?"[54] It is not clear whether Handelsman's cartoon was inspired by an older and unrecorded joke, or whether such a joke was derived from the cartoon and then recollected, or whether the joke was bred by mis-recollection of the cartoon. In any case it is clear that this line hit a nerve.

Remarkably, the jokes don't pursue this unequal justice theme, at least not directly, despite a large portion of the public subscribing to the unequal justice critique and holding lawyers to blame for their complicity in it. There is a widespread and abiding view that the legal system is biased in favor of top people. Twenty-five years ago 59 percent of a national sample agreed that "the legal system favors the rich and powerful over everyone else."[55] In 1985, when asked whether "the justice system in the United States mainly favors the rich" or "treats all Americans as equally as possible," 57 percent of respondents chose the "favored the rich" response and only 39 percent the "equally" response.[56] In a 1995 survey conducted by *U.S. News & World Report,* fully three-quarters of the respondents thought that the American legal system affords less access to justice to "average Americans" than to rich people—and four out of five of these thought "much less."[57] The same poll shows the public placing responsibility for this imbalance squarely on lawyers:

> Here are some things that people say about lawyers. Which one of the following comes closest to your views?
>
> Lawyers have an important role to play in holding wrongdoers accountable and helping the injured
>
> Lawyers use the legal system to protect the powerful and get rich.

Fifty-six percent affirmed the "protect the powerful and get rich" response; only 35 percent the "helping" response.[58] That ordinary people are denied the benefits of the legal system is attributed to lawyers.[59]

Yet compared to the elaborated repertoire of jokes that recite and embroider various grievances about lawyers, jokes that turn on the class bias of the legal system are rare indeed. As we have seen, a number of stories with the theme of lawyers fiddling the system on behalf of the rich have fallen out of the contemporary canon of lawyer jokes. Lawyers' depredations (lying, cheating, betraying, exploiting) in individual instances are vividly displayed, but there is little attention to their public or systematic failures and the deleterious consequences that flow from them. Older jokes that pointedly depicted lawyers as agents of public injustice (e.g., I12, *proved it constitutional*) have dropped out, perhaps because the notion of lawyers abruptly changing course or undermining the public interest for private advantage no longer violates our expectations with sufficient force. Lawyers are viewed as instruments of private will rather than as guardians of public weal. The *Scorn* and *Death Wish* jokes that have displaced these *Justice* jokes do not focus on specific misdeeds of lawyers, but take for granted a broad consensus that their presence is unwelcome and harmful and that their removal would be

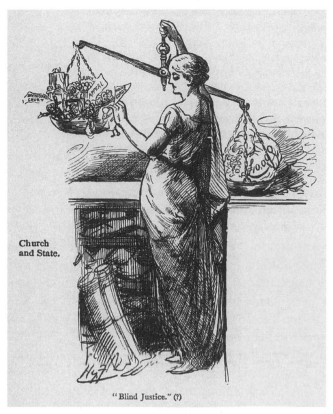

52a. "Blind Justice." Illustration by Harry Furniss for A'Beckett's *The Comic Blackstone*, 1887. Her blindfold removed, Justice notices that the entire legal process (from the jury to the House of Lords) is outweighed by £10,000.

52b. Cartoon by Ken Wilkie in S. Gross, ed., *Lawyers! Lawyers! Lawyers!* (© Ken Wilkie 1994)

beneficial. Their punch lines play off the tension between the lawyer's high status and our customary civility on the one hand and the explosive violence of the response to the lawyer on the other.

The jokes about lawyers' *Corruption of Discourse* and *Economic Predation* turn on the way that protagonists, acting in conformity with the practices of the profession, violate the expectations of fairness and justice which the profession is supposed to institutionalize. It is more acceptable to attribute this deviance to the failings of individuals (greed, opportunism, overreaching) than to systemic failure. It is easier to accept that society is infected with bad guys than that we have institutions so constructed that they cannot consistently produce just results. But the measures we take to restrain bad actors may have little to do with making our institutions realize their highest goals. Joel Best points out that "a society which is mobilized to keep child molesters, kidnappers and Satanists away from innocent children is not necessarily prepared to protect children from ignorance, poverty, and ill health."[60] Similarly it is more congenial to focus on individual villains (greedy lawyers, overreaching clients, even ruthless prosecutors, and brutal cops) than to address the structures that obstruct justice.

The *Justice* jokes are the only category that has not grown at all since 1982 (when the last few additions were registered). Indeed, virtually no new jokes have been added to this category since the Great Depression. Instead, it has shrunk over the years, with more than half of the items fallen out of circulation.[61] The corporate/wealth disparity stories are gone; perhaps because such disparities and their influence are no longer seen as deviant or surprising. Indeed my sense is that only three are in circulation (J1, *appeal at once;* J15, *expert in justice;* and J21, *how much justice can you afford*). We have moved from mocking deviations from our high expectations of legal equality to a world in which revelation of self-seeking, gamesmanship, and social contingency are expected, or at least no longer sufficiently surprising to support a punch line.

CHAPTER 11

❧

Only in America?

Our extended tour of the corpus of lawyer jokes has revealed dramatic changes. The tone of joking about lawyers has moved from mockery, sometimes gentle and sometimes caustic, to mean-spirited scorn and aggression. The core categories of jokes have endured and, with the exception of the justice category, flourished. The core has incorporated many new jokes; and even spawned whole new themes, such as the sexploitation cycle of *Economic Predation* jokes. Beyond the core categories, the change has been truly dramatic. Where twenty-five years ago there were only a scatter of stories, there are now large new clusters of jokes about lawyers' treachery, moral deficiency, public obloquy, and suitability for extermination.

Whether these new categories will continue to flourish and become as established as the core categories remains to be seen. Most of their inhabitants are jokes that were switched to lawyers from other targets. Some have found the new soil hospitable and appear robust; others seem likely to fall away as the demand for lawyer jokes slackens. But even if many do fall away, the accretion of new themes and new material, combined with new visibility as a genre, means that the contours of joking about lawyers will be very different than they were half a century ago.

The changes in joking about lawyers accompanied a decline in public esteem for lawyers and an increase in their presence and visibility. The number of lawyers has multiplied as the law has expanded and become more pervasive, casting its shadow in every corner of our lives. Patterns of joking appear to track changes in the ubiquity and invasiveness of lawyers and law rather than a worsening of lawyer behavior. After Vietnam and Watergate, public attitudes toward institutions and elites became less trusting and more critical. In conjunction with growing resistance to regulation, taxes, and "big government" starting in the late 1970s, many recoiled against what they viewed as the excessive reach and cost of the law. Some were disappointed that law failed to deliver on its promises of remedy and protection; others, including major sections of business, governmental, and media elites, embraced a jaundiced view of the legal system in which the problem was "too much law" and the perpetrators were lawyers.

Expression of the animus against lawyers through jokes was encouraged by developments in the wider world of joking. It became incorrect in many settings to aim jokes at ethnic minorities, women, the disabled, and other "victim" groups. Lawyers, however, remained fair game. Rather than victims, they are the quintessential antivictims. They are aggressive and domineering; they prosper on the woes of genuine victims. When the swell of broad public discomfort with the legalization of life met the great antilawyer antagonism among elites, lawyers were attractive targets of comic assault.

Jokes are only one of many channels through which legal culture is expressed. In longer narrative forms like movies, television, and novels, lawyers are more likely to be involved in the criminal process (as prosecutors as well as defense lawyers), the matter is more likely to involve a formal trial and more likely to deal with large public issues, than are the lawyers in jokes. In movies, on television, and in thrillers, lawyers are more glamorous and heroic than they are in jokes. In the novels of John Grisham and in films like *The Verdict* (1982), *Class Action* (1991), *The Firm* (1993),[1] *Philadelphia* (1993), and *The Rainmaker* (1997) lawyers are shown as triumphing through law. In these works "Justice is done!"—lawyers succeed in vindicating the right, at least locally and temporarily.

In contrast, the lawyers in jokes tend to be engaged in the pursuit of private interests. They may be clever and resourceful, but they are of (at most) middling moral stature. In movies, television, and novels, lawyers engage in tactical maneuver in order to serve their clients and vindicate high principles. In the jokes, the lawyer's clever stratagems are deployed mainly to serve the lawyer's interest. The tensions between law and justice remain unresolved. Lawyers in jokes function in the world of game-playing rather than in the world of weighty values and momentous events. The longer narrative media often show us the nobility of the law vindicated in the midst of the compromises of everyday life. But the jokes highlight the contrast between the seamy reality and the law's pretensions of nobility.

The distinctly skeptical representation of lawyers in jokes is fairly close to the public opinion revealed in surveys that show the public full of critical views about lawyers and cynical knowledge about the system. We have seen that it is widely believed that there are too many lawyers and that lawyers are deficient in ethics. In a recent survey, over half the public thought it a fair criticism of most lawyers that "they file too many lawsuits and tie up the court system."[2] Another survey found a resounding 74 percent who agreed that "the amount of litigation in America today is hampering this country's economic recovery."[3]

Public opinion tracks many aspects of the jaundiced view of the legal system, as does much in the joke corpus—including such emblematic jokes as *dogs* (B58), *chaos* (D4), *laboratory rats* (G26), *brass rat* (I21), and the whole categories of *Scorn* and *Death Wish* jokes. But while the jaundiced view targets claimants and their lawyers (under the rubrics of "trial lawyers," "contingency fee lawyers," and "class action lawyers"—i.e., those who launch legal attacks on corporate America), the joke corpus pays no special heed to claimants (and their lawyers) or to corporations (and their lawyers). Indeed the two distinctive clusters that have dropped out of the joke corpus are jokes about conniving claimants and jokes about lawyers frustrating justice at the behest of the powerful. Grassroots disaffection with lawyers is not focused on their alignment in the civil justice wars.

In many respects the grievances of ordinary people are distinct from those that animate the jaundiced view. Genuine grassroots legal reform groups, to the extent that they exist at all, are concerned about issues like excessive fees and the weakness of lawyer self-discipline.[4] They call for the abolition of self-regulation and the establishment of an open public procedure for grievances against lawyers. They want "plain language," do-it-yourself provisions, and higher limits in small claims courts—all to enable citizens to pursue their legal business without lawyers. They oppose the lawyer monopoly, enthusiastically urging nonlawyer practice. It is a consumerist perspective in which access is a major theme: they want a system that is user-friendly for ordinary people.[5] Interest in generic law reform is vastly overshadowed by interest in remedies for specific grievances, such as those involved in the "Patients Bill of Rights," which roiled political debate at the turn of the new

53. Cartoon by Mick Stevens (© The New Yorker Collection 1990, from cartoonbank.com. All rights reserved.)

century. Despite wide agreement that it is "overused," most people would like to enlarge access to the justice system rather than restrict access and curtail remedies. In a 1995 survey, 39 percent of the respondents preferred to retain the present balance between injured and insurers, another 39 percent favored reform that would "tilt things a little more in favor of those injured in accidents," and only 7 percent wished to tilt more the other way.[6]

Unlike the advocates of the jaundiced view, wider publics do not see the system victimizing the affluent. For all their misgivings about the legal system, most Americans do not share the sense that it oppresses large businesses. When asked which types of people were "not apt to be treated fairly by the law," respondents to a 1987 Roper survey identified the poor (54 percent), uneducated (47 percent), and blacks (33 percent); only 5 percent thought "top business executives" were treated unfairly. Indeed, when asked which types of persons "the courts are too lenient with," government officials and top business executives ranked, along with heroin users and frequent offenders, just below dope peddlers.[7] And this was long before the public became exercised about corporate flim-flam in the wake of the scandals, starting in late 2001, involving Enron, Arthur Andersen, Merrill Lynch, and other visible pillars of the economy. There is an abiding sense that the system favors the rich and powerful and that lawyers promote and benefit from this disparity.

Like much of the legal profession itself, proponents of the jaundiced view lament the disappearance of the good old days, that Golden Age of professionalism in which lawyers were paragons of civic virtue.[8] This decline scenario conveniently enables one to maintain allegiance to the law while deploring the excesses and deformities of our fallen time. In contrast, the jokes (and the broader streams of public opinion) are free of nostalgia. There is no sense of an earlier time when lawyers were better than those of the present day. Indeed, there is little sense of "history" or change in the jokes; they portray a timeless world of small practices and personal service to clients. The deficiencies of lawyers are portrayed as congenital to the profession, not a function of their involvement in the world of contemporary rationalized money-driven forms of practice. Their critique of lawyers is not "it ain't like it used to be," but "it ain't like it 'spozed to be."

Jokes carry us to a realm of what we know but at the same time don't want to know. They remind us that lawyers lie, cheat, bungle, and make disastrous miscalculations, and that judges are sometimes corrupt, somnolent, and dense. Within the joke frame we can affirm these uncomfortable truths without the explosive and demoralizing force of a factual accusation.[9] Jokes point to our cynical "second" or "shadow" knowledge that mirrors the prescriptively suffused knowledge that portrays lawyers and judges, husbands and wives, presidents and professors in the raiment of their benign, respectable, frontstage roles. Jokes reveal the underside, the backstage, of these normative constructions and relieve the tension of the duality of our knowledge.

Putting our awareness of the underside of the law within the joke frame not only makes it acceptable. It also enables us to forget or at least discount it. It is the nature of jokes to be intermittent discontinuous flashes, each a small whole, not connected with one another in a sequence or narrative. So jokes never cumulate to offer us an alternative picture of the role or institution. They may even reinforce the dominant normative picture by resolving the tension of deviance from it.

That jokes are rapidly forgotten by most people is an important part of the joke institution. It enables tellers to get much more mileage from their stock. And it means that listeners never assemble this shadow knowledge into an alternative vision of society that could challenge or displace the dominant normatively suffused picture of the social world. Jokes enable us to dissent without overt challenge and without a program for change.

This account has focused on lawyer jokes in the contemporary United States. When I have asked scholars and practitioners from other countries about the existence of a comparable body of jokes about lawyers, their unanimous response is that no such thing exists in their countries. I have visited Great Britain more than a dozen times since 1990 to conduct research that has involved interviews with lawyers, and with journalists, consultants, and scholars concerned with the legal profession. I found no evidence of the presence of a body of lawyer jokes of anything like the scope and intensity of the American variety. The few topical joke books about lawyers that have been published in Britain in the past twenty years are quite different from the American publications of the recent past.[10] The humor is far gentler. Lawyers are funny in the way that golfers and salesmen are funny; they are not demonized. The most prominent of these collections, published in 1989, contains many *Discourse, Economic Predation,* and *Conflict* jokes. Apart from a single *Death Wish* joke—the old story about the judicial curmudgeon who says "bury twenty-one of them" (I1)—there is not a single joke located in the "new territories" of lawyer joking.[11] The stories of *Betrayal, Moral Deficiency,* and *Scorn* that figure prominently in the American collections are entirely absent. When the kind of aggressive lawyer jokes that are so common in the United States do crop up in England, they are often characterized as "anti-lawyer jokes imported from the States."[12] This is not because the jokes are unknown; many of them are in the repertoire, but they are just not applied to lawyers—or at least to the local lawyers. For example, a 1992 book of jokes about then recently deceased Robert Maxwell contains a number of jokes that in the United States were then strongly associated with lawyers, including *professional courtesy* (B29), *dogs* (B58), and *check in the coffin* (F13).[13]

An excellent 1994 general joke collection from Australia bears a considerably closer resemblance to the American corpus.[14] Its section on lawyers contains a few *Death Wish* and *Scorn* jokes and more *Economic Predator* jokes—as well as a series of scathing attacks on judges that have no counterpart in the American literature. Many stories that were already told as lawyer jokes in the U.S. are told about others: *two plus two* (A33) about accountants, *dogs* (B58) about trade unionists, *chaos* (D4) about politicians. In 1996 each of these was published as a lawyer joke in Australia in versions derived from the Internet, but lawyers are still outnumbered by other protagonists. In that same year the first topical collection of lawyer jokes was published in Australia by a law professor with roots in the American poverty law movement and a definite reform agenda for Australian professionals.[15]

In India, too, we find an absence of *Death Wish* and *Scorn* jokes about lawyers. Again it is not that the jokes are unknown, but many are deflected to politicians— even *rats* (G26), one of the signature stories of American antilawyer sentiment, appears in India as a joke about politicians. In India, as well as in England and Australia, *chaos* (D4) is told about politicians rather than about lawyers.[16]

In each instance, the diffusion of print material, joined now by electronic materials, suggests the need for caution; jokes may be appreciated even where they are not thought reflective of local conditions, but instead are regarded as good jokes about American or generic lawyers. For example, in India there are jokes about lawyers arguing before juries even though juries have not existed in India for over a century.

In an era when so many aspects of American culture have been imported and imitated indiscriminately, how is it that the traffic in lawyer jokes has been so selective? Britain, which has similar legal institutions, unsurprisingly shares a very large part of what I call the enduring core of lawyer jokes. But despite an expansion in the number of lawyers even more dramatic than that in the United States, the jokes depicting lawyers as a pestilential affliction have not been taken up.[17]

Why has Britain been unreceptive to the new categories? In a richly elaborated depiction of English and American legal cultures, Patrick Atiyah and Robert Summers contrast a more formal, more certain, more strictly and evenly enforced English law with a more substantive, indefinite, and uneven American counterpart.[18] But not only is the law different in character, it plays a very different role. The fierce antilawyer animosity in early modern England, British historian Wilfred Prest explained,

> reflects the central relevance of the legal system and its practitioners to the everyday life of early modern England. . . .
>
> [In early modern England] proportionately more people were directly involved in legal proceedings conducted at a much higher emotional and psychological temperature than our modern, purpose-built, and public deserted courtrooms normally witness, except for the occasional *cause celebre*.[19]

Prest attributes the eclipse of antilawyer sentiment in England to the decline in the centrality of law:

> Private law and litigation now play such a relatively insignificant part in the life of most modern western societies that a major effort of imagination is required to grasp their central prominence in early modern times. The late sixteenth and early seventeenth centuries constituted possibly the most litigious era in English history, as well as a time when legal forms and institutions impinged upon almost every aspect of daily life.[20]

If it was possible in 1986 Britain to perceive the legal system as remote and not significant in daily life, certainly no one could have said this of the United States in 1986 or since. If law in contemporary England is a delimited sphere of institutional activity that impinges only indirectly on ordinary citizens, the United States is more like early modern England, where law has "central relevance" to everyday life. In the United States law is less a delimited sphere than a pervasive master control of controls.[21] I do not mean that law actually determines the course of all other social institutions, but rather that it is the site of debate about them and influences them as model, monitor, and intervener. It is this centrality and pervasiveness of law that is absent in Britain.

When we move outside the English-speaking common law world, the contrast with the American lawyer joke culture is even more pronounced. Where these jokes appear, they are often appreciated specifically as commentary on the "American situation" (as the Dutch call it), rather than assimilated to the local scene. Thus a 1999 German collection of lawyer jokes contrasts the integrity of the local bar with that in the U.S, where professionalism is stained by large awards, contingency fees, and ambulance chasing. The compiler alerts the reader that "some of the jokes printed here originate in the USA, and they are the most severe. In the nature of things many of these jokes about lawyers seem drastic to us, because here the income of lawyers in not a proportionate share as it is on the other side of the Atlantic. Also, in our parts there are no lawyers that chase

"Would everyone check to see they have an attorney? I seem to have ended up with two."

54. Cartoon by Michael Maslin (© The New Yorker Collection 1989, from cartoonbank.com. All rights reserved.)

ambulances to assist the victim—meaning to share the fat compensation. Then enjoy these raven-black *jokes* about the American lawyer guild. Perhaps it will come to us yet."[22]

Generally, there are many fewer jokes about lawyers outside the common law world. In civil law countries, with their smaller number of lawyers and larger contingents of judges, lawyers do not seem to play an important role in the public imagination. For example, Giselinde Kuipers, a Dutch sociologist, writes:

> I can assure you there are no lawyer jokes in the Netherlands. . . . It reflects the very different position of lawyers and legal practice in the Netherlands and the US. Dutch people tend to jokingly refer to the American practice of "suing" (even using the English word to stress the Americanness of the practice). . . . In the Netherlands, lawyers simply don't have the power and the social influence they have in the U.S.; as a result, [the] Dutch don't feel as ambivalent or even negative about lawyers. No need for jokes. [The] Dutch simply couldn't care less.[23]

The "power and social influence" of American lawyers derive from the American institutional setting of fragmented government and judicial review, but they also reflect the distinctive preeminence of law in American ideology. The central role assigned to law and courts by Americans, long a staple of lawyer rhetoric on civic occasions, is conceded and sometimes celebrated by others. For example, a journalist surveying "The Crisis in the Courts," for *Fortune* in 1961, before the intensification of discomfort about the law, finds the inefficiency of the courts troubling because "law is the authentic idiom of the American people in the struggle for the world, carrying within its wisdom much of the morality, the charity, the restraint and experience in the nation's heritage—all waiting for application to specific new cases. The great task is to bend and fashion the workings of justice to fit the nation's—and the world's—newest needs."[24] The nation, he concludes, is "hungry for the leadership of law," and if the courts succeed in reforming themselves "they can be the principal institution that gives point to American national development." This kind of nomo-centrism is idiosyncratically American and remains a puzzle and a wonder to European observers. A Danish scholar, Helle Porsdam, examining American legal culture, concludes that "the American legal system and American law . . . occupy a unique position in American culture and society. Americans may complain about litigiousness and overcrowded court dockets, about greedy lawyers and an adversarial system run wild, but if and when they have problems it is to their lawyers and their courts that they turn for help. . . . Countless are the cultural texts—books, films, and television series—that, after setting out to expose the sorry state of American law, then move on to affirm its promise."[25] Porsdam finds that in contrast to Denmark, where "the law is viewed solely as a technical means to achieving a certain end, for Americans the law, in addition to performing such a technical function, also carries a very important symbolic meaning. Unlike Danes, Americans are persuaded that the law, beyond protecting their rights and preserving their liberty, will provide them with trust and meaning—Justice of a higher kind."[26] Observers have long noted that lawyers in America occupied a distinctive position in relation to the central values of the society. They have been likened to the priests of ancient Egypt or of medieval Christiandom.[27] If lawyers are priests, law is the national church, its "secular religion."[28] America, as Canadian legal scholar William Bogart calls it, is "the land of law."[29]

The profusion of lawyer jokes in the United States is not an independent development driven by forces internal to the worlds of humor or entertainment. It is driven by the ubiquity, visibility, and centrality of lawyers in American life. They are, as one historian put it, "now the dominant profession in American society."[30] As law appears more and more the central arbitral and meaning-conferring institution in American society, it generates anxiety and consternation about the legalization of life.

America is a society that absorbs huge amounts of law and lawyering—both absolutely and compared to other industrial democracies. Even when we adjust for the different occupational structure and nomenclature of providers of legal services, it is clear that the United States supports far more lawyers per capita than do other rich industrial democracies.[31] This reliance on lawyers is the effect rather than the cause of a decentralized legal regime in which any activity is subject to multiple bodies of regulation; where the application of those rules depends on complex and perhaps unknowable states of fact; where decision-makers produce not definitive and immutable rulings but contingent temporary resolutions that are open to further challenge; where outcomes are subject to contestation in multiple forums by an expanding legion of organized and persistent players who invest increasing amounts in more technically sophisticated legal services. Robert Kagan observes that in the United States, popular demand for expanded remedies and regulatory protections

> have been filtered through a political culture that mistrusts "big government" and resists high taxes. In a political system that lacks strong national law enforcement, regulatory, medical care and welfare bureaucracies, the satisfaction of demands for "total justice" necessarily has been left in large measure to state and local judges and governmental agencies, even for the implementation of federally enacted programs and policies. Without the capacity for exercising centralized, "top down" control over local police officers, environmental inspectors, school districts and businesses, legislators and high courts have granted ordinary citizens and advocacy groups the right to haul errant officials and corporations into court. Lawyers and adversarial legalism thus substitute for hierarchical bureaucratic and political accountability mechanisms.[32]

The allegiance of the lawyers that provide these services is less to their guild than to their clients, whose views they absorb and whose interests they champion. Mark Osiel points out that American lawyers are different not only in their "unqualified partisanship" but also in the kind of knowledge that comprises their expertise.[33] They provide not only technical mastery of legal texts but "practical

THE POLICY OF THE LAW!

55. The Policy of the Law! Illustration by Harry Furniss for A'Beckett's
The Comic Blackstone, 1887. Powered by vast minions, the law, although made
of books and files and topped by a scarecrow in judge's ermine, crushes all
before it, rich and poor alike.

judgement: discernment in predicting how courts will balance, in light of under-lying policy and principle, the relative significance of particular features of a com-plex factual configuration."[34] The distinctive scope and role of American lawyers underlies their prominence in the American political and cultural scene. As the legend of lawyers undermining American competitiveness attests, they are seen as leading actors astride the main stage, who bear responsibility for the society's central failings, real and imaginary.

Through this decentralized, endlessly receptive, and very expensive system, we attempt to pursue our multiple and colliding individual and social visions of substantive justice.[35] We want our legal institutions to yield both comprehensive policy embodying shared public values and facilities for the relentless pursuit of individual interests. But we are suspicious of the concentrated authority required for the former and reluctant to support the elaborated public machinery required to provide the latter routinely to ordinary citizens. We prefer fragmented govern-ment and reactive legal institutions with limited resources, so that in large mea-sure both the making of public policy and the vindication of individual claims are delegated to the parties themselves, who are left to fend according to their own resources. In this complex system, lawyers form a major component of these resources. But lawyers, each attached to her own client, cannot fulfill the fatally divided promise of substantive justice.[36]

The lawyer joke corpus is a forum in which strands of popular and elite resis-tance to the law come together. Both are anxious whether the society and world we live in are just. We each know that in this or that familiar corner of things, wrong-doers prosper and there is lots of undeserved and avoidable suffering. We would like to think that nevertheless somehow it all adds up, that each gets his deserts, that there is a cosmic balance in which virtue is rewarded and evil punished. But there is a nagging feeling that the wicked flourish.[37]

What causes the shortfall? Law, courts, and lawyers seem deeply implicated. Even as we have more law, injustice seems to increase rather than dwindle. The amount of injustice increases, not because there is less justice but because the sphere of justice (and injustice) is expanding. As the law addresses new demands for justice it does not, paradoxically, reduce the amount of injustice. For our soci-ety produces new injustices at an ever increasing rate. Injustice is something bad that someone ought to do something about. As the risks of everyday life have de-clined dramatically, there is a widespread sense that science, technology, and gov-ernment can produce solutions for many of the remaining (and newly revealed) problems.[38] As more things are capable of being done by human institutions, the line between what is seen as unavoidable misfortune and what is seen as imposed injustice shifts. The realm of injustice is enlarged: hurricanes are misfortunes, but inadequate warning, insufficient preparation, and mismanaged relief efforts may be injustices.[39] Once, having an incurable disease was a misfortune; now a percep-tion of treatment bungled or withheld or insufficient vigor in pursuing a cure can give rise to a claim of injustice. As the scope of possible interventions broadens, more and more terrible things become defined by the incidence of potential intervention. Consciousness of injustice increases, not because the world is a worse place, but because it is in important ways a better, more just place.

Every addition to the human capacity for control and remedy enlarges the legal world. As resources increase and expectations rise, new vistas of injustice unfold and new demands for remedy are brought to the legal system. But as more justice is possible, more choices need to be made. Our pursuit of justice is not single-minded. We want lots of other things as well—affluence, security, and social acceptance to mention only a few. As with health care, the rationing of justice is inevitable. Demands compete for an inadequate supply, and possession of other resources helps capture some of that supply. We constantly encounter the "how much justice can you afford?" question.

Why should this anxiety about justice be so much more intense in the United States? Perhaps Americans can indulge immodest expectations with less constraint by ancestral notions of propriety. Or perhaps they lack the cushioning provided by highly developed welfare states. In any event, they clearly search for social justice in a different location—relying more on law (and correspondingly less on government) as a vehicle of justice.

So the swollen body of jokes about lawyers is another form of American exceptionalism, testimony to our vaunting expectations of law and our anxiety that they will be disappointed. The jokes reflect a mismatch that we cannot escape. Suspicious of government, we want impartial law to secure us the fruits of commonwealth. But that same law is a vehicle of individual assertion, at the service of every "special interest," including our own. Longing for fraternity, we find ourselves ever more dependent on those who zealously guard our self-interest and our less fraternal impulses, the lawyers. Critics point to the paradox of trying to achieve social or communal justice with legal tools suited to the assertion and defense of individual interest. And, of course, the invocation of community affords a ready disguise to those who seek to forward their own interests and dismantle the protections of others.

APPENDIX:
Register of Jokes

NOTES

REFERENCES

INDEX

56. The fake coat-of-arms is an old comic device. At the beginning and end of this appendix we see two specimens, separated by centuries, gravitate to a set of common themes and symbols. The 1692 English *Dum Vivo Thrivo* ("Where I live, I thrive") (BM 1284) depicts the lawyer as a fox in robes, spouting reams of legal jargon, taking fees from both sides, and emerging with clients' wealth . The verse reads: "Clients, Precarious Titles May Debate; / The Lawyer only Thrives, grows Rich and Great: / The Golden Fee alone is his Delight; / Gold make ye Dubious Cause go wrong or Right. / Nay; rather than his Modesty he'll hide, / He'll take a Privae Dawb o' t'other side: / Heraldry ne'er Devis'd a fitter Crest, / Than Sly Volpone so demurely drest: / Lawyers by subtle querks, their Clients fleece, / So when old Reynard Preaches, 'ware ye Geese. / Two Purse-proud Sots yt quarrel for a Straw, / Are justly ye Supporters of the Law: / As Fools at Cudgels, find it to their Cost, / The best comes off but with dry Blows at Most. / So wrangling Clients may at variance fall / But 'tis ye Lawyer Runs away with all."

APPENDIX
Register of Jokes

The Register of Jokes lists all the jokes in the archive that is the source of the lawyer jokes examined in this book. It includes some, but not many, that are not included in the text. The sources are presented in the notes to each individual joke. This register contains some summary information about these jokes and provides a name for each joke. In a few cases (e.g., ambulance stories) a set of related jokes are clubbed together under a single name. The register indicates in brackets [ ] the year of the joke's first known (to me) appearance as a lawyer joke. Jokes are classified as *indigenous* to the legal setting (I) or *switched* to the legal setting (S). In the case of switched jokes, the year of its first known appearance is identified in braces { }; if there is a predominant earlier subject it is indicated in parentheses, e.g., (politician). Cases in which a joke is shared with another group are indicated by an equal sign within the parentheses (=). Where I feel confident that the joke is not currently in wide circulation, I have marked it as a dropout (D).

A few items marked "Supp." are jokes that are not told about lawyers, but seem closely related to particular lawyer jokes.

Jokes that I was able to identify with a tale-type (Aarne-Thompson 1961) or motif (Thompson 1955) are indicated by AT or Motif.

The dates given should be read as dates by which the item was in circulation. They represent the earliest instance that I found, but some may have appeared in print earlier and most probably appear in the oral culture earlier—in some cases much earlier.

Codes

[ ] year of first appearance as lawyer joke
( ) predominant earlier subject
(=) shared subject
{ } first appearance with any subject
I indigenous
S switched
D dropout

A. DISCOURSE

Lying and Dishonesty

1. lips moving [1986] (husband){1935} S
2. lawyer = liar (play on sound) [1797] I
3. which side (play on lie/lay) [1669] I
4. death's door [1899] I
5. other play on lie/lay [1639]
6. either side [1945] (teacher) {1879}
7. don't need lawyer for truth [1913] I
8. lying clumsily [1923] I
9. lying as professional qualification [1541] I
   A9 supp. who will weigh coal {1916}
10. not too honest [1956] I
11. what's the difference? [1991] (politician) {1928} S
12. regular kind [1997] I
13. put in lies yourself [1850] I D
14. sometimes tell truth [1895] I
15. God works wonders [1793] I
16. scarcest
17. game laws [1909] I D
18. two in grave [1892] I
19. strange [1893] I
20. miscellaneous lying

Workers in the Mills of Deceit

21. professional advice [1942] I
22. juryman learns law is cheating [1873] I
23. lawyer objects to truth [1923] I
24. lantern [1902] I
25. oath [1889. Other versions to 1877] I

Eloquence, Persuasiveness, Resourcefulness

26. inconsistent defenses [1853] I
27. equally conclusive [1879]
28. client convinced [1871] I (AT 1860c; Motif X319.1 [Eloquent lawyer makes obviously guilty client doubt his own guilt])
29. what could he possibly say [1890] I
   A29 supp. Hear the evidence {1871} I
30. reversing course [1871] I
31. another doctor [1988] (Jew or patient) {1926} S
32. ghostwriter's revenge [1987] (speechwriter) {1965} S
33. two plus two [1982] (Communist functionaries) {1953} S

"Hot Air": Fakery and Bombast

34. telephone [1915] I
35. pound the table (1871) I
36. can't talk without thinking [1898] I

37. who's doing our thinking [1950] I
38. brain in jar [1988] I
39. winning in spite of argument [1926] I
40. refute any point [1995] I
41. gas works [1915] I
42. balloon [1990] (parliamentarian) {1954} (client version 1999; associate version 2001) S

Masters of Stratagem

43. overstate debt [1947] {1877} S
44. unscrew arm [1889] I
45. give clerk more [1853] [Cf. B3] I?
46. steal more [1925] I
47. jury selection [1997]
48. pay off low bidder [1993] {1979} S
49. train con (1997) S

Lawyer Outsmarted

50. measured it [1765] I
51. clock behind you [c. 1926] I
52. hit lawyer hard [1852] I
53. all wanted to acquit [1890] I
54. watching door [1992?] I
55. cow came home [1975?] I
56. gift to judge [1905] I
57. other side's story [1904] I
58. Pathelin (lawyer's winning strategy turned against him by client)[c.1480] I AT 1585
    [The lawyer's mad client]
59. outsmarted by blonde [2000] {1956} S
60. duck [1998]
61. cigar fires [2002] (men) {1897} S
62. misc. discourse

B. Economic Predators

Only the Lawyer Wins

1. law impoverishes [1742] I
2. fat lawyer, thin clients [1795] I
3. lawyer consumes stake [1742] I
4. sheep will be ours [1988] I
5. you'll get it all [1922] I
6. hard work to get money from lawyers [1910] I

Taking It All

7. won't move without fees [1832] I
8. lawyer takes residue of loot [1928] I
9. won't defend client who didn't steal [1967] I
10. innocent until proven broke [1999] I
11. nothing to offer [1879] I
12. entirely professional [1860] I

13. remainder a mistake [1898] I
14. newly discovered evidence [1915] I
15. go to prison broke [1968] I
16. lawyer takes legacy [1908]I
17. light bulb . . . afford [1981] S
18. light bulb . . . yours to his [1995] S

A Prodigious Predator

19. two fat wethers [1864] I D
20. sure to be fleeced [1864] I
21. client was rich [1915] I
22. fix up our home [1938] I
23. pockets [1871] I?
24. lawyer would steal more (1864) I
25. pirate [1902] I?
26. did he get anything? [1899] I?
27. pickpockets concede prey [1887] I
28. parasites/scavengers (tick, leech, vampire, vulture, buzzard) [1993] I
29. professional courtesy [1877] I
30. mistake shark for lawyer [1993] I

Fee Simple

31. contingency fee [1883] I
32. counterfeit dollar [1905] I
33. anyone can fall down manhole [1895] I
34. think you got hit by brick [1905] I
35. timesheets [1980] I
36. like buying a car [1940] [=doctor] I
37. didn't make much either [1979] (=doctor) {1975} S

Throwing the Meter

38. butcher and dog [1737] I AT 1589 [The Lawyer's Dog Steals Meat]
39. lawyer charges for "social" services (1830) I
40. bill for greeting [1739] I
41. doctor at party [1945] I
42. sequence of lawyers send bills [1993] I
43. charge for advice at dinner [1887] I
44. wake up at night [1900] I
45. crossing street [1945] (doctor) {1922} S
46. three questions [1976] (=fortune-teller) {1971} S

Sexploitation

47. spinster's estate [1910] I
48. really needed this case [1987] (friend) {1963} S
49. workaholic avoidance of romance [1997] {1915} S
50. clucks defiance [1962] I
51. choice of sins [1991] (suitor, various) {1945} S
52. screwing somebody already [1987] (Republican) {1945} S

53. screw out of what? [1992] I
    B53 supp. out of crooked business {1901}
54. multiply-married virgin [1995] {1964} S
55. screwing in queue [1994] {1976} S
56. screw partner's wife/repay $1000 [1988] (friend) {1953} S AT 1420C [Borrowing from the Husband and Returning to the Wife]
57. pay whore with client's debt [1992] (Israeli) {1968} S
58. dogs [1964] S?
59. misc. sexploitation

C. The Devil's Playmates

The Devil's Own [cf. A2]

1. St. Ives [1688] D
2. association with devil/hell/sin/irreligion [1756]
3. came to you [1871]
4. wicked practice law a while [1895] D

Headed for Hell

5. brimstone [1828] I D
6. my attorney'll be there [1788] I
7. chase lawyer in hell [1892]
8. retrieve from devil [1858] I
9. not out of danger [1986]
10. fire across street [1996](patient){1925} S
11. next to fire [1854] (=preachers) I
12. best lawyers in hell [1801] I

Absent in Heaven

13. no lawyers admitted to heaven [1793] I [Cf. AT 1738] [The Dream: All Parsons in Hell]
14. no prosecution in heaven because no lawyers [1854] I [Cf. AT 1738]
15. where will you get a lawyer? [1938] {1953} S? [Cf. AT 1738]
16. no lawyer in heaven to do divorce [1989] (parson){1953?} I [Cf. AT 1738]
17. first lawyer in heaven [1906] (=various) {1947} S AT 802 [The Peasant in Heaven]

A Kingdom of this World

18. reward in this world [1871] I
19. die like savior [1831]
20. opposite of Christian (1898)
21. too important for God [1892] I
22. religion not efficacious in legal realm [1904] I
    C22 supp. Akhnai's Oven (majority prevails over God) {2d cent. C.E.}
23. he's not, I am. [1961] I
24. chapter 11 [1998] I
25. judge more efficacious [1902] I

D. Conflict

Excess and Insufficient Combativeness

1. argumentative son [1923] I
2. fight over nothing [1859] I

3. fair to both [1958] I
4. chaos [1964] (politician) {1938} S

Promoters of Conflict

5. lest thy servant perish [1975] I
6. steal clothes [1915] I
7. town with two lawyers [1880] I
8. ambulance stories [1928] I
9. crutches [1913] I
10. need lawyer to know if injured [1905] I
11. lawyer advises conciliation [1916] I

The Conniving Claimant

12. determined litigant {1893}
13. strike blow to get damages {1907}
14. lie down beside you {1922}
15. compensation has set in {1942}
16. I'm on disability {1999}
17. victim thinks he is defendant {1911}
18. defense preemption {1894}
19. Jewish litigiousness {1923}
20. next week {1907}
21. why the delay? {1902}
22. other fire stories {1900}
23. misfortune as good fortune {1906}
24. gold digger {1902}
25. how do you make a flood {1925}
26. lift arm {1931}
27. Lourdes {1959}
28. spiteful litigant {1848}
29. litigious child {1959}

Litigation Fever

30. lawyer son wants me lame [1922] I
31. fore [1984] (Jew) {1915} S
32. orchard [1987] I
33. annuity for life [1853] I
34. won't settle [1952] I
35. virtuoso of delay I
36. doctor won't treat lawyer [1908] I
37. lawyer goes crazy when can't figure how to sue self [1994] I
38. spitting in shoes [1999] (waiter, cook) {1968} S

Lawyer as Champion

39. lawyer as heroic benefactor/compassionate champion [1877] I D
40. get money back [1943] I
41. OK to come to work late [1946] I

E. Demography

Women in Combat

1. pit bull [1990] {1988} S
2. female prosecutor and terrorist [1994] {1990} S
3. marry woman lawyer [1915] I
4. cross lawyer with feminist [1977] I
5. monomania [1992] (golf/political obsessive) {1971} S
6. feed gorillas [1990] {1971} S
7. promote one with biggest tits [1990] (boss) {1945} S
8. misc. woman lawyer

Jews and Other Outsiders

9. almost thou persuadest me [1905] I
10. yens goy [1928]
11. misc. Jewish lawyer
12. misc. ethnic lawyer

Seniors and Juniors

13. junior outsmarts senior [1795] I
14. senior exploits junior [1997]

F. Betrayal

1. collision and flask [1982] (various) {1917} S
2. outrun bear [1991] (outdoorsmen) {1982} S
3. payment during robbery [1993] (Jews) {1916} S
4. extra $100 bill [1988] (Jewish merchant) {1926} S
5. safe unlocked [1989] (partners, often Jewish) {1922} S
   F5 supp. put it back {1952}
6. mine died [1988] (partners) {1928} S
7. beautiful house too [1993] {1905} S
8. celebrity greeting spurned [1988] (various) {1971} S
9. sign language [1990] (translator) {1984} S
10. poisoned you [1987] (spouse, partner) {1928} S
11. trust me [1992] (Yiddish) {1982} S
12. partner undoes wishes [1997] (dumb guys) {1987} S Cf. AT 750A [The Wishes]
    F12 supp. just a cup of coffee{1980}
13. check in the coffin [1964] (Jew, Scot, Welsh, etc.) {1876} S Motif K231.13 [Agreement
    to Leave Sum of Money on Coffin of Friend].
14. misc. betrayal

G. Morally Deficient

Suspect Profession (criminal, prostitute, etc.)

1. don't expect much of them [c.1860] I?
2. who did he rob? [1832] I?
3. criminal lawyer [1913] I
4. how else get advice [1871] I
5. whose profession? [1964] (=doctor) {1932} S

6. prostitute by luck [1977] I?
7. prostitute: no difference [1989]
8. prostitute stops after you die [1995]
9. prostitute doesn't pretend to care [1996]
10. some things hooker won't do [1990] I?
11. other prostitute

Looking Out for Number One (indifferent to others)

12. baby grabs all [1989] (politician) {1907} S
13. my Rolex [1990] [=yuppie] S?
14. drag Harry [1990] (golf addict) {1964} S
15. Mother Theresa [1993] I?
16. what's the catch? [1990] (agent) {1988} S?
17. I don't see a problem [1993]
18. misc. indifference to others

No Redeeming Social Value

19. refund [1987] (rich miser) {1911} S AT 809 [Rich Man Allowed to Stay in Heaven]
20. don't give to any [1991] (rich miser, often Jewish) {1926} S
21. higher grass [2000] {1922} S
22. play at night [1994] {1977} S

"He Just Doesn't Get It"

23. a few more missteps . . . [1987] (bookkeeper) {1928} S
24. father sued for tuition [1982] I
25. just a suggestion [1987]

In the Laboratory

26. laboratory rats [1984]
27. misc. moral deficiency

H. OBJECTS OF SCORN

Circle of Scorn

1. throw lawyer back in mud [c.1475] Motif X317
2. skid marks [1985] I?
3. hostages [1992] (spouse, mother-in-law) (1895) S
4. cows protest [1990] (various ethnic) {1974} S
5. commemorative stamp [1992] (tyrannical ruler) {1958} S
6. saved from drowning [1992] (military officers, politicians) {1928} S

Sounding the Depths: "Lower than . . ."

7. prefer burglar, etc.[1905] I
8. piano player in whorehouse [1986] (various) {1976} S
   H8 supp. tell about source of shame {1963}
9. better a bastard[1987] (black) {1946} S
10. would ruin heaven [1995]
11. toxic-waste dumps [1987] (various ethnic) {1964} S
12. question her punishment [1990] (various) {1968} S

Into the Slime

13. spider[1822]
14. snake [1993]
15. blind rabbit [1988] I
16. sperm [1992] (black) {1991} S
17. catfish [1992]
18. Viagra {1998}
19. ten-inch prick [1994] {1971} S Viagra {1998}

The Anal Connection

20. cats bury [1988] (black) {1983} S
21. anal sex [1988] (various) {1953} S
22. enema [1990] (Irish/Texans) {1954. Expurgated versions from 1906} S
23. bucket [1990] (various) {1965} S
24. melting [1993] (various) {1983} S
25. taste worse [1993] (Texan, black) {1975} S
26. give up law practice [1995] (show business) {1956} S
27. misc. anal

I. Death Wish

Prehistory

1. bury twenty-one [1850] I (=undesirable immigrants/politicians, etc.)
2. rebate for killing lawyer [1887] I
3. hang lawyer instead [1895] (weaver) {1614} S AT1534A; Motif J2233.1 [Innocent Man Chosen to Fit the Stake (Noose)]
4. check with undertaker [1959] (office-seeker) {1922} S

The Contemporary Onslaught

5. more cement [1986]
6. good start [1988] (various) {1982} S
7. bus over cliff [1989] {1977} S
8. love to hear it [1988] (various) {1928} S
9. make sure he's dead [1993]
10. wanted to tell him [1998]
11. bury deep down [1989]
12. deathbed conversion [1995] (Jews, Catholics, etc.) {1926} S

Let's Kill All the Lawyers

13. get in line [1990] (wife, mother-in-law) {1469? from Cicero?} S
14. Doberman [1992] (black) {1983} S
15. alligator [1993] (Jews, blacks, etc.) {1967} S
16. lawyers get double [1995] S AT 1331 [The Covetous and the Envious]; Motif J2074 Twice the Wish to the Enemy]
17. got him with door [1995] (black) {1984} S
18. open season [1997] I

A Pestilential Affliction

19. more lawyers than people [1990] I

20. throw out of train [1993] (wife, Mexican, etc) {c. 1508} S
    I22 supp. make everyone happy (politicians) {1950}
21. brass rat [1990] (Chinese) {1966} S
22. misc. death wish

J. ENEMIES OF JUSTICE

Doing Justice

1. appeal at once [1910] I
2. two oppose hanging [1852] I D
3. consult to break law [1922] I D
4. cheaper to obey law [1922–30] I D
5. justice not enough [1915] I

Lawyer as Enemy of Justice

6. conveys physical threat [1854] I D
7. ensnares innocent [1871] I D
8. lawyer advises escape I [1936]
9. corporation law [1915] I
10. charge more to evade law [1922] I
11. no tricks this time [1897] I D
12. proved it constitutional [1915–45] I D
13. don't separate from lawyers[1889] I D
14. wonderful quality [1982] I
15. expert in justice [1982] I

What Does Law Deliver?

16. not courts of justice [1898] I
17. chief justice [1871] I D
18. pricy lawyer will win [1915] I D
19. courts open to all [1822] I D
20. not one law for rich [by 1856] ID
21. how much justice can you afford? [1973] I
22. misc. justice

K. META-JOKES

1. how many lawyer jokes [1994] I
2. didn't know they were jokes [1997] I
3. Research (academics) {1902}

A HINT TO THE BAR ASSOCIATION.
PROPOSED ESCUTCHEON FOR THE LEGAL FRATERNITY.

57. Two centuries later, in 1877, *The Daily Graphic*, a New York newspaper published, *Tout Pour Soi, Rien Pour Les Autres* ("All for me, nothing for the others"). Here the fox is joined by a vulture, the lawyer takes the oyster and leaves a shell for each of the litigants (a visual depiction of B3) and collects piles and bags of money. In addition to raking it in at clients' expense just as his predecessor did, a new and ominous claim is made: "Laws I make and destroy."

NOTES

ABBREVIATIONS

AML
    A Million Laughs. CD-ROM. Spring Valley, NY: Interactive, 1993.

AT
    Aarne 1961. Aarne, Antti. 1961. *The types of the folktale: A classification and bibliography.* Trans. Stith Thompson. 2nd rev. ed. Helsinki: Academia Scientarum Fennica

1995 Cal.
    365 uproarious lawyer jokes, riddles, and quotes: 1995 calendar. Riderwood, MD: Paramount Enterprises, 1994.

1996 Cal.
    The lawyer joke-a-day calendar [for 1996]. Lame Duck, 1995.

1997 Cal.
    The lawyer joke-a-day calendar [for 1997]. Lame Duck, 1996.

1998 Cal.
    The lawyer joke-a-day calendar [for 1998]. Lame Duck, 1997.

2000 Cal.
    Lawyers: jokes, quotes and anecdotes. Kansas City, MO: Andrews McMeel, 1999.

2002 Cal.
    Lawyers: jokes, quotes and anecdotes. Kansas City, MO: Andrews McMeel, 2001.

BM
    British Museum. 1870–1954. *Catalog of political and personal satires preserved in the department of prints and drawings in the British Museum.* Vols. 1–4 by Frederick George Stephens; vols. 5–11 by M. Dorothy George. 11 vols. London: The British Museum.

CLLH 1995
    Canonical list of lawyer humor (court jester). URL at on-line section of reference list.

CLMH 1995
    Canonical list of medica humor (funny bone). URL at on-line section of reference list.

Jhumor List
    Jewish humor list. E-mail humor list, date as indicated.

Lawyer Jokes
    various dates. URLs at on-line section of reference list.

Lawyer Jokes from Internet
    Unnamed collection on file with the author.

INTRODUCTION

1. Lawyer jokes from Internet 1994, no. 134; Brallier 1996: 102; 1998 Cal.: Oct. 29; Regan 2001: 108; Anon. 2001a: 162. Cf. Hobbes 2002b: 64 (woman jokes).

2. McCaslin 1997. The joke surfaced earlier in O'Dwyer's PR Services Report 1997: 1; Streiker 1998: 245.

3. Radin 1946.

4. Philip Stubbes quoted at Ives 1960: 137.

5. Tucker 1984: 11; Ives 1960: 130.

6. Ives 1960: 99.

7. Prest 1986: 286.

8. Brooks 1986: 138.

9. The "economic thinking of the day for the most part held that lawyers, instead of adding to the nation's wealth, siphoned their incomes from those farmers, merchants, and tradesmen who did." Brooks 1986: 134.

10. Veall 1970: 203, 208–9.

11. Chroust 1965: 17, in part quoting from John McMaster, *History of the People of the United States during Lincoln's Administration* (1927), 302. See also Bloomfield 1976: chap. 2; Gawalt 1970: 283; Warren 1911: chap. 10.

12. Adams 1902: 343, 359.

13. The presence and coexistence of the multiple and conflicting strands in American legal consciousness are richly documented in Ewick and Silbey 1998. From intensive interviews about the way that people construct "legality" in everyday life, they distill three widely shared perspectives on the legal: the law as majestic impartial authority; the law as a complex game of pursuing self-interest; and the law as oppressive constraint. These three perspectives are not the possession of different sets of individuals, but coexist in different mixes in most of us and are manifested in different settings. The vitality of law, Ewick and Silbey argue, lies in the combination of these multiple perspectives: "the majestic removal of law from everyday life inspires allegiance" while "the cynicism and pessimism expressed in a view of law as a game level our aspirations and set realistic expectations" (31).

14. Not only do the doings of imaginary lawyers inform our ideas about real ones, but the two are often conflated. The 1993 *National Law Journal* survey asked people to name the lawyer they most admired; the top ten included both Perry Mason and Matlock. Samborn 1993. Among legal intellectuals, this is paralleled by the struggle over the significance of *To Kill a Mockingbird's* Atticus Finch. See n. 22 below and chap. 1, p. 6–7.

15. The Gallup results are presented in American Bar Association Commission on Advertising 1995: 64.

16. On the literature of legal nostalgia, see Galanter 1996: 549.

17. Francis Nevins 1984 calls the late 1950s–early 1960s period the "first golden age of the law film" (3, 4).

18. Stark 1987: 255.

19. Chase 1986: 281, 284. Chase says this image coalesced in the period from 1957 to 1963 (Sputnik to Kennedy assassination). See also Asimow 1996: 1131.

20. C. Johnson 1994: 14.

21. Asimow 1996: 1138.

22. Many of the claims and counterclaims are recounted in C. Johnson 1994. Atkinson 1999 sets out an elaborated critique of Atticus as a model for lawyers. Steven Lubet 1999 propounded a revisionist take on the story. In Lubet's view, "Atticus was able to recognize and rise above the race prejudices of his time, but he was not able to comprehend the class and gender prejudices that suffused his work" (1359). Five other legal academics disagreed vigorously. Althouse et al. 1999. A controversy over Kenneth Starr's appropriation of Atticus Finch to reprove President Clinton is described at chap. 1, p. 39–40.

23. Looking back, Lipset and Schneider 1987 note that "the early 1960s turned out to be a high-water mark in the history of the American public's attitudes toward their key social, political and economic structures" (15).

24. Wolff 1971: 8, 12.

25. Lefcourt 1971: 15 ("collapsing"); Rostow 1971 (Is Law Dead?).

26. See, e.g., Sheppard 1975: "With the overflow of Watergate and the revelation that a great majority of the offenders were members of the legal profession, the public image of the Bar seems to have reached a low ebb. . . . There seems to be a rising tide of resentment to the entire profession who [sic] guides the legal system in our country" (184).

27. On public interest law, see generally Weisbrod et al. 1978; Council for Public Interest Law 1976. On access to justice, see Cappelletti 1978–79 and Cappelletti 1981.

28. Carter 1978. Earlier critiques include Blumberg 1967; Bloom 1968; Nader and Green 1976; Auerbach 1976; Lieberman 1978. Carter's address is the direct descendant of an unheralded Law Day speech he gave at the University of Georgia School of Law, four years earlier, as governor of Georgia. In that speech he traced his understanding about justice and "what's right and wrong in this society" to reading Reinhold Niebuhr and listening to the songs of Bob Dylan (Carter 1975). Cataloging the injustices of the legal system, he chastised lawyers for tolerating injustice, lacking fire to improve the system of which they were a part, avoiding the obligation to "restore equity and justice and to preserve or enhance it," and being distracted from the pursuit of justice by self-serving concern for their own well-being and authority. He closed with the reflection, echoed four years later, that the State could be transformed if the body of attorneys were deeply committed to abolishing the inequities of the system. Apparently the speech was from notes and no full text exists. The version that appears in his book of addresses was reconstructed from a tape recording.

Fortuitously, the audience that day included gonzo journalist Hunter S. Thompson, who reports Carter telling him in 1976, "That was probably the best speech I ever made" (Thompson 1976: 54, 64). Viewing it as "the heaviest and most eloquent thing I have ever heard from the mouth of a politician," Thompson extended an enthusiastic endorsement of Carter's candidacy for the Democratic presidential nomination.

29. Quotations are at Carter 1978: 842, 843, 844, 846.

30. The *New York Times* reported, "Leading lawyers around the country reacted with anger, bitterness, frustration and sadness yesterday to President Carter's assertion that the legal profession has been an impediment to social justice." Goldstein 1978. The *Wall Street Journal* noted that since "Washington itself has become the fountainhead of unnecessary laws and litigation," the president should spend "less time lashing out at lawyers in general and more time asking the government's lawyers just what it is they are trying to

do" (May 10, 1978). The *Washington Post* dismissed the president's remarks as "unfocused resentment" (May 7, 1978). Two-thirds of a sample of registered voters polled by Yankelovich, Skelly, and White thought the president's criticism of the legal profession was fair. A Roper poll of a national sample of adults found 53 percent who thought his criticisms were justified and another 16 percent who thought them partly justified (Roper 1989).

31. The American Bar Association's Special Commission on Evaluation of Professional Standards was known as the Kutak Commission, after its chair, the late Robert Kutak (National Organization of Bar Counsel, 1980). The impetus for a new ethics code, which was adopted on August 2, 1980, came in part from the damage to the bar's public image occasioned by Watergate. See Spann 1977: 2.

32. Schneyer 1989: 677.

33. Schneyer 1989.

34. Clark 1983: 79, 85.

35. The signal event in the crystallization of the "too much law" critique was the National Conference on the Causes of Popular Dissatisfaction with the Administration of Justice, held in April 1976, at the instance of Chief Justice Warren Burger. The proceedings are published at 70 F.R.D. 79 (1976). The conference, known as the Pound Conference, commemorated Roscoe Pound's 1906 address of the same title; the participants (like Pound) propounded "popular" perceptions unaided by any discernible consultation of the broader public.

36. *U.S. News & World Report* 1978.

37. Burger 1976.

38. These concerns antedate Carter's 1978 speech. Burger's address to the 1976 Pound Conference contains faint echoes of the public justice critique in the chief justice's observation of "the loss of public confidence caused by lawyers' using the courts for their own ends rather than with a consideration of the public interest." Burger 1976: 91. But the predominant theme of the chief justice's address is not a shortage of justice, but surfeit of law (91). Just a year later, the chief justice was warning that "unless we devise substitutes for the courtroom processes—and do so quickly—we may well be on our way to a society overrun by hordes of lawyers, hungry as locusts, and brigades of judges in numbers never before contemplated." Burger 1977: 8; Goldstein 1977.

39. These larger assertions about the civil justice system were embodied in oft-related atrocity stories about outrageous claims and monstrous decisions. See Daniels 1989; Hayden 1991; Brill and Lyons 1986: 1; Strasser 1987: 39.

40. In the United States, the population grew from 180 million in 1960 to 238.7 million in 1985. The median age increased from 29.4 in 1960 to 31.5 in 1985. Per capita income grew from $9,023 in 1960 to $15,029 in 1985. The median years of school completed increased from 10.6 years in 1960 to 12.6 years in 1985. U.S. Bureau of Census 1976: 224; U.S. Bureau of Census 1987: 14, 121, 419, 754. All dollar amounts in 1982 dollars. Current dollar amounts were converted into 1982 constant dollars using the annual GNP implicit price deflator of the given years. See *Economic Report of the President* 1987: 248–49, table B3; U.S. Bureau of Census 1987: 226, table 732.

41. Public spending on social welfare increased from $169.2 billion in 1960 to $653.9 billion in 1985. Public spending on health and hospitals increased from $17.0 billion in 1960 to $56.7 billion in 1985. Average life expectancy increased from 69.7 years in 1960 to 74.7 years in 1985. U.S. Bureau of Census 1976: 1120–27; 1987: 69, 25, 334. For discussion of higher expectations of institutional performance, see L. Friedman 1985.

42. Lipset and Schneider 1987.

43. The gross national product increased by 679 percent, from $515.3 billion in 1960 to $4,014.9 billion in 1985. U.S. Bureau of Census 1987: 421, table 685. Employment rose from 67 million in 1960 to 108 million in 1985. Workforce increased, due largely to greater participation by women, from 38 percent of the population to over 45 percent.

44. In 1960, 51.5 percent of GNP was in goods and 37.2 was in services. In 1985, goods made up only 40.9 percent of GNP while services made up 49 percent. U.S. Bureau of Census 1976: 228, series F; 1987: 423, table 688.

45. The percentage of wage and salary workers employed in the financial sector increased from 4.7 percent in 1960 to 6.8 percent in 1987. From 1960 to 1968, the ratio of interest income to pretax profits in the United States increased fivefold, rising from 9 percent to 51 percent. The ratio of external to internal financing used by nonfinancial corporations increased from 1.5: 1 to 4.6: 1. U.S. Bureau of Labor Statistics 1988: table A21; *Economic Report of the President* 1988: tables B12 and B89; Galanter and Rogers 1991: 54.

46. Exports and imports as a percentage of gross domestic product increased from 10.5 percent in 1960 to 23.3 percent in 1985. *Economic Report of the President* 1988: tables B1 and B8; Galanter and Rogers 1991: 14, table 2. U.S. assets invested abroad increased from $277.0 billion to $853.8 billion, while foreign assets in the U.S. increased from $132.4 billion to $949.8 billion. U.S. Bureau of Census 1987: 779, table 1389.

47. Galanter 1999 (lawyers); Caplow et al 2001: 31 (comparison with doctors).

48. Between 1960 and 1985, the share of the gross domestic product contributed by the legal services sector increased from 0.59 percent to 1.17 percent. The share of national income contributed by the legal services sector increased form 0.52 percent in 1960 to 1.23 percent in 1986. On the value of lawyers' work that is not counted in the legal services sector, see Sander and Williams 1989: 431, 435.

49. A rough measure of the sheer quantity of rules may be derived from the number of pages added to the *Federal Register* each year: in 1960, 14,477 pages were added; in 1985, 53,480. This is the gross addition for the year; some of it supplants or repeals earlier regulation and some is ephemeral. But making appropriate discounts for depreciation, it is clear that there has been a great increase in the "capital stock" of regulation. From 1961 to 1977, the number of pages in the *Federal Register* devoted to regulations increased from 14,000 to 66,000 with more than two-thirds of that growth occurring during the 1970s. Buhler 1978; Galanter and Rogers 1991.

There were comparable increases of regulation by state and local governments. The absence of direct measures makes it necessary to use the even rougher measures of expenditures and employment. State and local government expenditures increased from 9.7 percent of the GNP in 1960 to 12.9 percent in 1985. *Economic Report of the President* 1988: 248, 341. Total civilian employees of governmental units roughly doubled in this period, from 8.8 million in 1960 to 16.7 million in 1985. U.S. Bureau of Census 1976: series Y 272–89; U.S. Bureau of Census 1987: table 479. Not all of these employees were engaged in tasks connected directly with law making or regulation, but the figures are used here as a rough index of the increase in regulatory activity.

50. Less formal channels of legal information grew as well. For example, in 1989 nearly 1,000 newsletters were published in Washington (in addition to those published by the 3,200 Washington-based associations that mailed newsletters to their members). Weiss 1989: 10.

51. At the turn of the previous century, legal work was reshaped by the telephone, the typewriter, expanded legal publishing, and new research devices like digests and citators.

Apart from minor refinements like loose-leaf services, the technology of the law office remained essentially unchanged into the 1960s.

52. On the "trough" in American litigation from the onset of the Great Depression until the end of the postwar recovery, see Galanter 2001.

53. On the changing patterns of litigation in the federal courts, see Galanter 1988; Posner 1985; Clark 1981.

54. Curran 1985: 16. This figure includes lawyers as judges, court officials, and support personnel.

55. Employees in the federal judiciary increased from 4,992 in 1960 to over 18,000 in 1985 and 20,244 in 1987. U.S. Bureau of Census 1976: 1102; U.S. Bureau of Census 1987: 319. The number of lawyers employed by the judicial branches, federal and state, almost tripled, from 8,180 in 1960 to 22,276 in 1985. Weil 1968: 20; Curran 1986: 3.

56. Friedman 1987: 351, 355; see also Friedman and Russell 1990: 295.

57. Bergstrom 1992: 157.

58. Galanter 1990.

59. A reading of the magnitude of this change is provided by the analysis of Tillinghast, a firm of actuarial consultants, which has compiled data on the gross cost of the tort liability system and of other social systems from the 1930s to the present. Tillinghast found that "until shortly after World War II, growth in both tort costs and the GNP ran fairly parallel. Only in the late 1940s and early 1950s did the two diverge." Tillinghast 1992: 4. Tort costs have risen dramatically, from 0.6 percent of gross domestic product in 1950 to 2.3 percent of gross domestic product in 1991. Tillinghast 1992: 13. This includes the cost of insurance and self-insurance. Only a fraction of this goes to victims; Tillinghast estimates 25 percent (10). The compensation received is only a fraction of the economic losses of victims, leaving aside all other forms of loss, pain and suffering, etc. For example, a study of recoveries by victims of air crash fatalities from 1970 to 1984 found that decedents recovered about one-fourth of their economic loss and survivors about one-half of theirs. King and Smith 1988: viii.

60. Friedman 1985: 42.

61. Galanter 1990: 164; Speiser 1980.

62. Friedman 1985.

63. Gawalt 1984: vii.

64. Reich 1964.

65. Fleming 1974; Kirp 1976.

66. O'Neil 1970.

67. Dertouzos, Holland, and Ebener 1988; Geyelin 1989.

68. Cf. Edelman 1990.

69. Galanter 1981: 1.

70. Warren Miller in the *New Yorker,* July 24, 1978, 45.

71. E.g., Barton 1975; Galanter 1983; Galanter 1986.

72. Macneil 1984–85.

73. Teubner 1987.

74. Teubner 1987: 4, quoting Jurgen Habermas, *Theorie des kommunikativen Handelns,* 2 vols. (Frankfurt: Suhrkamp, 1981).

75. Yngvesson 1985.

76. As societies industrialize, serious disputes are increasingly between entities of different sizes—typically between individuals and large organizations—rather than between comparable entities. Coleman 1989, Coleman 1974.

77. Galanter and Rogers 1991. From 1967 to 1987, the portion of the receipts of the legal services industry contributed by businesses increased from 39 percent to 51 percent of a much enlarged total, while the share purchased by individuals dropped from 55 percent to 42 percent. Bureau of Census 1972: table 3; 1977: table 9; 1982: table 30; 1987: table 42. Figures for 1967 are estimates from Sander and Williams 1989: 435, 441. Large firms: Galanter and Palay 1991: chap. 4; Sander and Williams 1989: 447–51.

78. Galanter 2005.

79. Coleman 1993.

80. Galanter 1974.

81. An ever-increasing share of the ever-growing legal services "pie" is purchased by businesses and governments rather than individuals. In 1967, individuals bought 55 percent of the product of the legal services industry and businesses bought 39 percent. With each subsequent five-year period, the business portion has increased and the share consumed by individuals has declined. By 1992 the share bought by businesses increased to 51 percent and the share bought by individuals dropped to 40 percent. Individuals' expenditures on legal services increased 261 percent from 1967 to 1992, while law firms' income from business increased by 555 percent during that period. Even this more than double rate of growth understates the growth of business expenditures on legal services, for it includes only outside lawyers and does not include in-house legal expenditures, which greatly increased during this period. Bureau of the Census 1972, 1977, 1982, 1987, 1992. Figures for 1967 are estimates developed by Sander and Williams 1989. (The legal services category includes all law practices that have a payroll, which means virtually all lawyers in private practice.)

82. Heinz and Laumann 1982 estimated that in 1975 "more than half (53 percent) of the total effort of Chicago's bar was devoted to the corporate client sector, and a smaller but still substantial proportion (40 percent) is expended on the personal client sector." When the study was replicated twenty years later, the researchers found that about 61 percent of the total effort of all Chicago lawyers was devoted to the corporate client sector and only 29 percent to the personal/small business sector. Since the number of lawyers in Chicago had doubled, this meant that the total effort devoted to the personal sector had increased by 45 percent. But the corporate sector grew by 126 percent. To the extent that lawyers serving the corporate sector were able to command more staff and support services with their effort, these figures understate the gap in services delivered. Heinz et al. 1997.

83. Smigel 1969: 19.

84. Hoffman 1973: 71–2.

85. The Canons of Professional Ethics condemned as "unprofessional" various forms of advertising, solicitation, getting business through agents, and "furnishing or inspiring newspaper comments," as did its successor, the Code of Professional Responsibility.

86. *Bates v. State Bar of Arizona,* 433 U.S. 350 (1977).

87. This curiosity reflected the sharp increase in the number of lawyers and was manifested in the first prime time television shows about noncriminal law and lawyers, including *The Paper Chase* (1978–79) and *The Associates* (1979) and culminating in *L.A. Law* (1986–94). On lawyers on television, see Stark 1987; various contributions to Yale Law Journal Symposium on Popular Culture (June 1989); Rosen 1989; Jarvis and Joseph 1998. On lawyers in movies, see Chase 1986; Mastrangelo 1985–86; Denver 1998; Asimow and Mader 2004. On the impact of these media on law, see Sherwin 2000.

88. For a sketch of the new era of legal journalism, see Sherman 1988: 32.

89. Goldstein 1983; Powell 1985.

90. Goldstein 1979.

91. Dramatically marked by the publication of Woodward and Armstrong 1979, and elaborated by disclosures by the judges themselves. Wermiel 1986: 48; Taylor 1988: 20.

92. The Production Code of the Motion Picture Producers and Directors of America included a General Principle that "law, natural or human, shall not be ridiculed, nor shall sympathy be created for its violation." The text of the code can be found in Jowett 1976: app. 4. The weakening of censorship, starting in the 1950s, is detailed in Randall 1968; Jowett 1976: chap. 13.

93. Sherman 1991: 9.

94. On the history of this genre, see Robinson 1998.

95. A similar "downward trajectory" reappears in the portrayal of Supreme Court justices in the novel, drama, and film. Over the past fifty years, Laura Krugman Ray finds, there are "two related tendencies: an increasing familiarity with the Court and a declining reverence for the figure of the Justice." Ray 1997: 151, 153.

96. A 1992 study of network prime time found that television depictions of attorneys' character, composure, physical attractiveness, and presence were significantly higher than the public's perceptions. TV depictions and public estimation attributed to lawyers significantly more power than did lawyers themselves. Pfau et al. 1995: 307, 320, 321.

97. Pfau et al. 1995 at 325. Surveys provide no support for the belief, widespread among lawyers, that lawyer advertising is an important cause of lawyers' declining image. An ABA commission that assessed the evidence on this pointed out that "those who are most likely to have received information about lawyers through advertising have a relatively high impression of the legal profession." ABA Commission on Advertising 1995: 71.

98. In the legal academy, the relatively stable and comfortable consensus about law that had prevailed in 1960 was shattered. Schools and movements of legal thought displaying a variety and disagreement then unimaginable flourished in the legal academy and through conferences and journals—sociolegal studies, law and economics, alternative dispute resolution, critical legal studies, critical race theory, and feminist legal theory. For the most part, these bodies of thought, which are not built on legal categories, are remote from the views of practitioners. But in other ways, at least some of them are closer than rarefied analysis of doctrine, paying more attention to the practitioner's quotidian world of tactics, fees, and compromises.

99. In the ancient world "the lawyer was a close second to the doctor as a butt of jokes." McCartney 1931: 195.

100. Meadow 1986: 9.

101. Alan Dundes, quoted in Scanlan 1987.

102. MacLean 1988.

103. Shrives 1989 (joke books); Ringle 1989 (radio, etc.).

104. Harvey I. Saferstein, quoted at Torres 1993. His considered program for stopping lawyer bashing (which did not include hate-speech legislation) is at Saferstein 1993a. Saferstein and other commentators were concerned not only with jokes but with a set of prominent television advertisements demeaning lawyers, as well as the depiction of an obnoxious lawyer being devoured by a dinosaur, to great audience satisfaction, in the hit movie *Jurassic Park* (1993). Saferstein 1993.

105. See, e.g., Radin 1946: 734, 740–52.

106. The organization of "profoundly contradictory" popular attitudes toward lawyers around such polarities is insightfully explored in Post 1987: 379. Tensions among

contradictory images of lawyers are empirically documented in Mindes 1982: 177, 211 ("The lawyer finds himself in a conflicted world in which one must be both Tricky and Helpful to maximize admiration, while being helpful requires that one is not Tricky and being Tricky requires that one is not Helpful").

107. Calve 1994: 39.

108. Dundes 1987: vii–viii.

109. Myrdal 1944: 38.

110. Myrdal 1944: 39.

111. I base this coinage on the analogy with "discography," a 1930s word which in turn seems to be based on bibliography.

112. Also included are a few stories that are not about lawyers as such but about the legal realm in which they work (e.g., A22, *cheating;* A25, *oath;* J16, *courts of law,* etc.). Jokes that are specifically about judges rather than lawyers or law are not included.

113. Whether the jokes cross language barriers as readily as national borders must remain a question for another day. Jokes about lawyers are far less prominent, where visible at all, outside the English-speaking, common law world. See p. <000>.

114. Other observers have hit upon some elements of the classification (e.g., Bachman 1995) and naturally I deem them perspicacious.

115. Jokes comprise what Hayak 1973 calls a "spontaneous order" that is "the product of the action of many men, but not the result of human design" (37). Such an order "utilizes the separate knowledge of all its several members, without this knowledge ever being concentrated in a single mind or being subject to those processes of deliberate coordination and adaptation which a mind performs" (41–42). A similar notion is found at Davies 1998: 52.

116. While there is no bibliographical guide to lawyer jokes, guides to other genres of lawyer humor about law and lawyers can be found in Bander 1982; Bander 1985; Gordon 1992; Baker 2002.

117. Jan Brunvand 1978 defines an anecdote as "a short personal legend, supposedly true but generally apocryphal, told about an episode in the life of either a famous individual or a local character " (114). As noted below, many tellers are tempted to present jokes as anecdotes.

118. Hetzron 1991: 65–66. Adapting from James Humes he likens a joke to a balloon: "You pump it up with details and puncture it with a punch line" (66).

119. Many instances will be found below. A particularly striking example is the solicitude for clients found in item A33, *two plus two.*

120. The Register of Jokes (appendix) indicates the source of each joke. On the practice of switching see below at p. 23.

121. Folklorists sometimes refer to oicotypes [oikotypes, ecotypes] to make a related distinction. The term is elastic. It was borrowed from botany to refer to "a special version of a folktale, developed by isolation in a certain cultural area, by which on account of special national, political, and geographical conditions it takes a form different from that of the same tale in other areas." Bodker 1965: 220. It expanded to refer to "local forms . . . [of] any folklore genre . . . defined with reference to either geographical or cultural factors." Dundes 1984: 2. On the career of the concept see Cochrane 1987. The oicotype concept is of limited use in describing the lawyer joke corpus, for it involves localization to a group of carriers. But the present study is not of a group of carriers (at least not one narrower than all English-speaking tellers of jokes about lawyers). It is about a group of subjects. There may be ecotypification based on different groups of tellers—lawyers versus

nonlawyers, whites versus blacks, or Americans versus British—but most of the sources used here give little information about tellers, except for what can be inferred from the identity of the compiler and the place of publication. On the other hand, these sources provide abundant information about differences between the version of a joke told about lawyers and versions of the same joke told about Jews or politicians. In addition to eco-typification (i.e., the adaptation to a group of carriers), we require a notion of specification—i.e., the distinctive adaptation of a joke to a specific set of topics or protagonists.

122. See "What Do the Jokes Tell Us?" in chap. 6.

123. Richard Raskin traces the transformation of stories that began as anti-Semitic jokes about Jews into classic Jewish jokes told by Jews. Raskin 1992: chap. 3 ("ten commandments" joke); chap. 4 ("he had a hat").

124. Hetzron 1991: 66.

125. Wright 1939: 251. An extended discussion of switching by gag writers and professional comedians is found in Adams 1968: 35–42. The same process is called "spinning" by Miller 1991: 8–10.

126. Davis 1954: 117.

127. Thus, from "roasts and show business contacts," the major popularizer of Ole and Lena jokes "collected more and more bits of top rated humor, many of which were converted to Ole & Lena jokes." Stangland 1993: 46.

128. Before Wilde 1982, the last topical collection of lawyer jokes by a "professional" author was Golden 1953. In the interval, two "amateur" collections by a lawyer were published (May 1956; May 1964).

129. E.g., Shafer and Papadakis 1988; Steiger 1990.

130. This impression is strengthened by occasional traces of the incomplete switch. For example, when an old story told about bookkeepers or accountants was switched to lawyers by both Wilde (1987: 13) and Knott (1990: 103), telltale traces of an earlier origin remained (references to "the company" rather than the firm—see joke G23). Later editors got the switch smoothed out.

131. For the partner switches, see chap. 6. In the course of a discussion of the limits of "switchability," Davies 1986 observes that "there is . . . a significant stock of Jewish jokes, particularly those deriving their humor from a distinctively Jewish use of indirect and elliptical but relentlessly consistent reasoning that perhaps could be adapted to fit the circumstances of another group but in practice rarely are" (76).

132. For example, an Israeli journalist (Nesvisky 1987) presents as "quintessential Israeli humor" an easily switched joke of wide international currency (A48, *pay off low bidder*).

133. I refer to G22, *play at night*, which I heard in 1994, but it did not appear in print until 1999.

134. Explanations for the distinctive license to be nasty about lawyers are taken up in chap. 9.

135. Pierce 1995: 215–16.

136. Just four of these jokes—*lips moving* (thirteen times), *professional courtesy* (twelve), *laboratory rats* (nine), and *skid marks* (seven)—accounted for almost three-quarters of all the tellings. Each of these has appeared many times in print and electronic media. See A1, B29, G26, and H2, app.

137. E.g., the list version of B54 (*multiply-married virgin*), the "Art Buchwald" version of D36 (*doctor won't treat lawyer*) or the list version of G26 (*laboratory rats*).

138. E.g., A13 (*put in lies yourself*) seems to have suffered a seventy year gap in publication and A20 (the "stick to it" version of *oath*) a 66 years gap. D18 (*town with two lawyers*)

evaded print for 98 years. The longest gap in publication I have encountered is the 103 years between appearances of J11 (*no tricks this time*).

139. The arrival of contemporary antilawyer humor is traced in detail below. Little of the harsh antilawyerism of the present era can be detected in any of the specialized topical books of lawyer jokes published more than forty years ago (G. Edwards 1915; Milburn 1927; Cook 1938; Golden 1950; May 1956; May 1964) or even in the book that marks the beginning of the current period, Larry Wilde's *Official Lawyers Joke Book* (1982). The shift is fully in evidence in 1990s collections such as *Kill the Lawyers* (Steiger 1990), *Lawyers from Hell Joke Book* (Grossman 1993), and *First, Kill All the Lawyers* (Adler 1994).

140. On the other hand, in cases where my archive includes collected oral material that precedes the earliest published material, the gap is never more than a few years. Yet there are instances of gaps of forty years or more between published versions.

141. *Love's Labour's Lost* act 5, scene 2.

142. For these reasons, humorist George Mikes 1971 concludes that jokes are fated to "unavoidably always remain a minor art" (298–99).

143. Henry 1948: 163. Also Anon 1902: item 238 [=Williams 1949: item 2789 = Botkin 1957: xxi]; Fuller 1942: item 1168; Mandel 1974: 315. More simply, "if you steal from one author, it's plagiarism; if you steal from many, it's research." Allen 1945: item 2117. Butler (1862–1947) was President of Columbia from 1901 to 1945; Mathews (1852–1929) was a Professor there from 1892 to 1924 and a noted author.

1. Lies and Stratagems: The Corruption of Discourse

1. Oliver 1986; Knott 1988: 115; Rafferty 1988: 24; Novak and Waldoks 1990: 106; Knott 1990b: 120; Behrman 1991: 50; Brallier 1992: 48; Grossman 1993: 121; *Nolo's Favorite* 1993; Adler 1994: 114; 1996 Cal.: Jan. 2; 1997 Cal.: Mar. 26; Ross 1996: 48 [Australia]; POPULUS Jokes Top Ten Jokes, Dec. 1, 1997; Lyons 1998: 63; anon. Stanford law student, Mar. 10, 1998; Alvin 1999a: 80; Greene 1999: 163; Tibballs 2000: item 1158.

2. Husbands: Cantor 1943: 171; Meier 1944: 306; Golden 1972: 245; Pendleton [1979]: item 445; Murtie 1985: 128; Forbes 1992: 19; Topol [1994]: 95. Sartor 1989: 85 (woman); Rovin 1989: 266 (salesperson); Yermonee 1992 (Robert Maxwell); Leo 1996: 281 (criminal suspects: reported by researcher as "truism among detectives"); Barnett and Kaiser 1996: 99 (economist); Baddiel et al. 1999: 508 (men); Johnson 2000: 133. Politicians: Ginger 1974: 48 (Lyndon B. Johnson); Terrell and Buchanan 1984: 98 (Republican); Miller 1991: 136 (senator); Pease 1996: 299; Colombo 2001: 100 (Brian Mulroney).

3. Radin 1946; Pound 1914. The classic critique of the shortcomings of the lawyer's rhetorical art is Plato's *Gorgias* (Jowett 1937: 505).

4. The lawyer = liar equation is a favorite in India, where the vowel sounds are much closer in Indian English.

5. The version here is from Lurie 1928: 138. The story has changed little since it appeared in *The Town and Country Almanack, for . . . 1797* (Dodge 1978: 125). Also in Hupfeld [1871]: 166; Willock 1887: 77; Kieffer 1907: 24; Engelbach 1913: 132; Williams 1949: 1374; Woods 1967: item 96.1; Wilde 1982: 25; Scott 1984: 10 (attributed to Abraham Lincoln); Wilde 1987: 163; Adler 1992: 122 (attributed to Lincoln); Rovin 1992: 157; *Nolo's Favorite* 1993; Ross 1996: 86; Lawyer Jokes, Jan. 30, 1998;; Regan 2001: 24. A variant identifies the lawyer not as the devil's son but as the devil himself ("the devil was a lawyer from the beginning"): *The Farmer's Almanack . . . for . . . 1797* (Dodge 1987: 126; *Joe Miller's* 1903 I: 281). A vaudeville routine playing on the lawyer-liar equation leaves out the devil but

emphasizes, "Well, it's all the same thing; you've got to be one to be the other" (Kemble 1901: 172).

6. Grenville, *Witty Apothegms . . . [1669]* in Ashton 1884: 38; *An Astronomical Diary . . . for . . . 1789* (Dodge 1987: 125); *Joe Miller's* 1903 I: 185; Morton and Malloch 1913: 5; Engelbach 1913: 93; Lupton 1938: item 1229; Golden 1950: 177; Hay 1989: 33.

7. Nash et al. 1995: 54; Hay 1989: 33 ("more than fifty years ago"). Bigelow 1871: 166; Hupfeld [1871]: 102.

8. Edwards 1915: item 916; Mosher 1922: 296 (identical); Milburn 1927: 21 (identical); Copeland 1936: 236 (identical); Eastman 1936: 21 (identical); Wilde 1987: 14 (identical) Phillips 1989: 19; Lowdown Disk 1992: item 499 (= Edwards 1915); 2000 Cal.: Nov. 14.

9. Anon. 1902? [Cole's 2nd]: 232; Clode 1922: 141; Milburn 1927: 14 (identical); Copeland 1936: 233 (identical); Phillips 1989: 50. Cf. Landon 1883: 709 (lawyer like restless sleeper, lies first on one side and then on the other); 1997 Cal.: Nov. 27 ("last night I slept like a lawyer. First, I lied on one side, then on the other"); Alvin 1999b: 18; Mr. "K" 2001: 121. MacDonald [1985]: 76 tells an anecdote of a dying Canadian Q.C. who told his nurse, "I'm a lawyer and I'm used to lying on both sides."

10. Esar 1945: 173.

11. Berle 1989: 367; 2000 Cal.: Dec. 20. This joke has been more frequently published about the teacher applying for a job who assured the selection committee that he can "teach it round or flat." Brown [1879]: 24; Wynn 1950: 56; Friedman 1964: n.p.; Murdock 1967: 102; Tomlinson 1991: 38.

12. The "either side" theme reappears in J11 and J12 in chap. 10.

13. Johnston 1922: item 1148. Usually the defendant is an "old negro charged with robbing a hen-coop," often appearing before a newly appointed judge in the South: Morton and Malloch 1913: 230; Mosher [1922]: 293; Milburn 1927: 7; Case 1928: 66 (identical); Scruggs 1928: item 428 (college students); Eastman 1936: 23; Copeland 1936: 229; Lupton 1938: item 743; Williams 1938: item 900; Knox c.1943: 149; Meier 1944: 173; Esar 1945: 462 (village ne'er do well); Williams 1949: item 3949; Wilde 1987: 28. Cf. Nash et al. 1995: 5 (no race factor; told as anecdote about 1989 case in Middletown, OH). Race drops out in an Australian version: Ross 1996: 53. British versions omitted the story altogether and reduced matters to the crucial exchange: Aye 1931: 11; Ferguson 1933: 193; Phillips 1989: 25. A fine turn is added by the Irish defendant who argues, "Sure, if I was guilty I'd have a lawyer." McCann [1968]: 30; Desmond [1995]: 22.

14. Esar 1945: 261; Lawson 1923: 162; Moulton 1942: item 1438; Golden 1950: 69; Adams 1968: 334; Wilde 1982: 47; 1996 Cal.: Aug. 9 [= 1997 Cal.: June 16]; Mital and Gupta 1995: 101 (India).

15. Copeland 1936: 241; *Green Bag* 11: 437 (1899); Johnston 1925: item 1119; Scruggs 1928: item 419; Anon. 1971: item 454.50; B. Phillips 1986: 92; Wilde 1987: 8; Knott 1990: 97; Steiger 1990: 21; Rovin 1992: 3; Adler 1992: 91 (= Copeland 1936); *Nolo's Favorite* 1993; 1996 Cal.: Apr. 9; Streiker 1998: 271. Cf. CLLH 1995: no. 21; Ross 1996: 57 (afterlife for lawyers assured for "they lie still after death").

16. Johann Gast, *Convivalium sermonem liber* (Basel, 1541) at Bowen 1988: 75.

17. Anon. c.1860 [Uncle Sam's Jack-Knife]: 26; Anon. 1898: 73. Cf. Lean 1903: vol. 2, pt. 2:871 ("It is an old joke that a lawyer cannot be too bare-faced," citing Webster "As short as a lawyer's beard").

18. Lieberman 1956: 85; Lieberman 1975: 68 (identical); Behrman 1991: 70. Cf. the "client" version of this in Edwards 1915: item 1025:

LAWYER: "Are you—er—er—truthful?"

YOUTH: "Yes, sir, but I ain't so blame truthful as ter interfere with your business."

19. Other occupations also cultivate expertise in lying: "My father is a real estate man, and he knows more about lying than your father does." Edmund and Williams 1916: 373; Johnston 1922: 252; Aye 1933: 8; Holub 1943: 79; Berle 1989: 498; E. Phillips 1989: 7. Cf. Aye 1933: 49 (boys who don't tell truth get sent out as traveling salesmen when grown). A coal merchant is excused from jury duty as unable "to weigh a matter properly." *Green Bag* I: 224 (1889). Another coal merchant parries his brother's attempt to convert him with "If I join the church who'll weigh the coal?" Edmund and Williams 1916: 97; Masson 1922: 208 (wool merchants); Aye 1933: 40; Copeland 1936: 54; Williams 1938: item 1255; Jones 1944: 11; Esar 1945: 367; Droke 1948: 352. Cf. Johnston 1922: item 341. This version of the story expired in postwar America with the decline of coal heating of homes. In a recent appearance the brothers have become butchers and the worldly one asks, "If I get religion too, who's going to weigh the turkeys." Adams 1996: 476.

20. Shillaber 1854: 200 [= Hupfeld [1871]: 87 = Willock 1887: 292]; Gillespie 1904: 121 (American girl tells Scots lawyer, "Whenever we've a member of a family who is a bigger liar than another, we make him a lawyer"); Morton and Malloch 1913: 238 (do.); Lawson 1923: 163 (mother who doesn't want son to be lawyer because "a lawyer has to tell so many lies," embarrassed to realize she is speaking to wife of lawyer, proceeds, "That is—er—to be a *good lawyer*"); Pickens 1926: 141 (lying son becomes lawyer); Singh 1992: 34 (lawyer "professionally required to tell lies"); Jones and Wheeler 1995: 115 (man goes into ministry because "he was too weak to plow, too dumb to teach, too honest to law"). The theme recurs in this recent item:

A young girl curious about her later college years was asking her mother what college was like. She said "mommy, if I want to be a lawyer when I grow up, what do I do in college?" Her mother said, "you have to take special classes for that." She replied, "like what? Lying classes?" (A9)

POPULUS Jokes Top Ten Jokes, Oct. 14, 1997.

21. Schermerhorn 1928: 230. The resonance with the story of George Washington and the cherry tree is developed further in the story of the Texan George whose father responds, "We're moving to Virginia. With an attitude like that, you'll never make it in Texas politics." Scott 1984: 18; Ginger 1974: 133; Skubik and Short 1976: 99; Esar 1978: 138; Wilde 1984a: 58; Dole [1998]: 1; Brunsting 2000: 412.

22. Shillaber 1854: 92 [= Hupfeld [1871]: 93 = Willock 1887: 292]; Carrick et al. 1850: 98 [= Howe [1891]: 129]; Sprague 1895: 166 (Scot client); *Green Bag* 8: 474 (1896) [= *Green Bag* 11: 437 (1899)]; Anon. 1906b: 83; Morton and Malloch 1913: 220 (Scotch countrywoman); Johnston 1925: item 1111; Lurie 1928: 134; E. Phillips 1989: 54; Regan 2001: 190 (Scot). Shillaber's 1854 version has an English ring to it. Curiously this item seems to have been passed over in the general joke literature of midcentury and the great outpouring of lawyer joke publication after 1982.

23. Willock 1887: 404 [= *Green Bag* 12: 605 (1900)]. Cf. Franklin 1925: 77 (attorney's remark that action for a divorce "will not lie" provokes woman's response: "Not lie! It is you, sire, I engage for that purpose"); McIlwaine 1933: 57 (litigant brings solicitor only "in order that he need not tell lies himself").

24. Sprague 1895: 99; *Green Bag* 22: 368 (1910); Johnston 1922: 238; Franklin 1925: 123; Adams 1970: 181; Wilde 1982: 185; Wilde 1987: 4; Adler 1992: 106 [= Adler 1994: 112]; 1996 Cal.: June 16; Adams 1996: 393.

25. Brallier 1992: 45 (Franklin); *New-England Callendar: or Almanack, for . . . 1793* (Dodge 1987: 127); Anon. 1902? [*Cole's* 2nd]: 431; Aye 1931: 11 (Ben Jonson); Boatright 1949:

122 (Ben Jonson); Humes 1994: 99 (Franklin); Nash et al. 1995: 48 (Franklin). In an elaborated story, this is inscribed by St. Peter on the tombstone of "St. Evona, the patron saint of lawyers." Botkin 1957: 186 (from James J. MacDonald, 1907).

26. Hupfeld [1871]: 85; Kempt 1865: 86; Bigelow 1871: 332. Cf. Waters 1900: 138 (honest woman).

27. Patten 1909: 195; *Green Bag* 21: 424 (1909); Edwards 1915: 272; Heighton 1916: 211 (Judge Gary replies); Anderson 1922: 64 (Dallas); Anderson 1923: 185 (identical); Lawson 1923: 162 (Arkansas); Franklin 1925: 208 (Texas); Johnston 1925: item 1137 (identical); Lurie 1928: 136 (Alabama); Lupton 1938: 255 (Alabama); Moulton 1942: item 1427 (Arkansas); Prochnow 1942: 115 (Alabama); Anon. 1943: 252 (New York: game laws omitted); Esar 1945: 371 ("Southern state"); House 1948: 9 (Arkansas); Williams 1949: item 1765 (identical to Moulton 1942); May 1964: 183; Prochnow and Prochnow 1964 (identical to Prochnow 1942); Adams 1968: 411 (south). In Canada, the writer was a young politically ambitious liberal who left Quebec for Alberta (Shelley 1976: 44).

28. Aye 1931: 11; *Green Bag* 4: 186 (1892); Sprague 1895: 103; *Green Bag* 14: 201 (1902); Masson [1913]: 112; Franklin 1925: 290; Knox 1926: 141; Wood 1926: 59; Schermerhorn 1928: 143; Eastman 1936: 20 (marriage to lawyer and honest man is bigamy); Williams 1938: item 886; Copeland and Copeland 1940: item 4833; Meier 1944: 112; Esar 1945: 262; Cerf 1946: 174; Weiherman 1955: 92; Lieberman 1956: 124; Adams 1959: 147 [= Adams 1968: 343]; Hefley 1968: item 790; Adams 1970: 119; Morecroft [1974]: 50; Harris 1979: 66; Terrell and Buchanan 1984: 86 (lawyer and Christian gentleman); Leary 1991 [1987]: 187; Rovin 1989: 182; Berle 1989: 61; Jones and Wheeler 1989: 107; Phillips 1990: 86; Duncan 1990: 208; Rovin 1992: 41; Adler 1992: 47; 1997 Cal.: June 8; Richard Gordon, e-mail message to author, Feb. 20, 1997; Streiker 1998: 257; Dedopulos 1998: 237 [= Baddiel et al. 1999: 581]; Singh 1999: 16; Greene 1999: 155.

This joke has been switched to politicians (Parker 1978: 290; Cagney 1979: 20 (Irish); Wilde 1984: 150; Hill 1987: 8; Coote 1994: 335); liberals (B. Phillips 1994: n.p. [= B. Phillips 1996: 64]); investment bankers (Odean 1988: 143); estate agent (Schindler 1988: 84). Cf. Barry 1990: 23 (marriage to "stockbroker and honest man" is bigamy); King and MacNeil 1995: 16 (Irishman interprets as Scotch stinginess).

29. Anon. 1893: 429; Hicks 1936: 28; Henry 1948: 95; Fredericks 1953: 34; Adams 1970: 119; Lowdown Disk 1992; Adler 1992: 47; Adler 1994: 44 (identical); Anon. 1997c: 105 [= Baddiel et al. 1999: 104]; Streiker 1998: 273; Southwell 1999: 61; Baddiel et al. 1999: 104; Brunsting 2000: 203; Regan 2001: 95.

30. Clemons 1902: 73; Wheeler 1925: 12 (vaudeville routine); Dundes 1987: 153 (extended into Englishman joke, but Strange not a lawyer); Rovin 1992: 42; *Nolo's Favorite* 1993; CLLH 1995: lawyer humor no. 30; Rees 1995: 83 (man named Amazing dislikes name; wife puts inscription "here lies a man who was faithful to his wife for sixty years"); Ross 1996: 54.

31. Gallup poll conducted for *Newsweek,* Jan. 1987.

32. Mouton 1942; Lewis and Wachs 1966: 206; Wilde 1982: 154 (identical to Mouton 1942); Rovin 1992: 9; Harvey c.1998b: 76; 2002 Cal.: Feb. 2/3.

33. Lurie 1928: 131; Hood et al. 1873: 42; Esar 1945: 260; Wilde 1987: 97.

34. Anon. 1902?: 233.

35. Anderson 1923: 90; Rango 1944: 35; Braude 1958: 127; Prochnow and Prochnow 1964: 83; Boliska [1966]: 143; Berle 1989: 61; E. Phillips 1989: 16; Johnson 1991: 101; Regan 2001: 9.

36. Cobb 1923: 130. The earliest version is presented as an anecdote involving Senator

Daniel of Virginia as defense counsel. Anon 1902:126 [=*Green Bag* 14: 446 (1902)]; *Green Bag* 23: 552 (1911); *Green Bag* 26: 252 (1914); Edwards 1915: item 280; Anon. 1920: 95; Mosher 1922: 190; Kieffer 1923: 116; Milburn 1927: 8 [= Copeland 1936: 230]; Williams 1938: item 390; Smith 1941: 31 (New Englander); Cerf 1946: 14; Keene 1949: 341 (Joseph Choate perspicaciously anticipates crucial question); May 1964: 73; Wilde 1987: 38; Rovin 1992: 100; Regan 2001: 220. After World War Two, the watchman lost his black identity in most versions, but remained an old codger. The story migrated to the UK (Ashmore 1930; Aye 1931: 84; E. Phillips 1989: Southwell 1999: 74); Australia (Howcroft 1985: 374; Adams and Newall 1995: 290); and India (Vaidyanathan 1992: 74).

37. *Green Bag* 1: 267 (1889); Sprague 1895: 80; Patten 1909: 53; *Green Bag* 22: 368 (1910) (reported as anecdote about Southern Negro); Morton and Malloch 1913: 230 (same); Heighton 1916: 272; Milburn 1927: 18; Ferguson 1933: 188; Copeland 1936: 235; Estman 1936: 21; Hicks 1936: 133; Johnson et al. 1936: 257; Gilbert [1986]: 162 citing Maurice Healy (1939) (told as anecdote about Irish witness in father's case); Copeland and Copeland 1940: item 6867 (Australia: aborigine); Moulton 1942: item 1448; Cantor 1943: 170; Esar 1945: 462 (hillbilly); Golden [1950]: 52; Lieberman 1956: 92 [= Lieberman 1975: 75]; May 1956: 227; Bowker 1961: 105 (told as anecdote about child witness in English court); Jackson 1961: 54 (slight variation of Bowker 1961); Woods 1967: item 92.17; Adams 1968: 314; Wilde 1982: 61; Rosten 1985: 337; Dines 1987: 102; Wilde 1987: 37; Shafer and Papadakis 1988: 131; E. Phillips 1989: 68; Rovin 1992: 75; 1995 Cal.: Oct. 19; Mital and Gupta 1995: 101; 1997 Cal.: Dec. 15; Regan 2001: 104.

A child witness responds that she "would not be given any witnesses' expinses" (Knox ca.1943: 147) or sent to his room or "kicked out of Cubs" (MacDonald [1985]: 73). Other witnesses, asked what is "the value of an oath," respond with the sums they received as bribes. *Green Bag* 3: 386 (1891); *Green Bag* 19: 738 (1907); John 1995: 103.

38. Hupfeld [1871]: 106. In another variant, a witness who alludes to this possibility finds the judge has something else in mind:

In another court case, an old farmer was giving testimony that was so far fetched that the judge thought it best to warn him that he was in serious danger of perjuring himself.

"Are you aware," the judge asked, "of what will happen to you if you are caught lying under oath?"

"When I die I'll go to hell," the old man replied.

"Yes, but what else?" the judge asked.

The old man was puzzled for a moment. "You mean there's more?" (A20)

Scott 1984: 134 [= Adler 1992: 138].

39. Brown [1879]: 34; Franklin 1925: 5; Esar 1945: 310; House 1948: 147; Wilde 1987: 83; Humes 1993: 102.

40. Cf. Gregory Casey's (1974) finding that those with the most education, status, and political awareness are the most likely to embrace the mythic picture of the U.S. Supreme Court.

41. Curtis 1951: 20, 9.

42. Curtis 1951: 9, 12.

43. Drinker 1952: 349, 355.

44. Drinker 1952: 352.

45. Drinker 1952: 355.

46. Freedman 1975; Luban 1988; Applbaum 1997; Campos 1998; Simon 1998. For a sophisticated critique of the various justifications of lawyers' lying, see Wetlaufer 1990, who concludes that "lying is not the province of a few 'unethical lawyers' who operate on

the margins of the profession. It is a permanent feature of advocacy and thus of almost the entire province of law" (1272).

47. Starr 1998; *Washington Times* 1998.

48. Geoffrey Hazard cited in the *Economist* 1998: 32.

49. Lee 1960: chap. 30. See Johnson 1994: 106. Finch remains an icon for the bar and a site of considerable controversy. See p. 7 and note 22.

50. Anon. 1853: 215; Kempt 1865: 3; Andrews 1896: 249; Anon. 1905: 219 (criminal defense); Engelbach 1913: 76; Lawson 1923: 162; Knox 1926: 154; May 1956: 113; Jackson 1961: 114; Marquand 1977: 152; Pollack 1979: 13; Triverton 1981: 149 (identical to Marquand 1977); Wilde 1982: 166; E. Phillips 1989: 46; Adler 1992: 8; Phillips [1993]: 10.

51. Hupfeld [1871]: 99 (neighborhood joker in court); Anon. 1893: 64 (draftee); Anon. 1893: 95; Mosher [1922]: 47 (dunned customer); Anon. 1928 (Anecdota): item 445 (rape defendant); Ferguson 1933: 44 (drinker); Copeland and Copeland 1940: item 4498 (dunned customer); Knox ca. 1943: 135 (clergyman); Meier 1944: 116 (sued borrower); Levenson 1948: 48 (borrower); Spalding 1976: 153 (sued borrower); Chambers 1979: 74 (rape defendant); Anon. 1984: 87 (church elder at hearing before bishops); Phillips 1984a: 73 (dunned customer); Wilde 1987: 31 (sued dog owner); Schindler 1993: 76 (hotel guest accused by manager); Arya 1996a: 108 (wife accused by husband).

52. The notion of prevailing by the relative rather than absolute merit of performance also occurs in F2.

53. Brown [1879]: 45; *Green Bag* 13: 207 (1901); Anon. 1902: 203; Anon. 1902a: 128 [= Brown 1879]; Franklin 1925: 194 [= Brown 1879]; Spalding 1978: 301; Davidson 1998: 162 (told as anecdote about William Jennings Bryan, mistakenly attributed to Jackson 1961).

54. Brown [1879]: 84; Hupfeld [1871]: 85; *Green Bag* 1: 409 (1889); Sprague 1895: 176; Andrews 1896: 245 (English, two versions, one given as anecdote); *Green Bag* 12: 671 (1900) (client didn't realize how badly he was abused until he heard Rufus Choate); Landon 1901: 392; Anon. 1902?: 233; Patten 1909: 240; *Green Bag* 21: 259 (1909); *Green Bag* 22: 316 (1910) (client convinced of innocence before plea); Morton and Malloch 1913: 117; Edwards 1915: item 44 (accused changes plea when convinced of innocence by lawyer); Edwards 1915: item 673; Franklin 1925: 185; Pickens 1926: 69 (acquitted client convinced of innocence demands lawyer accept lower fee); Wood 1926: 43; Ernst 1930: 210; McIlwaine 1933: 3 (solicitor almost convinced defendant); Copeland 1936: 242; Johnson et al. 1936: item 107 (acquitted client answers "not that horse"); Johnson et al. 1936: item 906; Lupton 1938: item 1274; Williams 1938: item 352; Gee 1941: 73; Meier 1944: 171; Rango 1944: 35; Boatright 1945: 180; Esar 1945: 262; Boatright 1949: 125; Jackson 1961: 135; Wachs 1968: 22; Walser 1974: 81; Spalding 1978: 250 (Irish recasting of *Green Bag* 1900); MacDonald [1985]: 128 (told as anecdote about turn-of-century Calgary lawyer Patrick James Nolan); Jones and Wheeler 1989: 108; *AML* 1993: no. 464, no. 492, no. 781; Berle 1993: 150; Jones and Wheeler 1995: 90; 2002 Cal.: Apr. 9. This is tale-type no. 1860c; Motif X319.1 (Eloquent Lawyer Makes Obviously Guilty Client Doubt His Own Guilt). In spite of its continuing currency, the story is entirely passed over by the recent spate of topical books of lawyer jokes, a useful reminder that these do not represent the whole of the lawyer joke corpus.

In a lesser version, a witness cross-examined by defense counsel is no longer sure he ever owned the stolen horse or car: Allen 1945: item 1137; Howcroft 1985: 451; E. Phillips 1989: 72 (English); B. Phillips 1990: 88; MacDonald 1992: 28 (told as anecdote).

55. O. J. Simpson, Aug. 1. 1995: misc. jokes no. 55 (on-line; attributed to Jay Leno).

56. Adams 1970: 92; *Green Bag* 2: 183 (1890); *Green Bag* 2: 558 (1890); Downs 1903: 65; *Green Bag* 24: 160 (1912); Knox 1926: 149; Learsi 1941: 131; Learsi 1961: 220; Braude 1964:

item 525; Golden 1972: 155; Cagney 1979: 20; Wilde 1982: 139; Marks 1985: 197; Phillips 1989: 86; Berle 1989: 384.

57. Bigelow 1871: 33 (treatise); cf. J12, *proved it constitutional.*

58. Morton and Malloch 1913: 204–5; Hood et al. 1873: 535.

59. Cerf 1956: 195 [= Adler 1994: 17]; Milburn 1927: 10; Muller [1939]: 44.

60. Knox 1926: 173; Eastman 1936: 7; Davis 1954: 223; Youngman 1963: 93 (Jew); Blumfield 1965: 55 (Jew); Mindess 1971: 238 (Jew); Asimov 1971: item 40 (Jew); Rabinowitz 1986 [1973]: 195 (Jew); Mandel 1974: 120 (Jew); Humes [1975]: 126 (Israeli); Marquand 1977: 80; Spalding 1978: 206 (Irish); Pendleton [1979]: 85; Pollack 1979: 37 (Jew); Yarwood [1981]: 26; Baker 1986: 155 [collected 1970] (Jew); Murtie 1985: 132 (Irish); Berle 1989: 122 (Cajun); Schindler 1992: 95 (Jew); Topol [1994]: 247 (Jew); Jhumor List, Aug. 12, 1999 (Jew).

61. Knott 1990: 49 [= Knott 1990g: 81 = Knott 1993: 111 = Cohl 1997: 353]; Shafer and Papadakis 1988: 135; Humes 1994: 162.

62. Morton Sklaroff, e-mail message to author, May 22, 2000.

63. Stevens 1987: 179; Rodent 1995: 177. This is a wonderful adaptation from the story of the ghostwriter upending his rich or powerful client: Cerf 1965: 192; Gerler 1965: 194; Boliska [1966]: 26; Gingras 1973: 145; Humes [1975]: 199; Skubik and Short 1976: 100; Shelley 1976: 63; Schindler 1986: 50; Alverson [1989]: 64; Tomlinson 1991: 252; Rees 1994: 171.

64. Cited by Post 1987: 381, from Kupferberg 1978: 62.

65. Swift 1726: chap. 32.

66. Oral tradition (collected, Madison, WI, ca. 1992); collected by Edward Reisner, Madison, WI, ca. 1993; Adler 1992: 45 [= Adler 1994: 40] (corporation director); *Nolo's Favorite* 1993; Brallier 1996: 99; Cohl 1997: 284–85; 1998 Cal.: Jan. 30; anon. Stanford law student, Mar. 10, 1998; Streiker 1998: 258; Greene 1999: 168.

In addition to the "three candidates for the big job" variant, there is another and earlier appearing major variant of the story in which lawyers and members of other professions serially respond to a test or to a troubled questioner or in no context at all; Wilde 1982: 77; Rafferty 1988: 47; Knott 1990: 79; Behrman 1991: 78; Law and Politics (Jan. 1991) 11; *AML* 1993: no. 398; Grossman 1993: 45 [= *AML* 1993: no. 660]; 1995 Cal.: May 29; CLLH: lawyer humor no. 4, Mar. 2, 1995 [= Ross 1996: 46].

67. Many years earlier a lawyer repulsed a judge's use of "two plus two" as a model of indisputability by noting that it made twenty-two: Anon. 1898: 96.

68. Another possible contributor to the 1980s version—or possibly the ancestor of the Eastern European version—is a joke about Jews in which the response to the "two and two" question was "Am I buying or selling?" Rees 1994: 96 (told of impresario Lew Grade in 1962); Blumenfeld 1967: 105; Coote 1994: 221.

69. Dolgopolova 1982: 30; Kolasky 1972: 76; Dolgopolova 1982: 72; Banc and Dundes 1986: 95 and references there. The joke also existed earlier in the West with the same theme of the abnegation of truth before power:

A maid of honour, in old France, was once asked by the Queen what o'clock it was. She replied, with a curtsey: "Whatever your majesty pleases."

Laing 1953: 35.

Banc and Dundes (1986: 96) relate the "how much do you want it to be" story to the story in which the joke figure is not the candidate but the selector, who elicits responses to a numerical puzzle and then ignores the responses to pick the girl with appealing physical characteristics. See discussion of E7 in chap. 5.

70. Scott 1984: 100 (politician); MacHale 1989: 80 (candidate for Conservative Party information officer, responding to Margaret Thatcher); Rees 1994: 9 (accountant, dated to 1990); Warner 1993: 91 (applicant for job in bar); Lonigan 1993: 30 (accountant); Adams and Newall 1994: 443 (accountant); Adams and Newall 1995: 189 (economist); Two Fun Guys 1997 (accountant); Baddiel and Stone 1997: 289 (accountant); Singh 1999: 133 (municipal accounts superintendent); Anon. 2000a: 121 (economist); Anon. 2001a: 143 (economist).

71. This empathic receptiveness is also present in the troubled questioner version, where the lawyer's answer is accompanied by such gestures as the arm around the shoulder or "leaning forward" and "smiling compassionately" in the case of a woman lawyer.

72. Rees 1994: 9 (letter to the *Times,* Sept. 19, 1990); Baddiel and Stone 1997: 289.

73. Anon. 2000c: 270.

74. Adams and Newall 1994: 443. (The reference to "counsel's opinion" I take as meaning it would be advisable to consult a specialist on this rather than to act on the basis of my opinion.) In an American CPA version (Two Fun Guys 1997) the accountant checks to secure privacy.

75. Campos 1998: 13.

76. Rodell 1939: 166, 16, 19.

77. Rodell 1957: 131.

78. Rodell 1957: 108.

79. Riesman 1954: 450 [1951]. Compare Sally Engel Merry's observation in a contemporary urban court: "If a case progresses to a pretrial conference or to a trial, the prosecutors and defense attorneys play a critical role in translating complex, emotional problems into narrow legal cases. They serve as the front line, cleansing problems of their emotionally chaotic elements and reducing them to cold rational issues." Merry 1990: 148.

80. Lieberman 1975: 208–9.

81. Edwards 1915: item 472; Franklin 1925: 99; Scruggs 1927: item 469; Mosher 1933: 49 (told as anecdote); Mendelsohn 1935: 195; Williams 1938: item 45; Wright 1939: 216; Williams 1949: item 818; Weiherman 1955: 92; Braude 1964: item 527; May 1964: 123; Wilson and Jacobs 1974: 57; Shelley 1976: 90; Walker 1982: 34; Wilde 1982: 172; Chariton 1989: 71; Phillips 1989: 38; Behrman 1991: 7; Grossman 1993: 22 (firm setting rather than own practice); *Nolo's Favorite* 1993; 1996 Cal.: June 17 [= 1997 Cal.: July 6]; Subramaniam 1995: 76; CLLH 1995: lawyer humor no. 93; Pease 1996: 29; Cohl 1997: 285; Dedopulos 1998: 241 [= Baddel et al. 1999: 585]; Richard Gordon, e-mail message to author, Feb. 20, 1997; Brunsting 2000: 245; Regan 2001: 37 (woman lawyer); Anon. 2001b: 118. Although predominantly a lawyer story, this is also told of newly promoted military officers (*Laugh Book Magazine,* Aug. 1955: 57; Hefley 1968: item 1230; Wilde 1980a: 105 [Israeli major]; B. Phillips 1984: 7; Adams 1996: 59) and occasionally of a doctor (Blumenfeld 1970: 49), oil promoter (McManus 1948: 114), investment advisor (Rosten 1985: 455), theatrical agent (Topol [1994]: 171), young businessman (Berle 1989: 105; Kostick et al. 1998: 218; Tibballs 2000: item 383), a Democratic congressman (B. Phillips 1994: n.p.), and a Labour M.P. (Dale and Simmons 1999: 39). Cf. the story, now apparently dead, of the new doctor or lawyer shopping for a well-worn doormat or old magazines: Ernst 1930: 299; Copeland 1936: 251; Lupton 1938: 115; Hershfield 1938: 115 [= Hershfield 1964: 165].

82. Anon. [1967]: 187; Anderson 1923: 211; Braude 1955: item 1421; Droke 1956: 305; Reader's Digest 1958: 254 (quoted from W. S. Maugham); Hefley 1968: item 786 (attributed to Justice Oliver Wendell Holmes); Baughman 1974: 117; Walser 1974: 91 (attributed to Sen. Sam Ervin in 1956); Schock 1976: 96; Hay 1989: 176 (Maugham); Rovin 1992: 18;

Vas 1994a; 1998 Cal.: May 12; Reader's Digest 1997: 44; Mason 2001: 101 (told of U.S. prosecutors). It has been switched to congressmen (Parker 1978: 78) and clergy (Murray 1954: 245; Bouquet 1989: 45; Streiker 1998: 25).

83. Hupfeld [1871]: 95; Bigelow 1871: 392 (told of English barrister).

84. Johnston 1922: item 1133; *Green Bag* 19: 175 (1898); Waters 1900: 115; Edwards 1915: item 690; Anderson 1924: 215; Ernst 1930: 210; Williams 1938: item 883 [= Williams 1949: item 4070); Esar 1945: 452; Keene 1949: 348; Braude 1958: item 683; Readers Digest 1967: 694 (told of Sir Henry Irving); Woods 1967: item 92.6 (similar to Johnston 1922); Jessel 1973: 132; Phillips 1974a: 43; Wilde 1975a (black): 57; Wilde 1982: 58 (similar to Johnston 1922); B. Phillips 1984a: 43; Rosten 1985: 338; E. Phillips 1989: 36; Phillips 1990: 89; Steiger 1990: 23 (told of Henry Irving); Rovin 1992: 7; Lowdown Disk 1992: item 522; *AML* 1993: no. 494; Grossman 1993: 27; *Nolo's Favorite* 1993; 1995 Cal.: item 154; 1996 Cal.: June 23 [= 1997 Cal.: Dec. 10]; Burke 1997a: 52; Kostick et al. 1998: 334; 2002 Cal.: Jan. 15. This story is told exclusively about lawyers, but the need to talk without thinking turns up in a few stories about Mormon Elders (*Saints' Herald*, May 9, 1928, 554, quoted in Smith 1982: 264) and politicians (Esar 1945: 337; Humes 1993: 43 [attributed to Lincoln about Stephen Douglas]).

85. Golden [1950]: 165; Droke 1956: 98; Braude 1964: item 528; Murdock 1967: 108; Woods 1967: item 94.16; Shafer and Papadakis 1988: 71; Phillips 1989: 14; Knott 1990: 16; Behrman 1991: 111.

86. Barry Glassner, e-mail message to Cynthia F. Epstein, Nov 4, 1997 [= e-mail from Ann Althouse, Nov. 5, 1997 = e-mail from Sarah Galanter, Jan. 24, 1998 = e-mail from Bill Broder, Mar. 6, 2000]. An earlier "true story" version is found in Hay 1989: 166. The same story is presented as a joke in Shafer and Papadaikis 1988: 125; Knott 1990: 3; Cohl 1997: 278; 1998 Cal.: Feb. 8; Randy's Favorite Lawyer Jokes, July 24, 1997; Lawyer Jokes, Jan. 30, 1998; Streiker 1998: 248; Greene 1999: 160; Anon. 2000a: 113; Brunsting 2000: 249; Tibballs 2000: item 1168; Anon. 2001: 132; Regan 2001: 98; Mason 2001: 156; 2002 Cal.: Sept. 4. *Bangkok Post* (June 13, 1997, 12) is agnostic.

The ancestor of this tale may be the story of the arrogant emergency room intern who is scornful of the policeman who declares an arrival dead only to realize that it is "a decapitated body, its head tucked under its arm." Anon. 1963a: "Heads, you lose."

87. In addition to items A34 and A35 above about lawyers not thinking, lawyers have been frequent subjects of several "brain" jokes: if lawyer and another bang heads, only the other risks brain concussion (e.g., Case 1928: 60; Ashmore 1930: 52); lawyer's brain is very expensive for brain transplant because it has never been used (e.g., 1997 Cal.: Mar. 27); or because it is necessary to kill so many to get requisite amount (e.g., Greene 1999: 172).

88. Lupton 1938: item 2418; Williams 1926: item 771 (Harlan); Meier 1944: 171; Droke 1948: 149 (Harlan); Williams 1949: item 2189 (Harlan); Golden [1950]: 13 (Harlan); Behrman 1991: 99 (woman lawyer); *AML* 1993: no. 420 (similar to Behrman 1991) Related themes are examined Anon. 1902: item 332 (judge cuts off young lawyer and directs verdict in his favor because "I don't want to take any chances"); Foote 1911: 93 (appellate judge *still* concurs after hearing colleague's lengthy judgment).

89. CLLH 1995: no. 70; Regan 2001: 165. The "no lawyers in heaven" theme is taken up in chap. 4 at items C11–C16. Yarwood (1981: 84) anticipated the "refutation" point: "Charles [*sic*] Darrow, the noted criminal lawyer," unprepared for debate, says "I'll take the negative side. I can argue against anything."

90. Edwards 1915: item 91; Milburn 1927: 27 [=Eastman 1936: 22] (law school); Anderson 1925: 175; Wilde 1987: 21 (law school). Cf. Esar 1945: 173 (retainer to lawyer like quarter put in gas meter). Switched to politicians in Parker 1978: 116.

91. Adams and Newall 1994: 266; Foster 1998: 1; Steiger 1990: 2; Law and Politics 1991: 10; *Nolo's Favorite* 1993; CLLH 1995: lawyer humor no. 23 [= Streiker 1998: 265]; Brallier 1996: 37; anon. Stanford law student, Mar. 10, 1998; Brunsting 2000: 247; Regan 2001: 54; 2002 Cal.: July 5. It appears as a story about parliamentarians (Benton and Loomes 1977 [1976]: 26), diplomats (Schindler 1988: 99; Aspinall 1986: 3; E. Phillips [1993]: 30), accountants (Schindler 1986: 26; Subramanian 1995: 1; Two Fun Guys 1997; Mason 2001: 190), public relations men (Rees 1994: 156), Microsoft employees (Howard Erlanger, e-mail message to author, Jan. 31, 1997 [response identifies spot for lost helicopter pilot]), neurologists (Prasad 1998: 81), information technology workers (Greene 1999: 221), Dominicans (Blue 2001: 101 [man stuck in tree]), psychologists (Anon. 2002: 25).

92. E-mail message to author from Gretchen Viney, Aug. 20, 1999 (quotation marks supplied) = e-mail from Mia Cahill, Jan. 19, 2000 = e-mail from Bill Broder, Apr. 25, 2000. In its first published renditions the characters in the enlarged exchange are an information technology person on the ground and a corporate manager in the balloon. Greene 1999: 221; Anon. 2000a: 119; Anon. 2001a: 140; Colombo 2001: 418.

93. Mindes 1982: 191.

94. Lewis and Wachs 1966: 205; Keene 1949 [1947]: 452; Woods 1967: item 94.10; Rosten 1985: 287; E. Phillips 1989: 41; *AML* 1993: no. 536; Coote 1994: 245 [= Coote 1995: 227]. Although this has been a lawyer joke for half a century, it continues to be told of other advisors: Hupfeld [1871]: 837 (Baron Rothschild provides helpful advice to a money-lender); Robey 1920: 16 (millionaire); Meier 1944: 52 (friend); McManus 1948: 136 (friend); *Laugh Book Magazine,* Sept. 1951: 34 (Scot father); Braude 1955: item 500 (father); Reader's Digest 1958: 154 [= Reader's Digest 1972: 129] (John D. Rockefeller); Cerf 1965: 395 (businessman's friend); Yarwood [1981]: 84 (accountant father); Prochnow 1992 [1990]: 69 (father); E. Phillips 1994: 12 (executive).

95. Edmund and Williams 1916: 361; *Green Bag* 24: 497 (1916); Anderson 1923: 193; Williams 1926: item 321; Anon. ca.1930: 25; Copeland 1936: 240; Woods 1967: item 90.24; Wilde 1987: 72; E. Phillips 1989: 47 (English, told of barrister); Streiker 1998: 249. The sentencing of the offending body parts appeared some years earlier, attributed to "Judge Kent" (possibly James Kent, 1763–1847, Chancellor of the New York court of chancery and the first major commentator on American law): *Green Bag* 1: 504 (1889) (right arm, right shoulder and head sentenced to prison) [= Sprague 1895: 73 = Kieffer 1907: 19]).

96. Quoted at Arnold 1935: 101.

97. Golden [1950] 1953: 159; Edwards 1915: item 160; Wilde 1982: 168.

98. Dr. Merryman 1853: 546; Anon.1902: 31 [= Engelbach 1915: 161]. In Spalding 1978: 257 Curran also refuses to accept a fee.

99. Behrman 1991: 75 (note the substitution of the woman lawyer, which may be a report of what is circulating orally or the compiler's effort at correctness) [=*AML* 1993: no. 395]; Lieberman 1956: 118 [= Lieberman 1975: 58]; Wilde 1982: 169; Rovin 1992: 87.

100. Franklin 1925: 81. In May 1964: 213 the lawyer, on learning that the embezzler has "run through all the money," advises him to "get $5,000.00 more and then come back to see me."

101. Baddiel and Stone 1997: 305 [= Baddiel et al. 1999: 305]; D. Brown 1998f: 176; Keelan 1999: 203; FHM 2001: 32.

102. *Nolo's Favorite* 1993; Randy's Favorite Lawyer Jokes 1997; Streiker 1998: 270 (very similar to *Nolo's Favorite* 1993); 2000 Cal.: Aug. 19–20; 2002 Cal.: July 3.

103. Orso 1979: 55 (German, Englishman, Greek); Pietsch 1986: 256 (Pole, Italian, Jew); Anon. 1986: 83 (Kerryman, Welshman, Englishman); Stangland 1987: 316 [=Stangland

1989: 8] (Norweigan, Dane, Swede); Knott 1987: 33 (Pole, Italian, Jew); Nesvisky 1987: 13 (German, American, Israeli); Alvin 1988: 12 (Pole, Italian, Jew); Allen 1990 (Pole, Italian, Jew); Knott 1990b: 3 (Pole, Italian, Jew); Dover and Fish 1992 (Pole, American, Robert Maxwell); Muradi 1993: 101 (Sikh, Sindhi, Marwari); MacHale 1994: 11 (Englishman, Irishman, Scotsman); Coote 1994: 258 [= Coote 1995: 235] (Brisbane, Sydney, Melbourne contractors); Mital and Gupta 1995: 96 (Marathi, Marwari, Sindhi); Adams and Newall 1996a: 158 (Brisbane, Sydney, Melbourne); Cohl 1997: 162 (Pole, Italian, Jew); Jhumor List, July 9, 1998 (Florida, Missouri, New York contractors); Cohen 1999 (Polish, Italian, Chicago gardeners).

104. Major Grant Blowers, U.S. Forces in Korea, e-mail message, Mar. 5, 1997; Randy's Favorite Lawyer Jokes 1997 (lawyers outwit accountants).

105. Two Fun Guys 1997 (engineers con accountants); Anon. 1997b: 262 (engineers con accountants); Brown and Flynn 1998: 229 (one family cons another); Griest, posting on Novell community chat, Jan. 25, 1999 (engineers con lawyers); 2000 Cal.: Oct. 28 (paralegals con lawyers); e-mail from Jan Hoem, Nov. 25, 2004 (Bushes con Clintons); McFool 2000: 11 (engineers con lawyers); Columbo 2001: 24 (Canadians con Americans).

106. Wardroper 1970: item 154 (from *The Complete London Jester . . .* 2nd ed., 1765) [= Dodge 1987: 122 (from *Hutchin's Improved: Being an Almanack . . . for . . . 1776*)] = Dr. Merryfield 1795: 58]; Lemon 1864: 41; slightly modernized in Anon. 1867: 238; Bigelow 1871: 353; Hupfeld [1871] 71; Brown [1879]: 55 [= Burdette 1903: 441]; Downes 1903: 69 (German); Anon. 1905: 15 (told as anecdote by Philadelphia lawyer); Engelbach 1913: 43; *Green Bag* 25: 488 (1913); Edwards 1915: item 413; Clode 1922: 189; Milburn 1927: 9 [= Copeland 1936: 230 = Eastman 1936: 23 = Rango 1944: 232]; Aye 1931: 87; Johnson et al. 1938: 166; Muller [1939]: 118; Esar 1945: 483; Woods 1967: item 92.4; Adams 1970: 181; Wilde 1975a (black): 63; B. Phillips 1976: 57; Spalding 1978: 247; Wilde 1982: 60; Berle 1989: 470 (questioner is police lieutenant); E. Phillips 1989: 46 (British); Johnson 1989: 183; Phillips 1991: 5; Adler 1992: 139; Warner 1993: 171; Claro 2000: 17.

107. Arya 1996: 42; Wood n.d. [c.1926]: 55 [= Eastman 1936: 45 = Copeland 1936: 125]; Esar 1945: 175 (saw through hole in fence); Lieberman 1956: 100; May 1956: 62 (looked at clock on my dresser); Triverton 1981: 68; Wilde 1982: 54; Behrman 1991: 86; Rovin 1992: 8; Vas 1994: n.p.

108. Meier 1944: 172; Byrn [1852]: 248; Shillaber 1854: 257; Hupfeld [1871]: 104; *Green Bag* 4: 498 (1892); Engelbach 1913: 181; Milburn 1927: 11 [= Copeland 1936: 231]; Meier 1944: 172; Berle 1989: 239; E. Phillips 1989: 27; Rovin 1992: 155; 2002 Cal.: July 18. The early versions do not contain the multiplier, which first appears in Milburn 1927.

109. Moulton 1942: item 1410; *Green Bag* 2: 227 (1890) (German juror); Anon. 1900: 129 (quoted in Tidwell 1956: 357); Anon. 1902?: 306 (German juror); *Green Bag* 15: 95 (1903); Copeland and Copeland 1940: 479; Fuller 1942: item 2511; Cerf 1945: 40 [= Cerf 1945a: 29]; Esar 1945: 59; Boatright 1949: 126; Keene 1949: 353; Wilson and Jacobs 1974: 62 (elaborated Cajun version); Spalding 1978: 252; Yarwood [1981]: 39; Anon. 1987: 73; Claro 1990: 97; Behrman 1991: 14; *AML* 1993: no. 355; CLLH 1995: no. 100; CLLH 1995: no. 131; Adams and Newall 1995: 287; Claro 1996: 116; Brallier 1996: 34; Regan 2001: 223; 2002 Cal.: June 12.

In an equally popular variant, it is the defendant (or a relative) rather than the lawyer who bribes the juror: Kemble 1901: 11 (Jewish juror); Kelly 1906: 56 (Irish juror) [= Cahill 1906: 30 = Johnston 1922: item 1129 = Ernst 1925: 5 = Copeland 1936: 130 = Eastman 1936: 61 = May 1956: 215]; Engelbach 1913: 96; Robey 1920: 65; Franklin 1925: 18; Hershfield 1938: 144; Knox ca. 1943: 149; Thomas 1947: 27; Lehr et al. 1948: 31; Williams 1949: item

2107 [= Kelly 1906, etc.]; Golden [1950] 1953: 58; Kahn 1999: 158 (South Africa, citing Blackwell 1962); Hershfield 1964: 76; Adams 1968: 250; Adams 1975: 159; Hornby 1977: 42; Wilde 1982: 92 (Irish juror); Baker 1982: 37; Gardner 1982: 99; Scott 1984: 133; Rovin 1987: 206; Chariton 1989: 75; Knott 1991: 30; Knott 1992a: 100; Adler 1992: 79; Adams 1996: 208; Arya 1996: 14 (India [a jurisdiction with no juries!]); Cohl 1997: 272; Claro 2000: 55; Allan 2000: 118; Sharpe 2000: 167; Mason 2001: 139.

A civil version of this turnabout is found in *Green Bag* 24: 325 (1912) (lawyer's office boy obtains continuance as instructed although judge wanted to dismiss in his favor).

110. Brallier 1992: 65; Lisa Harinanan, e-mail message to author, Apr. 10, 1998; Sharpe 2000: 163; Mason 2001: 115; Alan Dundes, e-mail, Aug. 27, 2001; 2002 Cal.: Feb. 22.

111. Buford and Grabowski 1998: 50; Humes [1975]: item 305; Delf 1992: 97; Adams and Newall 1995: 262; Streiker 1998: 272; Kostick et al. 1998: 251.

112. Phillips 1990: 24; Anon. 1905: 168 (farmer client); Davidson 1913: 44 (Jewish client); Franklin 1925: 6 (Jewish client); Richman 1926: 233 (Jewish client); Ferguson 1933: 287 (Scots client); Johnson et al. 1936: 163; Old Commercial Traveler n.d.: 64 (Jewish client); Esar 1946: 278; McManus 1948: 75; Williams 1949: item 2093; May 1956: 141; Woods 1967: item 93.29; Morecroft [1974]: 51 (Maori client); Harris 1979: 50; Gillespie-Jones 1980: 123 (Chinese client); Johnston 1984: 72 [= Johnston 1994: 50] (farmer client); Wilde 1987: 75; Sood 1988: 56 (sent cheapest whiskey); E. Phillips 1989: 35 (farmer client); Behrman 1991: 73; Rovin 1992: 97 (Jewish client); *AML* 1993: no. 2; Coote 1994: 245 [= Coote 1995: 64]; Mital and Gupta 1995: 113. In a few instances it is the novice lawyer who upends his senior colleague (Cerf 1970: 311; Lawyer Jokes, Jan. 30, 1998; 2000 Cal.: Jan. 20) or an imported "Philadelphia lawyer" who outdoes the locals (*Green Bag* 21: 193 [1909]). In a single instance the joke is reversed: the lawyer sends the brandy over the objection of the client (Berle 1989: 61).

A similar story is told of politicians who cadge drinks or fail to tip and divert the opprobrium to their opponents. Wilson 1949: 257; Cerf 1959: 348; O'Neal and O'Neal 1964: 134; Boliska [1966]: 22; Shelley 1976: 48; B. Phillips 1994; Singh 1996: 97; Dole [1998]: 173.

113. *Debow's Review* 1855: 519.

114. Droke 1948: 385 [= Lupton 1938: item 432]; *Green Bag* 16: 264 (1904) (Scot); Edward 1915: item 16 (Scot); Heighton 1916: 60 (bad case, barrister happy to take it); Robey 1920: 152 (Scot); Franklin 1925: 155 (Scot); Ernst 1930: 287 (Scot); Johnson et al. 1936: 263 (Scot); Copeland and Copeland 1940: 481; Cerf 1945: 149 [= Cerf 1945a: 107 = Cerf 1956: 206]; Esar 1945: 261; Lieberman 1956: 114 [= Lieberman 1975: 53] (Jew); Cohen 1958: 25 (Jew); Braude 1964: item 524 [= Reader's Digest 1967: 76 = Davidson 1998: 219] (told of financier Russell Sage, 1816–1906); Crompton 1970: 33 (Jew); Wilde 1982: 147; Rosten 1985: 283 (Scot); Shafer and Papadaikis 1988: 29; Berle 1989: 385; E. Phillips 1989: 28; Allen 1990: 78 (Jew); Rosten 1990: 370 (Jew); Claro 1990: 98 [= Claro 1996: 98]; Duncan 1990: 148; Behrman 1991: 32; Rovin 1992: 142; Coote 1994: 246 [= Coote 1995: 227 = Coote 1996: 181] (Scot); Vas 1994: n.p. (Jew, two versions); 1998 Cal.: May 31; Brunsting 2000: 250.

115. Reproduced in London 1960: 1:472–94. This is AT1585 (The Lawyer's Mad Client). Pre-twentieth-century versions in many languages are surveyed in Oliver 1909. In addition to the versions cited below, see Zall 1962: 277 [1535?]; Zall 1963: 284 [1535]; Ashton 1884: 92 [1686] (lawyer enlisted to outwit himself by daughter's suitor); Brown [1879]: 67 [= Landon 1883: 405]; Lurie 1928: 140; Anon. 1988: 70 (daughter's suitor); Hochwald [1994]: 47.

116. Angelo Poliziano (1454–94), *Bel Libretto* [1477–79], reproduced in Speroni 1964: 148.

117. Pasquil's Jests . . . [1650?], reprinted in Ashton 1884: 223 = Willock 1887: 379; Zall 1963: 277 [1535?]; Brown [1879]: 67; Landon 1883: 405; Pickens 1926: 76; Hochwald [1994]: 47.

118. Lurie 1927: 148–9; Hupfeld [1871]: 79 (told of Luther Martin [1748?–1826], a prominent Maryland lawyer); *Green Bag* 18: 636 (1906) (young lawyer buys senior's houses at tax sale). This is an expansive American version of an English variant that features a lawyer and his clerk: Dr. Merryfield 1795: 41; Merryman 1853: 480; Willock 1887: 395; Anon. 1898: 76.

119. House 1948: 35; Pickins 1926: 76 (insanity); Lurie 1928: 40 (insanity); Elgart 1954: 120 (witnesses); Woods 1967: item 942 (same); Esar 1978: 554 (same); Harris 1979: 110 (same); Gardner 1982a: 109 (same); Wilde 1987: 82; Rovin 1992: 81 (same); Hochwald [1994]: 47 (imbecility).

120. McFool 2000: 41; Tibballs 2000: item 1153; Anon. 2000c: 361. Cf. Davis 1956b: 155 (professor and student); Delf 1992: 64 (banker and peasant).

121. Lawyer Jokes, Jan. 30, 1998; Edward A. Tiryakian, e-mail message to author, Sept. 17, 2000 (California lawyer in Texas); Baddiel and Stone 1997: 236 [= Baddiel et al. 1999: 236] (Scotsman kicks Englishman); Brown 1998e: 36 (same); Keelan 1999: 33 (two Irishmen).

122. Alan Dundes, e-mail message to author, Jan. 29, 2002. This is an adaptation of "cigar fire Insurance" at the AFU and Urban Legend Archive, Nov 4, 1997 (Charlotte man); Anon. 2001c: 29. But this up-to-date story is found in Sprague 1897: 113 ("cunning fellow"), where it is credited to a German tobacco trade paper.

123. de Tocqueville: 1:287.

124. Auerbach 1976b: 38.

125. Miller 1995: 162.

126. "The Money Trail" at http://www.pbs.org/newshour/bb/white_house/march97/fund-3–6.html.

127. Denby 1994: 52

128. *New Republic* 2000: 13.

2. The Lawyer as Economic Predator

1. Reprinted in Zall 1980: 27. Compare the wry observation, "'I never was ruined but twice,' said a wit: 'once when I *lost* a lawsuit and once when I *gained* one.'" Lemon 1864: 72. A capable lawyer confesses that he would not defend against a claim for his coat "lest in defending my *coat*, I should too late find that I was deprived of my *waistcoat* also." Lemon 1864: 91; Willock 1887: 41. That clients are emaciated and lawyers adipose is asserted by a joke about fat and lean horses. Merryfield 1795: 53; Hupfeld [1871]: 84; Anon. 1893: 36; Anon. 1898: 39; *Joe Miller's* 1903: I, 68. In a modern counterpart, "Gandhi look[s] more like a client than a lawyer to me." O'Neal and O'Neal 1964: 69.

2. Marks et al. 1908: 47.

3. Trubek et al. 1983: 93. The comparable figure for organizational parties was 98 percent.

4. The lawyer's economic incentive to encourage clients to proceed may be countered by professionalism and concern for reputation.

5. Croy 1948: 86 [1901]; Droke 1956: item 903 [= Subhash and Dharam 1995b: 83].

6. Rhodes 1890: 115.

7. Singh 1992: 86.

8. Tucker 1984: 47 cites this as a retelling by James Puckle (around 1700) of Nicholas Boileau's (1636–1711) celebrated tale and notes other eighteenth-century versions, including one by Alexander Pope. Also, Hupfeld [1871]: 81 (two boys quarreling over walnut); Edmund and Williams 1916: 261 [= Milburn 1927: 27 = Bonham 1981: 85]; Knott 1990: 105; Behrman 1991: 8; Berle 1993: 315; Streiker 1998: 264; Regan 2001: 12.

9. A prose version is May 1964: 38.

10. Johnston 1922: item 1145; Aye 1931: 149; Wilde 1982: 2; Phillips 1989: 15; Harvey ca.1998a: 96. Compare Anon. 1898: 76 (asked to prevent son from inheriting, lawyer overperforms).

11. Esar 1945: 241; *Green Bag* 22: 316 (1910); Wilde 1987: 132; Rovin 1992: 34.

12. Anon 1832: 72–73; Hood et al. 1873: 136.

13. For example, Willock 1887: 239 (poor man whose lawyer did not respond until he was given a lamb, thinks lawyers understand lambs' words better); *Green Bag* 7: 308 (1895) (Theophilus Parsons [1750–1813], the leading lawyer in the U.S. in the first years of the nineteenth century, says opinion "stuck in his throat" until client pays more); Engelbach 1913: 188 (Serjeant Davy [d.1780] can read no further in brief for two guineas).

14. *Green Bag* 21: 259 (1909).

15. Lurie 1928: 139; E. Phillips 1989: 90.

16. Woods 1967: item 93.16; Wilde 1987: 35; Berle 1989: 61; Knott 1990: 99; Rovin 1992: 97; Berle 1993: 148; Arya 1995: 32.

17. Alvin 1999: 95; Alvin 1999a: 37 ("Johnny Cochran's theory of law"); Green 1999: 166; 2000 Cal.: Jan. 18.

18. Brown [1879]: 86; *Green Bag* 1: 174 (1889); Klein 1903: 80 [= Anon. 1906a: 33]; Anon. 1906b: 60; *Green Bag* 20: 576 (1908); Edwards 1915: item 300; Anderson 1923: 73 (lawyer *and* "a couple of jurymen") [= Braude 1955: item 1402a]; Franklin 1925: 238; Gerler 1965: 40; Anon. 1971: item 454.51; Jessel 1973: 132; Wilde 1987: 87; Berle 1989: 368; B. Phillips 1990: 88; Rovin 1992: 12; Adams 1996: 393 [= 1997 Cal.: Oct. 29 = 1998 Cal.: Oct. 23]; Harvey 1998a: 176; 2000 Cal.: Jan. 25.

19. Lemon 1864: 123 [= Hupfeld [1871]: 80 = Burdette 1903: 474 = Ferguson 1933: 197]; Hood et al. 1873: 261; Landon 1883: 395 (told of Rufus Choate); Miles 1890?: 65 (took every farthing, told of "Serjeant" William Davy [d.1780], renowned as a master cross-examiner and a humorist); Miles 1890: 65 (adverting to custom that barristers' fees be paid in gold); *Green Bag* 4: 394 (1892) (Choate); *Green Bag* 7: 397 (1895); *Green Bag* 15: 148 (1903); Engelbach 1913: 145; Edwards 1915: item 434; Johnstone 1922: item 104 (told of Augustine Birrell [1850–1933]); Franklin 1925: 217 (Choate); Ferguson 1933: 197; Williams 1949: item 2206 (Rufus Choate in England); Ross 1996: 16 (Choate).

20. Gilbert [1986]: 66, citing Edward G. Parker, *Reminiscences of Rufus Choate* (1860). Presumably the incident occurred some years earlier.

21. In a related story a drayman accepted a measly fee from a poor widow for a sizable job for "I took all she had, sor; an' bedad, sor, a lyer could have done no better nor that, sor." Landon [1883]: 402 [= Burdette 1903: 396]; Mustlaff c.1900: 147; Boatright 1945: 179 [= Boatright 1949: 123].

22. Apart from appearing in the introduction to an Australian collection (Ross 1996: 16) as an illustration of the profession's long-standing preoccupation with money.

23. *Bates v. State Bar of Arizona*, 97 S. Ct. 2691 (1977).

24. Some medical examples are Anon. 1906; Claro 1996: 110.

25. Bierce [1898] (1972: 554) [= Behrman 1991: 121 = *AML* 1993: no. 438]; Spalding 1976: 233.

26. Edwards 1915: item 804 [= Lawson 1923: 162 = Gerler 1956: 40 = Lieberman 1956: 86 = True 1972: 58 = Lieberman 1975: 69 = Vas 1994]; Cerf 1959: 286 [=Adams 1968: 344]; Lewis and Wachs 1966: 206; Woods 1967: item 94.8; Wilde 1982: 76; Shafer and Papadaikis 1988: 93; E. Phillips 1989: 29; Knott 1990: 89; Lowdown Disk 1992: item 495; *Nolo's Favorite* 1993; 1997 Cal.: Mar. 19; Adams 1996: 207; Streiker 1998: 266.

27. Wachs 1968: 183; Droke 1956: item 909; Pendleton [1979]: 98; Wilde 1982: 175; Wilde 1987: 164; Allen 1990: 65; Knott 1990: 67; B. Phillips 1990: 88; Rovin 1992: 89; Vas 1994; Mital and Gupta 1995: 112; Adams 1996: 411; 1997 Cal.: July 18; *Nolo's Favorite* (on line, Sept. 19, 1997).

28. Scruggs 1928: item 406 [= Williams 1949: item 3197]; *Green Bag* 20: 480 (1908).

29. Lowdown Disk 1992: no. 470; Washington Post 1981; 1996 Cal.: Mar. 11; Rees 1995: 146 (quoting *Financial Times,* May 27, 1994); Lawyer Jokes, Jan. 30, 1998; Streiker 1998: 316; Greene 1999: 187; Regan 2001: 58.

30. 1995 Cal.: item 157; Ross 1996: 50.

31. Lemon 1864: 40; Anon. 1902: 232; *Joe Miller's* 1903: I, 171; Copeland and Copeland 1940: 475; E. Phillips 1989: 87. The medical counterpart may be found at Ferguson 1933: 226 (physician sends patient to colleague in Bath with letter that advises "keep the old lady three weeks and send her back again").

32. Halpert and Thomas 2001.

33. Lemon 1864: 223 [= Beeton 1880: 9 = Woods 1967: item 96.7]; Howe [1891]: 106, Williams 1949: item 2198 (rabbi).

34. Edwards 1915: item 720; Knott 1990: 111; Rovin 1992: 91 [= *AML* 1993: no. 186]; 1996 Cal.: July 6.

35. Williams 1938: item 904; Esar 1945: 223; Lehr et al. 1948: 124; Adams 1959: 147 [= Adams 1968: 344]; Cohen 1960: 107; Hefley 1968: item 788; Spalding 1969: 348; Wilde 1982: 169; Berle 1989: 384; E. Phillips 1989: 25; Behrman 1991: 55 [= *AML* 1993: no. 379]; Adler 1992: 95 [= Adler 1994: 99 = 2000 Cal.: May 23]; Mital and Gupta 1995: 112.

36. In addition the lawyer/other people's pockets trope occurs in various stories, such as Lemon 1864: 294; Engelbach 1913: 208.

37. Anon. 1900: 151; Hupfeld [1871]: 79; Werner 1893: 234; *Green Bag* 7: 42 (1895); Anon. 1898: 95; *Green Bag* 22: 659 (1910); Johnston 1925: item 1109; Williams 1938: item 885; Fuller 1942: item 2530; Boatright 1949: 122; Spalding 1978: 250; E. Phillips 1989: 15. The *portrait* version has occasionally been applied to bankers (Moulton 1942: item 999), politicians (Meier 1944: 211; Skubik and Short 1976: 28), and businessmen (Larson 1980: 23).

38. Edmund and Williams 1916: 259 [= Lawson 1923: 163; Milburn 1927: 24 = Copeland 1936: 277 = Eastman 1936: 15 = Copeland and Copeland 1940: item 5446 = McManus 1948: 99]; Zall 1985: 85 [versions from 1889 and 1900]; Anon. 1900: 151; Lurie 1927: 142; Scruggs 1928: item 219; Johnson et al. 1936: 180; Smith 1941: 174; Allen 1945: item 1143; Teitelbaum 1945: 341; Mendelsohn 1947: 177; Williams 1949: item 1811; Golden 1953 [1950]: viii; Rabinowitz 1986 [1973]: 209; Claro 1990: 131 [= Claro 1996: 155]; Nash et al. 1995: 106; 1997 Cal.: Nov. 5; 2002 Cal.: Mar. 4.

39. It is possible that Twain is the source of the *two speakers* version of *pockets*. Zall 1985: 85 reports a Twain version in 1889. Twain would probably have been familiar with the *portrait* version, which was published in 1877.

40. William Maxwell Evarts (1818–1901) was a prominent lawyer who served as attorney general of the United States (1868–69), secretary of state (1877–81), and a member of the United States Senate (1885–91). Louis Marshall (1856–1929) was a prominent American

lawyer and Jewish communal leader. The Yiddish writer and humorist Sholem Aleichem (1859–1916) spent 1906–7 and 1914–16 in the U.S., so an encounter with Marshall may have occurred.

41. Lieberman 1956: 96 [= Vas 1994]; Wilde 1982: 2; Rovin 1992: 100.

42. *National Law Journal,* May 20, 1996: A18; Ross 1996: 51; Cohl 1997: 280 (narrative version); 1998 Cal.: Aug. 9; Dedopulos 1998: 240; Alvin 1999: 96. These were anticipated by a version involving senators: Stangland 1994: 3.

43. Act 1, scene 9.

44. Lemon 1864: 84.

45. Shafer and Papadaikis 1988: 142; Dole [1998]: 153; Regan 2001: 110.

46. Puzo 1969: 51.

47. *Green Bag* 14: 200 (1902) [= Milburn 1927: 45]; Braude 1964: item 699; Adams 1968: 344; Wilde 1982: 147; E. Phillips 1989: 30; Adler 1992: 50; Robin 1992: 134 (be like Clyde Barrow); 1997 Cal.: June 23. This joke has also been applied to other callings: Davies 1954: 119; Amsterdam 1959: 15 (television repairman); Wilde 1981: 161 [= Wilde 1997: 101] (surgeon).

48. *Ellis v. Frawley,* 165 Wis. 381, 385 (1917).

49. Speiser 1980: 268.

50. Rovin 1992: 90; *Green Bag* 14: 400 (1902); *Green Bag* 16: 196 (1904); Fowler 1915: 111; Edwards 1915: item 696 [= Johnston 1922: 244 = Milburn 1927: 23 = Prochnow and Prochnow 1964: 144]; Franklin 1925: 133; Johnson et al. 1936: 238; Posner 1937: 60; Williams 1938: item 882; Knox c.1943: 153; Golden 1953 [1950]: viii; May 1956: 208; Wilde 1982: 128; Berle 1989: 60; Knott 1990: 86; *AML* 1993: no. 183; *Nolo's Favorite* 1993; B. Phillips 1996: 85; Alvin 1997: 111; Knott 1997: 33; 2000 Cal.: July 12.

51. Bierce 1946 [1899]: 585.

52. *Green Bag* 19: 559 (1907).

53. Robbers lose money in the course of spirited physical resistance from members of a lawyers' club: Delf 1992: 95; *Nolo's Favorite* 1993; Dedopulos 1998: 242 [= Baddiel et al. 1999: 586]; Tibballs 2000: item 1151; Regan 2001: 86. Cf. Cerf 1956: 196 (home for retired actors); MacHale 1988: 78 (Scots' boardinghouse).

54. Ernst 1930: 11 (attributed to *Boston Transcript*); Case 1928: 129.

55. Anderson 1922: 54 (insurance man sells policy to hold-up man); Schermerhorn 1928: 307 [= Rango 1944: 276] (real estate man sells lots to burglar). Similarly, a bishop extracts a contribution from a beggar (Lurie 1927: 167). And a Jewish insurance agent sells life insurance to a priest sent to convert him (Gurney 1987).

56. Willock 1887: 254; Franklin 1925: 193; Ernst 1930: 291.

57. Singh 1990: 93 (attributed to lawyer in Ludhiana).

58. 1995 Cal.: item 88; Ross 1996: 34; 1997 Cal.: Oct 27 (vampire bat is mouselike creature with wings, lawyer is diseased, bloodsucking predator); Alvin 1999a: 82; Tibballs 2000: item 1132. Another set of riddles compares lawyers with leeches (e.g., CLLH 1995: riddle no. 40; 2000 Cal.: Mar. 21; Tibballs 2000: item 1145) and ticks (e.g., Ross 1996: 38; Greene 1999: 165; Alvin 1999: 94 [= Alvin 1999a: 24]).

59. *Oxford English Dictionary,* s.v. "Shark." Partridge 1961: 751. Cf. Wentworth and Flexner 1975: 463.

60. Anon. 1900: 147. The same collection contains a similar story about lawyers being chased by a pack of wolves. Anon. 1900: 147. Earlier collections remarked on the identification of sharks as "sea lawyers" (Hupfeld [1871]: 106) and noted shark-bite as the source of antilawyer animus (Willock 1887: 411).

61. Reader's Digest 1949: 200 (attributed to Alex F. Osborn); Cerf 1945: 236; Taube-neck 1946: 176; Esar 1946: 254; Droke 1948: 30; Morecroft [1974]: 36 (speech in London, 1950); Braude 1955: item 1402; *Laugh Magazine* c.1960: 25; O'Neal and O'Neal 1964: 69; May 1964: 125; Rabinowitz 1986 [1973]: 143; Humes 1985 [1975]: 82; Baker 1982: 32; Wilde 1982: 22; Robin 1987: 213; Chariton 1989: 68; Phillips 1989: 48; Sartor 1989: 63; Berle 1989: 61; Knott 1990: 15; Novak and Waldoks 1990: 105; Steiger 1990: 44; Behrman 1991: 22; Rovin 1991: 268; Johnson 1991: 189; Brallier 1992: 62; Asimov 1992: 207; Grossman 1993: 30; *Nolo's Favorite* 1993; *AML* 1993: nos. 362, 645; Berle 1993: 326; Nick Larsen, e-mail message to author, Aug. 27, 1994; Adams and Newall 1994: 268; 1996 Cal.: July 1; CLLH 1995: riddle no. 47; E. Phillips 1996: 53; Goldstein-Jackson 1996: 86; Barnett and Kaiser 1996: 89; Ross 1996: 48; Van Munching 1997: 54; Streiker 1998: 250; 2000 Cal.: May 19; Greene 1999: 167; Alvin 1999a: 17; Anon. 2000a: 112; Claro 2000: 80. In many of the recent items, the narrative shrinks to a riddle. Occasionally the courtesy is not from sharks, but from snakes (*Maledicta* 9: 313 [1986–87]; Lawyer Jokes, Jan. 30, 1998) or thieves (1997 Cal.: Sept. 15; 1998 Cal.: Nov. 8).

62. Franklin 1925: 299 (lobbyist and burglar); Bonfonti 1976: 66 (Mafia capo); Rees 1994: 130 (Hollywood agent, attributed to Dick Vosburgh, 1979); Lyons 1987: 81 (Jewish American Princess and cobra); Knott 1991: 136 (Jewish mother); Miller 1991: 136 (politi-cian and thieves); Dover and Fish 1992 (Robert Maxwell); Yermonee 1992 (Maxwell); Alvin 1997: 102 (Jewish American Princess); Cohl 1997: 262 (Jewish mother); Two Full Guys 1997 (accountants).

63. E.g., Humes [1975]: 82; Wilde 1982: 22 ("immediately eight sharks formed a two-lane escort and helped him to the ship, and back").

64. For Counsel Product and Gift Catalog 1997: 24. A Dallas firm was reported to have mounted an eighteen-foot fibreglass shark, visible from the interstate. *National Law Journal*, Oct. 16, 2000, 5.

65. Advertisement of the Law Offices of Walter W. Moore, *San Francisco Chronicle*, Mar. 9, 1998.

66. 1997 Cal.: 76; Berle 1993: 181; Behrman 1995: 116; 1998 Cal.: Oct. 4; Regan 2001: 138.

67. Curran 1977: 231. Seventy-three percent of nonusers agreed, but only 65 percent of those who had used lawyers. Curran 1977: 235.

68. Roper Center 1984.

69. National Family Opinion Research, survey "How Do You Rate the Value You Get . . . Lawyers' Fees," available in Westlaw, Poll database.

70. Samborn 1993: 1.

71. Karsten 1998: 291. Much earlier, a Massachusetts polemicist against lawyer mis-deeds speaks in 1786 of the "pernicious practice . . . [of] making bargains upon the event of the cause. . . . Are the 'people' of this Commonwealth reduced to so dreadful a state, as to give one quarter part of their property to secure the remainder, when they appeal to the laws of their country?" Honestus [1819] 1969: 256.

72. Bergstrom 1992: 89

73. Karsten 1998; Auerbach 1976: 44–50; Bergstrom 1992: 91; Dornstein 1996: chap. 3.

74. Landon 1883: 386; *Green Bag* 5: 340 (1893); Sprague 1895: 33; Edwards 1915: item 435; Ernst 1930: 39; Franklin 1925: 5; Williams 1938: item 642; Esar 1945: 262; *Maledicta* 10: 240 (1988–89) (reporting 1964 telling); Wilde 1982: 175; Rovin 1989: 182; May 1989: 114 (Evarts, different case); Allen 1990: 65; Behrman 1991: 58; Rovin 1992: 44; Lowdown Disk 1992: item 461; *Nolo's Favorite* 1993; Berle 1993: 324; Vas 1994; 1996 Cal.: Mar. 13; CLLH 1995: lawyer humor no. 29; Ross 1996: 32; Greene 1999: 172; Regan 2001: 161.

75. Berle 1993: 324.

76. Anon. 1905: 190. Hamlin practiced law in Maine until 1848. Also, Edmund and Williams 1916: 261 [= Ernst 1925: 25]; Milburn 1927: 29 [= Copeland 1936: 238 = Smith 1941: 77 = Lowdown Disk 1992: item 468]; Rango 1944: 179; Esar 1945: 261; Boatright 1945: 180; Williams 1949: item 2200; Golden 1950: 180; Wilde 1982: 154.

77. Milburn 1927: 29.

78. Sprague 1895: 113; Edwards 1915: item 438; Johnston 1925: item 1105; Franklin 1925: 141; Ernst 1930: 210; May 1956: 31; Friedman 1960: 38; Cerf 1965: 263; Woods 1967: item 94.6; Wilde 1982: 78; Phillips 1989: 5; Rovin 1992: 40; Berle 1993: 326; Goldstein-Jackson 1995: 73; Adams 1996: 410.

79. Rovin 1992: 40.

80. *Green Bag* 17: 545 (1905) [= Williams 1938: item 884]. Aye 1931: 148 (scaffolding); Ferguson 1933: 188 (scaffolding); Braude 1955: item 1248 (car); May 1956: 102; Wilde 1987: 147 (car). A slight variation of the punch line to "you would think you started the fire" connects the joke with another line of jokes that are addressed in chap. 4.

81. Roper Center 1985.

82. Louis Harris and Associates 1987: 36.

83. But if the contingency fee is accepted as an institution, this does not mean that the public feels that the price is fair. The public regards lawyers' charges generally as excessive. I have been able to find very little on public response to contingency fee rates. In a 1954 Gallup survey, a national sample of adults were asked how much a lawyer should get "without going to court" for "mak[ing] the railroad pay damages of $10,000" to your friend badly hurt in a railroad accident. Of the 87 percent who had an opinion, 30 percent chose $1000—i.e., 10 percent (the median response); 34 percent thought the appropriate fee higher and 21 percent thought it lower.

84. Those who have actually made a claim are even more favorable to the contingency fee: in the 1982 Gallup poll, those with trial experience were more favorable (1982: 140); in the 1986 Louis Harris survey those who had a claim considered it more indispensable.

85. Karsten 1998: 27.

86. *Copeland v. Marshall*, 205 U.S. App. D.C. 390; 641 F.2d 880 (1980) (en banc, Judge Wilkey dissenting at 641 F.2d 929, n.53). Also, White 1983: 193; Dickson 1984: 22; Shafer and Papadakis 1988: 38; Knott 1990: 1; Novak and Waldoks 1990: 105; Steiger 1990: 21; Brallier 1992: 99; Asimov 1992: item 17 [= Humes 1993: 105]; Rovin 1992: 108; Delf 1992: 96; Lowdown Disk 1992: item 524; *AML* 1993: no. 340; Grossman 1993: 116; *Nolo's Favorite* 1993; Warner 1993: 187; Adams and Newall 1994: 263; 1996 Cal.: Feb. 4; *Funny Times,* May 1995, 3; Goldstein-Jackson 1995: 72; CLLH 1995: lawyer humor no. 8; CLLH 1995: lawyer humor no. 9; Barnett and Kaiser 1996: 149; Ross 1996: 31; 1997 Cal.: Sept. 3; Richard Gordon, e-mail message to author, Feb. 20, 1997; Cohl 1997: 279; Two Fun Guys 1997; Van Munching 1997: 128; 1998 Cal.: June 21; Streiker 1998: 255; Dedopulos 1998: 235 [= Baddiel et al. 1999: 579]; Greene 1999: 254; Claro 2000: 59; Tibballs 2000: 185; Mason 2001: 109; Regan 2001: 234. A recent English version switches to accountants (Anon. 2000b: 33 = Anon. 2001b: 109).

87. Observers of the current legal scene sometimes project hourly billing much further back, as does an advisor on dealing with lawyers, who reports, "U.S. President Thomas Jefferson—a lawyer himself—said in 1807 that 'It is the business of a lawyer to question everything, produce nothing, and bill by the hour.'" Dancing with Lawyers 1998 (on-line).

88. The joke, which is told only about lawyers, may derive from an older story about the job applicant who is asked to explain how his years of job experience can be greater

than his age and replies, "I put in a lot of overtime." Cohen 1960: 20; Blumenfeld 1967: 14; Hefley 1968: item 1551; Golden 1972: 196; Marks 1985: 86; Prochnow 1992 [1990]: 96; Phillips 1994: 93; Subramanian 1995: 93.

89. Copeland and Copeland 1940: 481; Esar 1945: 324; May 1956: 211; Wilde 1982: 7; Behrman 1991: 53; Grossman 1993: 14; *Nolo's Favorite* 1993; 1995 Cal.: item 3 [= 1996 Cal.: Jan. 28]; CLLH 1995: lawyer humor no. 79; Brallier 1996: 20; 1997 Cal.: Oct. 16; Ross 1996: 36; Streiker 1998: 269; Greene 1999: 172. The joke appears about doctors with about equal frequency: David 1954: 177; Cerf 1959: 156; Anon. 1971: item 232.44; Pendleton [1979]: 82; Wilde 1981a: 169; Rosten 1985: 151; Pietsch 1986: 28 [= Boskin 1997: 191]; Knott 1987: 112 [= Knott 1990b: 18]; Allen 1990: 70; Odean n.d.; Subramanian 1995: 30; Behrman 1995: 84; Claro 2000: 68; Sharpe 2000: 99 (dentist).

90. Green 1984: 40; Pendleton [1979]: 188; Berle 1989: 384; Metcalf 1993: 133; Rovin 1994: 4; Coote 1994: 431; Cohl 1997: 284; Greene 1999: 163; Brunstine 2000: 247; Regan 2001: 4. Blue collar guys triumph over other professionals, too: Humes [1975]: 132 (doctor); Hornby 1977: 10 (bank manager); Spalding 1978: 87 (brain surgeon); Foster 1986 (doctor); Warner 1993: 75 (doctor); Pietsch 1998: 266 (brain surgeon); Streiker 1998: 235 (doctor); Dance 1998: 150 (orthodontist); Prasad 1998: 106 (doctor, citing 1994 source); Kostick et al. 1998: 206 (brain surgeon); Southwell 1999: 108; Anon. 2000b: 20; Anon. 2000c: 276 (neurosurgeon); Anon. 2002: 81.

91. The jokes about the depreciation and neglect of social obligations in this section concern lawyers' fees, but a related set of jokes extend the charge into other areas. See the section "No Redeeming Social Value" in chap. 7.

92. *Joe Miller's* 1903: II, 134. Six shillings and eightpence (one-third of a pound) was the traditional minimum fee of English solicitors.

93. Richman 1952: 26. The butcher version is tale type AT 1589 (The Lawyer's Dog Steals Meat). *Joe Miller's* [1737]: item 169 [= K . . . 1797: 127] (judge offsets oath fee against coachman's charge); *Green Bag* 2: 92 (1890) (told of Gen. Ben Butler, 1818–93); Werner 1893: 250; Marks 1908: 157; *Green Bag* 21: 656 (1909) [= Anon. 1911: 78] (lawyer being dunned by tailor interprets his inquiry as request for legal advice); Engelbach 1918: 108; Anon. 1914: 20; Fuller 1942: item 486; Moulton 1942: item 1436; Esar 1945: 91; Keene 1949 [1947] (Ben Butler); Williams 1949: item 2190; Droke 1956: item 908; Wachs 1968: 27; Adler 1969: 33; Adams 1970: 181; Ranke 1972: item 213; Wilde 1982: 173; E. Phillips 1989: 70; Rovin 1992: 141 (baker); Subhash and Dharam 1995b: 53; CLLH 1995: lawyer humor no. 47; Ross 1996: 34; 1998 Cal.: Dec. 12; Streiker 1998: 266; Dedopulos 1998: 239 [= Baddiel et al. 1999: 583]; Greene 1999: 159; Tibballs 2000: item 1160; Regan 2001: 6.

94. *Joe Miller's* 1903: 1, 39 [= Tickleside 1788: 17 = Willock 1887: 378 = modernized language version of *Joe Miller* 1739: item 247]. The item resurfaces as Adams 1996: 410.

95. Shafer and Papadaikis 1988: 30. Samuel Untermeyer (1858–1940) was a prominent New York lawyer and name partner in the city's most prestigious Jewish firm. Also Hershfield 1932: item 149; Mendelsohn 1941: 163; Cerf 1945: 203; Ford et al. 1947: 48; Golden 1953 [1950]: 11; Murray 1954: 183; Braude 1955: item 1406; O'Neal and O'Neal 1964: 70; May 1964: 273; Lewis and Wachs 1966: 204; Boliska [1966]: 133; Crompton 1970: 47; Morecroft [1974]: 47; Wilde 1982: 81; Wilde 1986a: 168; Hay 1989: 117 (told of Max Steuer); Lowdown Disk 1992: item 513; Rovin 1992: 127; *AML* 1993: no. 127; *AML* 1993: no. 454; Cohl 1997: 284; Streiker 1998: 267. The joke has been extended to a few doctors (Fowler 1915: 171; Eastman 1936: 5; Davis 1954: 76) and to a public relations man in England (Rees 1994: 155 [cited to 1992 source]).

96. Case 1928: 249; Lawson 1923: 161; Hay 1989: 117. David Lloyd-George (1863–1945) served as prime minister of Great Britain from 1916 to 1922.

97. Kiser 1927: 119; Bell 1929: 76.

98. Nader and Smith 1996: 234.

99. Bonham 1981: 85. In the earliest versions the lawyer is asked to ascertain the genuineness of a coin. Lemon 1864: 282; Cole 1887?: 265. This variant is still extant (Phillips 1989: 54 [counterfeit note]). Another lawyer charges his daughter's suitor for "advice." Ernst 1930: 9. The doctor enters in 1945 and has occupied the field since. Cerf 1945: 26 [= Cerf 1945a]: 17]; Woods 1967: item 94.9; Esar 1978: 573; Newman 1979: 82; Yarwood [1981]: 123; Bonham 1981: 85; Wilde 1982: 161; Korale 1984; Anon. 1988: 65; E. Phillips 1989: 65; Claro 1990: 97 [= Claro 1996: 117] (combined with "bill for greeting"); Behrman 1991: 44; Adler 1992: 43; Brallier 1992: 48; Lowdown Disk 1992: item 497; AML 1993: no. 624; Robin 1993a: 80; Adler 1994: 39; Subramanian 1995: 77; CLLH 1995: lawyer humor no. 156; Behrman 1995: 33; Streiker 1998: 269; Kostick et al. 1998: 116; Regan 2001: 213.

100. Adams 1996: 410; Berle 1993: 325; B. Phillips 1996: 84.

101. Aye 1931: 149; Willock 1887: 269; Rhodes 1890: 264; Miles 1890?: 66 (attributes it to account of a Dublin lawyer in London Chronicle of 1781); Engelbach 1913: 112; Engelbach 1915: 49 (attributes story to London Chronicle of Jan. 11–13, 1781).

102. Williams 1949: item 2204; Anon. 1900: 145; Edwards 1915: item 699; Franklin 1925: 192; Lieberman 1956: 56; Wilde 1982: 82; Gardner 1982a: 109; Knott 1990: 100; Behrman 1991: 88; Nolo's Favorite 1993; Ross 1996: 40; 1998 Cal.: Mar. 28; National Law Journal, May 24, 1999, A17 (cartoon).

103. Petersen 1998.

104. Rodent 1996: 47.

105. Nader and Smith 1996: 234.

106. Richard Gordon, Esq., quoted in Budiansky 1995: 53.

107. Claro 1990: 99 [= Adler 1992: 104 = Adler 1994: 109 = Claro 1996: 118]; Cerf 1945: 174 [= Cerf 1945a: 130]; Droke 1948: 285; Bowker 1961: 117; Jackson 1961: 152; Hershfield 1964: 119; Shafer and Papadaikis 1988: 9; E. Phillips 1989: 77; Rovin 1992: 103; Nolo's Favorite 1993; AML 1993: no. 205; Metcalf 1993: 133; Ross 1996: 40; Cohl 1997: 278; Michael Cardinal posting at alt. gathering rainbow, Jan. 16, 1999; Anon. 2000a: 112; 2002 Cal.: July 22.

108. Anderson 1921: 39 [= Mosher 1922: 151]; Lawson 1923: 96 [= Knox 1926: 176 = Eastman 1936: 5 = Copeland 1936: 255 = Copeland and Copeland 1940: item 5049]; Allen 1945: item 1510; Keene 1949 [1947]: 432; Golden 1949: 36; Wilde 1986a: 168; Behrman 1995: 70.

109. Green Bag 4: 299 (1892).

110. Rafferty 1988: 11; Boliska [1966]: 133; Skubik and Short 1976: 77; Spalding 1976: 151; Wilde 1982; Jones and Wheeler 1989: 107; Knott 1990: 74; Stangland 1990: 10; Novak and Waldoks 1990: 105; Behrman 1991: 52; Lowdown Disk 1992: item 488; Robin 1992: 49; Brallier 1992: 50; Nolo's Favorite 1993; Metcalf 1993: 132; Berle 1993: 325; Faine 1994: 48; Coote 1995: 226; 1996 Cal.: Sept. 2 [= 1997 Cal.: Aug. 31]; Adams 1996: 411; Pease 1996: 25; Ross 1996: 32; Barnett and Kaiser 1996: 223; Cohl 1997: 283; Baddiel and Stone 1997: 261; Kostick et al. 1998: 247; Greene 1999: 166; Keelan 1999: 209; Anon. 2000a: 115; Anon. 2000c: 279; Brunsting 2000: 246; Claro 2000: 59; Tibballs 2000: item 1175; Anon. 2001a: 134; Regan 2001: 174; 2002 Cal.: May 27; Pritchard 2002: 119.

111. Friedman 1960: 287 (fortune teller); Anon. 1971: item 302.36 (Gypsy); Playboy 1972: 158 (Gypsy); McElroy 1973: 37 (crystal gazer); Philips 1987a: 67 (crystal gazer);

Peterson 1976: 36 (fortune teller); Pendleton [1979]: 115 (same); Murtie 1985a: 83 (Irish clairvoyant); Rosten 1985: 394 (clairvoyant); Rosten 1985: 504 (fortune teller); Brandreth 1986: 129 (same); Rovin 1987: 147 (same); Berle 1989: 302 (Gypsy fortune teller); Barry 1990: 105 (fortune teller); Delf 1992: 134 (gypsy fortune teller); a lone therapist turns up in Strean 1993: 203.

112. Playboy 1972: 314; Legman 1968: 359 (citing 1910 source); Scruggs 1928: item 434; Anecdota 1934: item 79 [= Anecdota 1944: item 124]; Murray 1954: 18; Gerler 1965: 217; Anon. 1968b; Roberts 1969: 113; Wilde 1975b: 33 [= Wilde 1982: 150]; Shafer and Papadaikis 1988: 154; Berle 1989: 538; Knott 1990: 50 [= Humes 1993: 103]; *AML* 1993: no. 309; Subhash and Dharam 1995b: 29; Amy Singer, e-mail message to author, Oct. 21, 1999; Jan Hoem, e-mail, Oct. 28, 2000; Anon. 2001c: 17. The story has occasionally been told about others: Anon. (Anecdota) 1928: item 491 (salesman); Anon. (rugby) 1968: 9 (doctor); Jones and Wheeler 1995: 58 (bank trust officer); Jhumor List, Sept. 11, 1999 (rabbi).

113. Wilde 1987: 120; Knott 1990: 87.

114. Playboy 1963: 162; Roach 1977: 29; Cleveland 1980: 98; Berle 1993: 144.

115. See the section "A Suspect Profession" in chap. 7 and item J15, *expert in justice,* in chap. 10.

116. Richard Gordon, e-mail message to author, Apr. 30, 1997. This story is more frequently told of scientists. See Two Fun Guys 1997 (physicist; lawyer is earlier in series); Anon. 1977c: 75 [= Baddiel et al. 1999: 75]; McFool 2000: 196. The basic idea has been around much longer. Engelbach 1915: 125 (man with two mistresses).

117. CLLH 1995: riddle no. 76; Dundes and Georges 1962: 222; May 1964: 298; Tobias 1982: 147; Wilde 1982: 80; Knot 1983: 92 [= Knott 1993a: 16]; Cruikshank 1987: 59; Lyons 1987: 99; Robin 1987: 212; Collected by Joshua Wynd in Berkeley, CA, Dec. 2, 1990; Rovin 1992: 65; Metcalf 1993: 133; *Nolo's Favorite* 1993; Barnett and Kaiser 1996: 89; Pease 1996: 28; Cohl 1997: 284. Dundes and Georges 1962 call this a spooneristic condundrum and provide many more examples of the type.

118. Richard Gordon, e-mail message to author, Feb. 20, 1997; Behrman 1991: 28 [= *AML* 1993: no. 367]. This apparently goes back to a story about the suitor, quizzed by his sweetheart's father whether his intentions are honorable or dishonorable, who asks, "Do I have a choice?" Cerf 1945: 165; Allen 1945: item 1240; Esar 1945: 247; Lehr et al. 1948: 15; Reader's Digest 1949: 134 (attributed to H. Hershfield); Anon. 1954; Hershfield 1959: 109; Playboy 1963: 8; Kowalski 1974: 13; Larkin 1975: 133. The shift to a choice among sinful pursuits comes in with Adams 1953 [1952]: 131 (attributed to Groucho Marx); Rees 1999: 230 (several versions, from 1958); Anon. 1961; Wachs 1968: 232; Adams 1970: 195 (Groucho Marx); Adams 1970: 222; Humes 1985 [1975]: 147 (Groucho Marx); Esar 1978: 440; Novak and Waldoks 1981: 95; Triverton 1981: 127; Lanigan 1988: 125; Breslin 1991: 105 (Brian Mulroney); Gross 1991: 66; Rovin 1991: 54; Warner 1993: 153; Berge 1993: 514; Johnston 1994: 69; Kahn and Boe 1997: 120; Reader's Digest 1997: 119; Forbes 1998: 85; Alvin 1999a: 89; Jan Hoem, e-mail message to author, Feb. 16, 1999 (Clinton and Jerry Falwell); Anon. 2000c: 89 (Clinton and Ian Paisley); Johnson 2001: 62. An alternative punch line makes the same point: when, reproved for smoking with the adultery comparison, the young woman replies, "I have only half an hour for lunch," etc. Playboy 1963: 76; Wachs 1968: 232; Anon. 1968b; Harvey 1998b: 60.

119. The association of the lawyer with gratification in this world rather than the next is taken up in the section "A Kingdom of This World" in chap. 3.

120. Brallier 1996: 24; Wilde 1987: 16; Knott 1990: 55; *Nolo's Favorite* 1993; 1997 Cal.: Mar 24; Anon. 1997: 10.

121. Anon. 1986: 87; Dorson 1960: 162; Dorson 1960a: 146; Legman 1975: 732 [collected 1963] (white ten minutes and hates Negroes); Gross 1991: 61; Eilbirt 1991: 194.

122. Legman 1975: 732 [collected 1945]; Keene 1949 [1947]: 501 (Republican, stealing); O'Neal and O'Neal 1964: 139 (Democrat, stealing); Wilde 1984: 120 (Republican, screwing); Miller 1991: 91 (Democrat, thief); Alvin 1993: 122 (Republican, screwing); Pietsch 1998 (Republican, screwing); Dale and Simmons 1998: 24 (Democrat, screwing). The switch here may be traceable. In 1984, Larry Wilde published a Republican version; three years later the first published lawyer version appeared in his topical collection of lawyer jokes.

123. Alvin 1993: 119; Lowdown Disk 1992: item 476; collected from Jerome Carlin, Berkeley, CA, August, 1995; CLLH 1995: lawyer humor no. 173; 1996 Cal.: Nov. 10; CLLH 1995: lawyer humor no. 117; Sethi 1995b: 149; Brallier 1996: 6; Clifford Westfall, e-mail message to author, Nov. 19, 1996; Cohl 1997: 283; Martling 1997: 111; Pietsch 1998: 41; Cohen 1999: 74; Keelan 1999: 202; Anon. 2001c: 227. This may be related to an older item that plays on the ambivalence of the phrase "out of," which can signify either departure or extraction:

> "As soon as I found it was a crooked business, I got out of it."
>
> "Did you?" said the other. "How much?" (B53 Supp.)

In Croy 1948 [1901]: 87, the speakers are just "two men." In more recent appearances (Wilde 1982: 80; Sood 1988: 55) they are lawyers.

Another possible ancestor (*Green Bag* 23: 381 [1911]) also turns on the notion of the lawyer as incorrigibly extractive:

> First Lawyer—Suppose we go out and take something.
>
> Second Lawyer—From whom?

124. A version about agents is at Alvin 1995a: 87; Mr. "K" 2001: 76.

125. May 1964: 118 ("Kennedy crowd who sit on the edge of the bed and talk about how good things are going to be"); Playboy 1972: 190 [= Humes 1985 [1975]: 202] Wilde 1982: 151; Alvin 1983a: 103; Rovin 1987: 218; Knott 1990a: 79 [= Knott 1990b: 55]; Forbes [1992]: 52; Phillips [1993]: 8; Sethi 1995b: 149; Thomas 1996: 86; Reader's Digest 1997: 173; Reginald 1997: 56; Pietsch 1998: 165 (lawyer is the third husband who "just kept saying, 'I'll get back to you next week!'"); Dole [1998]: 171; Lyons 1998a: 52; Johnson 2000: 92; Hobbes 2002a: 118.

126. CLLH 1995: lawyer humor no. 117; CLMH 1995: gynecologists no. 11; Baddiel and Stone 1997: 96 [= Baddiel et al. 1999: 96]; Alvin 1998a: 66; Tibballs 2000: item 1186. The joke has grown into an extended list: Mark Suchman, e-mail message to author, Nov. 26, 1996 (lawyer is tenth husband); Neil Smelser, e-mail, May 26, 1998 [= Lisa Harinanan, e-mail, Sept. 29, 1998] (lawyer is thirteenth husband); Amy Singer, e-mail, Apr. 20, 2000 (eleventh husband); Anon. 2000c: 275.

127. Kahn and Boe 1997: 172; Boskin 1997: 191 (collected 1994); CLLH 1995: lawyer humor no. 149; Clark Freshman, e-mail message to author, Sept. 20, 1996; anon. Stanford law student, Mar. 10, 1998; Greene 1999: 153; Keelan 1999: 203; Alan Dundes, e-mail, July 24, 2001. This was switched from a joke about a man with fourteen kids: Martling 1984: 89; Knott 1992: 77.

128. Knott 1990: 115–16; Shafer and Papadaikis 1988: 150.

129. AT 1420C; Motif K1581.3 (lover's gift regained; borrowing from the husband and returning to the wife). The theme surfaces in Boccaccio, *Decameron,* Eighth Day, nos. 1, 2; Chaucer, *The Shipman's Tale.*

130. Elgart 1953: 72; Anon. 1965a; Anon. 1968: 78; Adams 1970: 79; Playboy 1972: 67; Wilde 1975b: 70; Mr. J. 1976: 73; Wilde 1978a: 155; Orson 1979: 39; Walker 1981: 85; Rovin

1989: 153; Berle 1993: 447; Coote 1994: 43; Jhumor List, Nov. 1, 1996; Adams 1996: 169; Baddiel and Stone 1997: 70 [= Baddiel et al. 1999: 70]; Reginald 1997: 72; Pietsch 1998: 71; Alvin 2000: 81; Sharpe 2000: 355; FHM 2000: 39; Hobbes 2000a: 128.

131. Rovin 1992: 50 [= *AML* 1993: no. 304]; Pease 1996: 30 (sister in Sydney). Non-lawyer versions invariably involve a traveler entrusted with a large sum by a caring and supportive relative, whose generosity highlights the predatory opportunism of the emissary. Adams 1968: 400 (sister in Hungary); Novak and Waldoks 1981: 141 [dated to 1978] (grandmother in Israel); Wilde 1981: 154 (mother in Raleigh); Dolgopolova 1982: 67 (aunt in Tel Aviv); Ben Eliezar 1992 [1984] (brother in Israel); Barry 1990: 111 (friend in Brooklyn to "Becky" in Israel); Gross 1991: 55 (grandmother in Haifa); Telushkin 1992: 182 (brother in Haifa); Strean 1993: 73 (brother in Israel); Adams and Newall 1996a: 65 (brother in Brisbane); Goldstein-Jackson 1996: 107 (father in Edinburgh); Jhumor List, Nov. 14, 1997 [= Jhumor List, May 28, 1999 = Anon. 2001b: 122] (sister in Minsk); Brown 1998f: 59 (father in Edinburgh); Anon. 2000c: 331 (father in Melbourne); Joseph Thome, e-mail message to author, Apr. 22, 2002 (shift from Minsk to Louisiana).

132. CLLH 1995; lawyer humor: no. 51 [= Barnett and Kaiser 1996: 223 = Southwell 1999: 53]. Other lawyer versions are May 1964: 125 (lawyer's dog takes lion's share of bones); Knott 1982: 95 [= Knott 1990: 4 (edited version)]; Playboy 1982; Wilde 1982: 76 [= Tobias 1982: 299 = Wilde 1988: 174]; Behrman 1991: 43; Rovin 1992: 70; Brallier 1992: 88; *Nolo's Favorite* 1993; Grossman 1993: 15; *AML* 1993: nos. 155 (cats), 547; Adams and Newell 1995: 304; Clifford Westfall, e-mail message to author, Nov. 16, 1996; 1997 Cal.: Feb. 13; Ross 1996: 56; Cohl 1997: 277; Van Munching 1997: 27; Lawyer Jokes, Jan. 30, 1998.

133. See B38 above.

134. Jane Mansbridge, e-mail message to author, May 19, 1999. Other government worker versions are Singh 1990: 124; Jhumor List, Apr. 18, 1996; Greene 1999: 268; Tibballs 2000: item 2665; Jan Hoem, e-mail, Mar. 11, 2002 (cats). Union versions are Anon. 1980: 44 (collected in Southfield, MI, 1979); *Wisconsin State Journal,* Nov. 3, 1993 (letter to editor adapts joke to attack strike by Madison Teachers Union); Adams and Newall 1994: 299; Pease 1996: 260: The story is readily switchable and has also been told of actors (Alvin 1984: 48); musicians (Pietsch 1986: 71); Apple engineers (Wilde and Wozniak 1989: 124); Brian Mulroney (Breslin 1991: 62); Robert Maxwell (Yermonee 1992); bond salesmen (Knott 1993a: 109); radiologists (Prasad 1998: 99), and salesmen (Keelan 1999: 247). Many of the same story elements appear in a tale of a competition among Australian drovers to see whose dog is smarter that involves neither interprofessional competition nor destructive behavior (Gurney 1986; Coote 1995: 111).

135. Gigot 1992.

136. Peter D. Hart Research Associates 1993: question 22.

137. Peter D. Hart Research Associates 1993: 4–5. See chap. 9, p. 225–26.

138. Crevecoeur quoted in Warren 1911: 217.

139. Silberman 1978: 18, 21, 44.

140. Silberman 1978: 21. Silberman here anticipates an anxiety about the excessive number of lawyers in the United States that blossomed over the following decade and came to fruition in Dan Quayle's 1991 polemical question about why the United States had 70 percent of the world's lawyers. See "The 70 Percent Legend" in chap. 9.

141. Hacker 1978: 37. The annual total of law school graduates when this was written was about 36,000. Auerbach 1997: 43.

142. Magee et al. 1989: chap. 8. Magee's methods and findings are critiqued by Cross 1992; Epp 1992; Epp 1992a: 695.

143. On the polemical use of Magee's work, see chap. 9, n. 73.

144. Pitts 1843.

145. Pitts 1843: 11, 13.

146. Pitts 1843: 42. His argument that "lawyer legislating" is a major cause of bad policy anticipates Magee's concern.

147. Pitts 1843: 5, 33.

148. Radin 1946: 748.

149. Castelmen at 182, 184 (quoting Warner).

150. That the skill of the lawyer should be free to all is argued in the immensely influential *Piers Plowman* (Langland [1386–87]) and *Ship of Fools* (Brant [1494]).

151. Yunck 1960: 268.

152. Peter of Blois (c.1135–c.1205), quoted at Yunck 1960: 268. The final lines are from Psalm 34.

153. See "The Enlargement and Withdrawal of the Legal World" in the introduction; Galanter 1994.

154. Galanter and Palay 1991: 11, 36; Gordon 1988.

155. *American Lawyer* 1895: 84.

156. Kronman 1993; Glendon 1994; Linowitz and Mayer 1994.

3. Playmates of the Devil

1. On St. Ives, see *Green Bag* 6: 142 (1894); Axon at Andrews 1896: 24; Miller 1907: 10.

2. *Green Bag* 6: 143 (1894). See also *Green Bag* 18: 636 (1906). Radin 1930: 615 observes of several later lawyer-saints that "hagiographic tradition represents them as leaving the profession because of its moral dangers."

3. Tucker 1984: 72.

4. Anon. 1756: 12.

5. Anon. 1832: 5–6.

6. Crosswell's Diary: or The Catskill Almanack, for . . . 1800, reprinted at Dodge 1987: 126.

7. Hupfeld [1871] 85; Haslitt 1886: 75; Willock 1887: 76; Anon. 1898: 26; Edwards 1915: item 165; Milburn 1927: 23; Ashmore 1930: 56; Muller [1939]: 46; Esar 1945: 262; Teitelbaum 1945: 370; Wilde 1982: 26 (judge); E. Phillips 1989: 14; Rovin 1992: 81; Burke 1997a: 51 (magistrate); 1998 Cal.: Oct. 30. The jest (not specifically applied to lawyers) was present earlier, Anon. 1832: 197.

8. The Farmer's Almanack . . . for . . . 1797, reprinted at Dodge 1987:126 (emphasis in original). The lawyer-liar equation is discussed in the section "Lying and Dishonesty," chap. 1 .

9. Trachtenberg [1943]: 6.

10. Trachtenberg [1943]: 26.

11. Trachtenberg [1943]: 159.

12. Quoted at Yunck 1960: 268. See the section "The Justice Tariff," chap. 2.

13. Sprague 1895: 121; Anon. 1900: 146; Johnson et al. 1936: 147.

14. Hupfeld [1871]: 71. This follows closely an earlier English version (Anon. [1830?]: 4). Foote is presumably Samuel Foote (1720–77), English actor and comic playwright. In his history of the American legal profession, Anton-Hermann Chroust (1965: 2:100) reprints a version from the *Jefferson City* (*MO*) *Inquirer,* June 12, 1847, and describes the story as "widely circulated on the frontier." Also Lemon 1864: 326; Beeton 1880: 21; Willock 1887: 313; Aye 1931: 15; Phillips 1989: 88.

15. Milburn 1927: 49. The thought is anticipated by Tickleside 1788: 37. Also, Johnston 1922: 240; Mosher [1922]: 123; Schermerhorn 1928: 232; Eastman 1936: 16; Lupton 1938: item 1969; Anon. 1943: 254; Esar 1945: 261; May 1956: 167; Anon. [1967]: 177; Wilde 1982: 149; Wilde 1987: 20; Humes 1993: 106.

16. Johnston 1922: item 241; *Green Bag* 4: 242 (1892). The joke reappears later as a story about an unlucky gambler and a casino operator (Davis 1981: 50) and about a justice of the peace (Shafer and Papadaikis 1988: 106; Adler 1994: 22).

17. Woods 1967: item 24.5. This is a very close replication of Jerrold 1858: 23; Rhodes 1890: 252; and *Green Bag* 6: 349 (1894). Jerrold (1803–57) was a journalist, playwright, and renowned wit.

18. Wilde 1986a: 80.

19. Randy's Favorite Lawyer Jokes, July 24, 1997; *Star Tribune,* Sept. 2, 1996 (source noted as in Rio de Janeiro); Ross 1996: 86; 2000 Cal.: Mar. 15; Claro 2000: 60; Anon. 2000a: 113. The specification to lawyers is recent, but the joke had been around for a long time with little specification of the patient's occupation: Ham 1921: 205 (autobiographical anecdote); Johnston 1925: item 590 (attributed to Ham); Lupton 1938: item 619; Esar 1945: 315; Hefley 1968: item 1020; Anon. 1973a; Newman 1979: 67; Yarwood [1981]: 46; Wilde 1986a: 86; Duncan 1990: 147. More recently, it has been switched to Bill Clinton (Symons 1998: 19), Peter Mandelson (Dale and Simmons 1994: 14), and other British targets ((Baddlel et al. 1999: 108; Sharpe 2000: 209).

20. CLLH 1995: lawyer humor no. 20; Shillaber 1854: 179; Hupfeld [1871]: 83; Brown [1879]: 61 [= Willock 1887: 194 = *Green Bag* 2: 454 (1890)]; Landon 1883: 417; Willock 1887: 194; *Green Bag* 2: 454 (1890); Sprague 1895: 117; Edwards 1915: item 731; Johnson et al. 1936: 209 (Lincoln); Gardner 1937: 38 (Lorenzo Dow) [= Botkin 1957: 187]; House 1948: 112; Keene 1949 [1947]: 173; Golden 1953 [1950]: x (Lincoln); Wilde 1982: xiii (Lincoln); Studer 1988: 98; Knott 1990: 92 (Lincoln); Humes 1993: 43 (Lincoln); Grossman 1993: 78; *Nolo's Favorite* 1993 (Dow); CLLH 1995: lawyer humor no. 20 (Dow) [=Streiker 1998: 260]; CLLH 1995: lawyer humor no. 114 (U.S. Grant) [= Adams and Newall 1995: 228 = 1996 Cal.: Feb 11 = 1997 Cal.: Dec. 8]; 2000 Cal.: May 11; Regan 2001: 193 (Dow). The story has been switched to clerics: Boatright 1949: 142; MacGregor 195?: 122; McNeil [1978]: 119; Newman 1979: 67; Anon. 1984: 172; Phillips 1986: 31; Jones and Wheeler 1987: 41. And less frequently to "the rich" (Pickens 1926: 148), to whites using blacks as shields from the fire (Pickens 1926: 35), and to Democrats (B. Phillips 1994).

21. Cal.: May 1 [= 1997 Cal. Nov. 4 = 1998 Cal.: July 9]. A narrative version is at Knott 1990: 13. Or the abundance may be of judges: Shafer and Papadaikis 1988: 22; Streiker 1998: 259; 2002 Cal.: Oct. 31.

22. The New-England Almanack for . . . 1801, reprinted at Dodge 1987: 127 and Streiker 1998: 245; Bigelow 1871: 325 [= Hupfeld [1871]: 98] ("the people have the money"). In a jest attributed to Jonathan Swift, the devil would prevail in a lawsuit with the clergy because all the lawyers are on his side. Hood et al. 1873: 220; Anon. 1893: 42; Macrae [1904]: 268; Fowler 1915: 115; McCann [1968]: 105. Hell also has all the umpires (Peterson 1976: 41; Marquand 1977: 297; Streiker 1998: 87) and referees (Brown 1998b: 17).

23. Mendelsohn 1935: 157; Rywell 1960: 131; Spalding 1969: 350; Rabinowitz 1986 [1973]: 23.

24. *Green Bag* 6: 142 (1894).

25. Byrn [1852]: 147.

26. Anon. 1900: 151 [= Williams 1938: item 888]; Beer's Almanac . . . for . . . 1793, reprinted in Dodge 1987: 126.

27. Chance 1915: 54; Aye 1931: 13. Another lawyer gained admission when St. Peter concluded, "He's no lawyer; he only *thinks* he's a lawyer." *Green Bag* 24: 323 (1912).

28. Lisa Harinanan, e-mail message to author, Sept. 8, 1998; Tibballs 2000: 190; Regan 2001: 100; 2002 Cal.: Aug. 8.

29. Avery 1854: 18 [= Shillaber 1859: 18]; Hupfeld [1871: 82; Sprague 1895: 75; DeMorgan 1907: 158; Morton and Malloch 1913: 102; Johnston 1922: 237; Milburn 1927: 32 [= Copeland 1936: 240 = Rango 1944: 246]; Eastman 1936: 18; Moulton 1942: item 1439; Boatright 1945: 179 [= Boatright 1949: 122]; Williams 1949: item 2195; May 1964: 206.

30. Cook 1938: 26; Copeland and Copeland 1940: 474 [= Rango 1944: 163 = Berle [1945]: 97 = Friedman 1960: 69]; May 1956: 168; Braude 1964: item 521; Boliska [1966]: 142; Woods 1967: item 267.11; Adams 1968: 344; Jessel 1973: 132 (reprinted at Sartor 1989: 63); Spalding 1978: 216; Wilde 1982: xiv; Dickson 1984: 22; Singh 1987: 12; Rafferty 1988: 41; Rovin 1989: 135; Jones and Wheeler 1989: 112; Berle 1989: 133; Phillips 1989: 47; Knott 1990: 48; Novak and Waldoks 1990: 105; Phillips 1990: 89; Steiger 1990: 5; Behrman 1991: 62; Adler 1992: 101 [= Adler 1994: 105]; Dover and Fish 1992; Berle 1993: 264; *AML* 1993: item no. 30; Grossman 1993: 16; B. Phillips 1994; Faine 1994: 46; 1996 Cal.: Jan. 20; Subramanian 1995: 75; CLLH 1995: lawyer humor no. 28; Jones and Wheeler 1995: 91; Desmond [1995]: 30; B. Phillips 1996: 84; Brallier 1996: 52; 1997 Cal.: Dec. 17; *Charleston Gazette,* Sept. 18, 1996; Ross 1996: 84; Coote 1996: 211; Cohl 1997: 276; Streiker 1998: 252; Dedopulos 1998: 238.

31. Morton Sklaroff, e-mail message to author, July 3, 1997; Jack Ladinsky, e-mail, Apr. 16, 1997; Elissa, e-mail, Apr. 28, 1997; John McCaslin, *Washington Times,* Aug. 14, 1997, A6; Van Muching 1997: 53; Tibballs 2000: 194; Pritchard 2002: 152. This story provides a revealing glimpse of the sequential relation between "oral" transmission (represented by the e-mail messages), newspaper publication a few months later, and publication in book form after a further few months. The first edition of the Van Muching book is dated October 1997. The "improvements in Hell" theme appeared some thirty years earlier as a result of the sequestering there of Jews who, to Satan's displeasure, "already . . . raised $100,000 and want to air-condition the place." Blumenfeld 1967: 43; Alvin 1999: 12; Weston-Macauley 2001: 194 ("Hadassah Ladies"). Cf. Skubik and Short 1976: 105 ("Republican women"); Wright and Wright 1985: 250 ("club women"). This theme was anticipated even earlier in a story about magnates organizing and prospering in jail. *Green Bag* 20: 384 (1908).

32. Adams and Newall 1995: 289; Jones 1989: 33; Jhumor list, Apr. 21, 1996; 1998 Cal.: Dec. 5; Readers Digest 1997: 11; Streiker 1998: 254; Lauren Edelman, e-mail message to author, Aug. 8, 1998; Jhumor List, Apr. 2, 1999; Sarah Galanter, e-mail, Sept. 26, 1999; Southwell 1999: 72; Anon. 2000a: 68; Anon. 2000c: 277; Regan 2001: 199.

33. AT 1738 (The Dream: All Parsons in Hell). E.g., Dorson 1967: 175 (collected by 1953); Spalding 1978: 216 (verse); Stangland 1993: 44; Johnson 1994: 217. References to Jewish sources are at Schwartzbaum 1968: 345–46.

34. *Green Bag* 18: 636 (1906); *New York Times,* June 7, 1991, reprinted at Streiker 1998: 25.

35. Rafferty 1988: 38; Playboy 1982: 147 [= Tobias 1982: 299]; Knott 1983: 78; Terrell and Buchanan 1984: 142; Shafer and Papadaikis 1988: 32; Knott 1990: 7; Steiger 1990: 4; Behrman 1991: 15; Delf 1992: 92; Asimov 1992: item 409; Adler 1992: 89 [= Adler 1994: 92]; Rovin 1992: 25; *AML* 1993: no. 356; Grossman 1993: 105; Adams and Newall 1994: 460; 1996 Cal.: Mar. 16; CLLH 1995: lawyer humor no. 10; Coote 1995: 285; Pease 1996: 31; Brallier 1996: 60; Ross 1996: 58; Coote 1996: 243; Lawyer Jokes, Jan. 30, 1998; Jhumor

List, Aug. 3, 1998; Streiker 1998: 246 (St. Yves); Marigay Grana, e-mail message to author, Mar. 20, 1999; Claro 2000: 58; Anon. 2000a: 112; Regan 2001: 17; Colombo 2001: 445.

36. AT 802.

37. Botkin 1957 [1947]: 188 (admiral); Woods 1967: item 246.8 (admiral) [= Wright and Wright 1985: 249; Skubik and Short 1976: 79 (politician); Wilde 1984: 128 (Republican Senator)]; Dickson 1984: 17 (Congressman); Anon. 1986: 141 (congressman); Wilde 1986a: 164 (Doctor); Stangland 1988: 18 (Swede); Berle 1989: 319 (senator); Phillips 1990: 109 (congressman); Knott 1993a: 99 (sales manager); B. Phillips 1994 (Democratic congressman); Marsh and Goldmark 1997: 87 (jazz musician).

38. Bigelow 1871: 416. This is also told as an anecdote about Joseph Choate: *Green Bag* 20: 272 (1908); Edwards 1915: item 442; Williams 1926: item 743 [= Williams 1949: item 3196].; Also Wilde 1987: 162 (woman lawyer); Rovin 1992: 103; 2000 Cal.: June 20. Cf. Schindler 1986: 45.

39. Rovin 1992: 103.

40. A recent and comprehensive collection of attempts at rapprochement between religion and the practice of law will be found in *Fordham Law Review* 1998. In his foreword to the collection, Russell Pearce notes how different is the vision of the religious lawyering movement from "the standard conception of the lawyer's role." *Fordham Law Review* 1998: 1082.

41. For an account of this proverb, much used by Martin Luther, and its French and German versions, see Kenny 1903; Murray 1912: 170, 201.

42. *Green Bag* 12: 545 (1900); Anon. 1831: 13; Anon. 1900: 151; May 1956: 138. In recent versions, the lawyer has to share the thief role: Jones and Wheeler 1995: 116 (lawyer and doctor); Streiker 1998: 238 (lawyer and doctor); Tapper and Press 2000: 162 (doctor and priest); Regan 2001: 96 (lawyer and doctor); Alan Dundes, e-mail message to author, Sept. 4, 2002 (lawyer and IRS agent).

43. *Green Bag* 10: 83 (1898).

44. Burnett 1955: 66.

45. *Green Bag* 12: 53 (1900); *Green Bag* 4: 42 (1892); Cook 1938: 65; Edwards 1977: 41.

46. Heighton 1916: 272 (two versions); Kahn 1999: 42 (South Africa, citing 1995 source).

47. *Green Bag* 16: 335 (1904),

48. Hay 1989: 205 (told of Supreme Court Justice Harold H. Burton 1888–1964); Jackson 1961: 41; May 1964: 320; Morecroft [1974]: 18; Edwards 1976: 55; Esar 1978: 107; Yarwood 1981: 105; Baker 1982: 39; Foster 1988: 3; Rees 1999: 128; Kahn 1999: 9 (South Africa). Cf. *Green Bag* 22: 141 (1910) (judge sentencing prisoner to death counsels him to "get such consolation as he can [from priest] but the court advises you to place no reliance upon anything of that kind").

49. Knox c.1943: 148.

50. Williams 1926: 140.

51. Streiker 1998: 227; Strean 1993: 164 (rabbi); Brunsting 2000: 50.

52. Anon. 1902: 304; Engelbach 1913: 107; Fuller 1942: 267; Laing 1963: 81; May 1964: 53; Yarwood 1981: 36; Wilde 1987: 60.

53. Bialik and Ravnitsky 1992: 223. For a nuanced assessment, see Stone 1993: 855–65. The story now circulates in joke form as well: Jhumor list, Apr. 15, 1996 (when God gives sign, rabbi says, "Now its 3 to 2"); Jhumor list June 9, 1998 (synagogue elders outvote rabbi and God); Tapper and Press 2000: 96; Winston-Macauley 2001: 11.

54. Heinz and Laumann found that in 1975 28 percent of lawyers in Chicago agreed that "to lead a good life, it is necessary . . . to be guided by the teachings and beliefs of an

established religious group," while 60 percent disagreed. Heinz and Laumann 1982: 140. In a 1995 survey of partners in the highest-billing law firms, "84 percent . . . identify themselves as Catholics, Protestants, or Jews, [but] 57 percent never or only rarely attend religious services. . . . [A]bout 26 percent attend services once or twice a month, and 17 percent attend religious services every week." Black and Rothman 1998: 841.

55. Bouwsma 1973: 321, 322.

56. Bouwsma 1973: 321.

4. Conflict: Lawyers as Fomenters of Strife

1. B. Phillips 1976: 57; *Green Bag* 19: 386 (1907); Anderson 1923: 44; Prochnow and Prochnow 1964: 159; 1998 Cal.: Sept. 8.

2. Behrman 1991: 80; Shillaber 1859: 12 (dispute among judges); *Green Bag* 2: 502 (1890); Anon. 1905: 98; Engelbach 1913: 139; *Green Bag* 25: 455 (1913); Heighton 1916: 31; Hershfield 1932: 77; Mendelsohn 1941: 207; Rango 1944: 156; Thomas 1947: 12; Keene 1949 [1947]: 342; Williams 1949: item 4055; Richman 1952: 384; Lieberman 1956: 98; Woods 1967: item 92.13; Spalding 1969: 344; Golden 1972: 199; Lieberman 1975: 80; Harris 1979: 109; Wilde 1982: 68; Phillips 1989: 75; Adler 1992: 137, 139; Arya 1996: 47; 1998 Cal.: Jan. 28; 2002 Cal.: Oct. 15.

3. Blumenfeld 1967: 99 [= Adler 1992: 35 = Adler 1994: 31]; Braude 1958: item 682; May 1964: 143; Woods 1967: item 94.18; Reader's Digest 1967: 76 [= Reader's Digest 1972: 328]; Wilde 1982: 150 (dress manufacturers) Phillips 1989: 5; Claro 1990: 98 [= Claro 1996: 118].

4. Raskin's analysis is summarized in chap. 6, n. 51.

5. This pattern of lawyer as peacemaker/client as combatant recurs elsewhere in the joke corpus. See the client version of *appeal at once* (J1), where the lawyer is idealistic and the client cynical, or *gift to judge* (A56), where the lawyer tries to restrain the client from provocative tactics.

6. Macaulay 1979.

7. Blumberg 1967.

8. Sarat and Felstiner 1995: 111.

9. Hoenig (1977).

10. Communists: Williams 1938: item 190; Cerf 1942: 186 [= Cerf 1945a: 86]; Meier 1944: 32; Cerf 1945: 117. Politicians: Holub 1939: 100; Prochnow 1942: 115; Orcutt 1942: 55; Esar 1945: 336; Lehr et al. 1948: 61; McManus 1948: 119; Braude 1955: item 2017; Braude 1958: item 932; O'Neal and O'Neal 1964: 195; Gerler 1965: 153; Woods 1967: item 54.12; Murdock 1967: 80; Morecroft [1974]: 89; Mandel 1974: 96; Skubik and Short 1976: 142; Wilde 1976 (Democrat): 46; Bernnard 1977: 203; Bonham 1981: 116; Mr. O'S 1982; Baker 1982: 23; Phillips 1982b: 12; Wilde 1984: 31; Anon. 1986: 139; Lukes and Galnoor 1987; Rovin 1987: 262; William Grey 1990; Breslin 1991: 59 (Brian Mulroney); Gross 1991: 227; Humes 1993: 54; Allday 1993 (UK); Cooper, Oct. 22, 1993 (UK); Faine 1994: 31; Adams and Newell 1994: 238 (Australia); Bob Phillips 1994; Mittal and Gupta 1995: 148 (India); Behrman 1995: 94; Raasch, May 25, 1995; Bob Phillips 1996: 27; Adams and Newell 1996: 14 (Austrialia); Pretzer 1996; Goldstein-Jackson 1996: 135 (UK); Kostick 1998: 443; Streiker 1998: 288; Harvey ca.1998a: 153 (India); Dale and Simmons 1999: 113 (UK); Claro 2000: 145.

11. Cerf 1942: 186; Cerf 1945: 117; Meier 1944: 32; Lehr et al. 1948: 61.

12. Knott 1990: 13; collected by M. Caudill, Piedmont, CA., Sept. 1980; Behrman 1991: 37; Asimov 1992: item 16; Adler 1992: 132 [= Adler 1994: 138]; Builler 1992: 39; Rovin

1992: 10; *Nolo's Favorite* 1993; Grossman 1993: 126; Metcalf 1993: 133; 1996 Cal.: Apr. 1; CLLH 1995: lawyer humor no. 124; Morgan 1995; Marigay Grana, letter to author, Apr. 30, 1996; George Wright, letter to author, Sept. 25, 1996; Ross 1996: 75 (Australia); Cohl 1997: 278; Two Fun Guys 1997; Jhumor List, Jan. 22, 1998; Jhumor List, Mar. 7, 1999; Anon. 2000a: 72; Regan 2001: 34.

13. Hoenig 1977: 49. A simple doctor-engineer-lawyer version is found at May 1964: 83.

14. Pound Conference 1976. The National Conference on the Causes of Popular Dissatisfaction with the Administration of Justice, held in St. Paul, MN, in April 1976, was organized by Chief Justice Burger and sponsored by the Judicial Conference of the United States, the Conference of Chief Justices, and the American Bar Association. Needless to say, there was little to connect the discontents voiced there with popular dissatisfaction.

15. Samuelson 1992: A17.

16. Shafer and Papadakis 1988: 142; Humes [1975]: 79; Hay 1989: 112; Knott 1990: 114; Adler 1992: 62; Humes 1993: 102; Streiker 1998: 256.

17. Edwards 1915: 715; Milburn 1927: 13; Eastman 1936: 22; Copeland 1936: 232; Anon. 1959: 39; Wilde 1982: 185; Steiger 1990: 51; Harvey c.1998a: 99; 2002 Cal.: July 11.

18. *Nolo's Favorite* 1993. Lean 1904: 4:169 credits a barrister with the quip "Two attorneys can live in a town, when one cannot" in 1880. I have not found any printed versions between that and Esar 1978: 527. That same year it was described as "an ancient story which lawyers love to tell" by Silberman 1978: 20. Pietsch 1986: 26; Wilde 1987: 21; Rafferty 1988: 75; Chariton 1989: 65 (LBJ); Knott 1990: 77; Steiger 1990: 21; Behrman 1991: 114; Rovin 1992: 161; *Nolo's Favorite* 1993; Metcalf 1993: 133 (LBJ); *AML* 1993: no. 282 (long narrative version); Adler 1994: 101; 1995 Cal.: item 297; 1996 Cal.: July 3; 1997 Cal.: Apr. 28; Ross 1996: 99; 1998 Cal.: Dec. 20. Cf. Olson 1994: 364 (tort reform campaigner cites as "axiom" to explain liability crisis "happening throughout our system.") The internal attribution to Lyndon Baines Johnson (1908–73) by Chariton and Metcalf may evidence an earlier currency.

19. *Oxford English Dictionary*, 2d ed., s.v. "ambulance chaser."

20. Scruggs 1928: item 423; Brodnick 1976: 175; Wilde 1987: 145.

21. Adler 1992: 106.

22. Rafferty 1988: 86.

23. Daenzer 1974.

24. Braude 1958: item 680 (virtually identical to Lurie 1928: 188); Masson [1913]: 100; Johnston 1922: 199; Mosher 1922: 131; Williams 1938: item 20; Rango 1944: 299; Mendelsohn 1947: 99; Golden 1953 [1950]: 135; Davis 1954: 24; Hershfield 1964: 108; Larkin 1975: 183; Spalding 1976: 150; Wilde 1982: 152; Phillips 1989: 13; *AML* 1993: no. 281, no. 458; Grossman 1993: 132 (arm in cast); 1996 Cal.: Apr. 21; Mital and Gupta 1995: 113; Adams 1996: 410. Cf. Adler 1969: 75 (lawyer tells victim, "Don't get up"); Golden [1950]: 109 (sea voyage on advice of lawyer, not doctor).

25. Adams 1968: 343; *Green Bag* 17: 735 (1905); Anon. 1906a: 53; Brodnick 1976: n.p. (told of President Gerald Ford).

26. Behrman 1995: 116; Knott 1990b: 63; Rovin 1992: 60; Berle 1993: 324; Coote 1995: 3.

27. Heighton 1916: 206; Esar 1978: 266 (Choate reference dropped).

28. Edwards 1915: item 132.

29. Edwards 1915: item 395.

30. *Green Bag* 19: 70 (1907), attributed to *Harper's Weekly;* Edmund and Williams 1916: 128; Milburn 1926: 12 (more successful of Jewish claimants in railway accident "had

der presence of mind to kick my wife in der face"); Johnson et al. 1936: item 287 (man tells motorist he can have another go at wife if she was not injured); Lupton 1938: item 975 (woman volunteers to hit husband who was in accident if defendant has deep pocket); Brodnick 1976: 38; Esar 1978: 772; McHale 1988: 94; Sharpe 2000: 219.

31. Ernst 1925: 43.

32. Schermerhorn 1928: 218; Masson 1922: 18 (traveling salesman); Anderson 1923: 271 (Jew); Golden 1949: 154; *Laugh Book Magazine* (July 1951): 19 (tramp); Walker 1980: 205; Alvin 1983a: 11 (Jew); McHale 1988: 26 (Scot); Barry 1990: 73 (Jew); Coote 1995: 200 (Jew); Coote 1996: 141 (Jew). A similar opportunism in making claims is often attributed to Scots (collision of two taxis leads to a score of injuries) (Ferguson 1933: 129; McHale 1988: 85).

33. Dornstein 1996: 60–62, 93, 107, 108.

34. Moulton 1942: item 1021; Adams 1996: 390. Cf. May 1956: 53 ("legal mortis").

35. Jhumor List, Sept. 23, 1999; Greene 1999: 338 (third is Democrat); Southwell (English setting); Anon. 2000a: 176 (redneck); Tapper and Press 2000a: 118 (black); Harris 2002a: 146 (redneck).

36. *Green Bag* 23: 161 (1911); Edwards 1915: item 282; Edmund and Williams 1916: 129; Cobb 1923: item 134; Moulton 1942: item 1962; Peterson 1976: 83. Cf. Chance 1915: 21 (wife of injured man tells railroad it won't get a cent out of her); cf. Lupton 1938: item 1198 (injured Negro lying near railway disaster asked about damages denies hitting train: "You cynain't git no damages out ob me").

37. Anon. 1900a: 87. Cf. Anon. 1906b: 15 and May 1956: 159, where victims who sue for injuries sustained by fall into open coal chute are jailed for stealing coal.

38. Edwards 1915: 118–19; Edmund and Williams 1916: 370 (railroad director); Rango 1944: 99 (railroad director); Vaidyanathan 1992: 75 (Indian railroad official).

39. Phillips 1990: 85. As the coal chute and the working youngster suggest, this is a much older joke. I have seen, but am unable to locate, an earlier version. According to Anon. 1906b: 15 and May 1956: 159, this strategy may succeed. Cf. the preemptive strategy of the doctor:

Dr. Perlman was examining a patient when his nurse rushed into the room. "Excuse me, Doctor," she said, "but that man you just gave a clean bill of health to walked out of the office and dropped dead. What should I do?"

"Turn him around so he looks like he was walking in," replied the M.D.

Wilde 1981a: 183; Knott 1990b: 69; Stangland 1994: 40; Phillips 1996: 44.

40. Johnson et al. 1936: 171; Cobb 1923: 187.

41. When Douglas Rosenthal (1974: 189) studied personal injury claimants in New York City, he found no religious difference in activity/passivity as clients. However, this does not speak directly to the propensity to bring claims. Nor does Matthew Silberman's (1985: 101) finding that Jewish residents of the Detroit metropolitan area in 1967 were more likely to go to lawyers, but their small numbers in the sample did not support any firm conclusions. Silberman attributed greater Jewish involvement with the legal system to greater wealth and social integration rather than to religious or ethnic reasons. (These factors would not have been present during the period in which the conniving claimant jokes arose.) None of the studies of proclivity to claim has tested the religious/ethnic variable.

42. Allen 1990: 89. A related story tells of a collision in the desert between Arab and Israeli tanks: the Arab driver leaps out shouting "I surrender," the Israeli jumps out shouting "whiplash." Barry 1990: 74; Eilbirt 1991: 235.

43. Pietsch 1986: 2; Knott 1990: 9; Jhumor List, Nov. 20, 1997; Cohl 1997: 203. After a decade as a joke about Jews, the sushi bar shifted its clientele to lawyers: 1998 Cal.: Mar. 12; Southwell 1999: 51; Regan 2001: 140. Leo Rosten (1989: 502) credits the popularity of "so sue me" to the musical *Guys and Dolls* (1950) and Damon Runyon's earlier stories on which it was based. The phrase serves as the title of James Yaffe's book (Yaffe 1972) about the Jewish Conciliation Court in New York City.

44. Trachtenberg [1943]: 89–90.

45. On these Jewish fire stories, see Davies 1986: 85–87; Davies 1991: 197–201. An insurance publication advised, "There are honorable Jews and there are honorable Gentiles, but that the evil disposed among the race gravitate to incendiarism is a notorious fact." *Insurance Monitor* 55: 23 (1907), quoted at Baker 1996: 256, n.79.

46. Clode 1922: 190; Kieffer 1907: 105; Robey 1920: 228; Richman 1926: xiii; Knox ca.1943: 26. Long gone in the United States, the story survives in England: Mason 2001: 126 (West Riding businessman); Blue 2001: 15.

47. Johnston 1925: item 933; Ferguson 1933: 168; Cerf 1945a: 76; Berle 1989: 546. Curiously, the earliest instance of this story is an anecdote about a figure far removed from the pawnbrokers and dry goods proprietors that generally inhabit it, the president of Oberlin College, John Henry Burrows, D.D., printed in the *New York Times* at the turn of the century. Anon. 1902: 219.

48. Cohl 1997: 70; Alvin 1990: 41; Vas 1994: 70. Cf. Muller [1939]: 41 (merchant tells son marriage to wealthy woman almost as good as failure); Golden 1972: 231 (good luck if die before repayment due).

49. Anon 1906b: 34.

50. Murray 1954: 266; Kiser 1927: 100 (lucky customer broke arm); Ernst 1930: 197; Lupton 1938: item 2250 (lucky to have three accidents); Cerf 1945: 112 (lucky to lose arms and legs day after taking out policy); Murray 1954: 133 (lucky to break neck); Howcroft 1983 (good luck that wife was run over).

51. Anon 1997a: 141.

52. Anon. 1902: 86.

53. Kinser 1927: 233.

54. For a recent assessment of the "anti-heart balm movement," see Larson 1993: 83–99.

55. Eilbirt 1991: 71–72; Geiger 1928: 11 (quoted by C. Davies at Ziv and Zajdman 1993: 37) (French); Cobb 1925: 86 (tornado, not explicitly Jewish but "proprietor of a small retail clothing store"); Asimov 1971: 371 (hurricane, Jew); Anon. 1972 (flood, hillbillies); Novak 1977: 38 (earthquake, Jew); Walker 1980: 163 (flood, Jew); Tobias 1982: 108 (flood); Allen 1990: 79 (flood, Jew); Yermonee 1992 (hurricane, Robert Maxwell); E. Phillips [1993] (flood, factory owner): 74; Hochwald [1994]: 45 (hurricane, Jew); Vas 1994 (flood, Jew); Harvey ca. 1998b: 143; Tibballs 2000: 173 (storm, Jew). The joke also appears as a Hoja story, presumably at a much earlier date. Shah [1966]: 95.

56. Cohl 1997: 280; Adams and Newall 1995: 294 [= Randy's Favorite Lawyer Jokes, July 21, 1997]; Regan 2001: 15; 2002 Cal.: Oct. 9.

57. Such switches are particularly frequent among the *Betrayal* jokes discussed in chap. 6.

58. Aye 1931: 91. The story is told as an anecdote about Frederick Edwin Smith (1872–1930), first Earl of Birkinhead. Also Rango 1944: 251; Jackson 1961: 84 (Birkinhead defending bus company); Fadiman 1985: 513; Foster 1988: 110; Hay 1989: 160 (Birkenhead); Rovin 1992: 51; Davidson 1998: 46 (boy has grown into "young man"). Cf. Spalding 1976: 44 (Jewish grandmother displays arthritic condition).

59. Varon 1995: 28 (reported as told in late 1960s); Cerf 1959: 261 (Irish); Reader's Digest 1967: 74 [= Reader's Digest 1972: 322]; Mindess 1971: 141 (Jewish); Golden 1972: 20 (Jewish); McElroy 1973: 42; Humes [1975]: 74; Marquand 1977: 131 (Jewish) [= Pollack 1979: 152]; Wilde 1978: 158 (Jewish); Rosten 1985 (Irish); Berle 1993: 355; Coote 1995: 201; Coote: 1996: 251 (Irish); Mason 2001: 86; Colombo 2001: 194 (French Canadian going to Ste. Anne-de-Beaupré).

The Lourdes trope surfaced earlier in a joke about a Jewish immigrant who proposes to feign lameness to avoid working. Lipman [1991]: 172. Lipman records this story as circulating between 1933 and 1945 (164).

60. *S & A Restaurant Corp. v. Leal*, 892 S.W. 2d 855, 856, 857, 858; 1995 Tex Lexis 11; Tex. Sup. J. 38: 303 (1995). The strained distinction the court erected to reach this result was soon dismantled. In *Keim v. Anderson*, decided by the El Paso Court of Appeals on Apr. 4, 1997, the court explained that judgment is rendered not "when the trial court officially announces its decision in open court." *Texas Lawyer* 1997.

61. *U.S. News & World Report* 1978, 50.

62. Anderson 1985.

63. Galanter 1983: 6–8.

64. Galanter 1998; Brill and Lyon, 1986; Strasser 1987; Daniels 1989; Hayden 1991. A more recent crop of stories can be found on the "Loony Lawsuits" page of the Web site of the American Tort Reform Association, formerly called "Horror Stories: Stories That Show a Legal System That's Out of Control." The November 1997 batch is analyzed in Galanter 1998.

65. Lande 1998: 51.

66. Lande 1998: 51.

67. Quayle 1995: 312 [1994].

68. On these campaigns and their backers, see Daniels 1989; Chesebro 1993; Daniels and Martin 1995: chaps. 1, 2, 7; Daniels and Martin 1998.

69. Kritzer and Pickerill 1997: 21.

70. Dornstein 1997 concludes that the image of the personal injury faker "allows the honest claimant to believe that personal injury compensation is dirty in all its aspects" and thus liberates him to discount the immorality of "exaggerating a claim or authorizing their attorneys to make outrageous demands on their behalf or conspiring with a garageman to inflate the damage estimate and split the difference" (239).

71. Burger 1984.

72. Johnston 1922: item 943 [= Copeland 1936: 70 = Williams 1949: item 1129]; Berle 1993: 28.

73. 1995 Cal.: item 71. This was enlisted as a lawyer joke only recently—probably in the early 1980s. Originally, the joke figure was a Jew walking across the golf course: Edwards 1915: item 262; Johnson et al. 1936: 263; Hershfield 1938: 89; Copeland and Copeland 1940: item 6624; Ford et al. 1945: 18; Williams 1949: item 172; Golden 1953 [1950]: 154; Anon. [1967]: 87; Crompton 1970: 19; Pollack 1979: 59 [= Triverton 1981: 251]; Marks 1985: 86; Allen 2000: 121. The Jewish element is effaced in Hershfeld 1959: 43 ("city chap") and Matson 1990: 78 ("little old foreigner"). Scots also appear frequently—Knox 1926: 85; Larkin 1975: 110; Wilde 1977: 109; Rosten 1985: 221—along with a single Irishman (McHale 1994: 43). Those without ethnic specification turn up with Pendleton [1979]: 123; Rovin 1987: 156; McCune [1988]; Berle 1989: 294; Rovin 1991: 145; Streiker 1998: 254; Brown 1998c: 50.

Lawyers arrive in Green 1984: 40; *AML* 1993: no. 539, no. 627; Grossman 1993: 13;

Nolo's Favorite 1993; 1995 Cal.: item 71; King and McNeil 1995: 161; Brallier 1996: 75; Ross 1996: 39; Regan 2001: 36 [2002 Cal.: July 7].

74. Lawyer Jokes from Internet 1994: no. 154; Wilde 1987: 40; Phillips 1989: 81; Knott 1990: 119; Behrman 1991: 56; Rovin 1992: 149; *AML* 1993: no. 17.

75. Roper, no. 93.

76. Engelbach 1913: 18; Beeton 1880: 43; Dr. Merryman 1853: 531; Lemon 1864: 229; Willock 1887: 157; DeProses n.d.: 81; Andrews 1896: 252; Morton and Malloch 1913: 103; Heighton 1916: 145; Lawson 1923: 164; Franklin 1925: 121; Esar 1945: 261; Wilde 1982: 81; Phillips 1989: 10; *Nolo's Favorite* 1993; Lawyer Jokes 1995; 1997 Cal.: Feb. 8; Generic Lawyer Jokes, Sept. 19, 1997; Lawyer Jokes, Jan. 30, 1998; Streiker 1998: 272; Regan 2001: 88. I was told this story by my father in Philadelphia in the early 1940s. There is a medical counterpart story in which the doctor's son cures the patient whose illness put him through college, etc. Robey 1920: 88 (doctor can't afford to marry patient); Williams 1938: item 505; Rango 1944: 18; Meier 1944: 86 (can't marry); Wachs 1968: 168; Anon. 1973a; Pendleton [1979]: 84; Bonham and Gulledge 1989: 76; Berle 1993: 175; Stangland 1994: 45; Adams 1996: 270; Anon. 2001a: 149; Anon. 2002: 88.

77. Adams 1996; Cerf 1952: 92; MacDonald [1987]: 62 (told as anecdote about Canadian lawyer in 1930s); E. Phillips 1989: 10; Goldstein-Jackson 1995: item 290.

78. Thornberg 1995: 232, n. 31.

79. Thornberg 1995: 232–42.

80. Scruggs 1928: item 442; *Green Bag* 20: 432 (1908); Mosher [1922]: 325.

81. Leininger 1982: n.p.

82. I first downloaded this item in 1993. A Google search (June 26, 2002) for "lawyer kidney stone joke" found the story on some 522 web pages. Of these only three attributed the story to Buchwald. Art Buchwald, "The Case of the Lawyer's Kidneys," reprinted in Roth 1989: 157. Also at Internet 1993; CLLH 1995: no. 4; Redneck Humor, June 26, 2002.

83. Lawyer Jokes from Internet 1994: No. 99.

84. Amy Singer, e-mail message to author, July 14, 1999; Stephen M. Masterson, e-mail, Aug. 24, 1999; Ken S. Gallant, e-mail, Oct. 13, 1999. The roles are reversed in e-mail from Joseph R. Thome, Apr. 10, 1999. In Britain, the joke depicts different rivalries: Dale and Simmons 1999: 30 (old Labour / new Labour); Sharpe 2000: 333 (rival football supporters). The story is descended from an earlier joke about a group who tease and harass a waiter or cook; when they finally relent, their victim replies, "I'll stop pissing in your coffee." Anon. 1968b; Novak 1977: 113.

85. Mindes 1982: 204 discusses perceptions of the lawyer as hero. But this seems to be a misnomer. The major loadings of his "hero" factor are self-confident, competitive, aggressive, and energetic, a combination that includes neither the courage nor the beneficence associated with the lawyer heroes in contemporary fiction, television, and film.

86. This is distinctively, if not exclusively American. Narayana Rao 1990 notes that in India "what is significantly absent in movies, literature and folklore are stories of lawyers who stand out as heroes fighting for justice. India does not have hero characters like Perry Mason. There are no stories of skillful lawyers who work for innocent people in order to vindicate them" (205).

87. Anon. 1902 [Cole's 2nd.]: 234–36.

88. Lurie 1928: 143; Thomas 1947: 26. A version placed in nineteenth-century America appeared in an English collection (Phillips 1989: 94). Comparable stories depict the lawyer defending a streetcar conductor against an arrogant passenger (Anon. 1902: 255), confounding the schemes of an unjust seller (set in 1906 England [Cook 1938: 17]), intimidating an

oppressive and overbearing landlord (Keene 1949 [1947]: 582), and a Jewish lawyer turning the tables on a false accuser in nineteenth-century Petrograd (Rabinowitz 1986: 205 [1973]).

89. Allen 1945: item 1145; Fuller 1942: item 2544; Phillips 1989: 85 (England); Sartor 1989: 65; Adler 1994: 128; Streiker 1998: 250; Regan 2001: 35. A similar story, in which Lincoln refuses to press a claim against a widow with six children, is at Fuller 1942: item 2536.

90. Cantor 1943: 197. Wilde 1977: 169 (golf lessons); McDougal 1980: 74 (golf lessons); Phillips 1990: 151 (voice lessons); Rovin 1991: 274 (tennis lessons); Mital and Gupta 1995: 113 (singing lessons).

91. Knott 1992: 68 [= Knott 1992a: 114]; Taubeneck 1946: 223; Davis 1954: 79; Braude 1955: item 1352; Playboy 1963: 183 [= Playboy 1972: 180]; Anon. 1965a; Wachs 1968: 22; Austin 1968: 117; Adams 1970: 213 ; Wilde 1982: 5 [= Wilde 1987: 155]; Wilde 1986: 81 (lawyer and doctor—presumably she is pregnant); Rovin 1991: 257; Rovin 1992: 66; Knott 1993a: 86; Adams 1996: 447; Adams 1996: 487; Goldstein-Jackson 1996: 109; Harvey ca.1998a: 95; Alvin 2001: 11. While the receptionist's leverage may originally have been that of a scorned lover seeking "heart balm," the lawyer's presence takes on a different meaning in the era of sexual harassment suits.

5. The Demography of the World of Lawyer Jokes

1. See A6, *either side,* and A30, *reversing course,* in chap. 1.

2. Heinz and Laumann 1982: 56, 355; LoPucki 1990.

3. Rosen 1998:78.

4. In 1991, over 11 percent of lawyers worked for some governmental body (this includes judges); about 9 percent worked for private industry. Less than 2 percent were public defenders, legal aid, or public interest lawyers. Almost three-quarters of active lawyers were in private practice. Curran and Carson 1994: 7

5. Heinz and Laumann 1982: 42. Donald Landon did a comparable assessment of rural practitioners in the Midwest and found that 56 percent of the legal effort was devoted to individual and small business concerns. Landon 1990: 60.

6. Heinz et al. 1997: table 3. Since the number of lawyers in Chicago had doubled, this meant that the total effort devoted to the personal sector had increased by 45 percent. But the corporate sector grew by 126 percent. To the extent that lawyers serving the corporate sector were able to command more staff and support services with their effort, these figures understate the gap in services delivered.

7. U.S. Dept. of Commerce, Bureau of the Census, "Census of Legal Services," 1972: table 4, 1977, table 9; 1982, table 30; 1987, table 42; 1992, table 49. For 1967, only total receipts are available from the U.S. Census. Percentages for classes of clients are taken from the estimates of Sander and Williams 1989: 441.

8. Even this more-than-double rate of growth understates the growth of business expenditures on legal services, for it includes only "outside" lawyers and does not include in-house legal expenditures, which greatly increased during this period. For exclusion of in-house legal services from Census of Service Industries, see the introduction to U.S. Bureau of Census 1985: iii–vi.

9. Heinz and Laumann 1982: 319.

10. On the contrasting styles of ordinary lawyering and megalawyering, see Galanter 1983.

11. Heinz and Laumann 1982: 127.

12. In 1957, only 38 law firms in the United States had 50 or more lawyers and the largest firm had about 120 lawyers (Smigel 1969: 43). The total number of lawyers in these

large firms was less than 1 percent of all the lawyers then in practice. By 1991, 749 firms had 51 or more lawyers; the total number of lawyers in these firms was 105,236. Curran and Carson 1994: 16, 25.

13. Sander and Williams 1989: 440–41.

14. Firms: A32, A42 (associate and partner versions), A55, B17, E7, F12, J1, J14. Clients: A24, A33, D26, J1, J4, J9, J12, J13. This includes those where the client is identified as a "magnate" or a "tycoon."

15. Heinz and Laumann (1982: 40) estimate that in 1975 criminal defense absorbed 5 percent of the effort of the Chicago bar and prosecution 2 percent. In Landon's analogous estimate for midwestern rural locales, the total effort expended on criminal law was 6 percent on criminal defense and 4 percent on prosecution. Landon 1990: 60.

16. The exceptions include (much of) *L.A. Law* (1986–94) and movies like *The Fortune Cookie* (1966), *Kramer versus Kramer* (1979), *The Verdict* (!982), *Class Action* (1991), *The Rainmaker* (1997), *The Sweet Hereafter* (1998), *A Civil Action* (1998), and *Erin Brockovich* (2000).

17. On the history of the exclusion of women, see Epstein 1993; Garza 1996; Morello 1986.

18. Curran and Carson 1994: 4.

19. Internet collection e-mailed by Julian Killingly, Sep. 13, 1994: item 12; Steiger 1990: 2; 1995 Cal.: item 1 [= 1996 Cal.: Jan. 4 = 1997 Cal.: Mar. 23] (female *litigator*); 1998 Cal.: Sept. 6; Lawyer Jokes, Jan. 30, 1998; Alvin 2001: 85; Alvin 2001a: 98; Pritchard 2002: 118. The same comparison is made with other "difficult" women: Wilde 1988: 28 (Beverly Hills woman); Knott 1993a: 45 (woman selling used cars); Rhode (1997): 30 (woman with PMS); Alvin 1997: 31 (Hillary Clinton); Cohl 1997: 492 (PMS); Dedopulos 1998: 130 [= Baddiel et al. 1999: 473] (PMS); Symans 1998: 61 (Hillary Clinton); Hobbes 2002b: 79 (PMS).

20. Lawyer Jokes from Internet 1994: no. 33. Again, the comparison is made about other "difficult" women: Allen 1990: 10 (JAP); Adams and Newall 1995: 215 (soprano); Pease 1996: 45 ("woman with her period"); men's rights association newsletter, quoted by Rhode 1997: 229 (women's lib); Jewish Humor Issue no. 12 [e-mail from M. Weiss] (May 1997) (Jewish mother); Cohl 1997: 492 (PMS); Marsh and Goldmark 1997: 30 (vocalist); Pietsch 1998: 209 (PMS); Symons 1998: 87 (Hillary Clinton); Baddiel et al. 1999: 271 (PMS); Jhumor List, Mar. 29, 1999 (Jewish woman preparing for Passover).

21. Edwards 1915: item 1090.

22. Thus women lawyers become protagonists in some jokes in which lawyers are outrageously aggressive (e.g., *Steal more* [A46]; *Poisoned you* [F10]).

23. Epstein 1993: 280 [1981].

24. Epstein 1993: 280–81.

25. Epstein 1993: 280.

26. Pierce 1995: 137.

27. Cal.: Dec. 26. Cf. Alvin 1998: 25 (cross lesbian and lawyer).

28. Rovin 1992: 125; *AML* 1993: no. 243. This woman lawyer is the only female to be featured recently in this widespread monomania story, which appears in Boliska [1966]: 20 (sex-obsessed female hippie); Anon. 1968b (sex-obsessed Parisian girl); Asimov 1971: item 563 (golfer); Reader's Digest 1972: 123 (stockbroker); Wilde 1976: 72 (congressman); Wilde 1977: 198 (golfer); McDougal [1980]: 172 (golfer); Gardner 1982a: 37 (filmmaker); Wilde 1984: 82 (congressman); Caras 1985: 88 (military historian whose wife's off-the-shoulder outfit reminds him of Moshe Dayan); Wilde and Wozniak 1989: 124 (systems

designer); Rovin 1991: 113 (football fan); Berle 1993: 233 (football fan); Warner 1993: 127 (golfer); Forbes 1993a: 74 (golfer); Knott 1994: 63 (sports fan); Bar-Lev and Weis 1996: 38 (sex maniac); Cohl 1997: 442 (sports fan).

29. Knott 1990: 47. The same joke with a generic (nonlawyer?) "career woman" is at Knott 1989: 101. In other versions, the disinclination to "wear myself out" is not connected with the demands of career: Asimov 1971: item 277 (father/lion at zoo); Walker 1981: 123 (mother/tiger at zoo); Alvin 1993: 155 (WASP socialite/gorilla at zoo); Coote 1994: 75 (Tarzan/crocodile in jungle) [= Coote 1995: 73].

30. Epstein et al. 1995: 417–26; Hagen and Kay 1995: 97. For a nuanced account of how these pressures and preconceptions work out on the shop floor, see Reichman and Sterling 2002.

31. Knott 1990: 8. Other law firm versions in Grossman 1993: 31; 1995 Cal.: item 106.

32. This story is intimately connected to A33, another joke involving a contest, often about hiring for exalted rather than subordinate positions. The difference is not in the contest, but in the punch line ("How much would you like it to be?"). See the section "Eloquence, Persuasiveness, Resourcefulness" in chap. 1 for a discussion of that joke.

33. Some early versions do not have a formal contest: Anderson 1924: 80 (partners fix competition for pretty girl); Golden 1951: 74 (hire this girl for looking). Or they involve nepotism: Cerf 1946: 95 (hire wife's sister); Mendelsohn 1947: 211 (wife's cousin); Wilson 1949: 118 (same); Crompton 1970: 28 (wife's sister's daughter); Banc and Dundes 1986: 76 (Ceaucescu's cousin); Phillips 1994: 63 (wife's cousin). Or political favoritism: Esar 1978: 781; Anon. 1997d: 62.

The most typical contest is a quiz about is the sum of two and two: Allen 1945: item 1797 (3 + 3); Taubeneck 1946: 149; McManus 1948: 22; Kern 1949 [1947]: 126; Reader's Digest 1949: 217; Golden 1949: 62; Legman 1968 [1951]: 244; Elgard 1953: 18; Murray 1954: 143; Cohen 1958: 130; Woods 1967: item 3.5.; Blumenfeld 1970: 24; Playboy 1972: 185; Wilde 1974: 56; Cleveland 1980: 66; Triverton 1981: 234; Wilde 1984: 125; Caras 1985: 130; Banc and Dundes 1986: 94; Delf 1992: 139; Warner 1993: 62; Phillips 1994: 24; Anon. 1997a: 136. The more complex contest about caring for a sum of money, found in the law firm version listed in n. 28 above, appears in Shumaker 1983: 63; Pietsch 1986: 202 (man choosing wife); Knott 1992a: 40; Adams and Newall 1996: 113; Barnett and Kaiser 1996: 139 (wife); Adams and Newall 1996a: 34 (wife); Coote 1996: 324; Baddiel and Stone 1997: 197 (wife); Duck 1997 (wife); Leigh and LePine 1998: 86 (wife); Dale and Simmons 1998: 32 (Bill Clinton choosing new wife); Brown 1998b: 66 (wife); Keelan 1999: 306; Baddiel et al. 1999: 197 (wife); Jan Hoem, e-mail to author, Mar. 12, 1999 (wife); Lyons 1999a: 32 (wife); McFool 2000: 207 (wife); Johnson 2000 (wife); Mr. 'K' 2001: 44 (wife); Anon. 2001c: 174 (wife); Hobbes 2002a: 76 (wife); Hobbes 2002b: 182.

34. One example is *equally conclusive* (A27).

35. Auerbach 1976: 210. On the exclusion from the American Bar Association until the World War II era, see Auerbach 1976: 65–66, 216.

36. Smigel 1969: 45. Cf. the account in Gould 1979 of the obstacles to the rise of an Irish Catholic lawyer in a large New York firm in the late 1930s (xv–xviii).

37. The quote is from Rowe 1917: 593, 602. The campaigns are described in Auerbach 1976: chap. 4.

38. Henry S. Drinker, quoted at Auerbach 1976: 127.

39. Bloomfield 1980: 54. Curiously the term "shyster," which has been around since the 1850s, hardly appears in the lawyer joke corpus. See n. 51 below.

40. *Fortune* 1936: 9–10. Thirty years later, Jerome Carlin found that Jews made up 60

percent of the New York City bar, but a far smaller portion of elite law practice. Carlin 1966: 19, 28

41. *Yale Law Journal* 1964: 650.

42. Smigel 1969: 370.

43. Heinz and Laumann 1982: 112. The authors note that "'percentage Jewish' had a stronger negative correlation with prestige than did any of the other religious and ethnic categories."

44. In a National Opinion Research Center survey of the career plans of seniors graduating from American colleges in 1961, Jews made up nearly 20 percent of those aiming to be lawyers and 17.5 percent of those planning to attend law school. Greeley 1963: tables 3.16, 6.2. At this time just over 3 percent of the total population of the United States were Jews.

45. In Carnegie Commission surveys of graduate study, Jews composed nearly one-fifth of all law students in 1969 (and one-third of students in the twenty top-rated law schools). By 1975 "the proportion of students of Jewish origin dropped to twelve percent." Auerbach 1984: 50.

46. Black and Rothman 1998: 841.

47. Anon. 1905: 144; Anon. 1900a: 38 (two unnamed lawyers); Heighton 1916: 203 (Choate and Jewish client); Mendelsohn 1935: 211 (Choate and unnamed lawyer); Johnson et al. 1936: 115 [= Williams 1938: Item 235] (young Jewish lawyer consults Rufus Choate about fee in first important case); Fuller 1942: item 2545 (same, but *Joseph* Choate); May 1956: 143; Brodnick 1976: 42.

48. Joseph H. Choate (1832–1917), prominent lawyer, after-dinner speaker, and U.S. Ambassador to Great Britain, was the cousin of Rufus Choate (1799–1859), an equally famous lawyer of an earlier day, who frequently figured in the *entirely professional* story (B12) discussed in chap. 2.

49. Rosten 1985: 298; Topol [1994]: 165.

50. Anon. [Anecdota] 1928: item 361. "Yens" (or "yentz" or "yents") carries the same double meaning of "to copulate" and "to cheat or exploit" as the English "screw" and "fuck." See Rosten 1989: 551.

51. A false etymology links the term "shyster" to Jewish lawyers. In fact, the term, which goes back to the 1850s, antedates the visible presence of Jews in the American bar. On the derivation of the term from the German "scheisser," and the shift from its original meaning of bumbling incompetent to sleazy trickster, see Cohen 1982. In any event, the term "shyster" rarely appears in jokes.

52. Dornstein 1996: 142, 146. Lawrence Mitchell argues that the 1947 New York statute restricting stockholder's derivative suits was "adopted as the proximate (but almost certainly not the sole proximate) result of deeply ingrained antisemitism in the New York bar and corporate world" (2002: 4).

53. See D8 in chap. 4.

54. Alvin 1993: 19.

55. An outstanding older example is the young lawyer/older lawyer version of A58 (*Pathelin*). A32 (*ghostwriter's revenge*) anticipates the "large firm" instances discussed below.

56. On the demographic transformation of the profession and its implications, see Galanter 1999.

57. Rodent 1995: 161. The source of this story appears to be someone young enough not to have known that the firm in question (founded in 1909) was renowned many years before Dewey (1902–71) joined it, when it was known as Root, Ballantine.

58. Susan Bandes, e-mail message to author, June 2, 1999.

59. Dorothea Kettrukat, e-mail message to John Kidwell, Aug. 1, 2001.

60. Tutt is a fictional lawyer created by Arthur Train (1875–1945), one of America's most popular writers in the interwar years. Tutt, head of a small Manhattan law firm, "in almost every story . . . takes the side of a good person who is unfairly being disinherited, or in some other fashion being treated badly. Tutt uses his technical expertise in the law and/or his courtroom skills to come to the rescue." (Papke 2001: 211–12.) Between 1919 and 1945 eighty-six Tutt stories appeared in the *Saturday Evening Post,* the preeminent magazine of the day. The emblematic status of Tutt is described by Papke 2001, who observes that, like Perry Mason, Tutt works in a small, independent law office, enjoys professional autonomy and is "free of bureaucracy and hierarchy" (215).

6. Betrayers of Trust

1. Uslaner 1999; Putnam 1995; Fukuyama 1995.

2. Uslaner 1999: fig. 1.

3. Lipset and Schneider 1987; Uslaner 1993: 77ff.

4. Craig 1993: 11.

5. Newton 1997: 10–11. Presumably the meaning of trust to respondents may vary across times and settings: for example, whether it means confidence in others' competence, ability to help, or their allegiance and loyalty. Does trust mean I expect to be served, sustained, cared for? Not interfered with? Not betrayed? Or some or all?

6. Califano 1996.

7. Peters 1974: 37.

8. Denby 1994: 52.

9. Hurst 1950: 335–38 (security devices); Gilson 1984 (transaction costs); Suchman and Cahill 1996 (channeling and bonding).

10. The classic text on the limited role of legal controls is Macaulay 1963.

11. Princeton Survey Research Associates, Great American TV Poll no. 5 (1991), available on Westlaw, Poll Database. This is certainly not a new phenomenon. Back in 1949, when a national sample of adults was asked which of a list of professions and occupations they trusted the most, lawyers came in at the bottom (3 percent as opposed to 32 percent doctors, 26 percent professors/ teachers). Gallup Poll (1949), available on Westlaw, Poll Database.

12. Black 1984.

13. Peter D. Hart Research Associates 1993: table 7. A 2001 survey of a much smaller sample found a more negative view of lawyers' devotion to clients. Fifty-seven percent of respondents thought "most lawyers are more concerned with their own self-promotion than their client's best interests." Leo J. Shapiro 2002: 7.

14. *Nolo's Favorite* 1993; other lawyer versions include Wilde 1982: 160; Shafer and Papadakis 1988: 23; Berle 1989: 7; Rovin 1992: 140; *AML* 1993: no. 257; 1996 Cal.: May 6; CLLH 1995: no. 85 (= Adams and Newall 1995: 284); Ross 1996: 45; 1998 Cal.: Oct. 7; Kahn and Boe 1997: 172; anon. Stanford law student, Mar. 10, 1998; Greene 1999: 162; Regan 2001: 82.

15. Croy 1948 [1917]: 222; Taubeneck 1946: 29 (Jew outwits Scot); Cerf 1948: 673; Laing 1953: 28; Wachs 1968: 285; Anon. 1971: item 10.55; Schuster 1991: 75; Edwards 1993; Streiker 1998: 387.

16. Arneson 1981: 100 (townie outwits preppy); Wilde 1974: 6 (Irishman outwits priest); Hornby 1977: 53 (same); Howcroft 1985: 14 (farmer outwits city man); Jones and

Wheeler (farmer outwits tourist); Phillips 1991: 44 (Scotsman outwits Englishman); Reader's Digest 1997: 133 (local outwits tourist); Johnson 2001: 141 (woman outwits man); Hobbes 2002b: 31 (same).

17. May 1964: 195 (rabbi outwits priest); Walker 1980: 134 (same); Anon. 1987: 78 (same); Harris and Rabinovitch 1988: 228 (Soviet Jewish version featuring mutual accusations by a rabbi and an Orthodox priest); Jhumor list, Jan. 30, 1997 (rabbi outwits priest); Cohl 1997: 291 (one cleric outwits another); Baddiel and Stone 1997: 152 (rabbi outwits priest); Jhumor List, May 22, 1998 (same); Jhumor List, July 24, 1998 (same); Brown 1998a: 49 (same); Dale and Simmons 1999: 10 (Peter Mandelson outwits John Prescott); Baddiel et al. 1999: 152 (rabbi outwits priest); Tapper and Press 2000: 64 (same); FHM 2001: 107 (same). One early version has the rabbi's stratagem undone by the Irish cop, who asks the priest, "Father, how fast was this little fellow with the bottle going when he backed into your car." O'Neal and O'Neal 1964: 55. Cf. May 1964: 71 (Irish cop story without the flask).

18. Grossman 1993: 11. In most versions of this popular story, the animal sighted is a bear. Hence in the subsequent discussion, this joke is referred to as *outrun bear*. The first lawyer version appears in Jones and Wheeler 1991: 87; Lowdown Disk 1992: item 514; *Nolo's Favorite* 1993; Berle 1993: 288; Rabin 1993; Lawyer Jokes from Internet 1994: no. 118; Brallier 1996: 71; 1997 Cal.: July 7; Cohl 1997: 256; Lawyer Jokes, Jan. 30, 1998.

19. A Nexis search in November 1997 (something like "cougar or bear w/3 outrun") produced some seventy-six printed versions, starting with a telling by a Harvard Business School professor at the International Monetary Conference in Brussels (Trigaux 1983: 3) and including tellings by President Reagan (e.g., Smith 1986) and, by 1992, references to "that old joke about . . ."

20. Lawyer Jokes from Internet 1994: no. 118; Streiker 1998: 271; Greene 1999: 163; Regan 2001: 212; 2002 Cal.: Apr. 27/28.

21. CLLH 1995: lawyer humor no. 63. Other lawyer versions, almost identical: Ross 1996: 39; Cohl 1997: 283; 1998 Cal.: Jan. 19; Tibballs 2000: item 1187; Regan 2001: 78; FHM 2001: 170.

22. E.g., Masson [1913] 1:179 [= Milburn 1926: 10]; Edmund and Williams 1916: 130; Lurie 1928: 27; Mendelsohn 1935: 58; Eastman 1936: 69; Copeland 1936: 173; Johnson et al. 1936: 160 [= Williams 1938: item 1281]; Fuller 1942: item 2172; Esar 1945: 369; Gerler 1965: 119; Woods 1967: item 25.11; Crompton 1970: 23; B. Phillips 1974a: 57; Marquand 1977: 28 [= Pollack 1979: 54 = Triverton 1981: 249]. Apart from lawyers, no other new protagonists have appeared, apart from a single appearances by Robert Maxwell (Yermonee 1992), "two bosses" in topical collection (Phillips 1994: 94), and accountants (Anon. 2000a: 120 = Anon. 2001a: 141).

23. *AML* 1993: no. 273.

24. Knott, 1990: 73. Other lawyer versions at Steiger 1990: 39; Behrman 1991: 18; Rovin 1992: 73; Adler 1992: 51 [= Adler 1994: 49]; Grossman 1993: 39; *Nolo's Favorite* 1993; Humes 1993: 103 [= Knott 1990]; *AML* no. 158, no. 653; 1996 Cal.: July 2; CLLH 1995: lawyer humor no. 91; 1997 Cal.: July 2; Ross 1996: 28 (woman lawyer); 1998 Cal.: Oct. 5; Dedopulos 1998: 240; Greene 1999: 154; 2000 Cal.: Jan. 4; Tibballs 2000: item 1150; Regan 2001: 261; Anon. 2000c: 228.

25. A precursor has a Polish Jew defining honesty as sharing overpayment with partner. Knox 1926: 149; Hicks 1936: 124. Anon. 1927 (75) features a clothing merchant of unspecified ethnicity, but starting with Schermerhorn 1928 (144) it is overwhelmingly told about Jewish characters, although there are some nondenominational clothiers and an

occasional Scot: Hershfield 1932: item 52 (Jewish debaters); Johnson et al. 1936: 183; Hershfield 1938: 94 (Scots debaters); Williams 1938: item 591; Wright 1939: 51; Fuller 1942: item 290; Cerf 1945: 47 [= Cerf 1945a: 34]; Allen 1945: item 649 (Scots tradesman); Esar 1945: 155; Keene [1947]: 654; Jessel 1960: 163; McCarthy 1962: 167; Youngman 1963: 16; Gerler 1965: 77; Woods 1967: item 13.7; Asimov 1971: item 362; Anon. 1971: item 132.55; Youngman 1976: 110; Brodnick 1976: 17; Marquand 1977: 52; Wilde 1978: 156; Walker 1980: 178; Yarwood [1981]: 77; Aspinwall 1986: 107. Since the arrival of the lawyers in 1988, it has continued to flourish as a Jewish joke: Allen 1990: 71; Kramer 1994: 119; Coote 1994: 51; Coote 1995: 4; Pease 1996: 145; Coote 1996: 141; Keelan 1999: 149. It appears also in a deracinated form: B. Phillips 1990: 59; E. Phillips 1994: 14; Cohl 1997: 71 (first daughter!) Colombo 2001: 294 (Winnipeg merchants), but it has not been switched to any other group.

26. Lawyer Jokes from Internet 1994: no. 80. Other lawyer versions are found in Chariton 1989: 201; *Nolo's Favorite* 1993; Brallier 1996: 8; 1997 Cal.: Sept. 5; Streiker 1998: 264; 2002 Cal.: July 29.

27. The first appearances refer to "partners in a well-known Stock Exchange house" (Masson 1922: 96; Mosher 1922: 374; Ernst 1925: 57), but starting with Schermerhorn 1928 (276) the characters are almost invariably Jewish and continue to be so. Copeland and Copeland 1940: item 6574; Fuller 1942: item 2242; Moulton 1942: item 1694; Allen 1945: item 629 (Scots); House 1948: 76; Blumenfeld 1967: 100; Woods 1967: item 13.1; Adams 1968: 230; Asimov 1971: item 361; Golden 1972: 26; Anon. 1973a; Hornby 1977: 23 (Irish); McDougal [1980]: 64; Gardner 1982: 52; Berle 1989: 285, 460, ; Eilbirt 1991: 71; Harris 1994 (related as a tale about [the Jewish] Lord Grade, former head of the ATV network, and his brother); E. Phillips 1994: 51; Vas 1994; Kramer 1994: 86; Mital and Gupta 1995: 44; Arya 1995: 51; Adams 1996: 139; Cohl 1997: 412 (Italian restaurateurs). Again, the original Jewish protagonists live on, but apart from a few items, no other new identities are specified apart from lawyers.

28. Lawyer Jokes from Internet 1994: no. 139 (substantially identical to Behrman 1991: 16); *AML* 1993: no. 357. Versions with markedly less cooperation are at Knott 1988: 69 [= Knott 1990: 38 = Knott 1991a: 81]; Cohl 1997: 369.

29. The first version, about jewelry partners (Anecdota 1928: item 286 [= Anecdota 1934: item 269]) had none of the amity and cooperation of this version ("In their fright each tried to lay the onus of parenthood on the other"). Of course, there has been a dramatic reduction in the "onus" of out-of-wedlock birth in the past seventy years, so that the element of danger and shame is less salient. Legman 1968: 790 [1936]; Anon. 1954: n.p.; Davis 1956: 68; Youngman 1963: 83; Playboy 1972: 155; Marquand 1977: 50; Mr. J. 1979: 94; Triverton 1981: 154; Pietsch 1986: 67; Harris and Rabinovich 1988: 238 (Soviet Jewish version in which the Jewish assistant director bests the factory director); Sood 1988: 27. Versions about partners in stereotypically Jewish businesses or with stereotypically Jewish names remain current: Berle 1989: 285; Berle 1989: 495; Adams and Newall 1995: 87; Alvin 1995a: 9. Again, no new protagonists have emerged other than lawyers.

30. Lawyer Jokes from Internet 1994: no. 119. Other lawyer versions are Grossman 1993: 94; 1995 Cal.: item 255; Regan 2001: 226.

31. Anon. 1905a: 186; Lurie 1927: 4; Orcutt 1942: 65; Knox c.1943: 99; Rango 1944: 9; Allen 1945: item 1344; Ford et al. 1945: 148; Cagney 1979: 72; Pendleton [1979]: item 538; Wilde 1983: 96 (Irish woman: "what time does your husband get home"); Martling 1984: 130; Stangland 1987: 194 (Norwegian); Berle 1993: 125; Strean 1993: 77; Jones and Wheeler 1995: 140 (patient and doctor); Subhash and Dharam 1995a: 254; Coote 1995: 189;

Adams 1996: 166; Pease 1996: 369; Van Munching 1997: 51; Reginald 1997: 86; Harvey c.1998b: 83; Leigh and Lepine 1998: 31; Anon. 2000: 81; Anon. 2000b: 81; Anon. 2000c: 316; Tibballs 2000: item 4735; Sharpe 2000: 42, 47, 48; FHM 2001: 63; Hobbes 2002a: 155; Hobbes 2002b: 133.

32. E.g., Jones and Wheeler 1995: 140 (patient tells doctor, "By the way, you have a nice house"); Van Munching 1997: 51 (patient tells doctor, "You have a beautiful home").

33. Shafer and Papadaikis 1988: 31; Keelan 1999: 211 (Robert DeNiro).

34. Tulk 1971: 34 (Newfie and E. P. Taylor); Shelley 1976: 51 (young man and Pierre Trudeau); Harris 1979: 49 (young constable and M.P.); Walker 1981: 116 (salesman and Bob Hawke); Gurney 1986: n.p. (young executive and Rupert Murdoch); Ocker 1986 (same); Gurney 1987 (businessman and Sir Gordon Squire); Hill 1987: 52 (youth and Frank Sinatra); Strangland 1987: 31 (Ole and Clint Eastwood); Knott 1991: 54 (advertising executive and Donald Trump); Yermonee 1992 (Robert Maxwell and Paul Getty); Asimov 1992: item 552 (young man and Aristotle Onassis); Berle 1993: 214 (man and LBJ); Strean 1993: 25 (man and JFK); Knott 1993a: 89 (sales associate and Donald Trump); Knott 1994: 133 (advertising executive and Rupert Murdoch); Topol [1994]: 57 (young man and Sinatra); Phillips 1994: 6 (young man and Henry Ford); Adams and Newall 1995: 315 (Paddy and Sinatra); Healey and Glanville 1996: 147 (bloke and Sinatra); Coote 1996: 26 (yuppie and Rupert Murdoch); Cohl 1997: 180 (young advertising executive and Bill Gates); Lyons 1998a: 57 (Jewish tailor and fictitious celebrity).

35. Knott 1990: 27. Other lawyer versions are Brallier 1992: 58; *Nolo's Favorite* 1993 [= CLLH 1995: lawyer humor no. 98]; 1997 Cal.: Sept. 11; Lisa Lerman, e-mail message to author, Dec. 1, 1999; Tibballs 2000: item 189; Regan 2001: 52. The switch to the lawyer protagonist is palpably clear here: in the similar Knott (1986: 108) the mobster's employee is "a deaf-and-dumb accountant" who answers the summons "accompanied by his brother who could speak sign language." By 1990 the brother has acquired a law degree and the joke appears in a topical collection of lawyer jokes.

36. The lawyer as sign language interpreter incarnates Maureen Cain's (1983: 111) notion that the "day-to-day chore" of lawyers is to serve as translator between ordinary discourse and the "meta-language" of law. The joke also implies that the lawyer will end up with the entire stake over which the disputants are contending, an outcome celebrated in many jokes (see section "Only the Lawyer Wins" in chap. 2) and in the famous print that depicts contending litigants pulling a cow in opposite directions while the lawyer milks it.

37. From its initial 1976 appearance the faithless translator has mediated between the threatened victim and various heavies: Youngman 1976: 9 (Spanish conquistador); Wilde 1978: 178 (Mafia don); Thickett 1984: 83 (same); B. Phillips 1986: 112 (Spanish conquistador); Knott 1986: 108 (mobster); Rovin 1989: 178 (Mafia don, woman translator); Duncan 1990: 75 (Texas ranger); Rovin 1991 (Russian body-builder); Telushkin 1992: 67 (mob boss); Warner 1993: 189 (bank robbers); Adams and Newall 1995: 320 (Mafioso); Coote 1995: 201 (Godfather); Subhash and Dharam 1995a: 73 (Mafia underboss); Pease 1996: 133 (Godfather); Coote 1996: 136 (Mafia boss); Baddiel and Stone 1997: 258 (gambler) [= Baddiel 1999: 259 = Anon. 2000a: 174 = Anon. 2000b: 223]; Streiker 1998: 281 (Pinkerton detective); Greene 1999: 232 (mafia thugs); Claro 2000: 7 (Spanish conquistador); Tibballs 2000: item 185 (Texas ranger); McFool 2000: 124 (mafia hood); Sharpe 2000: 80 (gang boss); FHM 2001: 122 (mobster). These still outnumber the lawyer version, but the lawyer is the only professional identity given to the interpreter, apart from a single reference to a (Jewish) accountant (Telushkin 1992: 67).

38. Lawyer Jokes from Internet 1994: no. 147. Other lawyer versions are Behrman 1991: 31 (women lawyers) [= *AML* 1993: no. 369 (same with name changes)]; Grossman 1993: 73 (Wall St. lawyers) [= *AML* 1993: no. 685 with name changes]; 1995 Cal.: item 312; Regan 2001: 32. A client poisons lawyer version appeared a few years earlier (Wilde 1987: 124). The "partner" version presents treachery as the *modus operandi* of the legal profession; in the "client" version, the treacherous lawyer is repaid in kind by his client victim, joining the troop of jokes in which the tables are turned on the arrogant lawyer.

39. The husband poisoning wife version is in print by 1928: Anecdota 1928: item 474 (Baron poisons wife); Hershfield 1932: item 73 (Jewish husband poisons wife); Hershfield 1938: 92 (deracinated); Jones 1944: 53; Cerf 1946: 199; Playboy 1965: 104 [= Playboy 1972: 70 = Humes 1993: 113]; Adams 1968: 331 (Jewish); Anon. 1971: item 494.06; Asimov 1971: item 394 (Jewish); Marquard 1977: 119; Pollack 1979: 45 (Jewish); Triverton 1981: 146; Wilde and Wozniak 1989: 94; Coote 1995: 243; Pease 1996: 150; Thomas 1996: 42; Baddiel and Stone 1997: 39; Baddiel et al. 1999: 39; Allen 2000: 151 (Jewish); FHM 2001: 53; Hobbes 2000b: 132. The first wife poisoning her husband does not occur until Anon. 1973a; Dawson 1979: 77; Gardner 1982: 14; Savannah 1990: 75; Miller 1991: 102; Singh 1996: 137.

40. Berle [1945]: 65; Keene 1949 [1947]; Rezwin 1958: 27; Anon. 1963: n.p.; Anon. [1967] 46 (Jewish); Murdock 1967: 69; Spalding 1969: 79 (Jewish); Esar 1978: 86; Pendleton [1979]: 182; Wilde 1979: 23 (Jewish) [= Wilde 1986: 116]; Lyons 1987: 55; Ben Eliezar [1985]: 34 (Jewish); Rovin 1987: 95; Alverson [1989]: 67 (Jewish); Topol [1994]: 250 (Jewish); Barley/Weis 1996: 46; Harvey c.1998b: 137; Keelan 1999: 151 (Jewish); Anon. 2000c: 340 (Jewish).

41. Rovin 1992: 56; 1996 Cal.: Jan 8. Cf. 1996 Cal.: Apr. 22 ("I'm here to help" = lying). Earlier versions make the translation into various idioms: *Maledicta* 6: 298 (1982) (Jewish); Knott 1983: 6 (Los Angeles); Pietsch 1986: 184 (Yiddish); Barry 1990: 144 (Yiddish); Berle 1993: 41 (agent talk); Alvin 1998a: 103 (Hollywood); Keelan 1999: 145 (Yiddish); Lyons 1999a: 83 (Jewish).

42. Dan Steward, e-mail message to author, Feb. 28, 1997; 1997 Cal.: May 2; Anon. 2001c: 27; 2002 Cal.: Apr. 22.

43. E.g., Johnston 1984: 63 (Irishman); Cruikshank 1987: 39 (Alaska greenhorn); MacHale 1991: 12 (Irishman); Barnett and Kaiser 1996: 53 (Irishman); Cohl 1997: 171 (Russian); Buford and Grabowski 1997: 10 (redneck); Kostick 1998: 113; Brown 1998f: 102 (Irishman); Brown 1998d: 88 (same); Greene 1999: 85 (blonde); Tapper and Press 2000: 118 (rabbi); Colombo 2001: 218 (Newfie). This is a contemporary embodiment of tale-type AT 750 [The Wishes].

44. Cal.: May 2.

45. Berle 1993: 274; Baddiel et al. 1999: 99 (newspaper editor wants reporter and photographer "back here right now").

46. Oral tradition (collected by the author, Madison, WI, 1990).

47. The earliest version I have found is *Harper's Bazaar* (1876: 352). The trail breaks off at this point, but the *take it with you* variant bears a striking resemblance to a medieval story about a miser who wants to take his gold with him: "A certain usurer of Metz, drawing near unto his death, bound his Friends by oath, that in his grave they should put a purse full of Money, under his head; which [was] done accordingly. His sepulcher [being] afterwards opened, that it might be taken out, there was seen a Devil pouring melting gold down his throat with a ladle." *The Philosopher's Banquet*, 1614, reprinted in Hazlett 1864: 3:item 21. (I have modernized the spelling.) Here it is the deceased that is the object

of derision, not the survivor(s). But it starts from the same premise: the refusal to leave wealth to others and insistence on taking it with; the means is the same (deposit in the grave); the result is torment by the devil, replaced by frustration/betrayal by the clever Jew and then by the lawyer, both figures long associated with the devil in the popular imagination.

48. May 1964: 294.

49. Murdock 1967: 116 [= B. Phillips 1974: 141]. This represents a major change from earlier *check in the coffin* stories and seems to arrive full blown. Subsequent lawyer tellings of the *take it with you* version include: Moshman, *Trusts & Estates* 137 (10): 67 (Sept. 1998, quoting James McElaney, 1980); Wilde 1982: 23; Wright and Wright 1985: 276; Joel Hyatt in *Playboy* (April 1985: 20); Sorter 1989: 110; collected by Edward Reisner c.1990; Odean n.d.: collected from David Cheit, 1991; Long 1992; Adler 1992: 45 [= Adler 1994: 41]; *Arizona Republic,* July 17, 1992, C12; Delf 1992: 95; Grossman 1993: 37; *AML* 1993: no. 652; *Kansas City Star,* July 10, 1993; Kornheiser 1994; Lawyer Jokes from Internet. 1994: no. 11; Clark 1994; Dundes and Pagter 2000: 196 (collected 1994); CLLH 1995 lawyer humor no. 74 [= Adams and Newall 1995: 284]; Overton 1995: 1112; Carter 1996: 116; Marchal 1996; Dan Steward, e-mail message to author, Nov. 1, 1996; Ross 1996: 37; Henson 1997; letter to editor, *Cincinnati Enquirer,* Feb. 17, 1997; anon. Univ. of Iowa law student, Feb. 28, 1997; CLLJ 1997: no. 70; Funniest Darn Lawyer Jokes, May 21, 1997; A collection of lawyer jokes, May 21, 1997; Lawyer Jokes 1997; Pierleoni, *Sacramento Bee,* Aug. 17, 1998, C2; Greene 1999: 173; 2000 Cal.: Nov. 1; www.jokes-for-all.com, Nov. 26, 1999.

A distinctive adaptation is found in India where the lawyer who promises to transfer the client's assets to him in the hereafter places a check on the funeral pyre at the cremation. Singh 1990: 104.

50. Riesman 1954: 450.

51. The analysis that follows is inspired by Richard Raskin's wonderful *Life Is like a Glass of Tea: Studies of Classic Jewish Jokes* (1992), in which he develops three "interpretive frameworks" that he finds "useful for understanding many classical Jewish jokes." The first is *role fiasco* in which a character displays "outrageous incompetence in: a) performing or sustaining a given role; b) assessing what behavior or attitude a given situation calls for; or c) thinking logically and realistically (23)." A second comic perspective is *tactical manoeuvre* in which the character "is essentially a player who is out to get away with something, to pull something off, to evade a responsibility, to get more than his share of something he wants, to get the better of, or turn to tables on, someone else, to get around a prohibition, etc." (24). The third framework is *exemplary deviance* in which "the comic behavior on display in the punch-line is seen as a positive model we are implicitly invited to admire and emulate, even though it marks a break with conventional codes" (24). Thus we have outrageous failure to perform, crafty gamesmanship, and admirable deviance. Many lawyer jokes invoke one of these directly or indirectly. Raskin thinks that jokes that can be "understood in two (or three) of [these] perspectives . . . are the very best of the classic . . . [Jewish jokes]" because they generate an experience of "oscillation between two (or more) interpretive options" (29). For those who embrace such experiences, jokes that have this "open-endedness or reversibility . . . have an inexhaustible richness" (1992: 30). The *take it with you* version of the *check in the coffin* is the only lawyer joke I have encountered that invites analysis in all three of these perspectives.

52. Beyond the three versions discussed in the text, there are others that have not been switched to lawyers. These include versions in which the mourners deposit money neither as agents of the dead man (*take it with you*) nor as a gratuitous presentation to him

(*respectful gesture*). Instead they are repaying a debt, or complying with an explicit condition in his will. Yet another version involves a pact among friends that the survivor(s) will place money in the coffin to assist the next-worldly finances of whoever should die first. All of these apparently descend from the older *take it with you* story (or some common ancestor), most frequently told about Jews but also about other "canny" groups such as Scots and Ibos (see Davies 1990: 112).

53. I have found some thirty-six appearances of *take it with you* as a lawyer joke since it surfaced as one in 1964, thirty of these since 1990; fifteen versions of *respectful gesture* as a lawyer joke since it became one in 1990; and two appearances of *making amends,* the first in 1988. These fifty-three appearances are the basis for the assertions made below about the relationships described in the several versions of the joke.

54. Knott 1990: 70 [= Knott 1990b: 122 = Knott 1993a: 87 = Cohl 1997: 207]; Law and Politics 1991 [= Adler 1994: 37]. More frequently, the reason for the deposit is family tradition. Brallier 1992: 9; *Nolo's Favorite* 1993; Faine 1994: 56 (Australia); 1997 Cal.: Mar. 1 [= 1998 Cal.: Feb. 11]; CLLH 1995: lawyer humor no. 13; Starr, 1995; 1997 Cal.: Mar. 1; anon. Univ. of Iowa law student, Feb. 28, 1997; Lawyer Jokes, Sept. 19, 1997; Dedopulos 1998: 236; Southwell 1999: 65.

55. It was established as a joke about Scots and Jews by the 1920s. The first lawyer telling is Knott 1990 (70), a topical collection that has been influential in defining the canon of contemporary lawyer jokes.

56. Adler 1992: 50.

57. It first surfaces in an article by law professor Ronald Rotunda that appeared in several legal newspapers in early 1988 (Rotunda 1988a: 6; 1988b: 12). This article was based on a law review article dated the previous summer (Rotunda 1987). The newspaper article substituted this *make amends* story for an entirely different lawyer joke (A17, *two in grave*) that was included in the law review article. When I asked Professor Rotunda where he had heard what his newspaper article refers to as an "old joke" he could not remember whether he had heard it in that form or modified another story (possibly another version of the *check in the coffin?*). Telephone interview with Ronald Rotunda, Feb. 10, 1998. A topical collection of lawyer jokes (Adler 1992: 50) picked it up either from Rotunda or possibly from Rotunda's source (the wording is identical), but it was one of the few items omitted from the refurbished edition (Adler 1994) and has not surfaced since.

58. Of the thirteen *Betrayal* jokes discussed in this chapter, eight (*check in the coffin, collision and flask, mine died, safe unlocked, extra $100 bill, poisoned you, trust me, payment during robbery*) were predominantly or frequently told about Jewish protagonists before becoming lawyer jokes. Another (*sign language*) has been switched (at least once) to a Jewish protagonist as well as to lawyers. Of the others, two (*beautiful house, too* and *partner undoes wishes*) were "dumb" jokes. *Greeting spurned* hasn't taken as a lawyer joke. The remaining story (*outrun bear*) flourishes as a story about various sorts of outdoorsmen (fishermen, hunters, hikers, etc.) who are sometimes given various professional, business, and sports identities.

59. In popular imagination, the Jew is implicated in the archetypical betrayal, i.e., of Jesus by Judas. Trachtenberg [1943] details the medieval "picture of the Jew as an *enemy of the people,* never hesitating to betray his closest friend, or the city or nation that sheltered him" (182). The displacement of Jews in tendentious jokes is part of a larger post-Holocaust phenomenon of avoidance of joking about Jews, augmented by the more recent spread of "political correctness" taboos on ethnic, racial, and other characteristics as objects of jokes.

60. In two of these (*payment during robbery, poisoned you*) the initial switch to the legal setting is to a client-screws-lawyer format, but eventually the joke becomes more popular in the lawyer-screws-lawyer version.

61. In twelve of fifteen appearances of this variant, the relationship of lawyer to deceased is described as close friend; in only one appearance is the deceased identified as the lawyer's client.

62. The lawyer is so described in twenty-four of thirty-six appearances of this variant. In six, he is an "advisor" or "most trusted" friend; in six others he is characterized as a friend.

63. This profile would not be changed if we were to include as *Betrayal* jokes two of the economic/sexual *Predation* jokes discussed in chap. 2, *screw partner's wife/repay $1000* (B56) and *pay whore with client's debt* (B57). In the former, the victim is the lawyer's partner once more; in the latter, the lawyer extracts sexual favors from the opposing party. He uses the occasion of paying the client's debt to generate personal advantage for himself, but there is no evident harm to the client.

64. It may even be present in the insincerity of the lawyer's confession to his partner in the *make amends* story.

65. Galanter and Palay 1991.

66. Epstein 1997: 89.

67. On the literature of legal nostalgia, see Galanter 1996.

68. Simpson 1990: 825.

69. Warner 1992.

70. "Did You Hear the One about the Lawyer . . . ?" (undated mailer, ca. late 1991 or early 1992, from Indiana University School of Law); Anderson Kill Olick & Oshinsky, undated brochure; "Lawyer Jokes" (newsletter from Swanson & Gieser, Santa Ana, CA, 1993). A mail-order firm specializing in "products and gifts for lawyers" included in its Holiday 1997 catalog a large assortment of items based on lawyer jokes—for example, the shark T-shirt in fig. 11, chap. 2 (For Counsel: the Catalog for Lawyers, Wilsonville, OR, 1997: 24).

71. Davies 1991: 190.

72. Bennett 1964: 56. Middleton and Moland 1959, comparing southern white and black university students, found, "Not only did Negroes tell more anti-Negro than anti-White jokes, but they told significantly more anti-Negro jokes than Whites" (66). In a follow-up study, Middleton (1959) subjected Negro and white university students to a series of jokes including anti-Negro and anti-white ones. The Negroes, he concluded, "found the anti-Negro jokes quite as funny as did the whites" (178). Appreciation of these jokes was higher among middle-class Negroes (181). Appreciation by both Negro and white students bore no consistent relationship with acceptance or rejection of the stereotypes on which the jokes were based (180).

73. Katz and Katz 1971: 219. Cf. Bennett 1964, who observes that "race and nationality jokes are by far the most popular among the 'better' members of the ridiculed group. No one feels the need to be superior to the thickly accented 'ghetto' Jew more than the emancipated Jewish bourgeois, and nobody feels the need to separate himself from the ignorant, backward drawling Southern Negro more than the educated middle-class Negro" (56).

74. Ben-Amos 1973: 129.

75. Telephone interview with Brent Swanson, Esq., Santa Ana, CA, January 27, 1998.

76. Anderson Kill Olick & Oshinsky 1991. The agency that produced this brochure received a special recognition award from the Washington Advertising Club for work that "pushed the envelope on creativity." Myles 1992: B4. The jokes are also featured on the

firm's Web site. An administrator at the firm estimated that half the firm's lawyers were offended by the use of the jokes, but they are retained because "clients love it." Telephone interview with Maxa Luppi, Feb. 4, 1998. More recently, the Web site shows no sign of jokes. www.andersonkill.com (accessed Feb. 14, 2005).

77. Davies 1991 remarks on the capacity of members of a minority to "laugh at their own group in many different ways including those favored by the majority because of the high degree of social . . . differentiation [within the minority] . . . and through the ability of each individual member of a minority group to manipulate and slide between his or her majority and minority reference groups in such a way that the joke never applies to him or her personally" (192).

78. Legman 1968: 13–14.

79. Brandes 1983: 238.

80. Davies 1991: 202. Cf. Richard Raskin, who traces the transformation of stories that began as anti-Semitic jokes about Jews into classic Jewish jokes told by Jews. Raskin 1992: chap. 3 ("ten commandments"joke); chap. 4 ("he had a hat").

81. *Economist* 1997: 23. The examples cited are the *more cement* (I5) and *Doberman* (I14) jokes.

82. Shaw 1996: 60. As codified (and unintentionally caricatured) by Richard Delgado and Jean Stefancic 1994, joking should take aim at only higher-status targets: "Satire, sarcasm, scorn and similar tools should only be deployed upwards" (129, 116).

83. Simpson 1990: 825.

84. For a masterful discussion, see Luban 1988: esp. chap. 9.

85. Cramton 1996: 9.

86. Cramton 1996: 5.

87. Cramton 1996: 5, 4.

88. See, for example, *what could he possibly say* (A29); *two plus two* (A33), *fight over nothing* (D2).

89. The filial link to the devil was noted by Jonathan Swift and others. See chap. 3 at n. 4.

90. Much as did the woman lawyer in *The Client* (1994) who enfolds the endangered child client in maternal protectiveness.

91. In this film too, there is an ambiguous turn away from law practice at the end, when the hero decides that his ability to perform by identifying with his clients will eventually lead to his corruption. He proposes to become a legal academic, which presumably reduces the opportunity for corruption or confers immunity to temptation. For an assessment of the ethical perplexities of the film, see Mashburn and Ware 1996.

92. The 1993 *National Law Journal* survey asked people if a lawyer should represent a client that the lawyer knows is guilty of a crime. Fifty-seven percent answered that the lawyer should undertake the representation and 35 percent said the lawyer should not. But 62 percent thought that it would be wrong for a lawyer to "use . . . a technicality to free a client he knows to have committed the crime," and only 31 percent thought it would be right. Samborn 1993: questions 20, 21.

93. Thus, it is reported that prosecutors find juries unwilling to convict "private lawyers for getting too close to their clients' illegal conduct." Wittes 1997: A1. According to one former U.S. Attorney: "Juries expect lawyers to be manipulative, creative, and devious. . . . They have an appreciation of the role defense lawyers play. They take a long, deep breath and give these lawyers a wide berth—notwithstanding the fact that lawyers are held in ill repute and there are lawyer jokes."

94. Differentiation of ethical obligation by type of client appeals to some students of legal ethics. Thus, David Luban proposes that lawyers should have higher duties of protection toward individual clients than toward organizational ones. Luban 1988: chap. 10.

7. THE LAWYER AS MORALLY DEFICIENT

1. Anon. ca. 1860: 14.

2. Sandburg 1936: 154 (reprinted in Tidwell 1956: 363); Edwards 1915: item 693; Lawson 1923: 160; Johnson et al. 1938: 180; Cook 1938: 94; Fuller 1942: item 2535; Cerf 1945: 208; Esar 1945: 262; Weiherman 1955: 92; Murdock 1967: 108; Spalding 1978: 250; Bonham 1981: 85; Wilde 1982: 24; Rosten 1985: 337; Wilde 1987: 154; Phillips 1990: 87; Knott 1990: 4; Behrman 1991: 47; Brallier 1992: 15; Adler 1992: 50; Lowdown Disk 1992: item 464; 1995 Cal.: item 283; CLLH 1995: lawyer humor no. 103; Dedopulos 1999: 242 [= Baddiel et al. 1999: 587]; Brunsting 2000: 250; Regan 2001: 5. The confusion goes back even earlier: Anon. 1913: 52 (misplaced pity for woman whose son "turned out to be a criminal lawyer"); Johnston 1922: item 1139 (lawyer described as criminal lawyer isn't "specially so"). Finally, the difference between the lawyer and criminal may be that the former didn't get caught (Behrman 1991: 92; Lawyer Jokes, Jan. 30, 1998).

3. Boliska [1966]: 133; Phillips 1974a: 43 [= Phillips 1984a: 43]; Wilde 1987: 25; Rovin 1992: 53; 1996 Cal.: Apr. 25; B. Phillips 1996: 37; 1997 Cal.: Oct. 5.

4. Rovin 1992: 88; B. Phillips 1994; 2000 Cal.: June 1.

5. Seattle Sal 1994: 78; Lowdown Disk 1992: item 463; 1997 Cal.: July 24. Cf. Coote 1995: 227 ("up front"); Pease 1996: 28 ("honest").

6. Franklin 1925: 125.

7. Austin 1968: 69; May 1964: 319; Adams 1970: 164; Yarwood [1981]: 520. Doctor versions abound: Murray 1954: 24; Gerler 1965: 56; Boliska [1966]: 80; Blumenfeld 1970: 63; Powers and Powers 1973: n.p.; McElroy 1973: 35 (psychiatrist); Wilde 1981a: 169; Forbes [1992]: 73; Humes 1994: 157; Adams 1996: 168; Forbes [1992]: 73; Humes 1994: 157; Adams 1996: 168; Goldstein-Jackson 1996: 59; Reginald 1997: 82; Anon. 2006: 4. Cf. Berle 1989: 360 (husband of unspecified occupation met her in "business"); Coote 1995: 144 (bank manager). All of these husband versions are long predated by a story about the "Famous Wit . . . ambling down Hollywood Boulevard with the Current Female Attraction" who has an emotional reunion with another man who she describes as "a trouper I met years ago in the profession." Garnett 1932: 85; Spalding 1978: 282.

8. Tybor 1978: 18; Warren and Kelly 1978: 18.

9. Hindy Greenberg quoted in Arron 1988: 47.

10. Marquand 1977: 150 [= Triverton 1981: 28 except that the Corpus Juris (still misspelled) set is enlarged to forty volumes]. In subsequent versions the prostitute is the daughter of an ambassador (Berle 1993: 281) and graduate of Tufts, Columbia, and Oxford (Gruner 1997: 121). In a life-imitates-art variant of this story, the *Toronto Sun* reported that "hooking paid for her law degree" (Nov. 30, 1994). A reader responded to the story by asking: "As most of our politicians are lawyers and regularly prostitute themselves by lying, cheating, bedding down with any special interest group, etc., why would the Law Society of Upper Canada not consider her experience operating an escort service for prostitution as required training to become a future politician." *Toronto Sun,* letter to the editor, Dec. 7, 1994. Another route is suggested in Britain, where female lawyers may be seduced into prostitution by the possibilities of wordplay. For example: "May O'Hara became disenchanted with being a barrister so she dropped her briefs and started soliciting." Cagney 1979: 60.

11. Rovin 1992: 139; Knott 1993: 91 (gay prostitute). Cf. Chariton 1989: 71 ("results" to client are same). 1996 Cal.: Feb. 7 ("nothing" simpliciter).

12. Coote 1995: 226; 1996 Cal.: Mar. 30; Brallier 1996: 16; Pease 1996: 25; Duck 1997; Alvin 1998: 24; Mr. "K" 2001: 40; Hobbes 2002b: 54.

13. 1996 Cal.: Feb. 16 [= 1997 Cal: Dec. 23].

14. Knott 1990: 121 [= Adler 1992: 131 = Adler 1994: 137]; Rovin 1992: 139; Berle 1993: 325; 1996 Cal.: Sept. 28.

15. The "lower than" trope also surfaced on television in 1995. In the opening scene of the ABC sitcom *The Naked Truth*, "the lead character ends up in a bathroom and mistakenly assumes that two prostitutes are lawyers. And the prostitutes feel insulted." Pergament 1995.

16. Shaw 1905: xxx–xxxi. The play, banned from the London stage by the Lord Chamberlain, was first performed in 1902.

17. Campos 1998: 176.

18. Citations for this item are at n. 33 on p. 352, below.

19. Florynce Kennedy 1971: 81.

20. Fried 1976.

21. Dauer and Leff 1977: 582.

22. Curtis 1951: 18. This observation is accompanied by other comparisons with bankers, priests, and poets. Curtis 1951: 22–23.

23. Behrman 1991: 46; E. Phillips 1989: 44; Delf 1992: 93; anon. University of Southern California undergraduate, Feb., 1998; Greene 1999: 162.

24. Kieffer 1907: 56; Edmund and Williams 1916: 339; Williams 1938: item 1138; Copeland and Copeland 1940: item 5253; Meier 1944: 214; Rango 1944: 231; McManus 1948: 110; House 1948: 126; Williams 1949: item 2816; Laing 1953: 56; Braude 1955: item 2025 (the politician here is also a "successful lawyer"); Davis 1956: 189; Woods 1967: item 54.18; True 1972: 14; Skubik and Short 1976: 71; Marquand 1977: 221 [= Pollack 1979: 40]; Triverton 1981: 210; Wilde 1984: 210 (Republican); Berle 1989: 472; Harvey C. 1998a: 69 (diplomat); Dale and Simmons 1999: 1 (told of Tony Blair); Lyons 1999a: 106.

25. Other examples are D4, *chaos;* B52, *screwing somebody already;* H6, *saved from drowning.*

26. Rovin 1992: 28; Knott 1990: 22; *AML* 1993: no. 93; *Nolo's Favorite* 1993; Alvin 1993: 39 (Wasp attorney); CLLH 1995: no. 78; Ross 1996: 70 (yuppie barrister); Califano 1996; Streiker 1998: 261; Greene 1999: 156; 2000 Cal.: Oct. 3; Lisa Lerman, e-mail message to author, Mar. 29, 1999; Stephen M. Masterson, e-mail, Aug. 24, 1999; Tibballs 2000: item 1189; letter, *ABA Journal*, March 2002, 14.

27. Yuppie versions: Barry 1990: 18; Knott 1991: 104; Berle 1993: 503; Edwards 1993; Subhash and Dharam 1995a: 151; *Economist*, Dec. 20, 1997: 25 ("new Russian"); Reader's Digest 1997: 168; Jhumor list, June 1, 1998 (Jewish yuppie); Keelan 1999: 256; Anon. 2001c: 230; Blue 2001: 94. The term "yuppie" for young urban professional was coined around 1980.

28. Knott 1990: 31 [= Knott 1990b: 42]; Grossman 1993: 54; 1995 Cal.: item 97 [= 1996 Cal.: Sept. 14 = 1997 Cal.: May 24]; 2002 Cal.: Feb. 5.

29. Hershfield 1964: 132; Hefley 1968: item 623; Baker 1986: item 348 (colleted 1970); Asimov 1971: 7; Playboy 1972: 70; Schock 1976: 68; Wilde 1977: 43; Wilde 1977: 111; Walker 1980: 64; Tiverton 1981: 18; Anon. 1986: 12; Cruickshank 1987: 63; Strangland 1987: 44; Blumenfeld and Blumenfeld 1977; Berle 1989: 297; Rovin 1991: 139; Warner 1993: 127; Subhash and Dharam 1995a: 253; Subhash and Dharam 1995c: 246; Adams and

Newall 1996a: 134; Pease 1996: 305; Cohl 1997: 450; Streiker 1998: 198; Brown 1998c: 21; Jhumor List, Dec. 3, 1998; Kenworth 1999: 155; Alvin 2000a: 25; Brunsting 2000: 175; Claro 2000: 136; Hobbes 2002b: 57.

30. Grossman 1993: 84. 1995 Calendar no. 102. Two slightly different renderings of this story appear in the *Million Laughs* collection, both identifying the lawyer as a "corporate lawyer." *AML* no. 699, no. 758.

31. In a notorious 1974 instance two lawyers in upstate New York were led by an accused murderer to two bodies, which they found and photographed but kept to themselves for six months, provoking an outpouring of public indignation and professional soul-searching. See Freedman 1975; Luban 1988.

32. Warner 1993: 169 [= *AML* 1993: no. 338]; *Nolo's Favorite* 1993; Alvin 1993: 83; Adams and Newall 1994: 265; CLLH. 1995: Lawyer humor no. 159 [= Adams & Newall 1995: 292]; Coote 1996: 31; Lawyer Jokes, Jan. 30, 1998 [= Streiker 1998: 259]; 2000 Cal.: July 24; Anon. 2000a: 113; Claro 2000: 61; Tiballs 2000: item 1141; Anon. 2001c: 227.

33. Akst and Landro 1988 (agent Michael Ovitz); Barry 1990: 23 (commodity trader); Tucket 1992: 75 (golfer); Berle 1993: 41 (agent); Keelan 1999: 195 (lawyer working as Hollywood agent); Blue 2001: 78.

34. Novak and Waldoks 1990: 106; Knott 1990: 2; Steiger 1990: 1; Behrman 1991: 19; Brallier 1992: 44; Rovin 1992: 4; Lowdown Disk 1992: item 103; 1996 Cal: Aug. 8; 1997 Cal.: June 17, Alan Lerner, e-mail message to author, Oct. 16, 1998.

35. Other displays of indifference to wives are Wilde 1987: 115; Grossman 1993: 111 [= *AML* 1993: no. 729]; 1995 Cal.: items 224, 346.

36. CLLH 1995: lawyer humor no. 11. Other lawyer versions are Wilde 1987: 10; Behrman 1991: 60; Rovin 1992: 26 [= *AML* 1993: no. 89]; 1996 Cal.: May 28 [= 1997 Cal.: Nov. 5]; Ross 1996: 59; Cohl 1997: 281.

37. The story is a variant of AT 809 (rich man allowed to stay in heaven for single deed of charity, sometimes repaid and sent to hell). Jewish versions are discussed by Schwartzbaum 1968: 160. The story surfaces in Anon. 1911: 12 (Wall Street broker); Masson 1922: 1:155 (rich miser); Cobb 1923: 197 (rich miser); Copeland and Copeland 1940: item 4613 (Wall Street broker); Berle [1945]: 71 (Wall Street broker); Kern 1949 [1947]: 171 (Wall Street broker); Murray 1954: 158 (millionaire); Cohen 1958: 82 (dress manufacturer); Gingras 1973: 127 (rich man); Morecroft [1974]: 60 (stock broker); McNeil 1989 [1962]: 130 (miser); Woods 1967: item 267.2 (miser); Spalding 1969: 48 (miser dress goods manufacturer); Rabinowitz 1986 [1973]: 221 (miser); Humes [1975]: 135 (prominent businessman); Bonfanti 1976: 80 (Italian); Yarwood 1981: 59 (stockbroker); Dickson 1984: 16 (stockbroker); Anon. 1987: 142 (businessman); Hill 1987: 26 (Ballymena man); Breslin 1991: 12 (Brian Mulroney) [= Colombo 2001: 04]; Stangland 1993: 26 (skinflint); Coote 1994: 414 (stingy man); Subhash and Dharam 1995c: 159 (millionaire); Singh 1996: 103 (wealthy man); Streiker 1998: 82 (stockbroker); FHM 2001: 102 (Manchester United fan).

38. Lawyer Jokes from Internet 1994: no. 152 [= e-mail from Richard Gordon, Feb. 20, 1997]; Behrman 1991: 50 [= *AML* 1993: no. 377]; anon. Stanford law student, Mar. 10, 1998; 2000 Cal.: Mar. 13; Greene 1999: 165; Lauren Edelman, e-mail message to author, May 18, 1999; Alan Dundes, e-mail, Nov. 5, 2001.

39. Neches 1926: 85 (rabbi anticipates line and extracts contribution from rich miser); Mendelsohn 1935: 107; Learsi 1941: 100; Grossman 1944: 38; Teitelbaum 1945: 229; Rywell 1960: 147; Learsi 1961: 195; Eilburt 1991: 223. All of these explicitly or possibly take place in the Old Country. The same *a fortiori* trope is present in Ferguson 1933: 127 (Scot tells

hotel porter if he didn't tip bonnie chambermaid "what sort o' chance dae ye think ye've got"). Americanization sets in with Levenson 1948: 68 (collector is United Jewish Appeal representative); Cerf 1959: 128; Youngman 1966: 114 [= Youngman 1968: 59 = Youngman 1976: 15]; Asimov 1971: 239; Alvin 1991: 38; Telushkin 1992: 169; Kramer 1994: 142; Jhumor List, Aug. 21, 1999. The Jewish element is effaced in Woods 1967: item 27.3; Murdock 1967: 22; Adams 1968: 233 [= Adams 1996: 155]; Adams 1970: 199; Playboy 1972: 159; Humes 1975: 56; Wilde 1976 (Republican): 42; Anon. 1988: 91; Rovin 1989: 199; Fraser 1992: 36.

40. In 1993, the Hart Survey found that 63 percent of respondents thought that lawyers "make too much money." Only 14 percent disagreed and 23 percent were neutral. Fifty-nine percent thought lawyers were greedy and only 19 percent disagreed (14). (Curiously, the pollsters found "no relationship between unfavorable opinions of lawyers and perceptions of how much lawyers earn." Peter D. Hart Research Associates 1993: 15.) Although there was wide variation in respondents' estimates of lawyers' earnings, the median guess of the public fell very close to the median revealed by a concurrent 1992 survey of ABA members' income (about $90,000).

41. I do not regard this as a joke about a "Jewish lawyer" for the Jewishness enters through the attribution of thoroughness to Jewish communal fundraising; the qualities displayed by the lawyer (rich, clever, self-serving) are exactly those attributed to lawyers in general and derive nothing from the lawyer's Jewishness.

42. Jhumor List, Dec. 8, 1997.

43. Along with *what's the catch?* (G16), this joke echoes the themes present in many of the jokes in chap. 6, which emphasize betrayal of those to whom there are special obligations.

44. Amy Singer, e-mail message to author, Apr. 20, 2000; Clode 1922: 228 (housewife); Anon. 2001a: 207 (Republican).

45. Collected from Nancy Reichman, Phoenix, AZ, June 1994. It took five years for this to turn up in print *as a lawyer joke.* Alvin 1999: 115; Tibballs 2000: item 1163; 2002 Cal.: Oct. 4. The story appeared earlier with other protagonists: Adams and Newall 1995: 196 (economist); Jhumor List, July 1, 1996 (rabbi); Adams and Newall 1996a: 135 (rabbi); Van Munching 1997: 108 (golfer); Pietsch 1998: 163 (golfer). The story seems to derive from an earlier story about a golf enthusiast who accepts the challenge of a blind golfer and asks when they tee off, to be told "Two o'clock in the morning." Wilde 1977: 124 [= Wilde 1988: 190] (attributed to Bob Hope); Simpson 1988: 116 (Bob Hope); E. Phillips [1993]: 55; Coote 1994: 175; Barnett and Kaiser 1996: 74; Anon. 2001b: 47.

46. Cf. the observations by Riesman 1954 in chap. 1, p. 46.

47. Knott 1990: 103. Other lawyers versions are Wilde 1987: 9 (also incompletely switched); Rovin 1992: 24; *AML* 1993: no. 86; 1995 Cal.: item 351.

48. Anon. (Anecdota) 1928: item 473 (bookkeeper); Ferguson 1933: 211; Cerf 1945a (partner in fruit business); Ford 1945: 184 (bookkeeper); Golden 1951: 244 (partner); Elgart 1954: 52 (bookkeeper); Masin 1956: 124 (football player); Cohen 1958: 83 (accountant); Anon. 1963 (bookkeeper) [= Anon. 1970a: 137; Roberts 1969: 29; Anon. 1970: 112 (accountant); Anon. 1971: item 208.50; Jessel 1973: 36 (accountant); Gardner 1982a: 47 (movie director).

49. Rovin 1987: 212; Wilde 1982: 83; Rafferty 1988: 64; Berle 1989: 542; Knott 1990: 69; Behrman 1991: 32; Breslin 1991: 49; Miller 1991: 114; Rovin 1992: 62 [= *AML* 1993: no. 141]; Rovin 1993: 45; Berle 1993: 324; Subhash and Dharam 1995c: 134; Adams 1996: 411; Lauren Edelman, e-mail message to author, May 11, 1999; Anon. 2000c: 278; Brunsting 2000: 244; 2002 Cal.: Sept. 2. One possible ancestor is a story attributed to a New York

entertainment lawyer who claimed to have attended a correspondence law school that insured that its graduates would be good lawyers by cheating them out of the last three lessons. "The student would sue them, and if he won the case, they sent him the diploma." Fredericks 1953: 194.

50. Knott 1995: 109 = Cohl 1997: 280; Wilde 1987: 111 (not divorce lawyer); Brallier 1992: 50. A nonlawyer version is Berle 1993: 445.

51. Collected by the author in Madison, WI, 1989. Also (in addition to the various versions in nn. 53, 55, 56, 57, 58, 60 below) Kinchen 1985: sec. 8, p. 2; Hunter and Weaver 1985; Blair 1985b; Blair 1985a (told by Attorney General Ed Meese to Kiwanis Club); Pietsch 1986: 25 [= AML 1993: no. 344]; Lyons 1987: 52 [= Lyons 1998: 65]; Rafferty 1988: 66; Lafee 1988; collected by Leslie Millett, Berkeley, CA, Sept. 30, 1988; Johnson 1989: 106 (attributed to Harvard Law Professor Martha Minow); Jones and Wheeler 1989: 12; Chariton 1989: 67; Steiger 1990: 42; Novak and Waldoks 1990: 106; Carman 1990: 5 (citing Barron's); Behrman 1991: 107; Jack Germond, "McLaughlin Group," Aug. 16, 1991; Adler 1992: 130 [= Adler 1994: 136]; Lowdown Disk 1992: item 454; Brallier 1992: 22; Warner 1992; Star Tribune, Apr. 6, 1992 (told by former Surgeon-General C. Everett Koop; reporter describes it as "well worn joke"); Nolo's Favorite 1993; AML 1993: no. 429; Metcalf 1993: 133; Berle 1993: 325; Nash et al. 1995: 167; 1997 Cal.: Feb. 23; Populus Jokes, Oct. 20, 1997; Cohl 1997: 276; Streiker 1998: 254; Lyons 1998a; Greene 1999: 164; Claro 2000: 60; Tibballs 2000: item 1162.

52. E.g., Alvin 1983: 31 (pig won't mate with Puerto Rican).

53. Strasser 1986: 6.

54. Taylor 1995: 25.

55. Nolo's Favorite 1993; Adams and Newall 1994: 268; CLLH 1995: lawyer humor no. 15, no. 42; Pease 1996: 28; 1998 Cal.: Apr. 25, Sept. 1; Dedopulos 1998: 239; Baddiel et al. 1999: 583; Southwell 1999: 304.

56. 1998 Cal.: Jan 13, Feb. 17, Mar. 21, Apr. 25, July 2, Aug. 15, Sept. 1, Oct. 12, Oct. 17, Dec. 28.

57. CLLH 1995: lawyer humor no. 15.

58. Randy's Favorite Lawyer Jokes.

59. Pierce 1995: 215–16.

60. Anon. 1986: 116; Times, Mar. 7, 1990; Financial Times, Jan. 4, 1991,: 1:14; Jerusalem Post, July 4, 1991; Johnstone 1992; South China Morning Post 1992; Fotheringham 1992: 88; Herald (Glasgow), July 12, 1993: 10; The Independent, Jan. 26, 1994: 15; Donaldson 1994: 15; Adams and Newall 1994: 268; Macleans, Dec. 5, 1994; Subhash and Dharam 1995a: 234 (politicians); Adams and Newall 1996: 12 (politicans); Ross 1996: 24; Pease 1996: 28.

61. Rodent 1995.

62. Glaberson 2000.

63. Washingtonian 1995.

64. Lyons 1987: 85 (Mexicans) [= Lyons 1998: 99]; Odean 1988: 141 (Wall Streeters); Alvin 1988: 10 (Polacks); Jones and Wheeler 1991: 87 (politicians as well as lawyers); Rovin 1991: 167 (hockey players); Adams and Newall 1995: 221 (symphonic conductors); Adams and Newall 1996: 12 (politicians); Marsh and Goldmark 1997: 1 (guitarists).

8. Lawyers as Objects of Scorn

1. Mensa Philosophica ca. 1475: no. 37. This story is Motif X317. The same theme is the opening cartoon sequence of Wiley 1993 (sympathetic crowd gathers about body lying in gutter, but disperses when his business card reveals he is a lawyer).

2. Johnson 1997: 88–89.

3. Pietsch 1986: 254; *Los Angeles Times,* Dec. 7, 1985; Wilde 1987: 135; Rafferty 1988: 8; Johnson 1989: 208; Knott 1990: 64; Novak and Waldoks 1990: 106; collected by Andrew Green, Berkeley, CA, October 30, 1990; collected by Paul C. Korn, Los Altos, CA, Nov. 23, 1990; Behrman 1991: 23; Lowdown Disk 1992: item 500; Adler 1992: 129; Rovin 1992: 74; Grossman 1993: 55; *Nolo's Favorite* 1993; Berle 1993: 154; Adler 1994: 138; Bachman 1995: 86; 1996 Cal.: Jan 15 [= 1997 Cal.: Jan 12]; Ross 1996: 89; Coote 1996: 306; Cohl 1997: 276; 1998 Cal.: Sept. 19; Baddiel and Stone 1997: 291; anon. informant at Center for Advanced Study in the Behavioral Sciences, Stanford, CA, Jan. 4, 1998; Lawyer Jokes, Jan. 30, 1998; anon. Stanford law student, Mar. 10, 1998; 2000 Cal.: Jan. 31; Greene 1999: 171, 172; Baddiel et al. 1999: 291; Anon. 2000c: 277; Mr. "K" 2001: 31. All of these are in riddle form, but one student collector encountered and transcribed an equivalent narrative: "Well, there was an insurance investigator that went to investigate an accident—actually there were two accidents, one in which a lawyer had been run over and another was a dog that had been run over. And, um, he got there after they had, uh, removed the, the carcasses and he was trying to sort out what had happened. And he said which one was—uh, which one was it where the—where was the, the accident where the lawyer was run over and which one was the dog. And the people said, well the one with the, where the dog was hit is the one where there was skid marks." Collected and transcribed by Storm Watkins, Berkeley, CA, Nov. 25, 1990.

It has occasionally been switched: Rovin 1989: 208 (IRS agent and pothole); Rovin 1991 (Howard Cosell and pothole); Knott 1992a: 49 (brunette and blonde); Coote 1995: 298 (politician and kangaroo); Coote 1996: 306 (same). Several of these appear to be heroic responses to the need to produce material for a topical book of jokes.

4. Rovin 1989: 165 (IRS agent); Rovin 1991: 253 (Howard Cosell); Knott 1992a: 49 (brunette); Coote 1995: 298 (politician); Southwell 1999: 303 (guitar player).

5. Collected by Dana Gerstein in Berkeley, CA, Nov. 2, 1990. During the following weeks, similar versions were collected by Anna Berge, Catherine Corten, and Rachel Gerstein.

6. Cantor 1943: 195 [= Adams 1968: 369]; Larsen 1980: 84 (Khrushchev hijacked). In earlier versions the recipient responded that he/she did not have the money but was interested in the proposition, counted on the kidnappers to do their part, etc. Croy 1948: 30 [1895]; Edmund and Williams 1916: 296; Johnston 1922: item 1682; Schermerhorn 1928: 123; Lurie 1928: 69; Ernst 1930: 100; Fuller 1942: 159; Meier 1944: 226; Cerf 1945a: 90; Levenson 1948: 105; Adams 1953 [1952]: 109; Powes 1973; Dines 1987: 123; Hochwald [1994]: 41.

7. Gulf War versions: Adler 1992: 97; Knott 1992.

8. Brallier 1996: 47; CLLH 1995: riddles no. 57; Ross 1996: 65; Populus: Jokes, Oct. 14, 1997; Streiker 1998: 261; Alvin 1999a: 83; Greene 1999: 167; Baddiel et al. 1999: 587; Michael Saks, e-mail message to author, Jan. 10, 2000; Tibballs 2000: item 1167.

9. Warner 1993: 177; Steiger 1990: 31; Johnson 1991: item 366; Rovin 1992: 137; Grossman 1993: 118; Bachman 1995: 87; Brallier 1996: 35; 1997 Cal.: Aug. 7; Cohl 1997: 282; 1998 Cal.: Apr. 20; Populus Jokes, Dec. 20, 1997; Lawyer Jokes, Jan. 30, 1998; Streiker 1998: 257; Greene 1999: 169; 2000 Cal.: Dec. 6; Tibballs 2000: item 1134; Tapper and Press 2000: 168.

10. Wilde 1977a: 160; Spalding 1978: 316 (mayo men); Pietsch 1986: 162. Cf. Phillips 1974a: 95 (sheep come down from mountain because of smell of Smogarian). The theme is shared with this bit of late nineteenth-century Mormon antidrink propaganda: "In one

gutter I saw a pig; in another the semblance of a man. The pig was sober; the man was drunk. The pig had a ring in its nose; the other animal had one on his finger. The pig grunted, so did the man, and I said, aloud, 'We are known by the company we keep.' The pig heard me and walked away, ashamed to be seen in the company of a drunken man." Smith 1982: 124 (reproducing *Autumn Leaves,* Sept. 1890); also Williams 1926 (rhyming version).

11. Anon. 1988a: 64 (fund raiser); Berle 1993: 397 (politician); B. Phillips 1994 (politician); Coote 1995: 14 [= Coote 1995: 98 = Coote 1996: 2] (Australian); Adams and Newall 1995: 190 (economist); Pease 1996: 358 (Frenchman); Adams and Newall 1996: 42 (Australian premier Paul Keating); Jhumor List, May 26, 1998 (Bill Clinton); Simon Chapman, e-mail message to author, Nov. 10, 1998; Brown 1998a: 43 (Scotsman); Southwell 1999: 171 (Baptist); Colombo 2001: 254 (Newfie).

12. Levine 1994: 17; Rovin 1992: 80; *Nolo's Favorite* 1993; 1996 Cal.: Sept. 4; CLLH 1995: riddles no. 81; CLLH 1995: riddles no. 84; Brallier 1996: 43; 1997 Cal.: May 31; Ross 1996: 94; 1998 Cal.: Oct 18; Pietsch 1998: 266; Alvin 1999: 95; Tibballs 2000: item 1181.

13. Stokker 2000: 340 (Norwegian joke about Quisling during World War II occupation); Braude 1958: 54 (Balkan communist politician); Hershfield 1964: 23 (Mussolini); Peterson 1976: 87 (unnamed dictator); Orso 1979: 7 (Papadopoulos); Beckman 1980: 79 (Novotny); Zand 1982: 32 (Brezhnev); Raskin 1985: 226 (1970s joke about Israeli politician); Ruksenas 1986: 11 (Stalin); Rabinowitz 1986 [1973]: 48 (Hitler); Seigal 1987: 423 (Zia); Lukes and Galnoor 1987: 143 (Papadopoulos); Rovin 1989: 209 (Mussolini); Phillips 1990: 75 (Hitler); Anon. 1997d: 47 (Rákosi); Martling 1997: 87 (Al Sharpton); Gordon Baldwin, e-mail message to author, Aug. 24, 1998 (Bill and Hilary Clinton); Dale and Simmons 1999: 60 (Tony Blair); Alvin 1999a: 69 (Louis Farrakhan); Colombo 2001: 89 (Trudeau).

14. Rovin 1992: 103; 1997 Cal.: Feb. 6.

15. Luric 1928: 9 (army captain); Ernst 1930: 12 (naval officer); Raskin 1985: 226 (1930s German, Hitler); Wortsman 1963: 9 (Bobby Kennedy); Winick 1964: 60 (Stalin); Braude 1964: item 47 (naval officer); Blumenfeld 1965: 64 (Nasser); Asimov 1971: item 322 (Hitler); Rabinowitz 1986 [1973]: 204 (Sadat); Wilde 1976: 90 (Nixon); Benton and Loomes 1977 [1976]: 74 (Franco); Parker 1978 (mayor of city); Pollack 1979: 152 (Nasser) [= Triverton 1981: 277]; Larson 1980: 48 (Hitler); Lukes and Galnoor 1987: 143 (Franco); Berle 1989: 429 (Hitler); MacHale 1983a: 21 (Margaret Thatcher); Kilbirt 1991: 187 (Hitler); Breslin 1991 (Brian Mulroney); Yermonee 1992 (Robert Maxwell); Faine 1994: 12 (Paul Keating); B. Phillips 1994 (Clinton); Adams and Newall 1995: 182 (Clinton); e-mail from Lawrence G. Kahn, Nov. 11, 1996 (Clinton); Coote 1996: 308 (Clinton); Jhumor, Nov. 23, 1997 (Arafat); Streiker 1998: 308 (Clinton); Dale and Simmons 1998: 9 (same); Symons 1998: 22 (same); Jan Hoem, e-mail message to author, Apr. 4, 1999 (same); Dale and Simmons 1999: 24 (Tony Blair); Columbo 2001: 94 (Trudeau).

16. See A34, A48, A49, A50.

17. Kieffer 1923: 139; Anon. 1905: 103; Aye 1931: 66 (told as anecdote about Plowden, as in text above); Braude 1955: item 1430; Wilde 1982: 51; Philips 1990: 87; Anon. 1997a: 149.

18. *Green Bag* 18: 259 (1906) (actor); Morton and Malloch 1913: 97 (told as anecdote about minstrel George Clarke); Edwards 1915: item 737 (minstrel); Heighton 1916: 218 (Clarke); Scruggs 1927: item 260 (minstrel); Hershfield 1932: 85 ("blueblood lawyer" browbeats calciminer); Hershfield 1938: 83 (hod carrier); Lupton 1938: item 1381 (Clarke minstrel anecdote); Hershfield 1964: 77 (calciminer); Adams 1968: 344 (smuggler); Golden

1972: 55 (stripper); Marquand 1977: 152 (day laborer); Triverton 1981: 81 (ditchdigger); Wilde 1982: 74 (short-order cook); Wilde 1987: 27 (bricklayer); Adler 1992: 37 (stripper). The only switch out of the lawyer category is Berle 1993: 143 (garbageman challenging congressman says father was "cheap politician").

19. Wilde 1987: 13; Pietsch 1986: 25; Chariton 1989: 68 (bumper sticker); Knott 1987: 171 [= Knott 1990: 33]; Rovin 1992: 19; Adler 1992: 90; *Nolo's Favorite* 1993; Berle 1993: 107; CLLH 1995: lawyer humor no. 6; Ross 1996: 47; Alvin 1998a: 40; Tibballs 2000: item 1174. A mail order house specializing in merchandise for lawyers offered a sign with the inscription "Please don't tell my mother I'm a lawyer. She thinks I play the piano at the local bordello." For Counsel, Product and Gift Catalog 1997: 18.

20. Benton and Loomes 1977 [1976]: 136 [= Lukes and Galnoor 1987: 21] (Hungarian secret police major); Walker 1981: 103 (philosophy chair).

21. Odean 1988: 18 (bond salesman); Tucket 1992: 11 ("Don't tell my mother I'm in politics. She thinks I'm a prostitute"); Faine 1994: 47 (politician); Marsh and Goldmark 1997: 57 (record company). Curiously, a very similar joke with a longer history in the U.S. has not been enlisted as a lawyer joke. That is the story about the person with a long list of discreditable traits or associations who asks whether he is obligated to tell his fiancée about this brother or cousin who is a Republican (or whatever). Youngman 1963: 58 (used car dealer); Dundes and Pagter 1975: 15 (Republican); Tomlinson 1991: 201 (Democrat); Coote 1996: 4 ("Pom," i.e., Englishwoman, in this case).

22. Knott 1990: 53; Wilde 1987: 139; Behrman 1991: 45; Brallier 1992: 14; Rovin 1992: 151; Humes 1993: 104; *Nolo's Favorite* 1993; Faine 1994: 76; Ross 1996: 83; Alvin 1998a: 39.

23. Burma 1946: 713.

24. CLLH 1995: lawyer humor no. 99.

25. Rafferty 1988: 54; Newman 1987 (queers); *Maledicta* 10: 299 (1988); collected by Kim Nguyen, Berkeley, CA, Oct. 15, 1990; Novak and Waldoks 1990: 105; Knott 1990: 74; Behrman 1991: 102; Rovin 1992: 75; Lowdown Disk 1992: item 504; Adler 1994: 136; Bachman 1995: 86; 1996 Cal.: Apr. 3 [= 1997 Cal.: Nov. 14]; CLLH 1995: riddle no. 80; Streiker 1998: 258; Green 1999: 168; 2000 Cal.: Aug. 28; Claro 2000: 61; Anon. 2000a: 112; Tibballs 2000: item 1184.

26. Clements 1969 [1968]: 44 (Negroes chosen over Polacks); Larkin 1975: 102 (blacks chosen over Italians); Dalton 1982: 25 (Frenchmen chosen over North Dakotans); Knott 1983a: 27 (earthquakes chosen over blacks); Wilde 1984: 126 (mules chosen over Swedes); Thickett 1984: 58 (herpes chosen over real estate agents); Barry 1990: 147 (earthquakes chosen over blacks); Shocked and Harted 1992: 22 (toxic dumps chosen over stock brokers); Lyons 1998a: 63 (earthquake chosen over blacks).

27. The single exception is an Australian version (Ross 1996: 98) (flies).

28. *Nolo's Favorites* 1993; Knott 1990: 66; Adler 1992: 105; Brallier 1992: 101; 1996 Cal.: Apr. 4 [= 1997 Cal.: Apr. 23 = 1998 Cal.: Nov. 23]; Kahn and Boe 1997: 176; 2000 Cal.: Apr. 28; Tibballs 2000: item 1188.

29. Cerf 1959: 331 (sage); Wachs 1968: 154 (wise man); Draitser 1978: 73 (Brezhnev); Zand 1982 (same); Dickson 1984: 20 (senator); Ben Eliezer [1984] (rabbi); Terrell and Buchanan 1984: 136 (politician); Ruksenas 1986: 102 (Khruschev); Davidson [1988]: 61 (sage); Berle 1989: 311 (umpire); Breslin 1991: 103 (Brian Mulroney); Delf 1992: 109 (rabbi); MacHale 1991: 41 (Irishman); Topol [1994]: 248 (rabbi); Bar-Lev and Weis 1996: 35 (Sammy Davis Jr.); Goldstein-Jackson 1996: 45 (clergyman); Reginald 1997: 190 (same); Kostick et al. 1998: 432 (same); Southwell 1999: 173 (politician); Colombo 2001: 94 (Trudeau); Blue 2001: 81 (rabbi).

30. Veall 1970: 202, 208.

31. Anon. 1822: 248; Merryman 1853: 346; Hupfeld [1871]: 103.

32. Grossman 1993: 56 (old lawyer retires to snake farm to be among friends); Grossman 1993: 59 (zoo director summons lawyer to retrieve escaped snakes because "you need someone who speaks their language"); 1995 Cal.: item 125 (difference of snake and lawyer is that snake keeps dropping [shedding?] his briefcase); 1995 Cal.: item 127 (retire to snake farm); Funny Times fax from Bill Breslin, Apr. 25, 1995 ("you don't know difference either?"); Brallier 1996: 5 (crossing snake with lawyer is incest).

33. 1996 Cal.: May 11 [= 1997 Cal.: May 5]; Rafferty 1988: 29; Knott 1990: 71 [= Knott 1990b: 89 = Knott 1991: 95]; Steiger 1990: 6; Adler 1992: 99 [= Adler 1994: 102]; Delf 1992: 84; Grossman 1993: 17; Humes 1993: 107; CLLH 1995: lawyer humor no. 66; Brallier 1996: 38; Albert Alshuler, e-mail message to author, May 23, 1997; Cohl 1997: 277; Van Munching 1997: 106; Greene 1999: 161.

34. Only a few nonlawyer versions have appeared: Knott 1993: 63 (Puerto Rican); Adams and Newall 1995: 223 (conductor); Pietsch 1998: 54 (record company executive).

35. Rovin 1992: 52; Ignelzi 1992; Grossman 1993: 48; Nolo's Favorite 1993; 1996 Cal.: Oct. 20; Brallier 1996: 39. This version was earlier applied to blacks: Knott 1991: 28; Alvin 1997: 103.

36. 1995 Cal.: item 30; 1996 Cal.: Apr. 28; 1997 Cal.: Oct. 31; 1997 Cal.: Nov.16.

37. Lynne Henderson, e-mail message to author, Aug. 8, 1994; Bachman 1995: 86; 1996 Cal.: Aug. 31; Rees 1995: 145; 1997 Cal.: Aug. 3; Ross 1996: 68; Baddiel and Stone 1997: 27; Marsh and Goldmark 1997: 56 (concert promoter); anon. informant at Center for Advanced Study in the Behavioral Sciences, Jan. 14, 1998; Dedopulos 1998; Pietsch 1998: 143; Greene 1999: 171; Keelan 1999: 209; Alvin 1999: 105; Baddiel et al. 1999: 587; Tibballs 2000: item 1142. A "bloke" version is at Johnson 2000: 120.

38. See "Why Death Wish Jokes Flourish" in chap. 9.

39. Grossman 1993: 12; Warner 1992; Berle 1993: 325; Ross 1996: 93; Pease 1996: 27; Barnett and Kaiser 1996: 89. Cf. 1998 Cal.: Feb. 10 (female lawyer "slimy and has whiskers," etc.); 2000 Cal.: Mar. 27 (jellyfish); Tibballs 2000: item 1143 (haddock). Other applications include Bill Clinton (Dale and Simmons 1998: 41) and blokes (Dedopulos 1998: 171; Hobbes 2002a: 31). The same form is used in a comparison of a lawyer to a vampire bat ("One's a diseased, bloodsucking predator and the other is a mouselike creature with wings" 1997 Cal.: Oct. 27).

40. Ross Cheit, e-mail message to author, Dec. 15, 1998; Lisa Lerman, e-mail, Nov. 5, 1999; Deja News Viagra jokes, Feb. 5, 1999; Alan Dundes, e-mail, Aug. 26, 2001; Sarah Galanter, e-mail, Aug. 28, 2001. A bloke version is at Johnson 2001: 121.

41. Lawyer Jokes from Internet 1994: no. 101.

42. Asimov 1971: item 578; Wilde 1979a: 209; Gardner 1982: 36; Pietsch 1986: 158; Rovin 1987: 243; Lyons 1987: 26; Lanigan 1988: 77; Novak and Waldoks 1990: 301; Berle 1993: 41; Adams and Newall 1995: 55; Barnett and Kaiser 1996: 108–9 (genie's defective lamp produces ducks instead of bucks, etc.); Lyons 1998: 38; Keelan 1999: 91; Anon. 2001c: 26; FHM 2001: 31 (ducks); Hobbes 2002a: 153; Jan Hoem, e-mail message to author, Apr. 5, 2002 (ducks, 12-inch Bic).

43. Rafferty 1988: 30; Steiger 1990: 31; Lowdown Disk 1992: item 532; Brallier 1992: 11; Rovin 1992: 6; Grossman 1993: 92; Nolo's Favorite 1993; 1996 Cal.: Jan 11 [= 1997 Cal.: June 30]; Populus Jokes, Dec. 31, 1997; Greene 1999: 166. This seems to be a switch from a riddle: "Why don't their mothers let little black kids play in the sandbox?" Knott 1983: 112; Aman 1983: 294; Lyons 1987: 67 [= Lyons 1998: 82].

44. Lawyer Jokes from Internet 1994: no. 80; collected by Thomas Hunt in Moraga, CA, Oct. 11, 1988; *Maledicta* 10: 299 (1988–89); *AML* 1993: no. 606; Alvin 1995a: 9; 1998 Cal.: June 16; Richard M. Jaeger, e-mail message to author, Apr. 23, 1998; Alvin 1998a: 39; Dedopulos 1998: 215; Baddiel et al. 1999: 559; Mr. "K" 2001: 97; Pritchard 2002: 45. Cf. Adams and Newall 1995: 268 (same answer to child's question "Do prostitutes have babies?")

45. Legman 1968: 599 [1953] (bartenders, second lieutenants). More frequently the question was about birth from prostitutes rather than *ex ano:* Anon. 1961: n.p. (bartenders); Woods 1967: item 41.10 (traveling salesmen); Wilde 1975b: 90 (bartenders); Shumaker 1983: 105; Adams and Newall 1995: 224 (conductors); Goldstein-Jackson 1996: 114; Baddiel and Stone 1997: 106; Baddiel et al. 1999: 106; Tibballs 2000: item 389.

46. Knott 1990: 71.

47. Kelly 1906: 120 (Irishman); Fredericks 1953: 85 (Texans); Legman 1975 [1954]: 964; Anon. 1963 (Texan); Legman 1975 [1966]: 963 (Texan); Wilde 1976: 2 (Texas conservative politician); Mr. "J" 1979: 79 (Texan); Knott 1983a: 115 (Texan); Gurney 1986 (Australian); Knott 1988: 30 (Irishman); Duncan 1990: 139 (Texan); Dover and Fish 1992 (Robert Maxwell); Trevor 1992: 85 (Australian); Adams and Newall 1996: 350 (Australian); Adams and Newall 1996a: 146 (Australian politician Russ Hinze); Goldstein-Jackson 1996: 25; Colombo 2001: 123 (Ontario premier Mike Harris).

48. Knott 1991: 106.

49. Rovin 1992: 152.

50. CLLH 1995: riddle no. 83; Pease 1996: 27; 1998 Cal.: Mar. 27.

51. Collected by Andrew Green, Berkeley, CA, Oct. 30, 1990; Lowdown Disk 1992: item 501; 1995 Cal.: item 271; CLLH 1995: riddles no. 25; Ross 1996: 92; Alvin 1998a: 41; Greene 1999: 171; 2000 Cal.: June 28. Nonlawyer versions include Legman 1975 [1965]: 963 (Polack/Texan); Clements 1969: 14 [1968] (Polack); Knott 1983: 112 (mother-in-law); Thickett 1986: 48 (Libyan); Rovin 1987: 238 (mother-in-law); Knott 1990a: 2 (Pole); Dover and Fish 1992 (Robert Maxwell); Alvin 1994: 36 (Iraqi); Lyons 1999a: 111 (Libyan); Kuipers 2000: 166 (Turk in Netherlands).

52. *Nolo's Favorites* 1993 [= 1998 Cal.: Feb. 24]; 1997 Cal.: Mar. 4; Alvin 1999b: 13; Alvin 2001a: 32. Nonlawyer versions include Clements 1969: 14 [1968] (Polack); Knott 1983: 17 (black); Stangland 1987: 30 (Norwegian); Pietsch 1998: 112 (Hollywood agent); Lyons 1998a: 65 (Negro kid); Kuipers 2000: 161 (Negro in Netherlands).

53. CLLH 1995: lawyer humor no. 84; Grossman 1993: 98; *AML* 1993: no. 716; 1995 Cal.: item 339; CLLH 1995: lawyer humor no. 172; Brallier 1996: 59; Jhumor list, May 21, 1996; Southwell 1999: 48; Tibballs 2000: item 1169; Regan 2001: 253.

54. Legman 1975 [1963]: 963 (Texan); Wilde 1975: 98 (Pole); Brodnick 1976: 26 (Jew); Alvin 1983a: 50 (Mexican); Knott 1986: 108 (blacks); Lyons 1987: 99 [= Lyons 1998: 116] (African); Knott 1989: 38 (African); Coote 1995: 13 (Australian) [= Coote 1995: 98 = Coote 1996: 19]; Pease 1996: 131 (Englishman).

55. O'Neal and O'Neal 1964: 86. In Herron and Ivy (2000: 127) the dog "is a professional trained dog against politicians."

56. CLLH 1995: lawyer humor no. 161. A slightly modified version is at Adams and Newall 1995: 293.

57. In early versions, the subject, advised to quit show business, objects "I'm a big star." Cerf 1956: 20; McCarthy 1962: 105; Blumenfeld 1970: 26. The standard punch line arrives in a version about a Kennedy aide assigned to care for pet animals who asks "What? And give up politics?" Wortsman 1963: 19. Asimov 1971: item 22; Legman 1975 [1973]: 941; Kowalski 1974: 105; Scott 1984: 68; Wilde 1985: 128; Berle 1989: 363; Knott

1989: 109 [= Knott 1990b: 123]; Forbes 1990: 46; Claro 1996: 84; Dunn 1996: 71; Barnett and Kaiser 1996: 221; Cohl 1997: 493; Menchin 1997: 32; Martling 1997: 91; Baddiel and Stone 1997: 304; Keelan 1999: 111. Cf. Braude 1964: item 309 (despondent tramp won't seek job thus admitting he's a failure).

58. House counsel are present in J4 and J13.

59. Marks 1996: 69.

60. Luntz 1996?: 128–29 (emphasis in original). According to a report in *Roll Call*, "House Republicans and like-minded interest groups are listening." Eilperin and Vande Hei 1997. One "GOP source" was quoted as saying, "We'll unleash an attack on the trial lawyers never seen before. . . . The time is right to move from kicking the unions to hitting the lawyers." Eilperin and Vande Hei 1997.

61. Donohue 1997.

62. W. Miller 1997: 105. As it emerged the antilawyer campaign generated some misgivings, leading Donohue to specify that his problem was only with half of 1 percent of the nation's lawyers. Carter 1998: 70, 72.

9. "A Good Start!" Death Wish Jokes

1. E. Phillips 1989: 25. The guinea, an English gold coin minted until 1813, valued at twenty-one shillings, was replaced by the sovereign (pound), valued at twenty shillings, in 1817. But the guinea lived on as an honorific unit of measure for professional fees, race horses, works of art, landed property, and other transactions transcending commerce.

2. John Toler, Lord Norbury (1745–1831), chief justice of the Irish Court of Common Pleas from 1800 to 1827, was known as a "hanging judge" who "spared not his coarse jests to dying men." Engelbach 1915: 196.

3. Norbury (not always named) is the speaker in most instances: Lemon 1864: 193; Anon. 1867: 53; Hood et al. 1873: 292; Hazlitt 1886: 153; Willock 1887: 408; Burnette 1903: 465; Mosher 1922: 296; Knox 1926: 138; Milburn 1927: 22; Copeland 1936: 236; Eastman 1936: 21; Fuller 1942: item 2528; Spalding 1978: 202; Yarwood [1981]: 75; Wilde 1982: xii; Sortor 1989: 65; E. Phillips 1989: 25; Asimov 1992: 56; Brallier 1992: 59; Rovin 1992: 132; *AML* 1993: no. 251; CLLH 1995: lawyer humor no. 12; Ross 1996: 17; Dedopulos 1998: 236 [= Baddiel et al. 1999: 580]; Regan 2001: 160.

The joke predates the Norbury attribution. The earliest recorded cause of such expansiveness was a barrister's worry about the increased number of practitioners (Carrick et al. 1850: 178; Anon. 1867: 53). Later it was the eagerness of barristers to bury attorneys, i.e., solicitors (Engelbach 1913: 87; Aye 1931: 15).

4. Werner 1893: 248 (college porter, Dutch); Anon. 1913: 15 (police force); Edwards 1915: item 181 (bailiff); Schermerhorn 1928: 284 (politician); Meier 1944: 190 (violinist); Boliska [1966]: 27 (politician); Adams 1968: 198 (agent); Wachs 1968: 311 (hobo: take four friends away); Tulk 1971: 73 (Newfie: take four more); Baker 1985: 123 (Kentuckian in Indiana, collected 1973); Powers 1973 (doctor); Larkin 1975: 127 (Puerto Rican); Adams 1975: 146 (generic); Benton and Loomes 1977 [1976]: 12 (foreman); Kravitz 1977: 294 (Pakistani); Hornby 1977: 80 (Englishman); Wilde 1977a: 122 (Pole); Wilde 1981a: 161 (doctor); MacHale 1983a: 12 [= MacHale 1989: 20] (labor MP); Wilde 1984: 120 (Republican); Forster 1986 (doctors); Bonham and Gullidge 1989: 42 (doctor); Knott 1990a: 19 (Nigerian); Miller 1991: 9 (rap musician); Miller 1991: 10 (mother-in-law); Phillips 1994: 29 (foreman); B. Phillips 1994 (Democrat); Mital and Gupta 1995: 149 (politician); Adams and Newall 1995: 195 (economist); Wilde 1997: 100 (doctor); Bonham and Gulledge 1997: 28 (doctor).

5. Landon 1883: 385. Other stories about bounties for killing undesirables are Ginger 1974: 34 (Swede); Scott 1984: 20 (politician).

6. Sprague 1895: 101.

7. Hupfeld [1871]: 91. This is tale-type AT 1534A. Motif J2233.1.1. It appears in Kishtani 1985: 54 (citing Ibn Mammati [d. 1209], hang cage-maker, spare smith); Copley [1614] in Zall 1970: 11 (hang weaver, spare smith); K . . . 1791: 112 (same); Hood et al. 1873: 81; Freud [1905] 1960: 206 (hang tailor, spare smith); Lurie 1927: 145 (hang weaver, spare smith); Richman 1952: 268 (hang tailor, spare cobbler); Kumove 1985: 144 (same, condensed in reference to "Kulikov trial").

8. Chariton 1989: 73.

9. Shafer and Papadakis 1988: 5.

10. Clode 1922: 64; Mosher 1922: 367; Lawson 1923: 208; Lurie 1928: 273; Johnson et al. 1936: 157; Dionne ca. 1939: 143; Anon. [ca.1941]; Fuller 1942: item 1956; Knox ca.1943: 41; Rango 1944: 39 (daughter wants boyfriend to replace her father's partner); Esar 1945: 370; Lehr et al. 1948: 206 (bystander wants apartment); Fredericks 1953: 112; Braude 1958: item 919; Walser 1974: 150 [1967 item]; Adams 1970: 273; Phillips 1974a: 81; Shelley 1976: 42; Wilde 1976: 13 (Republican); Pendleton [1979]: item 331; Bonham 1981: 114; Rossiter 1981: 144 (told as anecdote about Woodrow Wilson and would-be senatorial appointee); Terrell and Buchanan 1984: 83; Claro 1990: 67 [= Claro 1996: 84]; Tomlinson 1991: 214 (Wilson anecdote); Delf 1992: 145; Warner 1993: 182; E. Phillips 1994: 84; Adams 1996: 238 (daughter's boyfriend); E. Phillips 1996: 88; Goldstein-Jackson 1996: item 357; Baddiel and Stone 1997: 342; Kostick et al. 1998: 208; Brown 1998b: 81; Dole [1998]: 33 (Wilson anecdote); Baddiel et al. 1999: 342; Anon. 2000a: 144.

11. Hershfield 1958: 93; Adams 1968: 395; Shafer and Papadakis 1988: 5; Brallier 1992: 8; 1996 Cal.: Feb. 3; 1998 Cal. Nov. 26; Regan 2001: 74.

12. Braude 1964: item 584; Adams 1970: 273 (President Roosevelt); MacHale 1978: 38 (English construction job already given to fellow who pushed him); Claro 1990: 155 [= Claro 1996: 181] (Lincoln); Phillips 1993: 67 (English mine job given to fellow who pushed him); Phillips 1994: 27 (English factory job given to fellow who pushed him); Dunn 1996: 32 (scarce room let to gentlemen who pushed her in). This seems to be that rare instance in which the English version is more violent than the American.

13. Pietsch 1986: 155; Rafferty 1988: 70; Conners 1989; Knott 1990: 67; Steiger 1990: 11; Phillips 1990: 87; collected by Andrew Green, 1990; collected by Jerry Salzman, 1990; Behrman 1991: 114; *Nolo's Favorite* 1993; Adler 1994: 136; 1996 Cal: June 3; CLLH 1995: riddle no. 18; Brallier 1996: 73; 1997 Cal.: Oct. 9; Ross 1996: 89; Kahn and Boe 1997: 175; Lawyer Jokes, Jan. 30, 1998; Lyons 1998: 63 (entertainment lawyers); Alvin 1999: 94; 2000 Cal.: Apr. 13; Anon. 2000a: 112; Claro 2000: 61; Tibballs 2000: item 1176.

14. Rovin 1989: 165 (IRS auditor); Phillips 1990: 81 (same); Rovin 1991: 253 (Howard Cosell); Dover and Fish 1992 (Robert Maxwell); Theaker 1997: 53 (conductors), 82 (banjo players). Cf. Pease 1996: 82 ("What do you call ten accountants buried up to their necks in sand? Soccer practice.").

15. Rafferty 1988: 14.

16. *Maledicta* 6: 311 (1982) (feminists); Knott 1983: 112 (blacks); Thickett 1986: 46 (Iranians); Dundes 1987: 80 (JAPs, collected 1985).

17. Phillips 1990: 87; Shapiro 1993: 264 (citing 1982 source); collected by Kim Nguyer, Hilary Ivancovich, Mark Caudill, Amy M. Emrich, Melinda Van der Reis, Meegan Amen, all in 1990; Behrman 1991: 14; Adler 1992: 131 [= Adler 1994: 137]; Brallier 1992: 57; Rovin 1992: 22; Grossman 1993: 20; Nick Larsen 1994; Alvin 1995a: 13; Bachman 1995: 86; Funny

Times 1995 (May): 3 (5000 lawyers in unemployment office); 1996 Cal.: Jan 1; Rees 1995: 145; Coote 1995: 226; Barnett and Kaiser 1996: 89; anon. informant at Center for Advanced Study in the Behavioral Sciences, Jan. 1998; anon. Stanford law student, Mar. 10, 1998; Lawyer Jokes, Jan. 30, 1998; Tibballs 2000: item 1129.

18. Rovin 1991: 253 (sportscasters); Barnett and Kaiser 1996: 138 (men); Two Fun Guys 1997 (accountants); Marsh and Goldmark 1997: 26 (harmonicas); Theaker 1997: 67 (baritones).

19. Phillips 1990: 87.

20. Before the lawyer version appeared in print in 1989 (Chariton 1989: 71), the bus was occupied by Pakistanis (for Enoch Powell [Kravitz 1977: 294]) or trade unionists (for Margaret Thatcher [MacHale 1983a: 9 = MacHale 1989: 14]). It resembles, and may have derived from, an earlier story about the difference between a misfortune and a calamity (Disraeli answers, "Well, if Gladstone fell into the Thames, it would be a misfortune. But if anybody dragged him out, ah! *that* would be a calamity!" Henry 1948: 170). It has flourished as a lawyer joke: Collected by Paul Korn, Nov. 23, 1990; Low Down Disk 1992: item 528 (difference between a pity and a shame); Brallier 1992: 34; Adler 1992: 131 = Adler 1994: 138; Metcalf 1993: 133; Grossman 1993: 11; 1996 Cal: Apr. 2; CLLH 1995: riddle no. 26 (difference between a shame and a crying shame); Barnett and Kaiser 1996: 89; Ross 1996: 94 (two versions turning on difference between shame and crying shame); anon. informant at Center for Advanced Study in the Behavioral Sciences, Jan. 14, 1998; Pietsch 1998: 42. The Disraeli-Gladstone story is still around: Claro 1996: 141 (Mario Cuomo says of Al D'Amato . . .).

21. Grossman 1993: 139; Nolo News 1988 [= *Nolo's Favorites* 1993]; *AML* 1993: no. 820; 1995 Cal.: item 18 [= 1996 Cal.: Mar. 28 = 1997 Cal.: July 27 = 1998 Cal.: Nov. 19]; Ross 1996: 84; Cohl 1997: 281; Alvin 1999b: 108; Keelan 1999: 206; Anon. 2000a: 119 (caller is former junior); Tibballs 2000: item 1180; Regan 2001: 162.

22. Lurie 1928: 221.

23. Periodicals: Beckman 1969: 65 [= Beckman 1980: 55]; Lipman [1991]: 96 (Nazi papers); Davies 1998: 99 (collected 1981); Jhumor List, July 9, 2000. Resignation: Bermant 1986: 161; Jhumor List, July 17, 1988 (rabbi); Hochwald [1994]: 130 (Ben Gurion).

24. Draitser 1998 (Stalin, collected 1953); Benton and Loomes 1977 [1976]: 106.

25. Shinkler 1993: 53 (bank manager); Coote 1995: 146 (same); Adams and Newall 1995: 221 (conductor); Adams & Newall 1996: 75 (bank manager); Theaker 1997: 56 (conductor); Marsh and Goldmark 1997: 38 (band leader); Southwell 1999: 70 (stockbroker); Mason 2001: 190 (bank manager); Colombo 2001: 399 (CBC producer).

26. Grossman 1993: 35 [= *AML* 1993: no. 650]; 1995 Cal.: item 63.

27. Pietsch 1998: 42. Cf. Anon. 2000: 11 (black doctors, white patient, in Capetown).

28. B. Phillips 1994 (liberal democrats); Two Fun Guys 1997 (accountants); Marsh and Goldmark 1997: 36 (Tupac); Theaker 1997: 30 (trumpet players); Theaker 1997: 52 (conductors).

29. Lowdown Disk 1992: item 460; Steiger 1990: 8; Phillips 1990: 86; collected by Lucy Leong, Oct. 29, 1990; Adler 1992: 129; collected from Eve Galanter, 1995; 1996 Cal: Oct 10; CLLH 1995: riddle no. 9; Coote 1995: 226; Brallier 1996: 48; 1997 Cal: Apr. 4; Pease 1996: 26; Kahn and Boe 1997: 174; Greene 1999: 171; Keelan 1999: 205; Alvin 1999a: 82; Tibballs 2000: item 1157; 2002 Cal.: Apr. 5. A few musician versions have appeared: Marsh and Goldmark 1997: 36; Theaker 1997: 30; Theaker 1997: 52.

30. Milburn 1926: 42 (Jew becomes Christian); Schnur 1945: 46 (Jew becomes Christian); Richman 1952: 351 (Jew becomes Mohammedan); Randolph 1967: 7 (Democrat

becomes Republican); Anon. 1970: 29 (Labour man becomes Conservative); Wilde 1975: 49 (Catholic becomes Protestant); Skubik and Short 1976: 132 (Republican becomes Democrat); Benton and Loomes 1977 [1976]: 43 (Irish Catholic becomes Orangeman); Schock 1976: 95 (man becomes Communist); Hornby 1977: 35 (Irish Catholic becomes Protestant); Gurney 1985: 13 (Irish Catholic becomes Mason); Pietsch 1986: 1 (Irish Catholic becomes Protestant); Knott 1987: 98 [= Knott 1990b: 93] (same); Lukes and Galnoor 1987: 34 (same); Rovin 1989: 238 (same); Eilbirt 1991: 204 (Jew becomes Christian); Asimov 1992: item 95 (Jew becomes Catholic); Rees 1995: 182 (Ulster Protestant becomes Catholic); Coote 1995: 100 (Irish Catholic becomes Protestant); Jhumor List, Apr. 29, 1996 (Jew becomes Christian); Goldstein-Jackson 1996: item 673 (socialist becomes Tory); Singh 1996: 71 (Irish Protestant becomes Catholic); Barnett and Kaiser 1996: 238 (American becomes Communist); Cohl 1997: 398 (Irish Catholic becomes Protestant); Jhumor List, Sept. 27, 1998 (Jew becomes Catholic); Colombo 2001: 200 (Quebecois becomes Anglo).

31. Lawyer Jokes, Dec. 18, 1995 [= Randy's Favorite Lawyer Jokes, July 24, 1997 = Generic Lawyer Jokes, Sept. 19, 1997 = Kahn and Boe 1997: 175]; Lawyer Jokes, Jan. 30, 1998; 2000 Cal.: Feb. 28. Notice the little dig about the lawyer "making sure his bill would be paid," a feature which does not appear in any of the older conversion jokes.

32. Act 4, scene 2. Apparently, Shakespeare modeled the targeting of lawyers on events in Wat Tyler's 1381 rebellion, two centuries earlier.

33. Steiger 1990: 11 (noted as "adapted from Henny Youngman"); Grossman 1993: 50; AML 1993: no. 664; Warner 1993: 181; 1995 Cal: item 315; Brallier 1996: 91; Lawyer Jokes, Jan. 30, 1998; 2000 Cal.: Sept. 9–10; Tibballs 2000: item 1147.

34. Copeland and Copeland 1940: item 2820; Cerf 1946: 202; House 1948: 2; Braude 1958: item 833; Gerler 1965: 136; Murdock 1967: 18; Jessel 1973: 161 [= Sortor 1989: 5]; Wilde 1978: 1 (dog); Walker 1980: 159; Triverton 1981: 23; Alvin 1983a: 46; Martling 1984: 45; Anon. 1984: 121; Pietsch 1986: 56; Phillips 1986: 119; Ocker 1986; Wilde 1986: 114; Berle 1989: 273; Asimov 1992: item 426; Millar and Keane 1994: 88; Adams and Newall 1996: 70; Cohl 1997: 209; Buford and Grabowski 1997: 93; Dedopulos 1998: 114; Dedopulos 1998: 145; Greene 1999: 30; Jan Hoem, e-mail message to author, Mar. 30, 1999; Baddiel et al. 1999: 489; Baddiel et al. 1999: 458; Gross 2000: 79; Mr. "K" 2001: 134; FHM 2001: 129; Hobbes 2002a: 5. Cf. B. Phillips 1994 (Ronald Reagan's bear ate liberal congressmen).

35. Lodovico Carbone (1469) in Bowen 1988: 17. Bowen 1988 (17 n. 3) traces this joke back to Cicero and the Gesta Romanorum and also supplies a modern Irish version. Thompson 1955 assigns this motif J1442.11 (the cynic and the fig tree).

36. Doberman was directed at blacks (Thickett 1983: 23); alligator was directed at Jews (Anon. [1967]: 157), Englishmen (Hornby 1977: 37; Ocker 1986), Irish Protestants (Hill 1987: 7), blacks (Knott 1983: 92; Alvin 1989: 68 [black customer]; Dedopulos 1998: 43), Kiwis (Trevor 1992: 74), IRS agents (Reader's Digest 1997: 181), Scots (Vas 1996), Catholics (Blue 2001: 112).

37. Rovin 1992: 57; Peas 1996: 25; Barnett and Kaiser 1996: 89; Ross 1996: 88; 1998 Cal.: Sept. 11; Pietsch 1998: 209; Lawyer Jokes, Jan. 30, 1998; Alvin 1999a: 82; Greene 1999: 168; 2000 Cal.: Aug. 22; Tibballs 2000: item 1131. The only other new subjects for this easily switchable item seem to be politicians (Alvin 1993: 53) and conductors (Theaker 1997: 53).

38. Brallier 1996: 58; Grossman 1993: 136; 1995 Cal: item 333 [= 1997 Cal.: Nov. 24]; Ross 1996: 94; Reader's Digest 1997: 181; Southwell 1999: 67; Regan 2001: 170.

39. Gotta Love Them Lawyer Jokes (last modified 8/30/95); CLLH 1995: lawyer humor no. 62 (man asks attorney genie to be beaten half to death); Dundes and Pagter

2000: 197 (kidney, collected 1996); Lawyer Jokes, Jan. 30, 1998 (kidney); Tibballs 2000: item 1130 (same); Regan 2001: 21 (same); 2002 Cal.: Feb. 8 (same); Jan Hoem, e-mail, May 1, 2002.

40. AT 1331. Some modern examples are: Drake 1956: item 200 (Irishman asks for one glass eye); Van Munching 1997: 68 (man asks for "*mild* heart attack"); Reader's Digest 1997: 127 (mate to get double, woman asks "scare me half to death").

41. CLLH 1995: lawyer humor no. 90 [= Adams and Newall 1995: 285]; Lawyer Jokes, Jan. 30, 1998; Greene 1999: 153; Tibballs 2000: item 1128.

42. Alvin 1984: 20. The joke is directed against Chukchis in Russia (Draitser 1998: 97) and Turks in Holland (Kuipers 2000: 156). A recent version targets talk-show hosts (Norrick 2001: 264).

43. John Kidwell, e-mail message to author, Nov. 25, 1997. A version about nerds is at Tapper and Press 2000: 64.

44. A four-item list of "regulations for the 1988 attorney season," including "The use of currency as bait is prohibited," was collected by Leslie Millett in Berkeley, CA, Oct. 19, 1988. A more elaborated eleven-item list entitled "Washington State Attorney Season and Bag Limits" is found on many Internet sites and includes both the "currency" item noted above and those that follow in the text.

45. Lawyer Jokes, Dec. 1, 1998. The same item was found at Gotta Love Them Lawyer Jokes July 22, 1997 (last modified 8/30/95). Further variants: e-mail messages to author from Lisa Lerman, Nov. 11, 1998; Alison Dundes Renteln, Oct. 7, 1998; Laura Macaulay, Aug. 12, 1999.

46. Daniel White quoted in Peterson 1990; Silber 1989: 213; Walker 1990; Beckham, 1990: 1; Sandra Day O'Connor as reported in Crawford, et al. 1991; Franklin 1992; Stephen G. Breyer in Rooney 1995.

47. Lawyer Jokes from Internet 1993 no. 113 [= CLLH 1995: lawyer humor no. 46 = Adams and Newall 1995: 295 = Ross 1996: 99] (switched from American to Australian) = e-mail from Richard Gordon, Feb. 20, 1997. Also, collected by Marc Louderback, Berkeley, CA, Nov. 2, 1988; Warner 1993: 156 [= AML 1993: no. 337]; Grossman 1993: 86; 1995 Cal: item 320; 2000 Cal.: Apr. 10.

48. Heinrich Bebel (1508–1512) in Bowen 1988: 43; Ludovico Demenichi (1548–1564) in Speroni 1964: 195; Robert Armin [1608] in Zall 1970: 100; Copley [1614] in Zall 1970: 6. The Renaissance story appears to be descended from a Roman joke about the passengers asked to lighten the ship in distress by throwing things overboard and the "egghead" takes his bank draft for 150 myriads and snips off the 50 (i.e., "L," I assume). Baldwin 1983: item 80 [ca. CE 500].

49. Murdock 1967: 109; Adams 1968: 200 [= Adams 1996: 60]; Berle 1989: 234; Knott 1990a: 25 [= Knott 1990b: 11]; Rovin 1991: 211; Alvin 1993: 46. By 1997, when the venue has shifted to a rafting expedition, the Mexican, anticipating the American's move, says, "Don't even think about it." Cohl 1997: 158.

50. Baker 1985: 123 [collected 1973]; Humes 1985 [1975]: 114 (Englishman throws Greek); Shelley 1976: 88 (Quebecker throws Ontarian); MacHale 1978: 25 (Englishman throws Irishman); Orso 1979: 50 (Greek throws American); Dalton 1982: 28 (Montanan throws North Dakotan); Dolgopolova 1882: 67 (Jew throws Arab); MacHale 1983a: 16 (Thatcher throws Irish PM); Stangland 1987: 206 (Norwegian throws Swede); Hochwald [1994]: 140 (Israeli throws Russian); Jones and Wheeler 1995: 23 (hillbilly throws social worker); Adams and Newall 1995: 309 (Oregonian throws Californian); Barnett and Kaiser 1996: 69 (New Zealander throws Australian); Barnett and Kaiser 1996: 73 (Maori throws

Japanese); Readers Digest Aug. 1997 (Seattle native shoots Californian and catches falling bottle. When asked why he did it, he replies, "We have lots of Californians . . . but I really feel I should recycle this bottle"); Kahn and Boe 1997: 105 (similar).

51. Steiner 1950: 80 (Israeli ministers); Mendelsohn 1951: 249 (same); Learsi 1961: 342 (same); Murdock 1967: 129 (politician); Benton and Looms 1977: 32 [1976] (Edward Heath and Margaret Thatcher); Kravitz 1977: 279 (Ian Paisley throws pope); Orso 1979: 7 (Greek Junta); Lukes and Galnoor 1987: 71 [1985] (Assad and brothers); Schuster 1991: 1 (president of Turkey); Adler and Adler 1992: 62 (Bush throws Quayle); Adams and Newall 1995: 180 (Clintons and Gore); Laurence G. Kahn, e-mail to author, Nov. 21, 1996 (Clinton, Dole, Perot); Jhumor list, May 10, 1997 (Israeli ministers).

52. Julian Killingley, Birmingham, England, e-mail to author, Sept. 7, 1994 (who reports that he had it from a U.S. internet site); Knott 1990: 44; Brallier 1992: 19; Adler 1992: 38 [= Adler 1994: 38]; Grossman 1993: 24; *AML* 1993: no. 639; Lawyer Jokes from Internet 1994: no. 26; Killingley 1994 [= CLLH 1995: lawyer humor no. 43 = e-mail from Len Riskin, May 9, 1996]; collected by Lara Kemper, Nov. 1995; 1996 Cal.: Mar. 31; presentation by Wilfred M. McKay at Heritage Foundation, Washington, DC, Dec. 13, 1995; Ross 1996: 101; 1997 Cal.: Mar. 10; Cohl 1997: 279; 1998 Cal.: Apr. 14; Lawyer Jokes, Jan. 30, 1998; Streiker 1998: 258; Dedopulos 1998: 232 (first publication in UK); Greene 1999: 155; 2000 Cal.: Feb. 15; Baddiel et al. 1999: 577.

53. Parry 1966: 38; Bregman 1967: 22; Banc and Dundes 1986: 142. Its first appearances on these shores were about Democrats (Pietsch 1986: 91) and "Niggers" (Knott 1987: 25); Alvin 1995a: 46. In these stories as in the Eastern European ones (but unlike the American lawyer joke), the "decoy" rat has a Pied Piper-like human proprietor.

54. Cited in Veall 1970: 208–9. "Caterpillar" at the time was used figuratively to designate "a rapacious person, an extortioner; one who preys upon society." *Oxford English Dictionary*, 2nd ed. 1989.

55. J. Jones (1652) quoted in Veall 1970: 202.

56. Murray 1996: 134. The 70 percent item is discussed in detail in the next section, "The 70 Percent Legend."

57. Burger 1977.

58. Gergen 1991: 72. Earlier, Colorado Governor Richard Lamm put forth various proposals to "de-lawyer" the American system. Larsen 1990; Sanko 1983.

59. Dee 1986: 3.

60. McCracken 1991.

61. Adelman 1996.

62. Wiemer 1998.

63. Viner et al.1994: unpaginated first page of text.

64. Quayle 1991, reprinted in Quayle [1994]. Quayle and his ample chorus were anticipated over five hundred years earlier by William Caxton (ca. 1422–ca. 1491, England's first printer), who used the same trope to express his exasperation with lawyers: "I suppose that in all Christendom are not so many pleaders, attorneys and men of the law as be in England only, for if they were numbered all that belong to the courts of the Chancery, King's Bench, Common Pleas, Exchequer, Receipt and Hell [record repository in Westminster Hall], and the bag-bearers of the same, it should amount to a great multitude. And how all these live, and of whom, if it should be uttered and told it should not be believed." W. Caxton, *Game and Playe of the Chesse* (1474), quoted by Baker 1986: 75.

65. The basis of this calculation and supporting documentation is presented in Galanter 1993: 77–83, 104–13.

66. For example, cabinet members Robert Mosbacher and Louis Sullivan and Senators Robert Dole, Mitch McConnell, and Charles Grassley, among many others. See Galanter 1993. This figure was also solemnly reported as fact by several media experts, such as David Gergen in Gergen 1991: 72. In the case of the knowledgeable William Buckley, Quayle's speech "reminded [!] us that 70 percent of the lawyers in the world are American." Buckley 1991. In the May 1992 issue of *Commentary*, Francis Fukuyama wrote that "there is something wrong with an economy that employs 70 percent of the world's lawyers." Berger et al. 1992.

Quayle's vice-presidential acceptance speech highlighted the 70 percent figure (Quayle 1992a), while the Republican platform inexplicably reverted to the two-thirds figure. Republican Party 1992: 75.

67. Quayle was presenting proposals of the Council on Competitiveness, of which he was chair. The council did not include the 70 percent figure in its *Agenda* (President's Council on Competitiveness 1991), but apparently there had been some consideration of it in the preparation of Quayle's ABA speech, for a week earlier "a Quayle spokesman" was reported as having "noted that the United States has 70 percent of the world's lawyers, and that the rising tide of litigation 'is a burden on our economy.'" Terry 1991.

68. Among the earliest sightings was a news magazine report that "the U.S. has 610,000 lawyers, two thirds of the world's total. . . . About 70 percent are in private practice." *U.S. News and World Report* 1982: 55. (Could this be the origin of the 70 percent figure?) A few months earlier, James Spensley, a practitioner and lecturer at the University of Denver Law School, was quoted as saying, "The U.S. has become the world's most litigious society, employing over two thirds of the world's lawyers." Salisbury 1982: 4. When I spoke with Spensley by telephone in January 1992, he could not recall the source of this information.

69. "It has been reported that about two-thirds of all the lawyers in the world are in the United States and of those, one-third have come into practice in the past five years." Burger 1984: 2. A very similar item appeared a few months earlier in a contribution to *Legal Times* by New York lawyer Peter Megargee Brown: "Two-thirds of all lawyers in the world are in the United States. One-third of the lawyers in this country have been in practice less than five years." Brown 1983: 10.

70. McLean 1984. Cf. a law school dean's op-ed in the *Wall Street Journal* that "two-thirds of the world's lawyers now practice in this country, and one-third of these were graduated during the past five years." Gellhorn 1984: 28.

71. E.g., Sanko 1983; Larsen 1990.

72. Quoted in Kleinfield 1990: 80.

73. On page 1 of the *Agenda*, there is an approving reference to "a recent report by a[n unnamed] Professor of Finance at the University of Texas . . . [that] estimated that the average lawyer takes $1 million a year from the country's output of goods and services." The report referred to is chap. 8 of Magee et al. 1989: 111–21. That source contains an incomplete listing of the number of lawyers in some thirty-four countries as of 1983. Magee et al. 1989: 120–21. Even this partial list enumerated enough lawyers that American lawyers could not have been more than 45 percent of the total. Magee et al. 1989. One can conclude that the council staff either did not examine the source they approvingly cite, or that they were aware that the 70 percent figure was spurious.

74. Quayle 1992: 17.

75. Quayle [1994]: 313, 316–17. A few years later, Quayle enlarged his indictment: lawyers not only burden the nation with excessive litigation, but the "aristocracy" of lawyers and judges is responsible for the nation's "cultural decline." Marinucci 1999.

76. Galanter 1993.

77. Columnist George Will noted as one of "the nation's most pressing problems . . . the suffocation of economic and social energies by regulations, and by litigation from the 70 per cent of the world's lawyers who are Americans." Will 1992. News host Barbara Walters solemnly reported that "70 percent of all the lawyers in the entire world are in this country." *Night-line* 1993. The president of Americans for Tax Reform concurred (Norquist 1994), as did columnist Herb Jaffe 1994, editorialist Bob Wiemer 1995, computer executive Charles Wang (Wintrob 1995), and an editorial "Really Stupid Lawyers' Tricks" (*Roanoke Times and World News* 1995). Even its citation by the left-wing *Monthly Review* as an explanation of why "in the United States, class struggle is expressed in legal terms" (Ehrenberg 1996) has not diminished its appeal to the right. Thus Rep. Bill Archer, proudly announcing the creation of "28 new taxpayer rights, including the right to sue the IRS for damages caused by negligence," expresses astonishment that in a country with 70 percent of the world's lawyers "anybody can complain that this may be adding a little bit more litigation." Federal News Service 1997: 7.

78. See the quotation from British commentator Ian Murray 1996: 134, above at note 56.

79. *Banker* 1994.

80. Cornwell 1995: 11; Carlin 1995: 17. A commentator in the same paper recently cited it in connection with dire warnings about the "litigation crazy" U.S. Puddephatt 1997: 25.

81. Nicoll 1995: 22; Johnson 1998: 6; Leslie and Gordon 1997: 16; Coleman 1997: 36.

82. Esler 1997: 90. The author's diatribe about America's legal morass (86–99) relies heavily on Olson 1991. Esler 1997: 325.

83. Totten 1994: 6.

84. Lim 1994.

85. De Alvarado 1995: 24. I am indebted to Lawrence Friedman for this reference.

86. See chap. 2, n. 143.

87. Much of the survey data reported in this section is derived from three national sample surveys, each conducted by telephone. Two of these surveys were conducted for the *National Law Journal,* the first in 1986 and the second in 1993. The third major survey was conducted for the American Bar Association in 1993.

The first of the *National Law Journal* surveys (n=1004) was published in Kaplan 1986. A second survey (n=815), which largely replicates the 1986 survey and thus provides a useful reading of recent changes, was conducted for the *National Law Journal* and the West Publishing Company by Penn & Schoen Associates, Inc. (Samborn 1993: 1).

The other 1993 survey (n=1202) was conducted by Peter D. Hart Research Associates, Inc., for the American Bar Association. It was reported in Hengstler 1993: 60. More extensive data can be found in Peter D. Hart Research Associates 1993.

88. Samborn 1993: 1. But this may not be very intense: when the ABA survey asked people to *volunteer* criticism of lawyers, only 5 percent volunteered that they were too numerous. Peter D. Hart Research Associates 1993: 13.

89. Samborn 1993: Question 22. A 57 percent majority thought lawyers had "too much influence and power in society." Samborn 1993: Question 4. Both public opinion and TV depictions attribute more power to lawyers than lawyers believe they have. Pfau et al. 1995: 321.

90. Hart Survey, 4–5. This pattern is not unique to present-day America. In early modern England, antagonism to lawyers and blaming them for excessive litigation was highest among top people. Brooks 1986: 136; Prest 1986: 313.

91. Kaplan 1986: table 9. In regard to lawyers' having too much power, the distribution again was skewed with more prosperous and powerful groups high (college graduates, 64 percent; professionals, 60 percent) and outsider groups low (blacks, 39 percent). Id. at table 6. The former were also among the most knowledgeable, least enthusiastic about mandatory pro bono service for lawyers, and most opposed to an elective federal judiciary. Id.

92. Overton 1995: 1104.

93. Trotter 1997: 190. Others concur that the intensity of abuse in the jokes is a direct reflection of ethical abuses by lawyers. Kolbe 1993; Puma 1995: 227; Drinan 1998: 112.

94. "The lack of attorney professionalism is a cause of both lawyer jokes and violence against lawyers." Puma 1995: 227. Often the notion of public outrage at lawyer behavior is combined with an assertion (or assumption) that lawyers behave more poorly than they did in the past (the premise of much recent writing on the profession). That there has been a significant decline in lawyer behavior seems doubtful, but such a development is not required, for an increase in public discontent could be produced by (1) the multiplication of contacts with lawyers; (2) greater visibility and salience of lawyer offenses; and (3) higher expectations of lawyer conduct. The first two of these have certainly occurred and probably the third as well.

95. Kaplan 1993: table 4.

96. Kaplan 1993: table 6.

97. Samborn 1993: graphs 4–5.

98. Samborn 1993 (containing a steady number of "very satisfied" responses).

99. Peter D. Hart Research Associates 1993: 25. More recent surveys in 1998 and 2002 report the same range of levels of satisfaction. Leo J. Shapiro 2002: 19.

100. A number of the narrative *Death Wish* jokes depict a recoil by client against "his" lawyer after (presumably satisfactory) continuing relations (I8, *love to hear it;* I9, *make sure he's dead*). As far as we can tell these people were using the system with satisfactory results, they are unhappy not with bad or abusive lawyering but with good lawyering. As Art Buchwald quipped, it is not the bad lawyers who are the problem but the good lawyers.

101. Trachtenberg 1993: 32. This explanation raises the expectation that there would be jokes targeting divorce lawyers, but there only a few and they have experienced no noticeable increase over the period in question.

102. Lipset and Schneider 1987; Uslaner 1993: 77ff.

103. As one distressed and indignant lawyer points out, the "fundamentally disturbing difference" between jokes about lawyers and those about other occupational groups is "the death of the lawyer" and its celebration—that is, the *Death Wish* and *Object of Scorn* jokes. Skladony 1996: 369.

104. Lewis 1997: 253.

105. See Dundes 1987: chaps. 1, 2; Sutton-Smith 1960; Abrahams 1961: 62.

106. Simon, 1995.

107. McDowell 1983.

108. A minority of the jokes switched to lawyers were previously directed principally at these no longer correct targets, including a number of those examined in this chapter: I6, *good start* (blacks); I7, *bus over cliff* (Pakistanis in UK); I8, *love to hear it* (wife); I12, *deathbed conversion* (religious groups); I13, *get in line* (wife/mother-in-law); I14, *Doberman* (blacks); I15, *alligator* (Jews, blacks); I20, *throw out of train* (Mexican); H3, *hostages* (wife/ mother in law); H16, *sperm* (blacks). Once established as lawyer jokes, some of those discussed here switched *to* such targets: I1, *bury twenty-one* (unwanted immigrants); but most

of the switching has been to other occupational groups: I5, *more concrete;* I6, *bottom of sea;* I8, *love to hear it;* I11, *bury deep down;* I14, *Doberman;* G26, *rats.* It is possible that this imbalance reflects a widespread inhibition of placing such material in the written record.

109. Wiley 1993.

110. Egan 1991.

111. Finer 1970: 45. The literary antecedents are traced in Tucker 1984: 4ff.

112. Bloomfield 1976.

113. [Jesse Higgins], *Sampson against the Philistines,* 2nd ed. (Philadelphia, 1805), 92, as quoted by Bloomfield 1976: 48. A late twentieth-century rendition, a drawing captioned "and on the eighth day God invented lawyers . . . and screwed it all up" displays less confidence in divine design. Bond 1990: 75.

114. G. Wistanley, quoted in Veall 1970: 209

115. MacIntyre 2000: 91–92.

116. Cf. Bachman 1995: 91–92: "The ugly turn in lawyer jokes is more a reflection of a mass feeling of self-revulsion towards certain trends in our society than a reaction to any change in lawyers' behavior or even to lawyers themselves."

117. Many of these were seemingly moribund but restored to life by the great outpouring of kindred jokes that started flowing in the mid-1980s.

10. Enemies of Justice

1. Davies 1990: 317.

2. Esar 1945: 253.

3. Of the sixty-some instances of *appeal at once* that I have collected, the phrase is uttered by the client in almost two-thirds. Other client tellings are: Knox 1926: 142 (UK, but told of U.S.); Aye 1931: 18 (UK); Copeland 1936: 242; Droke 1948: 279; Golden [1950]: 11; Richman 1952: 397; Lieberman 1956: 116; Bowker 1961: 114 (UK); Jackson 1961: 150 (UK); Woods 1967: item 94.11; Wachs 1968: 201; Golden 1972: 199; Bodine 1985 (told as anecdote); *Los Angeles Times,* Nov. 12, 1987 (reverse: lawyer tells client); Foster 1988: 113 (UK); *Accountancy Age,* May 12, 1988 (UK, accountant in tax case, told as anecdote at retirement dinner); Rafferty 1988: 26; Knott 1990: 83; Behrman 1991: 13; Dover and Fish 1992 (UK, client is Robert Maxwell); Rovin 1992: 143; Adler 1992: 143 [= Adler 1994: 13]; Berle 1993: 324; *AML* 1993: 872; *AML* 1993: no. 261; Murray 1993 (reversed); *Courier Journal,* Jan. 19, 1996, reporting Barbara Jordan's 1994 convocation address, citing Alan Dershowitz); Adams & Newall 1994: 117 (Australia); Coote 1994: 246 (Australia); CLLH 1995: lawyer humor no. 145; Subhash and Dharam 1995b: 127 (India, client is politician); Adams and Newall 1995: 291 (Australia); Ross 1996: 69 (Australia, woman lawyer); Streiker 1998: 260; Harvey ca.1998a: 80 (India).

4. Anon. c.1860: 45; Bigelow 1871: 339; Brown [1879]: 29; Landon 1883: 383; Johnston 1925: item 1132; Wood 1926: 43; Aye 1931: 137; Copeland 1936: 242; Esar 1945: 253. Cf. Aye 1931: 136 (counsel agrees with convicted client that he has not received justice, but "you'll get it all right tomorrow").

5. Mosher [1922]: 293 [= Milburn 1927: 5].

6. Ernst 1930: 210; Johnston 1922: item 1136.

7. Edwards 1915: item 659; Wilde 1987: 79.

8. *Green Bag* 22: 50 (1910). On the role of American lawyers and judges in intervention in Latin America in the era in which the joke emerged, see Noonan 1976; Lisagor and Lipsius 1988 (describing the notorious intervention of William Nelson Cromwell in securing the secession of Panama from Colombia in 1903).

9. The term is used, and very likely coined, by Roscoe Pound in 1908. "The leaders of the American bars are not primarily practitioners in the courts. They are chiefly client caretakers. . . . Their best work is done in the office, not in the forum. They devote themselves to study of the interests of particular clients, urging and defending those interests in all their varying forms, before legislatures, councils, administrative boards and commissions quite as much as in the courts. Their interest centers wholly in an individual client or set of clients, not in the general administration of justice." Pound 1909: 235.

10. Strong 1914: 378.

11. Strong 1914: 353–54.

12. E.g., D3, *fair to both,* where the client reproaches the lawyer for insufficiently serving his aggressive desires.

13. Shillaber 1854: 151; Avery 1859. Comparable tales appear in Gilbert [1986]: 21 (Irish lawyer in nineteenth-century England), and Engelbach 1913: 37 (Australian barrister).

14. Landon 1883: 376.

15. Behrman 1991: 41; Eastman 1936: 20; Lupton 1938: item 1510; Goldon [1950]: 109; O'Neal and O'Neal 1964: 72; Rovin 1992: 90; Arya 1996: 39; 2000 Cal.: Nov. 29.

16. Edwards 1915: item 203.

17. Dunne 1963: 35–36 [1905].

18. Clode 1922: 140; Milburn 1927: 46; Wilde 1987: 162; Knott 1990: 120.

19. Leo Cullum cartoon, *New Yorker,* July 7, 1997, 68.

20. The lawyer's readiness and ability to switch sides are also addressed in the sections "Lying and Dishonsty" and "Eloquence, Persuasiveness, Resourcefulness," chap. 1.

21. Sprague 1897: 206; *Green Bag* 10: 361 (1898); Regan 2001: 247 (reappearing in print after more than 100 years!).

22. Esar 1945: 260; Edwards 1915: item 183; Mosher [1922]: 295 ("railway magnate and prominent Philadelphia lawyer"); Milburn 1927: 14 (railway magnate and prominent attorney).

23. See Paul 1960; Shamir 1995.

24. David Corn, "Starr's Grand (Self-) Illusion," Loyal Opposition [http://www.american-politics.com/061998Corn.html].

25. Edmund and Williams 1916: 206–7 [= Lawson 1923: 163]; *Green Bag* 1: 455 (1889); Anon. 1902: 299 (secretary); Masson [1913]: 96; Lurie 1928: 137; Henry 1948: 72; Wilson 1949: 79.

26. This theme is addressed in "Headed for Hell," chap. 3.

27. In a curious cognate (or spin-off?) of this story, the magnate arrives at St. Peter's gate but refuses to answer questions about his life "by advice of counsel," whereupon Peter dispatches him to consult with counsel by dropping him "into the sulphurous depths." *Green Bag* 19: 325 (1907).

28. See text at notes 49–52 below.

29. Thus in *two plus two* (A33) the joke is intensified by the pointed contrast between the lawyer's elasticity and the fruitless literal-mindedness of the other candidates.

30. Marchal 1994: 1C. Other "partner" versions are: Cerf 1944: 175 [= Cerf 1956: 206]; Allen 1945: 1146; Adams 1968: 344; Jessel 1973: 133; Gillespie-Jones 1980: 50 (Australia, told of U.S.); Walker 1980: 203 (Australia); Wilde 1982: 160; Rosten 1985: 338 (U.S., told of UK); Judicial Conference (108 F.R.D. 465 (1985)); Phillips 1989: 21 (UK); Shulman 1993 (UK, told of U.S.); *Charleston Gazette,* Nov. 30, 1994; Coote 1994: 246 (Australia); Coote 1995: 227 (Australia, first fax).

31. Oral tradition, India 1958.

32. Wilde 1988: 171; Gardner 1982: 79.

33. Wilde 1982: 183; Wilde 1987: 4; Chariton 1989: 71; Knott 1990: 48; Berle 1993: 324; 1995 Cal.: item 33. Cf. Rovin 1991: 23 (baseball umpire). Other prostitute comparisons are in chap. 7, "A Suspect Profession."

34. Johnston 1922: item 1120; Kiser 1927: 118; Esar 1945: 106; May 1956: 48; MacDonald 1992: 6 (told by Canadian attorney as anecdote about 1976 U.S. criminal case); Kahn 1999: 185 (South Africa). Cf. Silbey 1997: 209 (comment allegedly made by Justice Oliver Wendell Holmes to young lawyer: "Young man . . . never forget that this is not a court of justice, it is a court of law").

35. Jackson 1961: 171. Deflecting the cynical message, the author labels the story one "which all laymen—particularly unsuccessful litigants—will relish." John Duke Coleridge, 1st Baron (1820–94), grandnephew of the poet Samuel Taylor Coleridge, was Lord Chief Justice of England from 1880 until his death.

36. Gary J. Aichele (1981) in Herz 1996: 147.

37. Robert Bork (1990) in Herz 1996: 111.

38. Herz 1996: 131. "I explore the ways in which people telling the story get it wrong." Herz 1996: 115.

39. I happened to be at the celebration of the fiftieth anniversary of the Supreme Court of India in New Delhi in January 2000. On the occasion, the president of India, K. Narayanan, recounted a story told by the first president of India, Dr. Rajendra Prasad (1884–1963), who left his law practice in 1920 to devote himself to the independence movement. Prasad "was appearing in a Patna court and told the judge, 'My Lord, justice in this case requires that etc.' The judge intervened and said, 'Judges are not here to do justice, but to decide cases according to evidence on record.'" *Times of India,* Jan. 29, 2000, 9; *Hindustan Times,* Jan. 29, 2000.

40. Landon 1883: 404; Bigelow 1871: 373 (elaborated English story told as anecdote about veteran lawyer responding to "new-fledged barrister").

41. Johnson et al. 1936: 116; Mosher [1922]: 72; Williams 1938: item 741; Esar 1945: 63; Droke 1956: 303; Humes [1975]: item 97; Pendleton [1979]: item 17; Yarwood [1981]: 99.

42. Edwards 1915: item 657.

43. Mendelsohn 1951: 234. According to one account, Steuer (1871–1940) was reputed to charge so much that "people began to suspect that anyone desperate enough to pay Steuer's going rate must have a shaky case, to say the least." Evans 1998: 228. But this theme antedated Steuer: Miles 1890?: 148 (if not guilty I would have defended myself); *Green Bag* 10: 83 (1898) (juror attributes conviction to defendant's hiring of lawyer).

44. Joe Miller 1832: No. 947, reproduced in Hazlitt 1890: 82 [= Anon. 1903: II, 64.]; Anon. 1822: 539; Lemon 1864: 11; Lean 1904: 4:129 (attributed to Sydney Smith [1771–1845]). John Horne Tooke (1736–1812) was a radical British politician who was tried for high treason in 1794, acquitted, and became a Member of Parliament in 1801.

45. Hazlitt 1890: 82.

46. Lord Birkett in Jackson 1961: 11.

47. Lemon 1864: 266; Cole 1887: 272; *Green Bag* 3: 354 (1891); *Encyclopaedia Britannica* 8: 339a (1911); Engelbach 1915: 136; Heighton 1916: 123–24; Aye 1931: 125; Alvarez 1981: 132; Hay 1989: 201.

48. *Encyclopaedia Britannica* 8: 339a (1911) ("final impetus"); Alvarez 1981: 132 ("precipitated").

49. Barrie 1983: 22 (aphorism). Others refer to a "saying" (Brazin 1993: 3) or an "adage"

(Anolik 1984: 14). Simmons 1992: 18 (libraries). Dershowitz 1991: 97. ("the cynical cartoon that now hangs in many a lawyer's office"); Hammel 1987: 101 (misremembered).

50. Goodman 1983.

51. Janofsky and Raven 1995.

52. Ladendorf 1996.

53. Morgan 1996.

54. Julius 1996. In the version given, the client is "Mr. Smith" as he is in Deborah Rhode's recollection of the cartoon several years earlier. Rhode 1994: 74.

55. Curran 1977: 234.

56. ABC News/*Washington Post* Survey 1985 (USACWP.196.R24) (on file with author).

57. *U.S. News & World Report,* news release, Jan. 21, 1995 (on file with author).

58. Robust majorities in a 2001 survey affirmed that "lawyers are more interested in winning than in seeing that justice is served" (74 percent), "lawyers spend too much time finding technicalities to get criminals released" (73 percent), and "lawyers are more interested in making money than in serving their clients" (69 percent). Leo J. Shapiro survey.

59. A comparable skepticism is displayed in surveys from other common law countries. In England, most of those with a view of the matter agreed that "the poor usually get the raw end of the stick in legal matters." Heavy majorities viewed lawyers as mercenaries: "Lawyers are mainly interested in making money" and "for a price lawyers will use every trick in the book to help their clients." Abel-Smith et al. 1973: 249–50). A quarter century later, 72 percent of English respondents agreed that "The legal system works better for rich people than for poor people." Only 13 percent disagreed. Genn 1999: 234. Canadian respondents agreed that "higher paid lawyers get better results for their clients; that lawyers are always finding loopholes to get around the law; that lawyers get too many guilty people off . . . that lawyers do not work as hard for poor clients as for clients who are rich; that lawyers are more interested in making money than in helping their clients." Moore 1985: 53. Comparable views in Australia are analyzed in Tomasic 1985.

60. Best 1990: 188.

61. In addition to the drop-outs listed in the Register of Jokes (appendix), the old (1871) version of A35, *pound the table,* can be accounted a lost *Justice* joke.

11. Only in America?

1. Where Grisham's book (1991) has the hero abandon the law and become a comfortable emigre as the price of his victory, the screenwriters devised a clever legal solution that enabled him to triumph and remain a lawyer.

2. Peter D. Hart Research Associates 1993: 16.

3. Samborn 1993: 20.

4. The "genuine" qualifier is needed because a great deal of the visible support for the jaundiced view is generated by simulated grassroots groups that promote "reforms" of the civil justice system. Thus Neal Cohen, of Apco Associates, a specialist in creating spurious "grassroots" tort reform organizations, gained notoriety when it was disclosed that he exhorted fellow lobbyists about "the importance of keeping the public in the dark about who the clients really are." Fritsch 1996; *O'Dwyer's PR Services* 1996.

5. Organized programmatic expression of popular, non-special-interest grievances is relatively uncommon. My characterization here is drawn from an examination of the publications of HALT, a reform organization founded in 1978, which indicate the sort of issues that engage that small section of the public that devotes attention and energy to challenging lawyers' practices. The name HALT was originally an acronym for Help

Abolish Legal Tyranny, but this was displaced by the less combative An Organization of Americans for Legal Reform. In early 1988, it was reported that the organization had a staff of 26 and nearly 150,000 "members." *Washington Post,* Jan. 21, 1988. Subsequently, economic constraints led to closing of field offices and cutting the staff to about a dozen; in 1992, membership was said to be about 100,000. Middleton 1992: 21, 22. Grassroots and militant offshoots such as Justice for All and the National Congress for Legal Reform charged HALT with being unresponsive to its membership and too amicable with the bar. In 2005, the organization's Web site (http://www.halt.org) claimed 50,000 members.

6. Yankelovich 1995: question 3.

7. Roper Report no. 87–7, July 1987, on file with author.

8. See Glendon 1994, Kronman 1993, Linowitz and Mayer 1994, and many other sources cited in Galanter 1996. Dissent from this frame breaks into print only rarely. See Galanter 1996: 553 n. 16.

9. As in the reaction to Charles Curtis's 1951 article, which frankly describes the ways in which advocates shade and obscure the truth. See "Workers in the Mills of Deceit," chap. 1.

10. Foster 1988; E. Phillips 1989; Mason 2001.

11. E. Phillips 1989. *Bury twenty-one* is at 25.

12. Webster 1994: 21.

13. Anon. 1992. *Check in the coffin* (F13) is also told of accountants in Britain.

14. Adams and Newall 1994.

15. Ross 1996. The author acknowledges the American provenance of the jokes ("our main source for jokes about lawyers came from the United States") and that he has "modified them to fit our local context" (2).

16. Subhash and Dharam 1995a: 234.

17. In 1960, the number of solicitors and barristers in England and Wales was 20,988. By 1997, it has grown to 101,752, an increase of some 385 percent. In the United States the number of lawyers grew from 285,933 in 1960 to 857,931 in 1995, an increase of 200 percent.

18. Atiyah and Summers 1987.

19. Prest 1986: 187, 303.

20. Prest 1986: 296.

21. Kagan 1988; Kritzer 1991; Kritzer 1996.

22. Golluch 1999 (translation by the author). Contrasting with *Witze* in the first line, the word "jokes" is in English.

23. Giselinde Kuipers, e-mail message to the author, Aug. 22, 2000.

24. Banks 1961: 198.

25. Porsdam 1999: 252.

26. Porsdam 1999: xii.

27. De Tocqueville: 1:287; Auerbach 1976b: 38; Miller 1995. See chap. 1, p. 62.

28. Porsdam 1999: 254.

29. Bogart 2002: 328.

30. Gawalt 1984: vii.

31. Galanter 1986: 151, 166. A calculation (August 1992: 72) that the U.S. has fewer "law providers" per capita than many other nations is seriously flawed. Based on international data on enrollment in law courses, it makes insufficient adjustment for differential rates at which students in various countries graduate and graduates become and remain suppliers of legal services. Galanter 1992a: 118.

32. Kagan 1994: 13–14.

33. Osiel observes, "The especially stringent duties of client loyalty now widely taken for granted by American lawyers, and embodied in their ethics codes, developed from the alliance struck in the late 19th century between large law firms and large companies." Osiel 1993.

34. Osiel 1993. See also Osiel 1990: 2009, 2056–64.

35. Atiyah and Summers 1987 regard the quest for substantive justice as a characteristic distinguishing American law from English law. Cf. Kagan 1991: 369, 392 (observing the inherent mismatch of attempting "to articulate and implement the socially transformative policies of an activist, regulatory welfare state through the legal structures of a reactive, decentralized, nonhierarchical governmental system").

36. Post 1987.

37. As in the familiar hymn "Farther Along":

> Tempted and tried, we're oft made to wonder
> How it can be so all the day long
> While there are others living about us
> Never molested, though in the wrong
> Farther along, we'll know all about it
> Farther along, we'll understand why
> Cheer up my brothers, live in the sunshine
> We'll understand it all by and by.

38. L. M. Friedman 1985.

39. Cf. Shklar 1990.

REFERENCES

Note: Dates are years of edition examined and, unless otherwise indicated, of original publication. Dates in brackets are years of original publication. I follow the title page in designating authors as editor or compiler.

Aarne, Antti. 1961. *The types of the folktale: A classification and bibliography.* Trans. Stith Thompson. 2nd rev. ed. Helsinki: Academia Scientarum Fennica. 588 pp.

ABC News/*Washington Post* Survey. 1985. Question ID: USACWP.196.R24. Available in Westlaw Poll Database.

Abel, Richard L. 1989. *American lawyers.* New York: Oxford Univ. Press. xv + 406 pp.

Abel-Smith, Brian, Michael Zander, and Rosalind Brooke Ross. 1973. *Legal problems and the citizen.* London: Heineman. xiv + 265 pp.

Abrahams, Roger D. 1961–62. Ghastly commands: The cruel jokes revisited. *Midwest Folklore* 11:235–46.

———. 1970. *Deep down in the jungle: Negro narrative folklore from the streets of Philadelphia.* 2nd ed. New York: Aldine. ix + 278 pp.

Adams, Joey. 1953. *Joey Adams' joke book.* New York: Popular Library. 224 pp.

———. 1955. *Strictly for laughs.* New York: Frederick Fell. 190 pp.

———. 1958. *Encyclopedia of humor.* New York: Bonanza Books. 481 + 17 pp.

———. 1959. *It takes one to know one: The Joey Adams do-it-yourself laugh kit.* New York: G. P. Putnam. 219 pp.

———. 1961. *The Joey Adams joke dictionary.* New York: Citadel. 342 pp.

———. 1970. *Son of encyclopedia of humor.* Indianapolis: Bobbs-Merrill. 309 pp.

———. 1975. *Joey Adams' ethnic humor.* New York: Manor Books. 192 pp.

———. 1996. *Joey Adams' complete encyclopedia of laughter.* Comp. Robert W. Cabell. West Hollywood, CA: Dove Books. 544 pp.

Adams, John Quincy. 1902. [1787–89]. Diary of John Quincy Adams. *Proceedings of the Massachusetts Historical Society,* 2nd ser., 16:295–464

Adams, Phillip, and Patrice Newall. 1994. *The Penguin book of Australian jokes.* Ringwood, Victoria: Penguin Books Australia. 482 pp.

———, comps. 1995. *The Penguin book of jokes from cyberspace.* (ingwood, Victoria: Penguin Books Australia. 450 pp.

———, comps. 1996. *Pocket jokes.* Ringwood, Victoria: Penguin Books Australia. 120 pp.

———, comps. 1996a. *The Penguin book of more Australian jokes.* Ringwood, Victoria: Penguin Books Australia. 510 pp.

Adelman, Ken. 1996. Litigious society in and out of court. *Washington Times.* Oct. 10.

Adler, Bill. 1969. *Jewish wit and wisdom.* New York: Dell. 144 pp.

———. 1992. *Great lawyer stories: From courthouse to jailhouse, tall tales, jokes and anecdotes.* New York: Citadel. 141 pp.

———. 1994. *First, kill all the lawyers: Legal proverbs, epitaphs, jokes and anecdotes.* New York: Citadel. viii +147 pp. (A republication of Adler 1992 with some slight variations.)

———, and Bill Adler Jr. 1992. *Quayle hunting: The Dan Quayle joke book.* New York: Carroll & Graf. xiv + 127 pp.

Adler, Eric. 1993. Trendy gags poke fun at professions; Lawyer jokes are part of latest cruel humor. *Kansas City Star.* July 10.

Adler, Larry. 1963. *Jokes and how to tell them.* New York: Doubleday. 138 pp.

Agarwal, Charu, comp. 1998. *The pocket book of funny jokes.* New Delhi: Hind Pocket Books. 138 pp.

Akst, Daniel, and Laura Landro. 1998. Preying for gain: In Hollywood's jungle the predators are out and feasting on stars. *Wall Street Journal,* June 20.

Allday, Richard. 1993. Letter to the editor. *Daily Telegraph.* Oct. 20.

Allen, Edward Frank, ed. 1945. *Modern humor for effective speaking.* New York: Dover. xii + 468 pp.

Allen, Jay. 1990. *500 Great Jewish jokes.* New York: Signet Books. 171 pp.

Allen, Steve. 2000. *Steve Allen's private joke file.* New York: Three Rivers Press. xvi + 411 pp.

Althouse, Ann, Rob Atkinson, Burnele V. Powell, William H. Simon, and Randolph N. Stone. 1999. Responses to Lubet (1999). *Michigan Law Review* 97:1363–84.

Altman, Sig. 1971. *The comic image of the Jew: Explorations of a pop culture phenomenon.* Rutherford, NJ: Fairleigh Dickenson Univ. Press. 234 pp.

Alverson, Charles. 1993. [1989]. *The world's best business jokes.* London: Fontana. 96 pp.

Alvin, Julius. 1983. *Gross jokes.* New York: Zebra Books. 159 pp.

———. 1983a. *Totally gross jokes.* New York: Zebra Books. 159 pp.

———. 1984. *Utterly gross jokes.* New York: Zebra Books. 158 pp.

———. 1986. *Doubly gross joke.* New York: Zebra Books. 172 pp.

———. 1988. *Awesomely gross jokes.* New York: Zebra Books. 159 pp.

———. 1989. *Painfully gross jokes.* New York: Zebra Books. 160 pp.

———. 1990. *Agonizingly gross jokes.* New York: Zebra Books. 142 pp.

———. 1991. *Excruciatingly gross jokes.* New York: Zebra Books. 143 pp.

———. 1993. *Intensely gross jokes.* New York: Zebra Books. 159 pp.

———. 1994. *Infinitely gross jokes.* New York: Zebra Books. 155 pp.

———. 1995. *Terribly gross jokes.* New York: Zebra Books. 155 pp.

———. 1995a. *Savagely gross jokes.* New York: Zebra Books. 159 pp.

———. 1997. *Insanely gross jokes.* New York: Zebra Books. 143 pp.

———. 1998. *Brutally gross jokes.* New York: Zebra Books. 156 pp.

———. 1998a. *Unbelievably gross jokes.* New York: Zebra Books. 156 pp.

———. 1999. *Obnoxiously gross jokes.* New York: Zebra Books. 128 pp.

———. 1999a. *Hilariously gross jokes.* New York: Zebra Books. 142 pp.

———. 1999b. *Frightfully gross jokes.* New York: Zebra Books. 128 pp.

———. 2000. *Fiendishly gross jokes.* New York: Zebra Books. 174 pp.

———. 2000a. *Offensively gross jokes.* New York: Zebra Books. 142 pp.

———. 2001. *Grossly gross jokes.* New York: Pinnacle Books. 124 pp.

———. 2001a. *Twistedly gross jokes.* New York: Pinnacle Books. 109 pp.

Aman, Reinhold. 1983. Kakologia: A chronicle of nasty riddles and naughty wordplays. *Maledicta* 7:275–307.

American Bar Association. 1999. *Perceptions of the U.S. justice system.* Chicago: American Bar Association. 118 + 14 pp.

American Bar Association Commission on Advertising. 1995. *Lawyer advertising at the crossroads: Professional policy considerations.* Chicago: American Bar Association. vi + 216 pp.

American Lawyer. 1895. The commercialization of the profession. Mar., 84–85.

Amsterdam, Morey. 1959. *Keep laughing.* New York: Citadel. 144 pp.

Anderson, Jack. 1985. U.S. has become a nation of lawsuits. *Washington Post,* Jan. 25.

Anderson, Stewart, comp. 1921. *Sparks of laughter: Suggestions to toastmasters how to tell a funny story.* 2nd ed. New York: Stewart Anderson. 96 pp.

———, comp. 1922. *Sparks of laughter.* 3rd ed. Newark, NJ: Stewart Anderson. 96 pp.

———, comp. 1923. *Sparks of laughter.* 4th annual comp. Newark, NJ: Stewart Anderson. 300 pp. (Items from p. 117 on are "Selections from Previous Editions.")

———, comp. 1924. *Sparks of laughter.* 5th annual comp. Newark, NJ: Stewart Anderson. 299 pp.

———, comp. 1925. *Sparks of laughter.* 6th annual comp. Newark, NJ: Stewart Anderson. 300 pp.

Anderson Kill Olick & Oshinsky. 1991? We are *not* the enemy. Unpaginated brochure.

Andrews, William. 1896. *The lawyer in history, literature and humour.* London: William Andrews. 276 pp.

Anolik, Alexander. 1984. Caveat emptor: Old saying also applied to those selling their travel agencies. *Travel Weekly,* Mar. 29, 14.

Anon. 1756. *The tell-tale: or, Anecdotes expressive of the characters of persons eminent for rank, learning, wit, or humour.* 2 vols. London: R. Baldwin. x + 432 pp.

———. 1822. *Anecdote library; Being the largest collection of anecdotes ever assembled in a single volume* by the editor of the "Vocal Library." London: Whittaker. 720 pp.

———. 1828. *The London jester; or, Museum of mirth, wit and humour* (London: Orlando Hodgson) 124 pp.

———. 1830? *Jestiana, or joke upon joke, comprising rich gems of humour and smart bon mots, extracted from the records of Momus.* London: D. Hodgson. 256 pp.

———. 1831. *The flowers of anecdote, wit, humour, gaiety, and genius* London: Charles Tilt. iv + 309 pp.

———. 1832. *The American jest book, being a chaste collection of anecdotes, bon mots, and epigrams, original and selected, for the amusement of the young and old of both sexes: By the author of the American Chesterfield.* Philadelphia: J. Howe. 216 pp.

———. 1853. *The American Joe Miller: or, The jester's own book, being a choice collection of anecdotes and witticisms.* Philadelphia: Leary & Getz. 219 pp.

———. 1855. Law and lawyers.—by the editor. No. III. *Debow's Review* 19:507–23.

———. [ca.1860]. *Chips from Uncle Sam's Jack-Knife; or Slices from the New York Picayune.* New York: Dick & Fitzgerald. 94 pp.

———. 1867. *The book of humour. wit and wisdom: A manual of table-talk.* London: George Routledge. vii + 365 pp.

———. 1893. *2000 Jokes and jests: Wit, humor and anecdote, native and foreign, classic and otherwise*. Chicago: Rhodes & McClure. 434 pp.

———. 1894. The legend of Saint Yves, the lawyers' patron saint. *Green Bag* 6:142–43.

———. 1898. [W. H. Howe?, comp.]. *English wit and humor*. Philadephia: George W. Jacobs. 220 pp.

———. 1900. *American wit and humor*. Philadelphia: George W. Jacobs. 246 pp.

———. 1900a. *Hebrew yarns and dialect humor*. New York: Popular Publishing. 90 pp. (Copyright by T. J. Carey.)

———. 1902. *"The Man in the Street" stories from* the *New York Times*. New York: J. S. Ogilvie. 310 pp.

———. 1902a. *Irish wit and humor*. Chicago: Frederick J. Drake. 151 pp.

———. 1904. *New jokes and monologues by the best jokers, no. 4*. Baltimore: I&M Ottenheimer. 95 pp.

———. 1905. *Wit and humor of the American bar*. Philadelphia: George W. Jacobs. 238 pp. (Librarian's notation: "Henry Frederic Reddall.")

———. 1905a. *New Hebrew jokes by the best jokers; Hebrew song parodies*. Baltimore: I&M Ottenheimer. 86 pp.

———. 1906. *Wit and humor of the physician*. Philadelphia: George W. Jacobs. 218 pp.

———. 1906a. *Wehman Bros. Hebrew jokes no. 1 containing side-splitting jokes, stories and dialect humor, as delivered by the celebrated humorists of the day*. New York: Wehman Bros. 58 pp.

———. 1906b. *Wehman Bros.' combination prize joker no. 1: Containing a collection of the latest and best vaudeville, Irish, Dutch and Hebrew dialect jokes*. New York: Wehman Bros. 91 pp.

———. 1907. *Wit and humor of women*. Philadelphia: George W. Jacobs. 249 pp.

———. 1911. *That reminds me: A book of after dinner stories*. New York: H. M. Caldwell. 96 pp.

———. 1913. *New drummer's yarns, no. 21 by a "knight of the grip."* Baltimore: I&M Ottenheimer. 58 pp.

———. 1914. *Anecdotes of the hour: By famous men*. New York: Hearst's International Library. 128 pp.

———. [ca.1920]. *Toasts and after-dinner stories*. New York: Barse & Hopkins. 96 pp.

———. 1927. *Bestlaffs of the year*. New York: Harper. xxvii (not numbered) + 313 pp.

———. [1928]. *Anecdota Americana*. The original "dirty" Anecdota, republished "in slightly different form" as Anon., *The classic book of dirty jokes: Anecdota Americana* (New York: Bell, 1981) xi + 201 pp. (William Passemon is identified at vii as the collector of the anecdotes. According to Legman 1992: 895, the original publication was in New York, printed by "Guy D'Isere"/Joseoph Gavorse for David Moss, Gotham Book Mart, 1927–28, and Passemon is a pseud. for Joseph Fliesler.)

———. ca. 1930. *Dr. Miles joke book*. Elkhart, IN: Dr. Miles Laboratories. 29 pp.

———. 1933. *Anecdota Americana: Five hundred stories for the amusement of the five hundred nations that comprise America*. New York: William Faro. 204 pp. (An edition published in 1934 [New York: Nesor Publishing House, 192 pp.] is identical except that the introduction and prologue at pp. 9–26 of the 1933 edition have been replaced by a different introduction at pp. 9–13. According to Legman, this volume was "expurgated and revised by Samuel Roth.")

———. [1934]. *Anecdota Americana: Series two*. (The original sequel to the 1928 *Anecdota*, republished "in a slightly different form" as Anon., *503 World's worst dirty jokes* [New

York: Bell, 1982], vii + 189 pp. The preface is initialed by "J. M. H." [identified by Legman as J. Mortimer Hall, pseud. of Vincent Smith]. Some items appear to have been updated, e.g., p. 22, "watching the football game on T.V.")

———. Before 1941. *Snappy jokes: A new collection of rich and rare jokes compiled by a jolly bartender for stag parties, smokers, etc.* Detroit: Johnson Smith. 32 pp. (Unpaginated, bound together with catalog material copyrighted 1941.)

———. 1943. *Laughter for the millions.* Rev. ed. New York: Larch Publications. 256 pp. (Original copyright by Louis Shomer, 1938.)

———. 1944. *The new* Anecdota Americana: *Five hundred stories for America's amusement.* New York: Greyson. vii + 171 pp. (According to Legman, a further revision by Samuel Roth of Anon. 1933a.)

———. n.d. 1945? *Humour and counter humour.* Shrewsbury, UK: Wilding. 112 pp.

———. 1953. *Sextra special.* New York: Scylla.

———. 1954. *Extra sextra special.* New York: Scylla.

———. 1955. *Open at your own risque.* New York: Scylla. 160 pp.

———. 1957. *Are you under sexty?* New York: Olympia House. 192 pp.

———. 1959. *The little joke book.* Mt. Vernon, NY: Peter Pauper Press. 60 pp.

———. 1961. *Jokes for the john.* New York: Kanrom.

———. 1961a. *That passing laughter: Stories of the Central South.* Birmingham, AL: Central South. 140 pp.

———. 1963. *More jokes for the john.* New York: Kanrom.

———. 1963a. *"It only hurts when I laugh": Cartoon classics from "Medical Economics" magazine.* Greenwich, CT: Fawcett.

———. 1965. *Laughsville U.S.A.* New York: Scholastic Press Services. 125 pp.

———. 1965a. *Jokes for the head.* New York: Kanrom.

———. 1968a. *The joke is wild.* Kansas City, MO: Hallmark Editions. 61 pp.

———. 1968b. *Can-a-rama: The john companion.* North Palm Beach, FL: Kamron.

———. 1970? *500 best Irish jokes and limericks.* New York: Wings Books. ii + 91 pp.

———. 1971. *Executive's handbook of humor for speakers.* Waterford, CT: Bureau of Business Practice.

———. 1972. *Hillbilly laugh book.* Amarillo, TX: Baxter Lane.

———. 1972a. [1967]. *Jewish jokes for the john.* New York: Pocket Books. 223 pp. (Originally published by Kanrom.)

———. 1973. *Cowboy laugh book.* Amarillo, TX: Baxter Lane.

———. 1973a. *Fisherman's laugh book.* Amarillo, TX: Baxter Lane.

. [Nasreddin Hodja]. ca. 1975. *202 jokes of Nasreddin Hodja.* Istanbul: Minyatur Yayinlari.

———. n.d., ca. 1980? *Tell me another.* St. Ives, UK.: Colourmaster International. 32 pp.

———. 1980. Union dogs. *Maledicta,* Summer, 44.

———. 1985. [1970]. *What rugby jokes did next.* Repr., London: Sphere Books. 138 pp.

———. 1987. *Rugby jokes score again.* London: Sphere Books. 146 pp. (Copyright 1987 by E. L. Ranelagh.)

———. 1988. *Hands up for rugby jokes.* London: Sphere Books. 165 pp. (Copyright 1988 by E. L. Ranelagh.)

———. 1988a. *Accent on humor: A look at the lighter side of philanthropy.* Washington: Philanthropic Service for Institutions. 84 pp.

———. 1990. [1970]. *Son of rugby jokes.* Repr., London: Sphere Books. 172 pp.

———. 1991. [1984]. *More rugby jokes.* Repr., London: Sphere Books. 187 pp. (Copyright 1984 by E. L. Ranelagh.)

———. 1992. *The Maxwell joke book.* London: Blake Paperbacks. 96 pp. (Also published as Yermonee 1992.)

———. 1993. [1986]. *Even more rugby jokes.* New York: Warner Books. 147 pp. (Copyright 1986 by E. L. Ranelagh.)

———. 1995. [1968]. *Rugby jokes.* Repr., New York: Warner Books. 175 pp.

———. 1996. *Disorder in the court: Legal laughs, court jests and just jokes culled from the nation's justice system.* Vienna, VA: National Court Reporters Assoc. vii + 298 pp.

———. [Four Anonymous Wall St. Guys]. 1997. *The Wall Street joke book: Raunchy humor from fast-lane financiers.* New York: St. Martin's. 82 pp.

———. 1997a. *Best of marriage jokes.* Bombay: Jaico Publishing House.167 pp.

———. 1997b. *The funny side of the law: Cop's clangers and courtroom classics.* London: Stevenson. 64 pp.

———. 1997c. *The best pub joke book ever.* London: Carlton Books. 351 pp.

———. 1997d. *Jokes of the (not so) humorous struggle against communism in Hungary.* Budapest: NOTESZ+K Ltd. 68 pp.

———. 1998. [1993]. *Favourite Yorkshire humour.* Skipton, UK: Dalesman. 64 pp.

———. 2000. *The raunchy joke book, vol. 2.* Mumbai, India: Magna. 134 pp.

———. 2000a. *A Prairie Home Companion pretty good joke book.* St. Paul, MN: Highbridge. 176 pp.

———. [The Laughter Lines Team]. 2000b. *Dirty jokes in a dinner jacket: After-dinner stories for speakers.* London: Foulsham. 128 pp.

———. 2000c. *E-tales: The best and worst of Internet humour.* London: Cassell. 398 pp.

———. 2000d. *E-tales two: More of the best and worst of Internet humour.* London: Cassell. 336 pp.

———. 2001. *Jokes, quotes and bar-toons.* Liberty Corner, NJ: Foley. 147 pp. (Copyright Raymond Peter Foley.)

———. 2001a. *A Prairie Home Companion pretty good joke book.* Rev. and exp. ed. St. Paul, MN: Highbridge. 224 pp.

———. 2001b. *The most outrageous after-dinner jokes and stories.* London: PPGS. 124 pp.

———. 2002. *The best doctor jokes ever.* New York: MetroBooks. 121 pp.

———. 2002a. *The best lawyer jokes ever.* New York: MetroBooks. 120 pp.

Applbaum, Arthur Isak. 1997. Are lawyers liars? The argument of redescription. Working Papers, Politics Research Group, Kennedy School of Government, Harvard Univ., July 3. 24 pp.

Arizona Republic. 1992. Short takes: You want more lawyer-bashing jokes?? (We thought so). July 17.

———. 1994. Hero or rogue?; J. J. gets celebrity-style justice. June 26.

Arneson, D. J. 1981. *The original preppy jokebook.* New York: Dell. 192 pp.

Arnold, Thurman. 1962. [1935]. *The symbols of government.* New York: Harcourt Brace & World. xv + 278 pp. (Originally published by Yale Univ. Press.)

Arron, Deborah L. 1988. Running from the law. *Law Practice Management* 14 (Sept.): 45–47.

Arrowood, Charles F. 1939. There's a geography of humorous anecdotes. In *In the Shadow of History,* ed. J. Frank Dobit, Mody C. Boatright, and Harry H. Ransom, 75–84. Austin, TX: Folk-Lore Society.

Arya, Sunil, ed. 1995. *Really funny jokes.* Delhi: Hind Pocket Books. 114 pp.

————, comp. 1996. *The really fantastic joke book.* Delhi: Hind Pocket Books. 108 pp.

————, comp. 1996a. *More really funny jokes.* Delhi: Hind Pocket Books. x + 114 pp.

Ashmore, A. C. Stevenson, comp. 1930. *Jokes from the courts.* London: T. Werner Laurie. 58 pp.

Ashton, John. 1884. *Humour, wit and satire of the seventeenth century.* New York: J. W. Bouton. viii + 454 pp.

Asimov, Isaac. 1971. *Isaac Asimov's treasury of humor.* Boston: Houghton Mifflin. xi + 431 pp.

————. 1992. *Asimov laughs again: More than 700 favorite jokes, limericks, and anecdotes.* New York: HarperCollins. 357 pp.

Asimow, Michael. 1996. When lawyers were heroes. *Univ. of San Francisco Law Review* 30:1131–38.

————, and Shannon Mader. 2004. *Law and popular culture: A course book.* New York: Peter Lang. xxvi + 273 pp.

Aspinwall, Jack, comp. 1987. [1986]. *Tell me another! A new collection of after-dinner stories from the House of Lords and the House of Commons.* London: Century. x + 113 pp.

Atiyah, Patrick, and Robert Summers. 1987. *Form and substance in Anglo-American law.* Oxford: Clarendon. xx + 437 pp.

Atkinson, Rob. 1999. Liberating lawyers: Divergent parallels in *Intruder in the Dust* and *To Kill a Mockingbird. Duke Law Journal* 49:601–748.

Attardo, Salvatore, and Jean-Charles Chabanne. 1992. Jokes as a text type. *Humor* 5:165–76.

Auerbach, Carl A. 1984. Legal education and some of its discontents. *Journal of Legal Education* 34:43–72.

————, comp. 1997. *Historical statistics of legal education.* Chicago: American Bar Foundation. 66 pp.

Auerbach, Jerold S. 1976. *Unequal justice: Lawyers and social change in modern America.* New York: Oxford Univ. Press. xv + 395 pp.

————. 1976a. From rags to robes: The legal profession, social mobility and the American Jewish experience. *American Jewish Historical Quarterly* 66:249–84.

————. 1976b. A plague of lawyers. *Harper's,* Oct., 37–44.

August, Ray. 1992. The mythical kingdom of lawyers. *ABA Journal,* Sept., 72.

Aurand, A. Monroe, Jr. 1946. *Wit and humor of the Pennsylvania Germans.* Harrisburg, PA: Aurand Press. 32 pp.

Austin, Jerry, comp. 1968. *Sock it to me.* Greenwich, CT: Fawcett. 128 pp.

Avery, Samuel Putnam. 1854. *Laughing gas: An encyclopaedia of wit, wisdom and wind.* 156 pp. (The copy I examined was bound together with Avery 1859 and lists no author or publisher; copyright was in name of Samuel P. Avery.)

————. 1859. *The book of 1000 comical stories; An endless repast of fun.* New York: Dick & Fitzgerald. 120 pp. (Also listed under Shillaber. The copy that I examined had no author's name on the title page, but Avery's name was pencilled in by a librarian. It was bound together with Avery 1854, which also had no author's name on title page, but was copyright in Avery's name. A second copy of these was identically bound.)

Aye, John [John Atkinson]. 1931. *Humour among the lawyers.* London: Universal Press. 158 pp.

————. 1933. *I am the joker: A collection of quaint and humourous incidents in the history of the tradesman.* London: Universal Publications. 122 pp.

————. 1933a. *Humour in our streets.* London: Universal Publications. 282 pp.

Bachman, Walt. 1995. *Law v. life: What lawyers are afraid to say about the legal profession.* Rhinebeck, NY: Four Directions Press. 140 pp.

Baddiel, Ivor, Ian Stone and Tim Dedopulos, comps. 1999. *The biggest pub joke book ever!* London: Carlton Books. 652 pp.

Baker, J[ohn] H[amilton]. 1986. *The legal profession and the common law.* London: Hambledon Press. xxvii + 495 pp.

Baker, Ronald C. 1986. *Jokelore: Humorous folktales from Indiana.* Bloomington: Indiana Univ. Press. xiii + 234 pp.

Baker, Thomas E. 2002. A compendium of clever and amusing law review writings: An idiosyncratic bibliography. *Drake Law Review* 51: 105–49.

Baker, Tom. 1996. On the genealogy of moral hazard. *Texas Law Review* 75:237–92.

Baldwin, Barry, trans. and ed. 1983. *The philogelos or laughter-lover.* Amsterdam: J. C. Gieben. xii + 134 pp.

Baldwin, John W. 1965. Critics of the legal profession: Peter the Chanter and his circle. In *Proceedings of the Second International Congress of Medieval Canon Law* [= *Monumenta Iuris Canonici,* Series C, Vol. 1], ed. Stephan Kuttner and J. Joseph Ryan. E Civitate Vaticana: S. Congregatio de Seminariis et Studiorum Universitatibus.

Baldwin, Joseph G. 1957. [1853]. *The flush times of Alabama and Mississippi: A series of sketches.* New York: Sagamore Press. xii + 244 pp.

Banc, C., and Alan Dundes. 1986. *First prize: Fifteen years! An annotated collection of Roumanian political jokes.* Rutherford, NJ: Fairleigh Dickinson Univ. Press. 182 pp.

———. 1990. *You call this living? A collection of East European political jokes.* Athens: Univ. of Georgia Press. 184 pp. (Republication of Banc and Dundes 1986 with new preface and enlarged bibliography.)

Bander, Edward J. 1982. Legal humor dissected. *Law Library Journal* 75:289–98.

———. 1985. A survey of legal humor books. *Suffolk University Law Review* 19:1065–71.

Banker. 1994. The bottom line. June, 80.

Banks, Louis. 1961. The crisis in the courts. *Fortune,* Dec., 87.

Bar-Hebraeus, Gregory John. 1899. [1333]. *Oriental wit and wisdom or the "laughable stories."* Trans. E. Wallis Budge. London: Luzac. xxvii + 204 pp. (Text as in 1333.)

Bar-Lev, Omri, and Joe Weis. 1996. *Jokes for your john.* New York: Barricade Books. 96 pp.

Barnett, John, and Lesley Kaiser in association with Brian Schaab, collectors. 1996. *The Penguin book of New Zealand jokes.* Auckland: Penguin Books. 261 pp.

Barrie, Joseph R., M.D. 1983. Letter to the editor. *New York Times,* Apr. 28. (Dated Apr. 13.)

Barron, Milton L. 1950. A content analysis of intergroup humor. *American Sociological Review* 15:88–94.

Barry, Marc. 1990. *Jokes my mother never told me.* New York: Shapolsky. 184 pp.

Barton, John. 1975. Beyond the legal explosion. *Stanford Law Review* 27:567–84.

Baughman, M. Dale. 1974. *Baughman's handbook of humor in education.* West Nyack, NY: Parker. 237 pp.

Beckham, Diane Burch. 1990. The lawyer machine. *Texas Lawyer,* May 14.

Beckmann, Petr. 1969. *Whispered anecdotes: Humor from behind the Iron Curtain.* Boulder, CO: Golem Press. 143 pp.

———. 1980. *Hammer and tickle: Clandestine laughter in the Soviet Empire.* Boulder, CO: Golem Press. 105 pp.

Beeton, Samuel Orchart. 1880. *Beeton's book of anecdote, wit, and humour.* London: Ward, Lock & Tyler. 140 pp.

Behrman, Sid. 1991. *The lawyer joke book.* New York: Dorset Press. 128 pp.

————. 1995. *The doctor joke book.* New York: Barnes & Noble. 128 pp. (Cover lists author as "Behrman," but title page reads "Berman.")

Bell, Aaron. 1995. The meaning of laughter in Jewish jokes. In *Laughter down the centuries,* ed. Siegfried Jakel and Asko Timonen, 2:235–42. Turku, Finland: Turun Yliopistoo.

Bell, J. J. 1929. *Hoots.* Dundee, Scot.: Valentine. 36 pp.

Ben Amos, Dan. 1973. The "myth" of Jewish humor. *Western Folklore* 32:112–31.

Bennett, D. J. 1964. The psychological meaning of anti-Negro jokes. *Fact* 1 (Mar.–Apr.): 53–59.

Benton, Greg, and Graham Loomes. 1977. [1976]. *Big red joke book: Laughs from the left.* New York: Two Continents. 154 pp. (First published in 1976 by Pluto Press, London.)

Berger, Arthur Asa. 1997. *The genius of the Jewish joke.* Northvale, NJ: Jason Aronson. xvi + 184 pp.

Berger, Bill, and Ricardo Martinez. 1988. *What to do with a dead lawyer.* Berkeley: Ten Speed Press. Unpaginated.

Berger, Paul L., et al. 1992. Is America on the way down? (Round two). *Commentary,* May, 20–21.

Bergin, Edward, ed. 1995. *The definitive guide to underground humor.* Waterbury, CT: Offbeat Publishing. 96 pp.

Bergstrom, Randolph E. 1992. *Courting danger: Injury and law in New York City, 1870–1910.* Ithaca, NY: Cornell Univ. Press. xi + 213 pp.

Berle, Milton. 1950. [1945]. *Out of my trunk.* Garden City, NY: Blue Ribbon Books. 224 pp.

————. 1989. *Milton Berle's private joke file.* Ed. Milt Rosen. New York: Crown Trade Paperbacks. xxiv + 642 pp.

————. 1993. *More of the best of Milton Berle's private joke file.* Ed. Milt Rosen. New York: William Morrow. 553 pp.

Bermant, Chaim. 1986. *What's the joke? A study of Jewish humour through the ages.* London: Weidenfeld and Nicholson. vii + 259 pp.

Bernhard, Edgar. 1977. *Speakers on the spot: A treasury of anecdotes for coping with sticky situations.* West Nyack, NY: Parker. 207 pp.

Bialik, Hayim Nahman, and Yehoshua Hana Ravnitsky, eds. 1992. [1908–11]. *The book of legends: Sefer Ha-Aggadah; legends from the Talmud and Midrash.* New York: Schocken Books. 897 pp.

Bierce, Ambrose. 1972. [1946]. *The collected writings of Ambrose Bierce.* 6th printing of paperback, Secaucus, NJ: Citadel. (Contains *The Devils Dictionary* [1911] and *Fantastic Fables* [1899].)

Bigelow, Lafayette J. 1871. *Bench and bar: A complete digest of the wit, humor, asperities and amenities of the law.* New York: Harper. 532 pp. (Reprinted 1970 by Johnson Reprint Co., New York.)

Black, Amy E., and Stanley Rothman. 1998. Shall we kill all the lawyers first?: Insider and outsider views of the legal profession. *Harvard Journal of Law and Public Policy* 21:835–60.

Blair, Tom. 1984. Tom Blair column. *San Diego Union-Tribune,* Oct. 18, B-1.

————. 1985a. Tom Blair column. *San Diego Union-Tribune,* Sept. 29, B-1.

————. 1985b. Tom Blair column. *San Diego Union-Tribune,* Oct. 3, B-1.

Bloom, Murray Teigh. 1968. *The trouble with lawyers.* New York, Simon & Schuster. 351 pp.

Bloomfield, Maxwell H. 1976. *American lawyers in a changing society, 1776–1876.* Cambridge, MA: Harvard Univ. Press. ix + 397 pp.

———. 1980. Law and lawyers in American popular culture. In *Law and American liter-ature: A collection of essays,* ed. Maxwell Bloomfield. Chicago: Commission on Under-graduate Education in Law and the Humanities, American Bar Association. 68 pp (separately paginated).

Blue, Lionel. 2001. *Blue's jokes: Ancient and modern, sacred and profane.* London: Hodder & Stoughton. 164 pp.

Bluestein, Gene. 1994. *Poplore: Folk and pop in American culture.* Amherst: Univ. of Mass-achusetts Press. xiii + 167 pp.

Blum, Andy. 1991. Victim group has crusader as its leader. *National Law Journal,* Mar. 25.

Blumberg, Abraham. 1967. The practice of law as a confidence game. *Law & Society Review* 1: 15–39.

Blumenfeld, Gerry. 1967. *Tales from the bagel lancers: Everyman's book of Jewish humor.* Cleveland: World. 128 pp.

———. 1969. [1965]. *Some of my best jokes are Jewish.* New York: Popular Library. 128 pp.

———. 1970. *Rx: Doctor's orders: Laugh!* New York: Popular Library. 127 pp.

———, and Harold Blumenfeld. 1987. *Hit the ball and drag Charlie and other great golf jokes.* Los Angeles: Price Stern Sloan. Unpaginated.

Boatright, Mody C. 1945. Law and laughter on the frontier. *Southwest Review* 30 (2): 175–81.

———. 1949. *Folk laughter on the American frontier.* New York: MacMillan. vii + 182 pp.

Boccaccio, Giovanni. 1982. [1353]. *Decameron.* 2 vols. Berkeley: Univ. of California Press.

Bodker, Lauritz. 1965. *Folk literature (Germanic).* Copenhagen: Rosenkilde and Bagger.

Bogart, William A. 2002. *Consequences: The impact of law and its complexity.* Toronto: Univ. of Toronto Press. xii + 405 pp.

Boliska, Al. 1968. [1966]. *The world's worst jokes.* New York: Pocket Books. 157 pp. (Orig-inally published by McClelland and Stewart.)

Bond, Donald F. 1935. The law and lawyers in English proverbs. *ABA Journal* 21:724–27.

———. 1936. English legal maxims. *PMLA* 51:921–35.

Bond, Simon. 1990. *Battered lawyers and other good ideas.* Toronto: HarperCollins. 75 pp.

Bonfanti, Joe. 1976. *Italian jokes.* New York: Nordon. 192 pp.

Bonham, Tal D. 1981. *The treasury of clean jokes.* Nashville, TN: Broadman Press. 160 pp.

———. 1986. *The treasury of clean country jokes* Nashville, TN: Broadman Press. 124 pp.

———. 1986a. *The treasury of clean sports jokes.* Nashville, TN: Broadman Press. 128 pp.

———. 1997. *The treasury of clean church jokes.* Nashville, TN: Broadman & Holman. xii + 112 pp.

———. 1997a. *The treasury of clean country jokes.* 2nd ed. Nashville, TN: Broadman & Holman. 108 pp.

———, and Jack Gulledge. 1989. *The treasury of clean senior adult jokes.* Nashville, TN: Broadman Press. 156 pp.

———. 1997. *The treasury of clean seniors jokes.* 2nd ed. Nashville, TN: Broadman & Hol-man. x + 117 pp.

Boskin, Joseph. 1997. *Rebellious laughter: People's humor in American culture.* Syracuse, NY: Syracuse Univ. Press. xii + 245 pp.

Botkin, B[enjamin] A., ed. 1957. *A treasury of American anecdotes.* New York: Galahad Books. xxix + 321 pp.

Bouquet, Betty Jane. 1989. *B. J.'s joke book.* Graham, WA.: Systems Company. vii + 73 pp.

Bouwsma, William J. 1973. Lawyers and early modern culture. *American Historical Review* 78:303–27.

Bowen, Barbara C. 1984. Roman jokes and the Renaissance prince, 1455–1528. *Illinois Classical Studies* 9:137–48.

———, ed. 1988. *One hundred Renaissance jokes: An anthology.* Birmingham, AL: Summa. xx + 107 pp.

Bowker, A[rchibald] E[dward]. 1961. *A lifetime with the law.* London: W. H. Allen. 217 pp.

Brallier, Jess M. 1992. *Lawyers and other reptiles.* Chicago: Contemporary Books. 102 pp.

———. 1996. *Lawyers and other reptiles II: The appeal.* Chicago: Contemporary Books. 108 pp.

Brandes, Stanley. 1983. Jewish-American dialect jokes and Jewish-American identity. *Jewish Social Studies* 45:233–40.

Brandreth, Gyles. 1985. *Cockburn's A-Z of after-dinner entertainment.* London: Pelham Books. viii + 149 pp.

———. 1986. *The ultimate joke encyclopedia.* Enfield: Guiness. 352 pp.

Brant, Sebastian. 1944. [1494]. *The ship of fools.* New York: Columbia Univ. Press. ix + 399 pp.

Braude, Jacob M. 1955. *Speaker's encyclopedia of stories, quotations and anecdotes.* Englewood Cliffs, NJ: Prentice-Hall. 476 pp.

———. 1958. *Braude's handbook of humor for all occasions.* Englewood Cliffs, NJ: Prentice-Hall. 378 pp.

———. 1964. *Braude's treasury of wit and humor.* Englewood Cliffs, NJ: Prentice-Hall. viii + 277 pp.

Brazin, Lionel I. 1993. Letter. *Illinois Legal Times,* July, 3.

Bregman, Alexander. 1967. Poking fun at Mao. *East Europe* 16 (3): 21–22.

Bremmer, Jan, and Herman Roodenburg, eds. 1997. *A cultural history of humor.* Cambridge, UK: Polity Press. xii + 264 pp.

Breslin, Mark, ed. 1991. *Son of a Meech: The best Brian Mulroney jokes.* Toronto: Ballantine Books. 113 pp.

Brill, Steven. 1989. The law business in the year 2000. *American Lawyer,* June, pull-out supplement.

———, and James Lyons. 1986. The not-so-simple crisis. *American Lawyer,* May, 1, 12–17.

British Museum. 1870–1954. *Catalog of political and personal satires preserved in the department of prints and drawings in the British Museum.* Vols. 1–4 by Frederick George Stephens; vols. 5–11 by M. Dorothy George. 11 vols. London: The British Museum.

Brodnick, Max, comp. and ed. 1976. *The international joke book #2.* New York: Leisure Books. 191 pp.

———, comp. and ed. 1976a. *The Jerry Ford joke book.* New York: Leisure Press. Unpaginated.

Brooks, C. W. 1986. *Pettifoggers and vipers of the commonwealth: The "lower branch" of the legal profession in early modern England.* Cambridge, UK: Cambridge Univ. Press. xiii + 396 pp.

Brower, Bill. 1952. *The complete traveling salesman's joke book.* New York: Stravon. 127 pp.

Brown, David, comp. 1998. *Really wicked dirty jokes.* London: Michael O'Mara Books. 96 pp.

———, comp. 1998a. *Really wicked drinking jokes.* London: Michael O'Mara Books. 95 pp.

———, comp. 1998b. *Really wicked football jokes.* London: Michael O'Mara Books. 95 pp.

———, comp. 1998c. *Really wicked golf jokes.* London: Michael O'Mara Books. 96 pp.

———, comp. 1998d. *Really wicked Irish jokes.* London: Michael O'Mara Books. 95 pp.

———, comp. 1998e. *Really wicked Scottish jokes.* London: Michael O'Mara Books. 95 pp.

————, comp. 1998f. *The truly terrible joke book.* London: Michael O'Mara Books. 195 pp.

Brown, Marshall. 1883. [1879]. *Wit and humor: A choice collection.* 18th ed., Chicago: S. C. Griggs. 340 pp.

Brown, Peter M. 1983. Profession endangered by rush to business ethic. *Legal Times,* Sept. 23, 10.

Brown, Ronald L., comp. 1988. *Juris-jocular: An anthology of modern American legal humor.* Littleton, CO: Fred B. Rothman. xix + 165 pp.

Brown, Yorick, and Mike Flynn. 1998. *The best book of urban myths ever.* London: Carlton Books. 320 pp.

Browne, Irving. 1876. *Humorous phases of the law.* San Francisco: Sumner Whitney. 190 pp.

————. 1883. *Law and lawyers in literature.* Boston: Soule and Bugbee. xv + 413 pp. (Reprinted, Littleton, CO: Fred B. Rothman, 1982.)

Brundage, James A. 1973. The ethics of the legal profession: Medieval canonists and their clients. *Jurist* 33:237–48.

————. 1988. The profits of the law: Legal fees of university-trained advocates. *American Journal of Legal History* 32:1–15.

————. 1988a. The medieval advocate's profession. *Law and History Review* 6:439–64.

Brunsting, Bernard. 2000. *The ultimate guide to good clean humor.* Uhrichsville, OH: Barbour. 440 pp.

Brunvand, Jan Harold. 1972. The study of contemporary folklore: jokes. *Fabula* 13:1–19.

————. 1978. *The study of American folklore: An introduction.* 2nd ed. New York: W. W. Norton. xvii + 460 pp.

Buckley, William. 1991. Invisible hand tripped up by burden of lawyer glut. *Austin American–Statesman,* Oct. 30.

Budiansky, Steve, et al. 1995. How lawyers abuse the law. *U.S. News & World Report,* Jan. 30, 50–56.

Buford, Jim Bob, and "Shotgun" Jack Grabowski. 1997. *The redneck joke book.* New York: Barnes & Noble Books. 112 pp.

————. 1998. *More redneck jokes.* New York: Barnes & Noble Books. 112 pp.

Buhler, Warren. 1978. *Calculating the Full Costs of Governmental Regulation.* Washington, D.C.: Office of the Librarian, Federal Register.

Burd, A. Harry. 1960. *New locker room humor.* Rev. ed. Chicago: Burd. 192 pp.

Burdette, Robert J., comp. 1903. *Masterpieces of wit and humor.* n.p.: American Home Reference Library. 514 pp.

Burger, Warren E. 1976. Agenda for 2000 A.D.—A need for systematic anticipation. *Federal Rules Decisions* 70: 83–96 (Address, National Conference on the Causes of Popular Dissatisfaction with the Administration of Justice, Apr. 7–9, 1976.)

————. 1977. Remarks . . . American Bar Association Minor Disputes Resolution Conference, Columbia University, New York, NY, May 27.

————. 1984. Annual Message on the Administration of Justice at the midyear meeting of the American Bar Association, Las Vegas, NV, Feb. 12.

Burke, J. C., comp. 1997a. *Five hundred years of Newfie humour (from Cabot to Crosbie).* Ottawa, Can.: Hermitage. 96 pp.

————, comp. 1997b. *Laughs from the rock: A collection of Newfoundland's funniest stories.* Ottawa, Can.: Hermitage. 98 pp.

Burma, John H. 1946. Humor as a technique in race conflict. *American Sociological Review* 11:710–15.

Burnett, W. B. 1955. *Scotland laughing: The humour of the Scot.* Edinburgh: Albyn Press. 95 pp.

Burns, Thomas A., with Inger H. Burns. 1975. *Doing the wash: An expressive culture and personality study of a joke and its tellers.* Norwood, PA: Norwood Editions. xvi + 359 pp.

Byrn, M. Lafayette. 1857. [1852]. *The repository of wit and humor; Comprising more than one thousand anecdotes, odd scraps, off-hand bits, and humorous sketches.* Boston: John P. Jewett. 392 pp.

Cagney, Peter, ed. 1980. [1979]. *The official Irish joke book no. 4.* Repr., London: Futura. 128 pp.

———, ed. 1980. [1979a]. *Positively the last official Irish joke book.* Repr., London: Futura. 128 pp.

Cahill, F[rancis]. J. 1906. *Rare bits of humor: After-dinner stories, convivial toasts and humorous anecdotes.* New York: George Sully. 156 pp. (Also published in that year by Sully under the title *A bunch of yarns and rare bits of humor.*)

Cain, Maureen. 1983. The general practice lawyer and the client: Towards a radical conception. In *The sociology of the professions: Lawyers, doctors and others,* ed. Robert Dingwall and Philip S. C. Lewis, 106–30. London: MacMillan.

Califano, Joseph A., Jr. 1996. The law: Once a noble profession. *Washington Post,* Jan. 28.

Calve, Joseph. 1994. The mock-pop-psycho-social-lawyer-joke-study article. *Connecticut Law Tribune,* Jan. 10, 39.

Campos, Paul F. 1998. *Jurismania: The madness of American law.* New York: Oxford Univ. Press. x + 198 pp.

Cantor, Eddie, ed. 1943. *World's book of best jokes.* Cleveland: World. 270 pp.

Caplow, Theodore, Louis Hicks, and Ben J. Wattenberg. 2001. *The first measured century: An illustrated guide to trends in America, 1900–2000.* Washington, DC: AEI Press. xv + 308 pp.

Cappelletti, Mauro, ed. 1978–79. *Access to justice.* 4 vols. in 6. Milan: A. Giuffrè; Alphen aan den Rijn, Neth.: Sijthoff and Noordhoff.

———, ed. 1981. *Access to justice and the welfare state.* With the assistance of John Weisner and Monica Seccombe. Alphen aan den Rijn, Neth.: Sijthoff. xiv + 365 pp.

Caras, Quentin. 1985. *Naughty jokes to make you blush.* Bombay: India Book House. vi + 153 pp.

Carlin, Jerome E. 1962. *Lawyers on their own: A study of individual practitioners in Chicago.* New Brunswick, NJ: Rutgers Univ. Press. x + 234 pp.

———. 1966. *Lawyers' ethics: A survey of the New York City Bar.* New York: Russell Sage Foundation. xxix + 267 pp.

———, Jan Howard, and Sheldon L. Messinger. 1966. Civil justice and the poor: Issues for sociological research. *Law & Society Review* 1:9–89.

Carlin, John. 1995. Last chance in America's ludicrous legal lottery. *Independent,* Mar. 10, 17.

Carrick, John Donald, William Motherwell, and Andrew Henderson, eds. 1850. *The laird of Logan, being anecdotes and tales illustrative of the wit and humour of Scotland.* London: Simpkin, Marshall, Hamilton, Kent. . 363 pp.

Carter, James E. 1975. *Addresses of Jimmy Carter (James Earl Carter), Governor of Georgia, 1971–1975.* Comp. Frank Daniel. Atlanta: Ben W. Fortson Jr., Sec'y of State. 304 pp.

———. 1978. Address at the 100th anniversary dinner of the Los Angeles Bar Association, May 4. Repr. in President Carter's attack on lawyers, President Spann's response, and Chief Justice Burger's remarks. 64 ABAJ 840.

Carter, Stephen L. 1996. *Integrity.* New York: Basic Books. x + 277 pp.

Carter, Terry. 1998. A lesson learned. *ABAJ,* May, 70, 72.

Case, Carleton B. 1928. *The big joke-book (new edition).* Chicago: Shrewsbury. 287 pp.

Casey, Gregory. 1974. The Supreme Court and myth: An empirical investigation. *Law & Society Review* 8:385–419.

Cerf, Bennett, ed. 1942. *The pocket book of war humor.* New York: Pocket Books. xi + 242 pp.

———. 1944. *Try and stop me: A collection of anecdotes and stories, mostly humorous.* New York: Simon & Schuster. ix + 378 pp.

———, ed., 1945. *Laughing stock: Over six-hundred jokes and anecdotes of uncertain vintage.* New York: Grosset and Dunlap. viii + 244 pp.

———, ed. 1945a. *The pocket book of jokes.* New York: Pocket Books. vi + 138 pp.

———, ed. 1946. *Anything for a laugh.* New York: Bantam Books. 220 pp.

———, ed. 1948. *Shake well before using.* New York: Random House. viii + 306 pp. (Also bound in *Bennett Cerf's bumper crop,* vol. 2, Garden City, NY: Garden City Books, n.d.)

———, ed. 1950. *Laughter incorporated,* bound in *Bennett Cerf's bumper crop,* vol. 2, Garden City, NY: Garden City Books, n.d.

———, ed. 1952. *Good for a laugh.* Garden City, NY: Hanover House. 220 pp. (Also bound in *Bennett Cerf's bumper crop,* vol. 2, Garden City, NY: Garden City Books, n.d.)

———. 1956. *The life of the party.* Garden City, NY: Doubleday. 352 pp.

———. 1956a. *Bennett Cerf's vest pocket book of jokes for all occasions.* New York: Random House. 320 pp.

———. 1959. *The laugh's on me.* Garden City, NY: Doubleday. 480 pp.

———. 1965. *Laugh day: A new treasury of over 1000 humorous stories and anecdotes.* Garden City, NY: Doubleday. xii + 496 pp.

———. 1970. *The sound of laughter.* Garden City, NY: Doubleday. xii + 463 pp.

Chambers, Garry, comp. 1979. *The complete Irish gag book.* London: W. H. Allen. 125 pp.

Chance, Norman H. 1915. *Chance hits.* Chicago: Saalfield. 157 pp.

Chariton, Wallace O. 1989. *Texas wit and wisdom.* Plano, TX: Wordware. xvii + 233 pp.

Chase, Anthony. 1986. Lawyers and popular culture: A review of mass media portrayals of American attorneys. *American Bar Foundation Research Journal* 1986:281–320.

Chesebro, Kenneth. 1993. Galileo's retort: Peter Huber's junk scholarship. *American Univ. Law Review* 42:1637–1726.

Chroust, Anton-Hermann. 1965. *The rise of the legal profession in America.* 2 vols. Norman: Univ. of Oklahoma Press. xxiii + 334, 318 pp.

Cicero, Marcus Tullius. 1970. [ca. 50 BCE.] *Cicero on oratory and orators.* Ed. J. S. Watson. Carbondale: Southern Illinois Univ. Press. li +379 pp.

Clark, Geoff. 1994. Officer can't claim spring break fame. *Orlando Sentinel,* Mar. 16 (*Osceola Sentinel*).

Clark, Gerald J. 1983. Fear and loathing in New Orleans: The sorry fate of the Kutak Commission's rules. *Suffolk Univ. Law Review* 17:79–91.

Claro, Joe, ed. 1990. *Random House book of jokes and anecdotes.* New York: Random House. vii + 232 pp.

———, ed. 1996. *Random House book of jokes and anecdotes.* 2nd. ed. New York: Random House. vi + 266 pp.

———, ed. 2000. *Get a laugh! Over 600 jokes and anecdotes about modern life.* New York: Random House. vii + 264 pp.

Clemens, Will M., ed. 1902. *The Depew story book.* Chicago: Thompson and Thomas. x + 207 pp.

Clements, William M. 1969. The types of the Polack joke. *Folklore Forum: A Bibliographic and Special Series,* no. 3, 45.

Cleveland, Andrew L. 1980. *Dirty stories for all occasions.* New York: Galahad Books. 160 pp.

Clode, Edward J. 1922. *Jokes for all occasions: Selected and edited by one of America's foremost public speakers.* New York: Edward J. Clode. 368 pp. (No author listed; Clode listed as publisher and copyright holder.)

Clouston, Al. 1978. *"Come 'ere till I tells ya": A collection of Newfoundland humor.* St. John's, NF: Dicks. 102 pp.

———. 1986. *"When I grow too old to laugh, shoot me!": A collection of Newfoundland humour.* St. John's, NF: Al Clouston. 103 pp.

Cobb, Irvin S. 1923. *A laugh a day keeps the doctor away.* Garden City, NY: Garden City. 246 pp.

———. 1925. *Many laughs for many days.* Garden City, NY: Garden City. 243 pp.

Cochrane, Timothy. 1987. The concept of ecotypes in American folklore. *Journal of Folklore Research* 24:33–55.

Cohen, Gerald Leonard. 1982. *The origin of the term "shyster."* Frankfurt am Main: Verlag Peter Lang. 124 pp.

Cohen, Myron. 1958. *Laughing out loud.* New York: Citadel. 190 pp.

———. 1960. *More laughing out loud.* New York: Gramercy. 218 pp.

Cohen, Sarah Blacher, ed. 1987. *Jewish wry: Essays on Jewish humor.* Bloomington: Indiana Univ. Press. ix + 244 pp.

Cohl, H. Aaron. 1997. *The Friars Club encyclopedia of jokes.* New York: Black Dog & Leventhal. 502 pp.

Cohn, Ted. 1999. *Jokes: Philosophical thoughts on joking matters.* Chicago: Univ. of Chicago Press. xi + 99 pp.

Cole, Edward William. 1887? *Cole's fun doctor: The funniest book in the world.* 1st ser. Melbourne: E. W. Cole. 512 + 28 pp.

———. 1902? *Cole's fun doctor: The funniest book in the world.* 2nd ser. Toronto: McClelland & Goodchild. viii + 441 pp. (This is a sequel to the preceding entry. The preface to the second series volume notes that "fifteen years have passed away" since the production of the first volume.)

Coleman, James S. 1974. *Power and the structure of society.* New York: W. W. Norton. 112 pp.

———. 1990. *Foundations of social theory.* Cambridge, MA: Harvard Univ. Press. xvi + 993 pp.

———. 1993. The rational reconstruction of society: 1992 presidential address. *American Sociological Review* 58 (Feb.): 1–15.

Coleman, Vernon. 1997. Don't swallow this butchered report! *The People,* Nov. 2, 41.

———. 1997a. Just what's going on in Britain with the long harm of the law? *The People,* Mar. 2, 36.

Colombo, John Robert. 2001. *The Penguin book of Canadian jokes.* Toronto: Penguin Books Canada. xv + 488 pp.

Connors, Tom. 1989. Up to their necks in sand. *Journal of Commerce,* Apr. 13, 8A.

Cook, Lyman E. 1938. *Comics in the law.* Chicago: Universal. 120 pp.

Cooper, Anna R. 1993. Notes and queries. *Guardian,* Oct. 22, 6.

Coote, George. 1994. *The serious joke book.* Kangaroo Pt., Qld., Austl.: Herron. 476 pp.

——. 1995. *The seriously rude joke book.* Norman Park, Qld., Austl.: Gap. xiv + 397 pp.

——. 1996. *The politically incorrect joke book.* Norman Park, Qld., Austl.: Gap. ix + 361 pp.

Cornwell, Rupert. 1995. Gingrich targets greedy lawyers. *Independent,* Mar. 10, 11.

Copeland, Lewis, ed. 1936. *The world's best jokes.* New York: Blue Ribbon Books. (Repr., Garden City, NY: Halcyon House, 1948, vii + 401 pp.

——, and Faye Copeland, eds. 1940. *10,000 jokes, toasts and stories.* Garden City, NY: Garden City Books. xi + 1020 pp. (The apparently identical volume published under the imprint of Doubleday in 1965 omits the "Negro" and "Jewish" sections [340 items] and substitutes a "Quotation Dictionary." Citations here are to the 1940 edition.)

Council for Public Interest Law. 1976. *Balancing the scales of justice: Financing public interest law in America.* Washington: Council for Public Interest Law.

Council on the Role of Courts (principal editor, Jethro K. Lieberman). 1984. *The role of courts in American society: The final report of the Council on the Role of Courts.* St. Paul, MN: West. xiii + 171 pp.

Craig, Steven C. 1993. *The malevolent leaders: Popular discontent in America.* Boulder, CO: Westview. xv + 223 pp.

Cramton, Roger C. 1996. What do lawyer jokes tell us about lawyers and lawyering? *Cornell Law Forum* 23 (1): 3–9.

Crawford, Jan, William Grady, and John O'Brien. 1991. Legal highlights of a lesser sort. *Chicago Tribune,* Dec. 31, Business, 3.

Cray, Ed. 1964. The rabbi trickster. *Journal of American Folklore* 77:331–45.

Crompton, Colin, comp. 1970. *More best Jewish jokes.* London: Wolfe. 63 pp.

Cross, Frank. 1992. The first thing we do, let's kill all the economists: An empirical evaluation of the effect of lawyers on the United States economy and political system. *Texas Law Review* 70:645–83.

Croy, Homer. 1948. *What grandpa laughed at.* New York: Duell, Sloan and Pearce. 255 pp.

Cruikshank, Hugh, Jr. 1987. *The Alaska book of jokes.* Bird Creek, AK: Fourth and Feather Productions. 107 pp.

Curran, Barbara A. 1977. *The legal needs of the public: The final report of a national survey.* Chicago: American Bar Foundation. xxxvi + 382 pp.

——. 1985. *The lawyer statistical report: A statistical profile of the U.S. legal profession in the 80s.* With Katherine J. Rosich, Clara N. Carson, and Mark C. Puccetti. Chicago: American Bar Foundation. xvii + 618 pp.

——. 1986. *Supplement to the lawyer statistical report: The U.S. legal profession in 1985.* With Katherine J. Rosich, Clara N. Carson, and Mark C. Puccetti. Chicago: American Bar Foundation. vii + 174 pp.

——, and Clara N. Carson. 1994. *The lawyer statistical report: The U.S. legal profession in the 1990s.* Chicago: American Bar Foundation. vii + 247 pp.

Curtis, Charles P. 1951. The ethics of advocacy. *Stanford Law Review* 4:3–23.

Dale, Iain, and John Simmons, comps. 1998. *The Bill Clinton joke book: Uncensored.* London: Robson Books. ii + 90 pp.

——, comps. 2000. *The Tony Blair new Labour joke book.* London: Robson Books. 133 pp.

Dalton, Mike. 1990. [1982]. *The North Dakota joke book.* New York: Carol Publishing Group. 160 pp.

Dance, Daryl Cumber, ed. 1998. *Honey, hush! An anthology of African American women's humor.* New York: W. W. Norton. xxxix + 673 pp.

Daniels, Stephen. 1989. The question of jury competence and the politics of civil justice reform: Symbols, rhetoric and agenda-building. *Law & Contemporary Problems* 52:269–310.

———, and Joanne Martin. 1995. *Civil juries and the politics of reform.* Evanston, IL: Northwestern Univ. Press. xii + 318 pp.

———. 1998. Punitive damages, change, and the politics of ideas: Defining public policy problems. *Wisconsin Law Review* 1998:71–100.

Dauer, Edward A., and Arthur Allen Leff. 1977. Correspondence: The lawyer as friend. *Yale Law Journal* 86:573–84.

David, Nelson. 2001. *The George (Dubya) Bush joke book: Uncensored.* London: Robson Books. 115 pp.

Davidson, Adolph. 1913. *Here's a new one: A book of after dinner stories.* New York: Dodge. 96 pp.

Davidson, Jim. 2000. *Too frisky: Wicked laughs with the ladies.* London: Robson Books. 144 pp.

Davidson, Lance S. 1998. *Ludicrous laws and mindless misdemeanors.* New York: John Wiley. xi + 244 pp.

Davies, Christie. 1986. Jewish jokes, anti-Semitic jokes, and Hebredonian jokes. In *Jewish Humor,* ed. Abner Ziv, 75–96. Tel Aviv: Papyrus.

———. 1990. *Ethnic humor around the world: A comparative analysis.* Bloomington: Indiana Univ. Press. x + 404 pp.

———. 1991. Exploring the thesis of the self-deprecating Jewish sense of humor. *Humor* 4:189–209.

———. 1998. *Jokes and their relation to society.* Berlin: Mouton de Gruyter. x + 234 pp.

Davis, Eddie. 1954. *Laugh yourself well.* New York: Frederick Fell. 224 pp.

———. 1956. *Stories for stags.* New York: Lion Books. 190 pp.

———. 1956a. *Playgirls, U.S.A.* New York: Pyramid Books. 125 pp.

———. 1956b. *Campus joke book.* New York: Ace Books. 159 pp.

Davis, Murray S. 1993. *What's so funny? The comic conception of culture and society.* Chicago: Univ. of Chicago Press. xiv + 386 pp.

Dawson, Les. 1979. *The Les Dawson joke book.* London: Arrow Books. 157 pp.

De Alvarado, Pedro. 1995. Hable con mi abogado. *Madrid & Compania,* Jan., 24.

Dedopulos, Tim, comp. 1998. *The best pub joke book ever! 2.* London: Carlton. 352 pp.

Delf, Jack P., comp. 1992. *Come laugh with me.* Richmond, BC, Can.: Jack P. Delf. ii + 152 pp.

Delgado, Richard, and Jean Stefanic. 1994. *Failed revolutions: Social reform and the limits of legal imagination.* Boulder, CO.: Westview Press. xix + 207 pp.

De Morgan, John, ed. 1907. *In lighter vein.* San Francisco: Paul Elder. xx (unpaginated) + 164 pp.

Denby, David. 1994. A motion to suppress. *New York* [magazine], Aug. 1, 52–53.

Denvir, John, ed. 1996. Legal reelism: Movies as legal texts. Urbana: Univ. of Illinois Press. xviii + 314 pp.

Dershowitz, Alan. 1991. Free speech and abortion. *Newsday,* June 4, 97, Nassau and Suffolk edition.

Dertouzos, James N., Elaine Holland, and Patricia Ebener. 1988. *The legal and economic consequences of wrongful termination.* Santa Monica, CA: RAND Institute for Civil Justice. xvi + 73 pp.

Desmond, Sean. 1997. [1995]. *A touch of the Irish: Wit and wisdom.* New York: Quality Paperback Book Club. 191 pp.

de Tocqueville, Alexis. 1945. [1835, 1840]. *Democracy in America.* Ed. Phillips Bradley. 2 vols. New York: Alfred A. Knopf Vintage Paperback, 1959. 1:xvi + 451 + xi; 2:xii + 518 + ix.

Dewees, Donald N., Michael Trebilcock, and Peter C. Coyote. 1991. The medical malpractice crisis: A comparative empirical perspective. *Law and Contemporary Problems* 54:217–51.

Dickson, Paul. 1984. *Jokes: Outrageous bits, atrocious puns, and ridiculous routines for those who love jests.* New York: Delacorte Press. xx + 236 pp.

Dingus, Anne, comp. 2002. "Yee-Ha!": 200 Texas jokes. *Texas Monthly,* Jan., 92–95, 145–54.

Dines, Michael. 1987. *The second Jewish joke book.* London: Futura. 128 pp.

Dionne, Jack, comp. ca. 1939. *"Lotsa" fun.* Houston, TX: Jack Dionne. 166 pp.

Diproses's anecdotes about lawyers, doctors and parsons. n.d. London: Diprose & Bateman.

Dodge, Robert K. 1987. *Early American almanac humor.* Bowling Green, OH: Bowling Green State Univ. Popular Press. 163 pp.

Dole, Bob. 2000. [1998]. *Great political wit: Laughing* (almost) *all the way to the White House.* New York: Broadway Books. xv + 202 pp.

Dolgopolova, Zhanna, ed. 1982. *Russia dies laughing: Jokes from Soviet Russia.* London: Andre Deutsch. 125 pp.

Donaldson, William. 1994. The benefits of being burgled. *Independent,* Apr. 30, 15.

Donohue, Thomas J. 1997. American business: The next agenda. *Vital Speeches of the Day,* Dec. 1. (Address to National Press Club, Washington, DC, Oct. 1, 1997.)

Dornstein, Ken. 1996. *Accidentally, on purpose: The making of a personal injury underworld in America.* New York: St. Martin's. vii + 452 pp.

Dorson, Richard M., ed. 1956. *Negro folktales in Michigan.* Cambridge, MA: Harvard Univ. Press. xiv + 247 pp.

———. 1960. Jewish-American dialect stories on tape. In *Studies in biblical and Jewish folklore,* ed. Raphael Patai, Francis Lee Utley, and Dov Noy, 111–74. Bloomington: Indiana Univ. Press.

———. 1960a. More Jewish dialect stories. *Midwest Folklore* 10 (3): 133–46.

Dover, Eileen, and Seymour Fish. 1992. *A drop in the ocean: The* official *Robert Maxwell joke book.* London: Corgi Books. Unpaginated.

Downs, Minna S. M. (Baumann). 1903. *German wit and humor.* Philadelphia: George W. Jacobs. 299 pp.

Draitser, Emil, comp. 1978. *Forbidden laughter (Soviet underground jokes).* Los Angeles: Almanac Publishing House. 85 pp.

———. 1998. *Taking penguins to the movies.* Detroit: Wayne State Univ. Press. 199 pp.

Drinan, Robert F. 1998. Joke's on us—but shouldn't be. *ABA Journal,* May, 12.

Drinker, Henry S. 1952. Some remarks on Mr. Curtis' "The ethics of advocacy." *Stanford Law Review* 4:349–57.

Droke, Maxwell, ed. 1935. *Anecdotes.* Indianapolis: Maxwell Droke. 48 pp.

———, ed. 1948. *The speaker's treasury of anecdotes.* New York: Grosset & Dunlap. 436 pp. (Originally published as *The anthology of anecdotes.*)

———. 1956. *The speaker's handbook of humor.* New York: Harper. ix + 464 pp.

Duck, B. S. 1997. *Bad boys' jokes: Jokes you wouldn't tell the woman in your life . . .* London: Michael O'Mara Books. Unpaginated.

Duncan, King. 1990. *King's treasury of dynamic humor.* Knoxville, TN: Seven Worlds Press. 250 pp.

Dundes, Alan. 1989. [1984]. *Life is like a chicken coop ladder: A portrait of German culture through folklore.* Detroit: Wayne State Univ. Press. xvii + 174 pp. (Originally published by Columbia Univ. Press.)

———. 1987. *Cracking jokes: Studies of sick humor cycles and stereotypes.* Berkeley, CA: Ten Speed Press. x + 198 pp.

———. 1989. *Folklore matters.* Knoxville: Univ. of Tennessee Press. xii + 172 pp.

———, and Robert A. Georges. 1962. Some minor genres of obscene folklore. *Journal of American Folklore* 75:221–26.

———, and Carl R. Pagter. 1975. *Urban folklore from the paperwork empire.* Austin, TX: American Folklore Society. xxii + 223 pp.

———. 2000. *Why don't sheep shrink when it rains? A further collection of photocopier folklore.* Syracuse, NY: Syracuse Univ. Press. xx + 332 pp.

Dunn, Clive. 1996. *Permission to laugh: My favourite funny stories.* London: Michael O'Mara Books. 192 pp.

Dunn, Thomas F. 1934. *The facetiae of the Mensa philosophica.* New Series, Language and Literature, no. 5. St. Louis: Washington Univ. 55 pp. (Study based on edition printed in Cologne in 1500.)

Dunne, Finley Peter. 1963. *Mr. Dooley on the choice of law.* Ed. E. J. Bander. Charlottesville, VA: Michie Co.

Dunworth, Terence, and Joel Rogers. 1996. Corporations in court: Big business litigation in U.S. federal courts, 1971–1991. *Law & Social Inquiry* 21:497–592.

Dymond, Jonathan. 1894. [1829]. *Essays on the principles of morality.* 9th ed. Dublin: Eason. xiv + 294 pp.

Earl of Funsborough. 1780? *The Covent Garden jester or lady's and gentlemen's treasure of wit, humour and amusement.* New ed. London: J. Roach.

Eastman, Max. 1936. *Enjoyment of laughter.* New York: Simon & Schuster. xviii + 367 pp.

Eastman, Rex R. 1936. *The jumbo joke book.* Girard, KS: Haldeman-Julius. 128 pp.

Economic Report of the President. 1987. Washington, DC: Government Printing Office.

Economist. 1997. Laughing Matters: You think that's funny? Dec. 20, 23.

———. 1998. The worrying zeal of Ken Starr. June 6, 32, U.S. edition.

Edelman, Lauren B. 1900. Legal environments and organizational governance: The expansion of due process in the American workplace. *American Journal of Sociology* 95:1401–40.

Edmund, Peggy, and Harold Workman Williams. 1916. *Toaster's handbook: Jokes, stories, and quotations.* 3rd ed. New York: H. H. Wilson Co. . xviii + 483 pp.

Edwards, Gus C. 1993. [1915]. *Legal laughs: A joke for every jury.* Edited with introduction and index by J. Wesley Miller. Buffalo: William S. Hein. liii + 437 pp. (Text is reproduction of 2nd ed. of 1915.)

Edwards, Kenneth, comp. 1976. *I wish I'd said that! An anthology of witty replies.* London: Abelard. 78 pp.

———. 1977. *I wish I'd said that too! An anthology of witty replies.* London: Abelard. 64 pp.

Edwards, Russ "The Flush." 1993. *The bathroom joke book.* Saddle River, NJ: Red-Letter Press. Unpaginated.

Egan, Elliott. 1992. *The lawyer's guide to cheating, stealing and amassing obscene wealth.* New York: St. Martin's. 95 pp.

Ehrenberg, John. 1996. The United States Constitution. *Monthly Review* 47 (Jan.): 43.

Ehrlich, Howard J. 1979. Observations on ethnic and intergroup humor. *Ethnicity* 6:383–98.

Eichinger Ferro-Luzzi, Gabriella. 1992. *The taste of laughter: Aspects of Tamil humour.* Wiesbaden: Otto Harrassowitz. xx + 218 pp.

Eilbirt, Henry. 1991. *What is a Jewish joke? An excursion into Jewish humor.* Northvale, NJ: Jason Aronson. xii + 293 pp.

Eilperin, Juliet, and Jim Vande Hei. 1997. Trial lawyers are new GOP villain for 1998 elections. *Roll Call,* Dec. 11.

Elgart, J. M., ed. 1951. *Over sixteen.* New York: Greyson. 174 pp.

———. 1953. *More over sixteen: Sequel.* New York: Greyson. 176 pp.

———. 1954. *Still more over sixteen.* New York: Greyson. 176 pp.

———. 1955. *Further more over sixteen.* New York: Greyson. 176 pp.

———. 1958. *Sixth over sixteen.* New York: Greyson. 176 pp.

Eliezer, Ben. 1992. [1984]. *The world's best Jewish jokes.* London: Fontana. 87 pp.

———. 1993. [1985]. *More of the world's best Jewish jokes.* London: Fontana. 94 pp.

Elliott, A., and B. Elliott. 1968. *Best Scottish jokes.* London: Wolfe. 64 pp.

Engelbach, Arthur H., comp. 1913. *Anecdotes of bench and bar.* London: Grant Richards. 270 pp.

———. 1915. *More anecdotes of bench and bar.* London: Grant Richards. 296 pp.

Epp, Charles. 1992. Do lawyers impair economic growth? *Law & Social Inquiry* 17:585–623.

———. 1992a. Toward new research on lawyers and the economy. *Law & Social Inquiry* 17:695–711.

Epstein, Cynthia Fuchs. 1993. *Women in law.* 2nd ed. Urbana: Univ. of Illinois Press. xvii + 491 pp.

———. 1997. Review of *The betrayed profession: Lawyering at the end of the twentieth century,* by Sol Linowitz. *Society,* May–June, 88–89.

———, Robert Saute, Bonnie Oglensky, and Martha Gever. 1995. Glass ceilings and open doors: Women's advancement in the legal profession. *Fordham Law Review* 64:291–378.

Ernst, Theodore R. 1925. *Laughter.* New York: Theodore R. Ernst. 63 pp. (Ernst is listed as publisher, not as author, but volume seems self-published.)

———. 1930. *Laughter: Gems of the world's best humor.* 1931 ed. New York: Theodore R. Ernst. 304 pp.

Ervin, Sam J., Jr. 1983. *Humor of a country lawyer.* Chapel Hill: Univ. of North Carolina Press. xii + 212 pp.

Esar, Evan. 1945. *Esar's joke dictionary.* New York: Harvest House. vii + 491 pp.

———. 1946. *The animal joker: A treasury of jokes and gags dealing with different kinds of beasts, birds, fish and insects.* New York: Harvest House. vii + 289 pp.

———. 1978. *The comic encyclopedia: A library of the literature and history of humor containing thousands of gags, sayings and stories.* Garden City, NY: Doubleday. lii + 831 pp.

Esler, Gavin. 1997. *The United States of anger: The people and the American dream.* New York: Penguin Books. 343 pp.

Evans, Colin. 1998. *Superlawyers: America's courtroom celebrities.* Detroit: Visible Ink Press. xi + 274 pp.

Ewick, Patricia, and Susan S. Silbey. 1998. *The common place of law: Stories from everyday life.* Chicago: Univ. of Chicago Press. xvii + 318 pp.

Faine, Jonathan. 1994. *The Jon Faine joke book.* Sydney: ABC Books. 118 pp.

Feder, Mark. 1948. *It's a living: A personalized collection of Jewish humor.* New York: Bloch. 96 pp.

Federal News Service. 1997. Press conference with Representative Bill Archer (R-TX). Oct. 21. Available in LexisNexis Library.

Ferguson, James. 1933. *The table in a roar or, if you've heard it, try and stop me.* London: Methuen. xvi + 303 pp.

Ferguson, John. 1968. *The wit of the Greeks and Romans.* London: Leslie Frewin. 144 pp.

Ferguson, Robert A. 1984. *Law and letters in American culture.* Cambridge, MA: Harvard Univ. Press. xi + 417 pp.

FHM. 2001. *FHM presents the best of bar-room jokes.* London: Carlton Books. 192 pp.

Finer, Morris. 1970. The legal profession. In *What's wrong with the law,* ed. Michael Zander, 44–51. Montreal: McGill-Queen's Univ. Press.

Fisher, Vardis, ed. 1939. *Idaho lore: Prepared by the Federal Writers' Project of the Work Projects Administration.* Caldwell, ID: Caxton Printers. 256 pp.

Flaherty, David. 1984. Right-wing firms pick up steam. *National Law Journal,* May 23, 1.

Fleischer, Matt. 2000. Sidebar: The talk of the profession. *National Law Journal,* Sept. 25, 5.

Fleming, Macklin. 1974. *The price of perfect justice: The adverse consequences of current legal doctrine on the American courtroom.* New York, Basic Books.

Foote, John Alderson. 1911. *"Pie-Powder" being dust from the law courts collected and recollected on the western circuit.* London: John Murray. xii + 216 pp. (Published anonymously by "A Circuit Tramp.")

Forbes, Ernest. 1988. *The world's best cricket jokes.* London: Angus & Robertson. 91 pp.

———. 1990. *The world's best acting jokes.* London: Angus & Robertson. 93 pp.

———. 1993. [1992]. *The world's best marriage jokes.* London: HarperCollins. 91 pp.

———. 1993a. *More of the world's best golf jokes.* London: HarperCollins. 89 pp.

Ford, Edward H. ("Senator Ed"), Harry Hershfield, Joe Laurie Jr. 1946. [1945]. *Can you top this?* Garden City, NY: Blue Ribbon Books. 237 pp.

———. 1947. *Cream of the crop.* New York: Didier. x + 271 pp.

Fordham Law Review. 1998. Symposium: The relevance of religion to a lawyer's work: An interfaith conference. 66 (4): 1075–1651.

Fortune. 1936. Jews in America. Feb. ["Slightly condensed version" in *Digest and Review.* 12 pp.]

Foster, Dr. 1986. *More of the world's best doctor jokes.* North Ryde, NSW, Austl.: Angus & Robertson. Unpaginated.

Foster, Timothy Roderick, comp. 1988. *The book of humourous legal anecdotes.* Ascot, Berks., UK: Springwood Books. 134 pp.

Fotheringham, Allan. 1992. Puzzled, perplexed, amazed, and boggled. *Maclean's,* Oct. 12, 88.

Fowler, Nathaniel C., Jr. 1915. *Witty stories and toasts for all occasions and how to tell them.* New York: George Sully. vii + 216 pp.

Franklin, Barbara. 1992. Remarks to the National Small Business Conference. Federal News Service, May 12. Available in LexisNexis Library.

Franklin, Max, comp. 1925. *Anthology of wit and humor.* New York: Max Franklin. 372 pp.

Fraser, Bob. 1992. *A guy goes into a bar.* Los Angeles: Price Stern Sloan. 52 pp.

Fredericks, Vic. 1955. [1953]. *Crackers in bed.* New York: Pocket Books. vi + 233 pp.

Freedman, Monroe H. 1975. *Lawyers' ethics in an adversary system.* Indianapolis: Bobbs-Merrill. xi + 270 pp.

Freud, Sigmund. [1905]. *Jokes and their relation to the unconscious.* London: Hogarth Press, 1960. v + 258 pp.

Fried, Charles. 1976. The lawyer as friend: The moral foundations of the lawyer-client relation. *Yale Law Journal* 85:1060–89.

Friedman, Edward L. 1960. *Toastmaster's treasury: A complete guide for the toastmaster, master of ceremonies and program chairman.* New York: Harper. x + 366 pp.

Friedman, Lawrence M. 1973. *A history of American law.* New York: Simon & Schuster. 655 pp.

———. 1985. *Total justice.* New York: Russell Sage Foundation. ix + 166 pp.

———. 1987. Civil wrongs: Personal injury law in the late 19th century. *American Bar Foundation Research Journal* 1987:351, 355.

———, and Thomas D. Russell. 1990. More civil wrongs: Personal injury litigation, 1901–1910. *American Journal of Legal History* 34:295–314.

Friedman, Lisa "Bunny." 1985. *Jewish American Princess jokebook.* Toronto: PaperJacks. ix + 145 pp.

Friedman, Philip R., ed. 1964. *Washington humor.* New York: Citadel. 128 pp.

Fritsch, Jane. 1996. Sometimes lobbyists strive to keep public in the dark. *New York Times,* Mar. 19.

Fukuyama, Francis. 1995. *Trust: The social virtues and the creation of prosperity.* London: Penguin. xv + 457 pp.

Fuller, Earl. n.d. ca. 1980s. *A life Fuller laughter.* n.p. 69 pp.

Fuller, Edmund, ed. 1942. *Thesaurus of anecdotes.* New York: Crown. xv + 489 pp. (Reprinted as *2500 anecdotes for all occasions.* New York: Avenel Books, 1980.)

Galanter, Marc. 1974. Why the "haves" come out ahead: Speculations on the limits of legal change. *Law & Society Review* 9:95–160.

———. 1983. Mega-law and mega-lawyering in the contemporary United States. In *The sociology of the professions: Lawyers, doctors and others,* ed. Robert Dingwall and Philip S. C. Lewis, 152–76. London: Macmillan.

———. 1983a. Reading the landscape of disputes: What we know and don't know (and think we know) about our allegedly contentious and litigious society. *ULCA Law Review* 31:4–72.

———. 1986. Adjudication, litigation and related phenomena. In *Law and the social sciences,* ed. Leon Lipson and Stanton Wheeler, 151–257. New York: Russell Sage Foundation.

———. 1988. The life and times of the big six: or, The federal courts since the good old days. *Wisconsin Law Review* 1988:921–54.

———. 1990. Bhopals, past and present: The changing legal response to mass disaster. *Windsor Yearbook of Access to Justice* 10:151–70.

———. 1992. Law abounding: Legalisation around the North Atlantic. *Modern Law Review* 55:1–24.

———. 1992a. Re-entering the mythical kingdom. *ABA Journal,* Nov., 118.

———. 1993. News from nowhere: The debased debate on civil justice. *Denver Univ. Law Review* 71:77–113.

———. 1994. Predators and parasites: Lawyer-bashing and civil justice. *Georgia Law Review* 28:633–81.

———. 1996. Lawyers in the mist: The golden age of legal nostalgia. *Dickinson Law Review* 100:549–62.

———. 1998. An oil strike in hell: Contemporary legends about the civil justice system. *Arizona Law Review* 40:717–52.

———. 1999. "Old and in the way": The coming demographic transformation of the legal profession and its implications for the provision of legal services. *Wisconsin Law Review* 1999:1081–1117.

————. 2001. Contract in court; or Almost everything you may or may not want to know about contract litigation. *Wisconsin Law Review* 2001:577–638.

————. 2005. Planet of the APs: Reflections on the scale of law and its users. Unpublished manuscript, on file with the author.

————, and Thomas M. Palay. 1991. *Tournament of lawyers: The transformation of the big law firm.* Chicago: Univ. of Chicago Press. xii + 197 pp.

————, and Joel Rogers. 1991. A transformation of American business disputing? Some preliminary observations. Institute for Legal Studies, Univ. of Wisconsin. Working Paper DPRP 10–3. 67 pp.

Gallup Organization. 1949. *Gallup Poll—A.I.P.O* (Roper Center for Public Opinion Research). Available in Westlaw, Poll database.

Gardner, Emelyn Elizabeth. 1937. *Folklore from the Schoharie Hills.* Ann Arbor: Univ. of Michigan Press. xv + 351 pp.

Gardner, Gerald, ed. 1982. *The I hate New York joke book.* New York: Ballantine Books. x + 147 pp.

————, ed. 1982a. *The I hate Hollywood joke book.* New York: Ballantine Books. viii + 120 pp.

Garnett, Tay. 1932. *Tall tales from Hollywood.* New York: Liveright. 96 pp.

Garza, Hedda. 1996. *Barred from the bar: A history of women in the legal profession.* New York: Franklin Watts. 224 pp.

Gawalt, Gerald W. 1970. Sources of anti-lawyer sentiment in Massachusetts, 1740–1840. *American Journal of Legal History* 14:283–307.

————, ed. 1984. *The new high priests: Lawyers in post–Civil War America.* Westport, CT: Greenwood. xiv + 214 pp.

Gay, John. 1923. [1728]. *The Beggar's Opera.* In *The plays of John Gay.* London: Simpkin, Marshall, Harrison, Kent. 1:127–226.

Gee, H. L. 1941. *Funnily enough.* London: Methuen. vi + 90 pp.

Gellhorn, Ernest. 1984. Too much law, too many lawyers, not enough justice. *Wall Street Journal,* June 7.

Genn, Hazel. 1999. *Paths to justice: What people do and think about going to law.* Oxford: Hart. xv + 382 pp.

George, Daniel, ed. 1958. [1957]. *A book of anecdotes.* N.p.: Citadel. xii + 445 pp. (Published in England in 1957.)

Gergen, David. 1991. America's legal mess. *U.S.; News and World Report,* Aug. 19, 72.

Gerler, William R. 1965. *Executive's treasury of humor for every occasion.* West Nyack, NY: Parker. ix + 243 pp.

Geyelin, Milo. 1989. Fired managers winning more lawsuits: Raising stakes, many now seek punitive awards. *Wall Street Journal,* Sept. 7.

Gibson, Dale, and Janet K. Baldwin, eds. 1985. *Law in a cynical society? Opinion and law in the 1980's.* Calgary: Carswell Legal Publications. xviii + 464 pp.

Gilbert, Michael, ed. 1989. [1986]. *The Oxford book of legal anecdotes.* Oxford: Oxford Univ. Press. xvi + 333 pp.

Gillespie, John. 1904. *The humours of Scottish life.* Edinburgh: William Blackwood. vii + 247 pp.

Gillespie-Jones, A. S. 1980. *The lawyer who laughed again.* Richmond, Vic.: Hutchinson Australia. xii + 123 pp.

Gilson, Ronald J. 1984. Value creation by business lawyers: Legal skills and asset pricing. *Yale Law Journal* 94:239–312.

Ginger, Ray. 1974. *Ray Ginger's jokebook about American history.* New York: New Viewpoints. 139 pp.

Gingras, Angele de T. 1973. *From bussing to bugging: The best in congressional humor.* Washington: Acropolis Books. 168 pp.

Glaberson, William. 2000. The legal profession smells a rat. *New York Times,* Oct. 22.

Glanz, Rudolf. 1973. *The Jew in early American wit and graphic humor.* New York: Ktav. 269 pp.

Glendon, Mary Ann. 1994. *A nation under lawyers: How the crisis in the legal profession is transforming American society.* New York: Farrar, Straus and Giroux. 331 pp.

Golden, Francis Leo. 1948. *For doctors only.* New York: Frederick Fell. 273 pp.

———. 1949. *Jest what the doctor ordered.* New York: Frederick Fell. 256 pp.

———. 1951. *Tales for salesman.* New York: Frederick Fell. 245 pp.

———. 1953. [1950]. *Laughter Is legal.* New York: Pocket Books. 280 pp.

Golden, Harry. 1972. *The Golden book of Jewish humor.* New York: G. P. Putnam. 252 pp.

Goldstein, Tom. 1977. Burger warns about a society overrun by lawyers. *New York Times,* May 28.

———. 1978. Carter's attack on lawyers. *New York Times,* May 6.

———. 1979. Demystifying the profession. *New York Times,* June 1.

———. 1983. Review of *The American Lawyer. Columbia Law Review* 83:1351–63.

Goldstein-Jackson, Kevin. 1995. *The public speaker's joke book.* Bombay: Jaico. 125 pp.

———. 1996. *Joke, after joke, after joke after joke . . .* Bombay: Jaico. 125 pp.

———. 1996a. *The right joke for the right occasion.* Kingswood, Surrey, UK: Elliot Right Way Books. 190 pp.

Golluch, Norbert, comp. 1999. *Neue Juristen-Witze.* Frankfurt am Main: Eichborn. Unpaginated.

Gordon, James D., III. 1992. A bibliography of humor and the law. *Brigham Young Univ. Law Review* 1992:427–56.

Gordon, Robert W. 1988. The independence of lawyers. *Boston Univ. Law Review* 68:1–83.

Gould, Milton S. 1979. *The witness who spoke with God and other tales from the courthouse.* New York: Viking. xxvi + 309 pp.

Gray, William. 1990. Speech to American Stock Exchange Conference. Federal News Service, Oct. 16.

Greeley, Andrew M. 1963. *Religion and career: A study of college graduates.* New York: Sheed & Ward. xvi + 267 pp.

Green, Milton D. 1984. *It's legal to laugh.* New York: Vantage Press. vii + 80 pp.

Green Bag. 1889–1908. Vols. 1–20. Boston: Boston Book Co.

———. 1909–14. Vols. 21–26. Brookline, MA: Riverdale Press.

———. 1894. The legend of Saint Yves, the lawyers' patron saint. 6:142–43.

———. 1906. The patron saint of the law. 18:636–37.

Greene, Mel. 1999. *The greatest joke book ever.* New York: Avon Books. 338 pp.

Grose, Francis. 1787. *A provincial glossary, with a collection of local proverbs and popular superstitions.* London: S. Hooper. Unpaginated.

Gross, David C. 1991. *Laughing through the years: A new treasury of Jewish humor.* New York: Walker. xvi + 232 pp.

Gross, S. 1994. *Lawyers! Lawyers! Lawyers! A cartoon collection.* Chicago: Contemporary Books. 100 pp.

Grossman, Ellie. 1993. *Lawyers from hell joke book.* New York: Signet Books. 140 pp.

Grossman, William. 1944. *Jewish humor.* New York: Bloch. 79 pp.

Grotjahn, Martin. 1966. [1957]. *Beyond laughter: Humor and the subconscious.* New York: McGraw-Hill. ix + 285 pp.

Gruner, Charles R. 1997. *The game of humor: A comprehensive theory of why we laugh.* New Brunswick, NJ: Transaction Books. 197 pp.

Gurney, John. 1986. *The world's best Catholic jokes.* London: Angus & Robertson. Unpaginated.

———. 1987. *The world's best salesman jokes.* London: Angus & Robertson. Unpaginated.

Hacker, Steven G. 1978. An abundance of lawyers. *National Underwriter* (Property & Casualty ed.), Jan. 23, 37.

Hagan, John, and Fiona Kay. 1995. *Gender in practice: A study of lawyers' lives.* New York: Oxford Univ. Press. ix + 235 pp.

Halpert, Herbert, and Gerald Thomas. 2001. Two patterns of an international tale: The lawyer's letter opened. *Fabula* 42:32–63.

Ham, George H. 1921. *Reminiscences of a raconteur: Between the '40s and the '20s.* Toronto: Musson Book Co. xvi + 330 pp.

Hammel, Frank. 1987. Drug testing: Now the grocery industry is under the glass. *Supermarket Business,* 42:101.

Handler, Joel. 1978. *Social movements and the legal system.* New York: Academic Press. xiv + 252 pp.

———, Ellen Hollingsworth, and Howard Erlanger. 1978. *Lawyers and the pursuit of legal rights.* New York: Academic Press. xvi + 272 pp.

Harrington, William G. 1984. A brief history of computer-assisted legal research. *Law Library Journal* 77:543–56.

Harris, G. A., comp. 1979. *A policeman's lot . . .* London: Police Review. 134 pp.

Harris, George. 1982. *Spare a copper.* London: Police Review. 146 pp.

Harris, Sidney. 1993. *So sue me! Cartoons on the law.* New Brunswick, NJ: Rutgers Univ. Press. 147 pp.

Harvey, James. n.d. ca. 1998a. *Goodwill's crazy jokes.* New Delhi: Goodwill. 176 pp.

———. n.d. ca. 1998b. *Goodwill's 1001 jokes.* New Delhi: Goodwill. 168 pp.

Hay, Peter. 1989. *The book of legal anecdotes.* New York: Facts on File. xiv + 322 pp.

Hayak, F[rederick] A. 1973. *Rules and order.* Vol. 1 of *Law, legislation and liberty.* London: Routledge & Kegan Paul. xi + 184 pp.

Hayden, Robert M. 1991. The cultural logic of a political crisis: Common sense, hegemony, and the great American liability insurance famine of 1986. *Studies in Law, Politics and Society* 11:95–117.

Hazlitt, W. Carew. 1864. *Shakespeare jest-books: Reprints of the early and very rare jest-books supposed to have been used by Shakespeare.* 3 vols. London. (Reprinted by Burt Franklin, New York, n.d., various paginations.)

———. 1887. *Jests, new and old.* London: J. W. Jarvis. xiv + 184 pp.

———. 1890. *Studies in jocular literature: A popular subject more closely considered.* London: Elliot Stock. viii + 230 pp.

Healey, Phil, and Rick Glanvill. 1996. *Now! That's what I call urban myths.* London: Virgin Books. xvi + 255 pp.

Hefley, James C., comp. 1968. *The sourcebook of humor.* Grand Rapids, MI: Zondervan Publishing House. 205 pp.

Heighton, Joseph, comp. 1916. *Legal life and humour.* London: Hodder and Stoughton. 318 pp.

Heinz, John P., and Edward O. Laumann. 1982. *Chicago lawyers: The social structure of the bar.* New York: Russell Sage Foundation / Chicago: American Bar Foundation. xxvi + 470 pp.

Heinz, John P., Robert L. Nelson, Edward O. Laumann, and Ethan Michelson. 1997. Chicago lawyers: Hemispheres, tectonic plate movements, and continental drift. Paper presented at the annual meeting of the Law and Society Association, St. Louis, May 29.

Hengstler, Gary A. 1993. Vox populi: The public perception of lawyers: ABA poll. *ABA Journal,* Sept., 60.

Henry, Lewis C. 1948. *Humorous anecdotes about famous people.* Garden City, NY: Halcyon House. viii + 215 pp.

Henson, Chris. 1997. On fire for hot peppers. *Roanoke Times & World News,* Jan. 2.

Herald (Glasgow). 1993. Against the law. July 12.

Herron, Roy, and L. H. "Cotton" Ivy. 2000. *Tennessee political humor: Some of these jokes you voted for.* Knoxville: Univ. of Tennessee Press. xvi + 156 pp.

Hershfield, Harry. 1932. *Harry Hershfield's Jewish jokes.* New York: Simon & Schuster. Unpaginated.

————. 1938. *Now I'll tell one.* New York: Greenberg. 159 pp.

————. 1959. *Laugh louder live longer.* New York: Gramercy. 174 pp.

————. 1964. *Harry Hershfield joke book.* New York: Ballantine Books. 173 pp.

Herz, Michael. 1996. "Do justice!": Variations of a thrice-told tale. *Virginia Law Review* 82: 111–61.

Hetzron, Robert. 1991. On the structure of punchlines. *Humor* 4:61–108.

Hicks, Seymour. 1936. *Laugh with me: Some of the world's best stories.* London: Castle. 218 pp.

Hildbrand, Rene, ed. 1987. *Tell me a Swiss joke.* Berne: Benteli. 96 pp.

Hill, Geoff, comp. 1987. *The Ulster joke book.* Belfast: Blackstaff Press. 77 pp.

Hobbes, Tom. 2002a. *Jokes men won't laugh at.* New York: Berkley Books. 182 pp.

————. 2002b. *Jokes women won't laugh at.* New York: Berkley Books. 185 pp.

Hochwald, Abraham. 1996. *The HarperCollins book of Jewish humour.* London: HarperCollins. ix + 150 pp. (Originally published in German in 1994.)

Hoeflich, Michael H. 2001. Lawyers, fees and anti-lawyer sentiment in popular art, 1800–1925. *Green Bag,* 2nd ser., 4:147–56.

Hoenig, Michael. 1977. The American manufacturer's problem: The question of design defects. Proceedings, First World Congress on Product Liability. London, Jan. 19–21.

Hoffman, Paul. 1973. *Lions in the street: The inside story of the great Wall Street firms.* New York: Saturday Review Press. 244 pp.

Holland, Norman M. 1982. *Laughing: A psychology of humor.* Ithaca, NY: Cornell Univ. Press. 231 pp.

Holloway, Gary. 1989. *Saints, demons, and asses: Southern preacher anecdotes.* Bloomington: Indiana Univ. Press. ix + 124 pp.

Holmstrom, John, comp. 1998. *The world's funniest pot jokes.* New York: High Times Books. 93 pp.

Holub, William M. 1939. *On the humor side.* Milwaukee: Bruce. x + 147 pp.

Honestus [Benjamin Austin]. [1819]. *Observations on the pernicious practice of the law.* Boston: True & Weston. (Articles published in *The Independent Chronicle* [Boston] in 1786, 60 pp. Repr, *American Journal of Legal History* 13: 241–302 [1969] with a comment by Erwin C. Surrency.)

Hood, Tom, Patrick Kennedy, and James Allan Mair, eds. 1873. *The book of modern anecdotes, humour wit, and wisdom. English—Irish—Scotch.* London: George Routledge. 570 pp.

Hooker, Randy. 1998. *Jokes for the rugby club from the blue team*. Slough, Berks., UK: Strathearn. 64 pp.

Hornby, Peter, ed. 1977. *The official Irish joke book*. London: Futura. 96 pp.

———. 1978. *The official Irish joke book: Book 3 (book 2 to follow)*. London: Futura. 94 pp.

Houck, Oliver A. 1984. With charity for all. *Yale Law Journal* 93:1415–1562.

House, Boyce. 1948. *Laugh parade of states: Star-spangled wit and humor*. San Antonio, TX: Naylor. 163 pp.

Howcroft, Wilbur G[ordon]. 1983. *The Bushman who laughed again*. Richmond, Vic.: Hutchinson Australia. 117 pp.

———. 1985. *Wilbur Howcroft omnibus*. Hawthorn, Vic.: Hutchinson Australia. vii + 504 pp.

Howe, Irving. 1951. The nature of Yiddish laughter. *New American Mercury* 72 (Feb.): 211–19.

Howe, Walter Henry. 1898 [1891]. *Scotch wit and humor; Classified under approriate subject headings, with, in many cases, a reference to a table of authors*. Philadelphia: G. W. Jacobs. 222 pp. (Originally published in London in 1891 as *Everybody's book of Scotch wit and humour*.)

Huggins, Leonard Victor. 1981. *Anecdotes*. Chapel Hill, NC: Leonard Victor Huggins. 315 pp.

Humes, James C. 1985. [1975]. *Podium humor: A raconteur's treasury of witty and humorous stories*. New York: Harper Perennial. xii + 298 pp.

———. 1993. *More podium humor: Using wit and humor in every speech you make*. New York: Harper Perennial. xii + 244 pp.

Hunter, Marjorie, and Warren Weaver. 1985. Briefing. *New York Times*, Aug. 2.

Hupfeld, Henry. 1897. [1871]. *Encyclopaedia of wit and wisdom: A collection of over nine thousand anecdotes . . . compiled during a period of fifteen years, with a special regard to merit and propriety*. Philadelphia: David McKay. 1008 pp.

Hurst, James Willard. 1950. *The growth of American law*. Boston: Little Brown. xiii + 502 pp.

Hylton, J. Gordon. 1991. The devil's disciple and the learned profession: Ambrose Bierce and the practice of law in gilded age America. *Connecticut Law Review* 23:705–42.

Ignelzi, R. J. 1992. The attorney market; And now—don't sue us!—for a few lawyer jokes. *San Diego Union-Tribune*, Feb. 6.

Independent [London]. 1994. No business like legal business? Jan. 26, 15.

Ives, E. W. 1960. The reputation of the common lawyers in English society, 1450–1550. *Univ. of Birmingham Historical Journal* 7 (2): 130–61.

Jackson, Stanley [Samuel Jackson]. 1961. *Laughter at law*. London: Arthur Barker. 141 pp.

Jaffe, Herb. 1994. Law schools crank out too many graduates. *Newark Star Ledger*, Dec. 20. (Repr., *New Jersey Lawyer*, Jan. 2, 1995.)

Janofsky, Leonard S., and Robert D. Raven. 1995. Justice for all—if they can afford it. *Los Angeles Times*, Aug. 4.

Jarvis, Robert M., and Paul R. Joseph. 1998. *Prime time law: Fictional television as legal narrative*. Durham, NC: Carolina Academic Publishers. xii + 323 pp.

Jerrold, Blanchard, comp. 1858. *Specimens of Douglas Jerrold's wit*. Boston: Ticknor & Fields. xi + 243 pp.

Jerusalem Post, 1991. Opinion. July 4.

Jessel, George. 1960. *Jessel, anyone?* Englewood Cliffs, NJ: Prentice-Hall. xi + 179 pp.

———. 1973. *The toastmaster general's favorite jokes: Openings and closings for speechmakers*. Secaucus, NJ: Castle Books. 217 pp.

Joe Miller's complete jest book. 1903. 2 vols. in 1. New York: William T. Henderson.

Joe Miller's jests or the wits vade-mecum. 1963. [1739]. London. Facsimile ed. New York: Dover. . xix + 70 pp.

John, Brian. 1994. *Pembrokeshire humour: Jokes and anecdotes from the Celtic fringe.* Newport, Pembs., UK: Greencroft Books. 144 pp.

Johnson, Claudia Durst. 1994. *To kill a mockingbird: Threatening boundaries.* New York: Twayne. xiv + 125 pp.

Johnson, Earl. 1984. *Justice and reform: The formative years of the OEO legal services program.* New Brunswick, NJ: Transaction Books. viii + 361 pp.

Johnson, Eric W. 1989. *A treasury of humor: An indexed collection of anecdotes.* New York: Ivy Books. viii + 278 pp.

———. 1991. *Humorous stories about the human condition: An indexed collection of anecdotes.* Buffalo: Prometheus Books. 229.

———. 1994. *A treasury of humor II.* New York: Ivy Books. 243 pp.

Johnson, J. H., Jerry Sheridan, and Ruth Lawrence. 1936. *The laughter library.* Indianapolis: Maxwell Droke. 279 pp.

Johnson, Louise, ed. 2000. *New woman bloke jokes.* London: Carlton Books. 143 pp.

———. 2001. *New woman bloke jokes 2.* London: Carlton Books. 143 pp.

Johnson, Luke. 1998. The lawyers will kill us. *Sunday Telegraph,* Mar. 29. (Review of the movie *Devil's Advocate.*)

Johnston, Brian. 1984. *Now here's a funny thing.* London: Methuen London. 122 pp.

———. 1995. [1994]. *I say, I say, I say.* London: Mandarin Paperbacks. viii + 117 pp.

———. 1997. [1996]. *An evening with Johnners.* Ed. Barry Johnston. London: Corgi Books. 147 pp.

Johnston, William T., ed. 1922. *Bill Johnston's joy book.* Cincinnati: Stewart Kidd. vi + 432 pp.

———. 1925. *Bill Johnston's second joy book.* Cincinnati: Stewart Kidd. viii + 345 pp.

Johnstone, Iain. 1992. Hooked on a Fallacy. *Sunday Times,* Apr. 12.

Johnstone, Ian M. 1992a. Taking lawyer jokes seriously. *Australian Folklore* 7:106–12.

Jones, Charley. 1944. *Charley Jones' famous laugh book.* Wichita, KS: Joste. 96 pp.

———. 1945. *Charley Jones' famous laugh book.* 2nd ed. [= *Laugh Book,* vol. 1, no. 2 (Oct. 1, 1945)]. Wichita, KS: Joste. 96 pp.

Jones, Loyal, ed. 1989. *The preacher joke book.* Little Rock, AR: August House. 109 pp.

———, and Billy Edd Wheeler. 1987. *Laughter in Appalachia: A festival of southern mountain humor.* Little Rock, AR: August House. 155 pp.

———. 1989. *Curing the cross-eyed mule: Appalachian mountain humor.* Little Rock, AR: August House. 211 pp.

———. 1991. *Hometown Humor, U.S.A.: Over 300 jokes and stories from the porch swings, barber shops, corner cafes, and beauty parlors of America.* Little Rock, AR: August House. 220 pp.

———. 1995. *More laughter in Appalachia: Southern mountain humor.* Little Rock, AR: August House. 218 pp.

Jones, Rodney R., Charles M. Sevilla, and Gerald F. Uelmen, eds. 1989. [1987]. *Disorderly conduct: Verbatim excerpts from actual cases.* Paperback ed. New York: W. W. Norton. 171 pp.

Jones, Rodney R., and Gerald F. Uelmen. 1993. [1990]. *Supreme Folly.* Paperback ed. New York: W. W. Norton. 205 pp.

Jowett, B[enjamin], trans. 1937. *The dialogues of Plato.* 2 vols. New York: Random House. xii + 879, 939 pp.

Jowett, Garth. 1976. *Film: The democratic art.* Boston: Little, Brown. xx + 518 pp.

Julius, Anthony. 1996. The butt stops here. *Guardian,* Oct. 26.

Junior, Allan. ca. 1930. *Aberdeen again!* 3rd ed. Dundee, Scot.: Valentine. 36 pp.

K . . ., G . . . 1797. *The festival of wit; or, Small talker, being a collection of bon mots, anecdotes &c of the most exalted characters.* 16th ed. Dublin, Ire.: P. Byrne and William
Porter. xvi + 270 pp.

Kagan, Robert A. 1988. What makes Uncle Sammy sue. *Law & Society Review* 21:717–42.

———. 1991. Adversarial legalism and American government. *Journal of Policy Analysis &
Management* 10:369–406.

———. 1994. Do lawyers cause adversarial legalism? A preliminary inquiry. *Law & Social
Inquiry* 19:1–62.

Kahn, Alice, and John Dobby Boe. 1997. *Your joke is in the e-mail: Cyberlaffs from Mouse-
potatoes.* Berkeley, CA: Ten Speed Press. ix + 181 pp.

Kahn, Ellison. 1991. *Law, life and laughter: Legal anecdotes and portraits.* Capetown, S.
Africa: Juta. xvi + 366 pp.

———. 1999. *Law, life and laughter encore.* Kenwyn, S. Africa: Juta. xvi + 320 pp.

Kaplan, David A. 1986. The NLJ poll results: Take heed, lawyers. *National Law Journal,*
Aug. 18, S2.

Karsten, Peter. 1998. Enabling the poor to have their day in court: The sanctioning of contingency fee contracts, a history to 1940. *DePaul Law Review* 47:231–60.

Katz, Naomi, and Eli Katz. 1971. Tradition and adaptation in American Jewish humor.
Journal of American Folklore 84:215–20.

Kearney, Paul W. 1923. *Toasts and anecdotes for all occasions.* New York: Edward J. Clode.
xviii + 299 pp.

Keelan, Brian, comp. 1999. The joy of the joke. Toronto: KAV Publishing. 360 pp.

Keen, Myra, ed. 1949. *The anthology of American humor.* New York: Magazine Digest.
767 pp.

Kelly, H. P. 1906. *Gems of Irish wit and humor.* New York: George Sully. 160 pp.

Kemble, John R., comp. and ed. 1901. *Four hundred laughs: or, Fun without vulgarity.* New
York: New Amsterdam Book Co. 183 pp.

Kempt, Robert, comp. 1865. *The American Joe Miller: A collection of Yankee wit and
humour.* 2d ed. London: Adams and Francis. xv + 226 pp.

Kennedy, Florynce. 1971. The whorehouse theory of law. In *Law against the people: Essays
to demystify law, order and the courts,* ed. Robert Lefcourt, 81–89. New York: Vintage
Books.

Kenny, Courtney. 1903. Bon jurista malus Christa. *Law Quarterly Review* 19:326–34.

Kenworthy, Kevin, comp. 1999. *The best jokes Minnie Pearl ever told (plus some that she
overheard).* Nashville, TN: Rutledge Hill. 160 pp.

Kieffer, Henry Martyn, ed. 1907. *It is to laugh.* New York: Dodge. x + 167 pp.

———, ed. 1923. *More laughs: Short stories and amusing anecdotes for a dull hour.* New
York: Dodge. 224 pp.

Kinchen, David M. 1985. Lawyers blamed for costly delays. *Los Angeles Times,* Apr. 21,
pt. 8, 2.

King, Elizabeth M., and James P. Smith. 1988. *Economic loss and compensation in aviation
accidents.* Santa Monica, CA: Rand, Institute for Civil Justice. xxi + 126 pp.

King, Paul, and Greg MacNeil. 1995. *The 200 funniest sports stories ever told.* Toronto: Seal
Books. 191 pp.

Kirp, David. 1976. Proceduralism and bureaucracy: due process in the school setting.
Stanford Law Review 28:841–76.

Kiser, S. E. 1927. *It is to laugh: A book of jokes.* New York: George Sully. ix + 261 pp.

Kishtainy, Khalid. 1985. *Arab political humor.* London: Quartet Books. xi + 203 pp.

Klein, Joe. 1903. *Good things.* New York: Kaufman. 94 pp.

Kleinfield, N. R. 1990. Silence is golden. *New York Times Magazine,* Apr. 29, 80.

Knott, Blanche. 1982. *Truly tasteless jokes.* New York: Ballantine Books. 116 pp.

———. 1983. *Truly tasteless jokes two.* New York: Ballantine Books. 113 pp.

———. 1983a. *Truly tasteless jokes three.* New York: Ballantine Books. 120 pp.

———. 1985. *Truly tasteless jokes V.* New York: Pinnacle Books. 115 pp.

———. 1985a. *Truly tasteless jokes IV.* New York: St Martin's. 115 pp. (Copyright 1984.)

———. 1986. *Truly tasteless jokes VI.* New York: St. Martin's. 110 pp.

———. 1987. *Truly tasteless jokes VII.* New York: St. Martin's. 121 pp.

———. 1988. *Truly Tasteless Jokes VIII.* New York: St. Martin's. 121 pp. (Copyright 1985.)

———. 1989. *Truly tasteless jokes IX.* New York: St. Martin's. 126 pp.

———. 1990. *Truly tasteless lawyer jokes.* New York: St. Martin's. 121 pp.

———. 1990a. *Truly tasteless jokes X.* New York: St. Martin's. 118 pp.

———. 1990b. *The very worst of truly tasteless jokes.* New York: St. Martin's. 132 pp.

———. 1991. *Truly tasteless jokes XI.* New York: St. Martin's. 116 pp.

———. 1991a. *Blanche Knott's book of truly tasteless anatomy jokes, vol. II.* New York: St. Martin's. 122 pp.

———. 1992. *Truly tasteless jokes XII.* New York: St. Martin's. 119 pp.

———. 1992a. *Truly tasteless blonde jokes.* New York: St. Martin's. 121 pp.

———. 1993. *Truly tasteless jokes XIII.* New York: St. Martin's. 115 pp.

———. 1993a. *Truly tasteless $alesman jokes.* New York: St. Martin's. 119 pp.

———. 1994. *Blanche Knott's treasury of tastelessness.* New York: St. Martin's. 178 pp.

———. 1994a. *Truly tasteless jokes XIV.* New York: St. Martin's. 117 pp.

———. 1995. *Truly tasteless jokes XV.* New York: St. Martin's. 116 pp.

———. 1997. *Truly tasteless disadvantaged white male jokes.* New York: St. Martin's. 116 pp.

Knox, D. B. 1926. *More quotable anecdotes.* London: T. Fisher Unwin. 220 pp.

———, comp. ca. 1943. *Laugh and grow fat: Seven hundred humorous stories.* London: James Clarke. 191 pp.

Kolasky, John, comp. 1972. *Look comrade—the people are laughing . . . Underground wit, satire and humour from behind the Iron Curtain.* Toronto: Peter Martin Assoc. 179 pp.

Kolbe, John. 1993. No joke; want respect? Earn it. *Phoenix Gazette,* July 14.

Korale, Raja. 1991. [1984]. *The world's best doctor jokes.* London: Fontana. Unpaginated. (First published by the author as *Laughter is the best medicine.)*

Kornheiser, Tony. 1994. Yuk yuk. *Washington Post,* Jan. 2.

Kornstein, Daniel J. 1994. *Kill all the lawyers: Shakespeare's legal appeal.* Princeton, NJ: Princeton Univ. Press. xvii + 274 pp.

Kostick, Anne, Charles Foxgrover, and Michael J. Pellowski. 1998. *3650 jokes, puns and riddles.* New York: Black Dog & Levanthal. 543 pp.

Kowalski, Mike, ed. 1974. *The Polish joke book.* New York: Belmont Tower Books. 179 pp.

Kramer, A. Stanley. 1994. *World's best Jewish humor.* New York: Citadel. xiii + 177 pp.

Kravitz, Seth. 1977. London jokes and ethnic stereotypes. *Western Folklore* 36:275–301. (Jokes collected 1974.)

Kristol, Irving. 1951. Is Jewish humor dead? The rise and fall of the Jewish joke. *Commentary* 12 (Nov.): 431–36.

Kritzer, Herbert M. 1991. Propensity to sue in England and the United States: Blaming and claiming in tort cases. *Journal of Law and Society* 18:452–79.

————. 1996. Courts, justice, and politics in England. In Herbert Jacob, Erhard Blankenburg, Herbert M. Kritizer, Doris Marie Provine and Joseph Sanders, *Courts, law, and politics in comparative perspective,* 81–176. New Haven, CT: Yale Univ. Press.

————, and J. Mitchell Pickerell. 1997. Contingent fee lawyers as gatekeepers in the American civil justice system. Institute for Legal Studies, Univ. of Wisconsin. Working Paper DPRP 12–3. 22 pp.

Kronman, Anthony T. 1993. *The lost lawyer: Failing ideals of the legal profession.* Cambridge, MA: Belknap Press. viii + 422 pp.

Kupferberg, S. 1978. An insulting look at lawyers through the ages. *Juris Doctor,* Oct.–Nov.

Ladendorf, Kirk. 1996. Battling plastics pirates. *Austin American-Statesman,* July 15.

Lafee, Scott. 1988. Lawyers come to the defense of the profession. *San Diego Union-Tribune,* Apr. 28.

Laing, Allan D., comp. 1953. *Laughter and applause: Anecdotes for speakers.* London: George Allen & Unwin. 192 pp.

Lande, John. 1998. Failing faith in litigation? A survey of business lawyers' and executives' opinions. *Harvard Negotiation Law Review* 3:1–70.

Landon, Donald D. 1990. *Country lawyers: The impact of context on professional practice.* New York: Praeger. xix + 167 pp.

Landon, Melville D. [Eli Perkins], ed. 1883. *Wit and humor of the age: Comprising wit, humor, pathos, ridicule, satires, dialects, puns, conundrums, riddles, charades, jokes and magic by Mark Twain, Josh Billings . . . Eli Perkins.* Chicago: Star. 774 pp. (No publication date given; copyright date is 1883. *Library of wit and humor: From the writings of the world's greatest humorists/ Mark Twain . . . and many others. . . .* [Chicago: Charles C. Thompson Co., n.d.; copyright dates 1883, 1901] consists of pp. 1–546 of the Star edition with new frontispiece and title page. Since all the material in the Thompson edition appears in the Star edition, and if all of the material there was copyright in 1883, then presumably all of this material was extant in 1883.)

Langland, William. 1981. [ca. 1377–79]. *The vision of Piers Plowman.* London: British Broadcasting Corporation. 287 pp.

Larkin, R. T., comp. and ed. 1975. *The international joke book #1.* New York: Leisure Books. 192 pp.

Larsen, Richard W. 1990. Time to restore logic to public policies. *Seattle Times,* Oct. 14.

Larson, Jane F. 1993. Women understand so little. They call my good nature deceit: A feminist rethinking of seduction. *Columbia Law Review* 93:374–472.

Laugh Book Magazine. 1951–55. Wichita, KS: Jayhawk Press. Various issues.

Laugh Magazine. ca. 1960. *Laugh at sea.* London: Laugh Magazine. 128 pp.

Lawson, J. Gilchrist. 1923. *The world's best humorous anecdotes.* New York: Harper. 275 pp.

The lawyer joke-a-day calendar [for 1996]. 1995. Lame Duck.

———— [for 1997]. 1996. Lame Duck.

———— [for 1998]. 1997. Lame Duck.

Lawyers: jokes, quotes and anecdotes. 1999. Kansas City, MO: Andrews McMeel. 2000 day-to-day calendar.

————. 2001. Kansas City, MO: Andrews McMeel. 2002 day-to-day calendar.

Lean, Vincent Stuckey. 1902–4. *Lean's collectanea: Collections of Vincent Stuckey Lean of proverbs (English and foreign, folk lore, and superstitiouns, also compilations toward dictionaries of proverbial phrases and worlds, old and disused.* 4 vols. in 5. Bristol: J. W.

Arrowsmith. 1 (1902): xvi + 509 pp.; 2 in two parts (1903): 940 pp.; 3 (1903): 512 pp.; 4 (1904): 481 pp.

Learsi, Rufus [Israel Goldberg]. 1941. *The book of Jewish humor: Stories of the wise men of Chelem and other tales assembled and retold.* New York: Bloch. 242 pp.

———. 1961. *Filled with laughter: A fiesta of Jewish folk humor.* New York: Thomas Yoseloff. 351 pp.

Leary, James P. 1991. *Midwestern folk humor.* Little Rock, AR: August House. 269 pp.

Lee, [Nelle] Harper. 1960. *To kill a mockingbird.* Philadelphia: Lippincott. 296 pp.

Lefcourt, Robert, ed. 1971. *Law against the people: Essays to demystify law, order and the courts.* New York: Random House. x + 400 pp.

Legman, Gershon. 1968. *Rationale of the dirty joke: An analysis of sexual humor.* New York: Grove Press. 811 pp.

———, comp. 1975. *No laughing matter: Rationale of the dirty joke.* 2nd ser. New York: Bell. 992 pp.

———. 1992. Bibliography. In Vance Randolph, *Blow the candles out: "Unprintable" Ozark folksongs and folklore.* Fayetteville: Univ. of Arkansas Press.

Lehr, Lew, Cal Tinney, and Roger Bower. 1948. *Stop me if you've heard this one.* Garden City, NY: Halcyon House. vi + 246 pp.

Leigh, Mark, and Mike Lepine. 1998. *The big Viagra jokebook.* London: MetroPublishing. 186 pp.

Leininger, Steve. 1981a. *The official Russian joke book.* New York: Pinnacle Books. 218 pp.

———. 1981b. *The official Iranian joke book.* New York: Pinnacle Books. 186 pp.

———. 1982. *The official doctors and dentists joke book.* New York: Pinnacle Books. Unpaginated.

Lemon, Mark, ed. 1864. *The jest book: The choicest anecdotes and sayings.* London: Macmillan. viii + 361 pp.

Leo, Richard A. 1996. *Miranda*'s revenge: Police interrogation as a confidence game. *Law & Society Review* 30:259–88.

Leo J. Shapiro & Associates. 2002. *Public perceptions of lawyers: Consumer research findings.* Chicago: American Bar Association, Section on Litigation. 38 pp.

Leslie, Ann, and George Gordon. 1997. For OJ, an open prison called LA. *Daily Mail,* Dec. 6.

Levenson, Sammy. 1948. *Meet the folks: A session of American-Jewish humor.* New York: Citadel. 128 pp.

Levine, Jack. 1994. Lawyers' hypocrisy disgusts public. *Arizona Business Gazette,* July 7, 17.

Levine, Lawrence W. 1977. *Black culture and black consciousness: Afro-American folk thought from slavery to freedom.* New York: Oxford Univ. Press. xx + 522 pp.

Lewis, George Q., and Mark Wachs. 1966. *The best jokes of all time and how to tell them.* New York: Hawthorn Books. xiii + 383 pp.

Lewis, Paul. 1997. The killing jokes of the American eighties. *Humor* 10:251–83.

Liebman, Ron. 2001. [2000]. *Shark tales: True (and amazing) stories from America's lawyers.* New York: Simon & Schuster. 281 pp.

Lieberman, Gerald F. 1975. *3,500 good jokes for speakers.* New York: Doubleday. ix + 468 pp.

Lieberman, Jerry, ed. 1956. *Off the cuff . . . from the private collection of Joe Laurie, Jr.* New York: Pocket Books. x + 165 pp.

Lieberman, Jethro K. 1978. *Crisis at the bar: Lawyers' unethical ethics and what to do about it.* New York: Norton. 247 pp.

————, and Tom Goldstein. 1990. The popular image of lawyers in America. Paper presented at the annual meeting of the Law and Society Association, Berkeley, CA, May 31.

Lim, Richard. 1994. The economic case for good behavior. *Straits Times,* Nov. 6.

Linowitz, Sol, with Martin Mayer. 1994. *The betrayed profession: Lawyering at the end of the twentieth century.* New York: Scribners. xii + 273 pp.

Lipman, Steve. 1993. [1991]. *Laughter in hell: The use of humor during the Holocaust.* Northvale, NJ: Jason Aronson. xiii + 279 pp.

Lipset, Seymour Martin, and William Schneider. 1987. *The confidence gap: Business, labor, and government in the public mind.* Rev. ed. Baltimore: Johns Hopkins Univ. Press. xxiv + 460 pp.

Lisagor, Nancy, and Frank Lipsius. 1988. *A law unto itself: The untold story of the law firm Sullivan & Cromwell.* New York: William Morrow. 360 pp.

London, Ephraim, ed. 1960. *The world of law.* 2 vols. New York: Simon & Schuster. xix + 654, 780.

Long, Steven. 1992. Lawyer jokes appeal to big audience. *Houston Chronicle,* Dec. 9.

Lonigan, Suds. 1988. *A man walked into a bar joke book.* New York: St. Martin's. 126 pp.

————. 1993. *Funny business.* New York: Barnes & Noble Books. 128 pp.

LoPucki, Lynn M. 1990. The de facto pattern of lawyer specialization. Institute for Legal Studies, Univ. of Wisconsin. Working Paper DPRP 9–10. 67 pp.

Los Angeles Times. 1985. Clippers run NBA team just like a law firm. Dec. 7.

Louis Harris & Associates. 1987. *Public attitudes toward the civil justice system and tort law reform.* Hartford CT: Aetna Life and Casualty Co.

Luban, David. 1988. *Lawyers and justice: An ethical study.* Princeton, NJ: Princeton Univ. Press. xxix + 440 pp.

Lubet, Steven. 1999. Reconstructing Atticus Finch. *Michigan Law Review* 97:1339–62.

Lukes, Steven, and Itzhak Galnoor. 1987. [1985]. *No laughing matter: A collection of political jokes.* Updated ed. London: Penguin Books. xiv + 177 pp.

Luntz, Frank I. 1996? *Conservatively speaking: How to use the language of the 21st century to win the hearts and minds of the American people.* Los Angeles: Center for the Study of Popular Culture.

Lupton, Martha, ed. 1938. *The treasury of modern humor.* Indianapolis: Maxwell Droke. 1079 pp.

Lurie, Charles N. 1927. *Make 'em laugh!* New York: G. P. Putnam. vi + 292 pp.

————. 1928. *Make 'em laugh again!* New York: G. P. Putnam. vi + 283 pp.

Lyons, Johnny. 1987. *#1 Joking Off.* Toronto and New York: Paper Jacks. 105 pp.

————. 1998. *Joking off.* New York: Kensington. 124 pp.

————. 1998a. *Joking off II.* New York: Kensington. 126 pp.

————. 1999. *More joking off.* New York: Kensington. 128 pp.

————. 1999a. *Joking off again.* New York: Kensington. 126 pp.

Macaulay, Stewart. 1963. Non-contractual relations in business: A preliminary study. *American Sociological Review* 28:55–67.

————. 1979. Lawyers and consumer protection laws: An empirical study. *Law & Society Review* 14:115–71

————. 1987. Images of law in everyday life: The lessons of school, entertainment, and spectator sports. *Law & Society Review* 21:185–214.

————. 1989. Popular legal culture: An introduction. *Yale Law Journal* 98:1545–58.

MacDonald, Peter V. 1988. [1985]. *Court jesters: Canada's lawyers and judges take the stand to relate their funniest stories.* Toronto: Stoddart. 208 pp.

———. 1988a. [1987]. *More court jesters: Back to the bar for more of the funniest stories from Canada's courts.* Toronto: Stoddart. 208 pp.

———. 1992. *Return of the court jesters: Back to the bar for more of the funniest stories from Canada's courts.* Toronto: Stoddart, 214 pp.

MacGregor, Forbes. n.d. 195–? *Doric spice: A selection of Scottish stories, humorous, philosophical, metaphysical, naive, fictitious and factual, from the cradle to the grave . . . and beyond.* Edinburgh: Pinetree Press. 135 pp.

MacHale, Des. 1983. [1978]. *Englishman jokes for Irishmen.* Repr. Dublin: Mercier Minibooks. 48 pp.

———. 1983a. *The official Margaret Thatcher joke book.* Dublin: Mercier Press. 48 pp.

———. 1989. *The world's best Maggie Thatcher jokes.* London: Angus & Robertson. 95 pp.

———. 1993. [1988]. *The world's best Scottish jokes.* London: HarperCollins. 96 pp.

———. 1994. *Paddy the Englishman, Paddy the Irishman, Paddy the Scotsman Jokes.* Dublin: Mercier Press. 48 pp.

MacIntyre, Alasdair. 2000. Theories of natural law in the culture of advanced modernity. In *Common truths: New perspectives on natural law,* ed. Edward B. McLean, 91–115. Wilmington, DE: ISI Books.

MacLean, Pamela A. 1988. Untitled UPI regional news dispatch. Sep. 26.

Macneil, Ian. 1984–85. Bureaucracy, liberalism, and community—American style. *Northwestern Law Review* 79:900–948.

Macrae, David. 1916. [1904]. *National humour: Scottish—English—Irish—Welsh—Cockney—American.* Paisley, Scot.: Alexander Gardner. 357 pp.

Macrobius. 1969. [ca. 400 CE]. *The Saturnalia.* Trans. Percival Vaughan Davies. New York: Columbia Univ. Press. xi + 560 pp.

MacTavish, Angus J., comp. 1931. *Scotch, or it's smart to be thrifty: A volume of the best Scotch jokes.* New York: Simon & Schuster, *sub nom,* MacSimon and MacSchuster. Unpaginated.

Magee, Stephen P., William A. Brock, and Leslie Young. 1989. *Black hole tariffs and endogenous policy theory.* New York: Cambridge Univ. Press. xx + 438 pp.

Maltbie, B. L. 1921. *Digs at doc and others: Second crop.* Newark, NJ: William W. Warner. 96 pp.

Mandel, Morris, ed. 1974. *A complete treasury of stories for public speakers.* Middle Village, NY: Jonathan David. 412 pp.

Mani, M. S. 1926. *The pen pictures of the dancing girl (with a side-light on the legal profession).* Salem, India. 127 + 32 pp.

Marchal, Terry. 1994. Marchal in the morning—junior high fitness. *Charleston Gazette,* Nov. 30.

———. 1996. Timing a dead horse. *Charleston Gazette,* May 13.

Marinucci, Carla. 1999. This time in S.F. Quayle blames the lawyers. *San Francisco Chronicle,* May 20, A1.

Marks, Alfred, comp. 1985. *I've taken a page in the Bible: A medley of Jewish humour.* London: Robson Books. 206 pp.

Marks, H. Stacy, et al. 1908. *Mr. Punch in wig and gown: The lighter side of bench and bar.* London: Carmelite House. 191 pp.

Marks, John. 1996. The American uncivil wars. *U.S. News & World Report,* Apr. 22.

Marquard, Ralph. 1977. *Jokes and anecdotes for all occasions.* New York: Galahad Books. 334 pp.

Marsh, Dave, and Kathi Kamen Goldmark. 1997. *The great rock'n'roll joke book.* New York: St. Martin's. xvi + 90 pp.

Martling, Jackie. 1984. *The only dirty joke book.* New York: Pinnacle Books. 149 pp.

———. 1997. *Jackie "The Joke Man" Martling's disgustingly dirty joke book.* New York: Simon & Schuster. 223 pp.

Mashburn, Amy R., and Dabney D. Ware. 1996. The burden of truth: Reconciling literary reality with professional mythology. *Univ. of Memphis Law Review* 26:1257–83.

Masin, Herman L., ed. 1956. *Sports laughs.* New York: Lion Library Editions. 186 pp.

Mason, Peter. 2001. *Next please (a judge's daybook).* Chichester: Barry Rose Law Publications. xvi + 201 pp.

Masson, Thomas L., ed. [1913]. *The best stories in the world.* Reprinted as *The Best of the World's Good Stories,* Vol. I, Doubleday, Page & Co. for Review of Reviews, 1922. Pp. vi + 244.

———, ed. [1918]. *Best short stories.* Reprinted as *The Best of the World's Good Stories,* Vol. II, Doubleday, Page & Co. for Review of Reviews, 1922. Pp. 258.

———. 1922. *Listen to these.* Garden City, NY: Doubleday, Page. vi + 275 pp.

Mastrangelo, Paul. 1986–87. Lawyers and the law: A filmography. *Legal Reference Services* 5 (4): 5–42.

Matthews, Joseph. 1998. *The lawyer who blew up his desk and other tales of legal madness.* Berkeley, CA: Ten Speed Press. xiii + 243 pp.

Mattson, Geoffrey, comp. 1990. *Golf stories and jokes for speakers.* London: Foulsham. 127 pp.

May, John G., Jr. 1956. *The lighter side of the law.* Charlottesville, VA: Michie. 228 pp.

———. 1964. *Courtroom kicktales.* Charlottesville, VA: Michie. 367 pp.

McArdle, Joseph. 1995. *Irish legal anecdotes.* Dublin: Gill & Macmillan. x + 230 pp.

McCann, Sean. 1990. [1968]. *Irish wit: Religion, the law, literature, love, drink, wisdom and proverbs.* Dublin: O'Brien Press. 144 pp. (Originally published in London by Leslie Frewin Publishers.)

McCarthy, Joe. 1964. [1962]. *In one ear.* New York: Pocket Books. xiv +209 pp.

McCartney, Eugene S. 1931. Ancient wit and humor. In *Classical studies in honor of John C. Rolfe,* ed. George Depue Hadzsits, 191–211. Philadelphia: Univ. of Pennsylvania Press.

McCaslin, John. 1997. Neither side amused. *Washington Times,* Nov. 14.

McCracken, Paul W. 1991. The big domestic issue: Slow growth. *Wall Street Journal,* Oct. 4.

McCraw, Thomas K., ed. 1981. *Regulation in perspective: Historical essays.* Cambridge, MA: Harvard Univ. Press. ix + 246 pp.

McCune, Robert. 1988. *The world's best golf jokes.* North Ryde, NSW, Austl.: Angus & Robertson. Unpaginated.

McDougal, Stan, comp. 1994. [1980]. *The world's greatest golf jokes.* Secaucus, NJ: Citadel. 175 pp.

McElroy, Paul S. 1973. *The little book of gentle humor.* Mt. Vernon, NY: Peter Pauper Press. 62 pp.

McFool, Alister, comp. 2000. *McFool's best Internet humor.* Tarentum, PA: Word Association Publishers. 227 pp.

McGrath, Phyllis S. 1979. *Redefining corporate-federal relations.* New York: Conference Board. ix + 102 pp.

McIlwaine, Colin, comp. 1933. *Laughter in court.* London: John Lane. 84 pp.

McLean, Milly. 1984. UPI, Regional News, Dateline: Hanover, NH, Apr. 9.

McManus, George. 1948. *Fun for all.* Cleveland: World Publishing. 144 pp.

McNeil, W. K. 1989. *Ozark mountain humor: Jokes on hunting, religion, marriage and Ozark ways.* Little Rock, AR: August House. 212 pp.

Meadow, Robin. 1986. The lawyer's image is no joke. *Los Angeles Lawyer,* Sept., 9.

Meier, Frederick, ed. 1944. *The joke tellers joke book.* Philadelphia: Blakiston. x + 323 pp.

Menchin, Robert. 1997. *101 classic Jewish jokes: Jewish humor from Groucho Marx to Jerry Seinfeld.* Memphis, TN: Mustang. 95 pp.

Mendelsohn, S. Felix, comp. 1935. *The Jew laughs.* Chicago: L. M. Stein. 222 pp.

———, comp. 1947. *Here's a good one: Stories of Jewish wit and wisdom.* New York: Bloch. xv + 255 pp.

———. 1951. *The merry heart: Wit and wisdom from Jewish folklore.* New York: Bookman. 260 pp.

———. 1952. [1941]. *Let laughter ring.* Philadelphia: Jewish Publication Society. x + 239 pp.

Merry, Sally Engle. 1990. *Getting justice and getting even: Legal consciousness among working-class Americans.* Chicago: Univ. of Chicago Press. x + 227 pp.

Merryfield. 1795. *Merryfield's jests, or, wit's companion.* London: J. Roach. 60 pp.

Merryman, Doctor, and Hilarius Le Gal. 1853. *One million of comic anecdotes, or flowers of wit and humour.* Paris: L. Passard.

Meyer, Philip N. 1996. "Desperate for love II": Further reflections on the interpenetration of legal and popular storytelling in closing arguments to a jury in a complex criminal case. *Univ. of San Francisco Law Review* 30:931–62.

Middleton, Martha. 1992. HALT: Rebels at a crossroad. *Student Lawyer,* Sept., 21, 22.

Middleton, Russell. 1959. Negro and white reactions to racial humor. *Sociometry* 22:175–83.

———, and John Moland. 1959. Humor in Negro and white subcultures: A study of jokes among university students. *American Sociological Review* 24:61–69.

Mikes, George. 1971. *Laughing matter: Towards a personal philosophy of wit and humor.* New York: Library Press. 133 pp.

Milburn, George. 1926. *The best Jewish jokes.* Girard, KS: Haldeman-Julius. 64 pp.

———. 1927. *The best jokes about lawyers.* Girard, KS: Haldeman-Julius. 64 pp.

Miles, Alfred H., ed. 1895. *One thousand and one anecdotes: Illustrations, incidents, episodes, yarns, stories, adventures, practical jokes, witticisms, epigrams and bon-mots, gathered from all sources, old and new.* New York: Thomas Whittaker. xvi + 388 pp.

Miles, C. W., comp. 1926. *Taffy tales from Welsh Wales.* Dundee, Scot.: Valentine. 36 pp.

Millar, Will, and Frank Keane. 1994. *Will Millar's Irish joke book.* White Rock, BC: Irish Publications. 156 pp.

Miller, J. R. 1991. *The 901 best jokes there ever was.* Nashville, TN: Rutledge Hill. 175 pp.

Miller, Lewis M. 1907. The lawyer's patron saint. *Green Bag* 19:10–11.

Miller, Mark C. 1995. *The high priests of American politics: The role of lawyers in American political institutions.* Knoxville: Univ. of Tennessee Press. xii + 228 pp.

Miller, William H. 1997. The chamber comes to life. *Industry Week,* Oct. 20, 105.

A Million Laughs. 1993. CD-ROM. Spring Valley, NY: Interactive Publishing. Contains 855 jokes that it labels as lawyer jokes.

Milner, Neal. 1989. The denigration of rights and the persistence of rights talk: A cultural portrait. *Law & Social Inquiry* 14:631–75.

Mindes, Marvin W. 1982. Trickster, hero, helper: A report on the lawyer image. *American Bar Foundation Research Journal* 1982:177, 211.

Mindess, Harvey. 1972 *The chosen people? A testament, both old and new, to the therapeutic power of Jewish wit and humor.* Los Angeles: Nash. 120 pp.

Mital, G. S., and Manju Gupta. 1995. *1221 World's choicest jokes.* Bombay: Jaico. 218 pp.

Mitchell, Lawrence E. 2002. Gentlemen's agreement: The antisemetic origins of restrictions on stockholder litigation. George Washington University Law School, Public Law and Legal Theory Research Paper Series No. 44 (Available at Social Science Research Network Electronic Paper Collection: http://ssrn.com/abstract_id=321680).

Moore, Robert J. 1985. Reflections of Canadians on the law and the legal system: Legal Research Institute survey of respondents in Montreal, Toronto and Winnipeg. In *Law in a cynical society?: Opinion and law in the 1980's,* ed. Dale Gibson and Janet K. Baldwin, 41–87. Calgary, Alta.: Carswell Legal Publications.

Morecroft, John H. 1981. [1974]. *White tie tales: A collection of after-dinner stories.* Folkestone, UK: Bailey Brothers & Swinfen. 101 pp.

Morello, Karen Berger. 1986. *The invisible bar: The woman lawyer in America 1638 to the present.* New York: Random House. xv + 271 pp.

Morgan, Dan. 1952. *The complete bartender's joke book.* New York: Stravon. 128 pp.

Morgan, David Gwynn. 1995. Directive does not extend to law degree. *Irish Times,* Sept. 25.

———. 1996. Tribunal may lack legal bite. *Irish Times,* Oct. 18.

Morton, George A., and D. MacLeod Malloch. 1913. *Law and laughter.* London: T. N. Foulis. 259 pp.

Mosher, Marion Dix, comp. 1932. [1922]. *More toasts: Jokes stories and quotations.* New York: H. W. Wilson. xii + 542 pp.

Moulton, Powers. 1942. *2500 jokes for all occasions.* New York: New Home Library. ix + 480 pp.

Mr. "J." 1979. *More of the world's best dirty jokes.* Secaucus, NJ: Citadel. 132 pp.

———. 1980. [1976]. *The world's best dirty jokes* New York: Ballantine Books. 112 pp.

———. 1994. *World's dirtiest dirty jokes.* New York: Citadel. 95 pp.

Mr. "K." 2001. *The dirty joke book.* New York: Citadel. 141 pp.

Mr. "O'S." 1982. *The world's best Irish jokes.* London: Angus & Robertson. Unpaginated.

Mr. "P." 1984. *The world's best Yiddish dirty jokes.* Secaucus, NJ: Citadel. 116 pp.

M[uller], F[rederick], ed. 1939. *Here's a good one! Over three hundred good stories.* London: Frederick Muller. 120 pp.

Mulligan, William Hughes, Jr., ed. 1997. *The wit and wisdom of William Hughes Mulligan.* New York: Fordham Univ. Press. xvii + 246 pp.

Murad, comp. 1993. *Bar room jokes and anecdotes.* New Delhi: UBS Publishers' Distributors. xvii + 120 pp.

Murdock, Clyde. 1967. *A treasury of humor.* Grand Rapids, MI: Zondervan. 159 pp.

Murray, David. 1912. *Lawyers' merriments.* Glasgow: James MacLehose. xiv + 303 pp.

Murray, Iain. 1996. Legal eagles swoop in for new kill. *Marketing Week,* May 10, 134.

Murray, Joe "Miller." 1948. *America's spiciest stories.* Hollywood, CA: Americana Press. Unpaginated.

Murray, Ken. 1954. *Ken Murray's giant joke book.* New York: Ace Books. 320 pp.

Murtie, Kevin. 1985. *At last! The official Irish joke book no. 2.* London: Futura. 160 pp.

Mustlaff, Hugh, ed. ca. 1900. *Side splitters: Fresh from our private joke factory.* Chicago: Stein.

Myles, Carolyn. 1992. First-place awards start addy-ing up for EPB. *Washington Times,* Apr. 13, B4.

Myrdal, Gunnar. 1944. *An American dilemma: The Negro problem and modern democracy.* With the assistance of Richard Sterner and Arnold Rose. 2 vols. New York: Harper. lix + 1483 pp.

Nader, Ralph, and Mark Green, eds. 1976. *Verdicts on lawyers.* New York: Crowell. xxx + 341 pp.

Nader, Ralph, and Wesley J. Smith. 1996. *No contest: Corporate lawyers and the perversion of justice in America.* New York: Random House. xxviii + 427 pp.

Narayana Rao, Velcheru. 1990. Courts and lawyers in India: Images from literature and folklore. In *Boeings and bullock-carts: Studies in change and continuity in Indian civilization,* ed. Yogendra K. Malik and Dhirendra K. Vajpeyi, 3:196–214. Delhi: Chanakya.

Nash, Bruce, and Allan Zullo, eds. 1995. *Lawyer's wit and wisdom: Quotations on the legal profession, in Brief.* Comp. Kathryn Zullo. Philadelphia: Running Press. 224 pp.

National Organization of Bar Counsel. 1980. *Report and recommendations on study of the model rules of professional conduct: Discussion draft of January 30, 1980 to the ABA Commission on Evaluation of Professional Standards (The Kutak Commission).* Honolulu, HI: National Organization of Bar Counsel.

Neches, S[olomon] M. 1926. *"As 'twas told to me": A hundred little stories of the old rabbis.* Los Angeles: Times-Mirror Printing and Binding House. 100 pp.

———. 1938. *Humorous talks of latter day rabbis "As 'twas told to me": A hundred little human-interest stories.* New York: Geroge Dobsevage. 127 pp.

Nelson, William E. 1990. Contract litigation and the elite bar in New York City, 1960–80. *Emory Law Journal* 39:413–62.

Nesvisky, Matt. 1987. Jokers all. *Jerusalem Post,* week ending July 25, international ed.

Neuhauser, Peg. 1993. *Corporate legends and lore: The power of storytelling as a management tool.* New York: McGraw. ix + 162 pp.

Nevins, Francis M. 1984. Law, lawyers and justice in popular fiction and film. *Humanities Education* 1 (May): 3–12.

Newman, A. C. H. 1979. *The select-a-joke book.* Kingswood, Surrey, UK: Elliot Right Way Books. 125 pp.

New Republic. 2000. Up and down by law. *New Republic,* Dec. 4, 13.

Newton, K[enneth]. 1997. Social and political trust. Paper for the Conference on Confidence in Democratic Institutions: America in Comparative Perspective, Washington, Aug. 25–27.

The New Yorker Book of Lawyer Cartoons. 1994. New York: Alfred A. Knopf. 87 pp.

Nicoll, Ruarridh. 1995. L.A. pleads insanity to OJ trial overkill. *Observer,* Sept. 17.

Night-Line, Aug. 4, 1993. Available in LexisNexis Library, ABCNEW file.

NOLO's favorite lawyer jokes. 1993. CD-ROM. Berkeley, CA: Nolo Press. .

Noonan, John T., Jr. 1976. *Persons and masks of the law.* New York: Farrar, Straus & Giroux. xvii + 206 pp.

Norment, John. 1971. *You've gotta be joking.* New York: Scholastic Book Services. 128 pp.

Norquist, Grover G. 1994. A winning drive. *American Spectator,* Mar.

Novak, Ned, ed. 1977. *The* new *Polish joke book.* New York: Leisure Press. 140 pp.

Novak, William, and Moshe Waldoks, eds. 1981. *The big book of Jewish humor.* New York: Harper & Row. xxvi + 308 pp.

———, eds. 1990. *The big book of new American humor.* New York: Harper Perennial. x + 342 pp.

Nye, Joseph S., Philip D. Zelikow, and David C. King, eds. 1997. *Why people don't trust government.* Cambridge, MA: Harvard Univ. Press. xi + 339 pp.

Ocker, A. N. [pseud.] 1986. *The world's best Aussie jokes.* North Ryde, NSW, Austl: Angus & Robertson. Unpaginated.

O'Connor, Sandra Day. 1998. Professionalism. *Washington Univ. Law Quarterly* 76:5–13.

Odean, Kathleen. 1988. *High steppers, fallen angels, and lollipops: Wall Street slang.* New York: Dodd Mead. xi + 212 pp.

———. n.d. Stupid patients, insensitive doctors (unpublished manuscript).

O'Dwyer's PR Services Report. 1996. Grassroots "weeds" need to be clipped, say angry activists. June.

——— 1997. IE pros rap corporate PR for poor media relations. July.

Old Commercial Traveller. n.d. ca. 1930s. *Breezy bits* London: Arthur H. Stockwell. 96 pp.

Oliver, Myrna. 1986. "Do-it-yourself" attorneys go to press, not court. *Los Angeles Times,* July 9.

Oliver, Thomas Edward. 1909. Some analogues of Maistre Pierre Pathelin. *Journal of American Folklore* 22:395–430.

Olson, Theodore B. 1994. The parasitic destruction of America's civil justice system. *Southern Methodist University Law Review* 47:359–68.

Olson, Walter. 1991. *The litigation explosion.* New York: Dutton. viii + 388 pp.

O'Neal, F. Hodge, and Annie Laurie O'Neal. 1964. *Humor, the politician's tool: Favorite stories of congressmen and other officials.* New York: Vantage Press. 210 pp.

O'Neil, Robert M. 1970. Of justice delayed and justice denied. The welfare prior hearing cases. In *The Supreme Court Review,* ed. Philip B. Kurland, 161–214. Chicago: Univ. of Chicago Press.

Orben, Robert. 1966. *The joke tellers handbook or 1,999 belly laughs.* New York: Bell. 212 pp.

Orcutt, William Dana. 1942. *Escape to laughter.* Norwood, MA: Plimpton Press. 95 pp.

Oring, Elliott. 1992. *Jokes and their relations.* Lexington: Univ. Press of Kentucky. xii + 171 pp.

Orso, Ethelyn G. 1979. *Modern Greek humor: A collection of jokes and ribald tales.* Bloomington: Indiana Univ. Press. xxiii + 262 pp. (Field work done through 1977.)

Osiel, Mark. 1990. Lawyers as monopolists, aristocrats and entrepreneurs. *Harvard Law Review* 103:2009, 2056–64.

———. 1993. Historical roots of adversarial legalism. Remarks at annual meeting of the Law and Society Association, Chicago, May.

Overton, Thomas W. 1995. Lawyers, light bulbs, and dead snakes: The lawyer joke as a societal text. *UCLA Law Review* 42:1069–1114.

Paley, Francis A. 1881. *Greek wit: A collection of smart sayings and anecdotes translated from Greek prose writers.* 2 vols. London: George Bell. 128, viii + 128 pp.

Papke, David Ray. 2001. Lawyer fiction in *The Saturday Evening Post:* Ephraim Tutt, Perry Mason, and middle-class expectations. *Cardozo Studies in Law and Literature* 13:207–20.

Parker, John F. 1978. *The fun and laughter of politics.* Garden City, NY: Doubleday. xi + 320 pp.

Parry, Albert. 1966. Russia cracks jokes about China. *New York Times Magazine,* June 26, 14–15, 38, 41.

Partin, Robert. 1973. *Lee County jokes 100 years ago.* Auburn, AL: Lee County Historical Society. 32 pp.

Patten, William, ed. 1909. *Among the humorists and after-dinner speakers: A new collection of humorous stories and anecdotes.* New York: P. F. Collier. 1:288 pp.

Paul, Arnold M. 1960. *Conservative crisis and the rule of law: Attitudes of bar and bench, 1887–1895.* Ithaca, NY: Cornell Univ. Press. viii + 256 pp.

Pease, Allan. 1996. *The ultimate book of rude and politically incorrect jokes: Stories to embarrass your mother.* Mona Vale, NSW, Austl.: Jarpen Pty. 391 pp.

Pendleton, Winston K. 1981. [1979]. *Complete speaker's galaxy of funny stories, jokes and anecdotes.* West Nyack, NY: Parker. 278 pp.

Penoyer, Ronald J. 1981. *Directory of federal regulatory agencies.* 3rd ed. St. Louis: Center for the Study of American Business.

Percelay, James L. 2000. *Whiplash: America's most frivolous lawsuits.* Kansas City, MO: Andrews McMeel. ix + 101 pp.

Pergament, Alan. 1995. One trial, one fine cast, one terrific new show. *Buffalo News,* Sept. 19.

Peter, Laurence J. 1977. *Peter's quotations: Ideas for our time.* New York: William Morrow. 540 pp.

Peter D. Hart Research Associates. 1993. *A survey of attitudes nationwide toward lawyers and the legal system.* 32 pp.

Peters, Charles. 1974. The screwing of the average man: How your lawyer does it. *Washington Monthly,* Feb., 33–42.

Petersen, Melody. 1998. The short end of long hours. *New York Times,* July 18.

Peterson, Karen S. 1990. The trials of lawyers. *USA Today,* Jan. 9.

Peterson, Mark A. 1987. *Civil juries in the 1980s: Trends in jury trials and verdicts in California and Cook County, Illinois.* Santa Monica, CA : Institute for Civil Justice. xix + 62 pp.

Peterson, Roland, comp. 1976. *The good humor book.* Santa Ana, CA: Vision House. vii + 147 pp.

Pfau, Michael, Lawrence J. Mullen, Tracy Deidrich, and Kirsten Garrow. 1995. Television viewing and the public perceptions of attorneys. *Human Communication Research,* Mar., 307–30.

Phillips, Bob. 1974a. *The last of the good clean jokes.* Irvine, CA: Harvest House. v + 121 pp.

———. 1974b. *More good clean jokes.* Irvine, CA: Harvest House. 132 pp.

———. 1974c. *World's greatest collection of clean jokes.* Eugene, OR: Harvest House. 172 pp.

———. 1976. *The all American joke book.* Irvine, CA: Harvest House. iii + 122 pp.

———. 1982a. *The all-new clean joke book.* Eugene, OR: Harvest House. 191 pp.

———, comp. 1982b. *The world's greatest collection of heavenly humor.* Eugene, OR: Harvest House. 190 pp.

———, comp. 1986. *The return of the good clean jokes.* Eugene, OR: Harvest House. 171 pp.

———. 1994. *The unofficial liberal joke book: For the politically incorrect.* Eugene, OR: Harvest House. Unpaginated.

———. 1996. *Jest another good clean joke book.* Eugene, OR: Harvest House. 175 pp.

Phillips, Edward. 1989. *The world's best lawyer jokes.* London: Angus & Robertson. 96 pp.

———. 1993. [1991]. *The world's best motoring jokes.* London: HarperCollins. 96 pp.

———. 1994. *The world's best boss jokes.* London: HarperCollins. 96 pp.

———. 1995. [1993]. *The world's best after-dinner jokes.* London: HarperCollins. 89 pp.

———. 1996. *The world's best sailing jokes.* London: HarperCollins. 91 pp.

Pickens, William. 1926. *American Aesop: Negro and other humor.* Boston: Jordan & More. xx + 183 pp.

Pierce, Jennifer L. 1995. *Gender trials: Emotional lives in contemporary law firms.* Berkeley: Univ. of California Press. xi + 256 pp.

Pietsch, Jim. 1986. *The New York City cab driver's joke book.* New York: Warner Books. 271 pp.

———. 1998. *The New York City cab driver's joke book, vol. 2.* New York: Warner Books. xv + 270 pp.

Pitts, John W. 1843. *Eleven numbers against lawyer legislation and fees at the bar.* n.p.: n.p. 48 pp.

Playboy [magazine]. 1965. *More Playboy's party jokes.* Chicago: Playboy Press. 192 pp.

———. 1972. [1963]. *Playboy's party jokes 1.* Chicago: Playboy Paperbacks. 192 pp. (Copyright is 1963.)

———. 1980. [1972]. *Playboy's complete book of party jokes.* Secaucus, NJ: Castle Books. 376 pp. (Originally published by Playboy Press, Chicago.)

Pollack, Simon R. 1979. *Jewish wit for all occasions.* New York: A.&W Visual Library. 191 pp.

Porsdam, Helle. 1999. *Legally speaking: Contemporary American culture and the law.* Amherst: Univ. of Massachusetts Press. xiii + 269 pp.

Posner, George. 1937. *This is good: Up-to-date jokes for all occasions.* New York: Diehl, Landau & Pettit. xii + 269 pp.

Posner, Richard A. 1985. *The federal courts: Challenge and reform.* Cambridge, MA: Harvard Univ. Press. xvi + 413 pp.

Post, Robert C. 1987. On the popular image of the lawyer: Reflections in a dark glass. *California Law Review* 75:379–89.

Pound Conference. 1976. Addresses at the National Conference on the Causes of Popular Dissatisfaction with the Administration of Justice, St. Paul, Minnesota, Apr. 7–9 *Federal Rules Decisions* 70:79–246.

Pound, Roscoe. 1909. The etiquette of justice. *Proceedings of the Nebraska State Bar Association* 3:231–51.

———. 1914. The lay tradition as to the lawyer. *Michigan Law Review* 12:627–38.

Powell, Chris, and George E. C. Paton, eds. 1988. *Humour in society: Resistance and control.* London: Macmillan. xxii + 279 pp.

Powell, Michael. 1985. The new legal press: Reflecting and facilitating changes in the legal profession. Paper presented at the annual meeting of the Law and Society Association, San Diego, June.

Power, Charlene, comp. 1984. *Leapin' Lena.* Crosby, ND: Journal Publishing. 59 pp.

Powers, Nick, and Wilann Powers, comps. 1973. *Booger Hollow's pill peddler's joke book.* Lindale, GA: Country Originals. Unpaginated.

Prasad, Che. 1998. *Physician humor thyself: An analysis of doctor jokes.* Winston-Salem, NC: Harbinger Medical Press. x + 119 pp.

Pratt, Will. 1996. *A funny thing happened on . . . the way!* Mukilteo, WA: WinePress. xxi + 217.

President's Council on Competitiveness. 1991. *Agenda for civil justice reform in America.* Washington, DC: Government Printing Office. 28 pp.

Prest, Wilfred R. 1986. *The rise of the barristers: A social history of the English bar.* Oxford: Clarendon. xvi + 442 pp.

Pretzer, Michael. 1996. What Washington plans for doctors. *Medical Economics* 73 (7): 57–60, 63.

Princeton Survey Research Associates. 1991. *Great American TV poll #5.* Roper Center for Public Opinion Research. Available in Westlaw, Poll database.

Pritchard, Jimmy. 2002. *The New York City bartender's joke book.* New York: Warner Books. xiii + 173 pp.

Prochnow, Herbert V. 1942. *The public speaker's treasure chest: A compendium of source material to make your speech sparkle.* New York: Harper. ix + 413 pp.

————. 1990. *Speakers and toastmasters handbook.* Rocklin, CA: Prima Publishing. vii + 357 pp.

————, and Herbert V. Prochnow Jr. 1964. *The public speaker's treasure chest.* Rev. ed. New York: Harper & Row. ix + 516 pp.

Puddephatt, Andrew. 1997. Liberty, equality and even dignity. *Independent,* May 18, 25.

Puma, Cris. 1995. The missing link: Does lawyer-bashing warrant additional protection for lawyers. *Journal of the Legal Profession* 19:207–34.

Putnam, Robert. 1995. Tuning in, tuning out: The strange disappearance of social capital in America. *PS: Political Science and Politics* 28:664–83.

Puzo, Mario. 1978. [1969]. *The Godfather.* New York: Signet Books. 446 pp.

Quayle, [J.] Dan[forth]. 1991. Address to the annual meeting of the American Bar Association, Aug. 13.

————. 1992. Too much litigation: True last year, true now. *National Law Journal,* Aug. 10.

————. 1992a. Text of Quayle speech accepting nomination. *New York Times,* Aug. 21.

————. 1995. [1994]. *Standing firm: A vice-presidential memoir.* New York: Harper Paperbacks. xiii + 466 pp.

Raasch, Chuck. 1995. Information explosion puts voters in touch with pols. Gannett News Service, May 25.

Rabin, Roni. 1993. Lawyer bashing has moved into prime time. *Newsday,* July 1.

Rabinowitz, H. R. 1986. [1973]. *Kosher humor.* Jerusalem: Ruben Mass. 224 pp. (Author's introduction dated 1973 seems to mark completion of manuscript.)

Radin, Max. 1930. Saints and lawyers. *Illinois Law Review* 24:614–16.

————. 1946. The ancient grudge: A study in the public relations of the legal profession. *Virginia Law Review* 32:734–52.

Rafferty, Michael. 1988. *Skid marks: Common jokes about lawyers.* Bolinas, CA: Shelter. 96 pp.

Randall, Richard S. 1968. *Censorship of the movies: The social and political control of a mass medium.* Madison: Univ. of Wisconsin Press. xvi + 280 pp.

Randolph, John. 1955. *The jokes on Texas.* 2nd ed. Tomball, TX: John Randolph. 64 pp.

————. 1967. *Texas grins and shares it.* Tomball, TX: John Randolph. 64 pp.

Randolph, Vance. 1944. *Funny stories about hillbillies.* Girard, KS: Haldeman-Julius. 24 pp.

Rango, Robert, ed. 1944. *The good humor book: A treasury of choice jokes and gags, cartoons and comic drawings . . .* New York: Harvest House. 319 pp.

Ranke, Kurt. 1972. *European anecdotes and jests.* Copenhagen: Rosenkilde and Baggar. 189 pp

Raskin, Richard. 1992. *Life is like a glass of tea: Studies of classic Jewish jokes.* Philadelphia: Jewish Publication Society. 263 pp.

Raskin, Victor. 1985. *Semantic mechanisms of humor.* Dordrecht, Neth.: D. Reidel. xix + 284 pp.

Ray, Laura Krugman. 1997. Judicial fictions: Images of Supreme Court justices in the novel, drama, and film. *Arizona Law Review* 39:151–203.

Re, Edward D. 1994. The causes of popular dissatisfaction with the legal profession. *St. John's Law Review* 68:85–136.

Reader's Digest. 1949. *Fun fare: A treasury of Reader's Digest wit and humor.* Pleasantville, NY: Reader's Digest Assoc. ii + 316 pp.

————. 1958. *Reader's Digest treasury of wit and humor.* Pleasantville, NY: Reader's Digest Assoc. 576 pp.

————. 1963. *Humor in uniform.* Montreal: Reader's Digest Assoc. (Canada). 95 pp.

————. 1967. *Fun and laughter: A treasure house of humor.* Pleasantville, NY: Reader's Digest Assoc. 832 pp.

————. 1972. *The Reader's Digest treasury of American humor.* Reader's Digest Press / McGraw Hill. xvii + 644 pp.

————. 1997. *Laughter, the best medicine.* Pleasantville, NY: Reader's Digest Assoc. 216 pp.

Rees, Nigel. 1994. *The Guinness book of humorous anecdotes.* Enfield, UK: Guinness. 219 pp.

————. 1995. *The Guinness dictionary of jokes.* Enfield, UK: Guinness. 272 pp.

————. 1999. *The Cassell dictionary of anecdotes.* London: Cassell. x + 307 pp.

Regan, Patrick, ed. 2001. *Lawyers: Jokes, quotes, and anecdotes.* Kansas City, MO: Andrews McMeel. viii + 264 pp.

Reginald. 1997. *Naughty jokes for big boys.* Noida, UP, India: Blossom Books. 224 pp.

Reich, Charles A. 1964. The new property. *Yale Law Journal* 73:733–87.

Reichman, Nancy J., and Joyce S. Sterling. 2002. Recasting the brass ring: Deconstructing and reconstructing workplace opportunities for women lawyers. *Capital Univ. Law Review* 29:923–77.

Reik, Theodor. 1962. *Jewish wit.* New York: Gamut. 246.

Republican Party. 1992. *The Republican platform, 1992: The vision shared; Uniting our family, our country, our world.* Washington, DC: Republican National Committee. 75 pp.

Rezwin, Max, ed. 1958. *Sick jokes, grim cartoons and bloody marys.* New York: Citadel. 64 pp.

————, ed. 1959. *More sick jokes and grimmer cartoons.* New York: Citadel. 62 pp.

————, ed. 1960. *Still more sick jokes and even grimmer cartoons.* New York: Citadel. 62 pp.

————, ed. 1962. *The best of sick jokes.* New York: Pocket Books. 174 pp.

Rhode, Deborah. 1994. The profession: Identity crisis. *ABA Journal,* Dec., 74.

————. 1997. *Speaking of sex: The denial of gender inequality.* Cambridge, MA: Harvard Univ. Press. 352 pp.

Rhodes, R. S., ed. 1890. *The world's wit and wits.* Chicago: Rhodes & McClure. 414 pp.

Richman, Jacob. 1952. *Jewish wit and wisdom.* New York: Pardes. 404 pp.

————. 1954. *Laughs from Jewish lore.* New York: Hebrew Publishing. xiii + 272 pp. (Reprint of 1926.)

Riesman, David. 1954. [1951]. Toward an anthropological science of law and the legal profession. In *Individualism reconsidered and other essays,* 440–66. Glencoe, IL: Free Press.

Ringle, Ken. 1989. Lawyer jokes abound, and the defense objects. *Los Angeles Times,* Sept. 4.

Roach, Hal. 1977. *Hal Roach's joke book for men only (women welcome).* Cork, Ire.: Mercier. 60 pp.

Roanoke Times and World News. 1995. Editorial: Really stupid lawyers' tricks. Nov. 27.

Roberts, Artie, as told to George Q. Lewis. 1969. *Dirty jokes for clean people.* New York: Bee-Line Books. 153 pp.

Robey, George. 1920. *After-dinner stories.* London: Grant Richards. 232 pp.

Robinson, Marlyn. 1998. Collins to Grisham: A brief history of the legal thriller. *Legal Studies Forum* 22:21–34.

Rodell, Fred. 1939. *Woe unto you, lawyers!* New York: Reynal & Hitchcock. xi + 274 pp.

The Rodent. 1995. *Explaining the inexplicable: The Rodent's guide to lawyers.* New York: Pocket Books. xxi + 198 pp.

————. 1996. Putting your bath on client's tab. *Legal Times,* Sept. 9.

Rodman, Richard, ed. 1968. *Flower power laff book #3.* Ft. Worth, TX: SRI. 190 pp.

Rooney, John Flynn. 1995. System faces serious problems, newest justice tells federal bar. *Chicago Daily News Bulletin,* Oct. 17.

Roper Center. 1984. The fees that lawyers charge are quite reasonable in light of the services they provide clients. Available in LexisNexis Library, RPoll file.

———. 1985. Do you think the present method of paying lawyers in personal injury cases is a good thing, or a bad thing, or doesn't it matter? Available in Westlaw, Poll database.

Rose, Jonathan. 1998. The legal profession in medieval England: A history of regulation. *Syracuse Law Review* 48:1–137.

Rosen, Milt. 1982. *The ugly joke book.* New York: Pinnacle Books. Unpaginated.

Rosen, Robert Eli. 1989. Ethical soap: *L.A. Law* and the Privileging of Character. *University of Miami Law Review* 43:1229–61.

———. 1998. Devils, lawyers and salvation lie in the details: Deontological legal ethics, issue conflicts of interest and civil education in law schools. In *Ethical challenges to legal education and conduct,* ed. Kim Economides, 61–81, Oxford: Hart Publishing.

Rosenbaum, Thane. 2002. Where lawyers with a conscience get to win cases. *New York Times,* May 12.

Rosenberg, Bernard, and Gilbert Shapiro. 1958. Marginality and Jewish humor. *Midstream* 4 (Spring): 70–80.

Rosenthal, Douglas E. 1974. *Lawyer and client: Who's in charge?* New York: Russell Sage Foundation. xi + 228 pp.

Rosenthal, Franz. 1956. *Humor in early Islam.* Leiden: E. J. Brill. x + 154 pp.

Ross, Stanley D. 1996. *The joke's on lawyers.* Sydney: Federation Press. 107 pp.

Rossiter, Leonard. 1981. *The lowest form of wit.* London: Book Club Associates. 154 pp.

Rosten, Leo [Calvin]. 1968. *The joys of Yiddish.* New York: McGraw-Hill. xxxix + 533 pp.

———. 1982. *Hooray for Yiddish: A book about English.* New York: Simon & Schuster. 363 pp.

———. 1985. *Leo Rosten's giant book of laughter.* New York: Crown. xi + 573 pp.

———. 1990. [1989]. *The Joys of Yinglish.* New York: Penguin Books. xxiv + 584 pp.

Rostow, Eugene V., ed. 1971. *Is law dead?* New York: Simon & Schuster. 416 pp.

Roth, Andrew, and Jonathan Roth. 1989. *Devil's advocates: The unnatural history of lawyers.* Berkeley, CA: Nolo Press. xi + 171 + 4 pp.

Rotunda, Ronald D. 1987. Lawyers and professionalism: A commentary on the report of the American Bar Association Commission on Professionalism. *Loyola Univ. Law Review* 1149–80.

———. 1988a. Demise of professionalism has been greatly exaggerated. *Manhattan Lawyer,* Mar. 29–Apr. 4, 12.

———. 1988b. Good old days not so great; challenging the ethics myths. *Legal Times,* Mar. 21, 6.

Rovin, Jeff. 1987. *1,001 great jokes.* New York: Signet Books. 318 pp.

———. 1989. *1,000 more great jokes.* New York: Signet Books. 318 pp.

———. 1991. *1,001 great sports jokes.* New York: Signet Books. 286 pp.

———. 1992. *500 great lawyer jokes.* New York: Signet Books. 169 pp.

———. 1993. *The first good news bad news joke book.* New York: Signet Books. 158 pp.

———. 1993a. *500 great doctor jokes.* New York: Signet Books. 171 pp.

Ruksenas, Algis. 1986. *Is that you laughing, comrade? World's best Russian (underground) jokes.* Secaucus, NJ: Citadel. 182 pp.

Runninger, Jack, comp. 1971. *Favorite jokes of mountain folks in Boogar Hollow.* Lindale, GA: Country Originals. 36 pp.

Rywell, Martin, comp. 1960. *Laughter with tears: A treasury of Jewish stories . . .* Harriman, TN: Pioneer Press. 222 pp.

Saferstein, Harvey I. 1993. President's message: Lawyers, lawyers, lawyers—What's the joke? *California Lawyer* 13 (Aug.): 91.

————. 1993a. These dead lawyers aren't part of a joke. *National Law Journal*, Aug. 2, 13–14.

Salisbury, David F. 1982. Colorado's quality of life fades in a changing West. *Christian Science Monitor*, July 30, 4.

Samborn, Randall. 1993. Anti-lawyer attitude up. *National Law Journal*, Aug. 9, 1.

Samuelson, Robert J. 1992. Hustling the system. *Washington Post*, Dec. 23.

Sandburg, Carl. 1936. *The people, yes.* New York: Harcourt Brace. 286 pp.

Sander, Richard H., and E. Douglass Williams. 1989. Why are there so many lawyers? Perspectives on a turbulent market. *Law & Social Inquiry* 14:432–79.

San Diego Union-Tribune. 1991. Across the nation. Aug. 13.

Sanko, John J. 1983. Governor addresses businessmen. UPI, Regional News, Nov. 3. Available in LexisNexis Library, UPSTAT file.

Sarat, Austin, and William L. F. Felstiner. 1995. *Divorce lawyers and their clients: Power and meaning in the legal process.* New York: Oxford Univ. Press. xii + 191 pp.

Savannah, Susan, ed. 1990. *Jokes for women only.* Cincinnati: Shenandoah Press. 109 pp.

————, ed. 1991. *More jokes for women only.* Cincinnati: Shenandoah Press. 107 pp.

Scanlan, Christopher. 1987. That's not funny—that's sick. *St Petersburg Times*, Dec. 2.

Schermerhorn, James. 1928. *Schermerhorn's stories: 1500 anecdotes from forty years of after dinner speaking.* New York: George Sully. vi + 397 pp.

Schindler, Phyllis, comp. 1986. *My lords, ladies and gentlemen: The best and funniest after-dinner stories from the famous.* London: Piatkus. 128 pp.

————, comp. 1988. *Raise your glasses: The best and wittiest anecdotes and after-dinner stories from the famous.* London: Piatkus. 128 pp.

————, comp. 1992. *100 best after-dinner stories.* London: Piatkus. 111 pp.

————, comp. 1993. *100 favourite after-dinner stories from the famous.* London: Piatkus. 107 pp.

Schneyer, Ted. 1989. Professionalism as bar politics: The making of the model rules of professional conduct. *Law & Social Inquiry* 14:677–737.

Schnur, Harry C., comp. 1945. *Jewish humour.* London: Allied Book Club. 64 pp.

Schock, Al. 1976. *Jokes for all occasions.* North Hollywood, CA: Wilshire. xii + 179 pp.

Schuster, Suzan Sayar. 1991. *One laugh two chops.* Walnut Creek, CA: SSS Press. 82 pp.

Schwartz, Alvin. 1973. *Witcracks: Jokes and jests from American folklore.* Philadelphia: J. B. Lippincott. 128 pp.

Schwarzbaum, Haim. 1968. *Studies in Jewish and world folklore.* Berlin: Walter De Gruyter. ix + 604 pp.

Scott, Willard. 1984. *Willard Scott's down home stories.* Indianapolis: Bobbs-Merrill. vi + 196 pp.

Scruggs, Ray, comp. 1927. *Five hundred laughs: An assortment of after-dinner stories and amusing anecdotes.* Houston, TX: Ray Scruggs. Unpaginated.

————, comp. 1928. *Ten hundred laughs.* Houston, TX: Ray Scruggs. 135 pp

"Seattle Sal." 1994. *Grungier jokes.* New York: Shapolski. 185 pp.

Sergeant, Elizabeth Shepley. 1926. Oliver Wendell Holmes. *New Republic*, Dec. 8, 59–64.

Sethi, Subhash C. 1995a. *Selected humorous jokes.* New Delhi: Crest. 256 pp.

————. 1995b. *Selected sex jokes.* New Delhi: Crest. 256 pp.

Seton, George. 1887. *A budget of anecdotes chiefly relating to the current century.* Edinburgh: William Blackwood. xii + 190 pp.

Shafer, Harry T., and Angie Papadakis. 1988. *The howls of justice: Comedy's day in court.* San Diego: Harcourt Brace Jovanovich. iii + 177 pp.

Shah, Idraes. 1983a. [1966]. *The exploits of the incomparable Mullah Nasruddin.* London: Octagon. xi + 107 pp.

———. 1983b. [1968]. *The pleasantries of the incredible Mullah Nasruddin.* London: Octagon. 169 pp.

Shamir, Ronen. 1995. *Managing legal uncertainty: Elite lawyers in the new deal.* Durham, NC: Duke Univ. Press. xiii + 252 pp.

Shapiro, Fred R. 1993 *The Oxford dictionary of American legal quotations.* New York: Oxford Univ. Press. xv + 582 pp.

Sharpe, Johnny. 2000. *The best adult joke book ever.* London: Arcturus. 390 pp.

Shaw, George Bernard. 1905. [1898] *Plays pleasant and unpleasant.* Vol. 1. Chicago: Herbert S. Stone. xxxi + 244 pp.

Shaw, Peter. 1996. Downward mobility and praise inflation. *Society* 33 (May): 59–61.

Sheppard, John W. 1975. Ethics. *Florida Bar Journal* 49:184.

Sherman, Rorie. 1988. The media and the law. *National Law Journal,* June 6, 32–34.

———. 1991. Small screen takes a shine to lawyers. *National Law Journal,* Feb. 4.

Sherwin, Richard K. 2000. *When law goes pop: The vanishing line between law and popular culture.* Chicago: Univ. of Chicago Press. xii + 323 pp.

Shillaber, Benjamin Penhallow. 1854. *Mrs. Partington's carpet-bag of fun.* New York: Dick & Fitzgerald. vi + 300 pp. (Librarian's notation of Shillaber's dates: 1814–90; copyright Samuel Putnam Avery.)

———. 1859. *The book of 1000 comical stories: An endless repast of fun.* New York: Dick & Fitzgerald. 156 pp. (Also listed under Samuel Putnam Avery.)

Shklar, Judith N. 1984. *Ordinary vices.* Cambridge, MA: Harvard Univ. Press. 268 pp.

———. 1990. *The faces of injustice.* Cambridge, MA: Harvard Univ. Press. vii + 144 pp.

Shocked, Hugh B. [pseud.] and Colt Harted [pseud.]. 1992. *Totally tasteless tragic jokes: Is nothing sacred?* New York: Shapolsky. 150 pp.

Shriver, Harry C. 1970. *What gusto: Stories and anecdotes about Justice Oliver Wendell Holmes.* Potomac, MD: Fox Hills Press. xi + 36 pp.

Shrives, Linda. 1989. There oughta be a law against these jokes—or should there? *Chicago Tribune,* Aug. 3, Tempo sec.

Shumaker, David. 1983. *Dirty Dave's 101 x-rated jokes.* New York: Bell. vii + 118 pp.

Siegel, Lee. 1987. *Laughing matters: Comic tradition in India.* Chicago: Univ. of Chicago Press. xvi + 497 pp.

Silber, John. 1989. *Straight shooting: What's wrong with America and how to fix it.* New York: Harper & Row. xvi + 336 pp.

Silberman, Laurence. 1978. Will lawyering strangle democratic capitalism? *Regulation,* Mar.–Apr., 15.

Silberman, Matthew. 1985. *The civil justice process: A sequential model of the mobilization of law.* Orlando, FL: Academic Press. xv + 200 pp.

Simmons, Luiz R. S. 1992. Justice by witnesses-for-hire. *Christian Science Monitor,* Jan. 14, 18.

Simon, Julian L., ed. 1995. *The state of humanity.* Oxford, UK: Blackwell. viii + 694 pp.

Simon, William H. 1998. Virtuous lying: A critique of quasi-categorical moralism. Draft. 32 pp.

Simpson, A. W. B. 1984. *A biographical dictionary of the common law.* London: Butterworths. xxv + 559 pp.

———. 1990. Legal iconoclasts and legal ideals. *Univ. of Cincinnati Law Review* 58:819–44.

Simpson, James A. 1986. *Holy wit.* Edinburgh: Gordon Wright. 79 pp.

———. 1990. *More holy wit.* Edinburgh: Gordon Wright. 127 pp.

Singh, Kushwant. 1987. *Kushwant Singh's joke book.* New Delhi: Orient Paperbacks. 155 pp.

———. 1990. *Kushwant Singh's joke book II.* New Delhi: Orient Paperbacks. 151 pp.

———. 1992. *Kushwant Singh's joke book III.* New Delhi: Orient Paperbacks. 143 pp.

———. 1996. *Kushwant Singh's joke book IV.* New Delhi: Orient Paperbacks. 143 pp.

———. 1999. *Kushwant Singh's joke book 5.* New Delhi: Orient Paperbacks. 143 pp.

Skubik, Stephen J., and Hal E. Short, eds. 1976. *Republican humor.* Washington: Acropolis Books. 195 pp.

Smigel, Erwin O. 1969. [1961]. *The Wall Street lawyer: Professional organization man?* Bloomington: Indiana Univ. Press. x + 386 pp.

Smith, Edna, ed. 1941. *The best I know.* Boston: Waverly House. x + 175 pp.

Smith, H. Alan. 1982. *Our heritage of humor: Humor in the reorganized church of Jesus Christ of Latter Day Saints.* Independence, MO: Herald Publishing House. 320 pp.

Smith, H. Allen. 1970. *Rude jokes.* Greenwich, CT: Fawcett. 207 pp.

Sood, P. S. 1994. [1985]. *Jokes for all occasions.* 4th paperback ed. Delhi: Hind Pocket Books. 142 pp.

———. 1994a. [1988]. *Everyday Jokes.* 4th paperback ed. Delhi: Hind Pocket Books. 144 pp.

Sortor, Toni. 1989. *The book of clean jokes.* Miami: P.S.I. 182 pp.

South China Morning Post. 1992. Greed is good for Gambians, but bad for Brits. Aug. 21.

Southwell, David, with Sam Wigand. 1999. *The best pub joke book ever! Book 3.* London: Carlton Books. 320 pp.

Spalding, Henry D. 1969. *Encyclopedia of Jewish humor: From biblical times to the modern age.* New York: Jonathan David. xix + 458 pp.

———. 1976. *A treasure-trove of American Jewish humor.* New York: Jonathan David. xv + 416 pp.

———. 1997. [1978]. *Joys of Irish humor.* Middle Village, NY: Jonathan David. 413 pp.

———. 1997a. [1980]. *Joys of Italian humor.* Middle Village, NY: Jonathan David. 340 pp.

Spann, William B., Jr., 1977. The legal profession needs a new code of ethics. *Bar Leader,* Nov.–Dec., 2.

Speiser, Stuart M. 1980. *Lawsuit.* New York: Horizon. v + 617 pp.

Speroni, Charles. 1964. *Wit and wisdom of the Italian renaissance.* Berkeley: Univ. of California Press. 317 pp.

Sprague, William C[yrus]. 1897. [1895]. *Flashes of wit from bench and bar.* 2nd ed. Detroit: Collector. 185 pp.

Stangland, Red. 1986. *Ole and Lena Jokes.* Sioux Falls, SD: Norse. 48 pp.

———. 1987. *More Ole and Lena Jokes.* Sioux Falls, SD: Norse. 48 pp.

———. n.d. 1987? *Norwegian Home Companion.* New York: Barnes & Noble. xi + 326 pp.

———. 1988. *Ole and Lena Jokes—Book III.* Sioux Falls, SD: Norse. 48 pp.

———. 1989. *Ole and Lena Jokes—Book 4.* Sioux Falls, SD: Norse. 47 pp.

———. 1990. *Ole and Lena Jokes—Book 5.* Sioux Falls, SD: Norse. 47 pp.

———. 1992. *Ole and Lena Jokes—Book 6.* Sioux Falls, SD: Norse. 45 pp.

———. 1993. *Ole and Lena Jokes—Book 7.* Sioux Falls, SD: Norse. 47 pp.

———. 1994. *Ole and Lena Jokes—Book 8.* Sioux Falls, SD: Norse. 47 pp.

Star Tribune (Minneapolis). 1992. Inside talk. Apr. 6.

Stark, Steven D. 1987. Perry Mason meets Sonny Crockett: The history of lawyers and the police as television heroes. *Univ. of Miami Law Review* 42:229–83.

Starr, John R. 1995. Untitled column. *Arkansas Democrat-Gazette*, Dec. 17, 5J.

Starr, Kenneth. 1998. Address, Mecklenberg County (NC) Bar Association, June 1.

Steiger, Sam. 1990. *Kill the lawyers.* Payson, AZ: Prickly Pear Press. vii + 95 pp.

Steiner, Paul. 1950. *Israel laughs: A collection of humor from the Jewish state.* New York: Bloch. vi + 166 pp.

Stevens, Mark. 1987. *Power of attorney: The rise of the giant law firms.* New York: McGraw Hill. x + 187 pp.

Stokker, Kathleen. 2001. Quisling humor in Hitler's Norway: Its wartime function and postwar legacy. *Humor* 14:339–57.

Stone, Suzanne Last. 1993. In pursuit of the counter-text: The turn to the Jewish legal model in contemporary American legal history. *Harvard Law Review* 106:813–94.

Storer, Edward, ed. and trans. 1928. *The facetiae of Poggio and other medieval story-tellers.* London: George Routledge. x + 172 pp.

Strasser, Fred. 1986. Bar meeting mixes work, play in Florida. *National Law Journal,* July 7, 6.

————. 1987. Tort tales: Old stories never die. *National Law Journal,* Feb. 16, 37.

Strean, Herbert. 1993. *Jokes: Their meaning and purpose.* Northvale, NJ: Jason Aronson. xv + 224 pp.

Streiker, Lowell D. 1998. *An encyclopedia of humor.* Peabody, MA: Hendrickson. 416 pp.

Strong, Theron. 1914. *Landmarks of a lawyer's lifetime.* New York: Dodd, Mead. 552 pp.

Studer, Norman. 1988. *A Catskill woodsman: Mike Todd's story.* Fleischmanns, NY: Purple Mountain Press. 122 pp.

Subhash and Dharam. 1995a. *More party jokes.* New Delhi: Crest. 256 pp.

————. 1995b. *Party jokes.* New Delhi: Crest. 256 pp.

————. 1995c. *Still more party jokes.* New Delhi: Crest. 256 pp.

Subotnik, Dan. 1998. The joke in critical race theory: De gustibus disputandum *est? Touro Law Review* 15:105–24.

Subramanian, M. 1995. *A to Z book of jokes.* Bombay: Jaico. xxix +154 pp.

Suchman, Mark C., and Mia L. Cahill. 1996. The hired gun as facilitator: Lawyers and the suppression of business disputes in Silicon Valley. *Law & Social Inquiry* 21:679–712.

Sunil, B. M. 1999. *Crackling jokes for all.* Mumbai: Jaico. 110 pp.

Sutton-Smith, Brian. 1960. "Shut up and keep digging": The cruel joke series. *Midwest Folklore* 10:11–22.

Swift, Jonathan. 1726. *Gulliver's Travels.* 3 vols. London: B. Motte.

Sydow, C. W. v. 1948. *Selected papers on folklore.* Copenhagen: Rosenkilde and Bagger. 259 pp.

Sykes, Adam, and Iain Sproat, comps. 1965. *The wit of Sir Winston.* London: Leslie Frewin. 93 pp.

Symons, Mitchell. 1998. *The Bill Clinton joke book.* London: Chameleon Books. 95 pp.

Tapper, Al, and Peter Press. 2000. *A minister, a priest, and a rabbi.* Kansas City, MO: Andrews McMeel. 247 pp.

————. 2000a. *A guy goes into a bar.* Kansas City, MO: Andrews McMeel. 197 pp.

Taubeneck, George F. 1946. *You'll love this one.* Detroit: Business News. 232 pp.

Taylor, Stuart. 1988. Lifting of secrecy reveals earthy side of justices. *New York Times,* Feb. 22.

———. 1995. Why so many lawyer jokes ring true. *Legal Times,* Sept. 18, 25.

Teitelbaum, Elsa, comp. 1945. *An anthology of Jewish humor and maxims.* Ed. Abraham Burstein. New York: Pardes. 462.

Telushkin, Joseph. 1992. *Jewish humor: What the best Jewish jokes say about the Jews.* New York: William Morrow. 237 pp.

Terrell, Bob, and Marcellus "Buck" Buchanan. 1984. *Disorder in the court.* Asheville, NC: Bright Mountain Books. ii + 206 pp.

Terry, Saundra. 1991. BCCI scandal a windfall for attorneys unlike any other. *Washington Post,* Aug. 12.

Teubner, Gunther, ed. 1987. *Juridification of social spheres.* New York: Walter de Gruyter. viii + 446 pp.

Texas Lawyer. 1997. Texas courts of appeals civil. Apr. 28, 11.

Theaker, Daniel G. 1997. *A working musician's joke book.* Toronto: Sound and Vision. viii + 88 pp.

Thickett, Maude. 1983. *Outrageously offensive jokes.* New York: Pocket Books. 127 pp.

———. 1984. *Outrageously offensive jokes II.* New York: Pocket Books. 126 pp.

———. 1986. *Outrageously offensive jokes III.* New York: Pocket Books. 123 pp.

———. 1987. *Outrageously offensive jokes IV.* New York: Pocket Books. 125 pp.

Thomas, John. 1996. *The world's best woman jokes.* London: HarperCollins. 95 pp.

Thomas, Rich. 1988. The magic of Reaganomics. *Newsweek,* Dec. 26, 40–41, 44.

Thomas, S. Evelyn, comp. 1947. *Laughs with the law: A symposium of world humour.* London: Temple Fortune Press. 48 pp.

———, comp. ca. 1948. *Good humour: An anthology of English humour.* London: S. Evelyn Thomas. 64 pp.

Thompson, Hunter S. 1976. Fear and loathing on the campaign trail '76: Third rate romance, low rent rendezvous. *Rolling Stone,* June 3.

Thompson, Stith. 1955. *Motif-index of folk-literature: A classification of narrative elements in folktales, ballads, myths, fables, mediaeval romances, exempla, fabliaux, jest-books and local legends.* 6 vols. Bloomington: Indiana Univ. Press.

Thornberg, Elizabeth G. 1995. Metaphors matter: How images of battle, sports, and sex shape the adversary system. *Wisconsin Women's Law Journal* 10:225–81.

365 uproarious lawyer jokes, riddles, and quotes: 1995 calendar. 1994. Riderwood, MD: Paramount Enterprises.

Tibballs, Geoff, ed. 2000. *The mammoth book of humor.* New York: Carroll & Graf. x + 614. (Originally published in UK by Constable & Robinson in 2000.)

Tickleside, Sir Toby. 1788. *The funny jester, or the cream of harmony and humour.* London: W. Lane. 72 pp.

Tidwell, James N. 1956. *A treasury of American folk humor.* New York: Crown. xx + 620 pp.

Tillinghast. 1992. *Tort Cost Trends: An International Perspective, 1992.* n.p.: Tillinghast-Towers Perrin. 16 + 23 pp.

Tobias, Andrew. 1982. Three horribly unfair jokes you can tell about lawyers. *Playboy.* March, 146–47.

Tomasic, Roman. 1985. Cynicism and ambivalence towards law and legal institutions in Australia. In *Law in a cynical society? Opinion and law in the 1980's,* ed. Dale Gibson and Janet K. Baldwin, 89–106. Calgary, Alta.: Carswell Legal Publications.

Tomlinson, Gerald. 1990. *Speaker's treasury of political stories, anecdotes and humor.* New York: MJF Books. x + 349 pp.

Topol, [Chaim], comp. 1995. [1994]. *Topol's treasury of Jewish humor, wit and wisdom*. New York: Barricade Books. 256 pp.

Torres, Vicki. 1993. Chief of bar assn. asks end to lawyer-bashing. *Los Angeles Times,* July 6, A1.

Totten, Bill. 1994. Why Japanese live better than Americans. *Daily Yomiuri,* Jun. 25, 6.

Trachtenberg, Joshua. 1983. [1943]. *The devil and the Jews: The medieval conception of the Jews and its relation to modern anti-Semitism*. 2nd paperback ed. Philadelphia: Jewish Publication Society. xvi + 278.

Trachtenberg, Stephen Joel. 1993. Lawyer jokes: What they tell us about today's America and today's world. *New York State Bar Journal* 65 (7): 32–33, 58.

Trevor [pseud.]. 1992. *The official New Zealand joke book*. Balmain: Ewe & I Press. 94 pp.

Trigaux, Robert. 1983. Quips, good food, a king, and Belgian hospitality. *American Banker,* May 23, 3.

Triverton, Sanford. 1981. *Complete book of ethnic jokes*. New York: Galahad Books. 319 pp.

Trotter, Michael H. 1997. *Profit and the practice of law: What's happened to the legal profession*. Athens: Univ. of Georgia Press. xix + 232 pp.

Trubek, David. 1984. Turning away from law. *Michigan Law Review* 82:824–35.

Trubek, David M., Austin Sarat, William L. F. Felstiner, Herbert M. Kritzer, and Joel B. Grossman. 1983. The costs of ordinary litigation. *UCLA Law Review* 31:73–129.

True, [G.] Herb[ert]. 1972. *Laugh oil*. Indianapolis: American Humor Guild. 96 pp.

Tubach, Frederic C. 1969. *Index exemplorum: A handbook of medieval religious tales* [= Folklore Fellows Communications No. 204]. Helsinki: Suomalainen Tiedeakatemia. 530 pp.

Tucker, E. F. J. 1984. *Intruder into Eden: Representations of the common lawyer in English literature 1350–1750*. Columbia, SC: Camden House. xiii + 141 pp.

Tucket, Nan. 1992. *The dumb men joke book*. New York: Warner Books. ix + 100 pp.

Tulk, Robert (Bob). 1971. *Newfie jokes*. Mount Pearl, NF: Robert Tulk. 82 pp.

———. 1973. *New Newfoundland Jokes [= Bob Tulk's Newfie Jokes Vol. 3]*. Corner Brook, NF: Newfie Jokes. Unpaginated.

Tybor, Joseph R. 1978. Ouster in Chicago: It ain't cheap. *National Law Journal,* Aug. 7, 18.

U.S. Bureau of Labor Statistics. 1988. *Bulletin 2307: Labor force statistics derived from the current population survey, 1948–87*. Washington, D.C.: U.S. Department of Labor.

U.S. Bureau of the Census. 1976. *Historical statistics of the United States: Colonial times to 1970*. Washington, D.C.: U.S. Department of Commerce.

———. 1972, 1977, 1982, 1987, 1992. *Census of service industries*. Washington, D.C.: U.S. Department of Commerce.

———. 1987. *Statistical abstract of the United States*. Washington, D.C.: U.S. Department of Commerce.

Uslaner, Eric M. 1993. *The decline of comity in Congress*. Ann Arbor: Univ. of Michigan Press. xi + 204 pp.

———. 1999. Democracy and social capital. In *Democracy and Trust,* ed. Mark E. Warren. New York: Cambridge Univ. Press. xi + 370 pp.

U.S. News and World Report. 1978. Why everybody is suing everybody. Dec. 4, 50.

———. 1982. Special section: the ABCs of justice. Nov. 1, 55.

Van Hoy, Jerry. 1997. *Franchise law firms and the transformation of personal legal services*. Westport, CT: Quorum Books. xii + 156 pp.

Van Munching, Philip. 1997. *How to remember jokes and 101 drop-dead jokes to get you started*. New York: Workman. 133 pp.

Varon, Benno Weiser. 1995. I made them laugh. *Midstream,* May, 27–29.

Vas, Gratian, comp. 1994. *A Consignment of business jokes.* New Delhi: Sterling. Unpaginated.

———, comp. 1994a. *Graduating with campus jokes.* New Delhi: Sterling. Unpaginated.

———, comp. 1994b. *Cupid's quiver of love jokes.* New Delhi: Sterling. Unpaginated.

———, comp. 1994c. *A feast of party jokes.* New Delhi: Sterling. Unpaginated.

———, comp. 1996. *Cuddle up with pet lover jokes.* New Delhi: Sterling. Unpaginated.

———, comp. 1996a. *Nosing around with neighbour jokes.* New Delhi: Sterling. Unpaginated.

Veall, Donald. 1970. *The popular movement for law reform 1640–1660.* Oxford: Clarendon. xxvi + 259 pp.

Viner, Michael, Susie Dotson, and Tim Foley. 1994. *Final exit for lawyers.* Beverly Hills, CA: Dove. Unpaginated.

Wachs, Mark. *The funniest jokes and how to tell them.* New York: Hawthorn Books. xii + 347 pp.

Walker, James T. 1980. *Have you heard? The after-dinner speaker's guide to being funny.* North Ryde, NSW, Austl.: Cassell. 216 pp.

———. 1982. *Leave them laughing: Confessions of an applause addict.* North Ryde, NSW, Austl.: Metheun. 176 pp.

Walker, Jerry. 1990. Wall Street Journal adds another law col. *Jack O'Dwyers Newsletter,* Jan. 24.

Wall Street Journal. 1978. Editorial: The law's delay, May 10.

Walser, Richard, ed. 1974. *Tar Heel laughter.* Chapel Hill: Univ. of North Carolina Press. xv + 310 pp.

Wardroper, John. 1970. *Jest upon jest: A selection from the jestbooks and collections of merry tales published from the reign of Richard III to George III.* London: Routledge & Kegan Paul. vii + 216 pp.

Warner, Karen. 1993. *500 great bartender's jokes.* New York: Signet. 202 pp.

Warner, Ralph. 1992. Readers find something to joke about in lawyers. *USA Today,* Apr. 1.

———, Tomi Ihara, and Barbara Kate Repa. 1994. *29 reasons not to go to law school.* Berkeley, CA: Nolo Press. 181 pp.

Warren, Charles. 1911. *A history of the American bar.* Boston: Little, Brown. xii + 586 pp.

Warren, James, and Brian J. Kelly. 1978. Reuben fights Kirkland and Ellis for lawyers, clients. *American Lawyer,* Aug. 11, 1, 14–16.

Washingtonian. 1995. Lawyers in turf war with rats. Aug. Available in LexisNexis Library.

Washington Post. 1978. Editorial: Mr. Carter's class struggle. May 7.

———. 1981. Bob Levey's Washington. District Weekly, Oct 29, 10.

———. 1988. Help from HALT. Jan. 21.

Waters, Robert. 1900. *Flashes of wit and humor.* New York: Edward S. Werner. 186 pp.

Webster, Sue. 1994. The professionals who prefer McJobs. *Independent,* Aug. 7, 21.

Weidenbaum, Murray K., and Ronald J. Penoyer. 1983. *The next step in regulatory reform.* St. Louis: Center for the Study of American Business.

Weiherman, William F. 1955. *That reminds me.* St. Louis: Concordia. xi + 129 pp.

Weil, Fred B., ed. 1968. *The 1967 lawyer statistical report.* Chicago: American Bar Foundation. x + 171 pp.

Weinstein, Henry. 1975. Defending what? The corporations' public interest. *Juris Doctor* 5 (June): 39–43.

Weisbrod, Burton A., Joel F. Handler, and Neil K. Komesar. 1978. *Public interest law: An economic and institutional analysis.* Berkeley: Univ. of California Press.

Weiss, Kenneth R. 1989. If there's a law, there's a newsletter. *New York Times,* June 2.

Wermiel, Stephen. 1986. Shroud of secrecy that veils the Supreme Court lifts as justices assume higher public profiles. *Wall Street Journal,* July 1.

Werner, A., ed. and trans. 1893. *The humour of Holland.* London: Walter Scott. xxiv + 398 pp.

Wheeler, H. H., ed. 1925? *"All star" joke book and complete minstrel guide.* Boston: Up-to-Date Publishing. xi + 102 pp.

White, D[aniel] Robert. 1983. *The official lawyer's handbook.* New York: Simon & Schuster. 241 pp.

———, and Philip R. Jenks. 1992? 1993? *The official lawyer's handbook (how to survive a legal career.* London: Harriman House. 207 pp.

Whitfield, Stephen J. 1978. Laughter in the dark: Notes on American-Jewish humor. *Midstream,* 24 (Feb.): 48–58.

Wickberg, Daniel. 1998. *The senses of humor: Self and laughter in modern America.* Ithaca, NY: Cornell Univ. Press. x + 267 pp.

Wiemer, Bob, et al. 1995. And furthermore. *Newsday,* Feb. 5.

———. 1998. It costs a lot to support cheap morality. *Newsday,* Mar. 2.

Wilde, Larry. 1973. *The official Polish/Italian joke book.* New York: Pinnacle Books. viii + 123 + 99 pp.

———. 1974. *The official Jewish/Irish joke book.* New York: Pinnacle Books. 116 +117 pp.

———. 1975. *More: The official Polish/Italian joke book.* New York: Pinnacle Books. xii + 92 + 108 pp.

———. 1975a. *The official black folks/white folks joke book.* New York: Pinnacle Books. 108 + 100 pp.

———. 1975b. *The official virgins/sex maniacs joke book.* New York: Pinnacle Books. 97 + 109 pp.

———. 1976. *The official Democrat/Republican joke book.* New York: Pinnacle Books. xix + 92 + 94 pp.

———. 1976a. *The official religious/not so religious joke book.* New York: Pinnacle Books. 102 + 98 pp.

———. 1977. *The official golfers joke book.* New York: Pinnacle Books. 206 pp.

———. 1977a. *The last official Polish joke book.* Los Angeles: Pinnacle Books. xiv + 209 pp.

———. 1978. *The complete book of ethnic humor.* Los Angeles: Pinnacle Books. xii + 246 pp.

———. 1978a. *The last official Italian joke book.* Los Angeles: Pinnacle Books. 204 pp.

———. 1978b. *The official cat lover's/dog lover's joke book.* Los Angeles: Pinnacle Books. 79 + 117 pp.

———. 1979. *More: The official Jewish/Irish joke book.* Los Angeles: Pinnacle Books. 98 + 104 pp.

———. 1979a. *The official book of sick jokes.* Los Angeles: Pinnacle Books. 215 pp.

———. 1980. *The last official Jewish joke book.* New York: Bantam Books. 177 pp.

———. 1980a. *More: The official Democrat/Republican joke book.* New York: Bantam Books. 98 + 102 pp.

———. 1981. *More: The official sex maniacs joke book.* New York: Bantam Books. 169 pp.

———. 1981a. *The official doctors joke book.* New York: Bantam Books. 188 pp.

———. 1982. *The official lawyers joke book.* New York: Bantam Books. xv + 188 pp.

———. 1983. *The last official Irish joke book.* New York: Bantam Books. 194 pp.

———. 1984. *The official politicians joke book.* New York: Bantam Books. 181 pp.

———. 1984a. *The official rednecks joke book.* New York: Bantam Books. 181 pp.

———. 1985. *Official book of john jokes.* New York: Bantam Books. 180 pp.

———. 1986. *The official executives joke book.* New York: Bantam Books. 185 pp.

———. 1986a. *More: The official doctors joke book.* New York: Bantam Books. 177 pp.

———. 1987. *The ultimate lawyers joke book.* New York: Bantam Books. 182 pp.

———. 1988. *The Larry Wilde library of laughter.* New York: Ivy Books. 264 pp.

———. 1988a. *The official all-America joke book.* New York: Bantam Books. 184 pp.

———. 1991. *The merriest book of Christmas humor.* New York: Bantam Books. 185 pp.

———. 1996. *The dumb, dumber, dumbest joke book.* New York: Pinnacle Books. 154 pp.

———. 1997. *You're never too old to laugh.* New York: Pinnacle Books. 172 pp.

———, and Steve Wozniak. 1989. *The official computer freaks joke book.* New York: Bantam Books. xix + 168 pp.

Wiley [David Wiley Miller].1993. *Dead lawyers and other pleasant thoughts.* New York: Random House. Unpaginated.

Will, George. 1992. Clinton: if he succeeds, it will be despite himself. *Daily Telegraph,* Nov. 12.

Williams, Larry. 1936. *Bombshells of laughter.* n.p. 152 pp.

Williams, Leewin B., comp. 1926. *Pungent paragraphs: A handbook of humorous illustrations, wit and wisdom.* Washington. Leewin B. Williams, xiii + 309 pp.

———, ed. 1938. *Master book of humorous illustrations.* New York: Abingdon-Cokesbury. 431 pp.

———, ed. 1949. *Encyclopedia of wit, humor, and wisdom.* New York: Abingdon-Cokesbury. 576 pp.

Willock, John. 1887. *Legal facetiae: Satirical and humorous.* London: London Literary Society. 442 pp. (Repr., Littleton, CO: Fred B. Rothman, 1982.)

Wilson, Earl. 1949. *Let 'em eat cheesecake.* Garden City, NY: Doubleday. xviii + 302 pp.

Wilson, Justin, and Howard Jacobs. 1982. [1974]. *Justin Wilson's Cajun humor.* Gretna, LA: Pelican. 133 pp.

Winick, Charles, comp. 1964. *USSR humor.* Mt. Vernon, NY: Peter Pauper Press. 62 pp.

Winston-Macauley, Marnie. 2001. *A little joy, a little oy: Jewish wit and wisdom.* Kansas City, MO: Andrews McMeel. 313 pp.

Wintrob, Suzanne. 1995. CA's Wang pleads case for Legent. *Computer Dealer News,* Aug. 9.

Wittes, Benjamin. 1997. Frustrating targets: Juries reluctant to convict lawyers who represent bad guys. *Broward Daily Business Review,* Nov. 4, A1.

Wolff, Robert Paul, ed. 1971. *The rule of law.* New York: Simon & Shuster. 254 pp.

Wood, Clement, ed. 1926. *The best American jokes.* Girard, KS: Haldeman-Julius. 64 pp.

———, ed. n.d. ca. 1926. *The best Negro jokes.* Girard, KS: Haldeman-Julius. 61 pp.

Woods, Ralph L., ed. 1967. *The modern handbook of humor.* New York: McGraw-Hill. xxii + 618 pp.

Woodward, Bob, and Scott Armstrong. 1979. *The brethren: Inside the Supreme Court.* New York: Simon & Schuster. 467 pp.

Wortsman, Gene. 1963. *The new frontier joke book.* New York: MacFadden Books. 112 pp.

Wright, Milton. 1939. *What's funny—and why: An outline of humor.* New York: Harvest House. 284 pp.

Wright, Rusty, and Linda Raney Wright. 1985. *500 clean jokes and humorous stories and how to tell them.* Uhrichsville, OH: Barbour. 305 + 22 unpaginated.

Wynn, William T. 1950. *Smile with me.* Milledgeville, GA: published by author. xii + 83 pp.

Yaffe, James. 1972. *So sue me! The story of a community court.* New York: Saturday Review Press. x + 275 pp.

Yale Law Journal. 1964. The Jewish law student and New York jobs—Discriminatory effects in law firm hiring practices. 73:625–60.

———. 1989. Symposium on popular culture. 98 (8).

Yankelovich Partners & Talmey-Drake Research & Strategy. 1995. *National Survey on Tort Reform.* Jan. x + 8 pp.

Yarwood, Mike, comp. 1982. [1981]. *Just joking.* London: Coronet Books. 146 pp.

Yermonee, Nick. 1992. *The Maxwell joke book.* London: Blake Paperbacks. 96 pp (unpaginated). (Also published by same publisher in same year anonymously.)

Yngvesson, Barbara. 1985. Re-examining continuing relations and the law. 1985 *Wisconsin Law Review* 623–46.

Youngman, Henny. 1963. *How do you like me so far?* New York: Gramercy. 127 pp.

———. n.d. *Henny Youngman's giant book of jokes.* Secaucus, N.J.: Citadel. Contains *How do you like me so far?* 127 pp., and *400 traveling salesman's jokes* (1966). 124 pp.

———. 1968. *Best salesmen's jokes.* London: Wolfe. 64 pp.

———. 1976. *Don't put my name on this book.* New York: Manor Books. 162 pp.

Yunck, John A. 1960. The venal tongue: Lawyers and the medieval satirists. *ABA Journal* 46:267–70.

———. 1963. *The lineage of Lady Meed: The development of mediaeval venality satire.* South Bend, IN: Univ. of Notre Dame Press. xiii + 350 pp.

Zall, P[aul] M., ed. 1963. *A hundred merry tales and other English jestbooks of the fifteenth and sixteenth centuries.* Lincoln: Univ. of Nebraska Press. 394 pp.

———, ed. 1970. *A nest of ninnies and other English jestbooks of the seventeeth century.* Lincoln: Univ. of Nebraska Press. xviii + 260 pp.

———, ed. 1980. *Ben Franklin laughing: Anecdotes from original sources by and about Benjamin Franklin.* Berkeley: Univ. of California Press. 204 pp.

———, ed. 1982. *Abe Lincoln laughing: Humorous anecdotes from original sources by and about Abraham Lincoln.* Berkeley: Univ. of California Press. xii + 193 pp.

———, ed. 1985. *Mark Twain laughing: Humorous anecdotes by and about Samuel L. Clemens.* Knoxville: Univ. of Tennessee Press. xxviii + 199 pp.

———, ed. 1996. *The wit and wisdom of the founding fathers.* Hopewell, NJ: Ecco Press. 171 pp.

Zand, Arie, comp. 1982. *Political jokes of Leningrad.* Austin, TX: Silvergirl. 82 pp.

Ziv, Avner, ed. 1986. *Jewish humor.* Tel Aviv: Papyrus. 215 pp.

———, and Anat Zajdman, eds. 1993. *Semites and stereotypes: Characteristics of Jewish humor.* Westport, CT: Greenwood Press. xix + 197 pp.

On-Line Collections

A collection of lawyer jokes. 1997. http://www.wfu.edu/~anderna5/laugh/lawyer.html. Last visited May 21, 1997.

American Tort Reform Association. 1997. Litigation horror stories: Stories that show a legal system that's out of control. http://www.atra.org. Last updated Nov. 7, 1997.

Canonical list of lawyer humor (court jester). 1995. Archived by Derek Cashman http://members.tripod.com/jokeyard/humor/lawyer.htm. Last modified Mar. 2, 1995.)

Canonical list of humor (funny bone). 1995. http://lithp.net/~mblake/textfiles/humor/medical.humor. Last modified Mar. 2, 1995.

Canonical list of lawyer jokes. 1997. http://wpi.edu/~tanis/lawyer.html. Last visited May 21, 1997.

Canonical list of medical humor (funny bone). 1995. http://www.im.pw.edu.pl/jokes/medical.html. Last modified Mar. 2, 1995. Could not be located Mar. 11, 2005.

Dancing with lawyers. 1998. http://www.dancingwithlawyers.com/freeinfo/lawjokes.html. Accessed June 1998.

The funniest darn lawyer jokes in the WDWW (Whole Darn Wide World). 1997. http://www.schober.com/~wwlia/jokes.html. Last modified Mar. 16, 1997.

Generic lawyer jokes. 1997. http://www.ruf.rice.edu/~kit/lawjokes.html. Accessed Sep. 19, 1997.

Gotta love them lawyer jokes. 1997. http://www.scroom.com/humor/lawyer.html. Last modified Aug. 30, 1995.

Jewish humor list. 1999.

Lawyer jokes. 1995. http://rever.nmsu.edu/~ras/lawyer.htm. Accessed Dec. 18, 1995.

———. 1997. http://www.conductor.com/lalas/kls/jokes.html. Accessed July 22, 1997.

———. 1997. http://www.ruf.rice.edu~kit/lawjokes.html. Accessed Sept. 19, 1997.

———. 1998. http://www.mpx.com.au/~danieln.lawyer.html. Accessed Jan. 30, 1998.

———. 1998. http://www.comedy.clari.net/rhj/jokes/91q2/colph.html. Accessed Jan. 30, 1998.

———. 1998. http://www.oipaz.net/V_LawyerJokes.html. Dated Dec. 1, 1998.

Long lawyer jokes. 1994. . http://hem.passagen.se/stenshmn/lawyer.htm. Accessed Aug. 16, 1994.

Movie/TV news—studio briefing. 2003. http://www.imdb.com/news/sb. Accessed Mar. 12, 2005.

O. J. Simpson: Canonical O.bligatory J.okes list. 1995. http://members.tripod.com/~Mysterium/ser0017.html. Dated Dec. 1, 1995.

POPULUS jokes. 1997. http://www.POPULUS.net. Accessed Oct. 14, 1997, Dec. 1, 1997.

Randy's favorite lawyer jokes. 1997. http://rever.nmsu.edu/~ras/lawyer.html. Accessed July 24, 1997.

Lawyer jokes from Internet. 1993. Unnamed collection. On file with author.

———. Sept. 1994. Unnamed collection. On file with author.

INDEX

413